COLLECTED ESSAYS IN LAW

The Great Juristic Bazaar

The Collected Essays in Law Series
General Editor: Tom D. Campbell

Law's Premises, Law's Promise:
Jurisprudence after Wittgenstein

Thomas Morawetz

ISBN: 0 7546 2013 1

The Jurisprudence of
Law's Form and Substance

Robert S. Summers

ISBN: 0 7546 2024 7

Regulation, Crime, and Freedom

John Braithwaite

ISBN: 0 7546 2005 0

Legal Rules and Legal Reasoning

Larry Alexander

ISBN: 0 7546 2004 2

William Twining

The Great Juristic Bazaar

Jurists' Texts and Lawyers' Stories

Ashgate
DARTMOUTH

Published by
Dartmouth Publishing Company Limited
Gower House
Croft Road
Aldershot
Hampshire GU11 3HR
England

Ashgate Publishing Company
131 Main Street
Burlington
Vermont 05401–5600
USA

Ashgate Website: http://www.ashgate.com

British Library Cataloguing in Publication Data
The Great Juristic Bazaar: Jurists' Texts and Lawyers' Stories. –
(Collected Essays in Law)
1. Jurisprudence. 2. Law – Philosophy.
I. Twining, William, 1934–
340

US Library of Congress Catalog-in-Publication Data:
The Great Juristic Bazaar: Jurists' Texts and Lawyers' Stories. –
p. cm. – (Collected Essays in Law)
Includes bibliographical references.
1. Jurisprudence. 2. Law – Philosophy. 3. Law – Interpretation and construction. I. Twining, William. II. Series.
K234.G73 2002
340–dc21 2001048712

ISBN: 0 7546 2211 8

Printed and bound in Great Britain by Antony Rowe Ltd, Chippenham, Wiltshire

Contents

To my students

Acknowledgements

Grateful acknowledgement is made to the following persons, editors publishers and institutions for their kind permission to reprint the articles included in this volume: Blackwells Publishers, Journals Division, Oxford; Sweet and Maxwell, London; *NYU Law Review*, New York; Professor R. Helmholz on behalf of the University of Chicago; The British Academy; London; Oxford University Press; Butterworths Publishers, London; Northwestern University Press, Evanston, Illinois; Kluwer Law International, The Hague; *South Texas Law Review*, Houston, Texas and Cornell Law Review, Ithaca, New York.

Series Preface

Collected Essays in Law makes available some of the most important work of scholars who have made a major contribution to the study of law. Each volume brings together a selection of writings by a leading authority on a particular subject. The series gives authors an opportunity to present and comment on what they regard as their most important work in a specific area. Within their chosen subject area, the collections aim to give a comprehensive coverage of the authors' research. Care is taken to include essays and articles which are less readily accessible and to give the reader a picture of the development of the authors' work and an indication of research in progress.

The initial volumes in the series include collections by Professors Frederick Schauer (Harvard), *Constitutional Interpretation*, John Braithwaite (ANU), *Regulation, Crime and Freedom*, Tom Morawetz, *Law's Premises, Law's Promise*, Robert Summers (Cornell), *Law's Form and Substance*, and Larry Alexander (San Diego), *Legal Rules and Legal Reasoning.* These collections set a high standard for future volumes in the series and I am most grateful to all of these distinguished authors for being in at the start of what it is hoped will become a rich and varied repository of the achievements of contemporary legal scholarship

William Twining was born in East Africa. He has taught in Sudan, Tanzania, Northern Ireland, and the United States as well as in England. He is Research Professor of Law at University College London (UCL), having been Quain Professor of Jurisprudence from 1983 to 1996. He writes from personal knowledge of the main subjects of these essays: Herbert Hart first aroused his enthusiasm for Jurisprudence; he was also taught by Karl Llewellyn whose papers he put in order, subsequently writing his intellectual biography. At UCL Ronald Dworkin is a colleague and Jeremy Bentham a brooding omnipresence. His other interests include evidence, law and development, and legal education. He rejects sharp distinctions between theory and practice. He loves teaching, writing, and travelling and believes that good stories are enjoyable, necessary and dangerous. Photo by Heather Brown and Daryl Everitt.

[1]
Introduction[1]

The Bazaar

Four images of the city pervade the literature of urban sociology: bazaar, jungle, organism, and machine. Each in different ways symbolizes 'organized diversity'.[2] Each can apply to legal orders.[3] Bazaars and machines are created and controlled by humans; jungles and organisms are natural. An organism is a naturally functioning entity; a machine symbolizes social engineering; a jungle suggests a dense, hostile environment beyond human agents' control; a bazaar, more user friendly and ordered by an invisible hand, represents pluralism, opportunity, eclecticism, freedom to choose.

The title of this book echoes *The Great Railway Bazaar* by Paul Theroux. It refers to the vast heritage of legal thought in the world throughout the ages. Here a bazaar represents an anti-reductionist view that catches some of the antimonies that pervade legal thought: law as natural and law as posited or man-made; unplanned evolution versus systematic planning; the free market and social engineering; top-down and bottom-up perspectives; order and anarchy; reason and imagination; unity in diversity. The metaphor of a bazaar also underlines the extent and variety of inherited legal thought and suggests some of the difficulties of reducing it to simple patterns of traditions, schools, movements, isms, and ists. A bazaar may have an underlying order, but its interest lies in diverse particulars.

In fact the focus of this book is deliberately narrow. Part A deals with reading and interpreting juristic texts with particular reference to a few key figures and texts in a single limited tradition, Anglo-American jurisprudence from 1750 to the present day. Part B deals with stories, a universal phenomenon, in relation to one specific context and topic: the role of narrative and background generalizations in relation to argumentation about questions of law and questions of fact in adjudication. The main links between these two themes are interpretation and the tensions between 'reason' and 'imagination'. In short, these essays focus in detail on two quite modest stalls in a huge bazaar. The purpose of this introduction is to set them in context.

When I was invited to contribute to this series, I was faced with a dilemma. The Editor suggested that I should treat the book as a retrospective exhibition of my work. The suggestion had some obvious attractions. However, I had already published three collections of essays, each centred on one general area.[4] A selection from all of my essays would have been mainly an anthology of anthologies, spread over a wide range of subjects and overlapping substantially with books that are still in print. The alternative was to construct a coherent book that would complement the others by focussing on one or two topics that were not central to them while keeping the amount of overlap to a minimum. I have chosen the second option. Only two of the essays included here are to be found in any of the other three collections. The relation of this book to the others will be indicated below.

The main intended audience for this book is legal theorists and students of jurisprudence and of evidence. Chapters 2–9 can be read as introductions to particular thinkers and, in most cases, as aids to reading particular texts in the original. Each essay stands on its own, so they can be read selectively and in a different sequence. Chapters 1, 4, 5, and 10 develop a pragmatic perspective on legal theory as a heritage and as an activity. The essays in Part B grew out of thinking and teaching about the theory of evidence, but they are relevant to any context in which the role of narrative and argumentation in law is under consideration.

This collection is directly rooted in teaching. I subscribe to the view that there can and should be an intimate reflexive relationship between teaching and research. In courses on jurisprudence I have regularly used nearly all of the texts discussed in detail in Part A. This has been one important way of learning from them and teaching about them. Similarly, in teaching evidence, my ideas about stories have been stimulated by using them in counterpoint with analytical approaches to the construction and criticism of arguments about questions of fact.

Part A: A pragmatic conception of jurisprudence

This book is a contribution to jurisprudence. Part A can be read as a series of critical introductions to the work of five particular jurists in the Anglo-American tradition, as an exploration of my views on realism, positivism, and post-modernism, and as reflections on and applications of a particular approach to reading juristic texts.

'Jurisprudence', 'Legal Theory', and 'Legal Philosophy' do not have settled meanings in either the Anglo-American or the Continental European traditions. So it may be useful to restate my conception of jurisprudence and of legal philosophy as one part of it.[5] My standpoint is generally that of a cosmopolitan English jurist who is concerned with the health of his discipline the purpose of which is advancing and disseminating understanding about law. I treat jurisprudence and legal theory as synonyms and legal philosophy as one part – the most abstract part – of jurisprudence. In this view, jurisprudence is the general or theoretical part of law as a discipline. A theoretical question is no more and no less than a question posed at a relatively high level of generality or abstraction.[6] The most abstract kinds of questions are conveniently characterized as 'philosophical'. Some topics, such as theories of justice, questions of metaphysics or of meta-ethics, belong to legal philosophy in this restricted sense. Some questions, such as 'what constitutes a valid and cogent argument on a question of law in the context of adjudication?' are in part philosophical, but they also involve elements about which philosophers have no special expertise, such as the nature of adjudication or the distinction between questions of law and questions of fact.

Jurisprudence, in this view, can be viewed as a heritage, as an ideology, and as the activity of theorizing, that is posing, reposing, answering, and arguing about general questions relating to the subject-matters of law as a discipline. The idea of heritage emphasizes continuity. The idea of ideology, in a non-pejorative sense, links one's beliefs about law to one's more general beliefs about the world – whether or not they are systematic; and in the Marxist pejorative interpretation of the term, the notion of ideology is a healthy reminder of the close connection between belief, self-interest, prejudice and delusion.

Jurisprudence has a number of jobs or functions to perform to contribute to the health of the discipline of law: constructing whole views or total pictures (the synthesizing or mapping function); elucidating, constructing, and refining concepts; developing normative theories, middle order hypotheses, and general working theories for participants; intellectual history; and critically examining the underlying assumptions of different kinds of discourse of and about law.

The selection of essays in Part A reflects the fact that, when teaching jurisprudence in the United Kingdom and the United States, I have deliberately focused on a few, usually short, texts in the Anglo-American tradition. 'The Great Juristic Bazaar' refers to a panoramic view of legal thought in the world as a whole. That is useful for setting a very broad context. But in teaching jurisprudence I have generally followed the precept: 'Think global, but focus local.' Concentrating on a few texts from one particular tradition has several advantages. First, it helps one to avoid the pitfalls of sacrificing depth to coverage. Second, it makes it possible to relate the texts to each other and to provide an historical perspective by telling a coherent story about the development of English, and later American, legal thought from about 1750 to the present day. This can supplement the provision of a more specific context for each text. Third, the relevance of a jurisprudence course to the rest of the curriculum is made clearer if it provides a coherent historical and theoretical background to the intellectual milieu in which the students are learning about law.

This is, of course, only one worthwhile approach among many to teaching jurisprudence. It involves some costs, not least in terms of omissions. However, the approach suits the particular learning objectives that I have tried to pursue. Here I have been a loyal disciple of Karl Llewellyn, who argued that the main function of a jurisprudence course should be to help each student relate his or her values, ideas and experience developed in other spheres of activity to their ideas about law.[7] In this view, such a course should be an exercise in self-definition. By providing an opportunity to integrate one's beliefs about law with one's religious, moral, political and other views, a successful course should result in a critical appraisal and development of both. It can lay a foundation, if not for a *waltenshaung*, at least for critical self-awareness about one's own 'legal philosophy'.[8]

Conversational Reading

This personal approach requires a particular method of using and reading juristic texts. For this purpose one reads not solely or even mainly to learn *about* particular texts or jurists. Instead one reads them dialectically or conversationally to clarify one's own views on significant general questions relating to law. To adopt an earlier formulation: '[I]t is the study of issues-via-texts, not intellectual history or the study of texts for their own sake, that provides the main educational justification for paying attention to our intellectual heritage.'[9]
Several of the essays included here develop ideas about method in relation to three main themes: First, in self-conscious reading of juristic texts, it helps to distinguish between genuinely historical reading, as exemplified by J. G. A. Pocock, Quentin Skinner and most contemporary Bentham scholars, and dialectical reading the purpose of which is to clarify one's own ideas. To 'converse' with Bentham or Llewellyn or even Hart in 2001 is inevitably to some extent anachronistic. Terms like 'contemporary significance' are seductive, but unclear.[10] For example, if one is reading Bentham's *Anarchical Fallacies* in 2001 in order to clarify one's own views on natural and other non-legal rights today, with whom is one conversing? The historical Bentham situated in a specific context? A modern Benthamite, who is familiar with the literature, debates and legal developments since Bentham's time? Or is one considering the implications of the text itself for contemporary issues? Each of these perspectives is significantly different and, as we shall see, each is problematic.
A second theme concerns charity in interpretation. Some of these essays can be read as a reaction against bad habits in jurisprudence: for example, caricaturing an author's or opponent's views; false generalization through talking inappropriately of 'schools', 'isms' and ists' without referring to any specific texts;[11] conflating disagreement and difference; and various

kinds of false polemics. If the purpose of reading a juristic text is to clarify one's own position, it is foolish to set up soft targets to attack. Debating with idiots is rarely fruitful. It pays to be fair to the author and 'true to the text'.

For purposes of conversational reading, one should give due regard to the historical context, the author's main concerns, what is actually said in the text, what makes the best sense of it, and what might be possible implications and applications of the ideas so interpreted.[12] So, conversational reading does not mean neglecting either history or careful scrutiny of the text, but it does involve choosing an interpretation that the reader thinks is the least vulnerable.

Charitable reading can draw one quite far away from both text and context. If one's starting-point is some such question as: 'Am I a utilitarian?' or 'Do I believe in natural rights?', then it is sensible to ask further: 'What do I think is the least vulnerable version of utilitarianism or natural rights theory?' For eaxample, the first six or seven chapters of Bentham's *An Introduction to the Principles of Morals and Legislation* are notoriously easy to criticize. One may conclude that the best historical interpretation of the text is not the least vulnerable version and that, for some purposes, one should focus on the latter rather than the former. If one is clear about what one is doing, this approach is both legitimate and more fruitful than careful historical exegesis or artificially speculating about what Bentham might have said if he were alive today.

A third, related theme is the importance of clarifying one's standpoint as a reader, analyst, or critic. This idea is elaborated at length in chapters 2 and 3, and informs most of the other chapters. The central thesis is that law is a participant-oriented discipline and a great deal of legal, including juristic, discourse assumes the standpoint of some participant in one or more kinds of legal action; that it is important to distinguish between different kinds of participants and observers and to avoid shifting standpoint unconsciously.

Four Jurists

Part A mainly deals with a few canonical figures and texts in the heritage of Anglo-American jurisprudence. Three jurists played a significant part in my intellectual development: at Oxford, Herbert Hart first aroused my interest in legal theory and provided a model for precision and clarity of thought; in Chicago, Karl Llewellyn opened my eyes to wider horizons, built important bridges between theory and practice, and treated reason and imagination in law as complementary. His law jobs theory provided a framework for a broad and flexible vision of law. For the past thirty years, in addition to teaching and writing about Jeremy Bentham, I have been closely involved with the slow process of producing a definitive edition of his *Collected Works*. Since moving to University College London in 1983, I have been surrounded by leading Bentham scholars and have been constantly reminded of his presence by Bentham's himself, sitting on display in South Cloisters.[13]

A fourth, more shadowy, figure is Oliver Wendell Holmes Jr. I have regularly used 'The Path of the Law' in teaching jurisprudence in several countries, exploring with my students the mysteries of this cryptic text and its even more enigmatic author.

I have been intimately involved with all four jurists over long periods of time as student, teacher, thinker and critic. I was taught by Hart and Llewellyn and later came to know each of them quite well – in Llewellyn's case largely through putting his papers in order and writing his intellectual biography. I have spent many hours with Bentham's manuscripts and more with problems connected with the preparation of *The Collected Works*. Like many others, I have been fascinated by the mysteries surrounding Holmes both as a person and a thinker.

The price of intimacy can be a loss of detachment. Discipleship can take many forms without necessarily being Oedipal.[14] I have generally used Bentham and Holmes as sounding-boards, Hart as a kind of analytical conscience, and Llewellyn as a stimulator. All have my respect, but I have not been an uncritical disciple. There are three main reasons for this. First, although they worked within a broadly shared intellectual tradition, all four are quite different thinkers. Hart and Llewellyn reacted differently to Holmes. Llewellyn distanced me from Hart and the kind of analytical philosophy that he represented.[15] Bentham is more systematic and more intellectually ambitious than Llewellyn. I share with many Bentham scholars a deep ambivalence towards their subject, for it is true to say that few Benthamists are Benthamites.[16] Much the same applies to Holmes' scholarship. Second, both as a scholar and a teacher I have regularly been involved in extended conversations with each of these mentors, who in my mind have also been in regular conversation with each other. My main concern has been to build on the work of my teachers, especially Hart and Llewellyn, but to go beyond them

Another factor contributing to a relatively detached stance in relation to the Anglo-American tradition is more personal. I was born in East Africa and early in my career I taught jurisprudence for almost seven years in Sudan and Tanzania. In such contexts, persistent questions arise about the relevance of Anglo-American jurists to African conditions and problems. From that kind of vantage point and perspective the Anglo-American tradition is just one among many and in some respects it can seem quite limited, parochial and even ethnocentric. Bentham, Holmes, Hart, and Llewellyn, despite their differences, all belong to a single tradition that is limited both geographically and temporally. They were, moreover, all white, male, positivist, and 'modern'. As a scholar I can justify focusing on a quite narrow tradition. It is also reasonable to require British students to study their own tradition in some depth especially if the main alternative is a superficial Cook's tour of Schools or Great Legal Traditions of the World.[17] However, it usually pays to locate specific texts in some broader context. Chapters 9 and 10 break out of the confines of a single intellectual tradition to view our heritage of legal thought from a global perspective.

Individual essays in context: Part A

The context of each chapter warrants a brief comment. Chapter 2 was written as a contribution to a series run by the *Journal of Law and Society* on 'a seminal work in one's intellectual development'. It is included here as it outlines some recurrent concerns, it summarizes my view of jurisprudence as an activity, and it introduces the concept of standpoint which is central to much of my work. Although it was written recently, the essay harks back to the start of my career as a jurist and gives some indication of where I am coming from.

'The Bad Man Revisited' was written in 1973, shortly after I had completed *Karl Llewellyn and the Realist Movement*. In that work I had approached Llewellyn on three levels – the historical, the analytical and the applied – but this essay was my first attempt to use this approach self-consciously. It was also an important vehicle for developing the concept of standpoint.[18]

Chapter 4 contains a general appraisal of Herbert Hart, written in 1978. Hart had resigned from the Corpus Chair of Jurisprudence in Oxford in 1968, initially to work on the Bentham edition and later to be Principal of Brasenose College, Oxford. To mark his seventieth birthday in 1977 he was honoured with a *festschrift* by some of his 'colleagues, former pupils, and devotees.' I had long felt it was unfortunate that after the publication of *The Concept of Law* in 1961, Hart had not moved on to deal with a wider range of issues. Instead, he had stayed with a fairly restricted vision of analytical jurisprudence and had been lured back into obsessive debates with his leading critics, especially Ronald Dworkin.[19] If Hart seemed to have stuck in a quite narrow groove, his most prominent disciples had done him no service by interpreting him even more narrowly in terms of a particular and recondite version of 'legal philosophy'.[20] The publication of the *festschrift* provided an opportunity to present a different assessment of Hart's contributions and to express concern about a growing gap between legal philosophy and the rest of academic law. This gap was doubly unfortunate at a time when the discipline was starting to diversify and to try to establish closer relations with social theory and the social sciences. If Hart had focussed his wonderfully clear mind on some of the issues raised by these new developments, he could have had a much greater influence on academic law in the English-speaking world at a crucial period in its history. Chapter 4 was written under some diplomatic constraints: it is not appropriate for a former pupil publicly to tell his teacher that he is not fully realizing his potential; in attacking the narrow perspective of some of Hart's disciples, I wanted to make clear that I was questioning neither the validity nor the quality of their work, but rather suggesting that there were many more things in jurisprudence than were dreamed of in their philosophy. The substance of the essay still represents my views, but, if it had been written today, it would have been more emphatic about the thesis that a healthy discipline of law needs to be able to draw directly on its theoretical underpinnings.

As Hart found to his cost, labelling theory applies to jurists. *Karl Llewellyn and the Realist Movement* was first published in 1973. For many years after that I was regularly invited to talk and write about Llewellyn, even though my interests had shifted. In 1986 the book was due to be reissued by the University of Oklahoma Press. I decided not to revise it because, echoing Llewellyn, 'the young fellow who wrote [this book] just isn't there any more.'[21] Instead, I used an invitation to give the annual Dewey lecture at New York University School of Law to revisit Legal Realism, to re-emphasize the dangers of generalizing about the Realists, and to gloss what I had said in the book. 'Talk about Realism' (Chapter 5) is the result.

Again, in 1993 I was invited to join in celebrations of the centenary of Llewellyn's birth in Leipzig, Chicago and Miami. On this occasion I decided to focus on one key idea in Llewellyn's law-jobs theory that had passed largely unnoticed – the job of juristic method. This brings into focus the idea of 'legal technology' which has generally been neglected in legal theory. Interpreted charitably, Llewellyn's theory is remarkably useful as a framework for asking questions about the ordering of any group. However, it is quite simple and one part of my unfinished agenda is to refine and develop it in the light of subsequent theorizing in the same broad intellectual tradition and my own experience of using it.[22]

Chapter 7, 'Reading Bentham', is an expanded version of the Maccabean Lecture in Jurisprudence delivered at the British Academy in October 1989. The Academy had for many years been the main external sponsor of the Bentham Project. I was invited specifically to talk about Bentham and, as Chairman of the Bentham Committee, which oversees the preparation of *The Collected Works*, it was appropriate for me to acknowledge the help and support of the Academy. However, the main point of the lecture was to comment on the evolution of Bentham studies from reconstructing and editing the original manuscripts, to textual exegesis, to contextual interpretation, to critical assessments of Bentham's historical and contemporary significance, to ongoing revisionist interpretations of Bentham and Benthamism. This provided an opportunity to link Bentham scholarship to different kinds of reading of texts. In expanded form this paper became the main vehicle for development of my general ideas about reading juristic texts.[23]

In 1996 the two hundred and fiftieth anniversary of Jeremy Bentham's birth was commemorated in several countries. 'Imagining Bentham' (Chapter

8) was a public lecture that launched the year-long celebrations at University College London. In examining both good and bad reasons for celebrating Bentham, the lecture picks up and develops themes from Chapter 7 relating to 'contemporary significance' and imaginary conversations. As it was addressed to a general audience, the lecture assumes less prior familiarity with Bentham than Chapter 7. For this reason some readers may find it easier to read these two chapters in reverse order.

The last section of Chapter 7 had briefly considered Bentham's universal jurisprudence and his claim to be a citizen and legislator of the world.[24] This was my first attempt to come to grips with the implications for legal theory of the increasingly fashionable idea of 'globalization'. This became my main project during much of the 1990s. Chapter 9, 'Globalisation, Pluralism and Post-Modernism: Santos, Haack, and Calvino', deals specifically with some themes that were only latent in my writings before the mid-1990s.In 1995, the Portuguese sociologist of law, Boaventura de Sousa Santos, published *Toward a New Common Sense: Law, Science and Politics in Paradigmatic Transition.* This is still the most ambitious attempt to deal with globalization and law. I found that I agreed with many of Santos' ideas about law, and learned a great deal from them, but the book was enveloped in a Utopian post-modern theory that seemed to involve some dubious philosophy. Struggling with this difficult but important book helped to clarify my own views about both post-modernism and globalization and to reconcile my attraction to the imaginative and complex vision of Italo Calvino with an attachment to a more down to earth form of pragmatic realism, here represented by my friend Susan Haack. Calvino represents an emphasis on imagination and complexity that counterbalances the tendency to hyper-rationalism and reductionism of a Bentham, without any necessary commitment to a dubious anti-rationalist version of post-modernism.[25]

Chapter 9 was first published in my *Globalisation and Legal Theory*, which was the culmination of the first stage of a project that is still in progress. Chapter 10, 'Reviving General Jurisprudence' looks to the future. It outlines an approach to the next stage which focuses on the question: To what extent is it feasible and desirable to generalize about legal phenomena – conceptually, normatively, empirically, or legally – across legal traditions, cultures or even jurisdictions?

The last essay in Part A is the original paper on 'The Great Juristic Bazaar' (Chapter 11). The story behind this may be of interest. In 1977 I had accepted an invitation to attend the World Congress on Philosophy of Law and Social Philosophy in Sydney. The theme of the Congress was 'A General Theory of Law for the Modern Age.' As the deadline for papers approached, I had not yet settled on a topic. Then, fired by some obscure excitement, I sat down and wrote my contribution in only a few days – a most unusual experience. The abstract of the paper read: 'While preparing to write a paper for the World Congress, the author lapsed into a dream. So he reports on what he saw in the dream.'

I was rather pleased with the result. The organizers had asked authors to classify their offerings according to a preliminary scheme that determined when the paper would be discussed. Tongue in cheek, I graded my paper A1. This meant that it would be scheduled for the very first substantive session of the Congress. I despatched the paper and thought no more about it.

I stopped in Sydney en route to Papua New Guinea three weeks before the World Congress was due to start. I then learned that some of the Organizing Committee had interpreted the paper as an offensive attack on the Congress and one member, a prominent judge, had recommended that it should be rejected. Rejection would have been embarrassing as I would have had to withdraw from the Conference, I was already in Australia, and the British Council had paid my fare. Happily, Professor Bill Morison of the University of Sydney, the one person who might reasonably have claimed to have been targetted in the paper, rescued me.[26] I was let off the hook, but Morison got his own back. The Committee had sensibly decided that, as authors could not be trusted to summarize their own work succinctly, each paper would be presented by someone else in 5–10 minutes. Morison arranged that he should be the person to present my paper and at the first session he did a splendid hatchet job in the form of a satire on a satire.
The Committee was not alone in interpreting the paper as offensive and subversive. A young radical judge had pirated it and circulated it to trade unionists and other left-wing circles in Sydney, suggesting that this was a direct frontal attack that showed up the Congress as a circus of bourgeois mystification. The judge had also arranged that she should be one of the co-chairs of the first session and she asked the very first question of the Congress, inviting me to confirm her interpretation. To her great chagrin I replied along the following lines: 'The paper reports a dream. The interpretation of dreams is a notoriously subjective matter. It is for readers rather than the author to interpret the text.' The judge was furious and for the rest of the Congress took every opportunity to berate me for a craven bourgeois liberal cop-out.

In retrospect, I think that my response was appropriate. I am not necessarily the best person to interpret the text or its motives. Of course, an author can provide some background facts. First, I was not consciously attacking the Congress as such nor the papers submitted to it, which I had not seen at the time of writing. I was critical of the pretensions and reductionism of its title, 'A General Theory of Law for the Modern Age', but my targets were much broader than that. Second, at the time, I was particularly irritated about the persistence of bad habits and false polemics in juriprudential writing generally – a recurrent theme in other essays in this book. But that alone does not fully explain the underlying passion of the piece. Third, the title 'World Congress' stimulated me to think about a total picture of legal theorizing in (rather than for) the world as a whole. This in turn sharpened my awareness of the parochialism and narrowness of much of the Anglo-American tradition of theorizing within which I was working, Bentham and Llewellyn excepted. This is illustrated by our collective ignorance of and indifference to other traditions of legal thought, in Europe, the Middle East and less favoured parts of the world. Later, when talk of 'globalization' came into vogue, I was stimulated to reinterpret the paper in such terms. Finally, my initial reaction to both the Organizing Committee and the judge was that they were being heavy and humourless. Perhaps a better sub-text is that jurisprudence can be fun.

These tid bits may provide a partial context for reading the paper, but they neither explain its motives nor provide a basis for a single interpretation. When I use it in teaching, I usually maintain a Sphinx-like demeanour, because unprompted student responses tend to be more varied and more interesting than any quasi-authoritative interpretation that I could provide. There is something to be said for the idea of the death of the author.

Part B: Narrative

The subject of narrative in law picks up a thread that was latent in most of Part A – the tension between reason and imagination in legal discourse. In 1986 the French philosopher and phenomenologist, Paul Ricouer, visited the University of Warwick as a Visiting Professor. His main legacy was a long-running workshop in 1986–87 on 'Narrative as an Instrument of Culture'. The organizers of the workshop, Cristopher Nash and Martin Warner, interpreted this largely in terms of the culture of academic disciplines. They invited a variety of specialists to discuss the role of narrative in their own field. For this purpose, disciplines could be roughly divided into obvious, moderately obvious, and not obvious. It is obvious that narrative and story-telling play a major part in literature, theology and history; it was not then obvious that narrative played any significant role in economics or mathematics or geography or the physical sciences. Law, anthropology and philosophy might be thought to fall somewhere in between. Several of the contributors reported that they had not thought about the topic before, but as soon as it was raised, they noticed narrative everywhere, including in some unlikely places.[27]

Stories had been considered in a variety of legal contexts, but never before in relation to law as a whole. At the time, there was not a widespread realization of the pervasiveness of narrative throughout most forms and contexts of discourse. Once asked, however, the question seemed interesting. This was certainly the case in law.

The story is told that the organizers first approached Lord Denning suggesting that, since he was the greatest legal story teller of his generation, it would be wonderful if he would visit Warwick to discuss the role of story telling in judging and advocacy and to share some of his secrets. Denning agreed with the premise, but declined the invitation on the ground that he was too old to travel to Warwick.[28] So the organizers had to look elsewhere.

Since it was clear that no one person could substitute for Lord Denning, they invited two academic lawyers: Bernard Jackson, who had done pioneering work in semiotics,[29] and myself, as an ex-Warwick person with an interest in proof and fact-finding. The question, 'What is the role of narrative in law?', was new to me. But as soon as I thought about it, I found stories and narrative everywhere: Lord Denning's famous card index of jokes for after dinner speeches, barristers' war stories, and accounts of *causes célèbres* were just the tip of the iceberg. Wherever I looked, narrative seemed to be pervasive, even in areas in which I had specialized. The law reports, Karl Llewellyn's idea of 'situation sense', Wigmore's substitution of charts for 'the narrative method', psychologists' accounts of how jurors decide, the distinction between atomism and holism, and my own use of stories in teaching were all familiar examples that I had not previously considered from this perspective.[30] 'Lawyers' Stories' was the first outcome of this new line of enquiry. I have continued to think, teach and write about the topic ever since, mainly in relation to evidence and proof.

Since the mid-1980s concern with narrative has become fashionable in many enclaves of academic law. As with new fashions, it has attracted its share of exaggeration and distortion: for example, 'narrative' is widely assumed to be a Good Thing; its importance and power have often been exaggerated; and terms like 'story', 'narrative' and 'scenario' have been used loosely and expansively, sometimes extending to cover almost any kind of discourse. Inadvertently, I found myself swimming against the tide: I insisted from the start on a thin definition of 'story' and on restricting 'narrative' to stories[31] – one does not narrate situations, scenarios, or chronological tables. It is also useful to distinguish conceptually between narrative and argument.[32] A central theme of the essays in Part B is that although stories may be psychologically necessary for making sense of some event or situation, in practice they are potentially very subversive. They can be used to sneak in unwarranted or invented facts by innuendo or confabulation or to fill in 'gaps' in the evidence; they tend to undermine conventional distinctions between fact and value and between questions of fact and questions of law; they mock important principles, such as 'Judge the act, not the actor' or 'every material fact should be warranted by evidence'. In short, we seem to need stories, but they are excellent vehicles for cheating.[33]

By criticizing some potential abuses of narrative, I may sometimes have given the impression that I am hostile to 'the narrative turn' in legal theory. This is not so. I fully accept that one reason why narrative is important is precisely because it challenges certain abstract formalistic and amoral tendencies in legal thought. As Gyora Binder puts it:

> Of course, while fiction is always narrative, narrative is not always fictional. Nevertheless, the association of narrative with fiction identifies it with imaginative literature. To call a story a narrative is

> to emphasize the imaginative activity of a narrator. We expect a 'narrative' account of events, even if factual, to reflect a particular, and often highly imaginative point of view.[34]

Similarly, while I have sometimes been critical of the more self-indulgent or dilettantish aspects of the 'law and literature movement', I think that it is generally a welcome development, not least because it can be interpreted as 'a humanist response to the perceived deficiencies in both law itself and its current interdisciplinary partner, economics.'[35] In my own work, Llewellyn and Calvino serve as counterpoints to Bentham and Hart, not so much as a humanistic response to hyper-rationalism, but rather to stress the point that reason and imagination are both integral to understanding law.

'Lawyers' stories' (Chapter 12) was a somewhat discursive preliminary exploration of this seductive subject. The next three essays deal with narrative specifically in relation to fact-finding in legal processes. Chapter 13 is an article on *Anchored Narratives*, the English version of a book by three prominent Dutch psychologists that had caused a furore when it was first published in the Netherlands in 1993. The authors had drawn heavily on Anglo-American literature relating to evidence and had applied it to a substantial number of actual cases in the Netherlands. The heat behind the criticism that they had encountered seemed attributable to the combination of (a) non-lawyers (b) presuming to criticize the Netherlands criminal justice system (c) on the basis of foreign theories. From the point of view of Anglo-American evidence theory, the book looked like a fairly straightforward application of familiar ideas to a civil law system and, if the author's accounts were correct, much of their critique seemed justified. However, some of the theorizing was a bit simple. In writing this comment, I was as anxious to suggest that much of the Dutch reviewers' criticism was misconceived as to point out faults in the book. The main interest in the present context is that *Anchored Narratives* illustrates how well some key common law ideas about evidence and narrative travel across the common law/ civil law divide.

One of the central themes of *Anchored Narratives* was that very often 'good stories push out true stories'. In Chapter 14 this is developed in a light-hearted vein, drawing on stories that I use in teaching. It is presented as a contribution to a *liber amicorum* for the distinguished Dutch psychologist, Hans Crombag.

Chapter 15 is a succinct restatement of the thesis that both stories and 'common sense' generalizations are 'necessary, but dangerous' in arguing about and deciding disputed questions of fact, but in different ways, and that each is directly connected to the interaction between the general and the particular.[36]

Generality and particularity are also the focus of the last chapter (Ch. 16), this time in relation to precedent. The central question is how far biblical parables and legal precedents can appropriately be interpreted as morality tales. A sub-text of this essay suggests that problems of interpreting theological texts, especially those to which some authority is ascribed, are at least as closely analogous to interpreting legal texts as the more fashionable literary texts.

Intellectual Development and Second Thoughts

> I have found there are only two attitudes I have been able to take toward my own work. The first is to think how shaming, how dreadful, how could I have written such drivel? The second is to think how clever, how witty, how original – I could never write anything so good again. There is nothing in between. (Auberon Waugh, *Will This Do?* (1998 US edn.)

Auberon Waugh was a polemicist and an extremist, but most authors will recognize the sentiment. I would not have selected essays for this volume unless I thought that they were worth republishing. My intellectual development is more clearly marked by shifts in my focus of attention rather than big jumps or sharp recantations.[37] Of course, some of my interests and specific projects have been concurrent, but my scholarly priorities fall fairly clearly into different periods: from 1958 to the late 1960s problems of institution building and legal development in Africa took up most of my energies.[38] Between 1962 and 1972 Karl Llewellyn engaged much of my attention, first putting his papers in order and then writing about him. My main project from 1972 until 1990 focused on theoretical aspects of evidence and proof. In the 1990s I returned to writing about jurisprudence under the general rubric of 'understanding law', with particular reference to globalization. This in turn led to a revival of my African contacts and interests. Throughout my professional life I have taken an active interest in issues of legal education and higher education, first as an activist and latterly writing about many aspects of law as an institutionalized discipline.[39]

Relationship to other works

Nearly all of the essays included here belong to the second half of my career. This book is closely related to four others: *Karl Llewellyn and the Realist Movement* and the three collections of essays mentioned above.[40] Relevant earlier works are cited in the footnotes of each essay, but it may be helpful to say something about the four books and relevant recent publications not included here.

Karl Llewellyn and the Realist Movement (1973) was published before all of the essays in Part A. Chapters 5 and 6 can be read as a gloss on that book. Some particular themes, e.g. on pluralism, precedent, standpoint and R/realism are developed further here. Since 1973 there have been many legal developments and a great deal of new writing about Realism, the

Uniform Commercial Code, and Llewellyn's ideas and personality. Some significant new archival material has been discovered in other collections of papers. There have also been notable intellectual developments in relation to socio-legal studies, economic analysis of law, critical legal studies and post-modernism. All of these are relevant to a reassessment of Llewellyn thirty years on, but they do not wholly supercede *Karl Llewellyn and the Realist Movement,* which is mainly a study of Llewellyn's writings that sticks quite closely to the texts.

Rethinking Evidence (1990) marked the culmination of almost twenty years devoted to exploring what might be involved in reconstructing a particular field as part of the general enterprise of 'broadening the study of law from within'.[41] The project, which continues as a secondary interest, was in part stimulated by the discovery that Bentham had written more about evidence than about any other subject; in part by the challenge of moving to Warwick in 1972, when I chose evidence in response to the question: 'What subject do you plan to Warwickize [– i.e., treat in some broader fashion than has been traditional]?'[42] However, the initial stimulus came from Jerome Frank, who was a hedgehog with one big idea: viz. that disputes about questions of fact are at least as important in practice as disputed questions of law in adjudication and litigation. It is ironic that having devoted almost ten years to working on a foxy jurist, Karl Llewellyn, I spent much of the next twenty years working through the implications of the one big idea of a lesser jurist, Frank's plea to take fact-finding seriously. The overlap between *Rethinking Evidence* and this volume is limited to 'Lawyers' Stories' (Ch. 12). Chapters 13–16 embody further reflections on the subject.

Law in Context: Enlarging a Discipline is a collection of essays dealing with the institutionalized discipline of law in respect of legal education, legal scholarship, and legal theory. The main overlap with this volume relates to the idea of legal theory as the general part of our discipline.[43] Although they are relevant, I have resisted the temptation to include such essays as 'Theory in the Law Curriculum' and 'Evidence and Legal Theory', partly because they are readily accessible, partly because the main ideas are restated in summary form in other essays included here. *Globalisation and Legal Theory* (2000) was written as a series of connected essays dealing with the implications of so-called 'globalization' for the discipline of law and for legal theory. The central argument is that even on a cautious or sceptical interpretation, globalization presents some clear challenges to legal theory. A revival of general jurisprudence and a rethinking of comparative law are needed to provide a coherent basis for the development of a more consistently cosmopolitan discipline.

Like this volume, *Globalisation and Legal Theory* deals in detail with canonical jurists in the Anglo-American tradition, including Bentham, Holmes, Hart, and Llewellyn – who are treated here – and Austin, Holland, Rawls, and Dworkin who are not. However, in *Globalisation and Legal*

Theory these thinkers are considered mainly in relation to the single idea of reviving general, or transnational, jurisprudence whereas here the treatment is broader. The main overlap is Chapter 9. Although published first, much of *Globalisation and Legal Theory* can be read as a sequel to this book. Chapter 10 is a bridge to my ongoing work in this area.

To conclude. This work is not a survey of the whole juristic bazaar, but rather a guided tour of part of his home territory by a specialist. This Introduction and chapter 2 are personal and semi-autobiographical, because it is useful to know something about the background, concerns and biases of one's guide. By now it should be clear that I am a jurist rather than a philosopher. That is to say, my primary discipline is law and law is my focus. Of course, philosophy has a direct bearing on the enterprise of understanding law, but so do many other disciplines. Of course, my own assumptions and presuppositions are subject to philosophical scrutiny. But I believe that many jurisprudential puzzlements are not primarily philosophical puzzlements.. I work within a recognizable Anglo-American tradition in which my main teachers have been three mainstream jurists. I am not an uncritical disciple of any of them, and legal anthropology, my African background, and contemporary intellectual trends have also influenced my views. Scratch me and you will find a common lawyer, a weak positivist (closer to Neil MacCormick than Herbert Hart), a modified consequentialist (again more modified than Hart), an innocent realist in the vein of Susan Haack and Charles Sanders Peirce and a fairly traditional, liberal intellectual in the tradition of John Stuart Mill, mildly sceptical, but I hope reasonably progressive. I am sympathetic to imaginative post-modernism in the style of Italo Calvino, but reject anti-rationalist post-modernism and strong versions of cultural, epistemological and ethical relativism. I am a legal realist in that I believe that understanding law involves studying it in context – historical, social, political, and cultural – and being concerned both with legal doctrine and the law in action, with what happens as well as what is meant to happen. This catalogue of my biases and background is relevant to interpreting what I say, and may be appropriate in a work that emphasizes a self-conscious approach to reading and using texts. But, unless one carries self-reflexivity to an extreme, a good guide fades into the background and focuses attention on the objects of the tour – in this case two stalls in a great bazaar set in the context of our vast heritage of legal thought.

Notes

[1] This Introduction contains cross-references to four other works: William Twining, *Karl Llewellyn and the Realist Movement* (Weidenfeld and Nicolson, 1973, U. Of Oklahoma Press, 1985) (hereafter *KLRM*), *Rethinking Evidence* (Blackwell, 1990, Northwestern UP, 1994), (hereafter *RE*), *Law in Context: Enlarging a Discipline* (Oxford University Press, 1997) (hereafter, *LIC*), and *Globalisation and Legal Theory* (Butterworth, 2000 and Northwestern UP, 2001) (hereafter, *GLT*).

[2] Peter Langer, 'Sociology – Four Images of Organized Diversity', in Lloyd Rodwin and Robert M. Hollister (eds) *Cities of the Mind* (Plenum, 1984) Ch.6.

[3] On analogies between cities and legal orders see further *GLT* Ch. 6.s.6, esp. pp. 170–73.

[4] Op. cit. n.1.

[5] For fuller accounts see further *RE* 343–5, *LIC* Ch. 6 and 7, and *GLT* 10–13.

[6] It is important to distinguish between generality in respect of levels of abstraction and of geographical reach. Mobile phones or the Internet have wide geographical reach without being very abstract; terms like 'due process' or 'seisin' are quite abstract but rather local. In the Anglo-American tradition the term 'general jurisprudence', contrasted with 'local' or particular jurisprudence, refers to geographical reach rather than level of abstraction. Often, however, generalization involves abstraction.

[7] K. N. Llewellyn, 'The Study of Law as a Liberal Art' in *Jurisprudence: Realism in Theory and Practice* (U. Chicago Press, 1962) Ch. 17 and 'A Required Course in Jurisprudence', (1940) first published in William Twining (ed.) *Legal Theory and Common Law*, (Blackwell, 1986) Ch. 14. See further *LIC* Ch.7, esp. 141–2.

[8] The much quoted statement by Filmer Northrop expresses this view well: 'To be sure, there are lawyers, judges and even law professors who tell us that they have no legal philosophy. In law, as in other things, we shall find that the only difference between a person 'without a philosophy' and someone with a philosophy is that the latter knows what his philosophy is and is, therefore, more able to make clear and justify the premises that are implicit in his statement of the facts of his experience and his judgment about those facts.' F. Northrop, *The Complexity of Legal and Ethical Experience* (Little, Brown, 1959) p.6.

[9] *LIC* 139.

[10] Chapter 7 below, n.53

[11] This point has recently been emphasized by Joseph Raz: '[O]ne of the unattractive tendencies of contemporary legal and political philosophy [is when a critic] does not discuss anyone's views, but a family of views. This allows one to construct one's target by selecting features from a variety of authors so that the combined picture is in fact no one's view, and all those cited as adhering to it would disagree with it.' 'Postema on Law's Autonomy and Public Practical Reasons: A Critical Comment', 4 Legal Theory, 1 (1998).

[12] See below, Chapters 3 and 45.

[13] On the 'auto-icon', see below Ch.8.

[14] See R. Tur and W. Twining (eds) *Essays on Kelsen* (Oxford University Press, 1986), Introduction.

[15] I would not presume to compare myself to John Stuart Mill, but there is one analogy. Mill found in Wordsworth and Coleridge important dimensions of human experience that were lacking in Benthamism. Similarly I found that Llewellyn gave play to imagination and intuition that were conspicuously absent from the English analytical tradition. In time Mill returned to a modified utilitarianism and to a more humane rationalism. After an initial phase of over-reaction, I did not completely reject the analytical approach represented by Hart; rather I devoted a good deal of energy to trying to reconcile Hart and Llewellyn.

[16] On 'Benthamic ambiguity' see Ch. 7, text at n.40.

[17] This is not intended as a criticism of the enterprise of constructing total pictures of law in the world (see *GLT* 150–53), nor of such works as H. Patrick Glenn's excellent

Legal Traditions of the World (Oxford University Press, 2000), but rather of approaches to the study of jurisprudence that sacrifice depth and accuracy to 'coverage'.

[18] 'The Path of the Law' is sometimes called 'the *Hamlet* of Jurisprudence'. I have returned to it again and again. At a conference to mark the centenary of its publication (1996/7) I revisited it once more. The resulting paper, 'Other People's Power', builds on and extends 'The Bad Man Revisited', with particular reference to positivism. It is not included here as it is readily available elsewhere (63 Brooklyn L. Rev.189 (1997) and *GLT* Ch.5).

[19] These debates continued until his death, culminating in his posthumous Postscript to *The Concept of Law* (Oxford University Press, 1994), perhaps his weakest work (discussed in 'General and Particular jurisprudence: Three Chapters in A Story', *GLT* Ch.2 and *LIC* Ch.8).

[20] See below Ch. 4. A recent example of the equation of 'jurisprudence' with a quite narrow conception of 'legal philosophy' is Brian Leiter, 'Patterns of American Jurisprudence' (book review) 17 Oxford Jo. Legal Studies 367 (1997).

[21] Echoing Llewellyn's Foreword to the second edition of *The Bramble Bush* (Oceana, 1951).

[22] See *GLT* 75ff.

[23] On my other writings about Bentham, see the footnotes of Ch.6 and *GLT* Ch.4.

[24] See now, J. Bentham, '*Legislator of the World': Writings on Codification, Law, and Education* (ed. P. Schofield, Oxford University Press, 1998) and P. Schofield, 'Bentham: Legislator of the World', (1998) 51 CLP Ch. 4.

[25] On Calvino see also *RE* 367–8, *GLT* Ch.7.

[26] Morison was a devotee of John Austin and, strangely, of Lasswell and McDougal, all of whom might be spotted in 'The Great Juristic Bazaar'. The link appears to be the Australian philosopher, John Anderson, see W. Morison, 'Law and Images of History' 11 Sydney L. Rev. 114 (1986).

[27] Some of the papers were collected in Cristopher Nash (ed.) *Narratives in Culture* (Routledge, 1986). On the role of narrative in a less obvious discipline see Donald McCloskey, id. Ch. 1 and *The Rhetoric of Economics* (University of Wisconsin Press, 1985).

[28] Subsequently four of us travelled to Lord Denning's home in Whitchurch to interview him about story-telling. The story of that memorable occasion has yet to be told in print.

[29] B. S. Jackson, *Semiotics and Legal Theory* (Routledge, 1985). Subsequently Jackson has developed his ideas in *Law, Fact and Narrative Coherence* (Deborah Charles, 1988) and *Making Sense in Law* (Deborah Charles, 1995).

[30] When I was invited to contribute to the workshop most areas of academic law had not yet been touched by 'the narrative turn'. To be sure, James Boyd White had done pioneering work on law and literature (1973) (1984), Bennet and Feldman (1981) and Hastie and Pennington (1983) had highlighted story construction by jurors, Bernard Jackson had done pioneering work in semiotics (Jackson 1985) and Robert Cover's 'Nomos and Narrative' (97 Harvard L. Rev. 5 (1974)) had already attracted a following. But these scattered efforts had not yet come together in a general movement focusing on law, literature and narrative. For bibliographical references up to 1989, see below, Ch.12.

[31] On temporality, connectedness, and particularity as necessary ingredients of 'story' see below Ch.12.

[32] For a similarly sceptical perspective, see Michael Bell, 'How Primordial is Narrative?' in Nash (ed. 1986), op.cit. Ch. 8.

[33] An interesting point, not developed here, relates to professional ethics. One teaches students *how* to construct and criticize arguments, but one talks *about* stories rather than teaching skills of story telling and construction. (E.g. D. Binder and P. Bergman, *Fact Investigation: From Hypothesis to Proof* (West, 1984), Anderson and Twining, *Analysis of Evidence*, (Little, Brown and Butterworth, 1991; Northwestern University Press, 1998). One possible reason for this may be that one instinctively feels that these are 'non-rational' means of persuasion. (cf. Plato's *Gorgias*) However, if the thrust of the narrative turn is correct in emphasizing the important role of stories and related discourses as aids to understanding and communication, then developing skill in constructing and presenting stories should be as desirable as developing skills of clear thinking and argumentation, provided of course that one distinguishes between ethical and unethical or dubious uses of both.

[34] Gyora Binder, 'The Law-as-literature Trope' in Michael Freeman and Andrew Lewis (eds.) *Law and Literature* (Current Legal Issues 1999, vol. 2, Oxford University Press).

[35] Anthony Julius, Introduction to Freeman and Lewis (eds.) (1999) op.cit.

[36] A longer treatment of this subject, in relation to the Netherlands, is 'Necessary but Dangerous? Generalizations and Narrative in Argumentation about 'Facts' in Criminal Process' in M. Malsch and J.H. Nijboer (eds.) *Complex Cases: Perspectives on the Netherlands Criminal Justice System* (Thela Thesis, Amsterdam, 1999) at 69–98

[37] My main regret is not to have been more forceful, or rather more persuasive, when diverging from the mainstream or subverting orthodoxy. I have been frustrated when my contemporaries have persisted in error after I have revealed certain widespread views to be fallacies: for example, the kinds of false generalizations and assumptions that occur when people think and talk in terms of schools and isms (such as the fallacy that American Realism was solely about appellate judicial processes – see Chapter 5); the continued use and over-use of terms such as 'thinking like a lawyer' and 'legal reasoning' to refer to questions of law, when it is clear that lawyers think and reason about many kinds of issues, especially questions of fact (*LIC* 20–21); and the tendency to underestimate the variety of conditions giving rise to doubt in interpretation and the rich variety of different techniques for 'handling' precedents in reasoning about questions of law (see Chapter 16).

[38] *LIC* Ch.1 contains a longer autobiographical sketch.

[39] In particular, *LIC* and *Blackstone's Tower* (Sweet and Maxwell, 1994)

[40] See n.1 above.

[41] This project has resulted in six books to date: *Facts in Law* (ed., Franz Steiner Verlag, 1983); Rethinking *Evidence* (Blackwell 1990, Northwestern 1994); *Theories of Evidence: Bentham and Wigmore* (Weidenfeld and Nicolson, 1985, and Stanford UP, 1986), *Analysis of Evidence* (with Terence Anderson, Weidenfeld and Nicolson, 1991, Little, Brown, 1991, Northwestern UP, 1998), *Evidence and Proof* (ed. with Alex Stein, Dartmouth, 1992) and *Evidence and Inference in History and Law* (ed. with I. Hampsher-Monk, Northwestern UP, forthcoming, 2002).

[42] *LIC* 13–15.

[43] In Continental Europe terms such as 'théorie génèrale du droit' and 'algemeine rechtstheorie' are often used to refer to an intermediate level of abstraction located between abstract philosophy and concrete doctrinal exposition and analysis. In the Anglo-American

tradition generality more often refers to geographical reach: for example, Bentham contrasts general or universal jurisprudence with 'local' (e.g. *An Introduction to the Principles of Morals and Legislation* (ed. Hart and Burns, Athlone Press, 1970) at 294–5). The two referents of generality overlap, but they are not co-extensive: for example, mobile phones are far from abstract but have a wide geographical reach, whereas such ideas as seisin or restitution are abstract, but quite local.

[2]
R.G. Collingwood's Autobiography: One Reader's Response

Once upon a time a workshop on legal and political theory was held at a famous hotel in Scotland. I was among those who allowed curiosity to trump potential political scruples about the provenance of the funding. Perhaps academics have a right to stay at Gleneagles once in a lifetime. And maybe such workshops need some ideological balance. Forget the dubious rationalizations. I was there.

The oldest and most eminent presence was Michael Oakeshott. In an interval before lunch he courteously invited two younger persons, both jurists, to join him. He started the conversation by turning to my colleague and asking: 'What work was seminal in your intellectual development?' John Finnis' response was immediate: 'R.G. Collingwood's autobiography. I read it when I was about twelve'.[1] Oakeshott turned to me with the same question. Resisting the urge to say 'snap', I replied almost as crisply: 'Collingwood's autobiography. I read it when I was almost twenty-one.'[2]

This series is an invitation to autobiography – in this instance, an unreliable memoir about reading the autobiography of a philosopher who warned of the dangers of relying on memory. Your importunate editor has made me reflect on this exchange. Why from many possibilities choose Collingwood? One thing is clear: I had been making the same claim for years, so this was not imitation nor was it necessarily a complete coincidence.[3]

1 R.G Collingwood, *An Autobiography* (1939). References are to the Oxford reprint of 1970 (hereafter *A.*)

2 This was an actual event. I have had to use what Collingwood called 'interpolation' to reconstruct the details – for example, I do not recall whether Oakeshott used the word 'work' or 'book'. Collingwood believed that it was the task of an historian to reconstruct the past on the basis of evidence, complemented by disciplined imagination. Whether he would have approved of the 'faction' of, for example, Simon Schama's *Dead Certainties* (1991) is unclear, but Schama's approach to history could be interpreted as an extension of Collingwood's ideas.

3 See, below, n. 16.

SOME POTENTIAL RIVALS

So why Collingwood? The first step is to consider some potential rivals. I fell in love with literature, especially Victorian novels, when my godmother read to me from *The Pickwick Papers*.[4] This was in Mauritius in 1940. Evelyn DuBuisson had come to stay with us for a few weeks, but was marooned there by the war for nearly five years. Her reading to me was a great treat, especially when I was allowed in her bed for the purpose. I fell for Mr Jingle, Sam Weller, Mr Tracy Tupman, and Mr Snodgrass – their names, the humour, and the language as much as the stories. Over the next four years she gently extended the range. We read to each other, but I much preferred being read to. I cannot remember what else we consumed, except that I developed a penchant for stories about desert islands, *The Swiss Family Robinson, Treasure Island, Robinson Crusoe*, and above all *The Coral Island*[5] – perhaps not inappropriate in an island cut off by U-boats and the setting for Bernardin de St Pierre's romance, *Paul et Virginie*, which we did not read.[6] My parents thought it a bit precocious for a five year old to have a taste for Dickens, but they treated the practice with amused tolerance. Later my father introduced a rival programme by bringing home from the office one at a time volumes of the eleventh edition of the *Encyclopaedia Britannica*, printed on rice paper and bound in shiny worn black leather. These I was allowed to browse through during tantalizingly short thirty-six-hour periods before each one had to be returned to the office. My systematic grounding in eclecticism started with 'A-Aus'.

In September, 1944 we braved the U-boats and escaped to Durban, which was not 'in the war'. I remember two things. First I was scornful of Durban's beaches which did not compare with Flic en Flac and Blue Bay; and, second, I saw my first book shop. During the war Mauritius had shops, but they did not rise to window displays, certainly not displays of books. That day I bought my first books that did not have to be stamped: 'Passed by the Censor of Mauritius'. Ever since I have spent my pocket-money on books rather than on cars or horses.

4 I still have the same copy: C. Dickens, *The Posthumous Papers of the Pickwick Club*. The edition was published in Wakefield by William Nicholson and sons. It is undated and has tiny print.

5 R.M. Ballantyne, *The Coral Island* (1857). The introduction to the Puffin Classics edition says that Balllantyne 'was one of the first writers to allow children their own adventures, free from adult control.' What I remember best was nude bathing, which was a novel and intriguing idea, but clearly taboo in my family; whether this symbolized liberation or was merely prurient curiosity is unclear. In the 1980s I did some work on localizing legal literature in small jurisdictions, that is jurisdictions with too small a market to sustain a local legal literature – a potentially lifelong project about an almost insoluble problem. It took me to many congenial places, including the Isle of Man, Barbados, Papua New Guinea, Australia, and back to Mauritius. I used to refer to it jokingly as 'my coral island project', but at the time did not make the connection with my childhood fantasies.

6 Mauritius was cut off by the war, but hardly deserted. It later became one of the most highly populous countries in the world, see V.S. Naipaul, *The Overcrowded Barracoon* (1972).

Back in England in late 1944 I suffered the standard fate of colonial waifs and was parked in a boarding-school. At my preparatory school I was unhappy, but this was hardly the school's fault. Indeed, it had some quite civilized ways and was really quite bookish. I remember with pleasure the Headmaster reading aloud to the whole school on Sundays: John Buchan, Dornford Yates, Conan Doyle, Agatha Christie, and P. G. Wodehouse; he even allowed older boys to sample his bookshelves for a quiet period on some evenings. I read the autobiography of a London cabby with the intriguing title *It's Draughty in Front*[7] and part of Virginia Cowles' account of the Spanish Civil War, *Looking For Trouble*.[8] The former did not affect my career plans; the latter was incomprehensible, but I still found it fascinating. We were also introduced to Shakespeare. I was cast as Macduff in scenes from Macbeth. We were each given our lines and cues for particular scenes, but no one told us that the play had a story or an ending. Only much later did I also learn that most of my best scenes had been censored, including drink as the provoker of nose-painting, sleep, and urine and 'Macduff was from his mother's womb untimely ripped'. My one big moment was announcing the discovery of Duncan's body:

> Oh horror, horror, horror!
> Tongue nor heart cannot conceive nor name thee.

On the day my horned hat got stuck in the scaffolding and the audience burst into delighted laughter and applause. I did an encore of those two lines, provoking more raucous applause. I retired from playing Shakespeare. This bizarre introduction to the Bard had the merit of focusing attention on the words and the imagery rather than on the story: caviar for the general instead of Lamb. I can still quote my lines *verbatim* and think of downy sleep as death's counterfeit – but it is doubtful whether this was really seminal in my intellectual development.

By the time I moved on to public school I was a poor scholar, but a committed bookworm. The next four years were painful. An enforced classical education may be good intellectual discipline, but it can kill both enjoyment and creativity. What I remember most is the terror and drudgery of a joyless study of the classics – almost the whole expanse of Greek and Roman literature treated as grammar, vocabulary, prosody, and form without regard to aesthetics or significance. What lingers is the vestiges of a puritanical idea that learning involves both discipline and suffering. Sadly, I also have an almost complete emotional block about most of the treasures of classical literature. There were a few exceptions. For example, I enjoyed *The Tempest* as a set book for School Certificate. I did not miss the absence of a story, I grasped that it was about closure, but at the time I failed to make connections with coral islands or colonialism. It is still for me the most resonant Shakespeare play.

7 H. Hodge, *It's Draughty in Front: The autobiography of a London taxidriver* (1938).
8 V. Cowles, *Looking for Trouble* (1941).

I needed to escape from the pains of studying. I soon learned that enthusiasm does not make up for lack of talent on the sports field. Encouraged by a literate older brother I took refuge in reading. This was a jealously guarded private world. Between twelve and twenty and beyond I made as many conquests of books as Don Giovanni boasted in respect of women – and sometimes in the same spirit. But reading was also a comfort, an intellectual adventure, a delight, sometimes even a taste of love. There was a sharp dichotomy between the public world of studying and private reading. Studying Cicero or Caesar or Virgil or Homer or Sophocles or Thucydides or even Aristophanes or Catullus was work and therefore painful. My own reading was voracious, untutored, and eclectic. I learned serendipitously, but I cannot identify one experience that was more significant than my first encounter with *The Pickwick Papers*.

And so to jurisprudence. When I went up to Oxford I had read widely, but not necessarily well. I was bookish, but in two quite different ways. Studying involved discipline and drudgery; reading was personal, exciting, liberating. I had to escape from classics. I had wanted to read history, but chose law to please my father and because my brother promised me his notes. For the first eighteen months, I continued my adolescent separation of reading and studying. I did not learn much law nor read much about it. Wolfgang Friedmann, and to a lesser extent Maine, d'Entrèves and C.K. Allen made an impression, but I did not associate my general reading with learning law. They were two separate worlds. And then in the spring of 1954 I encountered Herbert Hart and I became a jurist.

Hart was elected to the Chair of Jurisprudence in 1952. Soon rumours reached even undergraduate law students that something was afoot. In 1954 I attended Hart's lectures which were precursors of *The Concept of Law*, but it was his inaugural lecture, 'Definition and Theory in Jurisprudence',[9] that really made the difference. I first read it in pamphlet form – how I regret having missed the actual event! – during that summer term. It has been quite widely recognized as one of Hart's major achievements, perhaps more important even than *The Concept of Law*. It is difficult to evoke the impact of this short piece at the time, perhaps because most of the basic ideas are now treated as commonplace in jurisprudence: words do not have proper meanings; questions can be based on false or misleading assumptions and can be posed in ways that fail to express the concerns or puzzlements that may underlie them; many traditional questions in analytical jurisprudence – what is a state? what is law? what is a right? what is a corporate body? – suggest that they are requests for definitions of words, yet the words concerned are familiar; many puzzlements about abstract concepts can be dissolved by Bentham's technique of 'paraphrasis'; 'though theory is to be welcomed, the growth of theory on the back of definition is not'. And so on.

9 H.L.A. Hart, *Definition and Theory in Jurisprudence* (1953). This has been reprinted several times with slight variations.

My initial reaction to reading Hart's lecture was culture shock. It challenged many deeply embedded assumptions about language, meaning, definition, and theory. Not all of the ideas were original, but they were new to me, and generally to the culture of English academic law at the time. Apart from the specific ideas, *Definition and Theory* linked the study of law to what was then a more lively discipline and it informed the academic legal community about 'the revolution in philosophy'. With some guidance from two fellow undergraduates who were studying philosophy, I plunged into a reading binge on writings by members of the contemporary Oxford 'linguistic' school.[10] I spent much of that long vacation wrestling with Hart's lecture – at the time almost his only published work.

In retrospect my first encounter with Hart did at least three things: it persuaded me that the study of law, especially jurisprudence, could be intellectually interesting; it linked jurisprudence to contemporary philosophy; and, via Iris Murdoch, – a friend of Hart's – a further connection was soon made, this time between philosophy and literature.[11] The dichotomy between studying and reading began to break down.

It was because of Hart that I became a legal theorist. The key triggering event was reading his inaugural lecture. Surely that is as seminal as one can expect of any single work. So why did I choose Collingwood? I am not sure that I have the answer. But there are clues, some positive and some negative. The positive significance of Collingwood's *An Autobiography* we will come to shortly. The negative aspect is more difficult. Even though I still rate Hart's 'Definition and Theory in Jurisprudence' as one of the great classics of jurisprudence, in time it left me dissatisfied in important ways. I have written about this at length elsewhere and need not repeat the arguments here.[12] The crux of the matter is that Hart's lecture radically changed the *methods* of analytical jurisprudence, but it left the *agenda* largely the same. He argued that the traditional questions of mainstream jurisprudence needed to be reposed, but he assumed that these were by and large the questions that are at the core of the subject.[13] This assumption I fairly quickly rejected.

10 I was lucky in my guides: one, the late Michael Woods, became an excellent philosophy tutor at Brasenose; the other, Trevor Rutter, obtained a First, but shortly afterwards abandoned philosophy and Oxford for the public service. However, my self-education in philosophy had some harmful effects, on which see my *The Karl Llewellyn Papers* (1968) 5–8.

11 Iris Murdoch's *Under the Net* was first published in 1954, while she was still a Philosophy Fellow at St Anne's College.

12 See, especially, W. Twining, 'Academic Law and Legal Philosophy: The Significance of Herbert Hart' (1979) 95 *Law Q. Rev.* 557, and *Law in Context: Enlarging a Discipline* (1997).

13 In his article on 'Problems of Philosophy of Law' in *The Encyclopedia of Philosophy*, ed. P. Edwards (1967). Hart identified three main groups of problems belonging to the philosophy of law: problems of definition and analysis, problems of legal reasoning, and problems of criticism of law. Hart was careful to acknowledge that this classification was controversial and that no sharp distinctions could be maintained between philosophy of law and what he termed historical and sociological studies. Nevertheless I have consistently maintained that this conception of legal philosophy, let alone of legal theory, cannot provide a satisfactory theoretical foundation for law as a discipline.

Before moving on to Collingwood, let me deal briefly with some other contenders. Within jurisprudence, certain texts have been very important for me: Karl Llewellyn's 'The Normative, the Legal and the Law-jobs' and several of his other writings;[14] some of the works of Wolfgang Friedmann, Max Weber, and Jeremy Bentham; and in different ways writings by Holmes, Fuller, Finnis, Dworkin, and legal anthropologists. In this context I would give Hart's inaugural precedence. My godmother's reading made me into a bookworm, but the fact that she began with *The Pickwick Papers* rather than some other book was incidental. The book shop in Durban was an event rather than a book – and I was probably already hooked. Shakespeare, Shaw, Virginia Woolf, T. S. Eliot, Charles Morgan, Lewis Carroll, Jonathan Swift, *Catch 22*, and Africana in respect of history, exploration, nationalism, colonialism, and ethnography were all important, as were many others, but no one work stands out in its impact.[15] So Hart remains the leading contender. Against this background, we can turn to the Collingwood story.

COLLINGWOOD'S AUTOBIOGRAPHY

Once on a summer's day in 1955 I travelled from Westmoreland to London on a rather slow coach. I had just completed my final examinations at Oxford and was taking a break in the Lake District with my mother. On the journey I started reading R.G. Collingwood's *An Autobiography* and I finished it late that night. Something changed.

Collingwood was born in Coniston in 1889 and died there in 1943.[16] His autobiography was written in his fiftieth year after he had had a stroke and

14 K.N. Llewellyn, 'The Normative, the Legal and the Law-Jobs' (1940) 49 *Yale Law J.* 1355. On other favourites, see my *Karl Llewellyn and the Realist Movement* (1973).

15 This list is arbitrary and snobbish. Patrick Leigh Fermor's account of a similar stock-taking of his reading when he was eighteen takes up five pages (*A Time of Gifts* (1977) ch. 3). My list would in several ways be similar to his: 'The range is fairly predictable and all too revealing of scope, the enthusiasms and limitations . . . of a particular kind of growing up' (id., p. 84). The standard drops steeply after 'highbrow' favourites: in addition to Swift there was *Lilliput*; Biggles preceded Saint-Exupéry; and there was Dornford Yates as well as W.B. Yeats. We were both auto-didacts with a taste for English nonsense verse. The main differences are that I could not hope to emulate Leigh Fermor's prose and he was fortunate in not having his enjoyment of classical Greek and Roman literature killed by instruction.

16 Collingwood had a life-long association with the Lake District, but I did not know that, so this geographical connection is almost certainly a coincidence. It is more likely that I read the book at the suggestion of Michael Woods. Collingwood was not in vogue at the time, although *The Principles of Art* was still discussed. It was quite natural for an Oxonian to read *An Autobiography* early on in a philosophical self-education. Furthermore, Herbert Hart was familiar with Collingwood's work and there is some affinity in their perspectives on questioning. However, Hart and Honoré in *Causation and the Law* (1959) were quite critical of Collingwood's article on attribution of responsibility in causation. This article contains a classic example of differentiation of standpoint. I have found no other explicit citation of him in the indexes to Hart's own books. Robert Moles uses Collingwood's *An Autobiography* as a spring-board for criticizing Hart's reading of Austin: *Definition and Rule in Legal Theory* (1987) especially 2–5, 17.

believed, correctly, that he might not have long to live.[17] It is generally interpreted as providing a narrative of his intellectual development and a summary of work he had not finished in case he did not survive to complete it. That is why a great deal is devoted to the relationship between philosophy and history – his main work on the subject, *The Idea of History*, was edited and published posthumously.

The personal and 'external' lives of most academics are generally rather uneventful. Collingwood's was no exception. Apart from three years in the Admiralty Intelligence Division during the First World War, most of his life was spent as a philosopher in Oxford, except that during many summers he pursued a parallel career as a practising archaeologist, excavating sites to do with Roman Britain. He gained a considerable reputation as an archaeologist and epigrapher and wrote that he had come to realize that his life's work had hitherto been mainly 'an attempt to bring about a rapprochement between philosophy and history'.[18] *An Autobiography* follows his own principles in that it is a narrative reconstruction of the development of his thought – an internal history. It is short, lucid, vehement, and challenging. Controversy has surrounded the validity of his ideas and the accuracy and even the honesty of the book.[19] When I first read *An Autobiography*, I was innocent of these debates and of Collingwood's other writings. I probably did not understand much of it. Why did it make such an impact?

In preparing to write this essay, I jotted down notes on some aspects of my own work that I have associated with Collingwood. I still sometimes refer to particular passages in *An Autobiography*, but I had not read it through for some years. Having just re-read it, I find many more passages that are immediately familiar, with most of which I am in general sympathy.[20]

17 There is an extensive literature about Collingwood and there is an R.G. Collingwood Society which publishes *Collingwood Studies*. For this essay I have relied particularly on E.W.F. Tomlin, *R.G. Collingwood* (1953), A. Donagan, *The Later Philosophy of R.G. Collingwood* (1962), P. Johnson, *R.G. Collingwood: An Introduction* (1998) and S. Toulmin's introduction to the 1978 edition of the *Autobiography*. I cannot claim to be an expert on Collingwood, but over the years I read *The Principles of Art* (1938) and *The Idea of History* (ed. T.M. Knox, 1946), both of which I admired, and *The New Leviathan* (1942), which I disliked and did not finish.

18 *A.*, p. 77.

19 Stephen Toulmin (op. cit., n. 17) emphasizes the painful honesty of the work; Alan Donagan (op. cit., n. 17) claims that much of his narrative is untrue (see p. 619 below). They are probably focusing on different aspects of the work, and hence differing rather than disagreeing.

20 I have never felt much rapport with Collingwood's political views. At the time of its publication, *An Autobiography* caused a furore in Oxford because the author seemed to accuse some philosophers with whom he disagreed to have been 'the propagandists of a coming Fascism.' (p. 167) This was harsh, but Collingwood's strong opposition to appeasement in Oxford, which made him unpopular at the time, was later vindicated. Parts of the last chapter of *An Autobiography* still seem intemperate, but I can now read more sympathetically his accounts of the Spanish Civil War, his ambivalent reading of Marx, and his attack on philosophical detachment as a form of evasion. The general concern to undermine sharp distinctions between 'theory' and 'practice' I still find attractive.

I shall deal with some specific themes that I see as relevant to legal theory below. But the original impact of the book was far greater than the sum of these particular ideas. A Collingwoodian interpretation might be that the book addressed my own concerns in significant ways. At the time I was confused and worried by the fact that, as I moved in and out of several different milieux, people I respected and cared for in each had seemingly irreconcilable attitudes, values, and beliefs about politics, race, religion, and the worthwhileness of intellectual matters. I rationalized these conflicts in terms of 'The Problem of Belief' and it troubled me both emotionally and intellectually. Collingwood taught me that I had been focusing on the wrong question. I had been asking: 'Which of them is right?'; I should have been asking of each: 'What does it mean?'[21] Similarly, I was torn between my parents' concern with practical affairs and my private intellectual leanings. A similar tension is, of course, endemic within the discipline of law. Collingwood fiercely attacked any idea that philosophy, and in particular ethics, should be treated as a subject apart, detached from the world of affairs. He forcefully argued that theory and practice are interdependent. This too was immensely attractive.

On this recent re-reading I also realized for the first time how much Collingwood had anticipated ideas that have since become commonplace or ephemerally fashionable, often in forms that he would not have approved. For example, his 'theory of absolute presuppositions' – the idea that constellations of basic ideas and assumptions replace one another over time – soberly anticipates central aspects of Thomas Kuhn's theory of scientific revolutions, which has too often been vulgarized into equating every seemingly novel idea with a 'paradigm shift'.[22] Some of Collingwood's positions could even be interpreted as early examples of 'postmodernism', or mild cultural relativism, or anti-foundationalism, although he would almost certainly have been scathing about sillinesses associated with such ideas in much current fashion. More obviously, he is a clear precursor of the movement spearheaded by Quentin Skinner to put history back into the history of ideas.[23] And, in an important sense, he believed that historians construct

21 The first ray of light probably flashed at p. 27, where he is talking about teaching Aristotle: 'My plan was to concentrate on the question, "What is Aristotle saying and what does he mean by it?" and to forgo, however alluring it might be, the further question "Is it true?".' Later, in summarizing his theory of absolute presuppositions in relation to metaphysics (see below), he wrote: 'The question what presuppositions underlie the "physics" or natural science of a certain people at a certain time is as purely historical a question as what kinds of clothes do people wear. And this is the question that metaphysicians have to answer. It is not their business to raise the further question whether, among various beliefs on this subject that various peoples hold or have held, this one or that one is true' (p. 66). I am not sure that I understood this then, and I probably do not accept it unreservedly now, but at the time it was cathartic.

22 T. Kuhn, *The Structure of Scientific Revolutions* (1962).

23 Skinner openly acknowledges a general debt to Collingwood, for example, *The Foundations of Modern Political Thought* (1978) vol. 1, xi; compare x, fn. 2.

history using both evidence and imagination.[24] For me, this helps to explain why throughout much of my career many developments, fashions, and fads that have been presented as novel have seemed to me 'old hat'. Collingwood had been there already.

COLLINGWOOD AND LEGAL THEORY

There are other personal aspects that I still find appealing and some stridency of tone that I do not. Collingwood wrote almost nothing about law, but his work has implications for legal theory. Here I shall restrict myself to four particular themes.

First, thinking and other forms of scholarly enquiry are *activities* involving posing and trying to answer *questions*. Collingwood's particular targets were conceptions of history that ignored or obscured the questioning aspects: history as the mere collection and display of facts, or artefacts or other relics; archaeological digging done blindly, without guidance from clear, specific questions;[25] worst of all, 'scissors and paste' history, that is history conceived as knowledge of past events based on authoritative sources.[26] In respect of natural sciences, Bacon and Descartes 'had said very plainly that knowledge only came from answering questions, and that these questions must be the right questions and asked in the right order'.[27] Such questioning activity was not just a preliminary to achieving knowledge (or apprehension or compresence): 'it was only half (the other half being answering the question) of an act the totality of which was knowing'.[28]

Collingwood distinguished sharply between scientific and historical explanation, but he extended some classic ideas about enquiry in the natural sciences to philosophy, history, and thinking generally as activities. From these he developed, controversially, 'the logic of question and answer'.[29] Put simply, this is the thesis that every proposition is the answer to some question

24 See Collingwood, op. cit. (1946), n. 17.

25 '. . . long practice in excavation had taught me that one condition – indeed the most important condition – of success was that the person responsible for any piece of digging, however small or however large, should know exactly why he is doing it . . . "Let us see what we can find out about this site". . . is no more a "question" as I understand that term, than such pseudo-questions as "What is knowledge?", "What is duty", "What is the *summum bonum*?" "What is art?". Like them, it is only a vague portmanteau phrase covering a multitude of possible questions but not precisely expressing any of them.' (*A.*, p. 122). Compare the treatment of 'What is... ?' questions by Hart in his inaugural lecture, op. cit., n. 9. Collingwood's approach to excavation applies to other forms of empirical enquiry, such as criminal investigation. A 'scene of crime' officer who asks 'what have we here?' is less likely to find as much as one who approaches the scene with detailed, sharply focused questions. I am grateful to Detective-Inspector Richard Leary for this example.

26 *A.* throughout, especially chs. 7 and 8.

27 id., p. 25.

28 id., p. 26.

29 id., ch. 5.

and one can only understand and assess a proposition by working back to the question that the maker of the statement was trying to answer.[30] As jurists we do not need to accept Collingwood's thesis *in toto* in order to recognize the significance of the idea that legal theorizing is also in first instance a questioning-and-answering activity rather than a body of knowledge or a collection of 'theories' or even a theatre of debates. From this perspective 'a theory' is a purported answer to a question or a complex of questions; in order to understand the theory one must first identify the question(s).[31]

The second thesis, closely linked to the first, is that 'all history is the history of thought'[32] and 'historical knowledge is the re-enactment in the historian's mind of the thought whose history he is studying'.[33] To understand a naval battle involves understanding the tactics that were used, and to understand these the historian has to reconstruct what was going on inside the heads of key actors set in the context of the time, their perceptions of the situation, and the perspectives of people 'brought up in sailing ships armed with broad-sides of short-range muzzle-loading guns'.[34] This has a direct bearing on what is involved in understanding law. Similarly:

30 A key passage reads as follows: 'Whether a given proposition is true or false, significant or meaningless, depends on what question it was meant to answer; and any one who wishes to know whether a given proposition is true or false, significant or meaningless, must find out what question it was meant to answer.'

Now, the question 'To what question did So-and-so intend this proposition for an answer?' is a historical question, and therefore cannot be settled except by historical methods' (p. 39). The other part of the thesis that in the history of thought as well as action 'we can only know what the problem was by arguing back from the solution' (p. 70). I have never fully accepted the logic of question and answer, as set out in *An Autobiography*, because it seems to be overstated: for example, there are many propositions, such as speech acts, which are not sensibly treated as answers to questions. In most contexts, the statement 'With this ring I thee wed' is not an answer to such questions as 'What are you doing?' or 'What are you wedding me with?' or 'Who are you wedding?', it is a performative. For a balanced discussion of the controversy surrounding 'the logic of question-and-answer' see Johnson, op. cit, n. 17, ch. 5.

31 In this usage a theory can be a hypothetical or an asserted or a reasoned answer to one or more related questions. Collingwood should not be interpreted as being ultra-rationalistic in this context. He emphasizes imagination in history and he is quite explicit that the formulation or reconstruction of questions or problems is neither easy nor an entirely rational process. For example, he describes the early stages of thinking as often involving 'a formless and aimless intellectual disturbance, as if I was wrestling with a fog'. He continues: 'I know that this is what always happens when I am in the early stages of work on a problem. Until the problem has gone a long way towards being solved, I do not know what it is; all I am conscious of is this vague perturbation of mind, this sense of being worried about I cannot say what.' *A.*, pp. 4–5.

32 *A.*, p. 110.

33 id., p. 112.

34 id., p. 58. 'This way of treating other people's thoughts, though logically deducible from my "logic of question and answer", had been my habit long before I began working that logic out. . . . I dare say that I was not more than six or seven when I first saw that the only way to tackle any historical question, such as the tactics at Trafalgar, – I mention Trafalgar, because naval history was a childish passion of mine, and Trafalgar my pet battle – was to see what the different people were trying to do. History did not mean knowing what events followed what. It meant getting inside other people's heads, looking at their situation through their eyes, and thinking for yourself whether the way they tackled it was the right way.'

> Political history is the history of political thought: not 'political theory', but the thought which occupies the mind of a man engaged in political work: the formation of a policy, the planning of means to execute it; the attempt to carry it into effect, the discovery that others are hostile to it, the devising of ways to overcome their hostility and so forth.[35]

Some of the unqualified assertions in *An Autobiography* are vulnerable to quite cogent objections: for example, that Collingwood placed too much emphasis on individual actors, that the seemingly rationalistic psychology neglects the unconscious, and that the argument about inferring problems from solutions leads to an over-emphasis on winners' history. This is not the place to enter into such controversies.[36] However, there is one set of ideas that needs to be clarified, as it has a direct bearing on contemporary issues in jurisprudence. Unalloyed, this summary may suggest that Collingwood's idea of history focuses exclusively on internal events – the conscious thought processes of actors and writers. This is misleading. Collingwood in fact had an 'inside-outside' view of historical events, as is made clear in *The Idea of History*.[37] In brief, he argued that before one can get to the 'inside' of an event, one needs to know what was going on externally – its context. History involves reconstructing the thoughts of actors (including thinkers) in the context of the situation in which they found themselves, especially their own culture, upbringing and mental resources as well as their immediate vantage points and concerns. Collingwood's philosophy of history at the very least provides a starting-point for exploring distinctions between internal and external points of view and between the standpoints of observers and participants. These distinctions tend to be used uncritically rather like mantras in contemporary jurisprudence. They are not co-extensive and both are quite problematic.[38]

Collingwood's philosophy of history was probably the main inspiration for what, for me, has been a key tool of juristic analysis – the concept of standpoint.[39] Although I have written about this in many contexts and texts,

35 id., p. 110. On the participant orientation of much legal discourse, see p. 614 below.

36 See, for example, Donagan, Tomlin, and Johnson (all op. cit., n. 17).

37 'The historian, investigating any event in the past, makes a distinction between what may be called the outside and the inside of an event. By the outside of the event I mean everything belonging to it which may be described in terms of bodies and their movements: the passage of Caesar, accompanied by certain men, across a river called the Rubicon at one date, or the spilling of blood on the floor of the senate-house at another. By the inside of the event I mean that in it which can only be described in terms of thought: Caesar's defiance of Republican law, or the clash of constitutional policy between himself and his assassins.' (Collingwood, op. cit. (1946), n. 17, p. 213.)

38 The internal/external distinction arises in a variety of contexts which need to be differentiated. Closely related to this is the thesis that the tenability and utility of the is/ought distinction which is central to debates about positivism depend on context and standpoint. For example, for most participants normative concerns about role preclude sharp distinctions between is/ought, law/morals, fact/ value – as is illustrated by the normative element in adjudicative determinations of 'fact'. See W. Twining, 'Other People's Power: The Bad Man and English Positivism, 1897–1997' (1997) 63 *Brooklyn Law Rev.* 189, at 217–21 and the longer discussion in B. Tamanaha, *Realistic Socio-Legal Theory: Pragmatism and a Social Theory of Law* (1997) 153–95.

39 Subsequently, I also found much that was helpful in the work of Alfred Schutz, Percy Lubbock, and Erving Goffman.

it is so central to this story that something needs to be said about it. In almost every subject that I teach about – whether jurisprudence, introduction to law, legal method, analysis of evidence, or legal education – I almost invariably set my students to do a simple exercise. A standard version reads as follows:

> Consider the following limerick:
>
> There was a young student of Ealing
> Who got on a bus to Darjeeling
> The sign on the door
> Said 'Don't spit on the floor'
> So he lay back and spat on the ceiling.
>
> A. Write down in order of priority which three of the following propositions are closest to your initial reaction:
> 1. An above/below average limerick.
> 2. There are no buses from Ealing to Darjeeling.
> 3. What immature behaviour/ clever boy!
> 4. Why not spit out of the window?
> 5. The wisest course is to ignore such behaviour.
> 6. He has/ has not violated the rule.
> 7. An example of poor drafting.
> 8. Why 'lay back'?
> 9. What has this to do with law?

In the ensuing discussion, I try to bring out the following main points:
(1) There is a fundamental distinction between the situations of people on the bus (participants) and of those who are outside the limerick (observers).
(2) In legal contexts, as elsewhere, there are many different kinds of participants and many kinds of observers, with varying vantage points, roles, perspectives, resources, and agendas. Participants may watch and think and observers may be involved in action, but the distinction between being on the bus and outside the limerick is crucial, especially in studying law.
(3) Law is a strongly participant-oriented discipline in that a very great deal of legal discourse (both law talk and talk about law) assumes that the speaker is 'on the bus', that is, involved in action as a judge, law-maker, advocate, adviser, expositor,[40] witness, bad man, good citizen or other participant in legal processes or operations. Law students, either explicitly or implicitly, are called on to pretend to be, that is, to adopt the standpoint of, one or other kind of such actors. Less frequently they are asked to adopt various external points of view and these too need to be differentiated. In order to avoid confusion one needs to clarify what precisely is involved in a adopting a particular standpoint in a given context.
(4) In studying law the commonest form of stupidity consists in forgetting who one is pretending to be. Unless one is self-conscious about one's standpoint it is very easy to switch standpoint, inadvertently or imperceptibly, and this can be a great source of muddle for oneself and others. The limerick

40 On expositors as participants, see W. Twining, *Blackstone's Tower* (1994) at 130 ff.

exercise is designed to make it very difficult, but not impossible, to choose from the list three statements that comfortably fit a single standpoint and context.[41] In my experience, the great majority of law students shift from being outside the limerick to being on the bus without realizing that they have done so.

(5) Self-conscious clarification of standpoint is accordingly an important first step in almost any intellectual procedure concerned with law. How elaborate such clarification needs to be itself depends on context. In some contexts vantage point, role, situation, purpose, resources, and perspective (lenses) need to be differentiated in some detail – as I insist in teaching analysis of evidence. In other contexts it is often sufficient to ask: who am I (pretending to be)? At what stage in what process am I? What am I trying to do? Such ideas have been elaborated at length elsewhere.[42] I have always regarded them as Collingwoodian.

A further, related, theme also has important implications for juristic discourse. In *An Autobiography*, Collingwood outlined a 'theory of absolute presuppositions' that he later developed in *An Essay on Metaphysics* (1940). The basic idea, as set out in *An Autobiography* is that the content, forms, and structures of knowledge vary according to culture and time. All human thought is confined by constellations of presuppositions – very similar to Kuhn's idea of paradigms – which prevail in particular times and places. These constellations are continuously displaced. What they were and how and when they changed can only be ascertained by a form of historical enquiry that Collingwood called metaphysics. Questions can only be posed within these constellations. There are no universal questions and hence no universal answers and no timeless standards for evaluating the merits of these presuppositions.[43] Because the questions keep changing there are few closures.[44] This historicist position has clear echoes in the ideas of Vico, Marx, and Hegel. It has since been developed in different ways by, for

41 For example, if one asks: 'Who is most likely to have made statement 9 in what context?', a plausible answer is a law student confronted with this exercise in one of my classes. As with 1, 2, and 8 the person making the statement is 'outside the limerick'. On the other hand, statements 3, 4, 5, and 6 are at least as likely to be made by persons on the bus, that is, participants, but there is room for discussion about which kind of participant is the most likely and why? The provenance of statement 7 is less clear – it may be attributed to a law student doing this exercise or to a passenger observing events on the bus.

42 See, especially, W. Twining, 'The Bad Man Revisited' (1973) 58 *Cornell Law Rev.* 275; Twining, op. cit., n. 38; (with D. Miers), *How To Things With Rules* 1991, (3rd ed.), and (with T. Anderson), *Analysis of Evidence* (1991). See, also, D. Schum, *Evidential Foundations of Probabilistic Reasoning* (1994) at 71–5.

43 This interpretation closely follows that of Toulmin, op. cit., n. 17. The theory of absolute presuppositions represented a shift in Collingwood's views that has occasioned much controversy. Whether he became an extreme historical relativist, the explanation for the shift, and whether it was warranted need not concern us here. Collingwood rejected the idea of 'a view from nowhere'. (Johnson, op. cit., n. 17, pp. 121–5). On standpoint and relativism, see W. Twining, *Rethinking Evidence* (1990) 122–6.

44 *A.*, pp. 75–6.

example, Thomas Kuhn, Alisdair MacIntyre, and modern historians of ideas. Collingwood's version is contested, but it includes one message that is almost commonplace to day, except in jurisprudence:

> I soon realized that the history of political theory is not a history of different answers given to one and the same question, but the history of a problem that is more or less constantly changing, whose solution was changing with it.[45]

From such ideas Collingwood articulated some working rules. His practice as a teacher, archaeologist, and writer had just assumed that such precepts were basic to sound scholarship. The 'logic of question and answer' and 'the theory of absolute presuppositions' can be interpreted as *ex post facto* philosophical rationalizations of what he considered to be good practice, with the additional insight that the careful reading of philosophical and other theoretical texts is mainly an historical enterprise.[46] The metaphysics may be controversial, but the basic ground rules for reading and criticizing texts and for theoretical debate that flow from it are little more than elementary precepts of sound scholarship: in reading a text, first identify the author's underlying concerns and questions; 'never accept criticism of an author before satisfying yourself of its relevance';[47] in other words, see whether this is what he really said.[48] The implication for reading juristic texts is that one should not treat all theories of law or justice or rights as answers to identical questions – rather, one should distinguish between difference and disagreement; avoid indeterminate attribution and false polemics . . . and so on.

Throughout my career the predominant style of jurisprudential debate and criticism has often ignored such elementary precepts. Even the most respected thinkers, such as Hart and Dworkin, have sometimes failed to observe these precepts. Generalizations about 'schools' and 'isms', debates about positivism, and Non-Reading are rife. I have often railed against such

45 *A.*, pp. 62, 110. Compare scepticism about the functionalist approach to comparative law which suggests that what is being compared is the 'solutions' to shared 'problems' and that in Western societies these solutions or results tend to converge. The standard criticism of this approach is that it treats 'problems' as unproblematic.

46 Borrowing from literary theory, an historical approach to reading texts is sometimes dismissed as involving 'the intentionist' fallacy. It is presented as contrary to the idea that a text can be interpreted – or made the best it can be – independently of its provenance; or the critic can go one step further and talk of the reader creating the text; many jurists extend the practice to Non-Reading – 'criticizing' without reference to any texts – which opens the way to attacking ideas to be found in no text at all and which were probably not held by anyone. My position is that Collingwood was probably more a contextualist than an intentionist; that in some contexts, there are different kinds of legitimate readings and other uses of texts, such as anachronistic and conversational readings; but that serious literary theory does not legitimate practices of sloppy reading and non-reading of the kind I am criticizing. (See W. Twining, 'Reading Bentham' (1989) LXXV *Proceedings of the Brit. Academy* 97.)

47 *A.*, p. 74.

48 id., p. 27.

practices, to almost no avail.[49] They are a deeply rooted part of a culture of discourse and debate that is unscholarly because it is ahistorical.

The problem is most acute in teaching jurisprudence to undergraduates. Collingwood tells us that almost his whole teaching life 'was spent in showing pupils how to read a philosophical text'.[50] Reacting against colleagues who caricatured the views of past thinkers in order to demolish them, he insisted on strictly historical, or what he called scholarly, reading: 'Never think that you understand any statement made by a philosopher until you have decided, with the utmost possible accuracy, what the question is to which he means it for an answer.'[51] Criticism was allowed, but only if it was relevant to the author's problem. Collingwood rejected any distinction between historical and philosophical reading of philosophical texts. To understand a text involves thinking, but this thinking is historical, namely, reconstructing the problem and the answer of the author.

In teaching jurisprudence through texts, I have started with Collingwood but deviated from his approach. If the primary educational objective of reading a juristic text is for the students to clarify and develop their own ideas on important issues, then canonical or other texts can be used as a means to this end rather than as historical reconstruction for its own sake.[52] I call such exercises in self-definition, 'conversational' as opposed to historical reading.[53] I advise students to approach a juristic text, for this purpose, in three stages: the historical, the analytical, and the applied.[54] The first stage involves setting the text in the context of the author's life and work, the intellectual and political context of the time, and, above all, the author's immediate concerns (what was biting him/her?). The second stage involves analysing the text in terms of questions, answers, and reasons. First, what questions was the author addressing? What answers does the text propose? What reasons are given for the answers? Then the reader should ask: do I agree with the questions? do I agree with the answers? do I agree with the reasons? In short, reading a text in this way is an exercise in self-definition. The third stage is to consider possible implications and applications of the answers given in the text, as interpreted by the reader. This serves both to concretize the ideas and as a check on the interpretation of the text at a general level.

This kind of conversational or dialectical reading is Collingwoodian in spirit in respect of its emphasis on concerns, questions and answers and on

49 See, especially, W. Twining, 'Talk about Realism' (1985) 60 *New York University Law Rev.* 329; 'The Great Juristic Bazaar' (1978) 14 *J. of the Society of Public Teachers of Law (new series)* 185, and op. cit., n. 46.

50 *A.*, p. 74; compare pp. 72–3

51 id.

52 Collingwood took a more conservative view of canonical texts than many teachers of jurisprudence would accept today (id., p. 73).

53 Twining, op. cit., n. 46.

54 Twining, op. cit. (1997), n. 12, chs. 11 and 12.

setting a text in its historical context. Collingwood stressed that the ultimate aim of historical thinking is self-knowledge. However, conversational reading shifts the focus from the author's problems to those of the reader. This involves more than a difference of emphasis. For example, there can be a significant difference between an historical and a conversational reading of chs. 1–6 of Bentham's *Introduction to the Principles of Morals and Legislation*. A historical reading would focus on Bentham's views at the time he wrote: what were his concerns at the time? What were the central questions that he addressed? What is meant by 'pleasure' and 'pain' in this context? Was the felicific calculus conceived to be literal or metaphorical? What light do Bentham's other writings throw on the text? And many other questions about Bentham in the context of his times. Historians may differ on the propriety of applying concepts developed subsequently, such as the distinctions between preference and satisfaction, or act- and rule-utilitarianism, in such historical readings. However, the object is to reconstruct the historical text.

For a late-twentieth-century student of jurisprudence the main point of conversational reading of this text may be to address the question: 'Am I a utilitarian?' The text is just a resource in this enterprise. Setting it in its historical context may help to 'get on a wave-length', to avoid caricature and false polemics, to establish the relevance of the author's concerns to the reader's questions, and to bring out a range of possible interpretations and arguments about each. However, history can also be inhibiting in this context. For example, the modern reader may be well-advised to ask: 'What do I consider to be the least vulnerable form of utilitarianism?' In addressing this question it may be sensible to read the text anachronistically in the light of subsequent debates and to attempt a rational reconstruction of a sophisticated utilitarian position even if this cannot be supported by a strict reading of the historical text. For instance, Bentham may have been ambiguous or inconsistent. Or the reader may decide that 'pain' for Bentham meant 'satisfaction', but that preference-utilitarianism is less vulnerable to criticism, and hence deserves closer attention.

Similarly, conversational reading does not necessarily involve commitment to charitable interpretation or making every text 'the best it can be'. Caricature and false polemics are usually the route to begging hard questions. In dialectical reading it pays to construct worthy opponents, but this is not necessarily so. For example, if I am concerned to probe what it is that I find offensive about many Walt Disney publications, hostile or otherwise uncharitable interpretations – such as the Marxian satire *How To Read Donald Duck*[55] – may be more conducive to clarity of thought than laborious attempts to construct an apologia in terms of entertainment or family values. Asking nasty questions about how deviants, foreigners, ethnic minorities, and female characters are portrayed in Disney cartoons can be as revealing

55 A. Dorfman and A. Mittelart, *How to Read Donald Duck: Imperialist Ideology and the Disney Comic* (1975).

as interpreting 'the point' from the creator's point of view.[56] Using texts for one's own contemporary purposes may be different from scholarly historical interpretation, but it shares the idea that reading is an activity that involves asking questions of texts.

CONCLUSION

Can there be a distinctively Collingwoodian approach to legal theory? He wrote almost nothing about law and only indirectly about justice. He has received very little overt attention from jurists. However, from my own interpretation one might extrapolate the outlines of a general approach along the following lines: legal theory can be viewed as an activity, as a heritage, and as an ideology, that is a set of beliefs about law, which for anyone concerned with law is a form of self-knowledge. Legal theorizing is an activity directed to posing, reposing, answering, and arguing about questions directed to understanding law. This activity involves empathetic reconstruction of the thought both of past jurists and of significant participants in legal action. This perspective rejects any sharp differentiation between 'theory' and 'practice' because theory involves reconstructing the internal points of view of participants and is itself a basis for action. The heritage of past texts is an indispensable aid to the activity of theorizing about law. Reading such texts involves very precise identification of the questions addressed by the texts and the answers they provided, read in the context of their time. The reconstruction of internal points of view requires differentiation of the standpoints of various kinds of actors and thinkers. Such reconstruction is a historical activity directed to understanding and ultimately to self-understanding. On its own, this hardly constitutes a distinctive legal theory, in the sense of answers to central questions involved in understanding law, but it does have methodological implications for legal theorizing as an activity.

Whose autobiography is this, mine or Collingwood's? As a personal account of one reader's response to an autobiography it is clearly both. Neither should be treated as reliable. In the introduction to his critical study of Collingwood's later work, Alan Donagan wrote:

> The first obstacle to understanding Collingwood's later philosophy is his own narrative of its development, which is beyond doubt untrue . . . Only two years before he wrote it, he had warned autobiographers that in reconstructing their past thoughts 'recollection is a treacherous guide'.[57]

How can one know whether a work has been seminal? How much of the impact of my first reading was due to revelation, recognition or reinforcement?

56 Of course, if some classic text is found to have racist, sexist, imperialist, homophobic or other 'incorrect' elements, this involves difficult questions about editing and censorship.

57 Donagan, op. cit., n. 17.

How much have I read back into it from later readings or thinkings? I am not sure – but does it matter? That first reading on the coach certainly made an impact. This exercise has reminded me that a work can have resonance even if one may not have understood it and even if it can shown to be wrong. If one purpose of this series is to draw attention to books that are still worth reading, I can unhesitatingly recommend *An Autobiography*. Re-reading it more than forty years on, I find that it still resonates. However, let me end with a further recommendation.

If on a spring day in Miami in February 1998 a visitor is accosted by a colleague who says: 'Given what you said in yesterday's seminar, you ought to be using Calvino's *Invisible Cities*. It is my favourite book'[58] – what can the visitor do but buy a copy, be seduced, recommend it to everyone, and record that it is seminal in his continuing intellectual development . . .? There are few closures.[59]

58 I. Calvino, *Invisible Cities* (1974), on which see W. Twining, 'Mapping Law' (MacDermott Lecture, The Queen's University, Belfast, 1998), forthcoming in the *N. Ireland Legal Q*.
59 I. Calvino, *If on a Winter's Night a Traveller* (1981); compare *A.*, pp. 2–3.

[3]
The Bad Man Revisited

On the first day of my last visit to the United States I found myself with half-an-hour to kill in one of your most famous railroad stations. Naturally I visited the bookstore. One of the first items to catch my attention was a work entitled *The Bust Book*,[1] written by four young members of something called "the Movement," about which you probably know more than I. Most of the book is devoted to advice to participants in political demonstrations on how to behave when confronted with what is sometimes called "The Law," but which is referred to by a number of other terms in this particular work. The volume contains a good deal of information and advice not normally to be found in law books, ranging from what to wear in a demonstration to what factors to take into account when deciding whether to conduct one's own defense in court. It more than hints at a particular point of view. It also has pictures, the exact relevance of which is not entirely clear.

The subtitle of *The Bust Book* is "What to do Until the Lawyer Comes." It might well have been "The Bad Man—Modern Style."[2] Indeed, there seems to be emerging a new genre of writing for which such a title seems eminently suitable, including books on draft counselling, manuals—flippant, semi-serious, or professional—on the manufacture of homemade bombs and booby traps, radical critiques of the American judicial system, and miscellaneous pieces in the underground press. Confronted for the first time by this new fashion in literature, I could not help but wonder what Holmes would have thought of such works and whether they represent an application of his Bad Man theory. The spirit of these works does not seem to be the spirit of Holmes, but is the underlying premise so very different? Has the Bad Man theory now come into its own?

---

* This article is a revised version of a paper read to the Society for the Humanities at Cornell University in April 1971. I am indebted to Professors Robert S. Summers, James O. Freedman, and Geoffrey Wilson for valuable comments on an earlier draft. The present version does not necessarily represent their views.

1 K. Boudin, B. Glick, E. Raskin & G. Reichbach, The Bust Book (rev. ed. 1970).

2 The reference is to the Bad Man of Oliver Wendell Holmes's legal classic, "The Path of the Law." *See* Holmes, *The Path of the Law*, 10 Harv. L. Rev. 457 (1897) [hereinafter cited as *The Path of the Law*].

Shortly thereafter I had occasion to ask a class of about forty senior law students in a very prestigious institution how many of them had read Holmes's "Path of the Law."[3] Barely half-a-dozen claimed, or confessed, to have done so. This article represents a modest attempt to keep alive interest in this legal classic, since it would be a pity if concern for the Bad Man should be confined to subterranean circles. For it is a classic, and not only by Mark Twain's definition of that word as a work "which people praise and don't read." Holmes's piece has qualities which stand the test of time: it has the capacity to survive powerful, and sometimes valid, criticism; as circumstances change it invites reinterpretation and fresh criticism; it continues to strike a responsive chord among lawyers and law students who read it; and it contains memorable phrases which have achieved the double-edged distinction of becoming clichés. Moreover, either the Bad Man is very much alive today or there is some imposter about who deserves to be exposed for what he is.

I

"The Path of the Law"

Although "The Path of the Law" is often treated as a contribution to general jurisprudence, it was intended first and foremost as a discussion of legal education. In addition to the fact that much of it deals explicitly with legal education, the structure of the address, the occasion, and Holmes's concerns at the time justify such an interpretation.

Holmes begins as follows:

> When we study law we are not studying a mystery but a well known profession. We are studying what we shall want in order to appear before judges, or to advise people in such a way as to keep them out of court. The reason why it is a profession, why people will pay lawyers to argue for them or to advise them, is that in societies like ours the command of the public force is intrusted to the judges in certain cases, and the whole power of the state will be put forth, if necessary, to carry out their judgments and decrees. People want to know under what circumstances and how far they will run the risk of coming against what is so much stronger than themselves, and hence it becomes a business to find out when this danger is to be feared. The object of our study, then, is prediction, the prediction of the incidence of the public force through the instrumentality of the courts.[4]

[3] *Id.*

[4] *Id.* at 457.

The occasion was the dedication of a new hall at Boston University Law School, an appropriate site from which to launch a few thinly disguised missiles at a more renowned institution located across the river. Langdell had recently retired from the Deanship of the Harvard Law School and, as is well known, Holmes had been a persistent but discreet critic of Langdell's approach to law, which he considered to be generally too redolent of the ivory tower.[5] Holmes, who was at the time still on the Massachusetts Supreme Court, treats his audience as future practitioners of law. It is not unreasonable to suggest that the bulk of his address is directed to the question of what kind of legal education is best suited to the intending attorney's needs. It is also not unreasonable to interpret his answer to this question as being, in large part, a veiled attack on certain aspects of the philosophy of legal education which had become established at Harvard under Langdell's leadership and which was rapidly beginning to influence other law schools.[6]

> 5 I finished Langdell's *Equity Jurisdiction* yesterday . . . . It has his acumen and patient discussion of detail, but I think brings out the narrow side of his mind, his feebleness in philosophising, and hints at his rudimentary historical knowledge. I think he was somewhat wanting in horse sense . . . .

1 HOLMES-POLLOCK LETTERS 140 (M. Howe ed. 1941).

Holmes's ambivalent attitude towards Langdell is further illustrated in another letter to Pollock:

> [T]o my mind he represents the powers of darkness. He is all for logic and hates any reference to anything outside of it, and his explanations and reconciliations of the cases would have astonished the judges who decided them. But he is a noble old swell whose knowledge, ability and idealist devotion to his work I revere and love.

Id. at 17.

6 This statement is subject to a number of caveats. First, there was common ground between Holmes and Langdell which was as significant as their differences. Holmes did not seriously challenge Langdell's famous assertion that all the available materials for the study of law are contained in printed books. He echoes the view that "the number of fundamental legal doctrines is much less than is commonly supposed" (C. LANGDELL, A SELECTION OF CASES ON THE LAW OF CONTRACTS vi (1871) (Preface)); he shares, to a large extent, Langdell's case-law orientation; he accepts that the study of legal history can be of value, provided that it does not decline into antiquarianism (*The Path of Law* 474); he even concedes that there has been an improvement in modes of teaching, but hastens to add that "ability and industry will master the raw material with any mode." *Id.* at 477.

Second, not all of Holmes's barbs are directed against Langdell's Harvard. It would hardly have been appropriate to charge that institution with consistently failing to distinguish between law and morals, with overemphasizing the importance of Roman Law, or even with regularly succumbing to the pitfalls of antiquarianism. And when Holmes chides the "practical-minded" for undervaluing jurisprudence and the judges for failing adequately to weigh considerations of social advantage (*id.* at 478), he is explicitly spreading his fire quite widely.

A third, and final, caveat. Although the main focus of "The Path of the Law" is on legal education, it does not follow that the significance of the piece is limited to that relatively parochial topic. Worthwhile discussions of legal education often lead directly

"The Path of the Law" is diffuse and rambling. Much of its charm lies in its individual *aperçus* and obiter dicta. But there is a discernible central argument, for the core of the address is devoted to criticizing what Holmes considered to be two fallacies: the confounding of morality and law, and what he termed "the fallacy of the logical form."[7] Although the main targets of Holmes's criticism were certain ideas associated with Langdell's Harvard, at first sight only one of the two fallacies is attributable to Langdellism, and the Bad Man plays no part in its exposure. However, I propose to argue that in dealing with the alleged fallacies Holmes was attacking on three main fronts, not two, and that the main function of the Bad Man device was to expose a basic flaw in Langdellism.

We need not spend long on that part of the attack which deals with the idea that "the only force at work in the development of the law is logic."[8] In other contexts Holmes had quite explicitly associated this idea with Langdell;[9] here he is content to say that this is "the natural error of the schools, but it is not confined to them."[10] Holmes's arguments for bringing into the open the unarticulated policy assumptions embedded in legal reasoning and his plea for a closer integration of law and economics are well known.[11] For present purposes it is sufficient to note that the Bad Man plays no part in this particular argument.

---

to the questioning of accepted theoretical assumptions, and Holmes's address is not a unique example of provocative jurisprudential statements stimulated by educational concerns. There has been, especially in America, a close connection, both historical and analytical, between legal theory and discussions of legal education. It is not necessary to expound a theory of law every time one talks or writes about curriculum changes or professional training, but any such discussion presupposes at least some assumptions about law and lawyers (or law-trained people). *See* text following note 15 *infra*. Often introspection on the part of legal educators leads them straight back to consideration of fundamentals. Further, as a matter of history, a significant amount of legal theorizing in the United States over the past 100 years has been stimulated in large part by educational concerns—witness, for example, the early theoretical writings of Corbin, Llewellyn, Lasswell, McDougal, and, to a lesser extent, Jerome Frank. *See generally* Comment, *Legal Theory and Legal Education*, 79 YALE L.J. 1153 (1970).

7 *The Path of the Law* 468.

The relationship between law and morals and the place of logic in law are familiar topics to students of jurisprudence; some issues concerning them are perennial subjects of controversy. I do not propose to deal with these issues here, except as they have a direct bearing on the concept of the Bad Man.

8 *Id.* at 465.

9 *See* note 5 *supra*.

10 *The Path of the Law* 465.

11 "For the rational study of the law the black-letter man may be the man of the present, but the man of the future is the man of statistics and the master of economics." *Id.* at 469. "[E]very lawyer ought to seek an understanding of economics." *Id.* at 474.

Holmes's second line of attack deals with the confusion of law and morality, and the related, but not identical, error of failing to distinguish law as it is from law as it ought to be. Rather than identify particular offenders, Holmes is content to remark that the error "sometimes rises to the height of conscious theory, and more often and indeed constantly is making trouble in detail without reaching the point of consciousness."[12] The Bad Man is introduced ostensibly as a device to clear up the confusion. Holmes's point is that whereas the good and law-abiding citizen who looks to both morality and law to tell him how he ought to behave may not distinguish clearly between legal sanctions and "the vaguer sanctions of conscience,"[13] the Bad Man is indifferent to morality (including its sanctions) and is only interested in the actual consequences of his actions. He has a practical reason for observing the distinction between law and morality. In other words, while the Good Citizen asks "How should I behave?," the Bad Man inquires "What will happen to me if I embark on this course of action?"

Perhaps it is because the Bad Man's question is in the form of a request for a prediction that Holmes was led to link the distinction between law and morality to the idea of prophecy.

> The confusion with which I am dealing besets confessedly legal conceptions. Take the fundamental question, What constitutes the law? You will find some text writers telling you that it is something different from what is decided by the courts of Massachusetts or England, that it is a system of reason, that it is a deduction from principles of ethics or admitted axioms or what not, which may or may not coincide with the decisions. But if we take the view of our friend the bad man we shall find that he does not care two straws for the axioms or deductions, but that he does want to know what the Massachusetts or English courts are likely to do in fact. I am much of his mind. The prophecies of what the courts will do in fact, and nothing more pretentious, are what I mean by the law.[14]

This passage is one of the most quoted and criticized in all American jurisprudence. It is often treated as the *locus classicus* of the so-called prediction theory of law.[15] Given the context and Holmes's objectives, there is a suggestion of hyperbole in treating it as out-

---

12 *Id.* at 459. It is unlikely that Holmes considered Langdell to be a prime offender in this respect.

13 *Id.*

14 *Id.* at 460-61.

15 *See, e.g.*, E. PATTERSON, JURISPRUDENCE 118-22 (1953); W. RUMBLE, AMERICAN LEGAL REALISM 41-44 (1968); *cf.* H.L.A. HART, THE CONCEPT OF LAW (1961); G. PATON, JURISPRUDENCE (2d ed. 1951).

lining a general theory of law. By purporting to answer the question "What constitutes the law?," he could be said to have been advancing a definition of law or even an embryonic theory of law, and thus to have invited criticism on this basis. But it was not an essential part of his argument. It is not necessary to outline a theory of law every time one talks or writes about legal education, although it is often important to make one's assumptions explicit in such contexts. Holmes's main arguments did not depend upon defining law in terms of prophecies or predictions. The gist of his educational thesis would have been unaffected if he had adopted, for example, Austin's analysis of the concept of law.[16] The quoted passage, read in context, is best treated as a dramatic or rhetorical device rather than as a necessary step in Holmes's argument. Yet the Bad Man and the idea of prediction play an important part in his thesis. Holmes did not himself develop these ideas at length either in "The Path of the Law" or in his other writings. More recently, however, the idea of prediction has regained a central place in discussions of the concept of law, and the Bad Man has become a not inconsiderable character in juristic literature.[17] Accordingly, at the risk of being charged with reading too much into Holmes, I propose to consider first, the significance of the Bad Man for legal theory; second, the significance of the main arguments in "The Path of the Law" for legal education; and, finally, the connections, if any, between Holmes's Bad Man and the addressees of *The Bust Book*.

II

The Bad Man and Legal Theory

A. *Who is the Bad Man?*

In the present context, the Bad Man is not a revolutionary nor even a reformer out to change "the system." The Bad Man's concern is to secure his personal objectives within the existing order as painlessly as possible; he is not so much alienated from the law as he is indifferent to all aspects which do not affect him personally. Unlike Sartre's Saint Genêt, he is not one who has a problem of identity—who defines his being in terms of the system and who is driven to do acts *because* they are criminal or antisocial.[18] Nor is he a subscriber to

16 *See* J. Austin, The Province of Jurisprudence Determined 82-83 (1954).

17 *See* L. Fuller, The Law in Quest of Itself 92-95 (1940).

18 J.P. Sartre, Saint Genêt 66-67 (B. Frechtman transl. 1963).

some perverse ethic which turns conventional morality upon its head. The Bad Man is amoral rather than immoral. He is, like Economic Man and Bentham's "civilized" actors, a rational, calculating creature. In this and in other respects he does not necessarily reflect in a realistic manner the characteristics of actual deviants. Like Dahrendorf's *homo sociologicus*, he "can neither love nor hate, laugh nor cry. He remains a pale, incomplete, strange, artificial man."[19] Indeed, there appears to be no reason why the Bad Man should not be an artificial person, such as a corporation. In short, he is a theoretical construct with as yet unexplored potential as a tool of analysis.

Perhaps we can go a little further and suggest that the Bad Man can be defined in terms of prediction. He is the person whose only task is to predict what will happen to him if he embarks on some particular course of action. Here we may anticipate a possible objection. Although it may be granted that prediction is central to the role of the Bad Man, it is admitted that there are others who are similarly concerned—for example, the lawyer who has to decide whether it is worth appealing an adverse decision, the advocate who needs to predict how the personnel of a particular court will react to some line of argument or to the testimony of some witness, the judge who may wish to predict the likelihood of reversal on appeal or the possible effects of sending an offender to jail, the legislator who is concerned with the likely effects of a legal provision on patterns of behavior. And the scientist—is he not also concerned with prediction?

A simple response is that although these may all be valid observations, they are not objections to defining the Bad Man in terms of prediction. A comprehensive prediction theory would need to give a comprehensive answer to a question such as "Who is concerned with predicting what events at what point in time for what purposes using what means?" With the exception of the scientist, whose standpoint raises special difficulties, all the other characters are predicting as part of some other task; for example, the advocate predicts in order to perform the task of persuasion. For some purposes it may be useful to isolate the task of predicting *simpliciter;* for other purposes prediction is more usefully seen as part of a cluster of tasks. In other words, the Bad Man is a device for isolating for special consideration the task of predicting certain kinds of events.

The idea of prediction provides no basis for distinguishing be-

---

19 R. DAHRENDORF, *Homo Sociologicus*, in ESSAYS IN THE THEORY OF SOCIETY 76 (1968). This essay explores at length the relationship between constructs like *homo sociologicus* and actual people. *See also* H. LASSWELL & A. KAPLAN, POWER AND SOCIETY 78 (1950).

tween the standpoints of the Good Citizen and of the Bad Man. It is not incompatible with good citizenship to be concerned with predicting the likely consequences of one's actions. The Bad Man, however, is affected by guidance as to his actions *only* insofar as such guidance predicts the ultimate consequences of those actions. Take, for example, the situation of a law-abiding individual seeking advice on his liability to pay income tax. If his conscience permits him to make a clear distinction between tax avoidance and tax evasion (as far as the law recognizes such a distinction), he may ask what lawful course of action will leave him with the most money. If he has a tender social conscience, he may reject certain kinds of lawful avoidance devices as immoral; nevertheless, he may wish to predict what his net income is likely to be. There may also be occasions when the Good Citizen can be said to have a moral duty to predict the likely consequences of his actions. The difference between the Bad Man and the Good Citizen does not rest on the latter's indifference to prediction, but on the former's indifference to morality.

Of course, the distinction between law and morality is not exclusively the concern of the Bad Man. Bentham's legislator draws a sharp distinction between law as it is and law as it ought to be. Statements such as "This is a court of law, not of morals" are commonplace; typically, those who are concerned with analyzing and expounding legal doctrine draw similar distinctions. What distinguishes the standpoint of the Bad Man from the standpoint of the legislator, the judge, and the advocate is his exclusive concern with prediction; however, in this respect the standpoint of the Bad Man is very close to that of the Good Citizen and to that of the legal advisers of both of them.

Thus, the Bad Man has two characteristics: his badness and his citizenship.[20] The distinction between law and morality is related to the former characteristic, the idea of prediction to the latter. When Holmes advised his audience to adopt the standpoint of the Bad Man, he was not seriously urging them to use the Bad Man as an ethical model; rather, he was suggesting that they look at law from the perspective of a citizen who is concerned with predicting the consequences of his actions. He was in effect saying that as intending private practitioners of law they should put themselves in the shoes of the legal adviser of citizens, good or bad. From that standpoint their main concern should be with prediction.

---

20 "Citizenship" as used here refers to the condition of being subject to the laws of a particular legal system rather than to nationality or legal status.

B. *What Events Does the Bad Man Desire To Predict?*

According to Holmes, the Bad Man is anxious to predict what the "courts will do in fact."[21] Even if we allow that by "do," Holmes refers not only to judicial decisions on questions of fact and law, but also to the sanctions courts are likely to impose, this still seems to be an unduly restrictive answer. Such a response reflects, perhaps, a court-centeredness on Holmes's part, with possible overtones of "appellate court-itis."[22]

Suppose, for example, that our friend the Bad Man is in Boston (or Cambridge) wondering whether or not to do some specific act. He may ask, "What are the chances that a Massachusetts court would hold this type of act to be criminal?" But this is only one of a series of questions pertinent to the decision whether or not to do the act. He needs to estimate the likelihood of the authorities discovering the commission of the act; how energetically, if at all, they are likely to investigate it and other matters related to detection and apprehension; if apprehended, whether there will be a decision to prosecute and, if so, the likelihood of conviction; the likely effect of pleading guilty or not guilty; and the probable nature of the sanction if he is convicted. If he wants to follow the total process through, the Bad Man may also need to consider a whole range of possible post-conviction decisions. The decisions of courts are merely a single phase in what Lasswell terms a "flow of determinative activities" which go to make up the total process which may affect the Bad Man.[23] And, of course, if one is talking about actual people who are in danger of being "busted," not only do they need to predict a wider range of possible events, but they also need to perform tasks other than prediction.[24] A comprehensive picture of legal process on the Holmesian model would take all of these considerations into account.[25]

---

21 *The Path of the Law* 461.

22 *Cf.* J. FRANK, COURTS ON TRIAL 222-24 (1949). The broadening of the focus of attention to include all officials was suggested by Karl Llewellyn. *See* K. LLEWELLYN, *A Realistic Jurisprudence—The Next Step*, in JURISPRUDENCE 16-18 (1962).

23 H. LASSWELL & A. KAPLAN, *supra* note 19, at 81; *see* McDougal, *The Comparative Study of Law for Policy Purposes: Value Clarification as an Instrument of Democratic World Order*, 61 YALE L.J. 915, 921 (1952). *See generally* text accompanying note 42 *infra*.

24 Thus, for example, *The Bust Book* is addressed to people who are presumed to have political aims which they are advised to bear in mind at each stage of their encounters with "the system."

25 Holmes never fully developed such a comprehensive picture, although he is sometimes treated as if he had. At least he is treated, especially by critics, as being primarily responsible for the so-called prediction theory of law. The Bad Man passage (*see* text accompanying note 4 *supra*) is a somewhat slender pedestal for such a target, but it is not enough to dismiss the critics merely by suggesting that they have succumbed too easily to the temptation of elevating what they have sought to attack.

C. *Criticisms of the Bad Man Concept as a Theory of Law*

One standard criticism of the Bad Man passage is that concepts like "court" or "official" presuppose the idea of a legal system. They are, it is said, rule-defined concepts. To purport to define or elucidate "law" in terms of prophecies or predictions of what courts or officials will do involves an element of circularity, for the terms "court" and "official" must themselves be defined in terms of law. Thus Holmes's statement is inadequate as a general definition of law (and, if it deserves to be so treated, as a theory of law in the restricted sense).[26]

Another standard criticism of the so-called prediction theory of law is that it confuses the notion of prediction with the notion of rule. The point is simply illustrated by reference to the proposition "In circumstances X there is a duty not to . . . ." To say that such a proposition is a prediction or a prophecy involves a distortion of ordinary language and is likely to lead to confused thinking. In ordinary usage the statement "Y has a duty" means "Y ought"; it is a normative proposition, whereas a prediction is an empirical statement which is, *inter alia*, capable of verification. To equate rules with predictions blurs useful distinctions, such as the distinction between the existence of a rule and its actual enforcement. It also may lead to misdescription of situations in which rules in fact influence behavior. Furthermore, it obscures the point that many concepts take their meaning from legal rules.

Such an analysis is valid and important, but it is not necessarily applicable to "The Path of the Law," since Holmes limits his discussion to the standpoint of the Bad Man, who is, by definition, unconcerned with the normative. It may well be, however, that some followers of Holmes are vulnerable to this criticism. Another way of making the same point is to say that to equate rules with predictions is to confuse rules with roles or tasks involving the *use* of rules. Although a rule is a normative proposition, it can be used as an aid to making predictions. But rules have a variety of uses. The Bad Man may use propositions of law (statements of legal rules) as aids to predicting the likely consequences of his actions, but the Good Citizen also uses them as guides to correct behavior; the judge may use them as a guide to deciding and may invoke them to justify his decision; and the legislator may formulate rules to control, regulate, or guide behavior and expectations, and perhaps to educate or to assert some moral standard. Conversely, even in predicting the outcomes of court decisions the Bad

26 On "theory of law," see note 36 *infra*; on "officials," see generally the works cited in note 22 *supra*.

Man and his advisers may resort to other aids in addition to or instead of formulations of legal rules. When predicting other phases of legal process, such as decisions whether or not to prosecute a suspected offender, resort to other aids to prediction will be essential. Rules are only one of the Bad Man's aids to prediction, and predicting is only one of the uses of rules.

A third criticism, closely related to the others, is that the prediction theory is inadequate as a theory of law because it does not take into account the standpoints of other participants in legal processes, such as the judge, the advocate, and the legislator.[27] What is particularly interesting about this criticism is its assumptions about the concept of an adequate general theory of law and, related to this, its seeming acceptance of a switch from a traditional model of law as a system of rules to a model of legal process as a system of roles.

The first assumption is that an adequate general theory of law must take into account a variety of standpoints. What is meant by standpoint (or its approximate synonym "point of view") in this context? In ordinary usage it is possible to identify several primary, but related, meanings of these terms.[28] First, standpoint may refer to vantage point or point of view in an observational sense, for example, as "a vantage point of the sort that a photographer might seek."[29] Second, adopting a standpoint or point of view may be a matter of adopting some principle or ideology or intellectual system, as when someone approaches a subject from the standpoint of a utilitarian or a Marxist. Similarly, standpoints are sometimes distinguished by reference to disciplines or specialized fields of expertise, as in the expression "from the standpoint of an economist" (or an anthropologist or a moral philosopher). Typically in such usages the viewer is seeking to understand, describe, depict, interpret, analyze, or explain the subject of his viewing without necessarily having any immediate practical objectives in mind.[30] Third, standpoint may be defined in terms of some

---

27 As an indicator of some of the limitations of the Bad Man theory, this is obviously correct. It is another matter whether or not it is a fair criticism of Holmes, who identified himself with the Bad Man for a specific purpose. For an incisive account of Holmes's stance in other contexts, see Rogat, *The Judge as Spectator*, 31 U. CHI. L. REV. 213 (1964).

28 For a useful general discusion, see Moline, *On Points of View*, 5 AM. PHILOSOPHICAL Q. 191 (1968). *See also* Summers, *Notes on Criticism in Legal Philosophy*, in MORE ESSAYS IN LEGAL PHILOSOPHY 8-11 (R. Summers ed. 1971).

29 Moline, *supra* note 28, at 192; *see* note 33 *infra*.

30 We might categorize these first two usages as referring to observer standpoints, as contrasted with participant standpoints. The distinction between observers and participants is emphasized by Harold Lasswell and Myres McDougal in their forthcoming work, *Law, Science and Policy*. *See* H. LASSWELL & M. MCDOUGAL, LAW, SCIENCE AND POLICY

task or role or objective.[31] Often such tasks or roles or objectives are expressed as personifications, such as "the legislator," "the advocate," or "the judge."[32] The Bad Man, as here interpreted, is an example of such a construct. To investigate law "from the standpoint of the Bad Man" can mean to investigate what the Bad Man needs to know and to understand in order to be able to make effective predictions to further his own ends. Standpoint in this third sense implies some *criteria of relevance* determined by the conception of the task or role or objective in question. Thus, "the standpoint of the judge" assumes some more or less clearly defined notion of "the judge's role" which provides, *inter alia,* a basis for determining what the judge needs to know and to understand in order to do his job, as he or as others conceive it.

These three primary usages sometimes coalesce when the standpoint in question is that of an actual or imaginary person or class of persons. For example, "the standpoint of a typical Wall Street lawyer" may encompass not only what such a person needs to know in order satisfactorily to do his job, but also what he has the opportunity to observe by virtue of his special vantage point. Furthermore, for us to assume such a standpoint may (or may not) require that we adopt the ethos and attitudes of people who typically occupy such positions. It would be useful to treat this as a fourth and distinct usage of standpoint, if only to emphasize the lack of precision of ordinary usages of the term.[33] Moreover, it is only too easy to confuse notional constructs

(forthcoming). In some contexts the distinction is difficult to maintain. *See, e.g.*, L. Wilkins, Social Deviance *passim* (1964); The Participant Observer *passim* (G. Jacobs ed. 1970).

31 *See generally* M. Banton, Roles: An Introduction to the Study of Social Relations (1965); R. Dahrendorf, *supra* note 19; N. Gross, W. Mason & A. McEarchern, Explorations in Role Analysis (1958); Nieman & Hughes, *The Problem of the Concept of Role—A Re-survey of the Literature*, 30 Social Forces 141 (1951); Seidman, *The Judicial Process Reconsidered in the Light of Role-Theory*, 32 Modern L. Rev. 516 (1969).

32 For a typically confused example of such use of standpoint, see 2 R. Pound, Jurisprudence 129-32 (1959).

33 There is admittedly a close and complex relationship between the various usages of standpoint discussed in the text. Nevertheless, failure to distinguish between them in legal contexts may lead to confusion. For example, an English solicitor may in the course of his practice have an opportunity to learn a great deal about property values in his locality, yet he may not consider it as part of his role to advise a client on the value of a particular piece of property. Similarly, a solicitor may have ample opportunity to observe the functioning of property law in practice. On the basis of such observation he may conclude that the law is either in need of change or in need of preservation from attempts to reform it. In short, he may be qualified by his experience to contribute to law reform activities, and thus to share in the tasks of the legislator. He may, however, take the position that such reform is "none of his business," if in his opinion the job of the solicitor is to work within the existing system, not to change it; on the other hand, he may claim that when participating in law reforming activities he is acting in his capacity

which are defined in terms of some particular role or task (*e.g.*, the legislator defined in terms of the task of making rules of law) with stereotypes of actual people (*e.g.*, the legislator defined in terms of membership in some particular legislative body). This distinction, facilitated by an understanding of the fourth use of standpoint, is important because in real life few persons have roles which consist of a single type of task, and few functionaries have a monopoly on particular tasks. Thus, in the United States judges sometimes legislate (*i.e.*, participate in making legal rules), and legislators are often called upon to advise, persuade, and predict.

The concept of standpoint may be used with reference either to constructs personifying particular tasks or groups of tasks (*e.g.*, "the legislator") or to actual or imagined people (*e.g.*, Wall Street lawyers). The former conception is more intellectualized and accordingly more susceptible to rigorous development; the latter may be used to promote a more realistic identification with typical participants in actual processes. In "The Path of the Law" this distinction is glossed over. The latent function of the Bad Man in Holmes's argument is to support a plea for a more realistic identification on the part of law students and law teachers with the problems of practicing lawyers. But, as we have seen, the Bad Man is much more plausibly treated as a personification of the task of predicting decisions (which is only one of many tasks performed by practicing lawyers) than as a realistic stereotype of any kind of actual person.[34] Thus, the third and fourth usages of standpoint are directly relevant to an analysis of "The Path of the Law," although the first two should be kept in mind.

D. *The Significance of Standpoint*

The distinctions between the four usages of standpoint may help to clarify some obscurities in the expressions "the Bad Man theory (of law)" and "the prediction theory (of law)." Several possible meanings are attributable to these terms. First, either can be used to refer to a general definition of law in terms of prediction. Apparently this is what is meant when the prediction theory is criticized along the lines considered above.[35] The standard criticisms reveal some of the inadequacies of Holmes's dictum thus viewed, but it is stretching

as citizen and not *qua* solicitor. Alternatively, he may claim that by virtue of his experiences as a solicitor he is particularly well qualified to participate in law reform. One starting point for analyzing such claims is to clarify underlying assumptions about standpoint and role.

34 *See* notes 18-19 and accompanying text *supra*.

35 *See* notes 26-34 and accompanying text *supra*.

the term to treat this statement as encapsulating a theory of law.[36] A second possible meaning of the Bad Man theory, or the prediction theory, relates to standpoint in the third sense insofar as these theories attempt to provide a working theory for predictors. Taken this way the phrases represent a general account of what the Bad Man needs to know and to understand in order to make reliable predictions (including perhaps some general advice by way of guidelines or rules of thumb on how to go about the task of predicting). This is a perfectly plausible usage. Holmes, however, certainly did not produce such an account (nor drop more than the slightest of hints as to what it might contain), nor, as far as I know, has anyone else attempted to do so in a systematic fashion.[37]

A third possible meaning of the Bad Man theory (but less plausibly of the prediction theory) is a descriptive account of what law in general (or within a particular legal system) looks like from the standpoint of a Bad Man. Here, since standpoint is being used in the observational sense, it does not seem appropriate to define the Bad Man in terms of prediction;[38] indeed, there is considerable doubt as to who the Bad Man might be in this context and as to what exactly would be his vantage point. A work by Genêt or a professional burglar or a member of the I.R.A. might qualify under this heading, as might a descriptive work by the authors of *The Bust Book* or by a trained observer occupying a similar vantage point. Such worms' eye views are potentially of great interest since they represent perspectives which have been largely neglected by jurists. It is dangerous to generalize about such views, however, for there are many species of worms with different observational capacities who may be viewing for a variety of

36 One source of confusion relating to the prediction theory is attributable to the obscurity of the term "theory of law." Sometimes that term is restricted to attempts to elucidate the concepts of "law" and "legal system"; sometimes it is used vaguely to refer to the corpus of a jurist's more general ideas; sometimes it may be loosely equated with theorizing about law, or legal theory, and may be applied indiscriminately to any inquiry of a general nature about or related to law. Failure to distinguish between the restricted sense of a "theory of law"—or "theory of legal system" (*see* J. Raz, The Concept of a Legal System 1-4 (1970))—and legal theory (or theorizing about law) in general can be a potent source of confusion, not least because it easily leads to the error of assuming that all jurists have been addressing themselves to identical questions and that all legal theories are comparables. It is far from clear in what sense the prediction theory could be said to be a "theory of law," even if it were developed more fully than Holmes ever attempted to develop it.

37 Karl Llewellyn's *The Common Law Tradition* can be viewed as a handbook for predicting appellate court decisions, but not for predicting the outcome of legal processes in general. *See generally* K. Llewellyn, The Common Law Tradition (1960); W. Twining, Karl Llewellyn and the Realist Movement (forthcoming).

38 *See* text following note 19 *supra*.

purposes or who may, under the guise of viewing, be doing something else such as calling for help or advocating a cause. Thus, the Bad Man theory in the descriptive sense is an intriguing, if somewhat open-ended, category.

Finally, the Bad Man theory may be used in an ideological sense, corresponding to the second usage of standpoint. Again it is necessary to ask who exactly the Bad Man is in this context. He might be an ethical nihilist or a disciple of Nietzsche or de Sade or some kind of revolutionary or anarchist, labelled "Bad" because he is seen as an enemy of the established order. Certainly there is ample scope for theorizing from this type of standpoint, but such theorizing, perhaps not surprisingly, is not currently accorded much attention in orthodox Anglo-American jurisprudence. Thus, although this may be a plausible meaning of the Bad Man theory, it is not an adequate interpretation of Holmes.

We return, at last, to the criticism that the prediction theory is inadequate not because it is wrong, but because it is incomplete.[39] The argument is that while the Bad Man's desire is to predict, other participants have additional tasks, such as to persuade, to decide, to advise, to justify, to regulate behavior, and to channel expectations. What would a complete theory dealing with these points include? Without attempting a definitive answer, I would suggest that were we to take the idea of completeness literally, then the standpoints of all participants in legal process would need to be accommodated and the relationships among them indicated. In addition, we might wish to add the standpoints of people outside the process, as, for example, the observer who is not also a participant (*i.e.*, the scientist?), and ultimately (raising questions which here I deliberately bypass) the standpoint of God.[40]

---

39 *See* text following note 27 *supra*.

40 Another aspect of the argument about completeness assumes that a "complete" theory must accommodate a number of working theories. Presumably in this context an adequate theory for the Bad Man is one which provides him with the means to understand the nature of his situation, and furnishes him with an indication of the kind of information on which to base his predictions, and of the kind of skills requisite to making effective calculations. Terms such as "theory," "understanding," "information," and "skills" require further analysis, but in the present context it may suffice to define a working theory as a set of operative ideas which can give a participant at least general guidance on how he can most effectively perform his tasks or pursue his objectives. Without developing the point here, I think that the idea of a complete theory as one which accommodates not only the non-participant theories of observers and scientists (whoever they may be), but also the working theories of participants in legal process, is one which is worth developing in jurisprudence. Among other things, it may provide a basis for establishing a healthier relationship between theory and practice.

Developing such a model need not be as ambitious an undertaking as might at first sight appear.[41] It would be a very ambitious undertaking to attempt to provide a "complete" description of a legal system along these lines, let alone to provide a complete description of all legal systems. But to set up a model for describing and analyzing legal process in terms of the flow of decisions and of the varying tasks and roles of participants at each stage in the process is a more straightforward enterprise. Indeed, when we talk of "the legislator," "the judge," "the advocate," "the prosecutor," and "the citizen" (Good or Bad) and his advisers, we are assuming a crude version of such a model. This flowchart of the main decisions relating to the Bad Man's escapade in Boston[42] is an elementary example of a way of analyzing one type of legal process along these lines:

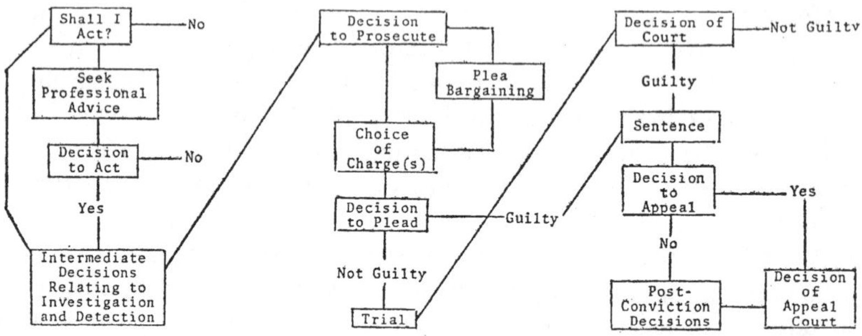

This is, of course, a very simple example of a model of one type of legal process. An adequate model for depicting and analyzing the totality of legal processes in the United States would obviously be much more complicated. I do not propose to develop such a model here, but it is worth making certain points about this kind of analysis. First, it is important in constructing such models and charts to bear in mind the distinction between general and particular jurisprudence. A chart may take certain things for granted which are not necessary or characteristic features of all legal systems. For example, it may assume that there are advisers and prosecutors, as well as the possibility of pleading guilty or not guilty, and provision for appeal. These are neither necessary nor universal features of legal process in all systems, although such features would be appropriate in most kinds of criminal process models in England and the United States. If a chart were to be expanded it

41 *See generally* H. LASSWELL & M. MCDOUGAL, *supra* note 30; Twining, *Pericles and the Plumber*, 83 L.Q. REV. 396, 412-15 (1967).

42 *See generally* text accompanying note 23 *supra*.

would tend to become more particularized and thereby more closely linked to one actual system. Indeed, the building up of more and more detailed charts of this kind would be a revealing way of comparing and contrasting criminal processes in two or more legal systems.

Analysis of legal process in terms of decisions, tasks, and roles is not an alternative to a model of legal system as a system of rules (or rules and principles).[43] It is not strictly speaking a theory of law, but rather presupposes such a theory; the concept of "legal process" assumes some concept of "law" and "legal system." Thus a "complete theory," as that term is used in criticizing the Bad Man theory, is best treated not as a theory of law, but as a model or ideal type of process within a legal system. As such it is a tool of analysis to be evaluated in terms of its utility.[44]

A model of legal system as a system of rules and a model of legal process as a system of roles need not be viewed as inconsistent or competing models. Each may be useful for certain purposes, although a particular model may, of course, be over-used or have an "overspill" effect which may be open to criticism. For example, much of the unease of American jurists with the rule model may be based on the feeling that it has exerted undue and unsalutary influence on the consideration of matters which are marginally related to basic questions about the nature of law, and that it has been used to provide criteria of relevance which are too narrow for particular purposes. A simple example of this overspill effect is found, once again, in legal education; the study of law has too often been equated with the study of legal doctrine. To suggest that it is important to study the role conceptions of lawyers and judges or the effects of laws is even today sometimes met with the reaction: "That's not law, that's sociology."[45] The identification of law solely with legal doctrine has led to literature, teaching, and talk that have repeatedly been characterized as "narrow," "sterile," or "unrealistic." Insofar as participants in legal processes and other affected people complain that too many of their concerns have been left unexplored, and that too many of their questions have been left unanswered by academic lawyers, their complaints are justified. The gist of their complaint is that for their purposes different criteria of rele-

---

43 *See* Dworkin, *Is Law a System of Rules?*, in ESSAYS IN LEGAL PHILOSOPHY 25 (R. Summers ed. 1968). The differences between Hart and Dworkin on this question are not at issue here.

44 *See* R. BENDIX, MAX WEBER: AN INTELLECTUAL PORTRAIT 274-75 (1962); *cf.* M. BLACK, MODELS AND METAPHORS 219-43 (1962).

45 Such statements may be more common in the United Kingdom than in the United States.

vance are required. A model of legal process developed around the concept of standpoint, it is suggested, is likely to provide a more satisfactory theoretical basis for such criteria than that provided by models of legal system as a system of rules (or rules and principles).[46] This is not to reject such theories. It is only to put them in their place.[47]

E. *Summary*

The "Path of the Law" is often treated as the *locus classicus* of the prediction theory of law. This theory, despite its ambiguity, is embryonic in character, and its vulnerability to elementary criticism seems to continue to attract at least two classes of persons: those who feel that the traditional approaches to law exhibited in juristic writing, legal literature, legal research, and legal education tend to be too academic or unrealistic or divorced from the realities of the law in action; and those who find that much of the theorizing of analytical jurists from Austin to Hart is narrow or sterile, or, again, remote from reality. Although demands for greater practicality and demands for a broader approach to law are by no means identical, they reflect a felt need for a theoretical framework which accords to such notions as process, role, function, official, institution, decision, and technique an important place in juristic analysis alongside traditional notions such as sovereignty, sanction, authority, rule, and duty.

A crucial reason for the continued attractiveness of "The Path of the Law" as a contribution to legal theory is that Holmes made an effective, although elementary, switch of standpoint; its main weakness as a contribution to legal theory is that his analysis was not developed in a systematic fashion. A key to finding a satisfactory theoretical basis for demands for more realistic or for broader approaches to law is to develop models of legal system and legal process which accommodate at least the principal standpoints of participants in legal processes. These standpoints can be defined either in terms of specific tasks (*e.g.*, rule-making, rule-interpreting, fact-finding, persuading, and predicting) or in terms of typical functionaries who in practice often have overlapping and imprecisely defined roles (*e.g.*, judges, legislators,

46 *See* Dworkin, *supra* note 43.

47 What is suggested here is not that attempts to elucidate the concept of law in terms of systems of rules—or rules-and-principles (*see id.*)—have been misconceived or mistaken, but rather that such theories of law have sometimes been used to provide or to justify inappropriately narrow criteria of relevance in other contexts. To conceive of law as a system of rules does not involve commitment to a narrow approach to legal literature or legal education as a matter of logical necessity, but it may in fact encourage such an approach.

and advocates). Such models of legal process are not an alternative to, but rather presuppose, a model of legal system as a system of rules (or rules and principles).

III

The Bad Man and Legal Education

In the United States concern with legal education has often been both a stimulus to and a testing ground for general theorizing about law. "The Path of the Law" exemplifies this tendency. Two major themes have dominated American discussions of legal education since Holmes: the search for ways of developing a more efficient and realistic system of preparation for legal practice, and the desire for a closer integration of law and the social sciences.[48] A close connection between these objectives is often taken for granted, although the exact nature of this connection is not always made clear. Both themes are recognizable in "The Path of the Law," where their compatibility is assumed rather than demonstrated. I propose to argue that in advocating a switch of standpoint, Holmes pinpointed a crucial weakness in Langdell's educational theory, but that largely because he failed to pursue the implications of such a switch, his own prescriptions for legal education did not provide the basis for a viable alternative. In particular, by failing to identify precisely what standpoint(s) might be suitable as the basis for a working theory of legal education, Holmes was able to beg some crucial questions, including questions about the relationship between these two themes.

Demands for a more efficient and realistic system of preparation for practice typically emanate from legal practitioners, who have not always been their own best advocates in this cause. Poor diagnosis, naive prescription, a lack of appreciation of educational problems—pedagogical, financial, and administrative—and more than a hint of anti-intellectualism have often spoiled the presentation of a potentially strong case. The American legal profession has been distinctive in having had over the years a number of men of stature, such as Holmes and Frank, who have performed the function of spokesmen for the profession in a manner which exempts them from charges of crude anti-intellectualism. From one perspective "The Path of the Law" is a powerful statement of the practicing lawyer's complaint against academic

48 *See generally* W. Twining, *supra* note 37; Stevens, *Two Cheers for 1870: The American Law School*, in 5 Perspectives in American History 405 (D. Fleming & B. Bailyn eds. 1971).

law in general and against Langdellism in particular. The essence of the complaint is that Langdell and his disciples adopted inappropriate criteria of relevance in their approach to teaching, research, and writing. In such an interpretation the Bad Man serves as a device for dramatizing a plea for the adoption of a more realistic standpoint.

What was the standpoint assumed by Langdellism? In his most famous formulation Langdell identified it with "the true lawyer," who has a mastery of legal principles and an ability "to apply them with constant facility and certainty to the ever-tangled skein of human affairs."[49] As has often been pointed out, Langdell's "true lawyer" is a far from realistic stereotype of actual private practitioners. His assumed criteria of relevance are almost identical with those adopted by appellate court judges in their task of expounding, interpreting, and applying the law to given sets of facts.[50] These criteria are different from, and generally much more restricted than, those of office or trial lawyers. In this context the charge of narrowness is apposite.[51]

---

49 C. Langdell, *supra* note 6, at vi (Preface).

50 *See* Megarry, *Law as Taught and Law as Practised*, 9 J. Soc'y Pub. Teachers L. 176, 176-78 (1966).

51 Of course, Langdell was not a lone offender in this respect. Indeed, his reforms at Harvard represent an important stride away from what might be termed the textbook tradition of legal education. As a product of a system which was in certain respects pre-Langdellian, I can give examples from personal experience of the consequences of adopting a standpoint which is closer to appellate court adjudication than to "Bad Mansmanship." For example, my only exposure as a student to the important subject of compensation for personal injuries occurred in a course called "Torts." We were encouraged to buy one of the leading textbooks on the subject, and to read a large number of reports of decisions of appellate courts as well as a few learned articles, almost all of which adopted similar criteria of relevance. The main textbook which I used was *Salmond*. *See* J. Salmond, The Law of Torts (11th ed. R. Heuston ed. 1953). It still flourishes and it is in many respects an admirable work. Salmond's treatise was quite informative and lucid about the ingredients of liability in the tort of negligence and about the various defenses, but it was silent on a great many matters that an English solicitor would want to know when handling a personal injury claim. There was, for example, no mention of the fact that in England only about 2% of such claims are determined by a judgment of a court and that the vast majority of the remainder (approximately 80% according to a recent survey) are settled or abandoned even before the issuance of a writ. *See* P. Atiyah, Accidents, Compensation and the Law 281-304 (1970); T. Ison, The Forensic Lottery 115, 155 (1967). There was no indication of the factors which make the pursuit of such claims what has been aptly called "a forensic lottery" (T. Ison, *supra*); there was almost no discussion of the relationship of the common law action for negligence to other compensation processes or to the social security system; and, most surprising of all, there was no discussion of the insurance factor. The latest editions of *Salmond* (the most recent edition is the fifteenth) make some concession on the last point (*see* J. Salmond, The Law of Torts 31-39 (15th ed. R. Heuston ed. 1969)), but the criteria of relevance remain essentially the same as before, with the result that most of the things which the injured citizen or his adviser or other participants in compensation processes need to know are treated as irrelevant. Thus, *Salmond* has limited value as a tool of prediction for participants in pro-

Up to this point there appears to be common ground between demands for more efficient professional training and the desire for a closer integration of law and the social sciences. Both involve the rejection of Langdellism as too narrow; both call for a broader approach; both evidence a concern with the law in action. But these seductive phrases all too easily conceal widely divergent standpoints and concerns. Broader in what respect(s)? Interest in the law in action from what standpoint(s)? The Wall Street lawyer, the gadfly reformer, the would-be pioneer of an Empirical Science of Law, and the representative of any one of the species of emerging legal worms might all give different answers to these questions.

Failure to recognize this point has probably helped to sustain the comfortable myth, central to the American Realist Movement, that the protagonists of improved professional training and the leaders of the integration movement were natural allies. The existence of a common enemy and some overlap between their concerns is not disputed. But the extent to which their criteria of relevance were shared and how far they diverged has never been adequately explored. Analysis along these lines may contribute something to explaining such phenomena as the split between the Scientists and the Prudents at Columbia in 1928, the disillusion and malaise that quickly succeeded the rise of the Realist Movement, and the continuing confusion and sense of dissatisfaction surrounding many contemporary debates about legal education, legal research, and legal literature.[52]

Recent developments in academic treatment of the law of torts

---

cesses involving claims for compensation for personal injuries. It is also questionable whether, without considerable supplementation, it is adequate as an educational work for intending participants in those processes or for those who wish to understand the way the system works in practice. Nor does it provide an adequate basis for evaluating the system. From a wide variety of standpoints its basic limitation is that its criteria of relevance are too narrow.

The authors (or editors) of such works may defend themselves by saying that they do not hold themselves out as doing more than expounding the law as it is in a particular field at a given moment in time. For example, in the preface to the first edition of Salmond's work, the author stated: "I have endeavoured in this book to set forth the principles of the law of Torts with as much precision, coherence and system as the subject admits of, and with as much detailed consideration as is necessary to make the work one of practical utility." *Id.* at v (1st ed. 1907) (Preface).

What is at issue is not whether such books achieve their objectives (although Salmond's assumptions about practical utility are debatable), but how dominant a place in a nation's legal literature and legal education should be accorded to works with such limited objectives, and whether it is a healthy situation for a high proportion of the energies of outstanding legal scholars to be devoted to the production of such works. *See generally* W. Twining, *Is Your Textbook Really Necessary?*, 11 J. SOC'Y PUB. TEACHERS L. 81 (1970).

52 *See generally* works cited in note 48 *supra*.

and accidents provide a concrete example of the unsystematic nature of the post-Langdellian reaction. Most torts books and courses even today provide striking examples of what Pound termed the divorce between law in books and law in action.[53] Yet the works and the courses survive and many of the responses to criticism of them look more like palliatives than cures. There has, however, recently been a spate of books on accident compensation which depart significantly from the traditional model. Many are of excellent intellectual quality.[54] These works are largely, but not exclusively, concerned with reform; thus, they represent a move away from the standpoint of the judge towards that of the legislator. Their criteria of relevance are closer to those of the Bad Man, although they are by no means identical. These works have generally been well received, but two contrasting lines of criticism have been leveled at some of them. On the one hand it has been pointed out that proponents of accident compensation schemes have not paid sufficient attention to the vested interests and political obstacles likely to prevent or delay the movement for reform.[55] On the other hand it has been suggested that they fail to provide sufficient guidance to those who wish to know how to operate within the existing system.[56] It is even arguable that traditional expository works are of more value to the intending practitioner than this new genre which claims, *inter alia,* to be more concerned with the law in action than were its predecessors. Thus, ironically, these ostensibly more realistic works are charged with lack of political realism from the standpoint of the legislator, and with neglect of immediate practical realities from the point of view of the practitioner. It is unnecessary here to treat the merits of these criticisms. The relevant point is that the movement away from the standpoint of the appellate judge or the expositor of legal doctrine has not involved a simple switch to the standpoint of the Bad Man or to any other single standpoint.

---

[53] There has been too much abstract reasoning from attractive analogies of the past and not enough testing of those analogies in the light of how they meet or fail to meet the exigencies of reasonable expectations of men in the time and place. Abstract ethics and abstract politics must be supplemented by comparative study of the social and economic conditions from which their abstract theories are derived and of those to which they are to be applied.

R. Pound, Law Finding Through Experience and Reason 47-48 (1960).

[54] *See, e.g.,* P. Atiyah, *supra* note 51; G. Calabresi, The Costs of Accidents (1970); T. Ison, *supra* note 51; R. Keeton & J. O'Connell, Basic Protection for the Traffic Victim (1965).

[55] *See, e.g.,* Greer, Book Review, 22 N. Ir. L.Q. 554, 559 (1971) (review of P. Atiyah, *supra* note 51).

[56] *See, e.g.,* Walker, Book Review, Jurid. Rev. 278 (1970) (review of P. Atiyah, *supra* note 51). *See also* Smith, *Authors and Authority,* 12 J. Soc'y Pub. Teachers L. 3 (1972).

A brief glance at existing literature, such as practical manuals on accident claims and defamation suits, which appears to be designed specifically for the Bad Man's legal adviser, conveys the impression that such literature is generally intellectually inferior to both the reform-minded books and traditional textbooks. For this reason, if for no other, this type of work is generally regarded as unsuitable for pedagogical purposes. Thus, even in an area in which significant intellectual advances have been made, the needs of the Bad Man's adviser have been catered to only incidentally.

What the Bad Man, the Good Citizen, and their legal advisers need to know in order to act out their roles as participants in legal processes is not coextensive with what other participants, such as judges and advocates, need to know. And much of legal theory and legal writing, as well as legal education, ignores their standpoints and their needs. Attempts to make adjustments in the light of such complaints have often been halfhearted and have tended to proceed on an inadequate theoretical basis. Nine pages on insurance in a recent edition of *Salmond on Torts*[57] represent little more than a placatory gesture. Holmes's Bad Man concept contained the germ of a theoretical basis for some practitioners' complaints. More fully developed, it could provide the basis for a systematic evaluation of and response to their demands. It represents a striking example of the influence of assumptions about standpoint on ways of approaching and thinking about law.

Holmes never developed a systematic theory for educating future practitioners. One may confidently infer from "The Path of the Law" and his other pronouncements that such an approach to legal education would have had little appeal to him. It seems likely that he would have rejected what might be termed "the rationalist model of formal legal education."[58] A mode of legal education which sets out methodically and single-mindedly to prepare students within the academy for tasks which they would be likely to perform in real life would almost inevitably have to contain a large element of the banausic. Even with the support of a romantic and inflated view of the role of lawyers in society (and backed by arguments that formal education should be seen as a long term investment in highly transferable skills), we cannot evade the fact that effective participation in legal processes almost always involves mastery of much that is specific, trivial, routine, dull, or any combination of these. Holmes, on the other hand, shared the prevailing high-minded and comfortable vision of the elite law school:

57 *See* J. Salmond, The Law of Torts 31-39 (15th ed. R. Heuston ed. 1969).

58 *See generally* What's Wrong With the Law? 124-26 (M. Zander ed. 1970).

"I say the business of a law school is not sufficiently described when you merely say that it is to teach law, or to make lawyers. It is to teach law in the grand manner, and to make great lawyers."[59]

Furthermore, it is doubtful whether Holmes would have agreed with those who believe that many of the lessons traditionally left to be picked up in practice can be learned more efficiently and more quickly within the academy. If any precise meaning can be attached to his cryptic aphorisms on the life of the law and the role of formal education, it is that the academy cannot and should not hold itself out as providing more than a start to a lifelong process of self-education. He believed that law schools should perform a role which is at once elevated, limited in scope, and not subject to precise analysis. A rationalist Bad Man theory of legal education would probably not have appealed to him.

Holmes never worked out in detail the implications of his pronouncements on legal education. His diagnosis was at best incomplete. His prescriptions were scattered and vague, and he dropped only a few very general hints about his views on educational priorities. He was correct in his perception that the main weakness of Langdellism was that it was too closely wedded to a single, and for many purposes inappropriate, standpoint. But he did not seriously attempt to identify what standpoint or standpoints would provide the basis for a more satisfactory theory of legal education. He probably sensed that an approach to legal education based exclusively on the standpoint of the Bad Man would be at least as defective as Langdellism. But he declined to provide a coherent alternative theory, perhaps because he was skeptical of theorizing about education. This omission enabled him to beg two of the most persistent questions facing American law schools: first, to what extent and by what means formal legal education should be wholeheartedly vocational in its orientation; and second, to what extent preparation for legal practice and the development of law as a social science are compatible objectives for a single institution. Much

[59] O.W. Holmes, *The Use of Law Schools*, in Collected Legal Papers 37 (1920).

> No result is easy which is worth having. Your education begins when what is called your education is over—when you no longer are stringing together the pregnant thoughts, the "jewels five-words-long," which great men have given their lives to cut from the raw material, but have begun yourselves to work upon the raw material for results which you do not see, cannot predict, and which may be long in coming,—when you take the fact which life offers you for your appointed task.

O.W. Holmes, *Profession of the Law*, in *id.* at 31.

Speaking before the Harvard Law School Association in 1886, Holmes remarked: "The main part of intellectual education is not the acquisition of facts, but learning how to make facts live." O.W. Holmes, *The Use of Law Schools*, *supra* at 36-37.

of the history of the American law school since Holmes's day could be written in terms of a recurring failure to face, let alone to resolve, these issues. "The Path of the Law" brings to the surface the two main ingredients of this central dilemma of American legal education: the Bad Man model of vocational training and the idea of law as a social science. Although Holmes identified the ingredients of the dilemma, he failed to resolve it.

IV

The Bad Man and the Bust Book

A pillar of the New England intellectual elite addressing potential members of the legal profession in 1897 and four young radicals giving practical advice to members of the underground in 1971 seem to belong to different worlds. The expressed aspiration of the former was to "catch an echo of the infinite";[60] that of the latter is to smash the system.[61] One function of Holmes's cynical acid is to strip value judgments from legal analysis; the acid of *The Bust Book* is directed at the whole structure of the legal system, not only at its claims to neutrality and impartiality. Holmes tended to dismiss radical socialism as empty humbug;[62] no doubt members of "the Movement" would use stronger language to characterize the social order and the attitudes represented by Holmes. To Frank, Holmes symbolized "the completely adult jurist";[63] the new radical jurisprudence is still in its infancy.[64] Despite these contrasts, I propose to argue that "The Path of the Law" may provide a starting point for a dialogue between the emergent jurisprudence of the radical left in the United States and the

---

60 The remoter and more general aspects of the law are those which give it universal interest. It is through them that you not only become a great master in your calling, but connect your subject with the universe and catch an echo of the infinite, a glimpse of its unfathomable process, a hint of the universal law.

The Path of the Law 478.

61 The judicial system in the United States is not a neutral institution. Although the courts hide behind a cloak of judicial impartiality, they are an apparatus for the preservation of the status quo—a society based on race, sex, and class exploitation. The cop and the judge wear different uniforms, but they both serve the same System we seek to destroy. Both the cop on the beat and the judge on the bench will attempt to crush our Movement; we must understand the function of each—and fight against both.

K. Boudin, B. Glick, E. Raskin & G. Reichbach, *supra* note 1, at 14.

62 Holmes's political views have been the subject of much debate. *See* S. Konefsky, The Legacy of Holmes and Brandeis 64-66 (1956).

63 J. Frank, Law and the Modern Mind 270-77 (1930).

64 It has, however, a formidable intellectual pedigree.

bourgeois jurisprudence (as radicals might categorize it) which has dominated American legal thought since Holmes.

It should not be necessary to labor the point that such a dialogue is worth encouraging. The genre of literature represented by *The Bust Book* presages the arrival of a new brand of radical jurisprudence which deserves the serious attention of jurists, whether radical, reformist, or reactionary.[65] Of course, manuals like *The Bust Book* tend to take for granted rather than to expound upon underlying ideological assumptions; even the more theoretical writings of radical lawyers presently tend toward exaggeration, crude simplification, and heavy use of emotive terms which obfuscate rather than assist rational discourse. But it would be foolish to make stylistic puerility an excuse for not taking seriously the challenging ideas that are emerging, or reemerging, from this quarter: that judicial impartiality is a myth which cloaks the essential function of the courts as apparatus for maintaining an unjust social order; that the function of bourgeois jurisprudence has been to legitimatize the existing order and to contribute to the mystification rather than the demystification of law; that all trials are political and that all prisoners are political prisoners; that talk of "civil liberties" is a species of the Big Lie; and that civil libertarian groups such as the American Civil Liberties Union function as paragovernmental organizations.[66] Such assertions deserve careful analysis, if only because they are gaining increasing currency among law students and lawyers. The challenge they present to traditional juristic discourse deserves, at the very least, a reasoned response. In the United States this response needs to be set in the context of American legal thought in general. The dominant historical position of Holmes in the American tradition makes him one, but not the only, suitable starting point for comparing and contrasting radical and bourgeois juristic ideas.[67]

It must be admitted that there are some important limitations to using "The Path of the Law" for this purpose. In many respects Holmes's essay and *The Bust Book* are hardly comparable;[68] the dates, the circumstances, the objectives, and the style of each work, their re-

---

65 The terminology adopted here is that of the radical left, who would probably characterize Jeremy Bentham (and the author of this essay) as "reformist" and Holmes as "reactionary."

66 *See generally* LAW AGAINST THE PEOPLE: ESSAYS TO DEMYSTIFY LAW AND ORDER AND THE COURTS (R. Lefcourt ed. 1971). This work also illustrates the tendency to rely heavily on emotive terms.

67 Jeremy Bentham has recently begun to provide a similar starting point in the United Kingdom. Lecture by Professor H.L.A. Hart, "Bentham and the Demystification of the Law," London School of Economics, June 28, 1972.

68 *See* notes 60-64 and accompanying text *supra*.

spective audiences, and the only semi-articulate major premises of their authors prima facie provide little basis for comparison. But on at least two points there are significant links between the Bad Man and the addressees of *The Bust Book*.

First, the criteria of relevance of the works are similar, although not identical. Both works are concerned with the practical realities of confronting the law as it is. There is a shared concern with predicting events at various stages in certain kinds of legal processes which mandates a realistic picture of how the legal system in fact operates. But there is an important difference between the works:

> The non-conformist challenges the legitimacy of the social norms he rejects while the criminal accepts the norms he violates. The non-conformist aims to change the norms and the criminal is primarily concerned with escaping the sanctioning force of existing norms without proposing substitutes. . . . The criminal and the revolutionary are linked by the inequities of society, the one reflecting and the other challenging them; the one deviant, the other defiant.[69]

At several points *The Bust Book* illustrates the dilemma of those who are obliged to participate in a system they seek to change. Conformance to the rules of the system may be seen as acceptance or even reinforcement of it, but refusal to conform may be counter-productive. This dilemma, although not shared by Holmes's Bad Man, is openly recognized in *The Bust Book*.[70]

A second point of contact between the Bad Man and *The Bust Book* relates to the Bad Man's amorality. As we have seen, one function of the Bad Man in Holmes's argument was to dramatize the distinction between law and morals. This distinction provides one basis for claims

---

69 Unpublished student essay by Timothy Chapman, University of Warwick, Coventry, England (quoted with permission of the author).

70 A conventional legal defense means using the facts and the law—technicalities, rules of evidence, Constitutional rights—to win a case. It can be used alone, or combined with a political defense.

> This approach is useful when a good plea bargain has not been offered or when you think you have a very good chance of winning.
>
> Legal technicalities have also been used to delay final judgment on a case until the political situation changed to the defendant's benefit. After the Columbia University busts, the defense lawyers stalled until the new University administration was appointed, which dropped the complaints against five hundred of the students.
>
> Using existing laws does tend to legitimate a legal system which we oppose. Asking the judge to enforce those laws on our behalf reinforces the myth that courts are neutral, and compliance with conventional courtroom procedures may add to the sanctity of the law.
>
> Nevertheless, at the present time, conventional legal defense does keep activists out of jail and free to organize.

K. Boudin, B. Glick, E. Raskin & G. Reichbach, *supra* note 1, at 92-93.

to neutrality in analysis and description of the law as it is. At first sight there appears to be a clash between this brand of legal positivism[71] and the ideas of radicals who pour scorn not only on claims that existing legal orders are in fact neutral or impartial, but also on the idea that legal analysis can ever be neutral or value-free. This raises extremely complex issues which have been much debated. Here I shall content myself with making two points. First, the positions of Holmes and the authors of *The Bust Book* are both more complex and closer to each other on this issue than might at first appear. Holmes's insistence on divorcing law and morals for the purposes of legal analysis did not preclude his acceptance of the point that judgments of value and considerations of policy have an important place in judicial reasoning. Indeed, he was one of the first to stress this theme.[72] Conversely, much of the information in *The Bust Book* could be said to be neutral in the sense that it is capable of verification by empirical means and that it could be useful to a variety of people with different values pursuing different objectives. These examples at least serve to make the elementary point that sweeping claims to, or denials of, neutrality need to be treated with caution.

Insistence on the distinction between prescription and description is indicative of a concern with demystification of law by jurists in the Anglo-American tradition of jurisprudence.[73] The main reason for this insistence has been a concern with clarity of thought as a precondition for describing, analyzing, and criticizing legal systems as they really are. In different ways demystification of law has been a prominent theme in the writings of jurists as varied as Bentham, Holmes, Frank, Llewellyn, and Hart. Here there is, prima facie, common ground between radical and orthodox jurisprudence. Ironically, the leading contemporary proponents of the demystification of the law (itself a eulogistic phrase) tend to be among the worst offenders in their mystifying use of question-begging epithets and other eulogistic and dyslogistic terms. Like Blackstone, their cardinal error is to confuse propaganda with analysis. If radical lawyers are to enter into meaningful dialogue

---

71 On the various meanings of "positivism," see Hart, *Positivism and the Separation of Law and Morals*, 71 HARV. L. REV. 593, 601-02 (1958).

72 I take it for granted that no hearer of mine will misinterpret what I have to say as the language of cynicism. The law is the witness and external deposit of our moral life. Its history is the history of the moral development of the race. The practice of it, in spite of popular jests, tends to make good citizens and good men. When I emphasize the difference between law and morals I do so with reference to a single end, that of learning and understanding the law.

The Path of the Law 459.

73 *See* Lecture, *supra* note 67.

with bourgeois jurists they could well add Bentham's *Book of Fallacies* to their shelf of handbooks, and could do very much worse than move on from that to "The Path of the Law" as part of their progress to a more mature radical jurisprudence.

Envoi

Invulnerability to criticism is not a necessary quality of a classic. Significant error is more characteristic of the genus. Does it contain important insights? Do its errors and exaggerations suggest further insights? Does it have something fresh to say to successive generations, or is it as ephemeral as most legal writing? Judged by these criteria, "The Path of the Law" easily passes the test. In arguing that legal education and legal theory could benefit from a change of standpoint, Holmes identified a persistent source of dissatisfaction and perplexity in American legal thought. He also provided a striking illustration of the potential of standpoint as a tool of juristic analysis. By exaggerating the importance of the task of prediction, he invited criticism which has itself been revealing. The protean qualities of the Bad Man in his subsequent existence serve to remind us of some neglected perspectives on law. *Floreat vir amoralis.*

[4]
Academic Law and Legal Philosophy: The Significance of Herbert Hart

WHEN the history of academic law in England during the past 200 years comes to be written, the uneven progress of jurisprudence will form an important subplot in the story. There will, no doubt, be differing interpretations of that subplot, but few are likely to dissent from the judgment that the election of Herbert Hart to the Chair of Jurisprudence at Oxford in 1951 was a very significant event and that during the next 25 years he was the single most influential jurist not only in this country, but also in many other parts of the Western World.

One version of the story might be condensed as follows: in the late eighteenth century Jeremy Bentham dealt some almost mortal blows to the metaphysical and conservative version of natural law exemplified by Blackstone. But Bentham was largely unsuccessful in his attempt to undermine the pragmatic and unsystematic modes of thought of the common law. His grand design for a science of legislation encompassed within a single theory both expository and censorial jurisprudence; his particular version of consequentialism emphasised the relevance of the detailed study of social facts to understanding and evaluating the actual operation and effects of particular laws and institutions. Bentham wrote at a time when the social sciences, in particular sociology, anthropology and social psychology, had hardly begun to emerge. He was ahead of his day in emphasising the need for reliable social data but, not surprisingly, by modern standards his ideas of what was involved in social research and his view of society and of social phenomena lacked sophistication. Even one hundred and fifty years after Bentham's death, the implications for the study of law of the broader perspectives of social theorists, such as Marx, Weber and Durkheim were as yet unexplored. To put the matter in a simplified form: English legal theory [1] had yet to be integrated with social theory.

For nearly two hundred years the mainstream of English (and to a large extent American) jurisprudence from Bentham to Dworkin flowed almost exclusively within the confines of liberal democratic thought; this was broad enough to include Harold Laski and the Fabians on the one hand and the free market economists, from Adam Smith to F. A. Hayek and Richard Posner on the other; but,

[1] The history of legal theory in Scotland is in many respects a separate story, see, for example, S. G. Kermack "Jurisprudence and Philosophy of Law" in *Sources and Literature of Scots Law*, The Stair Society, Vol. 1 (1936).

so far as academic law and its theoretical aspect, jurisprudence, were concerned, none of the major rivals to liberal democratic ideology, such as Marxism, Anarchism or Fascism, secured much of a foothold. Most, but not all, English jurists were positivistic in that they emphasised the importance of distinguishing law as it is from law as it ought to be, a distinction clearly reflected in the differentiation of expository and censorial jurisprudence.

Within this broad ideological mainstream English jurisprudence from the death of Bentham until the advent of Hart underwent a progressive narrowing of its focus of attention and a general loss of coherence. Austin narrowed down Bentham, and Austin's followers narrowed down Austin, in much the same way that some disciples of Maitland stuck with his period of history but lost sight of his vision. The leading academic lawyers of the next generation such as Pollock, Anson, Dicey and Vinogradoff were not, as has sometimes been suggested, indifferent to questions about what the law ought to be. But the systematic application of the principle of utility to the evaluation of laws was increasingly replaced by appeals to practical common sense and other often unstated criteria which Bentham would no doubt have relegated to the status of sympathy and antipathy.[2] There is even in the writings of Pollock and Vinogradoff a suggestion of a return to the unBenthamite view that the common law is not far from being the embodiment of pragmatic excellence. Historians may differ over the reasons for the decline in overt appeals to utility as a measure of laws, but it is not surprising that this was matched by a corresponding decline in interest in censorial jurisprudence as a serious intellectual pursuit.

From 1900 to 1950 the predominant mode of English jurisprudential writing and teaching was particular rather than general, expository and analytical rather than critical, and very largely apolitical, at least on the surface. During this period academic law was dominated by what may be conveniently referred to as the Expository Orthodoxy, that is to say that teaching, research and writing by academic lawyers were very largely concentrated on exposition and analysis of existing legal doctrine. As I have argued elsewhere, the predominance of analytical jurisprudence within legal theory and the domination of the expository orthodoxy within academic law are more plausibly interpreted as an example of symbiosis rather than of simple cause and effect.[3] In the prevailing

---

[2] See W. Morrison "Frames of reference for legal ideals" in E. Kamenka, R. Brown and A. Ehr-Soon Tay *Law and Society: The Crisis in Legal Ideals* (1978), pp. 18–20.

[3] W. Twining "Some Jobs for Jurisprudence," 1 British Jo. of Law and Society 149, 162 (1974). Bentham himself considered the Expositor to have a "humbler function" than the Censor. He also had no doubt about his own role: "The

climate of opinion it was not surprising that so much attention was devoted to analytical jurisprudence and that sociology of law and sociological jurisprudence were hardly developed at all. The narrowing of the focus of attention is illustrated by the extraordinary displacement of Bentham by Austin as "the Father of English Jurisprudence," a misjudgment that says much about the limitations of English academic law during the first half of this century.

Of course, analytical jurisprudence did not secure a complete monopoly of taught jurisprudence nor of juristic writing. Natural law did not go away; while noisy Americans like Frank and Llewellyn could be ignored or put down by caricature, jurists from Harvard such as Pound, Gray and Holmes were at least acknowledged with civility or accorded the dubious honour of being treated as reputable, but soft, targets for criticism. Hohfeld's analytical work was discussed as if he were almost an Englishman. Similarly, socially minded scholars, as diverse as Maitland, Dicey, Ginsburg, Laski, Stone, Friedmann and Montrose were too persistent to be ignored entirely; but, so far as jurisprudence was concerned, they were treated as belonging to the periphery rather than to the centre. The one major exception was historical jurisprudence as exemplified in the work of Maine and Vinogradoff, but somehow this fed relatively little into the mainstream of English academic law. From 1900 to 1950 nearly all chairs of jurisprudence in England were occupied by men who were lawyers first and foremost, often without very serious claims to being theorists of any kind. It would be churlish to dismiss the contributions to academic law of such outstandingly able men as Pollock, Salmond, C. K. Allen and Goodhart, but surely the judgment of history will be that their most important contributions were to particular studies rather than to general theory.

When the Chair of Jurisprudence at Oxford became vacant in 1951–52, the time was ripe for a change. Dissatisfaction with legal education and training was being expressed in some quarters; jurisprudence was clearly in the doldrums [4] and there were the beginnings of signs of unease about the expository orthodoxy within academic law.[5] The election to the Oxford Chair of a lawyer-turned-

business of simple *exposition* is a harvest on which there seemed no likelihood of there being any want of labourers: and into which therefore I had little ambition to thrust my sickle." *A Fragment on Government, Collected Works* at pp. 399, 404 (eds. J. H. Burns and H. L. A. Hart, 1977).

[4] See *e.g.* Hart's own assessment in "Analytical Jurisprudence in Mid-Twentieth Century: A Reply to Professor Bodenheimer," 105 U.Pa.L.Rev. 953, 957 *et seq.* (1957).

[5] See esp. L. C. B. Gower (1950) 13 M.L.R., p. 137, W. Friedmann *Law and Social Change in Contemporary Britain* (1951). There were also the beginnings of a new vitality in Jurisprudence: Julius Stone's *Province and Function of Law* (1946); Friedmann's *Legal Theory* (1944) and *Law and Social Change in Contemporary*

philosopher who had published little and who was virtually unheard of outside a narrow circle of philosophers must have come as something of a surprise, but in a very short time it was recognised that this was much more than just a good appointment. As an undergraduate at Oxford in the early 1950s, as I struggled with "Definition and Theory in Jurisprudence" and listened to the lectures that preceded the publication of *The Concept of Law*, I shared the sense of those around me that something new and significant was happening. Why it was significant and what exactly it signified were at that stage far from clear. A quarter of a century later it is at least worth trying to make a preliminary assessment.

The publication of a *festschrift* [6] to celebrate Professor Hart's seventieth birthday provides a suitable occasion. Unlike some *festschriften*, *Law, Morality and Society*, edited by Peter Hacker and Joseph Raz, is a substantial work in its own right. It contains a Preface, 16 essays, a bibliography of Hart's main writings (63 items) and no index. The authors of the essays are "colleagues, former pupils and devotees" of Herbert Hart. All are academics—seven philosophers, seven academic lawyers and two political theorists. With one or two possible exceptions, all could be said to be Oxonians in a fairly strong sense of the term and a clear majority were based on Oxford at the time of publication. They are reasonably representative of Hart's immediate successors. It would be tempting to categorise this book as an example of "English legal philosophising"; but the pitfalls of generalising are signalled by the fact that a majority of the authors have a close association with other jurisdictions, notably Scotland, the United States, South Africa, Israel and Canada. The collection both invites and resists generalisation: it is homogeneous, but not monolithic; there are differences of style, of perspective and of opinion, some subtle and some easily discernible. Yet the overall impression is of affinity; if the shared characteristics are merely family resemblances, then this is a not very extended family.

The difficulties of generalisation are illustrated by the range of topics addressed by the authors.[7] I shall not attempt here to do justice

Britain (1951); Glanville Williams' important articles on "Language and the Law" (1945–46) 61 and 62 L.Q.R. and his brave attempt to bring Salmond's *Jurisprudence* (10th ed., 1947) into line with modern techniques of conceptual analysis all preceded Hart's famous inaugural lecture, *Definition and Theory in Jurisprudence* (1953).

[6] P. M. S. Hacker and J. Raz (eds.) *Law, Morality and Society* (Oxford 1977, 312 pp. £7·50 hardback; £3·95 paperback, hereafter *L.M.S.*).

[7] The table of contents gives an indication of this: 1. "Hart's Philosophy of Law," by P. M. S. Hacker; 2. "Defeasibility and Meaning," by G. P. Baker; 3. "No Right Answer?," by R. M. Dworkin; 4. "The Phenomenon of Law," by J. R. Lucas; 5. "Real Laws," by A. M. Honoré; 6. "Naïve Instrumentalism and the Law," by R. S. Summers; 7. "Positivism, Adjudication, and Democracy," by G. Marshall; 8. "The House of Lords and the

to the book as a contribution to legal philosophy. Suffice to say that the general quality of the essays is almost uniformly good and that they clearly demonstrate the variety as well as the vitality of what I shall henceforward refer to as "Oxonian legal philosophy." [8] Only Hacker sets out to make a detailed critique of Hart's work and his essay concentrates largely on *The Concept of Law*. All of the contributors have paid Hart the compliment of preferring serious argument to ritual obeisance; several express their respect through open disagreement. The result is that this volume has rightly been praised as a significant contribution to the field. As Oxford's act of homage to its most eminent jurist it is both pleasing and apt.

However, as the editors would be the first to acknowledge, Herbert Hart is not exclusively an Oxford property. Despite its obvious merits both as a tribute and as a contribution to legal philosophy, this collection seems likely to provoke a sense of unease among many academic lawyers. The purpose of this paper is to explore two specific and related aspects of this unease. First, if the essays in this volume are representative of the work of Hart's disciples and successors, it seems that legal philosophy and academic law in this country may be moving in significantly different directions. At first sight, *Law, Morality and Society* suggests that Oxonian legal philosophy is tending towards increasingly sophisticated, often highly abstract, philosophical treatment of classical issues and concerns of analytical jurisprudence. Although several contributors explicitly treat law as a social phenomenon, the overall impression created by the collection is that this type of work is proceeding in almost complete isolation from contemporary social theory and from work in socio-legal studies, with little overt concern with the law in action.

Rules of Precedent," by R. Cross; 9. " Intention and *Mens Rea* in Murder," by A. J. P. Kenny; 10. " The Grounds of Responsibility," by J. L. Mackie; 11. " Rights in Legislation," by D. N. MacCormick; 12. " Promises and Obligations," by J. Raz; 13. " Approval and Disapproval," by P. R. Foot; 14. " Scepticism, Self-Refutation, and the Good of Truth," by J. M. Finnis; 15. " Justice Between Generations," by B. M. Barry; 16. " Harm and Self-Interest," by J. Feinberg.

8 It is reasonable to treat this as fairly typical of Oxonian legal philosophising. However it would be unwise to attach too much significance to a *festschrift*. The collection was intended as a tribute rather than as a representative anthology still less as a programmatic statement. It does not even set out to make a rounded assessment of Hart's achievements. Accordingly in developing my argument I shall, where appropriate, make reference to some other writings. *Law, Morality and Society* can usefully be seen as the third volume in the series of Oxford Essays in Jurisprudence, (A. G. Guest (ed.) *Oxford Essays in Jurisprudence* (1961); A. W. B. Simpson (ed.) *Oxford Essays in Jurisprudence*, 2nd Series (1973)). Taken together the three books contain thirty-seven essays; this is a somewhat better basis both for generalisation and for identifying trends in Oxonian legal theorising. In addition, I shall make occasional reference to two other works: *Taking Rights Seriously* (1977) by Ronald Dworkin, Hart's immediate successor in the Chair of Jurisprudence at Oxford, and two semi-popular books edited by Bryan Magee *Modern British Philosophy* (1971) and *Men of Ideas* (1978) which provide a convenient conspectus of the views of contemporary philosophers about the state of their subject.

Partly because of an increased philosophical sophistication, this kind of theorising is in danger of becoming further and further divorced from the central concerns of most academic lawyers and law students. Moreover, academic law in the United Kingdom and elsewhere is currently going through a period of rapid and significant change. One aspect of this is the movement to broaden the study of law, exemplified by the development of socio-legal studies and related activities. Such developments have stimulated interest in a much wider range of theoretical issues than were canvassed by mainstream jurisprudence up to 1950. To put the question bluntly: are academic law and Oxonian legal philosophy drifting apart?

A second question relates to the interpretation of the actual and potential significance of Herbert Hart's contributions. The editors of *Law, Morality and Society* interpret these exclusively in philosophical terms, summed up in the judgment that "[h]e has integrated [legal philosophy] into the mainstream of general philosophical thought." [9] None of the contributors to the collection diverges significantly from this interpretation. The question arises: is this an adequate assessment of the actual and potential significance of Hart's contribution? I propose to argue that this does less than justice to his significance as a jurist and that this is directly related to a missing element in the volume, *viz.* that it lacks a coherent conception either of academic law or of jurisprudence viewed as the theoretical sector of law-as-a-discipline.

I wish to dispose briefly of some obvious grounds for unease about, disagreement with or hostility towards the kind of approach which *Law, Morality and Society* represents. First, it is based on a particular conception of the nature and value of the philosophical enterprise. Those who do not accept this conception of philosophy or who are dubious of its claims, are likely to adopt a similar attitude to its legal manifestations. Oxonian legal philosophy, as represented by the work of Hart and nearly all of the contributors to *Law, Morality and Society,* falls clearly within the mainstream of contemporary British analytical philosophy. By and large they have adopted the techniques of analysis, some of the stylistic conventions and the predominant view of philosophical activity associated with it.

There are, of course, differences and disagreements within contemporary analytical philosophy. It is in a state of flux and is rather more varied than it was a few years ago. Yet, there appears to be a prevailing consensus among leading exponents about the nature of the enterprise. A concise statement of this consensus might be formulated in some such terms as these [10]: philosophy is concerned with

[9] *L.M.S.*, Preface, p. v.

[10] This statement is derived in part from passages in *Men of Ideas, op. cit. supra,*

the examination of fundamental assumptions and presuppositions underlying commonly held beliefs and specialised fields of discourse. The primary objective of philosophical analysis is to increase understanding, rather than to add to knowledge or to provide direct guidance for action. A characteristic of philosophical questions is that they resist categorisation as either empirical questions or as formal questions. Analytical philosophers are primarily concerned with elucidating concepts and with the critical examination of arguments. Philosophy does not have a distinctive subject-matter of its own, separate from other fields of discourse; rather it is concerned with analysing the fundamental concepts of and modes of argumentation appropriate to particular fields or disciplines; certain basic techniques of analysis can be applied to the subject-matter of any field of inquiry: the philosophy of linguistics or politics or physics is part of those disciplines as well as of philosophy. In this view, philosophical activiy is more concerned with analysing and elucidating than with synthesising or providing coherent frames of reference.

By and large the writings of Herbert Hart and of his immediate successors are based on some such view of the activity in which they are engaged. In *Law, Morality and Society* there is almost no explicit discussion of the nature of philosophical analysis in general or of legal philosophy in particular—the nature of the enterprise is taken for granted. Few are likely to disagree with the judgment that one of Hart's main achievements was to bring about a much closer integration of legal theory and contemporary British analytical philosophy, which the editors refer to as " the mainstream of general philosophical thought." This appears to equate one mode of philosophising with " general philosophical thought," a view which many would consider both narrow and parochial. For present purposes it is sufficient to note that Oxonian legal philosophy is based on a particular view of philosophy which is not universally accepted.

Another source of unease or disagreement may be based on misconceptions or outdated views about modern analytical philosophy. *Law, Morality and Society* could be used to counter some common myths about Oxonian legal philosophers: that they are all positivists in the sense that they deny any necessary connection between law as it is and law as it ought to be; that they believe that might is right; that they are indifferent to questions of value; that they are only concerned with analysing the meanings of words or

n. 8, especially dicta by Professors Berlin, Ayer, Williams and Hare. If these views are in some respects more characteristic of the nineteen-sixties than of the late nineteen-seventies, that may be appropriate in respect of prevailing views within contemporary legal philosophy. Allowance should be made for intellectual lag.

with the "ordinary usage" of inhabitants of North Oxford; that they are obsessed by a narrow range of over-worked questions; that they stand aloof from contemporary public debate on important moral, social and political issues; that they have nothing to say which is of direct relevance to practising lawyers or law reformers; that they all write in a style so recondite that it is beyond the reach of most academic lawyers, to say nothing of law students and practitioners.

It is not necessary for present purposes to explore whether there is any basis at all for any of these assertions. Suffice to say that *Law, Morality and Society* provides ample evidence that none of them is a *necessary* attribute of Oxonian legal philosophising and that such generalisations do not do justice to the diversity, the richness and the potential for illumination of this kind of work. Hacker writes of Hart: "The family of philosophical styles commonly referred to as 'linguistic' or 'analytical' (or occasionally even 'Oxford') philosophy has often been condemned as arid, superficial, and philosophically unilluminating—at best high grade lexicography. The *Concept of Law* provides a brilliant refutation of such nonsense." [11] In my view, a similar claim can be made for *Law, Morality and Society.*

Thirdly, almost without exception Hart and his immediate successors are either apolitical or accept some version of liberal democratic theory. Hart is a liberal in this sense.[12] Dworkin explicitly claims that the primary objective of *Taking Rights Seriously* is "to define and defend a liberal theory of law." [13] Most of the debates centred on the writings of Dworkin, Nozick and Rawls are debates within liberalism.[14] Recently various forms of political theory which are hostile to liberalism have become increasingly influential in this country. Quite clearly this is a central area of controversy within contemporary academic law as it is within our intellectual life generally. A possible criticism of some Oxonian legal philosophers is that they tend to write as if such controversies do not exist. But there are notable exceptions, of whom Dworkin

11 *L.M.S.* at p. 2.

12 *Cf.* Honoré (*L.M.S.* at p. 99): "One who wishes to take Hart seriously must approach his work as the neo-classical expression of a liberal social and political philosophy which the radical utilitarians first expounded but which he has, with sober eloquence and ingenious shift, remodulated and redressed for the eyes and ears of our age. To the liberal mainstream other aspects and characterisations of his work (analytical, positivist) are, I believe, no more than subordinate rivulets or embankments."

13 *Taking Rights Seriously* at p. vii.

14 There have, of course, been Marxist critiques, especially of Rawls and Nozick; but the reader of the four volumes of Oxonian essays (n. 8, *supra*) will find more references to Richard Nixon and Spiro Agnew than to Karl Marx. Some passages in *Men of Ideas* suggest that there is on the part of contemporary English philosophers a greater readiness to confront Marxism directly than was characteristic of the nineteen-fifties and sixties.

is the leading example. By and large contemporary legal theorising is much more overtly concerned with political and ideological issues than it was a few years ago. This reflects some more general trends, especially the revival of interest in political philosophy and the increasing influence of Marxist and Marxian ideas in academic life.

Ideological or political disagreement, antagonism to the prevailing English empiricist view of philosophy, misunderstanding and prejudice may all provide starting-points for suspicion or outright rejection of the Oxonian approach to legal philosophy. However, none of these account for the unease that seems to be felt by at least some of those who might be characterised as middle-of-the-road academic lawyers. What of the jurist who recognises both the therapeutic value and the standards of rigour of analytical philosophy; who accepts that this kind of activity involves a fairly abstract and intellectually demanding level of discourse; who welcomes the movement to broaden academic law, but who would not go so far as to acknowledge that the study of law must inevitably become a sub-discipline of sociology or of any other subject including philosophy; and who, whatever his personal political beliefs, accepts the liberal democratic intellectual tradition as a central part of his heritage? What if such persons are left uneasy by some recent trends in Oxonian legal philosophy? I wish to suggest that several further possible sources of dissatisfaction can be identified; that some are contingent rather than necessary features of contemporary analytical philosophy and its legal manifestations and that there are convergent as well as divergent tendencies between Oxonian legal philosophy and the movement to broaden the study of law. Without attempting a comprehensive account, I shall try to probe some interrelated reasons for dissatisfaction or unease which centre around the conceptions of morality, of society and of the study of law that may be suggested by the title *Law, Morality and Society.*

JURISPRUDENCE AND THE STUDY OF LAW

Perhaps the most important reason for this dissatisfaction is a tendency, discernible in *Law, Morality and Society,* to adopt a rather narrow and recondite view of jurisprudence and by implication either to treat jurisprudence as co-extensive with legal philosophy or to imply that philosophising in the Oxford style is the only intellectually worthwhile kind of jurisprudential activity. It is difficult to back this weak generalisation with hard evidence, because the authors' assumptions about the nature and scope of jurisprudence tend to be assumed rather than stated. But there are one or two examples. For instance in the Preface, the editors write:

"(Hart's) work provides the foundations of contemporary legal philosophy in the English-speaking world and beyond. His teaching in Oxford and elsewhere has inspired many a young philosopher to turn to jurisprudence in the reasonable expectation of a good harvest." [15]

Similarly in his interesting essay G. P. Baker not only seems to use the terms interchangeably but also suggests that "a systematic philosophy of law" [16] or "a developed synoptic view of jurisprudence" [17] would be to give "genuine explanations of legal concepts and legal statements." [18] Thus Baker seemingly restricts jurisprudence to the analysis of legal concepts and legal statements, the classic subject-matter of expository or analytical jurisprudence.

P. M. S. Hacker in his illuminating essay on "Hart's philosophy of law" is also careful to point out that Hart's jurisprudence has a sociological dimension.[19] He cites the tantalising claim that *The Concept of Law* may be regarded as "an essay in descriptive sociology," a claim that is echoed by Professor Honoré in his paper on "Real Laws," the most down-to-earth contribution in the book.[20] Hacker, quite rightly, suggests that an important part of the originality of *The Concept of Law* (and, no doubt, of many of Hart's other writings) lay in his perception of "the relevance of new analytic techniques and advances in general philosophy for classical questions in legal theory." [21] So far as one can tell Hacker uses "philosophy of law," "legal theory" and "jurisprudence" interchangeably. Hacker explicitly acknowledges that law is a social phenomenon and impliedly concedes a connection between social and legal theory. But neither from this essay, nor from any other contribution to the book, does there emerge a clear conception of the nature or scope of jurisprudence and of its relations to social theory, to philosophy in general and to legal philosophy in particular.

It is unlikely that any of the contributors to *Law, Morality and Society* would deny that law is a social phenomenon and that legal institutions are examples of social institutions. Indeed, this is implicit in the title of the book and explicit acknowledgement of such truisms is to be found scattered in other writings of, for example, Hart, Dworkin, Honoré, MacCormick, Raz and Summers. J. R. Lucas explicitly argues that law should be viewed as a social phenomenon [22] and Philippa Foot makes a similar plea in respect of morality.[23] Yet if law is to be viewed as a social phenomenon, it would seem to

15 *Id.*, p.v.

16 At p. 43.

17 *Ibid.*

18 At pp. 26, 43.

19 At pp. 8–10.

20 At p. 99.

21 At p. 2.

22 85 *et seq.*

23 229 *et seq.*

be worthwhile at least to explore the relationship between legal theory and social theory, in particular possible connections between theories of law and theories of society. Unfortunately *Law, Morality and Society* has no index, but in several readings of the book I did not discover a single reference to Marx, Weber, Durkheim, Parsons or Merton nor a single sustained discussion of any other major social theorist. In case a *festschrift* might in this respect prove to be unrepresentative of contemporary Oxford jurisprudence, I inspected the indexes to the two earlier series of *Oxford Essays in Jurisprudence.*[24] In the first series none of the five named thinkers secures a mention; in the second series there is a single passing reference to Marx. Again there is no sustained discussion of any thinker who might clearly be identified as belonging to the mainstream of modern social theory.

This suggests that the conception of legal philosphy that pervades the volume under review is still far removed from the mainstream of contemporary social theory. There is not only a gap, there is also a tendency to distortion, rather clearly illustrated by some passages in *Law, Morality and Society.* The first, though venial is illuminating. In a passage quoted above the editors write: "Herbert Hart has done for twentieth-century legal philosophy what Bentham did for eighteenth-century jurisprudence. He has integrated it into a mainstream of general philosophical thought."[25] This may be acceptable from a narrow philosophical perspective, but it is a dubious interpretation both of Bentham's central concerns and of his historical significance. It is not paradoxical to say of Bentham that he was a great jurist and reformer, but a rather uneven philosopher—a quite widely held view. For his "science of legislation" takes for granted, rather than explores, some of its key assumptions—for example, its epistemological assumptions. Its detailed development, which occupied so much of Bentham's attention, belonged to a level and demanded a range of techniques and knowledge which would generally be regarded as falling outside the scope of philosophy. It is one thing to say that Bentham made some important contributions to philosophy; it is quite another to suggest that his main significance is as a philosopher. Implicit in my argument is the judgment that Hart may be more of a philosopher than Bentham, but that he has contributed at least as much to jurisprudence as to philosophy.

Another revealing distortion is to be found in the casual references to American Realism which appear at various places in the book.[26]

---

24 *Op. cit. supra.*, n. 8.

25 *Op. cit. supra.*, n. 9.

26 At p. 4 (Hacker), pp. 26–27, 35 (Baker), p. 85 (Lucas). These all echo Hart's interpretation of Legal Realism, see *infra*, n. 56.

These all seem to accept the hoary and, one would hope, by now discredited interpretation of the Realists as a group of people whose main significance is that they perpetrated some philosophical howlers such as the belief " that talk of rules is a myth " or that propositions of law are mere predictions or can be reduced to simple statements of brute fact. This is not merely an irritating example of unscholarly practice or of unfair polemics. For the persistent repetition of such misinterpretations enables legal philosophers to avoid joining debate on an issue that was a central concern of American Realists—*viz.* what is the proper scope of law-as-a-discipline? [27] Jurists such as Holmes, Llewellyn, Cook and Frank have few claims to be treated as philosophers, yet they made significant contributions to jurisprudence. The equation of legal philosophy with jurisprudence almost inevitably leads to misunderstanding of those jurists who are not primarily philosophers.

The tendency to use terms like jurisprudence and legal philosophy loosely and interchangeably might be no more than an example of an uncharacteristically imprecise use of language. However, it is worth noting that one mark of Oxonian philosophy is a tendency to be impatient about programmes. It is not surprising that *Law, Morality and Society* does not set out to define a programme or launch a manifesto; for characteristic of this approach is an attitude, sometimes associated with J. L. Austin, of suspicion of or impatience with anything that smacks of a programme, a grand theory, of a Weltanschauung.[28] In this view there is no hierarchy of interesting or

[27] See William Twining, *Karl Llewellyn and the Realist Movement*, (1973) *passim*, esp. 70–83, 375–382, 405–411.

[28] One version of this attitude is illustrated by Iris Murdoch's account of Hugo Bellfounder in *Under the Net* (1954), pp. 65–66: " He was interested in everything, and interested in the theory of everything, but in a peculiar way. Everything had a theory, and yet there was no master theory. I have never met a man more destitute than Hugo of anything which could be called a metaphysic or general Weltanschauung. It was rather perhaps that of each thing he met he wanted to know the *nature*—and he seemed to approach this question in each instance with an absolute freshness of mind. The results were often astonishing. I remember a conversation which we had once about translating. Hugo knew nothing about translating, but when he learnt that I was a translator he wanted to know what it was like. I remember him going on and on, asking questions such as: What do you mean when you say that you think the meaning in French? How do you know you're thinking it in French? If you see a picture in your mind how do you know it's a French picture? Or is it that you say the French word to yourself? What do you see when you see that the translation is exactly right? Are you imagining what someone else would think, seeing it for the first time? Or is it a kind of feeling? What kind of feeling? Can't you describe it more closely? And so on and so on, with a fantastic patience. This sometimes became very exasperating. What seemed to me to be the simplest utterance soon became, under the repeated pressure of Hugo's ' You mean,' a dark and confused saying of which I no longer myself knew the meaning. The activity of translating, which had seemed the plainest thing in the world, turned out to be an act so complex and extraordinary that it was puzzling to see how any human being could perform it. Yet at the same time Hugo's enquiries rarely failed to throw an extraordinary amount of light on whatever he concerned himself with. For Hugo each

significant issues, just interesting questions awaiting resolution by the application of analytical acid. Philosophy is conceived more in terms of style and technique than of subject-matter. Legal philosophy, viewed thus, is this mode of analysis applied to questions of or about law, legal system and legal concepts.[29] There is no school with a generally agreed programme, no consensus about doctrine; it sets no boundaries in respect of subject matter or lines of inquiry; almost the only claim that is made is that this tradition of philosophising has developed a number of techniques of wide application for dissolving puzzlements and exposing errors. This is one reason why it is difficult to generalise about an Oxford or Oxonian school of philosophy or of legal philosophy.

In so far as it is true to say that Oxonian legal philosophising is anti-programmatic this at least signals a limitation. It suggests that one should not look to this quarter for coherent frames of reference nor even a reasonably flexible sense of direction for developing a coherent approach to a subject. We may expect an often healthy scepticism of the doctrinaire, the over-simple or the grandiose. We can look to this approach for some illuminating techniques of analysis but little help with synthesis.

The absence of a programme or a coherent conception of the field does not mean that the selection of issues to address or concepts to elucidate is entirely random. An unprogrammatic approach to a subject may be particularly susceptible to the stimulus of fashion: it is not unknown within jurisprudence for a book-of-the-moment, a robust debate, or some dramatic event to attract the *ad hoc* attention of swarms of jurists like moths to a flame.

Another influence that may be at work is the notion of "philosophically interesting questions." This notion can both attract and divert attention. It is natural for philosophers coming to law to seize on concepts, issues and examples which have a recognisable and direct bearing on their own home-grown concerns. Moral philosophers, for example, have found the law to be a rich source of examples for their own purposes; they have in turn usefully explored points of contact between individual ethics and law or jurisprudence. Often

---

thing was astonishing, delightful, complicated and mysterious. During these conversations I began to see the whole world anew."

29 In this, as in some other respects, Ronald Dworkin is something of an exception. In his own work he has fairly consistently been trying to develop a general theory. In *Taking Rights Seriously* his expressed aim is "to define and defend a liberal theory of law" and he goes on to indicate that a general theory of law must include, *inter alia*, a theory of legislation, a theory of adjudication and a theory of compliance (Introduction, pp. vii, viii). Dworkin sees legal philosophy as "parasitic" upon a number of branches of philosophy, notably ethics, the philosophy of mind and action, political philosophy, and the philosophy of language and metaphysics. (Introduction to *The Philosophy of Law*, 1977). Dworkin is not alone in this respect; see for example, G. P. Baker in *L.M.S.* at p. 43.

this has opened up lines of inquiry which have been relatively new for jurists. Notions of what is philosophically interesting may also have a limiting influence; at worst this may take the form of a kind of intellectual snobbery about what concepts or issues are worthy of attention. Techniques of conceptual analysis can be applied to elucidate a much wider range of concepts than those which have attracted the attention of philosophers. Within legal discourse there are many concepts, some highly abstract, some of a lower level of generality, which can benefit from careful elucidation whether or not they are philosophically interesting. To take some topical examples: "unmet legal needs,"[30] "lawyers,"[31] "dispute,"[32] "torture,"[33] are all concepts which have recently been the subject of a good deal of confusion in legal contexts. Whether or not they are philosophically interesting, they are legally or jurisprudentially interesting and that should be good enough for jurists. Sometimes it is appropriate to borrow techniques from a neighbouring discipline without borrowing their conceptions of what is important or significant.

If fashion, the interests of philosophers or intellectual snobbery have produced some imbalances or distortions within legal theory, these are faults which are quite easily corrected. Rather more important, in this context, is the potential influence of hidden assumptions about the nature and scope of jurisprudence and academic law. "The classical questions of jurisprudence" tend on inspection to turn out to be the questions which attracted the attention of post-Austinian analytical jurists. Similarly "fundamental" or "basic" legal concepts appear to have been identified by similar criteria. "Legal reasoning" is still used to refer almost exclusively to reasoning about disputed questions of law, as if there were not a whole range of contexts within legal processes and legal discourse in which different modes of reasoning may be appropriate and worthy of examination; decisions to prosecute, disputed questions of fact, decisions on sanctions in particular cases, are all examples involving "lawyers' reasonings" which have attracted remarkably little theoretical attention.[34] Why, one may ask is "legal reasoning" confined to reasoning about questions of law? Part of the answer surely

[30] *e.g.* P. Lewis, "Unmet Legal Needs," in P. Morris, R. White and P. Lewis, *Social Needs and Legal Action* 73 (1973).

[31] *e.g. Legal Education in a Changing World* (1975), pp. 14–16.

[32] e.g. R. Abel, "A Comparative Theory of Dispute Institutions in Society," 8 Law and Society Rev. 217, 226–228 (1974).

[33] *e.g. Republic of Ireland* v. *United Kingdom* (1978) 2 E.H.R.R. 25, W. Twining, "Torture and Philosophy" LII *Proc. Aristotelian Soc. Supp.* 143 (1978).

[34] *e.g.* D. N. MacCormick in *Legal Reasoning and Legal Theory* (1978), acknowledges that he has excluded extended consideration of such matters as the processes of reasoning from evidence "for quite arbitrary reasons of space and time" (at p. 88). *Cf.* William Twining and David Miers, *How To Do Things With Rules* (1976) at pp. 157–159.

lies in a narrow conception of academic law. If the study of law is equated with the study of rules it is natural that legal reasoning should be identified with reasoning about legal rules, just as the study of precedent is largely confined to the doctrine of precedent, the study of statutory interpretation to the rules and principles of interpretation, and, *mirabile dictu*, the study of evidence is restricted to the rules of evidence. Behind both American Legal Realism and the movement to broaden the study of law in this country lies the simple truism that the study of rules alone is not enough for the understanding of law.[35] To date Oxonian legal philosophy, largely because it has taken too much for granted the criteria of relevance of Austinian analytical jurisprudence, has contributed almost nothing to the systematic and persistent exploration of the implications of this truism.

In one important respect Hart and his successors have moved beyond identifying "the classical questions" with post-Austinian analytical jurisprudence. They have paid a great deal of attention to themes connected with "law and morals." It might be said that they have revived Bentham's censorial jurisprudence, but in an un-Benthamite form.

A prominent theme in several of the essays in *Law, Morality and Society* and in other recent writings is that moral concerns are central to legal philosophy. For example, the relationship between law and morals is widely recognised as one of the classical questions of jurisprudence; Hacker identifies censorial jurisprudence with "applying moral principles"[36]; for Lucas, the sceptic (with whom he seems to identify) "is forced to concede that . . . jurisprudence must be, as Vinogradoff terms it, a moral science, to be understood and reasoned about from the inside"[37]; Dworkin asserts that "Hart is a moral philosopher"[38] and he goes so far as to say that "jurisprudential issues are at their core issues of moral principle, not legal fact or strategy."[39] It is by no means clear in these or other passages how the terms "morality," "morals" and "moral" are being used and whether the various authors are all using them in approximately the same sense.

Words like "morality" and "morals" are notoriously ambiguous. Moral questions may be questions about the rightness or, more broadly, about the goodness of individual actions.[40] Sometimes the sphere of ethics is confined to guiding or evaluating the conduct of individual actors (how ought I to behave?), sometimes it is extended

35 Twining, *op.cit.* n. 27 at pp. 382–383.
36 *L.M.S.* at p. 8.
37 *L.M.S.* at p. 97.
38 *Taking Rights Seriously*, at p. 7.
39 *Ibid.*
40 See *e.g.* J. L. Mackie, *Ethics: Inventing Right and Wrong* (1977).

to cover choices, decisions and actions made by or on behalf of groups of individuals, institutions, or a whole community (*e.g.* how ought the legislator decide?). Bentham, for example, distinguishes between guidance to individual actors (morals) and guidance to the legislator (legislation), and it has recently been questioned whether he thought that the same principle applies to both.[41] On one view, the principle of utility as a guide to the legislator is considerably less vulnerable to criticism than the principle of utility as a guide to the individual moral actor.[42] It is characteristic of a great deal of modern writing about ethics that attention is largely directed to critical examination of utility as a principle of *individual* morality.[43] Whether the choices and actions of individuals and of "legislators" should be governed by different principles and, if so, what is the relationship, if any, between those principles are, of course, debatable questions. Phrases like "law and morals" obscure such distinctions. Typically morality is treated as falling within the sphere of the philosophy of action; but sometimes terms such as "morals" and "ethics" are applied in contexts where what is in issue is not the goodness or the rightness of the conduct of responsible actors or agents but the evaluation of institutions, laws, social consequences, or states of affairs.[44] There are good reasons for suggesting that the application of such terms to this broader kind of inquiry is a loose and potentially misleading extension. One reason is that concepts and standards appropriate to individual morality may be given undue emphasis in the evaluation of laws and other phenomena; for example, attention may be unduly focused on notions of fault and responsibility and insufficient consideration be given to factors such as fairness, cost effectiveness, and efficiency in achieving stated goals. This point is illustrated by the history of scholarly analysis of and public debate about policies underlying compensation for accidents and the law of torts. It has taken a long time to shift attention away from concern with fault, to concern with what constitutes just and equitable distribution of risk and thence to a broader framework in which due weight is given to other factors such as what percentage of a particular system of

---

41 See esp. David Lyons, *In the Interest of the Governed* (1973), J. Bentham, *An Introduction to the Principles of Morals and Legislation* (J. H. Burns and H.L.A. Hart, eds., 1970), Chap. 1.

42 *e.g.* A. J. Ayer, "The Principle of Utility," in *Philosophical Essays* (1954), at 254 *et seq.*

43 See *e.g.* J. J. C. Smart and Bernard Williams, *Utilitarianism: For and Against* (1973); Anthony Quinton, *Utilitarian Ethics* (1973). A notable exception is John Rawls, *A Theory of Justice* (1971).

44 See further Twining, "Torture and Philosophy," *op. cit, supra*, n. 33 at pp. 144–145. *Cf.* J. L. Mackie, "There is not, of course, just one ethical use. 'Good' can be predicated in moral contexts of a wide range of kinds of subject—results, states of affairs, people, characters or character-traits, actions, choices, ways of life." *Ethics: Inventing Right and Wrong* (1977), p. 59.

compensation is eaten up in costs of running the system. It is only fairly recently that it has been widely accepted that rational debate about compensation for personal injuries should be conducted in terms of effectiveness and cost efficiency as well as fairness and individual fault and responsibility.[45] It is misleading as well as loose to use terms like "morality" to include all such factors.

It is not necessary, for the present argument, to establish that all or even any of the contributors of *Law, Morality and Society* have themselves fallen into error by virtue of an uncharacteristic lack of clarity about how morality and related terms are being used. It is reasonably clear from the context that the term is being used quite broadly and it is rather unlikely that such precise and sophisticated thinkers will be unaware of the elementary points made in the previous paragraphs. It is sufficient for present purposes to point out that such loose usage may mislead others. Statements of the kind "jurisprudence is a moral science" are, at best, unclear; like claims that "law is a social science" or "jurisprudence is the study of fundamental legal conceptions," they are best treated as exaggerated statements of common-place truths. In order to put them in perspective it is important to have a coherent and balanced conception of legal theorising which can accommodate conceptual analysis, censorial jurisprudence, and concern with both detailed social fact and broad interpretations of law in society.[46]

It is tempting to say of *Law, Morality and Society* that its conception of law and of jurisprudence is narrow, its conception of morality is ambiguous and its conception of society undeveloped. But the collection of essays, and the kind of approach that it represents, is

---

45 See generally P. S. Atiyah, *Accidents, Compensation and the Law* (2nd ed., 1975).

46 It is sometimes forgotten that a consequentialist Science of Legislation is directly concerned with the actual operation of laws in society. The legislator must systematically concern himself with the social conditions he is trying to influence, the potential and actual effects and side-effects of particular laws, and the general relationship between legislation and its consequences. The Science of Legislation postulated an empirically oriented instrumentalist view of law which fell short of a broader sociological perspective. If this kind of instrumentalism may seem rather naïve to modern eyes, at least it clearly established the central relevance of social fact to the task of government. This lesson was learned by some of Bentham's successors in the field of Political Economy—most notably by the Fabians—but it was largely neglected within academic law. The revival of non-Utilitarian theories of justice and of rights may in practice divert attention away from the detailed study of social realities and the actual workings of institutions, processes, laws, etc. If one is in a position to say that torture or slavery or abortion is wrong in principle, one may be tempted to sit back as if there is nothing more to say. This is a mistake. A non-utilitarian concerned with "the problem of X," whether it be torture, abortion, slavery, alcohol or redistribution of income, if he is concerned with the implementation of his principles is as much concerned with situations, processes, means and effects as the utilitarian. A view of laws as solutions to problems, as means to ends, as instruments of policies does not necessarily entail a consequentialist position in ethics and social philosophy. It is not only consequentialists who are interested in consequences.

too varied, too subtle and too lively to be susceptible of such facile generalisation. There are, I have suggested, grounds for unease about some current trends in Oxonian legal philosophy. But there are also grounds for optimism, not least in the revival of interest in political philosphy and the relative lack of inhibition about developing theories on a grand scale that is characteristic of the work of some contemporary thinkers such as Rawls and Dworkin. There are thus signs both of divergence and convergence between the movement to broaden the study of law and current trends in Oxonian legal philosophy, but it remains to be seen whether what analytical philosophers have to offer in the way of conceptual clarification and rigour in argumentation will be assimilated into a broader or contextual approach to the study of law.

The Significance of Herbert Hart

Enough has been said at least to suggest that there is a tendency within "Oxonian Legal Philosophy," as exemplified by *Law, Morality and Society,* either to treat legal philosophy as being coextensive with jurisprudence or at least to suggest by implication that Legal Philosophy is the only part of Jurisprudence which is both intellectually respectable and educationally worth while. For the sake of brevity I shall postulate this trend as an ideal type which I shall hereafter refer to as the philosophical view. As an ideal type it may be more simple than, or even a caricature of, the actual views of many contemporary legal philosophers. The chief characteristics of this view are that it treats the philosophy of law as dealing only with questions which are both philosophically interesting and susceptible to analysis by the application of those techniques that are widely accepted as valid by contemporary English empirical philosophers. Since there is room for disagreement about what questions are philosophically interesting and what are acceptable techniques of analysis it is difficult to attribute to it a precise conception of the scope and methods of legal philosophising. But to date nearly all the work grounded on this view has been confined to expository and to a lesser extent censorial jurisprudence. Moreover it has tended to be more concerned with analysing and criticising legal doctrine *in abstracto* than with the systematic study and evaluation of law in action.

An alternative way of viewing jurisprudence can be summarised as follows: jurisprudence is the theoretical aspect of law-as-a-discipline (*i.e.* academic law); the nature and scope of academic law is itself a central question of jurisprudence and a controversial one at that. Within academic law jurisprudential activity can potentially perform a number of important functions.[47] The most important of these include:

1. the integrative function, that is to say, to explore and articulate frames of reference which provide a coherent basis for law-as-a-discipline and for legal discourse generally;
2. the conduit function, that is to say, the systematic exploration at a general level of the relationship between law and at least the more general aspects of all other disciplines relevant to law. This is approximately equivalent to Julius Stone's notion of jurisprudence as " the lawyer's extraversion." [48]
3. High Theory, that is to say, the exploration of fundamental general questions related to the subject-matter of law-as-a-discipline, for example, questions about the nature and functions of law, relations between law and justice, or the epistemological foundations of different kinds of legal discourse. Most questions that come within this sphere would generally be accepted either as philosophical questions or at least as sharing a philosophical dimension.
4. Middle order theorising, prescriptive as well as descriptive, in particular:
   (a) the articulation of general hypotheses about legal or law-related phenomena capable of being tested by empirical research, and;
   (b) the development of working theories for various kinds of participants in legal processes, such as prescriptive theories of legislation and adjudication.
5. Systematic study of the intellectual history and heritage of academic law, including the history of legal theory, and critical study of the work of individual jurists.

This rough prescriptive conception of jurisprudence provides, however crudely, a sharp contrast with the philosophical view. Two main differences between these views are worth emphasising. First, the former is very much broader than the latter, in that it includes both philosophical questions (including some neglected by philosophers) and questions which would not ordinarily be viewed as philosophical although they are of sufficient generality to deserve to be called theoretical. For example, a rounded theory of adjudication or a series of hypotheses about legal professions would clearly fall within this conception of jurisprudence although philosophers might have little or nothing to contribute to their formulation.

The second main difference is that this view treats jurisprudence

---

[47] See Twining, *op. cit.* n. 3 at pp. 156 *et seq.*
[48] J. Stone, *Legal System and Lawyers' Reasonings* (1964), p. 16.

as being *part* of academic law and as having some significant tasks to perform within it. Whereas the philosophical view is typically silent about the relationship between the philosophy of law and law-as-a-discipline. This is not to say that it denies any relationship; rather it has, at least to date, provided no systematic account of the role of theorising within academic law, in addition to having a much more limited conception of the potential scope and functions of jurisprudence. Moreover it would not be surprising to find at least some philosophers of law tending to write as if their primary audience were philosophers rather than lawyers. Thus it is probably fair to say that the majority of essays in *Law, Morality and Society* tend to assume a philosophically sophisticated audience.[49] This contrasts sharply with a considerable proportion of the writings of Herbert Hart who has regularly and quite explicitly addressed himself to legal audiences.

Of course, much more could be said about the relations between these two models, each of which is admittedly capable of considerable refinement. For present purposes it is sufficient to claim that this perspective provides a better basis than the philosophical view for assessing the significance and limitations of Hart's contributions to jurisprudence and academic law. What follows is a sketch for a preliminary assessment of Hart's significance from this point of view.

Hart's main achievement, it is generally agreed, has been to re-establish a sustained and particularly fruitful link between academic law and English analytical philosophy. He has done this more by applying techniques of philosophical analysis to a range of jurisprudential concepts and issues than by sustained theorising about the nature of the relationship. It is nevertheless possible to extrapolate from his writings a fairly clear and consistent view of what this kind of analysis can contribute to jurisprudence and more generally to legal thought (practical as well as theoretical).[50] This might be sum-

49 It is important to distinguish between two kinds of reason for theoretical writings being of little interest to a particular audience: a work may be of little interest to a non-specialist because he finds it too difficult, perhaps because it assumes prior knowledge that he does not have, because it uses unfamiliar symbols or specialised jargon or because it is written at a more abstract level than he is used to. A quite different reason is that he can see no direct implications for, nor applications to, matters in which he is interested. As legal philosophy becomes more sophisticated there is a danger that these two reasons may be confused. For example, lawyers may find Jonathan Cohen's *The Probable and the Provable* (1977) very difficult, but it may well have some important direct implications for the study of evidence and for legal practice; *per contra* the clarity and elegance of much philosophical analysis may bring it within reach of a non-specialist audience without making any claims that it will be *useful* for them to read it. As the entry under Philosophy in the *Warwick University Prospectus* is at pains to point out, perhaps with more clarity than elegance, " metaphysics boils no cabbages."

50 See in particular items 6, 7, 16, 19, 21, 26, 47, 48 and 62 in the " Bibliography of H. L. A. Hart " in *L.M.S.* at 309–312.

marised as follows: this kind of analysis is especially valuable for clarifying important concepts; for restating obscurely or misleadingly phrased questions in a form which makes them susceptible of clear answers; for exploring the nature of certain kinds of argument used in legal discourse; and generally for promoting clarity of thought through analysis of linguistic usage. Hart makes other claims: that he is more concerned with increasing understanding than knowledge [51]; that, following J. L. Austin, we may use "a sharpened awareness of words to sharpen our awareness of the phenomena," [52] and that many of the lessons to be derived from this kind of approach can be communicated to people with no philosophical training, such as lawyers and law students, freed from the incubus of obscure or questionable philosophical theories.[53]

By and large Hart has performed this role of a conduit more by example than by precept. Nearly all of his writings can be seen as models of the application of certain techniques of analysis to law-related concerns. To say that one of his contributions, perhaps the main one, has been to act as a conduit between law and another discipline should not be taken as implying that such a role is secondary and easy to perform and involves a lack of originality. The reverse is much nearer to the truth.

It is less easy to assess Hart's contributions to the integrative and synthesising functions of jurisprudence. It is widely acknowledged, and Hart's own views appear to support this, that English analytical philosophy has more to contribute to the clarification of particular issues and concepts than to the building of theories on the grand scale. It is, after all, more concerned with analysis than synthesis. It is better suited to debunking, or cutting down to size pretentious "macrotheories" than to promoting broad and coherent perspectives. That is not to say that this kind of analysis is necessarily restricted to destructive criticism and *ad hoc* theory. It could plausibly be argued that Hart's picture of a legal system as developed in the *Concept of Law* might provide a basis for a coherent and reasonably broad view of law as a discipline.[54] However, this has not been his main concern and it is probably closer to the truth to say that he has by and large been content to modernise and refine the content and methods of, rather than to redesign, the conception of jurisprudence inherited from Bentham.

Similarly while Hart has made significant contributions to particular

[51] *e.g.* "Analytical Jurisprudence in Mid-Twentieth Century," *op. cit.* n. 4 at pp. 953, 972; "Definition and Theory in Jurisprudence," *op. cit.* n. 5.

[52] *The Concept of Law*, Preface, p. vii (1961).

[53] "Dias and Hughes on Jurisprudence," 4 J.S.P.T.L.(N.S.) 143, 144 (1958).

[54] A recent example of such a claim is to be found in E. Colvin, "The Sociology of Secondary Rules," 28 U. of Toronto L.J. 195 (1978).

topics, which might be said to fall within the general area of middle order theorising—for example, his writing about theories of punishment and causation in English law—such matters have not tended to be among his central concerns. To say that one would not turn first to the writing of Hart if one were seeking for a fully developed theory of legislation or adjudication or fruitful hypotheses about the nature of legal professions is to indicate a limitation rather than to criticise him in terms of his own primary objectives.

Many of Hart's most important contributions can, not surprisingly, be said to fall within the realm of "High Theory." For this, after all, is peculiarly the realm of philosophers. It is not necessary here to examine in detail Hart's obviously important achievements in elucidating fundamental concepts like "legal system," "rule," "right," "responsibility" and in exploring the relationships between law and morals and law and other social phenomena. Nor would it be sensible to be artificially precise as to whether his analysis of particular concepts, such as causation and responsibility, are better characterised as "high" or "middle order" theorising. But it is worth making two points about his significance within the realm of "High Theory." First, by and large, he has tended to take analytical jurisprudence, as it was developed within the expository tradition of academic law, as his starting-point. This is illustrated not only by his criticisms of Austin and of other "traditional theories," but even more clearly by the range of concepts which he has chosen to analyse in detail: law, legal system, rule, causation, right, duty, responsibility, legal power, legal personality, intention, negligence, acts and justice. It is significant that all but the last of these are important concepts within the sphere of expository jurisprudence. In his writing on law and morals and related topics, Hart has, of course, ventured into the sphere of Bentham's censorial jurisprudence; he has expounded what, within contemporary legal thought, is perhaps the most developed form of liberal, modified utilitarianism or ethical pluralism; and he has tried to establish some kind of rapprochement with the natural law tradition, in his attempts to extract a core of truth from theories of natural law. What is particularly significant in the present context is that Hart has not in a systematic way attempted to proceed beyond the confines of Bentham's expository and censorial jurisprudence into the kind of broader perspective that is encompassed by phrases such as "sociology of law." He has not, for example, devoted sustained attention to analysis of key terms in the vocabulary of sociological theories about law such as society, group, class, function, process, dispute, social problem, institution or decision. He has clarified concepts, such as rule, habit and sanction, which are important in social theory as well as analytical jurisprudence; but he has, on the whole, been content to reformulate and refine issues posed by a fairly narrow tradition of academic law, rather than to raise or explore in a sustained way the kinds of questions which a broader social perspective is likely to treat as central or significant.

Hart has never denied the value or importance of broader approaches to the study of law, indeed he has more than hinted that he is sympathetic to attempts to develop this kind of approach. But his position has been that of sympathetic outsider rather than that of academic specialist. Accordingly, it need not be a matter of surprise nor serious criticism, if those who are concerned to develop the sociology of law or a significantly broadened conception of academic law do not treat him as quite so central a figure, for their purposes, as do legal philosophers in Oxford. The claims that *The Concept of Law* may be viewed " as an essay in descriptive sociology " can be defended on the grounds that terms such as " rule," " legal system " and " law " are key terms in legal sociology as well as in analytical jurisprudence. A sympathetic critic can be sceptical about the claim, not because it is wrong or misleading, but because the idea of a descriptive sociology of law is not developed in *The Concept of Law* nor in Hart's other writings. What, for example, is the scope of a " descriptive sociology " and how does it relate to other kinds of sociological enquiry? Why " descriptive " if the purpose is understanding? What within this field might be important concepts that might be usefully clarified by the kind of analysis of which Hart is an acknowledged master? Hart's individual concerns, and the intellectual tradition of academic law within which he has worked, have not led him to direct much attention to such questions. But it is important to recognise that while his focus of attention may have been relatively narrow, the philosophical techniques and approach which he has introduced into legal theory are capable of application to a much wider range of concepts and issues.

Finally, Hart has never claimed to be primarily an historian of ideas. For the most part he has chosen to address himself directly to issues rather than discuss the ideas of others. But he has, of course, inevitably, been involved in writing about other jurists, often with great clarity and insight.[55] Without attempting a detailed assessment of his work in this respect, it is relevant to my argument to make two specific observations, one critical and one complimentary. First, Hart has himself contributed to a misleading and unsympathetic interpretation of American realism, with some of the consequences mentioned above.[56] A more sympathetic interpretation of, for example,

[55] See the Bibliography in *L.M.S.*, *op. cit.* n. 50.
[56] Esp. *The Concept of Law* at pp. 133, 250.

Holmes and Llewellyn might have been particularly fruitful. For their broad and down-to-earth vision of the law in action, together with their many suggestive *aperçus*, were not matched by the analytical rigour and the capacity for developing a sustained argument that are the hallmarks of Oxford philosophy. Alas, we have been left with a legacy of artificial polemics rather than the refinement and development of a rich legacy of suggestive insights.

Secondly, it is rather surprising that no mention is made in *Law, Morality and Society* of Hart's very substantial contributions to what might be termed "the Bentham Revival." Through his criticism of Austin, Hart cleared the way for the overdue restoration of Jeremy Bentham as "the father of modern English jurisprudence." Through his work as editor, as commentator and, less visibly, as a key figure in the Bentham Committee, of which he is now Chairman, he has made crucial contributions to the development of Bentham studies. Since the time of his inaugural lecture he has consistently reminded us of Bentham's historical and contemporary significance. He has helped to demystify some of the central ideas of that great demystifier.[57] Like other Bentham scholars his admiration for Bentham's intellect has sometimes been tempered by a distaste for some of the attitudes and stylistic inadequacies of the "leather-tongued oracle."[58] Hart's contributions to Bentham scholarship alone would be a sufficient basis for a substantial academic reputation.

One way of summarising Hart's achievement to date is to say that he has restored expository and censorial jurisprudence to a position of intellectual respectability, analogous to but different from the position in which Bentham left it. I have suggested that Bentham's conception, while broad for its time, fell short of a comprehensive social theory and that his followers first narrowed his conception of the subject and then allowed it to deteriorate into incoherence. To suggest that Hart's main limitation is that he has not significantly broadened jurisprudence, and in its wake academic law, beyond the scope envisaged by Bentham is to put him in good company. It would indeed be unfortunate if Hart's successors, by treating legal philosophy as being coextensive with jurisprudence in a way which Hart himself would not condone, should once again contribute to a narrowing of the vision not only of jurisprudence but also of academic law.

---

[57] *e.g.* "Bentham and the Demystification of the Law" (1973) 36 M.L.R. 2.

[58] Karl Marx, *Capital* (Everyman edition) at p. 671.

[5]
Talk About Realism

In a recent lecture, Professor Twining updated his interpretation of American Legal Realism. This Article in large part recounts that lecture. Addressing jurisprudence as a multifunctional activity, Professor Twining begins by outlining his approach to textual interpretation. He then utilizes this approach to analyze the juristic texts which he characterizes as comprising the Realist legacy. Through this process, he reinterprets the Realist legacy in light of recent legal scholarship and reevaluates the Realists' roles, particularly that of Karl Llewellyn, in that legacy. Professor Twining continues by examining some parallels between the American Realist Movement and developments in academic law in the United Kingdom. He concludes by exploring the significance of "realism" and related concepts for contemporary jurisprudence.

Memoirs I

It may have been on a beach in Dar-es-Salaam that I heard the news of the death of Karl Llewellyn. It was quite possibly the same beach on which we later played frisbee with the late Wolfgang Friedman, who had come out to teach about Law and Economic Development . . . the same Wolfgang Friedman who in an earlier era had been a forerunner of the English Realist Revolution . . . if indeed England has undergone something that can be so described.

---

* Quain Professor of Jurisprudence, University College, London. B.A., 1955, Oxon.; J.D., 1958, University of Chicago; M.A., 1960, Oxon.; LL. D. (Hon.), 1980, University of Victoria, British Columbia. This is a revised and extended version of the Dewey Lecture delivered at New York University School of Law on October 23, 1984. I am grateful to Kenneth Casebeer, Jill Cottrell, Christopher McCrudden, David Nelken, James Paul, Jack Schlegel and Robert Stevens, among others, for helpful suggestions and comments, with the normal disclaimers. I also wish to thank Dean Norman Redlich and the Faculty of the Law School, and especially Graham Hughes, for their generous hospitality and the Editors of this Law Review, and especially Randal Milch, Jeff Dunoff and Gary Stein, for general help and exemplary restraint.

It was February, 1962. Academic news traveled fast in those days, for this was the peak period of American, indeed Western, interest in Africa . . . the brief era of the neocolonial honeymoon. This was the period in which a Scottish philosopher could justify his transfer to the Sudan on the ground that Khartoum was more central than Aberdeen. Almost every week we entertained at least one visiting fireman from the United States who was clocking up mileage, buying local carvings, selling American legal education, and passing gossip along the circuit.

I was upset by the news about Karl. I had found him an inspiring teacher; I was fond of him and I knew that his premature death meant that his final statement of his most general theory would never be completed. At the time I saw him as only one of a number of teachers from whom I had learned much. But Llewellyn's impact on me was growing as I reflected on the implications of his ideas for academic law in East Africa. They had more resonance than most other juristic ideas for young expatriates who were trying to make sense of the bizarre unrealities of the common law in a social context, nay a climate, that was not hospitable to Carbolic Smoke Balls.

As an expatriate Englishman I naturally subscribed to the airmail edition of the Times. *When it became apparent that the* Times *had not noticed Llewellyn's death, I quickly drafted an obituary and sent it off. In due course I received a curt rejection, which implied that readers of the* Times *were not interested in obscure American jurists. I was already well aware of the caricatures and sneering critiques of American Realism in English textbooks of the time. Incensed, I decided to convert the British public to Llewellyn by writing an article about him. Wishing to quote from his marvellously rich, if cryptic, course materials on Law and Society but retaining a gentlemanly concern for the niceties of copyright, I wrote to Soia Mentschikoff, Llewellyn's widow, for permission to quote from them. With a promptness never to be repeated, she replied almost by return, suggesting that I should come to Chicago to consult "one or two unpublished manuscripts." She would fix it. So in 1963 I set out from Dar-es-Salaam to Chicago, earning my fare by delivering a series of lectures on customary law in East Africa, a late example of armchair legal anthropology.*

The "one or two manuscripts" turned out to be the unprocessed hoards of paper that now occupy several filing cabinets in the University of Chicago Law School. During the next ten years the obituary notice swelled into several articles, two pamphlets, and a fat book. This last was transformed from a rather pedestrian intellectual biography into a more ambitious attempt at the contextual interpretation of a major jurist under the stimulus of the daunting criticism of an informal reading seminar at Yale. The group consisted of the late Arthur Leff and two precocious and uninhibited students, who if my memory serves me aright, were called Richard

Danzig and Duncan Kennedy. But I have never been good at remembering the names of students . . . .

Let us pause here and, following current fashion, pretend that we are literary critics. Let us adopt, therefore, some of the language and talk of texts and discourse, and talk about talk. From the standpoint of the audience or reader of this text let us ask: What are we to make of these opening paragraphs? Are they to be interpreted merely as a substitute for the statutory joke at the start of a public lecture? Are they a promotional preview from Twining's soon-to-be-long-awaited memoirs, possibly entitled *Go Further East, Young Man* or *Frivolous Liberal*? Could they be a spoof of barefoot realism—evocative, anecdotal, impressionistic, and not unduly concerned with factual accuracy? Might this be taken as a dig at the parochialism and isolationism of much American Jurisprudence? Could it be a bit of mythmaking, a story about Realism designed to tempt some future intellectual historian to recognize Swahili neocontextualism as the true forerunner of Critical Legal Studies—a frolicsome combination of beach shirts, African Socialism, and visitors from law schools on another East Coast? Or is it, anticlimactically, a belles lettrist device to introduce some themes in a serious lecture—perhaps an attempt to tease out some of the spirit of American Legal Realism?

All of these are possible interpretations. On one view my intentions as author are either nonexistent, unascertainable or irrelevant. Nevertheless I intend to state what I shall attempt in what follows. My primary objective is to present a personal assessment of some aspects of the contemporary significance of the legacy of American Realism for the discipline of law in the United States and the United Kingdom.[1] A secondary

[1] The text, with its footnotes, is intended to serve as a gloss on my book, Karl Llewellyn and the Realist Movement (1973) [hereinafter KLRM]. This has been reissued in 1985 with a new postscript, but without substantial revision.

Although I have retained the informal style of the original lecture in the text, I have taken the opportunity to include several substantial footnotes dealing with notable developments in interpretations of Realism since 1973. The lecture, however, represents a shift of perspective rather than any substantial changes of mind. It may be useful to indicate here what I consider to be the most significant developments in the study of Realism, in my own views, and in the general intellectual climate since 1970-1971.

There has been a substantial amount of research and commentary on American Legal Realism during this period. By and large this scholarship exhibits a greater sophistication and conern for accurate detail than did much of the earlier literature (although, as is indicted in the text, caricatures and overgeneralized interpretations still abound). A number of detailed studies have added considerably to our knowledge of the lives and work of individual Realists and their contemporaries. Outstanding is the historical research, still in progress, of J.H. Schlegel on Realism and empirical social science. Professor Schlegel's work already has done much to illuminate the "scientific" wing of Realism. See Schlegel, American Legal Realism and Empirical Social Science: From the Yale Experience, 28 Buffalo L. Rev. 459 (1979); Schlegel, American Legal Realism and Empirical Social Science. The Singular Case of Underhill Moore, 29 Buffalo L. Rev. 195 (1980) [hereinafter Schlegel, Underhill Moore]. Valuable detailed biogra-

aim is to explore material—some of the difficulties involved in observing

phies and critical studies have already appeared in the past 15 years on Brandeis, Douglas, Frank, Frankfurter, Fuller, Pound, and Wigmore among others.

At a more general level I have found the following works particularly helpful in interpeting the context of the Realist movement: L. Friedman, A History of American Law (1973); G. Gilmore, The Ages of American Law (1977) (although I disagree with some aspects of Gilmore's interpretation); E.A. Purcell, The Crisis of Democratic Theory (1973); R. Stevens, Law School: Legal Education in America from the 1850s to the 1980s (1983). Two important recent works are discussed in detail below: Robert S. Summers's Instrumentalism and American Legal Theory (1982) and Bruce Ackerman's Reconstructing American Law (1984). Other useful commentaries include A. Hunt, The Sociological Movement in Law (1978); G. White, The American Judicial Tradition (1976); and the interesting series of articles by Simon Verdun-Jones: The Jurisprudence of Jerome N. Frank, 7 Sydney L. Rev. 180 (1974); The Jurisprudence of Karl Llewellyn, 1 Dalhousie L.J. 441 (1974) [hereinafter Verdun-Jones, Jurisprudence of Karl Llewellyn]; Jurisprudence Washed in Cynical Acid: Thurman Arnold and the Psychological Bases of Scientific Jurisprudence, 3 Dalhousie L.J. 470 (1976); Cook, Oliphant and Yntema: The Scientific Wing of American Legal Realism, 5 Dalhousie L.J. 3 (1979) [hereinafter Verdun-Jones, Scientific Wing]. It is for others to judge how far these and the other works cited in this lecture complement, undermine, or supersede the relevant parts of KLRM. On the whole I have yet to be persuaded to change my mind on any major points.

I agree with the strictures, if such they were, that I could have said more about attempts to develop social to develop social scientific approaches in law schools, about the general intellectual and political climate of American thought in the period 1870-1940, and about whether Realist ideas were justifiably perceived as a threat to the Rule of Law, especially during the New Deal. By way of confession and avoidance, I would point out that KLRM was a book about Karl Llewellyn, set in the context of the story of the rise of the Realist Movement, rather than a book about Realism as a whole. Indeed, like this lecture, KLRM could be interpreted as a reaction against tendencies to overgeneralize about Realism. I acknowledged that I was not competent to do justice to Llewellyn's German writings and his contributions to commercial law. KLRM, supra, at xii.

In retrospect, I think it would have been fruitful to have explored in greater detail Llewellyn's relationship (at an analytical level) with functionalist thought and its critics and with Max Weber. In recent years, I have examined and written, perhaps at inordinate length, on problems of broadening the study of law from within, on the systematic study of highly transferable legal "skills" such as rule-handling and analysis of evidence, and on a number of other themes that owe much to Llewellyn. But, on the whole, as I indicate in the 1985 postscript of KLRM, I am prepared to stand by what I wrote.

Insofar as this lecture says anything new, this is due less to recent writings about Realism by others or changes of mind on my part than to changes and developments in the intellectual milieu of the Anglo-American law school. As I indicate in the preface to the new edition of KLRM, when that work was being written intellectual biography was seen as an eccentric indulgence for an academic lawyer. Jurisprudence in the United States was muted, and, at least in England, Realism was thought to be discredited. Neither Marxism nor economic analysis of law had many adherents in the law schools in either country. Terms such as "critical legal studies," "sociolegal," "contextual," "structuralism," and "phenomenology" all have gained currency in the law school world since then. The same period has seen major contributions to Legal Theory, broadly conceived, from Dworkin, Finnis, Fuller, MacCormick, Nozick, Rawls, Raz, Summers, Unger and many others. It has been a particularly rich period for the history and theory of contracts. Legal history has blossomed and diversified, and there have been interesting developments in legal anthropology. Particularly pleasing has been the revival of a contextual approach to the history of political thought by Skinner and others. The net effect of these and other developments is to create a different intellectual climate for interpreting and assessing the continuing significance of the Realist legacy. Hence the need for a fresh look.

minimal standards of scholarly accuracy when discussing in general terms any part of that immense heritage of texts, and texts about texts, that contains what we perceive as Western jurisprudence. The object is to identify and to criticize some pervasive bad habits in secondary juristic discourse and to suggest some ways of talking in general terms about juristic texts and our juristic heritage while avoiding at least the worst pitfalls and without descending into arid pedantry. Most of these pitfalls are attributed to problems of generalization.

The surviving corpus of Realist texts provides a suitable vehicle for such a discussion. For the Realists (assuming we can agree who they were) are generally regarded as an amorphous, individualistic, and loosely connected collection of persons linked together at least as much by historical contingency as by shared concerns and ideas. One of the few generalizations that can be confidently made about the Realists is that they were American, white, and male—and even then one hears the voice of Soia Mentschikoff growling "What about me?"

I propose to adopt the following strategy. I shall first restate a particular perspective on jurisprudence and an elementary strategy for approaching any juristic text or group of texts. I shall next identify five images of Legal Realism that can be constructed from recent writings and consider these images critically in connection with my own general assessment of the Realist legacy. I shall then proceed to address some specific questions, notably: Can "legal realism" be given any content as a juristic concept independent of the work of particular jurists, or is it best treated merely as a historical label?[2] What is the connection, if any, between "realism" and some analogous terms that have gained currency in recent years in the United Kingdom? In this respect, has academic law in the United Kingdom experienced a Legal Realist "Revolution" in any way analogous to the American experience? Finally, is there still some unfulfilled promise of Legal Realism within the discipline of law, especially in common law countries?

One way of looking at jurisprudence is as the theoretical part of the discipline of law.[3] Its main focus is on general questions relating to the

[2] In this lecture "Realism" and "Realist" refer to people, events, activities, or ideas that are attributable, at least in principle, to some specific historical context or text(s), such as the American Realist Movement as a historical phenomenon or some ideas shared by some or all of its members. The terms "realism" and "realist" are used only where the reference is divorced from any specific historical context: for example, exploration of the value of "realism" as a juristic concept. The distinction is problematic: indeed, the difficulty of constructing a satisfactory convention illustrates rather clearly some of the difficulties surrounding the relationship between the historical and analytical levels of secondary juristic discourse. I cannot claim to have solved the problem. When in doubt, I have adopted a presumption in favor of historical specificity. Accordingly, capital "Rs" predominate.

[3] This theme is developed in Twining, Some Jobs for Jurisprudence, 1974 Brit. J.L. &

underlying assumptions of legal discourse, both law talk and talk about law. These questions are of different kinds and are posed at different levels of generality. They are related to each other in complex ways. Legal theorizing is a specialized activity directed toward providing reasoned answers to these varied questions. This activity can be interpreted as serving a number of different functions, reflecting the diversity of the questions to which it is addressed. These functions include:

1. Intellectual history and the history of important legal and law-related ideas;
2. High Theory or Legal Philosophy *stricto sensu*;
3. Middle order theorizing, both prescriptive and descriptive: for example, Llewellyn's theory of Grand Style judging and appellate advocacy,[4] Bentham's Science of Legislation,[5] or a descriptive theory of lawmaking processes;
4. The conduit function, i.e., the exploration and development at a general level of relations between law and other disciplines—what Stone called "the lawyer's extraversion";[6] and
5. The integrative or synthesizing function, i.e., the construction of coherent frames of reference for legal discourse generally and for its particular parts, such as a general theory of Contract or of Evidence and Proof in Litigation.

This rough and ready way of depicting legal theorizing as an activity has implications that challenge some commonly held assumptions.[7] For example, it suggests that jurisprudence is not a one-question subject; that Legal Theory is very much broader than Legal Philosophy *stricto sensu*; that general theories of law and general theories about law are not the only, perhaps not even the most important, products of legal theorizing; and that many of those who participate in this activity either do not have explicit and developed general theories of or about law or that such theories as they have are not the most interesting or significant aspects of their contribution. It is arguable that Rawls assumes a theory of law very similar to Hart's[8] and that John Stuart Mill adopted his theory of law directly from Bentham and Austin.[9] Mill and Rawls are significant figures in jurisprudence, but we do not read them for their theories of law. To put this last point differently: a jurist may contribute ideas that are original, stimulating, penetrating, fertile, seminal, suggestive, inter-

Soc'y 149 [hereinafter Twining, Some Jobs] and Twining, Evidence and Legal Theory, 47 Mod. L. Rev. 261 (1984) [hereinafter Twining, Evidence].

4 See, e.g., KLRM, supra note 1, at 210-15.

5 J. Bentham, An Introduction to the Principles of Morals and Legislation (1789).

6 J. Stone, Legal System and Lawyers' Reasonings 16 (1964).

7 See Twining, Evidence, supra note 3, at 265-67.

8 J. Rawls, A Theory of Justice (1972).

9 W. Morison, John Austin (1982).

estingly wrong, mischievously nonsensical, or otherwise "significant" whether or not these ideas include clear or illuminating answers to general questions about the nature, functions, or uses of law.

If ideas or assumptions that are inconsistent with the above implications can properly be treated as fallacies, then it is fair to say that such fallacies are rife in juristic discourse. They underlie some of the standard misperceptions of "Realism."[10] Further, although our heritage of legal theorizing is immensely rich and varied, it is not matched by a strong tradition of intellectual historiography or textual interpretation. With a few honorable exceptions, we have inherited a collection of appallingly bad habits. Some of these unscholarly practices are both obvious and familiar: the inaccurate generalizations that accompany nearly all talk of schools, -isms, -ists, and movements; caricature, indeterminate attribution, and reification of -isms; treatment of texts out of context and referring to significant thinkers as if they had had only one thought. It would be tedious here to catalogue, analyze, and criticize these pervasive bad habits. Some of them deserve to be castigated for what they are: sloppy scholarship and unfair, usually obfuscating, polemics. Others need more careful diagnosis as inadequate responses to genuine problems: how, for example, to locate thinkers in some general overview of our intellectual heritage, to depict broad trends or patterns in legal thought in a particular time and place, or to present students with helpful maps of what they are studying.[11]

For the present purpose we do not need to employ some elaborate methodological apparatus nor to nail a flag to some particular theory of textual criticism. But in reading and talking about juristic texts, it is useful to have a method and a language to help us avoid being trapped by elementary fallacies and related bad habits.[12]

In warning undergraduates against the worst pitfalls, I advise them along the following lines. Any text or group of texts or the broader oeuvre of a particular jurist should be approached on three different levels:

---

10 Some of these fallacies are indicated in Twining, The Great Juristic Bazaar, 14 J. Soc'y Pub. Tchrs. L. (n.s.) 185 (1978); KLRM, supra note 1, at 70-83, 147-51.

11 I hope this makes clear that I do not subscribe to the view, seemingly attributed to me by Wilfred Rumble, that no kind of generalization (about Realists or other jurists), however careful and qualified, is possible. Rumble, The Legal Positivism of John Austin and the Realist Movement in American Jurisprudence, 66 Cornell L. Rev. 986, 988 n.12 (1981). My main targets are historical generalizations that are inaccurate or misleading and analytical statements masquerading as historical generalizations.

12 Some analogies between interpretation of literary and legal texts are at least suggestive. See, e.g., Symposium: Law and Literature, 60 Tex. L. Rev. 373 (1982); J. White, When Words Lose Their Meaning: Constitutions and Reconstitutions of Language, Character, and Community (1984). However, I generally find literature more illuminating than literary criticism. Cf. Miers, Legal Theory and Statutory Interpretation, in Legal Theory and Common Law (W. Twining ed. 1986).

the historical, the analytical, and the applied. The emphasis to be placed on each level depends on the reader, the text, and the purpose for which the text is being read. Thus, studying the historical context can range from the detailed particularistic history characteristic of the work of Quentin Skinner, J.G.A. Pocock, or John Henry Schlegel to a bare sketch of the immediate historical and personal context in which this text was produced.[13] At the very least a historical approach can provide a general orientation and help the reader to begin to get a handle on the central concerns of the author. This inquiry can be crudely expressed by the question: What was biting him?

The translation of concerns into questions provides a link between the historical and analytical levels. History deals with events, people, activities, and texts located in space and time. Analysis and interpretation deal with questions, answers, and ideas, which belong to a different sphere of discourse, that of logic, truth, and validity. A general problem of intellectual history and of the history of ideas concerns the precise relations between the historical and analytical spheres of discourse and how to avoid confusing or conflating them. Juristic discourse is at a rather more primitive stage of development in handling this kind of problem than is political theory, to say nothing of literary criticism or theology. But I suspect that interpreting juristic texts is often a more straightforward business than is interpreting poems.

One elementary kind of analysis—reading for plot—can be done in

[13] One particularly interesting recent development has taken place in political theory. I refer to the work of scholars such as Quentin Skinner, Richard Tuck, and Stefan Collini in England and J.G.A. Pocock in the United States. These scholars aspire to develop a genuinely historical history of political theory. In pursuing this aim they have not been committed to any rigid methodological doctrine. Skinner and others have produced a number of splendid works that at the very least provide models for historians of legal theory. See, e.g., S. Collini, D. Winch & J. Burrow, That Noble Science of Politics: A Study in Nineteenth-Century Intellectual History (1983); J. Pocock, The Machiavellian Moment: Florentine Political Thought and the Atlantic Republican Tradition (1974); Q. Skinner, The Foundations of Modern Political Thought (1978); Q. Skinner, Machiavelli (1981). These new intellectual historians have reacted against bad habits in their own received tradition, particularly intensive analysis of classic texts out of context; overconcentration on particular texts to the neglect of broader historical treatment of ideologies and ideas; the equation of history with the search for origins; and "writing history backward," i.e., imputing the concepts, issues, and concerns of one period to people who thought and wrote in a quite different intellectual environment.

Though the recent scholarship and history of political thought contain some healthy warnings and suggestive models, the world of legal theory is not identical with that of our neighbors in politics. One key difference lies in the relationship between theorizing and action. Departments of Politics are less intimately involved than are law faculties in such worldly affairs as vocational training, consultancy, and active practice. If we had a developed ethnography of knowledge it would surely confirm the hypothesis that the culture of academic law is more participant-oriented than that of political science. Jurisprudence is etymologically and historically, in theory as well as in practice, more intimately connected with *prudentia*—craft, skill, and know-how—than is political theory, Niccolo Machiavelli notwithstanding.

terms of questions and answers: What questions does this text address? How are these questions approached? What answers, if any, does it yield? History provides clues to the author's concerns; a "fair" interpretation is one that tries to establish a reasonably close connection between these concerns (historical) and questions extracted from the text (analytical). Criticism can be viewed in first instance as an analysis of the differences between the reader's own views and the interpretation he attaches to the text. Do I agree with the questions?[14] Do I agree with the approach to these questions, with the answers, and with the reasons for the answers? Criticism, in this view, is as much a matter of self-definition as of applying external criteria to a text. For surely one of the main reasons for reading juristic texts is to clarify one's own general ideas and assumptions about general issues relating to law. It should be a working precept of all jurisprudential criticism and polemics that before launching an attack one should first identify worthy opponents and attribute to them what one considers to be the least vulnerable interpretation of their views that the relevant texts will sustain. Intellectual debate is impoverished when one attacks caricatures; soft targets generally only suit weapons with correspondingly low firepower.

Finally, the "applied" level encompasses the study of the particular implications and applications of general ideas and answers for more specific or lower level questions. It is a broad, open-ended category that can be crudely expressed as covering all "So what?" questions. It includes an author's explicit application of his general ideas to particular topics, such as Bentham's application of utility to punishment or torture.[15] It includes the logical corollaries of adopting a general idea or theory, for example, whether utilitarianism necessarily leads to justifying conviction of the innocent or rejection of the values of due process. It also includes examining concrete examples of work inspired, influenced by, or derived in whole or in part from some general idea, method, or theory, such as analyzing the relationship between the Uniform Commercial Code and Realist jurisprudence,[16] or Peter Singer's application of utility to the treatment of animals.[17] It can include "the overspill effect"—that is, uses and abuses of general ideas in ways their progenitors neither intended nor desired, for instance some of the alleged consequences of Hegelianism[18] or the invocation of "realist" ideas to justify pure subjectivism.[19]

---

14 On misposed questions in jurisprudence see Hart, Definition and Theory in Jurisprudence, 70 L.Q. Rev. 37 (1954).

15 See J. Bentham, supra note 5.

16 KLRM, supra note 1, at 270-340; Danzig, A Comment on the Jurisprudence of the Uniform Commercial Code, 27 Stan. L. Rev. 621 (1975).

17 P. Singer, Animal Liberation (1975).

18 See, e.g., Hegel's Political Philosophy (W. Kaufman ed. 1970).

The general advice is to consider some of the particular implications and applications of general ideas that you have extracted from a given text. The appropriate way to interpret and follow this advice depends largely on the context. In teaching jurisprudence through study of original texts, I find it helpful for students to make matters concrete by considering such diverse questions as whether there could be a Kelsenite expository work on land law, whether a utilitarian is committed both to justifying torture and to becoming a vegetarian, and what kinds of legal artifacts were inspired by the ideas of Llewellyn and his contemporaries at Columbia and Yale.

In discussing Realism it is useful to keep in mind three elementary distinctions that fit in with this general strategy:

1. It is important to distinguish between historical generalizations of the kind "The Realists said . . . " or "Positivists believe . . . " and analytical statements such as "A Positivist is someone who insists on a sharp distinction between law as it is and law as it ought to be."[20] The first kind of statement is either true or false as a matter of historical fact (though typically with intervening textual interpretation); the second may be treated as a different logical type.[21]

---

[19] See text accompanying notes 65-76.

[20] See, e.g., Hart, Positivism and the Separation of Law and Morals, 71 Harv. L. Rev. 593, 601-02 (1958); cf. Summers, The *New* Analytical Jurists, 41 N.Y.U. L. Rev. 861, 889 (1966).

[21] Roberto Unger disarmingly acknowledges that his account of Liberal Theory is the analysis of a fiction: "[T]here is no one thinker who accepts the liberal theory, in the form in which I present it." R. Unger, Knowledge and Politics 8 (1975). Rather he is describing and criticizing the "deep structure" of liberal thought. Just as "ideal types" can be devices for describing the social world, so "deep structures" may legitimately be used in discussing ideas. At the level of analysis it is quite reasonable to construct hypothetical answers to questions and then consider them critically—for the validity or truth of a theory is, as a matter of logic, independent of its authorship or of the motives or other conditions that gave rise to it. There are advantages for readers in the simplicity and brevity of this kind of ahistorical approach. There are also advantages for authors: they need not read texts nor concern themselves with accuracy, fairness, or nuances of interpretation nor with elusive questions about "influence" or the relationship between ideas and actions.

Unger plays fair by giving a reasonably precise elucidation of his ideal type of "liberalism" and by making explicit disclaimers about historical examples; not all recent writers who discuss "liberalism" have been so clear or so sophisticated. In the introductory "kit" to Critical Legal Studies, for instance, after a long extract from Felix Cohen, there appears the following passage:

> Once it is realized that the *barrier* between law and politics depends on the reification of every purpose, every bit of politics, then the barrier disappears. To see it is to destroy it. To introduce a middle term we would not only have to change *our notions of law* but would also have to completely reshape the *liberal picture* of the *social world*. This insight is the source of one of the most fruitful lines of *scholarship*, both in terms of the projects *it* suggests and in terms of the perspective *it* gives on *main-stream legal theory*.

Critical Legal Studies: A Young Person's Guide 6 (J. Boyle ed. 1983) (unpublished manuscript) (emphasis added) [hereinafter Critical Legal Studies]. These sentences seem to contain several reifications. Usually these reifications are used for such targets as classical legal

2. One needs to distinguish between ideas that were shared by several thinkers or are common to a group of texts and the ideas of a particular thinker that were original or otherwise distinctive or significant. I shall argue below that some of Karl Llewellyn's most original contributions were not shared by other Realists and bore only a tenuous connection to his own statement of the starting points of Realism. Thus, Llewellyn's law-jobs theory[22] is passed over by Robert Summers in his brave attempt to present a rational reconstruction of pragmatic instrumentalism as a distinctive kind of legal theory.[23] By concentrating on the shared ideas of a number of American jurists, Summers is driven to construct an ideal type to which each individual only approximately conformed. Moreover, because it is based on the lowest common denominator, Summers's ideal type is neither as rich as the ideas of most of the individuals considered nor as historically distinctive as he claims.[24]

3. Finally, one must distinguish between what a jurist said and how

---

thought, liberal legalism, realism, and pluralism. One might deconstruct this passage by saying: "Once it is realized that the barriers between critical legal studies and its standard targets depend on the reification and consequent distortion and oversimplication of both CLS and of every one of its alleged targets, the barriers disappear."

22 The law-jobs theory was a central element of Llewellyn's legal thought. It is grounded in the proposition that human groups have certain needs that must be met for the group to survive or pursue common goals. These needs are a source of actual or potential conflict. As conflict poses a threat to group survival, the prevention and resolution of conflict are essential for group survival and effectiveness. E.g., K. Llewellyn & E. Hoebel, The Cheyenne Way 273-309 (1941); Llewellyn, The Normative, the Legal and the Law-Jobs: The Problem of Juristic Method, 49 Yale L.J. 1355 (1940) [hereinafter Llewellyn, Law-Jobs]; Llewellyn, Law and the Social Sciences—Especially Sociology, 62 Harv. L. Rev. 1286 (1949) [hereinafter Llewellyn, Law and the Social Sciences]. See also KLRM, supra note 1, at 175-84.

23 R. Summers, supra note 1.

24 Summers's *Instrumentalism and American Legal Theory* is the most important work relating to Realism published in the past 10 years. It is scholarly, clear, and contains much that is illuminating. I disagree with Summers on a number of points of detail, but find much of what he has to say on specifics unexceptionable. Here I wish to concentrate mainly on his conception of his enterprise.

Summers's primary objective is to reconstruct a general theory of law from the work of leading American jurists in the period 1890-1940 and to present this as "a meaningful and distinctive type of theory about law and its use." Summers, supra note 1, at 37. He concludes that this theory, which underlies the work of Holmes, Dewey, and Pound, as well as leading Realists such as Llewellyn, Frank, and Cook, represents a distinct American tradition alongside analytical positivism, natural law philosophy, and historical jurisprudence. Its distinctiveness lies in the facts that "this fourth tradition frontally addresses the instrumental and pragmatic facets of law," id. at 19, but unlike the other three traditions "the best is yet to be," id. at 281. In other words, the program of pragmatic instrumentalism represents a largely unfulfilled promise.

Summers has a clear and sophisticated conception of the nature of his project. He is concerned with the "general directions of thought" and the similarities of the thinkers he considers rather than with their unique specific contributions. Id. at 13. He acknowledges that "for many purposes the differences are more important than the similarities," and that some of the pragmatic instrumentalists' most important contributions were specific rather than general. Id. Unlike some commentators, he has read most of the classic texts carefully and

what was said was interpreted and used. For example, Bruce Ackerman's recent thesis that Realism provided legal practitioners with a means of coping with New Deal legislation by giving them license to intuit their way to justice is more a historical hypothesis about the reception of Realism by practicing lawyers than about what any partic-

---

discusses individual thinkers in detail, if selectively; but he is emphatic that the book "*is not primarily a historical study.*" Id. at 12 (emphasis in original).

Summers's "reconstruction" is closer to the texts and less explicitly ahistorical than Unger's interpretation of the deep structure of Liberalism. For both authors the approach seems to be prompted by two concerns: first, to give a clear and uncluttered account of a general theory; and second, to distance themselves from the theory as stated in order to be able to accept and reject it selectively. Unger is straining for a form of "protoliberalism"; Summers, influenced by Hart and Fuller as well as the pragmatic instrumentalists, is reaching for a theory that will "take the best in each of the four great traditions." Id. at 14.

The advantage of Summers's concession to history is that his account of pragmatic instrumentalism is richer and more detailed than Unger's account of liberalism. The weakness of Summers's work is that it is in certain respects misleading if taken as history because he has provided an answer to the question: "[I]f the following [eight] theorists had had a developed general theory of law, what would it have looked like?" His answer is, it seems to me, a combination of a utilitarian theory of value, a positivistic view of law as a means of furthering utilitarian ends, a concern with detailed empirical investigation of the operation of the law in action (especially, but not exclusively, in relation to its effects), and a particular concern with the systematic study of means, with legal technology worthy of attention in itself.

Let us leave aside the question whether the reconstruction can be interpreted as an Americanized, updated version of Bentham's program—which, if this is the case, would rather undermine the claim that it deserves to be seen as a distinctive fourth tradition. Rather, let us look at the consequences of trying to turn American pragmatic foxes into abstract theoretical hedgehogs. See id. at 13. The main weakness is that this can only be done by very largely ignoring the specific concerns of the individuals involved and their distinctive contributions, most of which were related to these concerns. It also means that, by and large, the most sophisticated versions of their ideas tend to be ignored or treated as deviations or glosses, and that statements that make sense at a fairly low level of generality (such as Holmes's and Frank's ideas about prediction) are elevated to a higher level of abstraction and are treated as if they are general theories of law. Thus Summers presents us with a chapter devoted to an exposition and critique of the prediction theory of law and "predictivism" as a theory of legal validity. See id. at 116-35. There is room for disagreement whether Holmes ever intended his famous statements about prediction and prophecy to have the status of a general theory of law. But today it is surely misguided to concentrate on reheating criticism of this most vulnerable interpretation of rash statements rather than exploring the implications of the lower order truism that predicting certain kinds of events and decisions is one of the main tasks of various participants in legal processes.

Defining law in terms of prediction is so thoroughly discredited as to be hardly worth further discussion: examining the nature, difficulties, and significance of prediction in a middle order theory of "lawyering" is still a relatively neglected theoretical task. Summers's approach results in a failure to discuss Frank's fact-skepticism (at either the level of philosophy or middle order theory), and Llewellyn's law-jobs theory (which surely must form at least part of his general theory of law); Summers only marginally deals with Cook's and Moore's notions of "science."

The debate between Summers and Michael Moore about some of these issues in Moore, The Need for a Theory of Legal Theories: Assessing Pragmatic Instrumentalism, 69 Cornell L. Rev. 988 (1984) and Summers, On Identifying and Reconstructing a General Legal Theory—Some Thoughts Prompted by Professor Moore's Critique, 69 Cornell L. Rev. 1014 (1984), came to my attention too late for extended comment here.

ular Realist actually said.[25] Similarly, H.L.A. Hart's criticisms of rule-skepticism and the alleged prediction theory of law[26] or John Dickinson's defense of the Rule of Law and principled decisionmaking[27] may have involved historically or textually dubious interpretations of the originals; yet their criticisms may in themselves be both valid and illuminating as arguments. Showing why some belief, proposition, or theory is wrong at the level of analysis does not necessarily imply commitment to a claim that anyone ever subscribed to such a belief as a matter of historical fact. Straw men have a role to play in legal theory. What is regrettable is the tendency to treat them as if they were historical characters and to give them leading roles as villains rather than walk-on parts.

Interpretations of Realism I

The Realist Legacy

Let us start then by outlining a broad total picture of the legacy of Realism viewed as a body of texts. These can be roughly divided into three categories: (a) original Realist texts; (b) works that were explicitly or arguably influenced by ideas expounded in original Realist texts; and (c) historical, interpretive, and critical secondary writings.

Let us include in (a) all the writings of individual authors who could reasonably be said to have been members of the Realist Movement. Let us treat that movement as a historical phenomenon and not quibble about precise conditions for membership:[28] let us admit all American jurists who were critical of "formalism" and who wrote in a particular period—on a broad view not earlier than 1870, and not much later than 1960; on a narrower, more manageable, view mainly between 1900 and 1940.[29] Almost everyone would agree to the inclusion of Arnold, Bingham, Cook, Douglas, Frank, Llewellyn, Moore, Oliphant, and Sturges as Realists. Most would treat Dewey, Holmes, Pound, Hohfeld, and Corbin as forerunners rather than as full members of the movement, but clearly each played a noteworthy part in the Realist story. Most historians would probably agree that it is sensible to treat figures like Beutel,

---

25 B. Ackerman, supra note 1, at 18-19 (1984).

26 H.L.A. Hart, The Concept of Law 121-50 (1961).

27 Dickinson, Legal Rules: Their Function in the Process of Decision, 79 U. Pa. L. Rev. 833 (1931) [hereinafter Dickinson, Function]; Dickinson, Legal Rules: Their Application and Elaboration, 79 U. Pa. L. Rev. 1052 (1931) [hereinafter Dickinson, Application].

28 On the difficulty of setting up precise criteria, see Rumble, supra note 11, at 987-88. Our only point of difference is that if one wishes to make any nontrivial generalizations about Realists it is particularly dangerous to follow Llewellyn's list of 20 Realists, who were selected for their diversity. See KLRM, supra note 1, at 73-77.

29 The year 1870 marks Langdell's appointment to Harvard and the start of his reforms, against which there was an almost immediate reaction. Frank died in 1958, Llewellyn in 1962.

Hoebel, Hurst, Mentschikoff, Levi, Hart, Sacks, and Schubert as successors or followers who belong to a different generation. Whether we include such diverse figures as Clark, Felix Cohen, Gray,[30] Green, Hutcheson, Hutchins, Patterson, Radin, Rodell, Yntema, and even Lasswell and Wigmore depends on the nature of the inquiry and the criteria employed.[31] What is clear is that the longer the list, the harder it is to make accurate, precise, and nontrivial general statements about Realism or the Realists. In order to simplify matters, for the purposes of this lecture I shall treat Llewellyn, Frank, and Cook as representative core Realists.[32] Any unqualified generalization that does not fit these three fails a

---

30 On the historical reasons for treating Gray as a forerunner rather than as a member of the Realist Movement, see KLRM, supra note 1, at 20-22. For a different view, see N. MacCormick, A Political Frontier of Jurisprudence: John Chipman Gray on the State, 66 Cornell L. Rev. 973 (1981).

31 If it is clear who exactly is being referred to, little hangs on classification as a "Realist." See KLRM, supra note 1, at 73-83. Wigmore is mentioned here because his *Principles of Judicial Proof* represents a pioneering attempt to rethink a field of law in broader and more realistic terms than had been traditional. See W. Twining, Theories of Evidence: Bentham and Wigmore (1985).

In conversation in 1980 or 1981, the late Soia Mentschikoff suggested to me that the 1928 Columbia crisis over the appointment of a new law school dean could, without much distortion, be interpreted as an attempt to "colonize" an eastern law school by people who had been affected by the intellectual milieu of the University of Chicago. The four leading scientists—Cook, Moore, Oliphant, and Marshall—had all been associated with the University of Chicago. Some of their key ideas were recognizably part of the Chicago ethos of the time: a community of scholars, the application of scientific method to the social sciences (a theme associated especially with the political scientists Bentley, Merriam, and later Lasswell), and the linking of law with economics and business studies. It could also be pointed out that the reaction against colonization of the Chicago Law School by Harvard (in the person of Joseph Beale, see Ellsworth, Law on the Midway 68-77 (1977)), had taken a different turn from the Yale-Columbia developments. It would be beyond the scope of the present paper to explore these differences in detail, but the following tentative hypotheses may be ventured:

1. The Chicago brand of realism was less practitioner-oriented than the Yale-Columbia brands.
2. At Chicago there was emphasis on law-government (especially in the person of Ernst Freund, see E. Freund, Standards of American Legislation (1917) (F. Allen ed. 1965); K. Llewellyn, Jurisprudence: Realism in Theory and Practice 378-79 (1962)) and on social reform; Yale was closer to the private law orientation of Harvard, but wanted to improve on it; Columbia was somewhere in between. This is reflected in different degrees of emphasis on fact-research as a basis for social reform (Chicago), and a more realistic understanding of what factors were influencing judges in deciding appellate cases (Yale).
3. Systematic empirical research into legal process and serious interdisciplinary cooperation between lawyers and sociologists are a relatively late gloss, without deep roots in any of these three law schools, at least before the late 1920's—except that the "scientism" of the Chicago school of politics may have had some influence.

32 Llewellyn and Frank are the two figures most prominently associated with "Realism." Cook was selected because he both represents the "scientific wing" and was associated with Yale, Columbia, and Johns Hopkins at important moments in the history of the Realist Movement. Summers also selects these three for special attention. R. Summers, supra note 1, at 36-37.

minimal test of historical and textual accuracy.

In recent months I have had occasion to read a great deal of relevant recent literature. I found very few sentences containing unqualified generalizations about Realism or the Realists that passed this minimal test. This is not to deny that such statements may have a role as rhetorical exaggerations, as interpretive myths, legends, or fictions, or as counters in rather abstract arguments. Sometimes they have a function as ideal types or as artificial targets or as aids in providing a general indication of the author's own position. Sometimes they represent little more than nostalgia, name-dropping, or name-calling that add nothing to the author's argument. What I am suggesting is that few, if any, such statements deserve to be taken seriously as historical or textual scholarship. Thus one of the few confident generalizations that one can make about Realism is that nearly all unqualified, nontrivial generalizations about Realism are false.

It would be neither instructive nor entertaining to establish this last assertion by detailed evidence.[33] It may be rather more helpful to reconstruct some of the more general interpretations that seem to be still current and to explore briefly how far they satisfy the minimal test of historical and textual accuracy with respect to Llewellyn, Frank, and Cook. One can identify at least five different perspectives on Realism that deserve comment:

1. A distinctive theory of or about law;
2. A theory of adjudication;
3. A negative or nihilistic critique of formalism;
4. A constructive search for alternatives to Langdellism; and
5. Various political or ideological interpretations.

These views, images, or interpretations of Realism are of different kinds and are by no means mutually exclusive. The first two are primarily analytical in that they purport to give an account of Realist writings as contributions to Jurisprudence. The last three are largely, but not entirely, historical interpretations of the concerns, activities, and achievements of the Realist Movement. I shall argue that there is some basis for all of them, but that each illustrates some of the pitfalls of generalization.

1. Realism and Legal Philosophy

Some commentators treat Realism as a general theory of or about law. This is exemplified by Robert Summers's reconstruction of the shared ideas of some Realists and their immediate precursors and successors in the form of "a meaningful and distinctive theory about law and its

[33] For specific examples of false or misleading generalizations, some of which are still current, see KLRM, supra note 1, at 30-31.

use," which he calls "pragmatic instrumentalism."[34] This view is also to be found in cruder interpretations that maintain that Realists deny any normative character to law and treat it merely as brute fact—for example, some criticisms of the alleged prediction theory of law.[35]

Did all or any of the core Realists have a general theory of or about law that was distinctive, original, or otherwise interesting? A brief answer is that of the chosen three only Llewellyn can be said to have advanced an explicit and developed theory of this kind. This was more developed with respect to some general questions about the functions of law than with respect to questions about the nature or definition of law.[36] Insofar as we can reasonably attribute such theories to Cook or Frank or reconstruct them from their steady assumptions, it is doubtful that their underlying ideas were particularly original or distinctive or even coherent. We can readily concede that nearly all of their theories have some recognizable affinity to Summers's model of pragmatic instrumentalism. However, Llewellyn, the most theoretically sophisticated of the three, deviated the most from this model, especially in his later work. Not only did Cook and Frank contribute almost nothing of value at this level, but the connections between their more original ideas and their more general underlying assumptions are neither uniform nor even very similar.

There is much more to this than pointing to differences between the epistemological views of Llewellyn, Frank, or Cook or to their more nuanced political, moral, and other differences and disagreements. More important are the differences in their central concerns and, related to this, the issues on which they are still worthy of attention. For example, Frank's most sustained concern was with litigation at first instance, its neglect as a focus of attention, the unpredictability of particular decisions on questions of fact, and, at a deeper level, the general practical and philosophical issue of the unreachability of fact.[37] I doubt that Frank was a genuine philosophical skeptic and I know that he was no philosopher.[38] Llewellyn doffed his cap to the importance of factfinding and

[34] R. Summers, supra note 1, at 11-14, 268-81.

[35] Summers presents a penetrating critique of "robust predictivism" as a theory of legal validity. R. Summers, supra note 1, at 116-35. His argument seems to be analytically sound, but historically dubious: was Holmes concerned with legal *validity* when he spoke of predictions and prophecies? See KLRM, supra note 1, passim; Twining, The Bad Man Revisited, 58 Cornell L. Rev. 275, 284-93 (1973).

[36] See Llewellyn, Law-Jobs, supra note 22; KLRM, supra note 1, at 175-84 (discussing *The Cheyenne Way* and *Law in Our Society*); Twining, Law and Anthropology: A Case Study in Inter-disciplinary Collaboration, 7 L. & Soc'y Rev. 561, 569-72 (1973) (discussing the differences between Llewellyn and Hoebel on definitions of law).

[37] For my views on Frank, see Twining, Some Scepticism About Some Scepticisms I, 11 J. L. & Soc'y 137, 159-61 (1984) [hereinafter Twining, Some Scepticism I]; Biographical Dictionary of the Common Law 190-93 (A.W.B. Simpson ed. 1984).

[38] Twining, Some Scepticism I, supra note 37, at 157-61.

threw out a few *aperçus*, but he was not consistently interested in this subject and contributed little to it.[39] Although Cook did some interesting analytical work on pleading and the distinction between law and fact, he hardly addressed Frank's central questions.[40]

Cook's late concern with the empirical scientific study of law resulted in naive answers to fundamentally important questions. Except perhaps in the specialized field of conflict of laws, his legacy of juristic texts is of limited significance.[41] Frank was rather unintellectually dismissive of empirical research about law.[42] Different assessments have been made of the value of Llewellyn's contributions to this topic. Some see him merely as a naive empiricist.[43] My own view is that, at their best, Llewellyn's discussions of law and social science method are sensible and perceptive, though not particularly original;[44] at their worst they are best forgotten.[45] Others have given them a higher rating.[46]

Less simple is the question whether a common theory of or about law can be *imputed* to the core Realists. In one sense all legal writers have a theory of and about law in that their legal discourse presupposes some answers to central questions about the nature of law. My personal view is that the underlying theories of law of Cook and Frank are of very limited interest. They were neither fully worked out nor as startling or original as has sometimes been suggested. Their concerns and their continuing significance, if any, relate to other issues in which their answers presuppose some not particularly interesting notions of law. Nor did Cook or Frank contribute much of lasting value to other philosophical

---

39 For Llewellyn's views on factfinding, see e.g., K. Llewellyn, supra note 31, at 431-50; K. Llewellyn, The Common Law Tradition 18, 359-60 (1960) [hereinafter K. Llewellyn, Common Law Tradition]; K. Llewellyn, Sacco and Vanzetti v. The Commonwealth: An Indictment of the Workings of Our Judicial Institutions (1928-35) Karl Llewellyn Papers, Chicago (unfinished, unpublished manuscript).

40 See W. Cook, Cases and Materials on Equity (3d ed. 1940); W. Cook, My Philosophy of Law 49, 66 (A. Kocoureck ed. 1941) (citing Cook, Scientific Method and the Law, 13 A.B.A. J. 303 (1927)) [hereinafter W. Cook, My Philosophy of Law]; W. Cook, The Logical and Legal Bases of the Conflict of Laws (1942) [hereinafter W. Cook, Conflict of Laws]; Cook, Book Review, 31 Colum. L. Rev. 725 (1931) (reviewing M. Cohen, Reason and Nature (1931)); see also KLRM, supra note 1, at 35-42; Verdun-Jones, Scientific Wing, supra note 1. For his views on scientific method Cook drew heavily on an article by Charles W. Morris in 1 International Encyclopedia of Unified Science (1920) and, rather simplistically, on Dewey's writings.

41 A more careful assessment of Cook must await the completion of Professor Schlegel's research. See note 1 supra.

42 See, e.g., J. Frank, Courts on Trial 190-221, 330-45 (1949).

43 See, e.g., Schubert, The Future of Public Law, 34 Geo. Wash. L. Rev. 593, 601 (1966).

44 See KLRM, supra note 1, at 188-96. Llewellyn's article The Theory of Legal "Science," 20 N.C.L. Rev. 1 (1941), still repays careful reading.

45 See, e.g., Llewellyn, On What Makes Legal Research Worthwhile, 8 J. Legal Educ. 399 (1956).

46 See, e.g., Verdun-Jones, Jurisprudence of Karl Llewellyn, supra note 1.

questions. They are more interesting as jurists than as philosophers of law.

Llewellyn is somewhat different in this respect. His law-jobs theory purports to be an outline of the functions of law-government as an institution. Its main interest lies in his insistence on not defining law-government and on making a virtue of the vagueness of the notion of "institution."[47] The general thrust of his work is to emphasize the *similarities* between law-government and other social institutions, and between legal skills and fundamental human skills, such as rulehandling, factfinding, and negotiating. This emphasis runs counter to the general tendency of legal theorists, especially positivists, to search for and emphasize the uniquely or characteristically legal.[48] Llewellyn deliberately refused to give general answers to questions posed in terms of *differentiating* law from morals or other social institutions.[49] In order to make the law-jobs theory operational in particular contexts, one needs to stipulate fairly precisely what is to count for this purpose as law-government, as opposed to other institutions. These stipulations can be confined to particular contexts and inquiries and they need not be treated as general. On this interpretation, the law-jobs theory can be operationalized by imputing to it some specific criterion of validity, such as Hart's rule of recognition or Kelsen's basic norm or possibly even a different kind of positivism such as Dworkin's institutionally imbedded principles. But Llewellyn's theory explicitly refuses to give *general* answers to questions about validity or distinguishing characteristics—that is one reason why he makes a significant contribution to the surprisingly neglected question of what is involved in understanding law. This aspect of Llewellyn's thought has taken us quite a long way from the concerns and views of Cook and Frank, not because they necessarily would have strongly disagreed with its tendency, but because they were primarily interested in different questions.

The argument so far can be restated as follows: whether we settle on

[47] Llewellyn, The Constitution as an Institution, 34 Colum. L. Rev. 1 (1934); Llewellyn, Law and the Social Sciences, supra note 22. See also KLRM, supra note 1, at 176-77; Hamilton, "Institution," in 8 Encyclopedia Soc. Sci. 84 (1932). In his later writings Llewellyn adopted the notion of "law-government" (or "law-and-government") as the organizing concept of the law-jobs theory, because law and government are primarily concerned with the same basic "job of producing and maintaining the groupness of a group." K. Llewellyn, supra note 31, at 357, discussed in KLRM, supra note 1, at 179-80.

[48] See Twining, Evidence, supra note 3, at 261, 264-65.

[49] See, e.g., K. Llewellyn, supra note 31, at 3-6; Llewellyn, Law-Jobs, supra note 22. Llewellyn's concern with empathetic understanding of the internal point of view of officials and other participants arguably has close affinities with Weber's *Verstehen*, but he never developed this very far. Note, however, his posthumously published work Recht, Rechtsleben und Gesellschaft (M. Rehbinder ed. 1977) (outlining Llewellyn's debt to Weber and his differences with Ehrlich); see also KLRM, supra note 1, at 418 n.90.

a short or long list of members of the Realist Movement, generalizations about their ideas are dangerous because such generalizations at best indicate little more than some vague intellectual affinities, and because the most significant contributions of the leading individuals are best treated as distinctive responses to concerns and questions that were not widely shared. For these reasons a sharp distinction has to be made between what they had in common and what is original or of continuing significance about their individual contributions.[50] Few if any of them made particularly important contributions to what may be termed the central questions of classical jurisprudence (for example, What is law? What is justice? What is the relationship between law and morals?).[51] This does not mean that they are not worth taking seriously as jurists. Their historical and contemporary significance lies in their concern with a range of rather different questions, many of which are most illuminatingly treated as being at lower levels of abstraction than the philosophical questions of high theory.

2. *A Theory of Adjudication*

A second image is that Realism presents a theory about the nature of judicial processes, rather than a general theory of law (if an American audience will accept such a distinction). The most common version of this image suggests that early Realists advanced a profoundly skeptical view of the rationality and predictability of adjudicative decisionmaking on questions of law and questions of fact, but that more balanced versions were subsequently advanced by Cardozo, Hand, and the later Llewellyn.[52] Examples of this interpretation include Professor Hart's picture of American jurisprudence as caught in perpetual tension between a "nightmare" and a "noble dream";[53] some critical legal scholars'

---

50 Professor Schlegel has suggested to me that this exaggerates the differences between leading Realists and does not allow for a tacit division of labor between individuals who were pursuing very similar goals. A "group portrait" that substituted the "greatest uncommon denominator" for the lowest common denominator would bring out the effectiveness of their critique of formalism and the impressive range of the sum total of their "constructive" achievements (private communication, Feb., 1985). The difference between us is one of emphasis. In this paper, I have been concerned to pinpoint the difficulties of generalizing about Realism; a brief sketch for such a group portrait can be found in KLRM, supra note 1, at 375-87. We are in agreement that the overall contribution of Realists on the "constructive" side was important—hence the rejection of the "negative" image. See notes 122-26 and accompanying text infra.

51 Nevertheless, both Llewellyn and Frank wrote extensively about Natural Law and Justice. See, e.g., J. Frank, supra note 42, at 346-73; 346 n.1; K. Llewellyn, supra note 31, at 111-58; KLRM, supra note 1, passim.

52 See, e.g., Heffernan, Two Stages of Karl Llewellyn's Thought, 11 Int'l J. Soc. L. 134 (1983).

53 Hart, American Jurisprudence through English Eyes: The Nightmare and the Noble Dream, 11 Ga. L. Rev. 969 (1977).

depiction of Realism as having irretrievably smashed the illusion of determinacy of rules in judicial decisionmaking;[54] Bruce Ackerman's interpretation, referred to above, that Realism offered practicing lawyers a particularistic and intuitive mode of discourse that made it easier for them to adjust to the New Deal;[55] and statements of many commentators

[54] See, e.g., Tushnet, Post-Realist Legal Scholarship, 15 J. Soc'y Pub. Tchrs. L. (n.s.) 20, 21 (1980):

> Imperfectly and with varying degrees of clarity, the realists developed a critique of classical legal analysis that led almost inexorably, and in general quite contrary to their own intentions, to what I have called legal nihilism . . . . The realist critique of rules was simple and deep. It held that law, which purported to be a set of rules that determined either behaviour, or more narrowly, outcomes in litigated cases, was in fact completely indeterminate.

See also Critical Legal Studies, supra note 21, at 3-5; Mensch, The History of Mainstream Legal Thought, in The Politics of Law 18 (D. Kairys ed. 1982). It is fair to say that Mensch, Kennedy and others are careful to qualify their generalizations about Realism and to emphasize the implications of "the Realist critique."

[55] B. Ackerman, supra note 1. Ackerman sets his argument in the context of an activist state that seems to be approximately equivalent to a mixed economy. His thesis is that "after fifty years of arguing out the particular meanings of bits and pieces of activist law, lawyers can begin to see larger patterns in the professional effort to make sense of our existing legal situation." Id. at 2. He discerns the birth of a form of legal discourse, Legal Constructivism, that is "prèmised on a distinctive set of attitudes toward fact and value." Id. at 3. Ackerman's new "language of power" incorporates a nonutilitarian approach to problems of distributive justice, along the lines advocated by Rawls and Dworkin, as well as an overt use of methods of economic analysis (represented by the welfare economics of Amartya Sen and Kenneth Arrow, rather than the more brutal version of economic analysis associated with Judge Richard Posner).

Developing his argument both as an interpretation of current trends and as a commendation of Constructivism, Ackerman reinterprets the historical significance of Legal Realism:

> During the 1930s, the Realists presented themselves, and were generally perceived, as the profession's *enfants terribles*—debunking cherished legal myths with devastating effect. This undeniable aspect of Realism, however, should not blind us to the paradoxical character of its ultimate contribution to legal discourse. With a half-century's hindsight Realism has come to seem profoundly conservative, not radically iconoclastic. Rather than transforming traditional legal discourse, the Realism critique allowed the profession to survive the New Deal without reconstructing its basic conceptual equipment. Rather than encouraging lawyers to confront the distinctive challenges posed by the rise of an activist state, Realists permitted the profession to evade them in good conscience.

Id. at 4-5.

The Realists encouraged a discourse that was intensely particularistic in dealing with facts and intuitive, rather than rational, in dealing with values. In contrast, the kind of legal analysis appropriate to a modern liberal activist state requires, in part, a broader and more systematic analysis of factual situations (as exemplified by economic analysis of products liability or landlord-tenant relations) and a systematic rational analysis of value choices on the basis of principle. In this view, going beyond Llewellyn's "situation sense" involves depicting the social context of the facts of a particular dispute as part of the statement of the facts in a less intuitive and particularistic way. See id. at 93.

Ackerman's notion of "constructivism" as a new "paradigm" for argument about questions about law (and, perhaps, more generally for academic legal analysis) deserves serious consideration as an intriguing attempt to synthesize deontological argument with economic analysis. Whether it is an appropriate model for such discourse in all or most kinds of cases is

who persist in talking of Realism as if it were solely concerned with the nature of adjudication on questions of law.[56]

The image of Realism as a skeptical theory about judicial processes fits each of the three core Realists quite differently. Frank gave currency to it by his division of Realists into rule-skeptics and fact-skeptics.[57] This interpretation emphasized two elements: the placing of judicial decisions at the center of the legal universe and a general skepticism about claims of the rationality and predictability of these decisions. Many commentators, however, equate judicial decisions with adjudicative decisions on disputed questions of law. Frank can at least take credit for trying to broaden the focus by including a range of other adjudicative decisions, especially those of first instance; and he was quite explicit that one of his main concerns was to increase the rationality of such decisions.[58] He may have done little more than substitute court-itis for appellate court-itis, but he can hardly be accused either of irrationalism or of mere obsession with the indeterminacy of rules.

The early Cook fits this image fairly well, except that the thrust of

clearly debatable. My concern here is with Ackerman's bold and rather freewheeling interpretation of "Realism." There clearly is a strong core of truth in the claim that there were particularistic and intuitionist strains in Realist approaches to legal argument and judicial decisions on questions of law. It may be pedantic to point out that the emphasis on narrower categories was a reaction to a legacy of abstract categories in private law (such as "title" in sales, and "master and servant" in torts) and that generalizing was also part of Llewellyn's program—for example, his development of the categories of secured transactions and unconscionability in the Uniform Commercial Code. It may also be pedantic to point out that what Ackerman refers to as "the situation sense in which the *Realists* took so much pride," id. at 93 (emphasis added), first given prominence in 1960 in *The Common Law Tradition*, created almost universal puzzlement among sympathizers and critics alike and is based on the idea of the notion of a *type of situation*. That is, stating the particular facts in general terms, with "the fireside equities" phased out. Llewellyn claimed that the Grand Style, of which situation sense forms a part, is more rational than the Formal Style; it is not based on individual intuition, but on an appeal to shared perceptions and values. The main difference between Ackerman's model of constructivism and Llewellyn's Grand Style is that the former appeals to more intellectually rigorous and abstract modes of analysis of a particular kind that is essentially contested. On this interpretation, constructivism is an intellectualization and formalization of some loose precepts rather than a substitute for "a shallow Realism that has outlived its time." Id. at 110.

There are, however, more fundamental differences. Ackerman's account of constructivism as a model for legal discourse in general rather than for argument about disputed questions of law leaves out some of Llewellyn's and Frank's central concerns: the institutional realities of the law in action; total processes rather than atypical stages of processes in atypical cases; the interaction between the general and the particular; a firm awareness of the limits of rationality and the irreducible personal element in law; and, in the case of Frank, problems of ascertaining the truth about *particular* past events rather than the more generalized kind of factfinding as a basis for policy and lawmaking that concerns Ackerman.

56 See, e.g., T. Benditt, Law as Rule and Principle 1-21 (1978); R. Dworkin, Taking Rights Seriously 3-7 (1977).

57 J. Frank, supra note 42, at 62-79; J. Frank, Law and the Modern Mind vi-xxvii (1949).

58 See, e.g., J. Frank, supra note 42, at 165-85; see also Twining, Some Scepticism I, supra note 37, at 158-61.

his critique was directed at the soft target of the deductive form in appellate judicial reasoning, and he was not necessarily committed to an extreme position on rationality, predictability, or indeterminacy.[59] The later Cook, however, does not fit the image so well: his empirical science of law focused more on judicial statistics at first instance and on the impact of legislation than on adjudication.[60] His approach was founded on a naively optimistic view of the possibility of applying methods borrowed from the physical sciences to the study of law, rather than a skeptical one. His most significant contribution to legal philosophy was neither exclusively focused on judicial processes nor skeptical in any strong sense of that term.

Llewellyn's law-jobs theory provides us with a lens for viewing appellate judicial processes in the context of all litigation and all dispute-settlement processes. This almost inevitably leads to a recognition of their relative marginality in law-government as a whole in most societies. It highlights the simple facts that only a tiny proportion of disputes ever reach or even get near the courts and that appellate judicial decisions in hard cases are only one phase in a realistic picture of the tiny minority of processes that reach adjudication.[61] It is a matter of muted textual debate among specialists whether or not Llewellyn retreated from a mild form of rule-skepticism to a version of optimistic rationalism in *The Common Law Tradition*, in which he emphasized the role of steadying factors in constraining indeterminacy.[62]

Thus the image of Realism as being mainly a skeptical attack on the rationality of judicial processes does not score high marks in the minimal test of historical and textual accuracy. Rather more significant is the point that some contemporary American jurists, as diverse as Dworkin, Ackerman, Kennedy, and Tushnet, are more vulnerable than are the core Realists to charges of being overconcerned with judicial decisions on disputed questions of law. The recently revived obsession with this traditional and narrow focus helps to give currency to this image of Realism:

---

59 See W. Cook, My Philosophy of Law, supra note 40.

60 Much of the early work of the Johns Hopkins Institute, of which Cook was the first director, was devoted to judicial statistics. See KLRM, supra note 1, at 60-67, 403-04 & n.20.

61 This runs counter to the tendency of many American jurists to place adjudication at the center of Jurisprudence. Contemporary adherents of this view include Ronald Dworkin, who acknowledges, however, that a general theory of law, in its normative aspects, "must have a theory of legislation, of adjudication and of compliance." R. Dworkin, supra note 56, at vii; cf. Moore, supra note 24, at 1013. The notion that judicial decisions cast a long shadow but are not necessarily *the* fulcrum of all legal processes is discussed in Twining, Some Scepticism About Some Scepticisms II, 11 J. Law & Soc'y 285, 298-300 (1984). Cf. Summers, supra note 1, at 1027-29 (effectively criticizing Moore's "concentration on adjudication as the core of legal theory").

62 K. Llewellyn, Common Law Tradition, supra note 39. Compare Heffernan, supra note 52, with KLRM, supra note 1, at 426 & n.12.

rationalists, like Dworkin, use the core Realists as targets,[63] whereas some critical legal scholars, such as Tushnet and Kennedy, claim them as predecessors in their emphasis on the indeterminacy of doctrine.[64]

3. *Realism as a Negative Force*

Perhaps the most common view is that the Realist Movement was a critical, essentially negative, sometimes nihilistic reaction against a prevailing academic orthodoxy that is generally depicted or caricatured as "Langdellism."[65] The Realists provided a powerful critique but failed to develop any constructive alternative. This iconoclastic interpretation of Realism approximates the predominant view that I encountered in England as an undergraduate: "They took us into the wilderness and left us there." It has been revived recently by some Critical Legal Studies (CLS) commentators who themselves emphasize the indeterminacy of rules and the subjectivity of interpretation, and who claim a close affinity with Realism in this respect.[66]

There are three distinct elements in this image: the conception of Realism as being essentially skeptical, irrationalist, and nihilistic; the suggestion that historically Realism's main target was an academic orthodoxy (Langdellism), or the ideology underlying this orthodoxy ("liberal legalism"), or more generally something referred to as "formalism"; and the allegation that the thrust of the Realist critique was negative rather than constructive. Some, but not all, commentaries combine all three elements with varying degrees of emphasis; others seem to concentrate on one or two of them.

It is not possible to do justice to this complex subject in a few paragraphs. But I shall argue that this composite image fails the minimal test of textual and historical accuracy in respect of all three elements. Thus, the negative image is not only inaccurate, but also seriously misleading.

The case for treating this as a misinterpretation of Realism can be

---

63 See R. Dworkin, supra note 56, at 3-4.

64 Tushnet, supra note 54, at 21; Critical Legal Studies, supra note 21, at 4.

65 See KLRM, supra note 1, at 80-81, 409-11 for references. Cf. J. Paul, The Legal Realism of Jerome N. Frank 129-42 (1959), which has a useful discussion of Frank's critics. A classic example of this view is Mechem, The Jurisprudence of Despair, 21 Iowa L. Rev. 669 (1936). Thurman Arnold seems to have taken this negative view retrospectively when he described Realism as "a good medicine for a sick and troubled society . . . [but] despite its liberating virtues . . . not a sustaining food for a stable civilization." Arnold, Judge Jerome Frank, 24 U. Chi. L. Rev. 633, 634 (1957).

For contrary views see, e.g., R. Summers, supra note 1, passim; W. Twining, The Karl Llewellyn Papers 5-6 (1968); KLRM, supra note 1, at 80-81; Note, Round and Round the Bramble Bush: From Legal Realism to Critical Legal Scholarship, 95 Harv. L. Rev. 1669, 1674-76 (1982). See also Schlegel, Underhill Moore, supra note 1, at 196.

66 See Tushnet, supra note 54; Critical Legal Studies, supra note 21.

briefly summarized as follows. First, few, if any, members of the Realist Movement were ever philosophical skeptics, nihilists, or pure subjectivists in any strong sense.[67] One would be hard put to find even a few passages in Llewellyn's extensive writings that could give color to such an interpretation. The great bulk of his work points in quite different directions.[68] I cannot claim an intimate knowledge of all of Cook's work, but it seems reasonably clear that the main target of his early "Realist" writings was the idea that most judicial decisions on disputed questions of law fit one standard model of deductive reasoning. This position was not fundamentally irrationalist; in respect of values Cook claimed to be a follower of Dewey, and his ideas about scientific method in law were the reverse of skeptical.[69] Frank's case is admittedly less straightforward. Frank undoubtedly made some skeptical noises and was taken seriously as a philosophical skeptic by Edmond Cahn, a perceptive commentator who knew him well.[70] However, as I have argued elsewhere, many of Frank's most important undertakings—to make judicial processes more "rational," to increase accuracy in factfinding, and to improve legal education—do not make much sense if we take his claims to philosophical skepticism seriously in respect of facts, values, or reasoning. Indeed, as a reformer he seems better characterized as an optimistic rationalist.[71]

Second, the main targets of Realist critiques were more diffuse and more varied than "Langdellism" (which is, in any case, a construct of later commentators). The slot-machine and declaratory theories of judicial decisionmaking, mechanical jurisprudence, the formal style of judging, "the myth of certainty," "lump concepts," appellate court-itis, the "unscientific" nature of legal scholarship, and some versions of Natural Law jurisprudence were among the main targets of one or more of the three core Realists, who also criticized each other.[72] Most, but not all, of

---

67 See generally, KLRM, supra note 1 passim; Twining, Some Scepticism I, supra note 37, at 142-43.

68 The Bramble Bush (1931) was probably the most common source of the view that the early Llewellyn was a "negative" critic. On why this is a misinterpretation see KLRM, supra note 1, at 140-52. Llewellyn could, however, be a harsh critic. See Nelson, Standards of Criticism, 60 Tex. L. Rev. 447, 457-61 (1982) (discussing Llewellyn's treatment of Richard Morris's Studies in the History of American Law (1930) in Llewellyn, Book Review, 31 Colum. L. Rev. 729 (1931)).

69 See K. Llewellyn, Jurisprudence, supra note 31, at 53 n.35, 103; KLRM, supra note 1, at 37-38, 40.

70 See E. Cahn, Confronting Injustice 269 (1967); Cahn, Jerome Frank's Fact-Skepticism and our Future, 66 Yale L.J. 824, 828 (1957).

71 See Twining, Some Scepticism I, supra note 37, at 157-61.

72 See, e.g., J. Frank, supra note 42, passim (on Llewellyn); id. at 316-25 (on Cook); K. Llewellyn, supra note 31, at 101-10, passim (same); K. Llewellyn, Common Law Tradition, supra note 39, at 104 n.135, 220 n.214 (on Frank); Llewellyn, supra note 45, at 400-01 (on Cook); Lecture by Karl Llewellyn 16-18 (May 9, 1955) (unpublished manuscript); K. Llewellyn, Law in Our Society 8, 34 (unpublished teaching materials 1958) [hereinafter Llewellyn,

these might be accommodated within a liberal interpretation of "Langdellism." To stretch the term this way, however, tends to obscure the diversity of the underlying concerns of individual members of the Realist Movement and the changing nature of these concerns at different periods. This diversity is particularly important when one considers the political significance of Realism.

Finally, the judgment that nearly all Realist endeavors and achievements were negative rather than constructive seems to me to be a travesty of history. With respect to temperament, aspirations, and achievements this just does not fit the Llewellyn I know. Ironically, apart from one or two intemperate book reviews, perhaps the most "negative" criticism he ever advanced in print was directed at some of the early programs of empirical research by Realists at Yale and Johns Hopkins.[73] Cook's work on scientific method and, perhaps more controversially, his radical rethinking of the Conflict of Laws can be interpreted as constructive rather than negative.[74] Frank may, admittedly, have enjoyed controversy and he may not have been particularly *successful* as a reformer. However, the overall thrust of his endeavors concerning judicial procedures and institutions, legal education, the SEC, and as a judge was surely in the direction of trying to improve things according to his particular version of the American Dream.[75] There may be some force in the thesis that the Realist Movement's achievements fell far short of its aspirations—for example, that it failed to destroy the dominant academic orthodoxy or to develop a coherent alternative to replace it.[76] Opinions may vary on the extent and value of the overall impact of Realist activities and ideas on American legal education, scholarship, literature, legislation, professional opinion, and so on. But the Uniform Commercial Code, *The Cheyenne Way*, Hurst's *Law and Economic Growth*, the Columbia casebooks, many developments in law and the social sciences, and numerous other specific legal artifacts can all be claimed as "products of Realism," all inspired or influenced to a significant extent by Realist ideas. If one adds the contributions of Holmes, Corbin, Douglas, Moore,

---

Law in Our Society]. I have not located any substantial discussion by Cook of the work of Llewellyn or Frank. This is not entirely surprising in that he belonged to an earlier generation and was concentrating on rather different issues in his later years.

[73] See Llewellyn, supra note 45, at 399-401.

[74] In his preface to *The Logical and Legal Bases of the Conflict of Laws*, Cook claims that his attack on the theories of Story, Dicey, Beale, and the Restatement was a "constructive" effort analogous to clearing a garden of weeds. W. Cook, Conflict of Laws, supra note 40, at ix (1942). His main thrust was directed toward over-broad rules; he argued for flexible guidelines based on narrower categories. Cf. Llewellyn, supra note 31, at 56-57 (No. 7 of Llewellyn's common points of departure); KLRM, supra note 1, at 97-98.

[75] For generally balanced assessments of Frank's achievements, see J. Paul, supra note 65; W. Volkomer, The Passionate Liberal: The Political and Legal Ideas of Jerome Frank (1970).

[76] See KLRM, supra note 1, at 375-87.

or whoever else you choose to include in the list of Realists, to claim that the sum total of their significant achievements was solely or largely negative seems an extraordinary judgment.[77]

It is not very surprising that this negative view has been quite widespread. Many Realist texts, including some by the core Realists, were critical in both style and substance. Some were aggressively polemical and indulged in overstatement. Llewellyn and Frank were self-styled "skeptics." All three core Realists were concerned, in different ways, with the limits of rationality, with misuses of "logic," and with the role played by "subjective" factors in legal decisionmaking. All three were dissatisfied with many loosely interrelated aspects of the theory and practice of academic law including legal education, legal scholarship, and general ideas and assumptions related to these. It is a convenient and legitimate simplifying device, for some purposes, to attribute these objects of dissatisfaction to a prevailing orthodoxy and to give this orthodoxy a label such as "Langdellism." In these and no doubt in other respects one can readily acknowledge some basis for the negative image. Nevertheless, it is not difficult to show that, as a global judgment on the ideas and achievements of members of the Realist Movement, it is so misleading as not to be salvageable by a few judicious caveats. It is better to shatter the image.

4. *Realism as a Constructive Search for Alternatives to Langdellism*

This interpretation is similar to the negative image in that it postulates that, at least in its early stages, the Realist Movement was united by its opposition to a perceived common enemy (variously characterized). However, it stresses that a great deal of the Realists' efforts, far from being negative, were directed to the constructive development of alternatives.[78] The Columbia curriculum discussions, the Johns Hopkins Institute, the Uniform Commercial Code, Llewellyn's Grand Style and the numerous other legal artifacts referred to in the previous section are thus seen as more or less conscious attempts to implement the Realist program at a concrete level. The story can be told with many variations and codas. The version that I tend to favor adds two general glosses. First, insofar as members of the movement perceived a shared enemy or set of targets in a newly dominant orthodoxy, there were several different kinds of reasons for their dissatisfaction: the illusion of the logical form or of so-called mechanical jurisprudence; the divorce between legal education

[77] For similar views of the constructive achievements of the Realists, see, e.g., R. Summers, supra note 1, at 278-81; Schlegel, Underhill Moore, supra note 1, at 195-99.

[78] This was the self-image of both Frank and Llewellyn, encapsulated in Frank's claim that they were "constructive skeptics." See J. Frank, Law and the Modern Mind vii (1949 ed.).

and private legal practice; the rather different divorce between law in books and law in action; the intellectual—and, separably, the political—conservatism of Langdellism; the nonempirical nature of Langdell's "science"; and the unresponsiveness of this kind of legal discourse to the needs of the American legal system. Thus, the concerns underlying the general sense of dissatisfaction were diverse and the suggested alternatives correspondingly diverse, but this diversity was obscured by internal interpreters of the movement, notably Llewellyn and Frank.[79] Second, in certain key respects the constructive Realists seriously underestimated the magnitude of the enterprises they had undertaken. The result was that though they produced many interesting particular legal artifacts, they failed to deliver on their promise of "a sustained and programmatic attack on the problems of law."[80]

5. *Ideological Interpretations: Realism as Reformist Politics and Liberal Ideology*

A rather different perspective sees the Realist Movement in political or ideological terms. Realism is sometimes depicted as a left-liberal movement—linked to the Progressive Movement in politics—that provided a critique of and rationale for the extension of discretionary powers in the judiciary and executive branches.[81] It thereby posed a threat to the Rule of Law and representative democracy. This threat in turn produced a political response—disguised or overt—in the form of defenses of the Rule of Law and neutral principles. Such a view of Realism probably motivated Pound's original attack in 1931,[82] as well as sophisticated defenses of the Rule of Law by people such as Dickinson[83] and Fuller,[84] and later by advocates of neutral or objective principles such as Wechsler[85] and Dworkin.[86] This interpretation is, not surprisingly, echoed with

---

79 See text accompanying notes 108-10 infra.

80 I advanced this thesis in *KLRM* and need not repeat it here. See KLRM, supra note 1, at 70-83. I reformulated this view with respect to the United Kingdom in Twining, Law and Social Science: The Method of Detail, New Soc'y 758, 759-61 (1974).

81 Few commentators discuss Realism solely in these terms. The best account of the political background of the Realist Movement is E.A. Purcell, supra note 1. See also L. Friedman, supra note 1, at 567-94; R. Summers, supra note 1.

82 Pound, The Call for a Realist Jurisprudence, 44 Harv. L. Rev. 697 (1931). The background to Pound's hostility to Realism is explored in D. Wigdor, Roscoe Pound 207-32, 249-81 (1974).

83 See, e.g., Dickinson, Function, supra note 27; Application, supra note 27. A more positive work is Dickinson's excellent Administrative Justice and the Supremacy of Law (1927), which *preceded* the debate between Llewellyn and Pound. See id. at 32-39, 105-56.

84 See, e.g., Fuller, American Legal Realism, 82 U. Pa. L. Rev. 82 (1934); see generally R. Summers, Lon Fuller 17-41 (1984).

85 Wechsler, Toward Neutral Principles of Constitutional Law, 73 Harv. L. Rev. 1 (1959). See also KLRM, supra note 1, at 456 n.247.

86 R. Dworkin, supra note 56.

different emphasis by Critical Legal Studies commentators, who see the core Realists as exemplars of what is expansively referred to as "liberalism" and who emphasize the inescapable connections between law and politics.[87]

[87] I was invited to explore the connections between the Realist Movement and Critical Legal Studies (CLS). This is clearly too large a subject for this occasion, even if one confines oneself to the juristic significance of the latter. I was tempted at least to comment on claims that members of CLS are true Daughters of the American Realist Revolution, but on examination, this also turned out to be a far more complex matter than it seemed at first sight. There are, however, a few themes in this paper that may have a bearing on such claims. I have already alluded to CLS tendencies to reification, the parochialism and isolationist tendencies of much American jurisprudence, and the relative deprivation of CLS scholars that results from the lack of a homogeneous orthodoxy, analogous to the myth of the slot-machine theory or the dominant legend of Langdellism, for them to react against. Let me here drop a few hints concerning historical parallels, perceived or claimed "influences," textual affinities, and similar tendencies toward self-interpretation and introspection.

1. *Historical "Parallels"*

Despite some obvious similarities (American scholar-teachers of law expressing in iconoclastic terms their dissatisfactions with prevailing orthodoxies), there are too many differences in the contexts (including the political and general intellectual climates, as well as developments in law schools, legal education, and other relevant disciplines), in the patterns of development (Realism's development was slow and spasmodic, whereas CLS's has been rapid and more coordinated), and in important triggering events to suggest much promise in the dubious enterprise of looking for historical parallels. One also wonders whether Realism and CLS are both "movements" in the same sense (CLS appears to be much more institutionalized, coordinated, clublike, and activist) and whether the complex differences in the degree and nature of their "movements," political motivation and commitment do not make the contrasts more interesting than the parallels, insofar as generalization is meaningful in either direction.

2. *Realist "Influences"*

Critical Legal Studies, supra note 21, includes an amusing "Identikit Paragraph from any CLS article" that adopts the central tenets of Realism as the starting point for CLS. This caricature of CLS does seem to fit quite a few CLS texts. It characterizes Realism as emphasizing the "vacuousness, circularity and medieval silliness of legal reasoning and . . . the role of policy rather than rules in judicial decisions." Such an interpretation is close to the "nightmare" image of Realism as nihilistic rule-skepticism and is at best exaggerated and highly selective. This revival of what one had hoped was discredited as a historical and textual interpretation of most writings of core Realists is mildly irritating. Whether such claims are intended to or in fact do serve as self-legitimating devices, as G. Edward White suggests, see White, The Inevitability of Critical Legal Studies, 36 Stan. L. Rev. 649, 650-51 (1984), or whether they are best treated as examples of nostalgia or sloppy scholarship is open to debate. One nevertheless wonders whether they may not serve to obfuscate the nature of various CLS enterprises for the participants, even if they do not fool many outsiders. It may, however, be worth noting one possible historical lesson of the Realist story: the enterprises of those Realists (such as Llewellyn and Frank) who consistently aspired to be accepted as "real lawyers" (insiders) were far more influential in fact than the efforts of those who aspired only to be committed scholars and thereby condemned themselves to be outsiders ("the scientists"). One would think that, given the economic base and social functions of nearly all law schools, if most efforts to transform them into serious centers of scholarship have failed, then surely the prospects for making them bases for genuinely radical political thought or action are rather slight.

3. *Textual Affinities*

One theme of this lecture has been that, at the analytical level, generalizations about Realist texts are dangerous not only because they tend to be inaccurate but also because much

Such accounts can often be fairly interpreted as responses to questions about the political significance of Realism rather than as rounded historical explanations of the rise of the Realist Movement or analytical interpretations of Realist ideas. I have no desire to set up this image as a straw man, but it is important to mention why it is misleading to exaggerate the political dimensions of Realism. It is doubtful that members of the Realist Movement were united by shared political concerns, especially during the movement's formative stages.[88] The political conservatism of Langdellism was probably one of the less important and certainly one of the least overt of the various grounds for dissatisfaction that were mentioned above. Except during the New Deal period,[89] most Realist writings did not directly address issues of national politics or general ideology. Some were strikingly apolitical. One reason for this may have been that some of these concerns were shared by people with significantly different political views and varying degrees of awareness and commit-

---

of the unfulfilled promise of Legal Realism is to be found in particular, often unique, contributions of individuals. The moral is, as always, to start with particular texts and to be skeptical of interpretations of general intellectual trends.

Based on a comparison of Realist and CLS texts, my strong impression is that there are remarkably few affinities or correspondences between familiar Realist texts and the more impressive contributions of such individual CLS scholars as Roberto Unger, Duncan Kennedy (The Structure of Blackstone's Commentaries, 28 Buffalo L. Rev. 205 (1979)), Morton Horwitz (The Transformation of American Law, 1780-1860 (1977)), or Robert Gordon (Historicism in Legal Scholarship, 90 Yale L.J. 1017 (1981) (despite his acknowledged debt to Willard Hurst)). This disparity can be taken as a compliment to the CLS scholars' originality, but the enterprises are also different. Did any Realist set out to develop a major social theory, apply techniques borrowed from literary criticism and linguistics to the interpretation of legal texts, or spawn a genuinely critical mode of legal historiography? Conversely, are we ever likely to get "critical" analogues to the Uniform Commercial Code, *The Cheyenne Way*, the Johns Hopkins Institute or even Frank's *Courts on Trial*? My conclusion is that neither the major achievements nor the examples of unfulfilled promise of Realist writings and ideas have very much to offer to CLS enterprises.

4. *Self-Interpretation and Introspection*

I have suggested that the leading internal interpreters of Realism, Llewellyn and Frank, tended to obfuscate the nature of their enterprises by glossing over significant differences and disagreements (Llewellyn), by introducing spurious distinctions (Frank's dichotomy between rule-skeptics and fact-skeptics), and by loose talk ("Realism is not a philosophy, but a technology."). K. Llewellyn, Common Law Tradition, supra note 39, at 509-10 (emphasis omitted). Some of the CLS interpreters from within (for example, Kennedy and Gordon) have been refreshingly open about internal differences and disagreements. Recent developments suggest a possible trend toward yet another convergence with literary criticism: a kilo of commentary for every gram of original work.

88 This is best treated as a hypothesis requiring further research and analysis of the political background, if any, of the relevant writings of, among others, Holmes, Gray, Bingham, Corbin, Cook, Hohfeld, Oliphant, and the young Llewellyn. For a perceptive critique of my failure to deal adequately with the broader historical context of the Realist controversy, see Purcell, Book Review, 19 Am. J. Legal Hist. 240 (1975) (review of *KLRM*).

89 Clearly political interpretations fit the writings of men like Arnold, Berle, Douglas, Frank, and Rodell during the period after about 1925. But the Progressive Movement and the concerns of the New Deal are widely regarded as starting much earlier.

ment. For example, Frank was a political activist and publicist, committed to a clear set of liberal principles that he openly proclaimed in his legal and other writings.[90] It is rather difficult to build a coherent profile of Llewellyn's political beliefs and postures at different times, perhaps because they are marked by a deep-rooted strain of ambivalence.[91] If Cook had strong political beliefs they are not apparent on the surface of his best-known writings.[92] The degree of overt political concern discernible in Realist texts varies considerably over time, rising to a peak during the New Deal, although not all Realists were New Dealers.

This is not to deny the close historical connection between Realism and politics. Rather, it is to suggest that the relations between the Realist Movement, the Progressive Movement, the New Deal, and political concerns about the growth of administrative agencies and threats to the Rule of Law were more complex than some commentators have suggested. Many of the original concerns discernible in Realist texts, especially in the period up to 1930, were strikingly apolitical. Indeed, this is one feature that distinguishes the early phases of the Realist Movement from the Critical Legal Studies Movement and from some recent developments in academic law in Britain. Furthermore, I would suggest that Realist texts are of only marginal interest to contemporary debates about administrative discretion or the Rule of Law or more general questions of ideology. If they are still interesting it is largely for other reasons.

To conclude: At the historical level "Realism" has been used as a label for the activities, ideas, and achievements of a group or movement which has never had an agreed list of members. This label has sometimes been used in connection with the totality of the achievements of all the relevant individuals—in this context the totality of texts by identifiable Realists. This is a rather rich heritage. The label has sometimes been used to designate either the ideas the "Realists" were supposed to have shared or some other shared similarity of these individuals. Given the "Realists' " diversity, attempts at accurate generalization tend to amount to little more than a shared opposition to formalism and some commitment to a broader approach to law than one that is confined to legal doctrine. The application of my minimal test to five reconstructed interpretations illustrates some of the dangers of talk about Realism in very general terms. The objection is not merely that each of them is

---

90 See W. Volkomer, supra note 75.

91 On Llewellyn's political views, see KLRM, supra note 1, at 87-93, 124-25, 418-19, 479-84.

92 But see Cook, The Privileges of Labor Unions in the Struggle for Life, 27 Yale L.J. 779 (1918); Cook, Book Review, New Republic, Aug. 30, 1922, at 22; Cook, The American Law Institute, New Republic, Mar. 21, 1923, at 87. I am grateful to Professor Schlegel for these references.

overgeneralized, but rather that such accounts tend to lead to impoverished, sometimes misleading, perceptions of the nature of the Realist legacy. This is so even though there is some basis for each interpretation.

So much for the Realist legacy viewed as a collection of texts. The next section addresses the question whether the term "realism" has any value either as a way of classifying jurists or as a juristic concept. This shift of perspective is introduced by a second anecdote.

Interpretations of Realism II

Memoirs II: The Camel in the Zoo

I began my teaching career in the Sudan. In my first year my responsibilities included teaching the English law of Torts. The English Common Law was treated as embodying "equity, justice, and good conscience." The students were bored, polite, and tolerant and they thought me a little crazy to be concerned about the unreality of what we were studying. Then one day we came to that complicated absurdity, the common law relating to liability for animals. We got through cases of horses jumping over hedges, stories of rabid monkeys and erring avers and circus elephants trampling dwarfs, cases with memorable and evocative names like Filburn v. People's Palace *and* Behrens v. Bertram Mills Circus. *We pondered whether cats and cocks were cattle. I even posed the question whether the owner of a talking parrot could be liable in defamation. Then we came to* McQuacker v. Goddard. *In that case a visitor to the London zoo fed an Arabian camel and was bitten. He sued the zoo. After hearing "expert" evidence Mr. Justice Branson held as a matter of law that camels are* mansuetae naturae. *That is, as he interpreted it, camels are both tame and harmless. He held that the zoo was not liable in the absence of proof of negligence. In order to provoke the class I read out a quotation from an alleged "expert," Sir F. Palgrave: "He is from first to last an undomesticated and savage animal, rendered serviceable by stupidity alone . . . never tame, though not wide-awake enough to be exactly wild."*

I threw down a challenge: Is that how Sudanese feel about camels? A hand went up. "Aha," I thought, "at least I have got a response." But instead I received a question: "Please, sir, why was the camel in a zoo?" *At that moment some scales fell from my eyes. What had a camel in a zoo to do with Sudan? Or circus elephants or performing fleas or slanderous parrots or carbolic smoke balls or the rule against perpetuities? What was I doing teaching all this artificial and irrelevant frippery to Sudanese students? Maybe I overreacted, but at least I got a discussion going. I had provoked a response by playing the nationalist card. Indeed, it was difficult to stop the students talking and I had subverted my own course.*

The discussion led to the conclusion that the English law of Torts was neither relevant nor suitable to the Sudan. To be sure, there were roads and factories where accidents might happen. People could be defamed or insulted. There was even a zoo—but how many people actually sued? And did English rules and values make sense in this kind of situation? What of liability for animals? What happened in practice when someone's goat or bull or camel (or some animal in the Khartoum zoo) caused damage? "It is governed by custom," said the students. But how could one find out about custom in order to teach it? "Ask the people," came the reply.

In solving one problem (for now I could hardly stop the students from talking) I had uncovered another. How could anyone, let alone a too-young expatriate, teach about the realities of the law-in-action in the Sudan? If customary law was important—as it clearly was—surely years of research would be needed before anyone could be qualified to teach it.

Shortly after this first incident one of the students invited me to visit a village in the desert outside Khartoum. The local headman (omda) *was present. He had heard that I was interested in customary law and he intimated that I could put some questions to him through an interpreter. I was doubly unprepared: I had no training in fieldwork and had prepared no questions. But I was, after all, a pupil of Karl Llewellyn. However, I had not learned all that he had to teach. Instead of asking the* omda *to tell me about some actual disputes about animals that had recently occurred in the village and how these had been handled, I improvised a series of formalistic hypotheticals based on the English law of Torts. What happens if* A*'s goat wanders onto* B*'s land and butts* C*, a trespasser? What happens if* X*'s bull escapes onto the highway and gores* Y*'s camel? He answered all my questions promptly, confidently, and with a straight face. At the end he said: "Very interesting, but we have no bulls or camels in this village and our goats do not behave like that—no such cases ever arise." Like my mentor, I decided that I was not equipped for fieldwork.*

Realism and Related Concepts

Whatever else one reads into this fable, at the very least it identifies a kind of problem that confronted expatriate law teachers in postcolonial Africa in a striking way.[93] Of course, it confronts law teachers everywhere, though not all of them confront it. Whether the issues are posed in terms of the relationship between law in books and law in action, theory and practice, paper rules and real rules, or relevance or realism, they relate directly to one of the main underlying concerns of Realist Jurisprudence. This is one reason for its continuing attraction. But does the

[93] For interpretations and implications of this experience, see W. Twining, Academic Law and Legal Development (1976) and W. Twining, The Camel in The Zoo (Dec. 1981) (unpublished lecture delivered at University of Khartoum).

term "realism" in law aptly describe a distinctive kind of theory about, or approach to, law? Does it provide any guidance for dealing with this or any other kind of problem at the level of theory?

Robert Stevens has recently referred to realism as an "amorphous state of mind."[94] That is a suggestive phrase, which rightly emphasizes the vagueness of the term. "Realism" is also ambiguous: it has several distinct meanings in philosophy, none of which is necessarily identical with "realism" in art or law or film.[95] It is little more than a coincidence that the same term was appropriated by followers of Hagerstrom in Scandinavia as by Llewellyn, who was interpreting quite separate and different developments in the United States.[96] Moreover, juristic labels are susceptible to liberal interpretation. It is unlikely that many of those who reject Realism, Liberalism or Critical Legal Studies would acknowledge that they are thereby open to serious charges of being unrealistic, illiberal or uncritical. Similarly not all critics of "common sense" views, in sociology or philosophy, can be said *ipso facto* to "lack common sense."

The first Dewey lecturer, my good friend Neil MacCormick, has admitted in public that sometimes, while he is shaving, he looks at himself in the mirror and asks, "Am I really a positivist?"[97] As I use an electric shaver, I am normally able to evade such matutinal introspections. But were a modern would-be realist to look at herself in the mirror and ask, "Am I positively a realist?" I suspect that she would require a different approach to answer this question than MacCormick uses. Linguistic analysis has helped to expose, if not to eliminate, some myths about positivism, but it seems to be of less use in deciding whether any meaning can usefully be attributed to the notion of "realism" in law.[98] In my experience, most efforts along this line have proved unfruitful, except perhaps to reemphasize the obvious ambiguity and vagueness of the term. Some have led to gross misreadings of Realist texts.

There are several other possible approaches to the problem of giving the concept of realism some specific content. Some of these have proved to be *pis allez*. One is to compare the historical and analytical relationship between Scandinavian and American Realism; this is hardly more rewarding than subjecting a not very good pun to laborious analysis. An-

---

94 R. Stevens, supra note 1, at 134.

95 For some reasons why "Legal Realism" may be misleading as a label even for core Realists, see R. Summers, supra note 1, at 36-37.

96 See KLRM, supra note 1, at 522 & n.7.

97 N. MacCormick, Address at W.G. Hart Workshop on Legal Theory (July 1984) (cited with permission). An introspective critical legal scholar might be expected to chant:

"Mirror, mirror on the wall,
Am I *really* critical?"

98 E.g., Hart, supra note 20; Summers, supra note 20.

other is to detach the term from its particular historical context and to try to construct generalizations about such diverse characters as Roger Bacon, Niccolo Machiavelli, John Dewey, and Bob Woodward.[99] A more interesting line is to take the notion of legal skepticism seriously. Though a good deal of attention has been devoted to rule-skepticism in jurisprudence, the implications of various kinds of value-skepticism, fact-skepticism, political agnosticism, and other skepticisms for the study of law have not attracted as much direct attention—at least in these terms—as one might have expected.[100]

Yet another approach is to take a fresh look at such common ground as can reasonably be attributed to the original American Realists, especially on the constructive side, and to try to analyze some of its implications. To some extent this has been done by Robert Summers in his reconstruction of "pragmatic instrumentalism."[101] My main reservation about this approach is that it filters out some of the most fruitful contributions of individual Realists; Summers, however, at least brings out clearly the strengths and limitations of the central Realist ideas, as he interprets them, and in his own work he has succeeded in developing some of these ideas well beyond the crudities of naive instrumentalism.

Even thinner interpretations of shared Realist ideas have some potential for development. For example, the notion of "broadening the study of law from within"[102] can be restated in terms of a general proposition such as "in order to understand law the study of rules alone is not enough." Elucidation of the meaning and implications of this proposition opens up some potentially fruitful lines of inquiry. For example, to ask "What is involved in *understanding* law?" is a suggestive way of posing or reposing a central issue of legal philosophy. If the study of rules is not enough for this purpose, what else is enough? At a more specific level, if the study of the *rules* of contract or criminal law or evidence is not sufficient to obtain an understanding of these fields, what more is required or desirable in each instance? What is involved in constructing coherent frames of reference for such broader studies? Are there any

---

99 On whether *The Brethren* deserves to be treated as a product of Realism, see Twining, Book Review, 44 Mod. L. Rev. 739 (1981) (reviewing B. Woodward & S. Armstrong, The Brethren (1979)). Cf. G. Anastaplo, Comment, Legal Realism, the New Journalism, and *The Brethren*, 1983 Duke L.J. 1045. Other candidates for recognition as prototypical realists include Biron in *Love's Labour's Lost*, Brother William in Umberto Eco's *The Name of the Rose*, and Louis Agassiz as described in G. Highet, The Art of Teaching 241-45 (1950).

100 See Twining, Some Scepticisms I, supra note 37, passim.

101 See R. Summers, supra note 1, at 20-37.

102 The phrase "broadening the study of law from within" was for a time associated with the ethos of the Warwick Law School and its first chairman, Professor Geoffrey Wilson. See Folsom & Roberts, The Warwick Story: Being Led Down the Contextual Path of The Law, 30 J. Legal Educ. 166 (1979); Twining, Some Jobs, supra note 3, at 167-70.

criteria for selecting organizing concepts for particular "fields" of law? What "nonlegal" dimensions deserve to be given a special emphasis in a broadened approach to a particular field? By what criteria is one to make such selections? And so on. Some recent efforts to "rethink" criminal law, torts, contracts, evidence, and other fields can be interpreted as examples of attempts to perform the synthesizing function of the theorist within a broadened conception of the discipline of law.[103] Have these attempts been sufficiently systematic? Can any *general* guidance be given to one about to embark on the enterprise of rethinking his particular specialty along broader or more realistic lines?

Thus even the thinnest interpretation of realism can be developed in such a way as to suggest an ambitious theoretical program. As I have suggested, those members of the Realist Movement who took on tasks of this kind did not on the whole fulfill the promise of their enterprise, partly because they often underestimated the magnitude of their tasks, and partly because they were not sufficiently systematic at a general or theoretical level.

Enough has been said to make the point that the possibilities for analytical development of the notion of "realism" are by no means exhausted, even at this very general level. However, it may be even more fruitful to consider potential meanings and implications of "realism" and related notions more concretely in specific contexts. Accordingly, by way of illustration, I propose to look at two particular examples: first, at some of Karl Llewellyn's pronouncements about "realism" as they apply to his own ideas rather than to the Realist Movement as a whole; then, at the emergence of "law in context" and "sociolegal studies" as labels in the United Kingdom in the late 1960's.

1. Llewellyn on "realism"[104]

Karl Llewellyn is generally regarded as the leading internal interpreter of the Realist Movement. He neither coined the term nor founded the movement, but he is acknowledged as its first labeler and publicist. As early as 1925 he had begun work on a paper entitled "A Realist Jurisprudence." This emerged in 1929 at a round table of the American Association of Political Science as a paper on "Modern Concepts of Law." It was published in 1930 as "A Realistic Jurisprudence—The Next Step."[105] Pound echoed this title in his broadside on "The Call for a

[103] See, e.g., G. Fletcher, Rethinking Criminal Law (1978); H. Gross, A Theory of Criminal Justice (1979); MacNeil, The Many Futures of Contracts, 47 S. Cal. L. Rev. 691 (1974); Twining, Evidence, supra note 3. See also Legal Theory and Common Law (W. Twining ed.) (forthcoming 1986).

[104] This topic is explored at greater length in KLRM, supra note 1, at 70-83, 517-23.

[105] 30 Colum. L. Rev. 431 (1930).

Realist Jurisprudence,"[106] which in turn provided the opportunity for Llewellyn's famous reply. "Some Realism about Realism—Responding to Dean Pound"[107] immediately became, and deservedly remains, the classic text of Realist self-interpretation.

One lesson of the history of talk about realism is the need to treat internal or self-interpreters and spokesmen with caution. Llewellyn's riposte to Pound should have effectively buried some unfair accusations; but it almost as effectively obscured the split between those who were concerned to broaden legal education and training from within and those who wished to develop an empirical science of law in ways which would inevitably divorce it almost completely from vocational training for private practice.[108] Jerome Frank's equally famous division of Realists into rule-skeptics and fact-skeptics was also misleading in several ways. It exaggerated the extent and the depth of the skepticism involved, including his own, suggested that Realism was concerned only with the predictability of judicial decisions, and, modestly or immodestly, disguised the fact that there was probably only one committed fact-skeptic—himself, a one-person school.[109] Similarly Llewellyn's later pronouncements—such as the idea that realism is a technology, not a philosophy[110]—served to pinpoint some of the more original aspects of his own contribution rather than to interpret the movement as a whole.

Although Llewellyn's nine "common points of departure" have been very extensively cited and discussed, this passage from "Some Realism about Realism"[111] has never been subjected to as systematic and comprehensive exegesis as it deserves. Though not based on as rigorous an analysis of texts as Llewellyn had employed to refute Pound's original charges, it nevertheless was a masterly attempt to generalize about the shared ideas of a diverse group. It still repays careful textual study both as a basis for attempting to construct an ideal type of Realist thought and as an aid to interpreting Llewellyn's own ideas. On the whole the work skillfully avoids most of the pitfalls of generalization. At the same time it is sufficiently carefully written to escape many later charges levelled at the Realists.

---

106 44 Harv. L. Rev. 697 (1931).

107 44 Harv. L. Rev. 1222 (1931).

108 See KLRM, supra note 1, at 56-83.

109 See J. Frank, supra note 42, at 74. Frank listed Leon Green, Max Radin, Thurman Arnold, William O. Douglas, and, tentatively, E.M. Morgan as fact-skeptics. It is debatable whether any of these, except Leon Green, completely fit Frank's account of "fact-skepticism," which is a statement of his own views. Rumble confines his useful discussion of fact-skepticism almost entirely to Frank and his disciple, Edmond Cahn. W. Rumble, American Legal Realism 38, 107-36 (1968).

110 K. Llewellyn, Common Law Tradition, supra note 39, at 509-10.

111 44 Harv. L. Rev. at 1235-38.

"Some Realism about Realism" is in many respects a model of juristic interpretation. Nevertheless, it must be treated with caution. In particular, the nine points were only a list of common points of departure for a sample of twenty individuals selected for their diversity, many of whom were at relatively early stages in their careers. Nearly all of these points reflect aspects of Llewellyn's thought at the time, but on their own they were far from a rounded statement of his most general theory, even in 1931.[112]

In his later general statements about realism, the most important of which appears in *The Common Law Tradition*, Llewellyn was as concerned to say what realism was not as he was to give it a specific positive content.[113] He denied that realism, on its own, constituted a rounded approach or a general theory of law. It was only one part of his jurisprudence. In his unfinished work *Law in Our Society*, Llewellyn was trying to develop his own "Whole View" based on, but reaching beyond, his law-jobs theory.[114] He was emphatic that realism could not ground such a "Whole View": "If, as I think, jurisprudence contains [seven] sub-disciplines, then realism deals with two out of the seven: craft techniques and descriptive sociology. . . ."[115]

In particular, he explicitly distinguished realism from any particular theory of value—that is part of what he meant by the dictum "realism is not a philosophy."[116] He was especially concerned to separate the notion of realism from his own values, partly because it related solely to the "Is" part of his famous "Temporary divorce of the Is from Ought for purposes of study,"[117] and partly because in his later years he was involved in rather more than a flirtation with Natural Law, so he wished to dissociate himself from unqualified utilitarianism or any form of nihilism or skepticism about values.[118] He was also concerned to separate realism from any particular conception or theory of law. In a 1954 letter he wrote: "The drive of Realism, on the other hand, is to establish an effective legal technology. To this such a question as that of the nature of law

112 On Llewellyn's early attempts to develop a general sociology of law see KLRM, supra note 1, at 170-71. Especially significant in this respect are his "Mechanisms of Group Control" (unpublished paper on file at the University of Chicago Law School) started in 1927, and *Recht, Rechtsleben und Gesellschaft*, written mainly in 1932 and published in 1977.

113 K. Llewellyn, Common Law Tradition, supra note 39, at 508-21.

114 K. Llewellyn, Law in Our Society, supra note 72, reprinted, in part, in KLRM, supra note 1, at 497-516; see also KLRM, supra note 1, at 170-202.

115 K. Llewellyn, Babel versus Teamwork: Jurisprudence since 1900 (1942-43) (unpublished manuscript), cited in KLRM, supra note 1, at 519.

116 For various versions of this idea, see KLRM, supra note 1, at 517-23.

117 K. Llewellyn, supra note 31, at 55-56.

118 KLRM, supra note 1, at 123-26, 185-88; Casebeer, Escape From Realism: Fact and Value in Karl Llewellyn, 1977 Duke L.J. 671.

is accidental or incidental, or even immaterial . . . ."[119]

Whether or not this position is defensible, it is clear that Llewellyn wanted to keep separate the notion of realism, which he claimed to share with others, and his distinctive approach to a general theory of and about law *stricto sensu*. Llewellyn's approach involved the substitution of the institution of "Law-and-government" for "Law" as the central concept of his jurisprudence and a repeated refusal to *define* "law," on the grounds that definitions leave too much out and place too much emphasis on unique and differentiating elements rather than on the continuities and similarities between social institutions.[120] In making these denials about realism, Llewellyn was emphasizing aspects of his thought that separated him from most if not all other Realists.

So much for what Llewellyn's version of realism was not. On the positive side he saw it as dealing with two parts of jurisprudence: descriptive sociology and what he variously characterized as legal technology, craft techniques, and method.[121] This is loose talk. It requires rather generous interpretation to save him from the criticisms of "descriptive sociology," barefoot empiricism, and crude instrumentalism that have sometimes been levelled against him.[122] A defense could be made, but I shall not attempt it here. Let us concede that some of these criticisms have force and press on.

In discussing realism as a method and a technology, Llewellyn seems to have succumbed to the vulgar error of conflating method and methodology, or techniques and technology. That is, he confused the *exercise* of a method or technique with its *study*. Here, with a bit of generosity, Llewellyn can be interpreted as making two distinct claims: one about legal technology as a focus of attention, the other about some precepts for a realistic approach. Both deserve comment.

One of Llewellyn's most distinctive and potentially fertile contributions to legal thought centers on his notion of the job of juristic method as one of the law-jobs. He rightly claimed that the study of that job—legal technology in a strict, but a broad sense—was an important but neglected part of legal theory. The focus of attention is *how* the law-jobs get done. This includes not only the study of craft techniques of individual practitioners and judges, but also a wide range of questions about institutions, legal inventions, craft traditions, and much else. Llewellyn's own work at an applied level is pervaded by his concern with such *how*

119 Letter from Karl Llewellyn to Graham Hughes (May 10, 1954), quoted in KLRM, supra note 1, at 522.

120 See K. Llewellyn, supra note 31, at 3; see also KLRM, supra note 1, at 148-50.

121 See K. Llewellyn, Law in Our Society, supra note 72, reprinted, in part, in KLRM, supra note 1, at 505-12; K. Llewellyn, Common Law Tradition, supra note 39, at 509-10.

122 See, e.g., Schubert, supra note 43.

questions—Cheyenne law-ways, the Grand Style of judging and advocacy, the "beauty" of the letter of credit, the direct teaching of basic legal skills, and much broader questions about commercial practice, bureaucratic organization, and institutional design. Bits and pieces of this have been picked up,[123] but the broader implications of the thesis that legal technology is an important focus for *theoretical* attention, both descriptive and prescriptive, have neither been widely perceived nor systematically followed through. There is clearly some loose connection with the notion of "realism," but to treat the theory of legal technology as necessarily associated with "realism" obscures rather than illuminates this aspect of Llewellyn's contribution.

This point needs to be clearly separated from the claim that "realism was, and is, a method," the main tenets of which are "see it fresh," "see it clean," and "come back to make sure."[124] Llewellyn fleshed out these general precepts with a plethora of homely metaphors: the child in the story of the Emperor's new clothes;[125] John Dewey's childlike, clear-eyed vision;[126] the horse sense of an experienced horse trader looking at the

123 Llewellyn's ideas on the crafts of law, job analysis and the teaching of professional skills directly influenced the work of a number of people. See, e.g., T. Anderson & W. Twining, Analysis of Evidence (preliminary circulation draft 1984); C. Kelso, A Programmed Introduction to the Study of Law (1965); S. Mentschikoff & I. Stotzky, The Theory and Craft of American Law (1981); W. Twining & D. Miers, How To Do Things With Rules (2d ed. 1982); W. Twining, Taking Skills Seriously (forthcoming 1986); Rutter, A Jurisprudence of Lawyers' Operations, 13 J. Legal Educ. 301 (1961). However, despite very extensive activity and literature in this area, especially in the United States, many of the implications of Llewellyn's theory of legal technology (of which the idea of law-crafts is only a part) remain largely unexploited.

124 See, e.g., K. Llewellyn, Common Law Tradition, supra note 39, at 510.

125 See W. Twining, supra note 65, at 15-16 (1968).

126 For Llewellyn, John Dewey was both the model realist and a symbol of the unfulfilled promise of Legal Realism. Llewellyn had reservations about several of Dewey's ideas: he was ambivalent toward Dewey's theory of value, somewhat indifferent to his logic, and critical of what was done by his followers in the name of "progressive education." What was to be admired was Dewey's cast of mind and "method."

In a 1959 lecture, Llewellyn said: "Since Thomas Jefferson or Benjamin Franklin there has been nobody with the sweet, childlike, open eye to see things fresh that Dewey had." Lecture by Karl Llewellyn (Mar. 31, 1959) (unpublished), quoted in KLRM, supra note 1, at 423. Earlier, Llewellyn had written: "[Dewey's] method of dealing with problems is still and always will be the great and needed method: Take a fresh look, look to see what is there, and what it is about, and re-pose your issues in those terms." K. Llewellyn, John Dewey and Our Law (1949) (unpublished manuscript).

Although these statements anticipate the spirit and even some of the words of Llewellyn's last attempts to distill what he meant by "realism," he also expressed disappointment about Dewey's contributions to jurisprudence. In his writings and his seminar with Edwin Patterson at Columbia, Dewey tended to concentrate on abstract philosophical questions—on logical method in the law, on fundamental questions of ethics, and on Austin's theory of sovereignty—rather than bringing his "childlike vision" to bear on actual legal processes and the law in action. Rather as Jeremy Bentham aspired to become the Martin Luther of jurisprudence, Karl Llewellyn's private ambition was to be seen as its John Dewey.

In an undated manuscript fragment, Llewellyn wrote:

mouth of a potential purchase;[127] and, perhaps, the Russian sculptor Sergei Konenkov's way of seeing shapes and patterns in driftwood.[128] Without pushing these metaphors too hard one still can reasonably extract some precepts from this sort of general prescription: use your eyes and ears and all your other faculties, including empathy; keep close to the particularities of practice; do not allow your expectations, wishes, and preconceptions to blur or distort your vision; test any generalization against your own firsthand experience; keep an open mind. These precepts could be interpreted as advocating distrust both of all abstract theorizing not grounded in experience and of purity of method. Push this interpretation further and it easily becomes anti-intellectual, anti-scientific, and anti-theory. There is no need, and little justification, to brand Llewellyn as this kind of extremist.

These homely precepts sound like an invitation to "use one's common sense." If so, this must be distinguished from the notion of common sense that is *démodé* in intellectual circles. Followers of Marx and Freud, phenomenologists, structuralists, and other ironic sociologists typically claim to be subversive of common sense. The priesthood of learning has a vested interest in the counterintuitive, and the academic world would indeed be duller if most theories and research findings con-

---

> John Dewey's philosophy is not a "complete" philosophy. It does not contain much to rest on. Dewey did not rest on it, he gives [no] invitation or excuse for others to rest on it. Its essential aspects are indeed compatible with any ultimates and with any faith by which the working out of what to do next is left to individual effort and responsibility; [but they are compatible with no ultimate or faith]. Dewey does not challenge the institution of authority, and he does not challenge the value of tradition; he has been much too wise to do either. What he does is to insist that authority and tradition go dry and wither unless they are from day to day in every generation fed with the sap of man's eternal struggle to make man's institutions meet man's present and emergent needs. The wisdom of the fathers was wisdom to the fathers because it was vibrant with life-experience of the fathers; and to the children it can be similar wisdom only as it becomes equally vibrant with the life-experience of the children. The verbal expression of old wisdom must not lose its tone, it must ring clear to living experience, or the warped or cracked bell of words must be recast to make its fine metal give true tongue again. This, to Dewey, is man's duty, man's necessity, man's glory.

Cf. K. Llewellyn, John Dewey and Our Law, supra.

Perhaps all this reveals more about Llewellyn than about Dewey. For the leading American Realist to criticize the only genuine philosopher in the movement for concentrating on philosophical questions could be taken as further evidence of the intellectual poverty of the American Realist contribution to jurisprudence. Alternatively it could be cited as a morality tale in support of the view that all worthwhile legal theorizing needs to grow out of intimate knowledge of the particularities of the law—a view very much in tune with the spirit of pragmatism.

127 K. Llewellyn, Law in Our Society, supra note 72, reprinted, in part, in KLRM, supra note 1, at 503.

128 K. Llewellyn, Common Law Tradition, supra note 39, at 222-23; see KLRM, supra note 1, at 447 n.51.

firmed mere common sense. Consider for example, this quotation from a rather engaging book by a radical literary theorist:

> The fact that structuralism offends common sense has always been a point in its favour. Common sense holds that things generally have only one meaning and that this meaning is usually obvious, inscribed on the faces of the objects we encounter. The world is pretty much as we perceive it, and our way of perceiving it is the natural, self-evident one. We know the sun goes round the earth because we can see that it does. At different times common sense has dictated burning witches, hanging sheep-stealers and avoiding Jews for fear of fatal infection, but this statement is not itself commonsensical since common sense believes itself to be historically invariable.[129]

Is this, then, what is really implied by a plea for common sense in law? If we are talking of Frank or Moore or Llewellyn, clearly not. Frank was a disciple of Freud and devoted many of his efforts to attacking the "common sense" beliefs, in Eagleton's use of the term, of the legal profession. Moore was concerned with developing scientific methods of observing human behavior in relation to rules in order to test and refine hypotheses that were derived from common sense as well as psychological theory. Llewellyn anticipated the debasement of the term "common sense" by switching to "horse sense," by which he meant "the kind of

---

[129] T. Eagleton, Literary Theory: An Introduction 108 (1983). This passage appears in a sympathetic, but not uncritical, account of structuralism. What is being attacked under the rubric of "common sense" in this context are (a) empiricist epistemologies that hold that all knowledge is derived from firsthand "experience," and (b) widely held beliefs that belong to "the stock of knowledge" in a given society at a given time. Llewellyn and Cook were probably type (a) empiricists, but it is doubtful whether Frank was. It is even more doubtful whether any Realist was committed to uncritical acceptance of beliefs of type (b). However, there is a considerable body of literature in the theory of evidence about the inevitable role played by "common sense generalizations" and "general experience" as a basis for making inferences from evidence in coming to judgments about disputed questions of fact. More sophisticated accounts recognize that a society's "stock of knowledge" changes over time, is not always based on a general cognitive consensus, and is likely to be made up of a mixture of scientific generalizations, beliefs based on first hand experience, speculative hypotheses, prejudices, myths, and oldwives' tales. One theme in the literature of the theory of evidence, from Bentham to L. Jonathan Cohen, is the unavoidability of basing many judgments on the existing "stock of knowledge," however fallible it may be. See W. Twining, Theories of Evidence: Bentham and Wigmore (1985).

Many evidence theorists emphasize that common sense generalizations often represent "the best knowledge that we have got." This links up interestingly with Llewellyn's theme that "knowledge does not have to be scientific to be useful and important." The evidence theorists emphasize the inevitability of basing many practical decisions on "common sense"; Llewellyn argues against confining empirical research to questions which will be susceptible to "scientific" answers, many of which may not be very helpful to practical decisionmaking. Neither of those approaches is fundamentally incompatible with "the message of contingency." Mensch, supra note 54. For a plea for common sense empiricism that goes much further than either Llewellyn or Frank would have done, see W. Morison, supra note 9, 178-205.

highly informed, distinctly *un*common, better-than-common, expert 'but not scientifically demonstrable' know-what and know-how which a David Harum had about horses and other horse traders."[130]

This kind of horse sense realism leads to a plea for a kind of theorizing that is derived from and continually checked and rechecked against firsthand experience of the real world. Its natural tendency is toward the particularistic and the earthy, and it is naturally suspicious of abstract theorizing. It does not, however, necessarily involve a commitment to narrow categories and other forms of resistance to abstraction. To Llewellyn a key concern was to reflect on experience and to accept the idea that "[k]nowledge . . . does not have to be scientific, in order to be useful and important."[131]

From this interpretation of the concept of realism one can extract many implications. For example, several interesting and important questions can be raised about the how, the what, and the why of "the lessons of practical experience"—questions which are, inter alia, central to any serious attempt to make legal training more systematic and efficient. But Llewellyn's own caveats and denials themselves suggest that any legal theorist who wishes to develop a whole view or a general theory of and about law needs to go beyond this brand of realism. On this view, "horse sense" may provide an important test of the acceptability of a particular example of theorizing—a test that many contemporary texts would prob-

130 K. Llewellyn, Law in Our Society, supra note 72, reprinted, in part, in KLRM, supra note 1, at 497. See also N. Westcott, David Harum (1898) ("the story of the shrewdest and the most crotchety banker who ever tended horses or brought young lovers together").

Of course, this does not take one very far. For, on its own, the notion of "horse sense realism" is open to the criticism that it assumes rather than explores what is involved in understanding reality or being realistic. Neither Llewellyn nor any other core "Realist" intended the term to be interpreted in a philosophical sense, as a form of epistemological theory to be contrasted, for example, with nominalism. But Llewellyn's explications of the term still seem to beg some of the central questions of interpretive sociology: What is social reality? How is it constructed? By whom? What is involved in describing, interpreting, or explaining it? The horse sense of the most experienced and brilliant horse dealer does not equip him to make contributions to either veterinary science or the sociology of horse dealing. Llewellyn was one of the first to attempt to translate Max Weber into English; this fact, together with *The Cheyenne Way* and his other writings about the law-jobs, should be enough to exempt him from charges of total illiteracy about the puzzles of interpretive sociology. Those writings represent his attempts to go beyond the elementary precepts of horse sense realism. Perhaps his espousal of a horse sense approach to Jurisprudence for the hundred thousand should be interpreted as coming down to three precepts: build on the best experience available; use it as a check; and recognize that it is often the nearest that we can approximate to understanding or knowledge at this stage in the development of our discipline.

131 Llewellyn, supra note 44, at 22; see KLRM, supra note 1, at 188-93. This last precept is part of a strategy for advancing a discipline. It is not a rejection of systematic and rigorous research in advancing knowledge. Similarly, I hope that my espousal in this lecture of a horse sense approach to reading juristic texts will not be taken as an outright rejection of analogies from literary criticism and theology.

ably fail. It does not, however, provide an adequate or clear way of identifying a type of legal theory. On this interpretation, realism is not a distinct brand of legal theory, and as a concept it can only bear a limited amount of intellectual traffic.

REALISM IN THE UNITED KINGDOM

"Law in Context" and "Sociolegal Studies"

In 1966 Professor Abraham Goldstein of Yale, comparing empirical research into legal processes in the United States with similar work in the United Kingdom, expressed doubt about prospects for advance on a broad front until "English law teaching, and the conception of law which animates it, has had its 'legal realist' revolution."[132] What does the situation look like eighteen years later?[133] During recent years, academic law in the United Kingdom has been transformed beyond recognition. The scale of the enterprise has greatly increased, and the structure and methods of professional training have been significantly changed. Academic curricula have diversified, as have legal research and literature. Some modest developments in such fields as clinical legal education, continuing legal education, and law and economics reflect direct American influence. Other innovations, such as our peculiar four-stage process of legal education and training, are distinctly non-American. Some of Professor Goldstein's projection has come to pass: the dominance of the expository orthodoxy has been generally undermined, although it has by no means been destroyed. No one can seriously claim that it has been replaced or threatened by a single rival orthodoxy. Rather, what has developed is an extraordinary—and perhaps temporary—degree of diversification in legal scholarship and legal education.[134]

Despite many differences between the two contexts one can reconstruct a story that brings out some parallels between these developments in the United Kingdom and the American Realist Movement. One version might go as follows:[135] during the early 1960's dissatisfaction with the dominant expository tradition became widespread. As in the United States forty years earlier, the reasons for such dissatisfaction were di-

---

132 Goldstein, Research into the Administration of Criminal Law: A Report from the United States, 6 Brit. J. Criminology 27, 37 (1966).

133 For more extensive accounts, see generally Twining, The Benson Report and Legal Education: A Personal View, in Law in the Balance 186 (P.A. Thomas ed. 1982); Twining, supra note 80; Twining, Some Jobs, supra note 3. For contrasting interpretations, see, e.g., Z. Bankowski & G. Mungham, Images of Law (1976), and the useful series of articles on relationships between law and other disciplines in the *British Journal of Law and Society* (now *Journal of Law and Society*) (1981—).

134 See Committee of Heads of University Law Schools, Law as an Academic Discipline (1984), reprinted in Summer 1984 Soc. Publ. Tchs. L. Newsletter and Commonwealth Legal Educ. Assoc. Newsletter No. 39 (Oct. 1984).

135 See Twining, supra note 80.

verse. Some were similar to those that provoked the early Realists—a concern over the distance between academic law and the realities of private legal practice; a desire to build bridges with some social sciences; a call for a more systematic approach to law reform so that the legal system could keep pace with social and political change; and so on. There were, however, some differences. For example, the complaint of the liberal educator against the anti-intellectualism of the prevailing tradition had more bite in the United Kingdom than in the United States. This was due in part to the fact that British law faculties had fewer professional responsibilities and were more closely integrated into universities, and in part because the Langdellian orthodoxy was more intellectually stimulating and demanding than the textbook orthodoxy in England. Further, some of the dissent from the prevailing approach was more overtly and profoundly political, from an earlier stage in our revolt against formalism, than was the case with the early phases of American Realism. The intellectual atmosphere in England in the late 1960's, and after, was much more tolerant of overt commitments to various brands of socialism and Marxism than has ever been the case in the United States. Although several bandwagons were rolling by the late 1960's, there was never a time when there was any substantial basis for claiming that those who were seeking change were members of a single movement. In short, we moved from a monolithic orthodoxy to a new pluralism in academic law without ever experiencing the illusion of a single movement of revolt or reaction. Nevertheless, a few terms, analogous to "realism," have gained some currency as labels. Let us consider just two of these: "law in context" and "sociolegal studies."

Memoirs III: "Law in Context"

It is more like a confession than a boast to claim responsibility for popularizing a new label in academic discourse. Still, I must acknowledge paternity, at least putative and partial, for the terms "law in context" and "a contextual approach" in the United Kingdom. This is how it came about.

Early in 1965 Robert Stevens, who was then at Yale, was approached by an English publisher for advice about how to break into academic law publishing. The stimuli behind this original request were a general sense of dissatisfaction with academic law and legal literature and a specific suggestion by John Vaizey, an economist, that academic law books as produced by the specialist law publishers were so narrow, hidebound, formalistic, and boring that others could hardly fail to do better. Stevens and I had got to know each other as part of the Dar-es-Salaam—New Haven axis. Because I was visiting Yale at the time and we had shared negative views about academic law in the United Kingdom, he invited me to join the discussions. We made what now seems a rather elementary analysis of the state of academic legal literature in England and put forward a number of proposals to the publisher. One of them was accepted. This was for a series of what we called "counter-text books," substantial works directed primarily at the student market, which would better satisfy the values of a liberal education and embody a "broader" approach to law than traditional student works. In trying to develop a rationale for the series two years later, we treated the orthodox textbook and the nutshell as symbolizing the enemy: "[a]s educational tools textbooks fly in the face of some of the fundamental values of university education and at the same time they are primitive as means of training effective practitioners; as works of scholarship they may be accurate but are rarely exhaustive; they are rarely sufficiently comprehensive to be efficient as works of reference; as works of the intellect they are, with rare exceptions, unimaginative; they have no pretensions to be works of art."

In retrospect, what seems to me to be striking about this critique, apart from the forcefulness of its rhetoric and the judiciousness of its caveats, is the emphasis on classical values of liberal education and the concern with self-consciously developing alternative kinds of literary form *in academic law. The relevance of jurisprudence was perceived, but given only limited emphasis. The same applies to political and ideological dimensions. Analytical jurisprudence was specifically not rejected; instead, the perceived challenge was to find ways of "exploiting the strengths of both analytical and sociological jurisprudence." The section on the juristic aspects of our enterprise ended as follows: " 'Law in Context' must proceed from a broader jurisprudential base than does* Salmond on Torts, *yet it must seek to preserve as far as possible the rigour associated with the narrower approach."*

As with most new projects the issue that gave rise to the most protracted discussion and disagreement was that of nomenclature. What should the series be called? We were consciously looking to American models and experience. Clearly anything associated with "realism" was out. In the United States the word had become meaningless; in Britain it was a term of abuse. Similarly, there were too many jokes and puns conflating sociology with socialism for "sociology" or "social" or "socio-" to be usable. "Law in Society" had been preempted by another publisher. Eventually I proposed "Law in Context," borrowed from Addison Mueller's Contract in Context, *in which Mr. Blandings's dreamhouse replaced Blackacre as the paradigm property beset by legal problems. This was accepted* faut de mieux. *I must admit that I rather liked the phrase and for a period I made some half-hearted attempts to popularize it as a term for a new, broader, and more realistic approach to law than the prevailing ortho-*

doxy. Whether it was in fact new, broad, or realistic remains a matter for perpetual debate.[136]

Twenty years later the "Law in Context" series is sufficiently well-established to be almost respectable, but I am glad to say that the terms "a contextual approach" or the deliberately avoided "contextualism" have not really caught on.[137] Why glad? Partly because the original impulse was genuinely liberal—to free academic law from some hidebound constraints and not to replace one orthodoxy by another; partly because the term "context" can hardly bear even as little intellectual weight as "realism" can.

Still, one may ask whether "context" is entirely devoid of content. If one subjects a phrase like "Law in Context" to close scrutiny can one attribute any precise propositions to it? To study a word in context includes studying it in relation to the words that immediately precede or succeed it in a phrase or sentence or longer passage—in other words, in relation to its neighbors.[138] Similarly, to study a legal rule or doctrine in context implies looking to its neighbors, as opposed to studying it in isolation.[139] But who are its neighbors? As the phrase has been used in the United Kingdom, the prescription is not restricted to the suggestion that one should look at either neighboring or analogous rules within an alleged "system." "Law in context" is typically used in contrast to one or other kind of legal dogmatics. Standard general phrases tend to be "in its historical or social or political or economic context" or "in the context of

[136] The first attempt to substitute "a contextual approach" for "realism" appears in Twining, Two Works of Karl Llewellyn, 30 Mod. L. Rev. 514, 530 (1967). The document quoted in the passage is R. Stevens & W. Twining, Law in Context: A Tentative Rationale 1 (1967) (unpublished manuscript) (on file at New York University Law Review); cf. P. Atiyah, Accidents, Compensation and the Law xi-xii (1st ed. 1970) (the first book in the "Law in Context" series). See also Folsom & Roberts, supra note 102.

[137] I have not always managed to avoid using such terms as "contextualist" and "contextualism." See, e.g., W. Twining & D. Miers, supra note 123, at xix, 113.

[138] This is, of course, by no means exhaustive of what may be involved in studying a word or phrase "in context." In jurisprudence, unlike law, the question "Who is my neighbor?" receives an almost unrestricted reply.

[139] Compare this to Bentham on circumstantial evidence:

> Circumstantial evidence is that deduced from the existence of a fact, or a group of facts, which, being directly applicable to the principal fact, lead to the conclusion that the latter exists. This conclusion is an operation of judgment. The distinction between *fact* and *circumstance* regards only a given case. Every fact may be called a circumstance in relation to another. That it thundered or hailed on the day a murder was committed, is an event extremely independent of the principal fact, but it may be a circumstance worthy of being remarked, and may lead to evidence. Circumstances, then, are facts placed round some other fact; each fact may be considered as a centre, and all others as ranged round it.

J. Bentham, A Treatise on Judicial Evidence 143 (M. Dumont ed. London 1825) (emphasis in original).

problems or policies behind the rule(s)" or "in the context of its underlying moral or ideological assumptions" or "in the context of the actual operation of the rules." Perhaps even more than for "realism," one of the abiding attractions of the phrase has been its openendedness; the advice is to open things up, to broaden the focus, to make connections with nonlegal materials, factors, or ideas, and to relate legal doctrine to actual circumstances and events.[140]

The price of openendedness is vagueness. Not surprisingly, the notion of "a contextual approach," like that of "realism," has attracted a number of criticisms directed at this vagueness. Let us consider just two of these.[141] First, the phrase "a contextual approach to law" cannot itself sustain anything sufficiently precise or coherent to count as a theory of law that presents a distinctive answer to questions of the "What is law?" kind. On this view, which I accept, neither the terms "realism" nor "a contextual approach" are sufficiently precise and substantial to satisfy the criteria of what one might call the minimum content of a full-fledged theory of and about law.[142]

There is a second criticism that is related, but separate: the term "law in context" and admonitions such as "laws should be studied in their historical/social/political context" do not merely fail to advance a theory, they *presuppose* a particular theory of law, namely positivism.[143] Thus, it might be argued, to advocate studying the law of evidence or contract in context not only implies a distinction between law and its context, but also assumes that the subject consists of rules: for example, that the subject of evidence is coextensive with the law of evidence.[144] More generally, "law in context" assumes a view of law as a body of rules; this is similar to the kind of positivist theory of law advanced by Hart or Kelsen. This is a tenable interpretation, and some supporters of a contextual approach would readily acknowledge that they are positivists in this sense. However, this involves an unnecessarily literal reading of the term. I prefer a more liberal interpretation: the original purpose of coining the phrase was to break away from a narrow version of positivism in which studying positive law in isolation, as a thing in itself or as a system of rules, was considered unsatisfactory for a variety

[140] R. Stevens & W. Twining, supra note 136.

[141] These criticisms are selected and reconstructed from a number of papers presented at the first U.K. Conference on Critical Legal Scholarship, held at The University of Kent at Canterbury in April, 1981. Especially interesting in this respect are Cotterrell, Notes on the Progress and Prospects of "Contextualism" in Legal Education (1981) and Thompson, Law and the Social Sciences—The Demise of Legal Autonomy (1981). It is not possible to do justice to their arguments here.

[142] Cotterrell, supra note 141.

[143] See Cotterrell, supra note 141; Thompson, supra note 141.

[144] See Twining, Evidence, supra note 3, at 267-69.

of reasons. In this view, to favor broadening the study of law did not necessarily involve either rejecting or sticking with a particular conception of law. In order to study law in context, it is not necessary to define "law" as context nor to accept a restricted, positivistic conception of law, such as that of Hart.

The term "law in context" was originally coined for a particular publishing purpose. We were motivated by liberal ideals of education and intellectual collegiality and edited texts on the basis of the liberal principle that authors should be encouraged to write the books they want to write. In view of these motives, the vagueness of "context" has been a source of strength. Although the books in the "Law in Context" series clearly share a family resemblance, any strong generalization about their juristic, ideological, or philosophical assumptions is almost certain to be either trivial or false or both. The contributors span a fairly broad ideological spectrum, with a slight left-liberal bias, and include positivists, Dworkinians, Marxists, and a number of excellent scholars whose work involves no explicit commitment to a clear set of specific juristic assumptions. Outside this particular context of a series of books, examples of a contextual approach are likely to be even more varied; generalization is accordingly even more dangerous.

Yet a general admonition to study law in context *can* be transformed into some specific precepts. We have already touched on the value of reading a juristic text in the context of the author's immediate concerns, his other writings, his personal background, and the intellectual climate of his time. Clarification of standpoint is a useful tool of contextual analysis.[145] It is almost commonplace to state that in interpreting a particular statutory word or phrase one should at the outset consider it in the context of the sentence, clause, or section as a whole, and that section should be interpreted in the context of the statute's general design, its other relevant parts, and its stated objectives, underlying policies, and historical genesis. Most disagreements and doubts worth debating arise *after* this advice has been followed. Many of these relate to the relative weight or priority to be given to different kinds of reasons advanced in favor of competing interpretations of a particular text.

A rather different piece of advice is to gloss Llewellyn's precepts "See it fresh, see it clean, see it as it works" with a fourth admonition, implicit in many of his writings: "See it whole."[146] This is an invitation to think in terms of total pictures. This precept mandates that one

[145] See generally W. Twining & D. Miers, supra note 123; Twining, supra note 61, at 296-300.

[146] The passages most obviously supporting this interpretation can be found in his accounts of the law-jobs theory, especially those emphasizing "The Entirety." See, e.g., authorities cited in note 22 supra.

should set any rule, case, text, decision, or other phenomenon that one is considering in the context of some broad picture that provides a basis for mapping its relationship to other phenomena, and for assessing how typical or untypical it may be. We are all familiar with the value of seeing some particular decision (for example, a decision to prosecute or settle, a jury verdict, or a parole decision) in the context of an overall picture of the total process of which it forms a part, and, if we follow Harold Lasswell, of plotting that total process as a sequence or flow of interrelated decisions and events.[147] Similarly, viewing appellate cases in the context of all litigated cases and litigated cases in the context of all disputes in a given society is a simple way of reminding ourselves how atypical and randomly selected most reported cases are. Such demographic perspectives can be applied to almost any legal phenomena in a wide variety of contexts. For example, my former colleague Patrick McAuslan found it helpful, when trying to break away from traditional approaches to teaching Land Law in England, to begin with an atlas and to build an elaborate demographic profile of land, its uses in England and Wales, and the various legal relations and transactions typically affecting land.[148] One thing that immediately became apparent was that such matters as racial and sexual discrimination in Council house queues and decisions by Building Societies to offer mortgages were much more pressing problems than curtailing the spendthrift propensities of heirs of Blackacre.[149]

Thinking in terms of total pictures seems to me to be a good intellectual habit, and not only for jurists. It is particularly valuable as an antidote to the myopia and tunnel vision of which lawyers frequently are accused. But, as with the precepts of realism, it is surely a mistake to

---

147 See H. Lasswell & A. Kaplan, Power and Society 81 (1950).

148 For further details, see Folsom & Roberts, supra note 102, at 182.

149 Similarly, Patrick Atiyah broke with tradition by starting his analysis of the common law action for negligence by presenting a total picture of all accidents in our society and of the different compensation systems for accidents that had emerged haphazardly at different times. He then analyzed and criticized the common law remedies by comparing and contrasting them with those other compensation systems. His presentation of this traditional topic in Torts in the context of a total picture of compensation for accidents has revolutionized academic thinking on the subject in England. See P. Atiyah, supra note 136.

I advise first-year law students to interpret their immediate situation in the context of two total pictures: first, a picture of the total process of their own education from cradle to grave (and especially the five-year periods preceding and succeeding their undergraduate law degree) and second, a picture of the variety of courses that are offered in law schools in Britain and elsewhere. The first context helps them to get some sense of what are reasonable expectations for a first-year course and for a three-year degree in the context of a ten- to twenty-year time span; the second provides them with some basis for interpreting and evaluating a particular program of legal education in the broader context of the varied and confusing system of legal education and training that we have in England and Wales. I have found this perspective to be valuable in dealing with such varied subjects as statutory interpretation, intellectual history, confessions, eyewitness identification, and legal literature and information.

inflate particular intellectual ploys, however valuable, into a whole approach or an -ism, let alone a philosophy. When McAuslan had completed his demographic picture of land and legal relations affecting it in England and Wales, he had taken only the first step towards rethinking his chosen field in a "realistic" manner. Indeed, one function of this picture was to bring home just how selective he would have to be in his treatment of this vast subject. Context provided him with only a few initial criteria for making selections. Posing the question "Am I being realistic?" was one check, but this was not and could not be enough. The precepts of realism and contextual thinking can provide stimuli and can serve as useful checks, but they do not purport to do any more than that.

Sociolegal Studies

In a well-known article published in *Law and Society Review* in 1976, Campbell and Wiles set out to interpret recent developments in the study of law in society in Britain.[150] They constructed a picture of two different intellectual orientations competing for resources and intellectual prestige under the banners "sociolegal studies" and "sociology of law." "Sociolegal studies" were narrowly empirical, reformist, liberal-democratic, and untheoretical, taking the legal order for granted and concentrating on formulating policies and recommendations for reform from within. On the other hand, supporters of "sociology of law" tended to be antipositivistic, critical (in several senses), and interested in developing broader macrotheoretical perspectives on law that would be exogenous to the system. Such contrasts between empiricist social engineering approaches and critical macrotheoretical perspectives are, of course, familiar. Campbell and Wiles perceptively identified a pattern of differences among those who were seeking to develop specifically sociological approaches to law, but as an interpretation of developments in law and social science in Britain generally, this dichotomy was seriously misleading.

Campbell and Wiles admitted that their pictures of the two sides in the alleged debate were caricatures.[151] But such disarming admissions do not generate total immunity from criticism. It is difficult, but not impossible, to criticize an ideal type. The model of sociology of law presented in *The Study of Law in Society* seems to be derived from an

[150] Campbell & Wiles, The Study of Law in Society in Britain, 10 Law & Soc'y Rev. 547 (1976). For a recent general review, see Harris, The Development of Sociolegal Studies in the United Kingdom, 3 Legal Stud. 315 (1983).

[151] Campbell & Wiles, supra note 150, at 559. Professor Campbell has modified his views since the publication of the article. See, Campbell, Research Into Legal Services, in Law in the Balance 217, 232, 239 n.17 (P. Thomas ed. 1982) (especially in respect of the "gap" between law and society). *The Study of Law in Society* is, however, widely cited in the United States.

important development in many British sociology departments in the 1960's: a switch to emphasizing macrotheoretical perspectives in reaction to the kind of narrowly focused, particularistic empiricism that tended to dominate research in sociology and criminology at that time. It is also historically correct that the new emphasis on grand theory in sociology was taken up by some people interested in the sociology of law as well as by the exponents of the new criminology.

The provenance of "sociolegal studies," was quite different. This ugly term reflects its bureaucratic origin. It was coined for a government-backed funding agency, the Social Science Research Council (SSRC), to cover the area in which it would give grants for interdisciplinary work in law and the social sciences.[152] The Council's remit was to deal with all of the social sciences, including economics, economic and social history, human geography, linguistics, management and industrial relations, planning, political science (including political theory), psychology, social anthropology, social administration, and statistics. In short, the "socio-" in "sociolegal" referred to all social sciences, and there was nothing in the remit or the policies of the original Committee on Social Sciences and the Law to give any special priority either to sociology or to any particular kind of research. About half of SSRC's budget on sociolegal studies was allocated to one institution, the Centre for Socio-Legal Studies at Wolfson College, Oxford; its brief was to develop sociolegal research in areas other than criminology. The most striking characteristic of this Centre has been its emphasis on *multi* disciplinary teamwork, in which sociologists as such have played a relatively minor role.[153] This is partly because two of the most prominent sociologists at the Centre—J. Maxwell Atkinson and Anita Pomerantz—have been specialists in conversation analysis, a field that barely fits either of the Campbell-Wiles models.[154] Anyone sensitive to the ethnography of knowledge will recognize the implausibility of a claim that developments in relations between law and such diverse intellectual cultures as departments of anthropology, economics, industrial relations, social history, psychology, and ur-

[152] The establishment of both the Centre for Socio-Legal Studies at Wolfson College, Oxford and the original Committee on Social Sciences and the Law was announced officially in 1972. Soc. Sci. Research Council Newsletter No. 14 (1972). The original intention was that the Committee would "complement the work" of the Centre for Socio-Legal Studies. In 1982 the Committee was reconstituted as a subcommittee of the Government and Law Committee, but the subcommittee was abolished in December 1984. In 1983 the Social Science Research Council was renamed the Economic and Social Science Research Council.

[153] On the achievements and problems of the Centre for Socio-Legal Studies, see its Annual Reports; see also Harris, supra note 150.

[154] For general accounts, see Atkinson, Our Masters' Voices: The Dynamics of Oratory (1984); Atkinson, Ethnomethodological Approaches to Socio-Legal Studies, in Sociological Approaches to Law (A. Podgorecki & C. Whelan ed. 1981).

ban planning could readily fit a single model of reformist empiricism. To contrast sociology of law with sociolegal studies is to commit the category mistake of contrasting attempts to develop macrotheoretical perspectives in one social science with a bureaucratic umbrella-term covering the relations between law and a dozen disciplines. This led Campbell and Wiles to obscure the rich and rather uncoordinated pluralism of what passes for sociolegal studies in the United Kingdom.[155]

If this criticism of Campbell and Wiles's analysis sounds harsh, you may attribute this to the frustration of one who feels that a good case is being spoiled by poor advocacy. For underlying their presentation are some concerns that I share: concern with the poverty of our stock of grand style social theorizing; with the threat that too high a proportion of limited funds for research will be devoted to short-term, officially approved inquiries into narrowly defined problems; even that emphasis on broadening the study of law from within could delay the development of genuine interdisciplinary and multidisciplinary studies. But a persuasive argument incorporating these concerns and interests has to be based, among other things, on a recognition of the complexity of academic law (and of its institutional base, the law school) and the diversity of the other disciplines with which we aspire to build relationships. To deny this pluralism and complexity is naive unrealism.

Conclusion

This lecture has concentrated on two main themes: a personal assessment of the contemporary significance of American Legal Realism, and some comments on the difficulties and dangers of making generalizations about any group of thinkers, texts, or intellectual trends. On the latter theme I have hinted at the outlines of a horse sense approach to intellectual history and textual criticism in jurisprudence. I have done little more than suggest a few robust maxims for avoiding some of the bad habits that still impoverish and obfuscate much juristic discourse. The most important maxims are really rather elementary. Approach any juristic text or group of texts on three levels: the historical, the analytical, and the applied. Do not confuse or conflate the historical and analytical levels of juristic discourse. Do not invoke past thinkers unnecessarily when addressing issues at the analytical level. Whenever

155 See Harris, supra note 150. For criticisms of the analogous tendency of critical legal scholars to draw too sharp a line between macro- (sociological) and micro- (empirical) approaches to law, concentrating mainly on sociology, see Trubek, Where the Action Is: Critical Legal Studies and Empiricism, 36 Stan. L. Rev. 575 (1984); cf. Nelken, The "Gap Problem" in The Sociology of Law: A Theoretical Review, 1 Windsor Y.B. of Access to Just. 35 (1981); Nelken, Law in Action or Living Law? Back to the Beginning in Sociology of Law, 4 Legal Stud. 157 (1984).

possible anchor discussion of past thinkers in one or more specific texts; classifying ideas and thinkers is notoriously difficult. If you must classify, ask: What is the purpose of this classification? Also ask: Is your -ism really necessary? Is that -ism defined precisely at the analytical level? When criticizing, choose worthwhile targets to attack, and err on the side of generosity in interpreting opponents. Such elementary precepts are by and large enough to undermine the most common bad habits. One does not need a sophisticated critical apparatus, nor need one join some faction within literary criticism, in order to avoid slovenly scholarship and false polemics.

To sum up my personal views on the contemporary significance of American Legal Realism is a less straightforward task. Let me restrict myself to five main points:

First, the Realist Movement is of enormous historical significance and interest, in the United States and beyond, in terms of both particular achievements and a general but extremely elusive kind of "influence." The Realist legacy is still relevant in interpreting many aspects of contemporary legal thought throughout the common law world, but its importance in this respect is sometimes exaggerated. Concern with practical realities in jurisprudence has never been an American monopoly.

Second, Realism and individual Realists are still frequently misrepresented, partly through overgeneralization, but more significantly through comment on and criticism of their alleged answers to questions that were remote from or peripheral to their concerns.

Third, insofar as one can reconstruct an ideal type of a Realist theory of law from ideas and assumptions that fit the general views of leading Realists, the result is neither particularly original nor distinctive. I disagree with Robert Summers's judgment that pragmatic instrumentalism, as he interprets it, deserves to rank as a fourth great tradition in Western legal theory alongside analytical positivism, natural law, and historical jurisprudence. The most important contributions of Realists to legal theory were of a different kind: they were by and large particular contributions by different individuals that addressed questions other than the classic questions of legal philosophy. Few, if any, of the Realists were accomplished philosophers, and insofar as they shared similar philosophical assumptions these are generally neither original nor interesting.

Fourth, we have outgrown most of the Realist texts. For example, contemporary interdisciplinary work in law and sociology or psychology or economics or anthropology or political theory or linguistics or social history has generally advanced beyond the pioneering attempts of Realists to perform the conduit function of reintegrating law and the social sciences, a task that in any case has to be tackled afresh in every generation. Similarly, contemporary juristic debates on such topics as judicial discretion, legal reasoning, and legal interpretation make the pre-World War II debates seem rather unsophisticated.

For these reasons I think that relatively few particular Realist texts deserve to be treated as timeless classics. Among these I would include Holmes's "The Path of the Law," Llewellyn's "The Normative, the Legal and the Law-Jobs," his historical articles on sales and, with reservations, his "Theory of Legal 'Science,' " perhaps Felix Cohen's "Transcendental Nonsense and the Functional Approach," and, if it counts as a Realist text, the analytical parts of Wigmore's *Science of Judicial Proof*. *The Cheyenne Way*, although showing its age, is sufficiently rich in fundamental insight to continue deserve attention. That is a personal Great Pieces list for what it is worth. It seems to me that *The Bramble Bush*, *Courts on Trial*, and *Woe Unto You Lawyers* are still fun to read, but on the whole are best treated as period pieces.

Fifth, to say that we have outgrown most Realist texts does not imply that the realist enterprise is complete nor that the Realist Movement ever really fulfilled its promise. That is very far from the case and is much too simple both as history and as an assessment of our present situation. One can look at this at three different levels.

1. Efforts to broaden the study of law from within, to maintain and develop systematic links with other disciplines, and to keep law teaching and legal research in touch with the actual experiences of "real" people who encounter the law (that is, everyone) are perennial aspirations. One of the jobs of jurisprudence is to further these efforts at a general level. It would be a bold person who would claim that any of these aspirations has been satisfactorily realized on a broad front at any time in history in your country or mine. Even if one could point to past successes, this does not get one very far. Dwelling nostalgically on past victories is not the best way of fighting present battles. Many contemporary references to Realism seem to me to be little more than nostalgic. To paraphrase Holmes, one role of intellectual history is to free oneself from the incubus of dead debates.

2. There are many particular ideas, arguments, and suggestive *aperçus* advanced by individual Realists that have yet to be followed through satisfactorily. These include Llewellyn's notion of "legal technology" (including a systematic theory of the crafts of law and a skills analysis of lawyers' operations); Frank's plea to take fact-handling more seriously;[156] possibly Underhill Moore's most sophisticated thoughts on

156 See Twining, Taking Facts Seriously, 34 J. Legal Educ. 22 (1984).

empirical method;[157] and Llewellyn's emphasis on the similarities of law to other human activities and phenomena, in contrast with dwelling on its unique or differentiating characteristics. This is illustrated by the notion of Law-Government as an institution and the related themes that legal skills are in large part basic human skills, that legal problem-solving is a particular form of ordinary problem-solving, and that legal experience is and should be very close to general human experience. This is a selection from my personal list of particular items that represent the unfulfilled promise of Legal Realism.

3. Finally, there is the elusive "spirit of realism"—what Stevens called "an amorphous state of mind."[158] Some of this can be reduced to specific precepts such as: in order to understand law the study of rules alone is not enough; clarify standpoints; see it fresh, see it as it works; think in terms of total pictures and total processes.

I do not believe that such precepts can sensibly be used to provide the basis for a general theory of law or of a general approach to its study. On the other hand, any approach or theory that ignores or is inconsistent with them is likely to be vulnerable to charges that it fails some elementary tests of adequacy. If being a realist means trying to see law as a practical human activity, trying to use one's horse sense and, yes, trying to be realistic about it, I have no hesitation about nailing my flag to that mast.

But, it may be objected, what has that to do with theory? Surely any reasonably sensitive and intelligent law teacher could have perceived and responded to the situation regarding the camel in the zoo without needing a lot of theoretical baggage? I disagree. Interpreting the situation, and the problems of teaching and studying law in the specific legal, political, and educational context of the Sudan in the late 1950's involved a wide range of theoretical tasks, as I have interpreted theory in this lecture. Similar jobs for jurists arise in all jurisdictions. One does not need to be committed to a crassly utilitarian view of theory to set a value on looking critically at the assumptions of the prevailing modes of discourse of one's immediate environment. In that context and in many others where the nature of academic law has been in issue I have found the legacy of American Legal Realism, and especially of Karl Llewellyn, to be particularly helpful on both the critical and constructive sides. The reason is simple: Realism addressed questions central to these practical

157 See Schlegel, Underhill Moore, supra note 1.

158 R. Stevens, supra note 1, at 134. Cf. J. White, supra note 12, at 287-88 (1983):

> Much of what is wrong about modern critical discourse seems to me its assumption, probably borrowed from a social science, that one's basic positions can be stated, in a single sentence or two, as a set of propositions that one supports, which can then be subjected to argument defense and attack.

concerns directly and at an appropriate level of generality. On the whole, jurists who addressed the classical questions of legal philosophy in the Anglo-American tradition have tended to be less immediately helpful in these respects. At the very least Realism helped to bridge the divide between abstract philosophizing and "macro-" social theory, and day-to-day practical concerns of participants in particular situations. On this horse sense view of legal theorizing, as a diverse activity that addresses many questions at many levels, it is surely almost always the case that we have too little theory in the law rather than too much. Maybe that is an appropriate note to end a/this/my/some talk about R/realism.

[6]
Karl Llewellyn's Unfinished Agenda: Law in Society and the Job of Juristic Method

INTRODUCTION

It was largely by chance that I came to write about Karl Llewellyn. I was teaching in Dar-es-Salaam in March 1962, when the news of his death reached me. It came as a shock and I was saddened, not least because I knew that he had not completed his projected magnum opus on the Sociology of Law. At the time, like a typical British expatriate, I subscribed to the airmail edition of the *London Times*—the rice-paper edition that might have been ironed by a P. G. Wodehouse butler, or a Burmese servant in a story by George Orwell or Norval Morris. When, after a couple of weeks, no obituary of Karl had appeared, I wrote one and sent it off to the editor. In due course I received a curt note of rejection, which implied that readers of the *Times* were not interested in obituaries of obscure American jurists, especially if submitted by persons from Dar-es-Salaam. Incensed, I decided to write an article introducing Karl to my countrymen. At the time, his image in Britain was pure caricature: an eccentric spokesman for a form of jazz age, digestive jurisprudence that perpetrated the fallacy that talk of rules is a myth.

In drafting my article, I drew quite heavily on Llewellyn's materials for his Jurisprudence course at Chicago, entitled *Law in Our Society*.[2] Some of you may recall this fascinating, if cryptic document which, alas, remains unedited and unpublished. It contained among other things

---

* Quain Professor of Jurisprudence, University College, London. This is a revised and expanded text of the Maurice and Muriel Fulton Lecture, delivered at the University of Chicago Law School on May 14th, 1993, to celebrate the centenary of the birth of Karl Llewellyn on May 22nd, 1893.

passages that could well have been attributed to Mr. Alfred Jingle of *The Pickwick Papers*. To give just one example:

> The plain wrong of today (Norman Conquest; White invasion of America; Napoleon's consolidation of German petty states) may prove to be a wisdom for tomorrow, for a greater whole. Or it may prove to have no such value, and remain wholly wrong. (Some of Genghis' massacres? Hitler's invasions? *Gould v. Harriman*, re railroads? our Alien and Sedition Laws?) Or the question of ultimate wisdom may be dubious (the destruction of the Albigensian culture, or the Hussite; Southern Pacific operations, re railroads; English Conquest of Ireland)

Later the passage continues:

> For *purposes of the legal and of Justice at any given moment of action*, however, it seems safe to state . . . (iii) that any personal application to personal action of ethical test by way of prospective "verdict of history" or of personal view calls for either effrontery, low ethical threshold, or inspiration. (John Brown, Thoreau, Cesare Borgia, Al Capone, John Fox, Napoleon, John Wilkes, and any rebel saint or prophet or political leader: e.g., Washington, Bolivar, Lee, Garibaldi, Lenin, Hitler.)[3]

At the time of his death Llewellyn had been planning to give a series of lectures in Germany after an interval of almost 30 years. He hoped that in due course these would be transformed into a definitive statement of his most general ideas, his "last work on jurisprudence." The course materials were the intended starting-point of this project, but they were clearly incomplete, as well as unfinished. Whether he would ever have produced a systematic final statement of his "working whole view of law-government" is a matter for conjecture. He was neither by temperament nor practice a systematic thinker, and the surviving manuscripts raise doubts about the likelihood of his writing anything that might have been called "definitive."[4]

In 1962, I was fascinated by *Law in Our Society*. Being young and inexperienced about copyright, I wrote to his widow, Soia Mentschikoff, requesting permission to quote from it. To my perpetual amazement I received a reply almost by return. In effect it said: "Hold on, there are one or two other manuscripts in Chicago that you ought to look at before you rush into print."

The bait was cast and I was hooked. So I arranged to give some lectures on customary law in East Africa for Dennis Cowen's New Nations Program and I duly returned to Chicago in the Spring of 1963, some fourteen months after Karl had died. I was, I believe, practically the first person to enter his office in the Law School since his death. Certainly no one had been in to tidy or clean it. A glutinous layer of typical Chicago grime lay over all the surfaces.[5] On the top of one pile of unopened letters and other papers on his desk was the draft in pencil of a poem in both German and English . . . almost certainly his very last work and possibly an exercise for returning to writing in German.[6] Lacking both the inhibitions and skills of an archivist and with Soia's even less inhibited encouragement, I ransacked the office for manuscripts and indeed found a few, as well as some typed transcripts of recent tape-recorded lectures. I reported to Soia that my mission had succeeded. "Hold on," she said, "He had a study at home. There might be something there." So I duly visited their house at 4920 Kimbark, where, equally duly, I moved from study to bedroom to attic to spare room to various cupboards. Eventually, in desperation, I waited until Soia was out and cased the joint systematically from roof to basement, where, *inter multa alia*, I found some boxes that had probably remained unopened since the move from New Haven to New York in 1924. About two years later, the Llewellyn Papers were in some sort of order and I started work first on a thin book and then on a fat one.

Over a period of about seven years, I visited Chicago fairly regularly, including a period of six months as a visiting member of the faculty. My former teachers became my colleagues and many more became my friends. The Chicago faculty in the 1960s was, as ever, friendly, hospitable, and sharply inquiring. I sensed that I was considered to be something of a curiosity, not so much because I was British or from Dar-es-Salaam—neither attribute was unprecedented or even unusual at the time—but rather because intellectual biography was not then included in prevailing conceptions of legal scholarship. I was regularly asked about what I was up to and why. At first, I took this to be a gentle way of hinting that young scholars should engage in more serious pursuits. But it soon became clear that behind some of these enquiries was an unspoken question: "Why Karl?" And, irreverently, I began to wonder whether there might not be a further, unspeakable question: "Why not me?"

Now that it is out in the open, let me give a direct answer to that last question. Law students do not usually judge their teachers by their reputation as scholars. Rather, they gossip about their classroom style, the insanity of their expectations of students, their eccentricities, and their grading curves. When I first came to Chicago as a callow Oxford graduate, I had heard of Karl Llewellyn mainly through *The Bramble Bush* and, on advice, I had also read Edward Levi's *An Introduction to Legal Reasoning* while crossing the Atlantic in the bowels of a liner. I had never even heard of Francis Allen or Walter Blum or William Winslow Crosskey or Aaron Director or Allison Dunham or Harry Kalven or Wilber Katz or Philip Kurland or Bernard Meltzer or Soia Mentschikoff or Nicholas deBelleville Katzenbach or Max Rheinstein or Malcolm Sharp or Roscoe Steffen or Sheldon Tefft or Hans Zeisel, let alone such striplings as Roger Cramton or Jo Desha Lucas.[7] (Dallin Oaks, Kenneth Dam, Kenneth Culp Davis, and even Ronald Coase, George Stigler, and Richard Posner had not yet appeared on the scene). I had no conception that this was perhaps the most star-studded law school faculty in the history of American legal education and that our class was privileged to be exposed to this galaxy of talent in its prime. The facts that nearly all of those who taught me cared about teaching and were accessible and especially hospitable to foreign students may further have obscured their greatness as scholars. When I am asked by younger colleagues, in the UK as well as in this country, who taught me at Chicago, it is not uncommon for my questioners to be familiar with every name on the list. There is only one answer to the question: "Why not me?" It is: "Why not indeed?" Frank Ellsworth's *Law on the Midway* serves as a useful account of the origins of the law school, and

Edward Shils's *Remembering the University of Chicago* has good pen-portraits of Kalven, Levi, and Rheinstein,[8] but Edward Levi's team clearly deserves not only a house history but also more than one intellectual biography.

From the vantage point of 1993, the question: "Why Karl?" is also quite easily addressed. His reputation is secure for at least four reasons:[9]

First, Llewellyn will be remembered as the outstanding commercial lawyer of his time. The Uniform Commercial Code, his seminal casebook on sales, and at least a dozen articles on different aspects of commercial law and contracts are all lasting monuments to his achievements. It is worth remembering that for much of his career commercial law took priority over jurisprudence. It is hardly surprising that most of his theoretical work reflected his private law orientation and exercised a strong magnetic pull towards particular jurisprudence.

Second, he made outstanding contributions to the anthropology and sociology of law. The central thesis of this lecture is that the full significance and potential of this aspect of his work were not fully realized in his lifetime and have yet to be recognized, especially in the United States. The seminal influence of *The Cheyenne Way* on the development of legal anthropology has been acknowledged.[10] But as we shall see, his contribution extends far beyond that.

Third, Llewellyn was extremely influential as a teacher, educator and general stimulator. He was one of the great characters of the law school world. Not all students appreciated his teaching and, it has to be said, his classroom performances tended to be uneven. That conceded, it is clear that he had a seminal influence directly on more than one generation of practitioners, judges, and law teachers. I shall refer in due course to the significance of his ideas on the direct teaching of legal skills. Sixty years on, the continuing appeal of that extraordinary, fascinating, and irritating lyric, *The Bramble Bush*, is indicative of a much wider influence. It has been my contention that this particular work has regularly been misperceived as an iconoclastic and skeptical attack on the very idea of legal rules.[11] It is more likely that its success is due in large part to a feeling that it encapsulates in quite compelling rhetoric a romantic and aspirational vision of mainstream legal education and idealized legal practice. It embodies one version of the Great American Law School dream. In this, as in some of his other communications, Llewellyn was a traditionalist thinly disguised in skeptical clothing.

Fourth, Llewellyn is remembered as a leading interpreter and prophet of the American Realist Movement. Here, I think, his influence has not been entirely salutary. I agree with Morton Horwitz and some others that his famous debate with Pound in 1930-31 obscured as much as it illuminated.[12] It inadvertently blurred the continuities with the wider Progressive Movement to which the young Pound was himself an important contributor. It also glossed over the diversity of concerns and perspectives within the so-called Realist Movement. As a European, I find it very strange that most commentators continue to assume that a concern with being realistic about law is an American exclusive, limited furthermore to a particular phase of your legal history.

In my view, Llewellyn's pronouncements on R/realism in *The Common Law Tradition* further confused subsequent interpreters by failing to distinguish clearly enough between contemporary or historical interpretation of certain trends in American legal thought up to about 1940 (Realism with a capital R) and the place of realism (with a small r) in Llewellyn's own, especially later, thought.[13] It is a truism of intellectual history that the least satisfactory aspects of a jurist's thought tend to attract the most attention. To me, Llewellyn as an interpreter of the American Realist Movement should be sidelined, if not entirely forgotten, but his ideas on what constitutes a realistic perspective on law still have something to say to us within the context of his broader theory or, as he called it, his Whole View.

When I was invited to deliver this celebratory lecture, I had some difficulty in settling on a theme. Karl's many achievements have been extensively documented and at least some of them have received due recognition since his death. Merely to rehearse them or to attempt a nostalgic evocation of the man would not be worthy of the event. Nor on such a happy occasion would it be appropriate to emulate Kipling's Disciple and climb on the shoulders of my guru in order to stab him in the back.[14] So I looked for a topic which would at once be historically significant and of contemporary interest. From several possible candidates I chose to focus on an aspect of his work which has been relatively neglected and which not only is relevant to interpreting his legacy but also has unfulfilled potential for application and development. The subject is the idea of "Juristic Method" or legal technology as part of his law jobs theory.

There are two special reasons for choosing this topic. First, most contemporary discussions of Llewellyn in the United States centre on the Uniform Commercial Code and his place in the Realist Movement, which is interpreted, wrongly in my view, as having been concerned almost entirely with issues of adjudication. Apart from some acknowledgment of his historical role in the development of legal anthropology, Llewellyn's sociology of law is largely ignored.[15] This contrasts with his reputation in Germany, as is illustrated by the fact that his centenary was celebrated in Leipzig in May 1993 by a colloquium, about half of which was devoted to this aspect of his work.[16] These two reputations reflect an unresolved tension between his concern to develop a general sociological theory and his strong personal identification with American legal practice and the common law. Nowhere is this more apparent than in his last published magnum opus, *The Common Law Tradition*. This is, I believe, flawed in large part because Llewellyn failed to use his own general theory to set a specialized study of American state appellate courts in a broad institutional context.[17] This tension suggests a possible discontinuity between Llewellyn's general and particular jurisprudence. This occasion provides an opportunity to correct an imbalance and to explore the relationship between these two aspects of his thought.

Another reason for choosing my topic is that Morton Horwitz, in an important book, has recently argued that Llewellyn, by virtue of his commanding position in the American Realist Movement, has persuaded historians to see a concern with value-free social science to be both the essence and the fatal flaw of Realism.[18] Horwitz sets out, in his own words, "to dispute the view put forth by its most important spokesman, Karl Llewellyn, that Realism was simply a methodology or 'technology' unrelated to substantive intellectual disputes or to social and political struggle."[19] Horwitz presents Llewellyn's emphasis on craft and method as being a late, conservative, even reactionary, sell-out of the critical thrust of his earlier Realism:

> In much the same way that scholarly fields as disparate as literary criticism and philosophy turned inward to technical questions of professional craft and technique, Llewellyn appears to have continued to do "open penance" for the destabilizing consequences of realism. In a period in which it was common to deplore the loss of a sustaining faith in legal objectivity, Llewellyn offered a new basis for belief in professional craft as the source of predictability and stability in law.[20]

I admire Horwitz's book and I find much of his story illuminating. But his attempt to depict Llewellyn as a radical who, like Pound in an earlier generation, sold out to conservative forces late in life is, I believe, quite misleading in a number of respects. I wish to put forward a different interpretation of Llewellyn's interest in method and technology and its significance in his thought. First, it is easy to show that Llewellyn's fascination with "how" questions was a constant theme throughout his life and that there is an essential continuity in his thought in his emphasis on tradition and craft as stabilizing factors.[21] If interest in craft and technique is a symptom of conservative tendencies (which I doubt), then Llewellyn was always a conservative (which may well be true). Second, and more important, I suggest that Llewellyn's ideas on juristic method represent one of the most original, fruitful and under-appreciated aspects of his contribution. Third, I agree with Horwitz and others that Llewellyn's interpretations of American Realism were, in important respects, profoundly misleading. However, our reasons for saying this are quite different. Horwitz depicts pre-war Realism as a legal wing of the Progressive Movement and as such essentially politically motivated. I think that it is correct to stress the connections with Progressivism, which have sometimes been underplayed or obscured;[22] but in his enthusiasm to emphasize the political and ideological roots of some parts of the Realist Movement, Horwitz (like Llewellyn) obscures the diversity of concerns– educational, scholarly, technical, and professional– which account for the diversity of the reactions to an earlier tradition in both their negative and constructive aspects. I have argued elsewhere that it is dangerous to generalize about American Realism just because of the diversity of concerns that stimulated the reaction against the predominating Langdellian orthodoxy and which led to a corresponding variety of prescriptions on the positive side.[23] Today, I shall focus on one aspect of Llewellyn's thought and merely content myself with a few sideswipes at Horwitz.

THE LAW-JOBS THEORY

Concerns and Provenance

The law-jobs theory was developed and restated over a period of more than 30 years. It dates back at least as far as 1927 to a paper on "Mechanisms of Group Control."[24] It features in the *Bramble Bush* and it provided the theoretical basis for his collaboration with Hoebel on the Plains Indians which culminated in *The Cheyenne Way* in 1941. Almost contemporaneously Llewellyn wrote "The Normative, the Legal and the Law-jobs: the Problem of Juristic Method," published in the *Yale Law Journal* in 1940.[25] This remains the most detailed and elaborate statement of the general ideas in print. The theory was restated in summary form in a number of other essays and lectures, published and unpublished, up to his death in 1962. In order to make my presentation manageable and to root it in specific texts, I shall confine my interpretation of the more general theory to four works: the *Law in our Society* teaching materials; the *Yale Law Journal* article, *The Cheyenne Way* and his short but revealing essay published in the volume entitled *My Philosophy of Law* in 1941.[26] In considering juristic method I shall have to range more widely.

The numerous sources from which one can reconstruct Llewellyn's sociology of law were written at different times and for a variety of purposes. Nevertheless, it is fair to say that the main ideas had stabilized by 1940 and that, with three notable exceptions (his general conception of jurisprudence, the idea of the parental, and the crafts of law) most of the later texts contain only minor variants or particular applications.

The provenance and concerns behind the 1940-41 version of the law-jobs theory are quite varied and complex. For present purposes one can perhaps isolate five rather different concerns that fed into the project.

(1) From an early stage, Llewellyn was keen to construct a general framework for his ideas, what he called a "working Whole View."[27] He chose to root this in social theory.

(2) An underlying concern was with inter-disciplinary co-operation and in particular with developing a picture of law and a theoretical vocabulary which might bridge the divide between law and other social sciences, especially sociology and anthropology, but also economics and political science.[28]

(3) A source of concern was with the law-in-action and hence with "realistic" jurisprudence. Here it is worth making two points: Llewellyn's interest in general social theory and his paper on "Mechanisms of Group Control" ante-date the Realist controversy and his first published attempts to develop an explicitly "realistic jurisprudence." Even more important is the point that from the outset Llewellyn was quite explicit that the ideas associated with "R/realism" formed only one part of his "Whole view." In a later formulation he put it as follows: "If Jurisprudence of necessity includes a study of ideals for law, then realism is not [co-extensive with] Jurisprudence. If, as I think, Jurisprudence contains [seven] sub-disciplines, then realism deals with two out of the seven: craft-techniques and descriptive sociology."[29]

This is worth emphasizing in order to counter two fallacies that are still widely prevalent: first, the idea that Llewellyn's "R/realism" was a theory of adjudication.[30] A realistic perspective on law deals with all legal phenomena and, indeed, in my view it is unrealistic to treat courts and litigation as the focal point of law, even in the United States. An obsession with courts tends to produce a distorted and hence an "unrealistic" vision of law. A second fallacy is the idea that Llewellyn's "realism" was co-extensive with his general theory of law.[31]

(4) A fourth concern that underlies the law-jobs theory is central to my theme. Throughout his life Llewellyn was fascinated, some might say obsessed, by method. This is a statement about the man as well as his ideas. Even his contemporaneous accounts of his German war adventure in 1914 tell us much about logistics, tactics, process and atmosphere and almost nothing about his perception of the ideological issues surrounding the war.[32]

Llewellyn's earliest formulations of his general sociology of law quite explicitly make the point that "science" (*Wissenschaft*) develops out of useful real world practices (*praktische Lebenskunst*) and institutionalized group responses to problems (*Handlungsgefüge*) . . . and that a primary notion of "law" encompasses a variety of skills.[33]

The Cheyenne Way is about Cheyenne *law-ways*, in particular how they resolved the eternal tension between established form and felt justice, the same tension that he later claimed is resolved by the Grand Style of appellate judging and advocacy.[34] The famous report of the Committee on Curriculum chaired by Llewellyn in 1944 had skills development as its central theme, as we shall see later.[35] His most important published version of the law-jobs theory is subtitled "The Problem of Juristic Method." Llewellyn's work is shot through with how questions . . . he is par excellence the jurist of the How. While some of Llewellyn's cryptic late statements about "R/realism" as technology are problematic, it is clearly wrong to treat his interest in method and technology as a late development.

(5) A fifth concern was more immediate. His first meeting with Hoebel in 1933 and his involvement in three studies of the Plains Indians, which began with the Shoshones and the Comanches and culminated in the classic study of the Cheyennes, provided an immediate stimulus to solve a particular problem. It is worth recalling Hoebel's account of their first meeting, as it illustrates how a quite specific problem generated a solution that in time suggested answers to questions of much wider significance.[36]

In 1933, Hoebel was a graduate student in the anthropology department at Columbia that was adorned by Franz Boas, Ruth Benedict, and Margaret Mead, among others.[37] Hoebel's proposal that he should study the law of the Plains Indians was met by extreme skepticism on two main grounds: First, the Plains Indians had no courts, no sovereign, no centralized sanctions, and hence no law "properly so called"– a revealing example of the disastrous influence of Austinian jurisprudence. Second, the Plains Indians were perceived as unable or unwilling to articulate their "customary" rules or norms in general terms.[38] When asked about what would happen in particular hypothetical situations, the standard reply was: "It all depends." Whether this was an accurate perception is neither here nor there. This combination of a particular conception of law with a perception of the Plains Indians as informants was considered to be a fatal bar to Hoebel's project. Fortunately, Franz Boas was sufficiently open-minded to suggest that there was someone in the law school who might hold a different view.

According to Hoebel, Llewellyn solved his problem at their first meeting in June 1933. The solution was simple: all societies and groups have disputes and the need to prevent and settle them. One can find out how a given group deals with these needs or "jobs," not by asking general questions which in any case invite misleading answers, but by asking detailed questions about particular cases and how they were dealt with, by whom, in what arenas, with what results, and how far these ways of solving problems of order were institutionalized. Later, Llewellyn recognized that myths and stories were almost as useful in getting at institutions and law-ways as historically accurate accounts. Thus, according to this version of history, the case-method was introduced into anthropology and Llewellyn, already conscious that method is dependent on theory, was stimulated to develop a rounded statement of the law-jobs theory.

Of course, a detailed exegesis of the relevant texts would reveal a multitude of other concerns, questions, and themes. But these five general concerns– the quest for a whole view, interest in inter-disciplinary co-operation, realism, the focus on method, and Hoebel's presenting problem– are enough for our purposes. It is worth noting that all five are theoretical or academic in the sense that they are directly connected with a vision and methodology for the discipline of law. They are less directly connected with legal education or providing practical guidance to practitioners, judges, law reformers, and other participants in legal processes. This enterprise was more concerned with legal scholarship than with legal training, practice, or reform.

The Theory Outlined

At this point it is appropriate to provide a summary restatement of the bare bones of the law-jobs theory.[39] All of us are members of groups, such as a family, a club, a teenage gang, a sports team, a school, a commercial organization, a trade union, a political party, a nation state, the world community. In order to survive and to achieve its aims, in so far as it has aims, *any* human group has to meet certain needs or ensure that certain jobs are done. These can, for purposes of convenient study[40] be broken down into five or six rough categories.

First, and the most unmistakably "legal," is adjustment of the Trouble-case (dispute, grievance, offense).[41] When conflict or other trouble arises, it has to be resolved or at least kept to a tolerably low level, or else the group will disintegrate or its objectives will be frustrated or impaired.

The second, and perhaps the most important, job is the preventive channeling of conduct and expectations to avoid trouble.

Third, as needs, conditions, and relations change, so the conduct and expectations of the group have to be re-channeled.

Fourth, there is the job of "Arranging for the Say and the Manner of its Saying," that is, the advance allocation of authority and the advance regulation of authoritative procedure. This job is prototypically the primary function of a "constitution" of a club, or organization or a nation-state. Where power and authority diverge, as any realist knows, there tends to be a gap between what in fact happens and what is meant to happen. Giving a realistic account of a constitution as a kind of institution is accordingly problematic.[42]

Fifth, there is the job of "providing Net Positive drive: Integration, Direction, Incentive for the whole."[43] Llewellyn, like Bentham, explicitly linked positive and negative sanctions (rewards as well as punishments, for example) within his conception of law-government.

Finally, in any group— but especially in complex groups— techniques, skills, devices, practices, and traditions need to be developed, institutionalized and adjusted if the first five needs or jobs are to be dealt with adequately or well. This is what Llewellyn called the Job of Juristic Method. He considered this to be his most original contribution to the sociology of law and I wish to consider it in detail below.[44]

Uses, Limitations and Criticisms

The law-jobs theory has been subjected to remarkably little sustained or detailed criticism in the Anglo-American literature.[45] Alan Hunt treats it as an example of "extreme functionalism" and argues that, as such, it is vulnerable to the standard criticisms of structural-functionalism of the inter-war period;[46] Roger Cotterrell suggests that it is too vague and general to be of much value, while acknowledging that functional analysis still has a place in contemporary sociology;[47] Julius Stone, in a generally sympathetic account, impliedly criticizes Llewellyn for failing to say much of significance about the differences between groups and about social and legal change, both of which points signal important limitations to Llewellyn's account;[48] I have suggested that on one interpretation the basic ideas can be reduced to a near tautology, but this is to clarify the nature of the theory rather than to condemn it.[49] In the light of modern developments in sociology and social theory, it may be open to criticism that it underplays the importance of power, structure, and discourse; and there are some familiar conceptual problems associated with the use of such terms as "function," "need," and "group."[50]

Without wishing to exempt Llewellyn from all such criticisms, it is my view that the law-jobs theory can be interpreted in a way which rescues it from nearly all of these criticisms, and that it could be usefully refined and supplemented in the light of subsequent developments in social theory within the same intellectual tradition.[51] A detailed treatment of these issues requires another occasion. Suffice to say here that Llewellyn anticipated and side-stepped most of the charges against "extreme functionalism" (e.g. of the kind associated with Talcott Parsons); that if it is considered not as an empirical theory but rather as a perspective and a heuristic theory that suggests a rich series of basic questions to ask about the ordering of any human group, then the charge of tautology is unimportant; and, insofar as Llewellyn's version lays relatively little stress on discourse,[52] structure, and power, it can quite easily be supplemented for a given enquiry by additional questions.

Its simplicity and generality are, in my view, a source of strength. It is easily grasped and extremely flexible; its claim to be applicable to any human group from a one-parent family to the world community is breathtakingly ambitious and has, indeed, raised quite a few eyebrows. Among the groups used in his course to test out and apply the theory were a submarine, a boy's camp, and the world of the bee-hive as described by Maeterlinck.[53] On the whole, outside legal anthropology, the use of the law-jobs theory, as such (as opposed to specific aperçus), has been rather limited. It provided the framework for the Chicago Arbitration Project,[54] which was never completed, but it has been conspicuously underused in recent work on "alternative dispute-resolution."[55] It was fairly unobtrusively the basis for the study of the Pueblos of New Mexico which was never completed.[56] In one project, that was never started, Llewellyn and Mentschikoff planned to compare dispute-settlement among the tiny Pueblos and in the Soviet Union, a bold, but abortive enterprise, which, through the work of Harold Berman, had an important influence on studies of Soviet law.[57] Llewellyn did not really exploit its potential for setting a broad context for his particular studies of American appellate courts, or his courses on Elements and advocacy.[58]

The main claims for the value of the law-jobs theory may be summarized as follows:

(1) It roots a general theory of law-government in an established and rich tradition of social theory;

(2) It is general in that it claims to apply to all human groups;

(3) It can be interpreted and used as a flexible perspective and set of concepts for asking open-ended questions about any human group. It is open-ended in that it makes almost no universal empirical assumptions about human nature or methods of group ordering beyond the proposition that all groups are susceptible to internal conflict and to changing conditions which may give rise to conflict. It makes no necessary normative or empirical assumption that conflict and dispute are inherently bad, nor that there are uniform or universal ways of doing the law-jobs;

(4) It is holistic or contextual in that it provides a lens for looking at particular institutions, devices, traditions, events, and other phenomena in the context of a total picture or whole view of an entirety; it makes no assumption that any entirety is self-contained, nor that a group or entirety is necessarily to be equated with a "system";

(5) It draws the semantic sting of obsession with definitions of law and related concepts by emphasizing focus without artificial confines . . . thereby sidestepping definitional problems at the most general

level and emphasizing the continuities between legal and other social phenomena;[59]

(6) By focusing on actual events, disputes, practices etc. it provides a basis for giving concrete, particularized accounts of the relationships between what is meant to happen (aspiration, official views, the law in books) and what happens in fact ("empirical reality," interposed norms and practices, actual consequences and effects, the law in action);

(7) It is entirely compatible with the axioms of interpretive sociology that (i) descriptions and explanations are constructed by interpreters with different standpoints and perspectives; and (ii) that such interpretations have to include both an external interpretive conceptual scheme (etics) and the internal concepts and ways of thought of actors (emics);[60]

(8) It allows for change and for the consideration of dynamic processes, with participants, choices, contingencies, institutions, traditions viewed over time, and it allows scope for questions about "the social functions of conflict" in such processes;

(9) It gives a place to rules and other norms (and principles and discourses and concepts) as an important element in legal phenomena without making them paramount; it is always an open question: to what extent are the law-jobs in fact being done by rules or other norms (paper or real) and/or by other means?

(10) It takes "how" questions seriously and these have often been neglected in legal theory; it links legal sociology with general rationalistic ideas about problem-solving, on the one hand, and unconscious, or semi-conscious patterns of behavior and ways of thought within a general concept of group culture, including legal culture;

(11) It is easily understood and applied in a wide variety of contexts.

Law-Jobs and Legal Records

The value and flexibility of the law-jobs theory can be illustrated by reference to a research project in which I was recently involved.[61] The Commonwealth Legal Records Project is concerned with archival policy relating to the preservation and disposal of legal records of all kinds in what is now referred to as "the Old Commonwealth," that is most anglophone countries that were at some stage under British rule and that have preserved a vestigial link with the Crown. The project arose out of three main concerns: first, many modern legal records of great potential archival value are in danger of being lost by virtue of neglect, oversight, or over-enthusiastic destruction by a new generation of cost-conscious records managers; second, it was felt that historians and other scholars have not adequately faced up to the imperatives and dilemmas of selection in the face of the massive proliferation of paper and the costs of its preservation; and, thirdly, archivists have tended in the past to equate "legal records" with court records, only occasionally and unsystematically extending the category to some other classes, such as land records and the papers of some private practitioners. They have lacked a coherent conceptual framework for devising systematic policies of selection and retention in respect of records other than court records.[62] To put the matter rather simply, archivists have tended to adopt a narrow and not very coherent conception of law and an outdated, often court-centered, conception of legal scholarship. There are also many law-related categories of records which have either been generally overlooked in archival policy or have been treated simply as administrative records. Examples include non-litigious business of law-firms (other than formal land transactions), alternative dispute resolution, the legal departments of public corporations or large private sector enterprises, and law-related non-governmental organizations such as civil liberties groups, legal awareness programs, and neighborhood law offices. In most countries there is an almost complete vacuum in archival policy in respect of such institutions. Furthermore, historiography has moved away from top-down, great man, winners' history to more diverse sets of perspectives, including greater emphasis on the ordinary, the routine, on modes of discourse and the perspectives of women, minorities and underprivileged groups. So selection criteria and priorities need to adjust to changing conceptions of scholarly significance. In respect of legal records, what contemporary and future historians and other scholars may consider to be significant has to be anticipated so far as is feasible. It is quite clear that the records of superior courts and formal land transactions will no longer be considered to be the only or even the main kinds of records demanding a high priority.

In designing the project we found that from the available stock of legal theories Llewellyn's law-jobs theory was the one that best fitted our purposes. It offered a broad and flexible perspective on law and legal institutions that enabled us to include records relating to customary law and religious law in plural legal systems; to law-making and law-enforcement; and to alternative dispute-processing and non-contentious professional legal work in public, parastatal, and private sectors in a variety of countries with very different state legal systems and cultures.

Further, by substituting "institutions specialized to law" for "legal records" and by refusing to provide a formal, general *definition* of the term, we killed two birds with one stone; in characteristic Llewellyn style, we side-stepped the definitional problem which had troubled many archivists by "drawing the semantic sting."[63] We merely treated an institution as being specialized to law if it pragmatically fitted the objectives of this project.

At the same time, focusing on institutions rather than classes of records fitted in well with the archival principle of provenance: that records are to be collected, appraised, and classified by reference to their creating institutions rather than their content. Furthermore, orthodox archival and records management theory has strong functionalist tendencies. For example, in Schellenberg's classic text "records" are explicitly related to institutions having functions that are mainly exercised through transactions.[64]

In a case-study of legal records in Accra, as part of the larger project, we started by compiling as comprehensive a profile as possible of all institutions which might be included in our survey . . . a demographic "total picture" of law-related institutions.[65] As we trawled Accra in a mini-bus reading signs on buildings (in the absence of up-to-date directories), we added to our list a women's legal advice center, the Ombudsman, some important administrative and military tribunals, the Legal department of the Volta River Authority, the Ga House of Chiefs (which exercises important judicial powers), the Ghana Law School, letter-writers outside the law courts, and even the Committee for the Redistribution of Sequestered Property. Almost none of these had previously attracted the attention of the National Archives.

This is an example of the law-jobs theory, in its broader aspects, providing a simple, broad, coherent, inter-disciplinary perspective for an enquiry that crossed national and cultural boundaries and which, it is hoped, may change perceptions of the extent and value of legal records as part of the national heritage. It was also enormous fun and a good way of learning about law in Ghana.[66]

Juristic Method

The list of five or six law-jobs was, in fact, almost commonplace rather than novel. Llewellyn claimed that the most original aspect of the law-jobs theory was the isolation of "the job of juristic method" as an explicit focus of attention worthy of sustained study from a sociological point of view. The concept of juristic method in this context is very broad indeed. It is not confined to the skills and techniques of individual specialists (the crafts of the lawyer, styles of judges, the skills of different kinds of negotiator). It includes but is not confined to craft-traditions (for example, the organization and ways of work of English Chancery barristers in Dickens' time or in 1993);[67] legal inventions (such as the trust, the letter of credit, legal fictions, the ombudsman);[68] institutional design (different models of constitution, different architectural styles of code, types of procedural system, or more specific institutions, such as modern ADR devices like rent-a-judge or the mini-trial); and any kind of machinery or institutionalized way of doing any of the law-jobs. Juristic method is "the *ways of handling* legal tools to law-job ends and of the ongoing upkeep and improvement of both ways and tools."[69]

The term "juristic method" can easily be confused with "legal method," a much narrower category in ordinary legal usage, that is typically confined to that narrow range of skills relating to interpreting and arguing about questions of law—what is commonly referred to by that justly-criticized phrase "thinking like a lawyer." Llewellyn was among those who have emphasized that such rule-handling skills represent only one phase of the skills of the lawyer, but because he had a special interest in the crafts of judging and lawyering, his idea of "juristic method" can easily be interpreted too narrowly. Just as the concept of "law-jobs" is very much wider than "lawyer-jobs," so "juristic method" is very much wider than "lawyer-crafts,"[70] which in turn transcends individual skills to include craft traditions, practices, and settled ways of thought. Furthermore, the theory of crafts is not confined to "lawyers,"[71] but extends to all participants in legal action. "Juristic method" encompasses all aspects of institutional machinery which, said Llewellyn, includes "ways *and* personnel *and ideology* about both."[72]

From now on I shall occasionally substitute the term "legal technology" for Juristic Method and try to keep narrower categories such as "law-crafts," "lawyer- crafts," skills, and techniques conceptually distinct.[73] In this context "technology" is broader than the systematic study of the practical or industrial arts. It refers to the sociological study of everything used in performing the law jobs, especially institutionalized ways and means, including thought-ways and the organization and management of work.[74]

The breadth of the general conception of legal technology is illustrated in *Law in Our Society*, which contains sketches for a series of sub-theories linked to Llewellyn's idea of Juristic Method: a general theory of law-crafts, with a sub-theory of lawyer-crafts; theories of problem-solution in general;[75] of dogmatics in general and legal dogmatics;[76] of legal aesthetics;[77] and working theories on appellate judging, appellate advocacy, and counseling; there are also promises of chapters on legislation and codification, viewed from this perspective. Even this is not comprehensive on Llewellyn's own terms. For example, in the late 1930s, he had drafted a major part of a book, provisionally called *The Theory of Rules*, in which rules are treated as one of the main instruments for doing the law-jobs.[78] It is ironic that the jurist who considered the development of better rules and more sophisticated methods of rule-handling to be one of the central tasks of legal technology and who was himself the chief draftsman of a major code, should still be referred to as a rule-skeptic.[79] It is strange that the "theory of rules" is not explicitly included in *Law in Our Society*.[80]

To develop a comprehensive theory of legal technology is an ambitious venture. In *Law in our Society* we have a series of more or less complete sketches, one of the most developed being the theory of crafts.[81]

This reflects Llewellyn's own interests, both generally and in his specialized work on judging, advocacy, drafting, and skills training. However, he tried, not always successfully, to differentiate between his general theory and his own particular contributions. He maintained that the idea of crafts was central to the law-jobs theory and was his own most important contribution to a particular intellectual tradition. His specific claim was that he was filling a gap in the work of Max Weber. It is worth quoting a key passage from *Law in Our Society* at length. After acknowledging the contributions of many forerunners, including Petrajitsky, Ehrlich, Sumner, Bentley, and Wigmore, he continues:

> *Max Weber* did the deepest cutting of all (except, of course, Dewey), because he saw at once, in a sort of intellectual counterpoint, four things . . . and managed to keep them clear: first (the thing which nobody before had adequately stressed) the machinery of the man-stuff to get the jobs done (the "bureaucracy"); second, the impact of the prevailing (conditioning, but possibly helping) realm of ideas and views-of-goals; third, the different sources of ideas and ideals and the differing factual results according to their sources (e.g. "unquestionable," "rational"); fourth, the *method* of operation (e.g. "rational"—though with his curious failure to keep clear consistently the difference between "*really* rational"—as *we* now see it—and "rational on the given premise"—i.e. in *their* terms).
>
> Weber's descriptive range (with its accuracy) is unmatched. His analytical power I rate the same. Yet it is amazing that the man who could build a sociology of music on the nature of available instruments ("leaving out," says Morris Cohen, with partial justice, "what makes music Music") could overlook, in the deep and needed idea of the man-stuff (bu<reau>cracy) the *craft-skills*, and the *key-position of the individual*. I think, only because he was not a lawyer. But with these, the whole, though the finest job one can really hope to see, still has to miss contact with life. The *craft-skills, and the tradition of the craftsman* and those men's judgment and uprightness (Weber got adequately only the second and a part of the third) *are the place where all of Jurisprudence, and all of Law, comes together in its impact*: The stuff for analysis, the focus for improvement, the place of key-meaningfulness.[82]

This strong emphasis on personnel and on the individual craftsman could be interpreted as a form of extreme individualism. This, I think, would be a mistake. Llewellyn's craftsman is not an atomistic, isolated unit. He or she is part of, and is created and constrained by received ways of thought, accepted practices, and bureaucratic organization. Rather, this is a plea to focus on the human element, especially the conscious and unconscious ways of thought and ideologies of individual craftsmen as social actors.

The theory of crafts is thus given a central place in Llewellyn's sociology of law. I shall not attempt here to expound the theory in detail. In *Law in Our Society* Llewellyn considers, inter alia, what a craft is, the ways (i.e. the institutionalization) of crafts, stability and change, the economic base, the law-crafts, and spokesmanship as illustrative of a craft which can be divided up into any number of sub-crafts. The text of this section is available in print and many of the ideas are extensively developed in other writings, published and unpublished.[83] Rather, by way of illustration, I shall consider the potential of the theory of crafts in relation to recent developments in two areas: the sociology of the legal profession and skills development in legal education and training. Then, I shall briefly deal with criticisms of the craft concept as either a form of romantic nostalgia (Hayakawa) or as a retreat from engagement with serious political issues (Horwitz).

Technology and Studies of the Legal Profession

In 1968, Robert S. Merrill wrote:

> Given the long history of concern with the social consequences of technology, it is puzzling that technological systems, like similar aspects of culture as political, legal, economic, social, and magico-religious systems, are not the focus of an established specialty in any of the social sciences. The academic institutionalization of the social study of technology does not even approach that recently attained by its sister subject, science. One reason for this discrepancy is that technologies are not thought to be very interesting.[84]

Merrill specifically excepted two pioneering scholars whom Llewellyn greatly admired: Bronislaw Malinowski and William F. Ogburn. Thanks in part to Merrill's own work, the study of technology is now an established field in the social sciences, but this does not seem to be the case in the sociology of law. For example, the sociology of legal professions (including comparative studies) has made enormous strides in the past thirty years. We now know much more than we did about stratification, recruitment, access, socialization, professionalization, and the demography, economics, ideologies and power relations of lawyers in many countries. The work of Carlin, Johnstone and Hopson, Heinz, Flood, Abel, and Lewis and many others illustrates this.[85] Yet, we do not know very much more systematically about what lawyers do in their daily work and how they go about doing it. At the start of one of five substantial volumes on lawyers in society, Richard Abel acknowledges as much:

> Except for a handful of very recent ethnographic studies of lawyer-client interaction (e.g. Cain, 1979; Griffiths, 1986; Sarat and Felstiner, 1986), we know little more about what lawyers do than how they allocate their time among different subject-matters. One reason for writing this book is my hope that its description of the social organization of the legal profession will enable and stimulate others to undertake the more difficult task of studying the content and form of their daily work activities.[86]

This is a remarkable admission to make near the completion of a five volume study, which is widely recognized to represent the state of the art. However there is one area in which Abel's admission might be said to be over-stated. For a great deal of work, including some empirical research, has been done in relation to direct teaching of professional legal skills. So let us consider this currently fashionable concern in the light of Llewellyn's ideas.

Skills and Legal Education

Skills and competency are currently high on the agenda of debates about legal education in the common law world. From British Columbia to New Zealand, from Zimbabwe to Hong Kong, from Melbourne to London

(England and Ontario), the merits of direct versus pick-it-up learning, of holistic versus abstracted approaches, of clinical versus simulated training, of the balance between know-how and know-what, are being vigorously debated in a plethora of experimental programs.[87] In the United States the history of the skills movement is variously told: some, with short memories, start with CLEPR or the competency debates of the 1970s;[88] some go back to an historic meeting in Asheville, Tennessee in 1965;[89] some treat the Lasswell-McDougal plan of 1943,[90] or the report of the AALS Committee on Curriculum, chaired by Llewellyn in 1944,[91] or a job-analysis by Wigmore in 1922[92] as marking the start of the modern skills movement; some trace the story back to the first law school clinics or to Langdell's switch from an emphasis on knowledge to rigorous, single-minded focus on a single set of intellectual skills.[93] Some of us would even trace the story back through the long history of rhetoric to Quintillian, Cicero, and Aristotle.[94]

The recent rapid increase in interest in the common law world outside North America is sometimes known as "the Gold Rush" in tribute to the influence of Professor Neil Gold first in developing ideas (largely derived from American models) in British Columbia and Ontario and then disseminating them to a number of jurisdictions in Africa, Australasia and South East Asia, and most recently, and rather belatedly, to England.[95] There, in 1989, the Inns of Court School of Law, in a remarkably radical move, substituted a year-long skills-based course for the traditional knowledge-based one that had fallen into disrepute.[96] The Law Society of England and Wales is in process of introducing a new Legal Practice Course from September 1993, which aims to move in a similar direction while maintaining a balance between knowledge and skill.[97]

Some academic lawyers fear that the profession will seek to off-load some of the substantive law topics that have been discarded at the vocational stage onto the undergraduate degree. To counter this "knowledge-backlash" they are vigorously claiming that, as liberal educators, "we are in the skills business, too," at least in respect of intellectual skills.[98]

For the past five years a very active Legal Skills Research Group has been stimulating and co-ordinating empirical research in this general area.[99] Interestingly, the recent ABA Task Force on Legal Education and Professional Development (the MacCrate Committee) acknowledged that "the Commonwealth programs are perceived to be far more effective than our existing bridge-the-gap programs."[100] If this is true, which is debatable, it is largely because more time is available in the Commonwealth courses: most of them involve 6-9 months full-time study after the completion of the first law degree. Some American "bridge-the-gap" courses last less than a week.

The modern skills movement is diverse and controversial. However, a predominant orthodoxy can be discerned. This is exemplified by the MacCrate Report in 1992, the much skimpier Marre Committee Report in England in 1988, and the writings of Professor Gold.[101] The basic tenets of this orthodoxy can perhaps be restated as follows: one of the primary objectives of legal education and training is to enable students to achieve minimum standards of competency in basic skills before being let loose on the public; what constitute such basic skills depends on a job analysis of what lawyers of different kinds in fact do; lawyer-jobs can be analyzed into transactions or operations, which can be further broken down into tasks or sub-operations;[102] a skill or skill-cluster denotes the ability to carry out a task to an acceptable, specified standard. Minimum acceptable competence is to be distinguished from excellence and it is the main function of law schools and bridge-the-gap programs to ensure that all entrants to the profession satisfy minimum competence in a range of skills, measured by actual performances which satisfy articulated criteria under specified conditions. Problem-solving is, in this view, seen either as one of the most important basic skills or, as some would have it, the master skill under which all lawyering tasks can be subsumed.[103] Finally, there is an ethical dimension: not only does the standard list of skills include ability to recognize and to resolve ethical dilemmas,[104] but issues of ethics, values, and professional responsibility need to pervade the learning of each skill—hence the idea of a pervasive approach to professional responsibility.

At first sight this looks like a restatement of Llewellyn's views. In 1941 he wrote: "[S]ound sociology of law is the precondition to sound legal technique."[105] The Lasswell-McDougal plan of 1943 and the 1944

AALS Report, which was mainly drafted by Llewellyn, are widely recognized as pioneering attempts to relate legal education to what lawyers in fact do in a systematic fashion and to move from one rather narrow set of intellectual skills to a broader and more systematic preparation for all important aspects of legal practice. Llewellyn helped to set the fashion of drawing up lists of skills, although his modest list of six looks rather meagre compared to MacCrate's list of ten skills groups (each with sub-divisions) and Lady Marre's twenty-four. "Problem-based learning" is now in fashion, Significantly, Llewellyn's *Law in Our Society* had a substantial section devoted to "Theory of Problem-solution in General."[106] His courses on Elements and Appellate Advocacy at Chicago were clear attempts to develop direct teaching of specific skills;[107] and he summed up the importance of the ethical dimension in the much-quoted aphorism: "Technique without ideals may be a menace, but ideals without technique are a mess."[108]

Undoubtedly many of the developments in skills-based legal education since 1944 in North America and beyond could be interpreted as attempts to implement, refine, and develop Llewellyn's own program. Contemporaries, such as Frank Strong and David Cavers, and former students, such as Irvin Rutter, Charles Kelso, and Terence Anderson explicitly acknowledged his direct influence, which could also be seen in particular programs at Cincinnati, Antioch, and Miami.[109] Mentschikoff and Stotzky edited and expanded the Elements materials which are still used as the main book for the first-year foundation course at Miami and a few other schools.[110] In my own work on interpretation and fact-analysis and more generally in legal education I am happy to acknowledge Llewellyn as a seminal influence.[111]

Thus, Llewellyn clearly has a place as an important pioneer in this area and his influence lives on. Yet one wonders whether the powerful modern orthodoxy is entirely in tune with his vision and ideas. If Karl Llewellyn were to return today and read the MacCrate and Marre reports, one suspects that he would react with a mixture of enthusiasm and dismay. On the one hand, he would probably welcome the broadening of the focus of legal education and training, the concern to be more realistic about what lawyers do, the increased educational professionalism, the emphasis on professional responsibility and problem-solving and recent attempts to develop an empirical base for skills training.[112] However, let me on his behalf, express some concerns.

First, let us consider the precept that "sound sociology of law is the precondition to sound legal technique."[113] It is very doubtful whether compiling lists of discrete skills which practitioners say they think are important goes very far in the direction of a sound sociology of law. This is not to denigrate the work of Zemans, Rosenblum, and Garth in Chicago,[114] nor that of Joanna Shapland in England.[115] However, the outcome to date seems to be longer and longer check-lists, with little analysis of interconnections, and only rather primitive efforts at setting priorities. As the lists get longer, the time available for study stays the same or even decreases. The almost inevitable result is the sacrifice of detail, depth, and transferability to the dragon of "coverage"— in this case coverage of longer and longer lists in the name of a mechanistic form of bureaucratic rationalism that is threatening to engulf legal education.[116]

In my country, perhaps even more than in the United States, the legal profession has been obsessed by coverage, that is the idea that there are certain fields of law that every student should have covered, however superficially, before being admitted to practice. This has been most obviously exhibited in the old style bar and solicitors' examinations– not very different from State Bar Examinations– which have traditionally tested short-term memory of masses of technical detail. The shift to skills has not reduced the obsession. Once competence has been defined in terms of a list of skills, the gate-keepers may even feel that they have to adopt a position that someone who has failed on even one item on the list has to be treated as incompetent. As the list grows, so detail, depth, repetition, and skillfulness are sacrificed. At one institution having persuaded the powers-that-be that "fact-management" was an important skill-set, I learned that within two years it had been squeezed into three hours of classroom instruction. One symptom of this tendency is to be found in disclaimers for the new-style skills courses. The Inns of Court School of Law claims that its one-year full-time course is no more than a preparation for pupillage, i.e. apprenticeship.[117] Similarly "bridge the gap" increasingly means the gap between law school and apprenticeship or starting practice under supervision. What is at risk in this primary school model is the idea of formal legal education as a long-term or lifelong investment.[118]

In his passionate plea for "The Study of Law as a Liberal Art," Llewellyn commented on Langdell's contribution which involved an historic switch from emphasis on substantive knowledge to emphasis on one set of case-law skills as follows: "The resulting skills, though sharp and well-instilled were narrow, and remained so. The wherewithal for vision was not given."[119] There is a danger that a future historian of the modern skills movement might write: "The resulting technical skills were broad, but they were neither sharp nor well-instilled and there was a total neglect of the vision thing."

Technology and Crafts: An Excursus

Words ending in -ology tend to be used loosely to refer to the science or study of a subject, or to the subject itself, or even to the products of a process of applied science. Thus "methodology" often conflates the study of method with method.[120] The word "technology" is commonly used to refer to the study of the practical arts, to the practical arts themselves, and to their products, such as machines, for example in such phrases as "new technology." Similarly, "legal technology" can refer to the study of the law-ways, to the law-ways themselves, and to the products of the law-ways, such as particular legal inventions and devices. Llewellyn was interested in all three, but the emphasis was on the *study* of juristic method: the law-jobs theory treats "juristic method" as a focus of study and includes a methodology *stricto sensu*; "the job of juristic method" refers to the law-ways (i.e. to method in a broad sense); but the study of juristic method encompasses practical arts (techne), practices, and legal artifacts or products, such as codes, devices, and institutions (means as well as ways).

"Legal technology" (my term) has a modern, industrial ring. "Craft", Llewellyn's favorite, is old-fashioned, even quaint and mildly embarrassing. As one Japanese commentator shrewdly observed, Llewellyn's emphasis on craftsmanship conjures up a nostalgic image of legal practice as a kind of tradition-bound, cottage industry at a time when it was moving into an era of factory mass production.[121] There is something awkward about the term, but it revealingly links some central strands in Llewellyn's own thought: the importance of tradition as a steadying factor; the idea of the craftsman who is both an individual and yet who is formed by and is part of a communal enterprise. The craftsman occupies a middle-brow position between the technician and tradesman on the one hand and the scientist, statesman, or artist on the other (Llewellyn's self-image was of "a half-way artist").[122] Legal aesthetics was explicitly, perhaps fancifully, part of the theory of the crafts of law, but the idea of beauty is quite functional and down-to-earth: the images and analogies are most commonly with carpentry, architecture, and sculpture;[123] Llewellyn himself was a versifier rather than a poet. The craftsman is neither a plumber nor Pericles; he or she is more than just a technician, but only exceptionally aspires to greatness. The distinguishing mark of the craftsman is pride in a job well done for its own sake. Money and fame are secondary. Craftsmanship is more akin to a form of love.[124]

"Craft" also suggests licensed craftiness, the ethically ambiguous Odysseus as none-too-scrupulous hero. Here one finds a deep ambivalence in Llewellyn's attitudes. "[C]rafty," he says, "reflects abuse by the craftsman unless, as in negotiation or war, maneuvers and even deception are part of the craft."[125] Llewellyn regularly proclaimed the importance of ideals and ethics, the quest for beauty and the quest for justice, but in his course on advocacy he was not above teaching the tricks of the trade, including some that might be thought to be ethically dubious. His model advocate puts the interest of the client first, plays the adversary game hard, and seemingly treats the idea of the role of "officer of the court" as an important, but secondary, side-constraint.[126]

In 1993, the idea of a theory of law-crafts seems not just quaint, but dubious and outdated. The associations of craft, craftsman, craftsmanship, are largely positive; they suggest a vision of legal practice that is optimistic, sentimental, uncritical. When Llewellyn writes in this vein, we are a long way from washing the law in cynical acid or even mild skepticism. When he waxes lyrical about the Grand Style or Cheyenne "legal genius" or revels in the skills and tactics of Elihu Root or John W. Davis or R. Muir, Q.C. (who prosecuted Crippen), has he not succumbed to an uncritical form of romanticism?

Jeremy Bentham, no lover of the legal profession or judges, referred to the perversion of sensibility that occurs when sportsmen or craftsmen or professionals become attached to techniques and technicalities as ends in themselves as "the technical prejudice":

> What sensation is ever produced in the breast of an angler by an impaled or writhing worm? in the breast of a butcher, by a bleeding lamb?... in the breast of an undertaker, by the death of the father or mother of an orphan family? If a fly were to be put on the hook, in a month when a worm is the proper bait—if the lamb were to be cut up into uncustomary joints, . . . if, in the decorations of the coffin, the armorial bearings of the deceased were to be turned topsy turvy... these are the incidents by which, in the several classes of professional men, a sensation would be produced; meaning always a sensation of the unpleasant kind.[127]

This in more forceful terms than he himself used is the essence of Horwitz's challenge. Llewellyn sold out to an uncritical and romantic view of law and legal practice by taking refuge in the study of crafts.

Can Llewellyn be rescued from such charges? He is clearly not guilty on some counts: first, his craftsman is not an isolated individual, as Hayakawa suggests. "The fact and idea of *crafts focus as nothing else does* (except the rearing of the young) *the homely daily processes of interaction between individuals and closer groups and the larger society around them.*"[128]

Second, and related, Llewellyn consistently emphasized that crafts were means to ends, that had to be considered in relation to goals and ideals; he reinforced this by explicitly linking his theory of crafts to his theories of justice and aesthetics: the quest for justice and the quest for beauty.[129] He may be vulnerable to charges of viewing some aspects of the common law tradition and American legal practice through rose-tinted spectacles, but only at the margins (for example, in some remarks on advocacy and negotiation) does he get so carried away with enthusiasm for skill or tactics or virtuosity that he can be said to have succumbed to "the technical prejudice." But what lover of the law is immune from such charges?

Third, insofar as Llewellyn idealizes the honest craftsman, the Grand Style judge or advocate, the beauty of the letter of credit, he is clearly in the sphere of the normative and the aspirational. At the very point at which we may be tempted to be skeptical, Llewellyn is a romantic enthusiast rather than the arch-positivist and the behavioral scientist that Horwitz depicts.[130]

This point is worth developing. If ever Llewellyn was at all attracted to positivistic social science it was when he was relatively young: he flirted with behavioral psychology for a time, but never espoused it. In one of his most thoughtful, but neglected essays he considered "legal science" to be at most a remote aspiration, while sociology and psychology were at a "pre-pre-science stage."[131] Early on he distanced himself from the empirical work of Cook and Moore, as he did later with jurimetrics and other forms of "number-crunching."[132] Max Weber was Llewellyn's main hero in social theory and interpretive sociology; especially in Llewellyn's rather free-wheeling, empathetic interpretation, this is hardly to be equated with Comteian positivism. Weber was of course concerned about rationality and objectivity, but the tensions between rational method and subjective meaning were for him the central problematic, as Stuart Hughes has elegantly shown.[133]

What of legal positivism? Llewellyn was a legal positivist of a kind, but a rather weak one. In the much-quoted statement of a positivist starting-point for Legal Realism (1931), he includes two qualifiers, one in italics: "The *temporary* divorce of Is and Ought for purposes of study."[134] His later statements of a legal positivist position are even more guarded. Llewellyn was never as unequivocal a positivist as Bentham or Holmes or Hart. But it is fair to say that he belongs to that tradition.[135]

Llewellyn's tendency to don rose-tinted spectacles was in spite of rather than because of his positivism. Here we come to the nub of the difference between Horwitz's and my interpretations. Horwitz sees Llewellyn as a young, critical radical who retreated from some of the ideas of his youth into a form of romantic conservatism and took refuge in "a new basis for belief in professional craft as the source of stability and predictability in law."[136] He associates this, strangely, with his "later advocacy of a 'temporary divorce' between the empirical and the normative,"[137] although the most famous formulation of this was in 1931, only a year after the publication of *The Bramble Bush*. Horwitz seems to suggest that Llewellyn's "austere positivism" (surely an overstatement) was in some way incompatible with "the intellectually fertile alliance between reformist social science and Realism."[138]

The three major points of difference in my alternative interpretation are: first, that the continuities in Llewellyn's thought are much greater than Horwitz suggests; second, that he was never as austerely positivistic or wedded to science as Horwitz asserts; and, third, like many other American commentators, Horwitz omits from his account both Llewellyn's concern to develop a general sociology of law as the unifying element in his thought, and the tensions between this aspect of his work and his close personal identification with the American legal profession and the common law.[139]

On the first point, it is easy to show that Llewellyn was always centrally concerned with method, technique, and technology; that he was never a committed political radical and he always had a romantic conservative streak; and that most of the ideas in *The Common Law Tradition* are anticipated in his Leipzig lectures of 1928. The arguments about positivism and science have already been dealt with. The important point is the tension between his particular and his general jurisprudence.

The sociology of the legal profession and skills training are just two examples of specialized areas in which the idea of legal technology provides a potentially illuminating perspective and a crucial link to broader social theory. I could as well have taken some other examples of contemporary interest to make similar points: constitution-making and constitution-mongering; alternative dispute resolution; the comparative study of procedural systems (as illustrated by the work of Damaska) were all possible candidates.[140] Llewellyn had suggestive things to say about such matters as recruitment and the career-development of legal personnel, specialization, the sociology of dogmatics and legal writing.[141] But his own specialized interests focused largely on more parochial concerns of American law teachers, such as appellate courts, teaching basic lawyering skills, and arguments about questions of law. Here it is probably fair to say that there was a tension between the general ideas of Llewellyn as sociologist of law and some of the specialized work of Llewellyn, the professionally oriented, American scholar-teacher of law. While the two phases of his work often fed into each other, the transition from sociologist to technologist to technician was not always easy. There is, I think, sometimes an awkward disjuncture between Llewellyn's more general ideas and some of his particular work. This point has already been made about *The Common Law Tradition*, but it might also be applied to his materials on *Elements* and to their development by Mentschikoff and Stotzky, in which the idea of "the theory and craft of American Law" gives the impression of being mainly concerned with litigation, arguments about questions of law and Llewellyn's own version of case-law skills.[142]

At one level, there should not be a sharp divide between insider and outsider perspectives. Interpretive sociology teaches that in order to understand a social practice one has to grasp the perspective of the actors: in order to describe chess one must understand the rules, moves, strategy, and tactics as the players see them; in order to understand Tiv or Barotse legal processes one must grasp the concepts of the actors (the emics) as well as the language of the external observer (the etics).[143]

Conversely, it often helps participants to have some understanding of the context in which they are operating, the role expectations, the factors that constrain and allow leeways of discretion, the economic realities of one's situation, the likely consequences of one's actions and so on. Such awareness may not always be a necessary condition for effective action, but it is often a useful part of the equipment of the reflective practitioner. A degree of empathy with actors is a necessary part of interpretive sociology, but the standpoint and role of the sociologist are different from those of the participant. The sociologist of food does not need to become a skilled cook nor vice-versa.

Llewellyn wanted to be both an observer and a participant and a trainer of participants. A capacity for empathy was one of his strengths. In a private note about *The Common Law Tradition* he wrote: "If the book is to convey its message, somebody from inside must echo Loughran: 'It reads as if you had been present at the consultations.'"[144] The concern to catch the "flavor" of the law in action is sometimes closer to that of a novelist than a social scientist. This is a far cry from the kind of positivistic scientism attributed to him by Horwitz. It is no coincidence that when addressing German audiences Llewellyn claimed to be adopting an anthropological or a sociological perspective, but even then he was giving a particularistic and evocative insider's account to a foreign audience, rather than a genuinely social scientific interpretation.[145]

Llewellyn's theory of the crafts of law was a sub-theory of his law-jobs theory. Even so, it was much broader than orthodox studies of judges and private practitioners in that it encompassed all personnel involved in operating and developing institutionalized machinery for performing the law-jobs in any group. It includes not only clerks and paraprofessionals and debt-collectors in American society, but also functionaries like the *I fugao monunkalon* and letter-writers and professional witnesses in Ghana. Even more important is the point that many law-ways are institutionalized as part of the practices of ordinary citizens or non-legal specialists, such as teachers, social workers or parents. *Au fond* the law-jobs theory is a broad, humanistic theory which, unlike most legal theories, emphasizes the continuities between legal and other phenomena rather than concentrating on what is uniquely or characteristically "legal." For example, everyone interprets rules; everyone weighs evidence; everyone is involved in negotiation; everyone applies rules to facts. Lawyers and jurists often speak as if they are the only people to do such things or as if the path to wisdom is to isolate what is unique or special about the application of such skills in legal contexts. Llewellyn's refusal to define law, his rejection of the idea of law as an autonomous discipline, the bold claim to universality of his basic theory, and his faith in horse sense are all part of a vision of law as a basic human enterprise which, in its essentials, is quite easily understood. Specialization, local knowledge, historical contingency, professional peculiarities are, of course, important, but in this context they are particular glosses on phenomena which are mostly part of "general experience".[146]

CONCLUSION

From the nineteen-twenties until his death in 1962, one of Llewellyn's main projects was the development of a general, horse-sense sociology of law. This concern to develop a coherent "Whole View" was in constant, often healthy, tension with his particularistic and practical projects. *Rechts, Rechtsleben und Gesselschaft*, several major essays and many minor ones, and in particular *The Cheyenne Way*, were published outcomes of this continuing interest in developing a general theory. Several more projects, including a book on the theory of rules, a translation of parts of Max Weber, the Pueblo study, and the project on Soviet law were left unfinished or were aborted. That he himself considered he had an unfinished agenda is quite clear from the record.

The 1950 edition of *Law in Our Society* acknowledged that this version fell short of even a semi-popular summation of his position: "The ten years which would have been needed for a proper full canvass and assessment . . . those years have gone instead into the Uniform Commercial Code."[147] Much of the next ten years were invested in *The Common Law Tradition*. One wonders whether the stimulus, detachment, and discipline of giving a series of formal lectures in Freiburg would have in fact resulted in a systematic, rounded statement that matched his ambition. Could he, in his sixties, have had the single-mindedness and energy to go beyond a restatement to further development of key ideas and new issues?[148]

We are left then with the fragments of an unfinished draft and a rather mixed bag of supplementary materials, published and unpublished, including a substantial collection of transcripts of informal lectures delivered over several years. *Law in Our Society* is almost entirely in note-form: a collection of fragments, some quite detailed and rich, some little more than headings for topics yet to be developed. Even the table of contents is sketchy and unsystematic. The emphasis and arrangement make too many concessions to an audience of American law students oriented to private practice and appellate courts for it to be satisfactory as a systematic outline of Llewellyn's most general theory.

In considering this fascinating legacy today it is important to distinguish a number of different, but related, tasks. There is first the editorial project of reconstructing from a number of sources an accurate and reasonably comprehensive compilation of Llewellyn's own words. Although incomplete and uneven, the course materials for *Law in Our Society* deserve to be treated as one of his most important works. In 1971, I decided with some regret not to undertake the challenging task of working the material up into publishable form. Unfortunately, twenty years on, the challenge remains unanswered.

The task, though difficult, is clearly worthwhile. Apart from topics touched on in this lecture—and I have not done justice to the detail—*Law in Our Society* contains Llewellyn's most developed views on Jurisprudence as a subject, on Justice, and on the heritage of Western Legal Theory, including many comments and asides on particular thinkers. It also contains a great deal of specific material that glosses his published writings. Perhaps more important, it provides a basis for interpreting his work as a whole. While falling short of a Germanic "system"— and who would want that of Karl?— *Law in Our Society* provides a general context for relating and, in some cases, reinterpreting his particular contributions. Above all, it confirms the importance of a sociological-cum-ethnographic perspective as the unifying element of all his work.

On its own, however, the text of *Law in Our Society* has some important limitations. It is incomplete. Much of it consists of initial contemplations rather than final thoughts. And it is a text geared to a specific educational context: it is difficult to sell a full-blooded sociological theory of law to a class of vocationally oriented American law students, even in Chicago. In my view, the organization and emphasis of the text reflect rather clearly an unresolved tension between a concern to develop an overarching Whole View and the gravitational pull of the immediate context and of Llewellyn's own personal identification with one rather special phase of American legal practice. One reason why Llewellyn still claims our attention is precisely because of this tension in his own work between the general and the particular, the scientific and the pragmatic, the search for understanding and the desire to be immediately useful.

Resurrecting reliable texts of the work of past thinkers is a worthy scholarly enterprise. A second task is more ambiguous. This is the job of reconstructing and constructing a coherent statement of what Llewellyn's general theory of law might have looked like had he been able to complete it to his own satisfaction. Even if true to the surviving texts, this task would involve a considerable amount of extrapolation, construction, and imaginative invention. Like any jurist worth studying, much of Llewellyn's thought is open to different interpretations, especially at points of tension. The leeways for interpreting his general sociology of law are quite wide not only because the record is incomplete, but also because he was not by temperament or practice a systematic thinker. At least one critic has taken me to task for failing to construct a coherent account of Llewellyn's "system". On my interpretation, he did not have one.[149]

The study of past jurists is not solely a matter of editing texts, intellectual history, or exegesis, still less of hagiography. Jurists also have their uses. Our heritage of juristic texts and ideas is one kind of resource that can aid the process of posing, refining and addressing questions of current concern. When we read texts for their "contemporary significance"– a dangerous, question-begging term– it is quite important to distinguish clearly, though not too sharply, between historical, exegetical, and conversational readings and what might be called polemical non-reading.[150]

A third task, then, is to move beyond our heritage of texts to develop fresh answers to questions that are of contemporary significance. One can debate with Llewellyn or any other thinker as an aid to developing one's own ideas.

At first sight, the law-jobs theory looks like a simple version of 1930s functionalism and, interpreted as such, it could easily be dismissed as outdated or even discredited.[151] I have suggested that Llewellyn's theory can be interpreted in a way which rescues it from most, if not all, of the charges that have been leveled against "extreme functionalism." I have also suggested that it still has heuristic value as a starting-point for asking basic questions about the ordering of any group and about institutionalized legal phenomena. One can readily concede that in Llewellyn's formulations rather little attention was paid to questions about power, structure, change, discourse, and meaning. It is, indeed, a rather simple and unsophisticated theory. How far it can be fruitfully developed within Llewellyn's own framework is too large a question for me to address here. Suffice to say that I would defend the view that a sound understanding of law as a social phenomenon needs to be rooted in a sound sociology and social theory and as part of such understanding, concepts such as group, order, need, norm, conflict, problem, process, institution, tradition, and even function, are as fundamental and in as much in need of elucidation as "fundamental legal conceptions" such as right, obligation, principles, sanction, state, sovereignty, and law. The vocabulary of social theory is as necessary to legal theory as the vocabulary of analytical jurisprudence and political philosophy. The tradition of sociology within which Llewellyn worked has been enriched and refined by Merton, Goffman, Giddens, Geertz, and Turner, among others. In constructing a sophisticated sociology of law as part of a general jurisprudence for an interdependent world, one would need to draw on ideas from many, quite diverse thinkers within a broad intellectual tradition. It is my contention that Llewellyn's law-jobs theory still has something of unique value to offer to that enterprise and that a large part of this is inherent in his idea of juristic method.

FOOTNOTES

1. This lecture builds on and develops themes treated in a number of earlier works by the author: *The Karl Llewellyn Papers* (1968) (hereafter KLP); *Karl Llewellyn and the Realist Movement* (1973, 1986) (hereafter KLRM); "Law and Anthropology: A Case Study in Inter-Disciplinary Collaboration," 7 *Law and Soc'y Rev.* 561 (1973) (hereafter LA); "Talk about Realism," 60 *N.Y.U. L. Rev.* 329 (1985) (hereafter TAR); "Reading Bentham" (Maccabean Lecture), 75 *Proceedings of the British Academy* (1989) 97-141 (hereafter RB); *Rethinking Evidence* (1990) (hereafter RE).

The following abbreviations are used in the footnotes for works by Llewellyn:

BB .... *The Bramble Bush*
CLSA ...... *The Case Law System in America* (*Praej.* ed. P. Gewirtz; trs. M. Ansaldi, 1989)
CLT .... *The Common Law Tradition: Deciding Appeals* (1960)
CW .... *The Cheyenne Way* (with E. Adamson Hoebel, 1941)
JRTP .... *Jurisprudence: Realism in Theory and Practice* (selected essays, 1962)
LiS .... *Law in Our Society: A Horse-sense Theory of the Institution of Law* topical syllabus. (Unpublished materials, University of Chicago Law School. 1950 edn., parts updated 1950-58)
MPL .... "My Philosophy of Law" in A. Kocourek ed., *My Philosophy of Law* (1941) 181
NLLJ .... "The Normative, the Legal and the Law-Jobs: The Problem of Juristic Method," 49 *Yale L. J.* 1355 (1940)
Praej .... *Praejudizienrecht und Rechtsprechung in Amerika* (1933)
PSLE .... "The Place of Skills in Legal Education" (Report of Committee on Curriculum), *Handbook of The Association of American Law Schools* (1944), 159; 45 *Columbia L.Rev.* 345 (1945)
RRG .... *Recht, Rechtsleben und Gesselschaft*, (M. Rehbinder, ed. 1977, based on MSS developed during two visits to Leipzig in 1928-29 and 1931-32)
UCC .... The Uniform Commercial Code

2. LiS. The materials were originally developed for a course given at Harvard Law School in 1948-49 and subsequently on a fairly regular basis at Chicago from 1951-62. Various editions and supplements survive in the Llewellyn papers in Chicago. The version used here is the set used in 1957-58 in a course taken by the author as a postgraduate student. Most of this work is still unpublished. A few extracts were printed in KLRM, appendix C. at pp 497-516. These represent about one sixth of Llewellyn's text (excluding supplementary course materials by other authors).

3. LiS at 26.

4. KLRM ch.9. N. E. H. Hull has suggested that Pound and Llewellyn were "jurisprudential bricoleurs" rather than original or systematic thinkers: "The concept of

bricolage comprises two important components: first, the idea of taking things or ideas at hand and using them in a new way or in a new context; second, the elevation of the practical over the formal . . . Pound and Llewellyn, like many other American craftsmen, used all the tools at hand—inherited European legal philosophies and American social scientific theories and methodologies—to innovate jurisprudential approaches of their own. It was thus inevitable that the new American jurisprudential voice that they adopted would inevitably resonate with a pragmatic or realistic timbre." See N. Hull, "Networks and *Bricolage*: A Prolegomenon to a History of Twentieth Century American Academic Jurisprudence" 35 *Am. J. Leg. Hist.* 307, at 321-22 (1991). There is evidence from personal papers that Llewellyn himself doubted whether he would ever complete a rounded statement of his Sociology of Law-Government to his own satisfaction. (see below n. 148)

5. See further KLP ch. 2.

6. KLP 11-12; the poem is printed in KLP at 113.

7. *University of Chicago Law School Announcements*, vol. LVII, no. 9. (1957)

8. F. Ellsworth Jr., *Law on the Midway: The Founding of the University of Chicago Law School* (1977); *Remembering the University of Chicago: Teachers, Scientists and Scholars*, Edward Shils ed. (1992). On the uses and limitations of "house histories," see A. Konefsky and J. Schlegel, "Mirror, Mirror on the Wall: Histories of American Law Schools," 95 *Harv. L. Rev.* 833 (1982).

9. For a longer answer to the question "Why Karl?" written in 1967, see KLP 18-23.

10. See KLRM 167-9 and 433, notes 37-40. For a general appreciation of Llewellyn and Hoebel's contribution to legal anthropology, see the Festschrift for Hoebel, in 7 *Law and Soc'y Rev.* (1973).

11. KLRM 140-52.

12. M. Horwitz, *The Transformation of American Law, 1870-1960* (1992) (hereafter TAL), ch. 6; cf. TR, KLRM ch. 5.

13. The distinction between Realism and realism is developed in TAR.

14. R. Kipling, "The Disciple," in *Rudyard Kipling's Verse, Inclusive Edition, 1885-1926* (1940) 774.

15. Striking examples of ignoring the law-jobs theory are Horwitz, TAL; R. Summers, *Instrumentalism and American Legal Theory* (1982). Wilfred E. Rumble, Jr., *American Legal Realism: Skepticism, Reform and the Judicial Process* (1968) focuses

almost entirely on judicial decision-making, as the sub-title suggests, and almost entirely ignores the law-jobs theory; see esp. 3-4, 145-54, and ch. 6. Theodore M. Benditt, *Law as Rule and Principle* (1978) distinguishes between Realism and Legal Sociology. It treats Llewellyn solely as a Realist and makes no reference to the law-jobs theory, despite an extended discussion of functional concepts in legal theory (see id. at 100, 112-3).

Llewellyn's sociology of law has been given rather more prominence by British and Australian writers, e.g. J. Stone, *Social Dimensions of Law and Justice* (1966); A. Hunt, *The Sociological Movement in Law* (1978); R. Cotterrell, *The Sociology of Law* (2nd ed. 1992); D. Lloyd and M. Freeman, *Introduction to Jurisprudence* (5th ed. 1985), ch. 8; H. Davies and D. Holdcroft, *Jurisprudence: Texts and Commentary* (1991), ch. 15. See also S. Verdun-Jones, "The Jurisprudence of Karl Llewellyn," 1 *Dalhousie L. J.* 441 (1974); Kenneth A. Warner "Trouble-cases and Socio-legal processes", *Am. J. Jurisprudence* 171 (1987).

Of course, apart from works specifically on legal anthropology, some American commentators have discussed the law-jobs theory: A notable example is Roscoe Pound, who generously stated: "In his paper on the problem of juristic method [Llewellyn] gives us much the best outline of a sociology of law and of the way of going about it which has appeared." II *Jurisprudence* (1959) 196. William C. Heffernan, "Two stages of Karl Llewellyn's Thought," 11 *Int'l J. Soc. L.* 134 (1983), in advancing an interpretation similar to that of Horwitz, (a sharp break between the earlier and the later thought in which emphasis on technique is a new element) treats *The Cheyenne Way* as marking the watershed in Llewellyn's intellectual development. The interpretation is unconvincing, largely for reasons stated in the text in relation to Horwitz. Heffernan ignores *Praej* and treats CW as a late work, even though the research began and the law-jobs theory was developed within three years of the publication of BB. If Llewellyn did "retreat," it was very much later, the main text being CLT (perhaps backed by accusations of a "sell-out" on the UCC).

Paul Gewirtz in his useful introduction to the translation of *Praej* by Michael Ansaldi (CLSA), emphasizes the continuity of Llewellyn's thought and his sociological perspective. I disagree, however, with his statement: "But as *The Case Law System in America* suggests, for Llewellyn realism meant, above all else, a set of beliefs about courts and their methods." This is to conflate Llewellyn's special interest in American appellate courts (of which this is one example) and his concern to be realistic about all "legal" institutions as part of a general sociology of law. For a valuable discussion of *Praej* and RRG see M. Ansaldi, "The German Llewellyn" (forthcoming, 1993).

16. The Symposium held in Leipzig 21-23 May 1993, to celebrate Llewellyn's centenary included nine papers on "Rechtssoziologische Themen," but some of these focussed largely on adjudication or the UCC. (M. Rehbinder, ed., forthcoming).

17. KLRM ch. 10, esp. 268-9.

18. Horwitz, TAL at 5, 247-50.

19. id. at 5.

20. id. at 250.

21. The most cogent evidence of continuity is *Praej* (trs. CLSA). The argument is developed in W. Twining, "Review of Ansaldi," 100 *Yale L. J.* 1093 (1991), and corroborated by Gewirtz op. cit. and by R. Cotterrell in an incisive review of the same book in 54 *Modern L. Rev.* 594 (1991).

22. E. Purcell, *The Crisis of Democratic Theory: Scientific Naturalism and the Problem of Value* (1973). Unfortunately, KLRM was published in the same year as this excellent book, which has helped greatly in explicating the political context of the time.

23. See especially TAR.

24. "Mechanisms of group control" (unpublished, started 1927, final version 1932-34?) KLP.B.II.22; the first developed statement was significantly in German: RRB, finished in 1932, but not published until 1977.

25. NLLJ, op. cit. n.1.

26. MPL.

27. E.g. LIS at 9-12.

28. Two of his general papers signal this explicitly in their titles: "Law and the Social Sciences . . . Especially Sociology." The offprint of this article contained an Introduction and was sub-titled "Being also an Effort to Integrate the 'Legal' into Sociological and Political Theory." Llewellyn was conscious that inter-disciplinary communication requires a shared vocabulary: that was one reason for adopting such terms as group, institution, function, role, dispute, process, legitimacy, ideology, power, and authority, which were commonplace, if problematic, in social science; some terms such as legal, imperative, supremacy, and normative he borrowed from contemporary jurisprudence; and some, such as law-jobs, law-ways, law stuff, and juristic method, to say nothing of some others that are best forgotten, he tried to introduce into both social science and juristic discourse—on the whole with limited success.

29. KLRM 519-21, cf. 184. It is not absolutely clear what the other five sub-disciplines were. They probably included fundamental questions about the Good , the True, and the Beautiful (legal philosophy, legal science and legal aesthetics) and the study of the relationship between means and ends (impact and engineering), but Llewellyn adopted different formulations in different contexts, see KLRM 172-84.

30. TAR at 347-51.

31. op. cit. n. 29.

32. KLRM at 482-7.

33. RRG at 32-34, discussed by Ansaldi, op. cit. n.15.

34. CLT 513, KLRM 169.

35. PSLE, discussed below.

36. KLRM 153-5, LA. These accounts are based largely on interviews with Hoebel, who published a shorter version in "Karl Llewellyn: Anthropological Jurisprude," 18 *Rutgers L. Rev.* 735 (1964).

37. Llewellyn had extensive contacts with Franz Boas and other members of the anthropology department at Columbia. Margaret Mead was a graduate student during this period but it is not known whether Llewellyn knew her personally.

38. CW at 275-6 contains a penetrating analysis of the deficiencies of "custom" as a concept.

39. For a more extended exposition see KLRM 175-84.

40. LiS 24.

41. Llewellyn's choice of "trouble" is a good example of his use of deliberately vague terms in some contexts to avoid definitional problems. "Dispute" is an example of a term that is problematic in legal anthropology and in discussions of "alternative dispute resolution" because there is a temptation to extend the term to cover such diverse phenomena as welfare claims, criminal prosecutions and clashes of interest of which one or more of the parties are not aware. The broader "trouble" can accommodate a much wider range of situations than "dispute" and it can easily be linked to the idea of "problem-solving." See further RE 353-6 and my "Alternative to What?" 56 *Modern L. Rev.* 380 (1993).

42. Llewellyn explicitly included procedures for decision as part of this law-job, but he did not himself develop ideas of procedural justice and due process very far in this context. On different conceptions of a "constitution," see below n. 140.

43. LiS 25.

44. E.g. LiS 78, NLLJ.

45. Some criticisms were advanced at the 1993 Leipzig Colloquium, the papers of which contain useful references to the German literature (op. cit. n. 16).

46. A. Hunt, op. cit. n. 15, ch. 3 (perhaps the most sustained critique of Llewellyn from a Marxist perspective).

47. R. Cotterrell, op. cit. n. 15, ch. 3. Cotterrell's first edition contains a more extended discussion.

48. J. Stone, op. cit. n.15, 646-51 and passim.

49. KLRM 180-4.

50. It is beyond the scope of this paper to consider in detail how far standard criticisms of traditional functional analysis apply to the law-jobs theory. On a charitable interpretation, Llewellyn's position can be reconciled with the account given by Robert Merton in his classic essay on "Manifest and Latent functions," *On Theoretical Sociology* (1949, 1967) ch.III. In particular Llewellyn can be exempted from the charge that some functionalists conflate "use, utility, purpose, motive, intention, aim, consequences" (id. 77); Llewellyn's "jobs" refer to group needs which can be interpreted in objective terms, i.e., without reference to human purpose, motive, or intention ("if the group is to survive, then certain needs must be met . . . somehow"). Similarly, the law-jobs theory involves no necessary commitment to the fallacies dealt with by Merton: the postulate of functional unity of society (i.e., strong integration); the postulate of universal functionalism (that all institutions, customs, etc., must have functions); and the postulate of indispensable items (that some items have indispensable functions). The law-jobs theory can probably also be interpreted as not involving ideological commitment to the status quo or to the assumption that group-survival is always desirable and disputes are always undesirable (e.g., Llewellyn explicitly recognized the social functions of conflict); but it is probably fair to say that some passages in Llewellyn tend in this direction and that he sometimes tended too readily to assume a consensus about values, and generally to be drawn more towards the consensual end of the conflict-consensus continuum of social theories (see, e.g., KLRM 219-26). I am inclined to agree with Irwin Stotzky that Llewellyn and Mentschikoff tended to have an overly optimistic vision of the role of law, especially in American society. Soia Mentschikoff and Irwin Stotzky, "Law—The Last Universal Discipline," 54 *University of Cincinnati L. Rev*. 695 (1986), 705 at n.14 (dissent by Stotzky). In my view the law-jobs theory can be separated from this personal bias of Llewellyn and Mentschikoff, but that is a theme for another occasion.

51. E.g., Robert Merton, Clifford Geertz, Anthony Giddens, and, perhaps, Victor Turner. Llewellyn was, in my interpretation, closer to Merton than to Parsons, and I suspect that he would not have been very sympathetic to the more formal "systems" approach of Luhmann and Teubner. In this connection, Charles Sampford's *The Disorder of Law* (1989) is suggestive, but he takes the more formalized theories of Parsons and Bredemeier (at 104) in his sustained attack on the "systematic" nature of law and does not explore in detail the implications of his thesis for the law-jobs theory.

52. Hoebel later admitted that they could fruitfully have submitted Cheyenne concepts and discourse to more intensive analysis (personal communication to the author; cf. KLRM 163).

53. Some copies of student papers are preserved in KLP PX, including one on law-government in a submarine entitled "The Shining Way." As a student in Llewellyn's course, I tried, not very successfully, to apply the law-jobs theory to Maeterlinck's *The Life of the Bee* (1901). This led me to conclude that the theory was not empirically falsifiable in any significant respects and contained an element of tautology (KLRM 180-81).

54. Ex rel. Soia Mentschikoff.

55. See "Alternative to What?" op. cit. n. 41. The law-jobs theory offers a framework for setting so-called "ADR" institutions in a broader perspective than standard litigation-oriented treatments by lawyers; it is also suggestive in respect of questions that might be asked about "the state of the art" from a broad technological perspective (see below).

56. KLRM 361-3.

57. KLRM 356-65, 475 n.92; H. Berman, *Justice in Russia* (2nd ed., 1963).

58. RJTP 3-6, KLRM 148-50, 177-79, 437-9.

59. LA 577-79.

60. Ward Goodenough, *Description and Comparison in Cultural Anthropology* (1970).

61. William Twining and Emma Varnden Quick eds., *Legal Records in the Commonwealth* (forthcoming, 1994).

62. Some records of governmental institutions specialized to law (e.g., ministries of justice) have been treated as administrative records for archival purposes and have not been entirely neglected, but this is less true of parastatal and private sector institutions. See op. cit. n. 61, ch. 1.

63. On Llewellyn's reasons for refusing to commit himself to a general definition of law in most contexts see KLRM 177-80.

64. T. R. Schellenberg, *Modern Archives Principles and Techniques* (1956, 1975).

65. On "total pictures" see TAR 376-78.

66. The results of the study are reported in Pino Akotia, Harry Akussah, and Victor Dankwa, *Legal Records in Accra: A Case Study* (1992); a shorter version is included in Twining and Quick eds. (1993), op. cit. n. 61.

67. Notable studies in Britain include J. Flood, *Barristers' Clerks: The Law's*

Middlemen (1983); John Morison and Philip Leith, *The Barrister's World and the Nature of Law* (1992).

68. On aesthetics and "beautiful" inventions, see KLRM 197-9, and refs at 443 at n. 112; on fictions, LiS 36ff, 5.6.3-5.6.6.

69. NLLJ 1392, which contains an excellent general formulation.

70. id.1393, CW 309. Examples of conflating "law-jobs" and "lawyer-jobs" include R. Stevens, *Law School* (1983) at 9.

71. The concept of "lawyer" is context-dependent and quite unsatisfactory as a tool for cross-cultural study. Abel and Lewis's major comparative study, *Lawyers in Society* (3 vols, 1988-89) recognized the problem (e.g., vol. II at 2-5) but never resolved it satisfactorily. Llewellyn's "theory of crafts" is suggestive in linking "the law-crafts" to a general sociology of law and identifying certain tasks that "center on eternal human needs, in all human groups: spokesmanship, decision, advice: trouble-shooting, generally, in regard to the team-work of people" (KLRM 510, LiS 18). But one task for general jurisprudence is to develop a more precise meta-language and conceptual framework for the comparative sociology of legal professions (or legal work).

72. NLLJ 1392.

73. A "skill" refers to mastery of one or more techniques and competencies in performing a task or series of tasks (an operation) to a given level of performance (i.e., skilfully). A craft refers to a congerie of skills and techniques institutionalized around the doing of certain "jobs" which typically involve more than one operation. This terminology is developed by K. Mackie in N. Gold, K. Mackie and W. Twining, eds. *Learning Lawyers' Skills* (1989) at 11. Llewellyn recognized some of the conceptual difficulties surrounding "skills" and did not rely heavily on the concept (e.g., KLRM 506-7).

74. Llewellyn sometimes subsumed "technology" under "craft," e.g., KLRM 506 line 6. I am using it here as a generic term which includes but is broader than "craft."

75. LiS, Lecture 13.

76. LiS, Lecture 14 "Theory of Dogmatics" (Sketch for perhaps a half) (LiS 1952) is the fullest statement; cf.JRTP,369-71; CLSA passim, esp. 89-95, 104-5.

77. KLRM esp 156-7, 197-9; 443n. 112-114 ; RTP 171-96 and 389-94

78. Lecture 13 of the 1953 edition of LiS is entitled "Building Materials for a Control structure: Theory of Rules." However, this is quite thin compared to the unfinished book, which survives in KLP.BII. 40; Ch. 4 on "Rule of Thumb and

Principle" is printed in full in KP at 81ff. For an attempted restatement of Llewellyn's theory of rules, see KLRM App.B

79. KLRM 200-2. Writers continue to repeat Frank's misleading distinction between "rule-skeptics" and "fact-skeptics": recent examples include Davies and Holdcroft, op. cit. n. 15. and Morison and Leith, op. cit., n. 67 at ch. 9.

80. See above, n. 78.

81. Lis, Lecture 2, reprinted in KLRM at 505-16.

82. The passage is quoted from LiS 78. Some of this is developed in transcripts of lectures. The allusion to Morris Cohen has not been traced. Llewellyn's precise relationship to Max Weber deserves closer study. Llewellyn started to translate Weber into English about 1935 and regularly acknowledged him as a major influence. However, apart from using Weberian "ideal types" and some ideas about bureaucracy and legal personnel, it is not entirely clear what specifically Llewellyn took from Weber. Llewellyn's copy of Rheinstein's edition of *Law in Economy and Society* (1977) was found in Professor Soia Mentschikoff's library and has been deposited with the Llewellyn Papers in Chicago. For about 60 pages there are quite detailed marginal comments by Llewellyn. Quite a few of these are critical: for example (Llewellyn's marginal comments, at 47, in square brackets):

"Parliament arose originally as a judicial body [Nuts] and, in France, it becomes such to the exclusion of all other activities. This confusion [KNL: Fusion first] between legislative and judicial functions was conditioned by political circumstances. The budget, which is a purely administrative matter [KNL: Crass anti-realism!], is also treated as a legislative act, in adherence to a pattern established in England as well for political reasons." Llewellyn reviewed the book: 24 *University of Chicago L. Rev.* 151 (1957) and 2 *Zeitschrift für auslandisches und internationales Privatrecht*, 720-1 (1957).

83. op. cit. n. 81 and KLRM, passim.

84. R. Merrill, "Technology" in 15 *Inter. Encyclopedia of Social Science* (1968), 576-98. There is a useful bibliographical essay in Thomas DiGregori, *A Theory of Technology* (1985), 191.

85. Useful bibliographies are to be found in R. Abel, *American Lawyers* (1989) and *The Legal Profession in England and Wales* (1988).

86. Abel, op. cit. (1988) at 3; cf. Abel (1989) at 14; cf. Lawrence Friedman, in Abel and Lewis, op. cit. n. 71, vol. III, ch.1.

87. A useful, international bibliography of the literature in English (mainly about particular skills) up to 1988 is Jeanine Watt, *The Legal Skills Sourcebook* (College of Law, St. Leonards, New South Wales, 1989).

88. On CLEPR see William Pincus, *Clinical Legal Education for Law Students* (Council on Legal Education for Professional Responsibility, 1980). On the competency debates, see for example, W. Burger, "The Special Skills of Advocacy: Are Specialized Training and Certification Essential to Our System of Justice?" 42 *Fordham L. Rev.* 227 (1973); ABA, *Report and Recommendations of the Task force on Lawyer Competency: The Role of the Law Schools* (the Cramton Report, 1979); and works cited in the extensive bibliography in the MacCrate Report, n.100, below.

89. H. Sacks ed., *Proceedings of the Asheville Conference of Law School Deans on Education for Professional Responsibility* (Council on Education in Professional Responsibility, 1965).

90. H. Lasswell and M. McDougal, "Legal Education and Public Policy: Professional Training in the Public Interest," 52 *Yale L. J.* 203 (1943).

91. *Report* of the AALS Committee on Curriculum (Chair, K. N. Llewellyn), PSLE n. 1. Interestingly, the Committee gave credit to Wigmore for pioneering the idea of making a job-analysis of lawyers' operations a basis for skills training, but considered his version too elaborate to be practical: J. Wigmore, "The Job-Analysis Method of Teaching the Use of Law Sources," 16 *Illinois L. Rev.* 499 (1922); 4 *American Law School Review* 787 (1922); cf. 30 *Harvard L. Rev.* 812 (1917).

92. id.

93. This theme is developed by Llewellyn in "The Study of Law as a Liberal Art" (1960), reprinted in JRTP ch. 17.

94. The tension between skills training (know-how) and study about (know-what and know-why) runs through contemporary treatments of narrative, rhetoric and reasoning in legal contexts. Given doubts about the validity and acceptability of "non-rational means of persuasion," few law-teachers openly claim to be directly teaching rhetorical and narrative skills. Practitioners' handbooks are only a little less inhibited. On the inevitability and potential abuses of story-telling in advocacy, see RE ch.7.

95. For accounts of some of these developments see Gold, Mackie, and Twining, op. cit., n. 73. Although the quip about the "Gold Rush" points, inter alia, to the delusion that one can get-wise-quick through short doses of skills training, Neil Gold should be exempted from any responsibility for this. He has regularly warned against expecting too much of direct teaching of skills and has pioneered important basic research into what constitutes excellence in advocacy and how it might be developed. (See below n. 101).

96. A good description and evaluation of the first year of this course is V. Johnston and J. Shapland, *Developing Legal Training for the Bar* (1990).

97. The Law Society of England and Wales, *Training Tomorrow's Solicitors* (1990), *Legal Practice Course —Written Standards* (1991), *Training Tomorrow's Solicitors — Second Report* (1992).

98. William Twining, "Legal Skills and Legal Education," 22 *The Law Teacher* 4 (1988); "Intellectual Skills at the Academic Stage: Twelve Theses," in P. Birks ed. *Examining the Law Syllabus: Beyond the Core* 93 (1993).

99. Institute of Advanced Legal Studies, London, *Legal Skills Working Papers* (1992).

100. American Bar Association, *Legal Education and Professional Development-An Educational Continuum* (MacCrate Report, 1992) at 405.

101. MacCrate, op. cit, n. 100; Lady Marre, A *Time For Change: Report of the Committee on the Future of the Legal Profession* (1988); N. Gold, numerous articles and reports for New Zealand (1986,1989), Zimbabwe (1986), England and Wales (Bar) (1987), Hong Kong (1989-92); Gold, Mackie, and Twining, op. cit. n. 73, ch. 11; J. Kilcoyne and N. Gold, "Instructional Technology: The Systematic design of Legal Education," in R. Matas and D. J. McAwley eds., *Legal Education in Canada* (1987); research project on exemplary performance of advocates for the Advocates Society Institute (Ontario), reports by A. G. Tobin and D. Rusnell, *Advocacy Training Project* (1987).

102. I. Rutter, "A Jurisprudence of Lawyers' Operations," 13 *J. of Legal Education* 301 (1961).

103. E.g. S. Nathanson, "The Role of Problem-solving in Professional Legal Education," 2 *J. of Legal Education* 167 (1989); P. Jones, "Skills Teaching in Legal Education—the Legal Practice Course and Beyond," in P. Birks ed., op. cit. n.98, at 102-4; cf. Lasswell and MacDougal, op. cit., n. 89; C. Kelso, "In Quest of a Theory of Lawyering: Some Hypotheses and a Tribute to Dean Soia Mentschikoff," 29 *University of Miami L. Rev.* 159 (1975); A. Amsterdam, "Clinical legal Education—A 21st Century Perspective," 34 *J. of Legal Education* 612 (1984).

104. E.g. MacCrate Report, op. cit. n. 100, at 203 (and passim).

105. MPL 197.

106. LiS, Lecture 13, 93-104.

107. Extensive teaching materials for both courses survive: Elements KLP M; Legal Argument KLP, N. The Elements materials provided the basis for S. Mentschikoff and I. Stotzky, *The Theory and Craft of American Law: Cases and Materials* (1981).

108. With slight variations in wording: e.g. PLSE at 162; "The Adventures of

Rollo," 3 *University of Chicago Law School Record* 23 (1952); LiS 26.

109. Examples include: F. Strong, "The Pedagogic Training of a Law Faculty," 25 *J. of Legal Education* 226 (1973); D. Cavers, "Skills and Understanding," 1 *J. of Legal Education* 396 (1949); I. Rutter, op. cit. n. 102; C. Kelso, *A Programmed Introduction to the Study of Law* (1965); T. Anderson and R. Catz, "Towards a Comprehensive Approach to Clinical Education: A Response to the New Reality," 59 *Washington U. L. Q.* 727 (1981); H. Russell Cort and Jack L. Sammons, "The Search for 'Good Lawyering': A Concept and Model of Lawyering Competencies," 29 *Cleveland State L. Rev.* 397 (1980).

110. op. cit. n. 107.

111. E.g. W. Twining and D. Miers, *How To Do Things With Rules* (3rd ed., 1991); T. Anderson and W. Twining, *Analysis of Evidence* (1991).

112. V. Johnson and J. Shapland, op. cit., n. 96; N. Gold, op. cit. n. 101; and the Legal Skills Research Group, op. cit. n. 99.

113. MPL 197.

114. e.g., F. Zemans and V. Rosenblum, *The Making of a Public Profession* (1981); B. Garth, D. Landon, and J. Martin, ABF Surveys (preliminary findings summarized in the MacCrate report, Appendix B, 379-84).

115. op. cit. n. 96.

116. op. cit. n. 97.

117. Statements about the course indicate that it aims to prepare students to perform adequately in work they might do in their second six months of pupillage and for this reason "the course aims to be extremely general, aiming at more or less the lowest common denominator for the practising bar." (Council of Legal Education, *The New Vocational Course, Introductory Paper* (1988). Johnston and Shapland, op. cit., interpret the objective somewhat more broadly to cover "most of the work a junior barrister might expect to obtain in the first few years after call" (at 2).

118. This theme is explored in W. Twining, "Developments in Legal Education in the Commonwealth: Beyond the Primary School Model," 2 *Legal Education Review* 35 (1990).

119. JRTP 377.

120. TAR 366.

121. T. Hayakawa, "Karl N. Llewellyn as a Lawman from Japan Sees Him," 18 *Rutgers L. Rev.* 717 (1964).

122. BB 126.

123. KLRM 117-23.

124. KLRM 197.

125. LiS, quoted KLRM 505.

126. Materials for the Course on Legal Argument (1957 edn.), passim (copy in possession of the author). Several annotated versions survive in the Llewellyn papers..

127. J. Bentham, 1 *Rationale of Judicial Evidence* (J. S. Mill, ed. 1827) at 10-11.

128. LiS, quoted KLRM 506.

129. See the table of contents for LiS, KLRM 497-8.

130. TAL, especially, 5, 210-11, and ch. 6.

131. LiS 8-10 (printed KLRM 501-3). Llewellyn's most important discussion of "science" is "Theory of Legal 'Science' " (a review of Huntington Cairns, *Law and the Social Sciences*), 20 *North Carolina L. Rev.* 1 (1920); see generally, KLRM, 53-5, 188-196, 452n.

132. KLRM 53-5, 103-4.

133. Stuart Hughes, *Consciousness and Society* (1959), ch. 8 and 430-31; cf. RE, 127.

134. e.g., JRTP 55.

135. LiS is a rich source for a reappraisal of Llewellyn's later relationship to positivism.

136. TAL 250.

137. id. 248.

138. id. 5.

139. Horwitz gives a perceptive account of some of the tensions and polarities in Llewellyn, as man and thinker (TAL 185-7). These, of course, open the way to multiple interpretations. On my interpretation, Horwitz, by ignoring the law-jobs theory, downplays the tension between Llewellyn's particular commitments and his continuing concern to develop a "Whole view."

140. On constitutions, see William Twining, "Constitutions, Constitution-making and Constitution-mongering," in Irwin Stotzky ed., *Transition to Democracy in Latin America: The Role of the Judiciary* (1993); on alternative dispute resolution, see n. 41 above. On procedural design, see M. Damaska, *The Faces of Justice and State Authority* (1986).

141. See especially LiS and NLLJ. Few of these ideas are developed very far.

142. The Elements materials, like *The Bramble Bush*, need to be read in the specific context of courses that purport to be building-blocks for particular degree programs that continue to emphasize litigation and appellate cases. It has been my experience in teaching "Elements" at the University of Miami that the gravitational pull of the context greatly inhibits radical broadening of the concept of "legal method," which here means the perspectives, methods, and techniques of *law students* in *this* program. Any deviation from the traditional materials of law study tends to strengthen student resistance to the direct study of theory and method. That said, Llewellyn, Mentschikoff, and their followers are vulnerable to charges that this is a sell-out to a tradition that is difficult to reconcile with the broad perspective of the law-jobs theory. For a fairly cautious attempt to break out, see William Twining, "Reading Law," 24 Valparaiso *L. Rev.* 1 (1989).

143. Above n. 60.

144. MS, quoted KLRM 456-7.

145. Gewirtz, op. cit. n. 1, Editor's Introduction to CLSA. At the Leipzig Colloquium, Lawrence Friedman argued that neither CLSA nor *The Common Law Tradition* could be claimed as truly sociological studies of judicial decision-making; I agree, cf. KLRM ch. 10.

146. Lis 8-11.

147. Lis 9.

148. A recently discovered private manuscript fragment, addressed to himself and almost certainly written shortly before he died, suggests that Llewellyn had some severe self-doubts as to whether he still had "the gumption" for "the hard labor of squeezing a Big Job into clean form." It ends: "I know I'm fading. . . . I know also that—thank God—it is I who uncorked more than any other man except Langdell in American legal education".

149. E.g. Manfred Weiss, review of KLRM in 174 *Archiv für die civilistische Praxis* 90 (1974).

150. RB 116 ff.

151. See above, n. 50.

[7]
Reading Bentham

WHEN I was honoured with an invitation to deliver the Maccabean Lecture, it was suggested that it should be on a Benthamite theme. Conscious of the maxim that few Benthamists are Benthamites I offered a Benthamic title. That offer was accepted. I was also conscious that I would be here as a representative of the Bentham Committee which has had a close relationship with the British Academy since the early days of the Bentham Project. In choosing a topic to suit the occasion I decided that it would not be appropriate to render an account of the Project to our most important sponsors. That is best left to annual reports. However, this is an opportunity to make a public acknowledgement of our indebtedness to the Academy for its continuous and vital support for one of the most ambitious enterprises of its kind in the world. Not only has the annual grant provided essential core funding, but through the rigour of its enquiries, the wisdom of its advice and the prestige of its imprimatur, the Academy greatly enhances our capacity to raise funds from other sources, both public and private, in this country and abroad. The Bentham Project still lives a precarious existence in a climate that is unfriendly to long-term research, but we are now more stable, more efficient and more productive than at any stage in our history. There have been times when the whole enterprise was at risk; but we now have the experience, the infrastructure and the momentum for there to be a realistic prospect of completion within a reasonable time; perhaps, with increased support, even by the year 2000. All that is lacking is the funding needed to complete the task. When that happy release comes, the Academy

[1] I am grateful to James Burns, Cyprian Blamires, Stephen Conway, John Dinwiddy, Patrick Gudridge, Stephen Guest, Paul Kelly, Fred Rosen, Philip Schofield and Alex Stein for comments and suggestions. All errors and opinions are my responsibility.

will rightly be able to claim a great deal of the credit for its contribution to an unfashionable, but important, endeavour and for keeping the values of fundamental scholarship alive. Thank you.

An obvious topic for such an occasion would be a general re-assessment of Bentham's contemporary significance or a critical stock-taking of the state of Bentham scholarship. Two former chairmen of the Bentham Committee, Professor Herbert Hart in 1962[2] and Lord Robbins in 1964,[3] delivered important lectures of this kind. They are still read today. Since Professor Hart's 'Master-mind' lecture there have been very significant developments in both primary and secondary Bentham studies. Sixteen volumes of the *Collected Works* have been published, two are in the press, and at least ten more are at various stages of preparation. There have also been over twenty specialized monographs devoted wholly or mainly to Bentham and, of course, a mass of shorter writings. There is now an established Bentham 'industry' with a postgraduate course on his legal and political thought, a regular Bentham seminar, research students, and an International Bentham Society. Perhaps the progress of Bentham studies since the lectures by Hart and Robbins can be symbolized by the fact that this year the annual *Bentham Newsletter,* launched in 1978, has been replaced by a biennial journal published by Oxford University Press entitled *Utilitas, A Journal of Utilitarian Studies.* This, one hopes, marks the advent of a new phase in which Bentham scholarship will be more fully integrated into broader intellectual currents.

These extensive developments in Bentham studies include their share of revisionism, criticism and debunking. There is plenty to take stock of. However, I have decided not to attempt this today for two main reasons. First, there have been several such stock-takings recently;[4] there have also been some useful surveys of

[2] H. L. A. Hart, 'Bentham', Lecture on a Master Mind, *Proceedings of the British Academy,* **48** (1962), 297.

[3] Lord Robbins, 'Bentham in the Twentieth Century', Address to the Assembly of Faculties, University College, London, 1964 (Athlone Press, 1965).

[4] E.g. Stephen Conway, 'The Bentham Project and Bentham Studies', unpublished paper, delivered Moscow, April, 1988; Fred Rosen, 'Jeremy Bentham: Recent Interpretations', *Political Studies,* **30** (1982), 575; 'Elie Halevy and Bentham's Authoritarian Liberalism', *Enlightenment and Dissent,* **6** (1987), 59; Michael Freeman, 'Jeremy Bentham: contemporary interpretations', in R. Faucci (ed.), *Gli Italiani E Bentham, Economia Del Benessere,* **7** (Milan, 1982), 19; L. J. Hume, 'Revisionism in Bentham Studies', *The Bentham Newsletter,* **1** (1978), 3; David Lieberman, 'From Bentham to Benthamism', *Hist. Jo.* **28** (1985), 199.

recent literature; I gave my personal answer to the question 'Why Bentham?' as part of the Shearman Lectures in 1983.[5] Furthermore, John Dinwiddy's recent monograph in the *Past Masters* series gives a splendid summary and assessment of current understandings of Bentham.[6] Dr Dinwiddy is both a more learned Benthamist and a more committed Benthamite than I am, but I have no reason to dissent from his succint and cogent answer to the question: why the *Collected Works*? His statement is worth repeating for non-specialists:

> The case for producing a new edition of Bentham's works rests partly on the importance of his thought, and partly on the inadequate and incomplete fashion in which his works were previously published. His writings are remarkable for their range, originality and influence. He was one of the greatest reformers, perhaps the greatest, in the history of English law. He was a legal philosopher of major importance, being one of the founders of the theory of legal positivism. In ethics he provided the classic exposition of the utilitarian theory which has been a major strand in moral philosophy since the eighteenth century. In political thought he was important both as a critic of established doctrines such as that of natural law, and as the originator of one of the main theoretical justifications for democracy. In the fields of public administration and social policy, he arguably had more influence than any other thinker on the process of administrative and social reform in Victorian Britain. In economic thought, his ideas about the measurement and utility lie at the root of modern theories of cost-benefit analysis and welfare economics. He has been recognized, too, as a pioneer in other fields ranging from international law and the birth control movement to motivational psychology and deontioc logic. He has been described by C. K. Ogden as 'the greatest social engineer in history', and by A. J. P. Taylor as 'the most formidable reasoner who ever applied his gifts to the practical questions of administration and politics'.[7]

Another reason for not attempting a magisterial appraisal of the state of Bentham scholarship today involves invoking what Bentham fallaciously treated as a general fallacy; the Procrastinator's Argument.[8] Bentham scholarship is approaching a point when it will be open to some significant new directions. But a substantial number of the manuscripts are still undeciphered and inaccessible. These include some of the most important writings

[5] William Twining, 'Why Bentham?', *The Bentham Newsletter*, **8** (1984), 34.

[6] J. Dinwiddy, *Bentham* (Past Masters, Oxford, 1989).

[7] Bentham Executive Committee, 'The Bentham Project: Past, Present and Future', University College, London (unpublished, 1983).

[8] J. Bentham, *The Book of Fallacies, Works,* Vol. 2, p. 432.

on logic and language, religion, economics, politics, law, sex and war. Any of these may contain important clues to unravelling some of the arcana of his thought and the apparent ambiguities of his character. It is significant that all of the leading Bentham scholars of the present generation have drawn back from attempting a full-scale biography or intellectual biography, several of them, like myself, claiming that the time is not yet ripe for a general appraisal. This seems to me to be a valid reason which will no longer apply when the *Collected Works* are complete or nearly complete and reliable texts of all Bentham's writings are available.

Another possibility was to take a theme related to the sponsorship of this lecture. This lecture series was endowed by the Maccabeans, a society of Jewish professional men with a particular interest in law, to mark the tercentenary of the Jewish settlement in England under Cromwell. There is here an important Bentham connection. My own College, the so-called 'Godless institution of Gower Street', was the first university institution in this country to admit non-Anglicans to its courses.[9] Jeremy Bentham was a spiritual rather than a material founder of University College. This crucial first step towards the secularization of higher education was based not on overt materialism, but rather on the principle of religious toleration. It is a strange form of godlessness for an institution to open its doors to Roman Catholics, Quakers, other dissenters, Hindus, Muslims, Jews and, eventually, to women. The Jewish connection with Bentham's College has been a strong one since its foundation and remains so today. Bentham may or may not have been a materialist in a strong sense ... that is one aspect of the fascinating theme of Benthamic ambiguity ... but he was a staunch and unequivocal supporter of religious toleration.

Bentham's concern for the oppressed ... women, homosexuals and animals as well as religious and ethnic minorities ... has been the subject of a valuable study by Lea Campos Boralevi.[10] This topic provides one ground for treating him as a modern thinker. Such claims to 'modernity' will be one of the themes of this lecture, but I propose to consider them from a somewhat different perspective.[11]

[9] N. Harte & J. North, *The World of University College 1828–1978* (1978), pp. 10–15.

[10] Lea Campos Boralevi, *Bentham and The Oppressed*, European University Institute (1984).

[11] E.g. the 'astonishing topicality' of Bentham's jurisprudence is a central theme of P. Gerard *et al.*, *Actualité de la pensee juridique de Jeremy Bentham* (Brussels, 1987).

In telling you what I am not going to talk about, I have, of course, sketched a context for my theme. Proceeding on the optimistic assumption that we are at least within sight of achieving a complete and definitive version of his *Collected Works,* I propose to explore some possible ways forward in Bentham studies during its next phase. One of the main functions of Bentham scholarship is rightly to make his thought more accessible through accurate exposition as well as through the production of reliable texts. In looking beyond this, I shall first consider some different ways of approaching Bentham, and indeed any important thinker, in the light of some recent developments in the history of ideas and in theories of interpretation. In the final section, I shall advance some particular reasons for the view that the time is ripe for Bentham to be restored to his rightful place as the Father of Modern English Jurisprudence.

On Reading Bentham

Bacon wrote:

> 'Some books are to be tasted, others to be swallowed, and some few to be chewed and digested: that is some books are to be read only in parts; others to be read, but not curiously; and some few to be read wholly and with diligence and attention. Some books also may be read by deputy, and extracts made of them by others; but that would be only in the less important arguments and the meaner sort of books; else distilled books are like common distilled waters, flashy things'.[12]

As one contemplates the prospect of seventy or so substantial volumes in *The Collected Works,* it is natural to wonder how Bacon's wisdom applies to reading Bentham. Most of you will have spotted the not-so-light irony in my title. For, on most interpretations of 'reading', Bentham is thought to be unreadable. The difficulty of deciphering his script; the deficiencies of the Bowring edition; the convolutions of the prose, especially in the later works; and the relentless concern for detail have all been sources of frequent complaint. The splendid volumes of *The Collected Works* do elegantly furnish a room ... as in the Fellows Library of this institution ... but one may ask: what other uses might they have? Many quote with approval the famous statement by Sydney Smith that '(n)either gods, men nor booksellers can doubt the

[12] Francis Bacon, 'Of Studies'.

necessity of a middleman between Mr Bentham and his public... The great mass of readers will rather choose to become acquainted with Mr Bentham through the medium of the reviews ... after the eminent philosopher has been washed, trimmed, shaved and forced into clean linen'.[13]

Strangely, this was written of one of Bentham's most enjoyable texts, *The Book of Fallacies.* Sydney Smith was writing about the general reader. Several commentators have tried with varying degrees of conviction to point to the witty aphorisms and pungent phrases that adorn many of his works, although as Professor Hart admits, they are like daisies among the thorns.[14] In teaching about Bentham, especially at postgraduate level, my impression is that students find him less obscure and no more tedious than most other jurists and philosophers. There are, however, two main obstacles to getting to grips with Bentham texts for the first time. First, it is helpful to distinguish between his 'popular' and his 'arcane' writings.[15] The 'popular' are generally more lucid, but the 'arcane' tend to be more precise and more profound. Thus most students are familiar with his treatment of utility and some of his other basic ideas through *A Fragment on Government* and *An Introduction of The Principles of Morals and Legislation,* two early relatively 'popular' works. One finds much more subtle and thorough treatments of the same topics in the *Deontology,* the *Constitutional Code* and other less inviting writings, some of which have now appeared in *The Collected Works.*[16]

Another obstacle is the sheer vastness of the terrain to be covered. In my own special area of interest, Evidence, the *Rationale of Judicial Evidence* filled 3000 admittedly small pages in the John Stuart Mill edition;[17] this represents less than a half of his extant writings, published and unpublished, on this subject alone. In order to grasp many of his ideas on particular topics and concepts one has to turn to cognate writings of similar extent.

[13] Sydney Smith, 'Bentham's Book of Fallacies' (review) *Edinburgh Review,* **42** (1825), 367.

[14] H. L. A. Hart, *Essays on Bentham* (Oxford 1982), p. 126.

[15] Mary Mack, *Jeremy Bentham: An Odyssey of Ideas 1748–1792* (London, 1962).

[16] A. Goldworth (ed.), *Deontology, together with A Table of the Springs of Action and Article on Utilitarianism* (Oxford, 1983); F. Rosen & J. H. Burns (eds), *Constitutional Code* (Oxford, 1983), Vol. 1; P. Schofield (ed.), *First Principles Preparatory to The Constitutional Code* (Oxford, 1989), all in the *Collected Works* (hereafter CW).

[17] J. Bentham, *A Rationale of Judicial Evidence,* ed. J. S. Mill, 5 vols (London) (reprinted *Works,* Vols 6 and 7).

In respect of this basic kind of reading, with due respect to Bacon, I belong to the clean linen school. In order to get to grips with Bentham's general ideas or his treatment of a particular topic one is often well-advised to start with one or more middlemen, when they are available. In his lifetime he was singularly well-served, especially by Dumont, whose *rédactions* so elegantly captured the best of Bentham's style and substance that several were translated into English. Some, such as Dumont's *Treatise on Judicial Evidence* remain to this day the best starting-point for becoming acquainted with Bentham's ideas on a given subject.[18] They do, however, contain pitfalls for the unwary, because Dumont and others not only simplified but also sometimes censored some of the less tactful or acceptable sentiments to be found in the original. Dumont's Bentham, and even more so Bowring's, is too well scrubbed to be reliable for scholarly purposes.

Here, however, let me put in a word in defence of the Bowring edition. It is standard for Benthamists to disparage both the work and the man. And, indeed, there is much to criticize: the small print; the inaccuracies; the omission or bowdlerization of passages or even whole works which might have offended Victorian attitudes in respect of sex, politics or religion.[19] All of these help to provide a justification for a more scholarly and comprehensive edition of the works. Bowring's personal failings are also well-known, although he is now recognized as a figure of sufficient consequence to have been the subject of a recent colloqium. Yet as Bentham's literary executor Bowring succeeded in organizing the publication of the eleven volume edition within twelve years of Bentham's death. For over 150 years this has been by far the most extensive and accessible source of Bentham's writings and in many respects remains so today. One of the most useful features is the analytical index in the eleventh volume. This was the work of John Hill Burton. It fills almost 400 pages and is an indispensable tool for both specialists and non-specialists. There is one good reason why this is especially valuable in respect of Bentham.

[18] The full title of the original was *Traité des Preuves Judiciaries*, ouvrage extrait des Manuscrits de M. Jeremie Bentham, Jurisconsulte Anglais, Par Et. Dumont, 2 vols (Paris, 1823). The translation appeared as *A Treatise on Judicial Evidence*, extracted from the manuscripts of Jeremy Bentham, Esq. by M. Dumont. Translated into English, 1 vol. (London 1825). The translator has not yet been identified.

[19] E.g. Mack, op. cit. n. 15, at p. 21. Some of the omissions were due to financial constraints rather than censorship.

On the one hand, the range of topics on which he wrote is truly extraordinary; on the other hand, the general framework of his thought is remarkably coherent and consistent. So it is relatively easy for the non-specialist to locate Bentham's treatment of even the most specific topic within the general framework of his ideas, the key ingredients of which are his version of utility, the theory of fictions and the pannomion. The Bowring edition is still the nearest approximation we have to a Bentham Encyclopedia. An extension and revision of the Analytical Index to cover all the published and unpublished writings should, in my view, be one of the highest priorities in the next phase of Bentham studies.

Getting acquainted with Bentham's general ideas and particular texts and using the Bowring edition as a work of reference are, of course, only first steps for the student of Bentham. To proceed to the next stage it may be helpful to bear in mind some recent trends in neighbouring disciplines, especially in literary theory and the history of ideas.

Excursus: On Reading and Interpretation in General

Four types of reading

Literary theory is currently in fashion in jurisprudence. James Boyd White has elegantly explored the apparently paradoxical idea of 'the legal imagination' in literary terms;[20] Ronald Dworkin and others have debated analogies between interpretation of legal and literary texts;[21] deconstruction and related French ideas are à la mode in the otherwise extraordinarily insular form of critical legal studies that has established some bases in the United States; and there is, in that country, even said to be a nascent 'Law and Literature Movement', which may be rather more than an inflated way of signalling that some academic lawyers are experimenting with using *Billy Budd,* or *The Trial* or *Crime and Punishment* in their teaching.[22]

[20] J. B. White, *The Legal Imagination* (Boston, 1973); *When Words Lose Their Meaning* (Chicago, 1984); *Heracles' Bow: Essays on the Rhetoric and Poetics of the Law* (Madison, 1985).

[21] E.g. R. Dworkin, *A Matter of Principle* (London, 1985); *Law's Empire* (London, 1986); Stanley Fish, *Doing What Comes Naturally* (Durham, N. Carolina, 1989); David Miers, 'Legal Theory and the Interpretation of Statutes', in William Twining (ed.), *Legal Theory and Common Law* (Oxford, 1986), Chap. 7.

[22] These developments are surveyed in Elizabeth V. Gemmette, 'Law and Literature: An Unnecessarily Suspect Class in the Liberal Arts Component of the Law School Curriculum', *Valparaiso L. Rev.*, **23** (1989), 267..

To the outsider, literary theories seem to fall into three main groups: those that emphasize the text; those that focus on context, whether that be the author's concerns and 'intentions' or the broader historical setting; and those that focus on the reader's experience of reading, reacting to and constructing interpretations of texts. Current modes of reading Bentham, and juristic texts generally, seem (on the surface) to follow a similar pattern: close textual reading; historical or contextual reading; and reading or conversing with the text in relation to present-day issues. In jurisprudence another mode of discourse about texts has been especially prominent: this is the discussion of particular jurists, or so-called schools or isms, without reference to any texts at all: what might be called 'Non-reading'.[23]

A similar, but not identical pattern, is to be found in recent developments in the history of ideas.[24] These are more directly relevant to my present purpose. The central issue in the debates about law and literature is to what extent interpretation of statutes, law reports and other *authoritative* texts is analogous to interpreting novels, poems and other literary artefacts. Intellectual historians, on the other hand, have been concerned mainly with questions about interpreting and using texts by philosophers

[23] It has been suggested to me by Stephen Guest that one cannot draw a sharp distinction between text and context 'because words take much of their meaning from "context"' and 'text' and 'context' are too vague to do much work on their own. I do not disagree. However, I am using 'context' here to refer to matters external to a given written text that may be relevant to answering questions about the text. Such questions could relate to biographical or linguistic or other historical information or to other texts by the same or different authors. Such information could provide extrinsic aids to interpreting the text or illuminate the text in other ways. Some of this information might be gleaned directly or by inference from the text itself, but a great deal of it may not. For present purposes it is sufficient to use 'textual' reading to refer to approaches that concentrate mainly or entirely (so far as that is possible) on single texts as historical products (asking certain kinds of questions *of* the text), whereas contextual reading draws on a wider range of sources (asking questions *about* the text). My terms ('textual', 'contextual', 'conversational') are intended to suggest no more than a rough typology of general strategies for approaching texts (whereas 'non-reading' is freed from the anchorage of particular texts). The terms are inadequate for giving detailed accounts of the extraordinarily complex processes of reading and interpreting particular texts. The difference between the strategies is mainly one of emphasis ... of course, nearly all particular reading is multi-layered and no reading is innocent.

[24] See, for example, R. Rorty, J. B. Schneewind & Q. Skinner (eds), *Philosophy in History* (Cambridge, 1984); James Tully (ed.), *Meaning and Context: Quentin Skinner and his Critics* (Oxford, 1988).

and political theorists, that is to say the kind of texts that Bentham wrote. These debates have barely touched directly on juristic texts as such, but they are hardly different in kind. The central issues concern methods of interpretation without the complicating factor of questions about the validity of analogies between different species of text. There tends to be more at stake politically between rival theories of interpretation of authoritative texts. One can usefully differentiate interpretations which emphasize text, context, conversation and not reading, provided that the distinctions are not drawn too sharply. Against this background let us look briefly at each perspective with reference to some recent writings about Bentham.

Textual reading

It is probably fair to say that in philosophy and political theory the predominant tradition of scholarship emphasized close textual reading of text that belonged to some conventionally prescribed canon of classic works. When exegesis and interpretation spilled over into 'criticism' this was often ahistorical so that it has not always been easy to differentiate criticism that might have been made by an author's contemporaries or on his own terms, such as charges of inconsistency, inaccuracy, ambiguity or fallacious reasoning; criticisms which invoke the wisdom of hindsight of the 'we know better now' variety; and more crudely anachronistic criticisms in which the essence of the charge is that the critic is arguing that the text provides defective answers to 'today's problems', which may or may not have been questions that the original author had addressed or even considered. Of course, all criticism of past thinkers is anachronistic in a weak sense, in that the concerns, vantage points, perspectives and values involved are those of the critic.[25] However, just as historians need to discriminate between different kinds of evaluations and assessments of past events and actions, so do those who talk about ideas need to distinguish between different kinds of criticism.

One of the outstanding examples of recent Bentham scholarship

[25] Cf. Skinner in Tully, op. cit. n. 24, at pp. 286–8. Skinner acknowledges that one role of intellectual history is to provide 'an additional means of reflecting on what we believe ... [However], it is only by refusing the vulgar demand for relevance that we can hope to indicate the serious way in which the study of intellectual history is indeed relevant to the assessment of our present beliefs' (ibid.).

is Gerald Postema's *Bentham and The Common Law Tradition.*[26] While it does not neglect context, it is primarily based on a close reading of the original texts. An important aspect of this excellent work is the thesis that Bentham had a direct utilitarian (in modern parlance act-utilitarian) theory of adjudication according to which judges are not strictly bound by positive law, but should apply the principle of utility to every case.[27] Because the main function of codified law is to provide a basis for settled expectations and 'to define and maintain a framework for social interaction', in nearly every case the strict application of law would promote utility.[28] But, when in a particular case, taking into account all the circumstances, utility requires a departure from the law, the judge should follow utility. This thesis challenges the orthodox view that Bentham, the arch-codifier and opponent of judge-made law, advocated that the role of the judge in respect of substantive law should be to apply codified substantive law strictly and to refer any perceived defects in enacted law for determination by the legislator.[29] His interpretation leads Postema to conclude that there is a deep conflict between Bentham's theory of law and his theory of adjudication.[30]

Postema's interpretation has been challenged on textual grounds and is likely to be the subject of protracted controversy among specialists. It is not possible to pursue the textual niceties here. My own view is that, if Postema's interpretation is correct, far from pointing to a fundamental incoherence in Bentham's thought it helps to reconcile his treatment of substantive and adjective law and his general commitment to direct or act-utilitarianism. Indeed this is a very clear statement of what kind of theory of adjudication is entailed by act-utilitarianism. However, Postema's interpretation is difficult to reconcile with all the texts.[31]

[26] Gerald J. Postema, *Bentham and the Common Law Tradition* (Oxford, 1986).

[27] Ibid., esp. Chap. 12.

[28] Ibid., p. 448.

[29] For details, see the discussion of Postema's book by John Dinwiddy in 'Adjudication under Bentham's Pannomion', *Utilitas,* I (1989), 283.

[30] Op. cit., at p. 453.

[31] E.g. Dinwiddy, op. cit. n. 29; Dr Paul Kelly, in a recent review of *Bentham and the Common Law Tradition* (History of Political Thought, 1989, pp. 366–70) takes issue with Postema on two grounds; first he challenges Postema's view that Bentham was a consistent act-utilitarian. Rather, he argues that Bentham was committed to some indirect utilitarian strategies, especially in respect of codification, and the evidence for this is largely the same material that Postema uses in Chapter 5 as evidence of Bentham's commitment to 'security of

expectation as the object and principal consequence of a legal system' (ibid., p. 369). Secondly, Kelly suggests that Postema's argument for the thesis that Bentham intended to allow scope for direct utilitarian reasoning by judges is based almost entirely on the adjective law writings in which Bentham advances a strong anti-nomian thesis. Kelly suggests that Postema fails to establish that Bentham was anti-nomian in respect of substantive law. In short, Kelly implies that Bentham adopted different models of reasoning for questions of fact and questions of law: the purpose of the former is to ascertain the truth, the purpose of the latter is a correct interpretation of positive law, i.e. to implement the will of the legislator. However, Kelly agrees that if Postema's premises are accepted, then Postema is right in arguing that Bentham's position is incoherent, for judicial decisions will inevitably become a basis for expectations, even if they are not intended by the judges to serve as precedents or to make law.

I differ with Postema and Kelly on the inevitability of decisions on questions of law being treated as precedents, for these reasons: first, in designing a system it is open to the legislator to declare that decisions on questions of law, no more than on questions of fact, should have no authority beyond the particular case. Secondly, a direct-utilitarian model of reasoning on questions of law is more closely analagous to judicial reasoning on questions of fact than Kelly suggests. In both great emphasis is laid on the specific circumstances of the particular case. The main basis for Bentham's anti-nomian thesis was his view that the best judgments on questions of fact are case-specific and beyond formal regulation by rigid rules; this is also the basis for a direct utilitarian approach to judgments of value. Thirdly, specific decisions by officials on questions of fact can provide some basis for predictions concerning future decisions without thereby becoming authoritative precedents. The same applies to decisions on questions of law and decisions by officials on other questions. For the knowledge that an official will decide consistently in a direct-utilitarian way in all cases, on a given version of utility, can itself be an aid to prediction and hence a basis for expectations. One might add that modern jurists recognize that the lawyers' distinction between questions of fact and questions of law is artificially sharp and that many 'questions of fact involve judgements of value' (e.g. Adrian Zuckerman, 'Law, Fact or Justice?', *Boston U.L. Rev.*, **66** [1986], p. 487), although Bentham did seem to draw a quite sharp line between adjective and substantive law.

I agree with Kelly that the textual evidence for Postema's interpretation is tenuous; I also agree that Bentham adopted some indirect utilitarian strategies in relation to codification, but disagree that this is incompatible with the kind of residual direct/act-utilitarianism that Postema identifies: generally we will follow the code, but all things considered, including long-term consequences, the right action is the one that furthers utility in the circumstances of the particular case. On this view the distinction between direct and indirect utilitarianism collapses in favour of direct utilitarianism. I differ from both Postema and Kelly on their view that an act-utilitarian theory of judicial reasoning is incompatible with giving a very high priority indeed to settled expectations in respect of law. However, 'the non-disappointment principle', in Bentham's thought while commanding a high priority is ultimately a principle subordinate to utility.

In the present context, the interesting question is methodological: what counts as the best interpretation of Bentham? Postema explicitly differentiates between contextual, historical and philosophical perspectives on Bentham and makes it clear that this work is primarily historical, but is conceived of as part of a wider enterprise that is philosophical and critical.[32] These differentiations correspond almost exactly to the distinctions between textual, contextual and conversational readings as they are used here. On my reading of Postema's interpretation, at the very least it tells us what Bentham should have said if his treatment of substantive and adjective law, his theory of adjudication and his act-utilitarianism were all coherent. In so far as there are some texts which seem not to fit Postema's account of Bentham's theory of adjudication, these might be accounted for on one or more grounds for example: (a) that Bentham changed his mind over time; (b) that Bentham contradicted himself or made statements with inconsistent implications; (c) that some texts deal with special situations or exceptions; (d) the seemingly deviant texts are open to alternative, less obvious interpretations; or (e) that the issues raised by the commentator were not central to the author's original concerns.[33]

Without claiming to have made an exhaustive study of all relevant passages, my view is that Postema's interpretation of Bentham's theory of adjudication is difficult to reconcile with at least some texts, but that is hardly surprising given that they were written in different contexts over a long period of time in response to varied, often quite specific, concerns. In short, Bentham was not entirely consistent and Postema's interpretation, while scrupulously honest to the texts (his phrase), goes beyond what Bentham said to construct or reconstruct a more coherent general theory than Bentham in fact articulated. Postema acknowledges as much in the Preface.[34] In this Postema, while being careful to try to avoid anachronism, was aided by consideration of recent debates about act- and rule-utilitarianism and the nature of judicial reasoning. Bentham did not use the term 'theory of adjudication' and constructing one from his texts, however scrupulously, reflects modern American juristic concerns more than Bentham's own.

Where Postema and I differ is that he concludes that he

[32] Preface.
[33] Cf. Skinner in Tully, op. cit. n. 24, at pp. 244–6.
[34] Preface.

has revealed a fundamental conflict within Bentham's thought, whereas I believe that he has achieved the Dworkinian result of making the text 'the best it can be'[35] (at least in respect of internal coherence) even if this involves rather liberal interpretation of some passages.

The immediate relevance of all this is that even the most scrupulous textual interpreter may be drawn into constructing interpretations in the light of subsequent debates. This illustrates how easy it is to move almost imperceptibly from historical to conversational readings.[36]

In recent years structuralists, post-structuralists, deconstructionists, semioticians and even narratologists have invaded jurisprudence. They have not yet made significant incursions into Bentham studies. We have an ambitious attempt at deconstruction of Blackstone's *Commentaries,* but so far nothing comparable on *Of Laws In General* or *The Constitutional Code.*[37] No doubt this will happen in due course. Whatever one thinks of the quality and value of recent attempts to apply the methods of Derrida or Barthes or Ricoueur or Greimas or Lacan to legal texts and ideas, such exercises serve to remind us of the almost infinite possibilities of interpretation and re-interpretation of any past thinker of substance, especially when one acknowledges or assigns a major role to the reader or commentator in constructing the text.

There is one general reason why Bentham is particularly susceptible to varying interpretations and re-interpretations. At one level he is a remarkably straightforward thinker who gives clear and precise answers to sharply posed questions. Some of the answers seem as shocking as they are unequivocal. Are there any non-legal rights? No. Which rules of evidence promote rectitude of decision? None. What is wrong with torture? Its susceptibility to abuse. Is the common law 'law'? No. As one digs deeper one becomes more conscious of what I have called Benthamic ambiguity.[38] This refers to a complex combination of tensions within Bentham's own thought and ambivalences on the part of his readers. At the root of utilitarianism lies an ambiguity as to whether 'pleasure' refers to satisfaction or desire or preference; it is reasonably clear that Bentham's usage is closer to the first, but

[35] R. Dworkin, *A Matter of Principle,* cit. n. 21; cf. *Law's Empire* (1986), Chap. 2.

[36] See further below n. 71.

[37] Duncan Kennedy, 'The Structure of Blackstone's *Commentaries*' *Buffalo L. Rev.,* **28** (1979), 209.

[38] This theme is developed in 'Why Bentham?' cit. n. 5 and in *Michigan L. Rev.,* **86** (1988), pp. 1523, 1536–9.

the last—i.e. preference—is thought by many modern commentators to be the least vulnerable.[39] We have already seen that there is room for doubt as to whether he was a consistent act-utilitarian and whether his treatments of codified substantive law and discretionary adjective law are consistent with each other. Both Fabian socialists and free-market economists claim him as an important ancestor; he was a genuine political radical, yet he placed a very high value on security; his belated conversion to democracy tempered neither his authoritarian and centralist tendencies nor his sensitivity to the potential for abuse of power nor his concern to combat misrule in all its forms. The architect of the seemingly inhuman Panopticon scheme was a life-long opponent of all forms of cruelty; his theory of adjective law transcends conventional distinctions between adversarial and inquisitorial models of procedure; he was deeply ambivalent about both the American and French revolutions; he satirized political fallacies of Left, Right and Centre; he was sexually ambiguous; ambitious, vain and socially diffident; a prolific writer who was notoriously reluctant to publish; and the inventor of schemes that range from the inspired to the nutty, sometimes combining both elements in a single proposal, as in the case of the auto-icon. Given all these seeming contradictions and tensions in his character and thought, it is hardly surprising that much Bentham scholarship at least appears to involve the pursuit of the ambiguous by the ambivalent.[40] I happen to think that quite a few of these seeming inconsistencies can be resolved by detailed attention to the texts. But even if one makes the slightest concession to the idea that the reader constructs the text the floodgates are open for multiple interpretations. I shall return to this in due course.

Contextual reading

So much for readings that place the primary emphasis on the text itself. Let us now turn to those that emphasize the importance of context in interpretation.

The movement to put history back into intellectual history or to develop a history of ideas which is 'a genuinely historical recreation of the past',[41] can be interpreted as a reaction against

[39] E.g. A. J. Ayer, 'The Principle of Utility', in *Philosophical Essays,* London (1963).

[40] This passage is adapted from *Michigan L. Rev.*, **86** at pp. 1536–7 (1988).

[41] Stefan Collini, Donald Winch & John Burrow, *That Noble Science of Politics* (Cambridge, 1983) p. 5; cf. Quentin Skinner, *The Foundations of Modern Political Thought* (1978), Vol. 1, p. xi.

what these new intellectual historians considered to be bad habits in their received tradition:[42] for example, intensive analysis of classic texts out of context; overconcentration on a narrow and arbitrarily selected canon of classics to the neglect of broader sweeps of ideologies and ideas and of lesser figures; the equation of history with the search for origins; or 'writing history backwards', that is anachronistically imputing concerns, questions, and even concepts to people who lived and wrote in a quite different intellectual environment; and a tendency to construct rather artificial 'continuities' and chains of influence. Bentham scholarship is almost entirely free from crude versions of these bad habits. It is standard to set almost any sustained discussion of one of Bentham's works in the context of his immediate concerns and agenda, of his intellectual development and of the general corpus of his ideas. It is also part of the convention to identify, so far as is feasible, the main sources on which Bentham relied or against which he reacted. This is often difficult in practice. Bentham read quite widely, but a great deal of the time he seems to have written largely from his head, drawing on what he had assimilated rather than constantly referring back to original sources. In many of his works, as exemplified by the *Rationale of Judicial Evidence,* citations are very sparse.

In writing a largely expository essay on the *Rationale* I attempted to observe these conventions of what might be termed moderate contextual scholarship.[43] One asked: when was the text written? Why did Bentham concentrate on evidence *then?* What were his central concerns? In particular, what explains the virulence and repetitiousness of his attacks on the legal profession in this work? When did he start to think about adjective law? Did any of his views in this area change significantly over time? What is the relationship between *The Rationale* and his other writings on evidence? How do his ideas on adjective law relate to other aspects of his thought? What was the state of the law of evidence at the time and of secondary writings on the subject? How much of this literature had Bentham studied carefully and how did he use it? and so on.

Such commonplace questions may have been sufficient for the modest task of setting a largely expository study of a major work in its immediate general context. Moreover, in one respect I was

[42] See generally, Tully, op. cit. n. 24.

[43] William Twining, *Theories of Evidence: Bentham and Wigmore* (London and Stanford, 1985).

more ambitious: I explored how far Bentham contributed to and conformed with an ideal type of assumptions about adjudication and proof that I argued were shared by most specialized secondary writings about evidence over a period of nearly 200 years.[44] However, as my work proceeded I became increasingly aware of many specific questions that remain unanswered about the biographical, intellectual, political and linguistic context of the *Rationale* and cognate writings. To give a few examples: the rules of evidence had been going through a phase of relatively rapid development at the time Bentham wrote and similar considerations apply to procedure and what he called judicial organization. While the legal context has been sketched in broad terms there are many specific lines of enquiry that still await the attention of orthodox legal historians. There are also many unanswered questions about the extent to which Bentham was reacting to debates and controversies and particular incidents that took place while he was writing. We need to know much more about such matters before we can make confident judgments about the extent and nature of his originality in this area as well as about the meaning and significance of many specific passages. Similar considerations apply to the intellectual context: for example, thanks to the work of Ian Hacking, Barbara Shapiro and others[45] we have some knowledge of the development of ideas about probability and inference before and after Bentham wrote and it should be relatively easy to locate Bentham's rather undeveloped ideas on probabilities in this story.[46] However, the connection between the seemingly simple empiricism of the *Rationale* and his theory of fictions, which is often presented as being highly original and ahead of its time is more problematic; as is the relationship between Bentham's treatment of reasoning about evidence and John Stuart Mill's *A System of Logic*.[47]

The new intellectual history has by no means been confined to negative criticism; it has produced some splendid scholarship as well as theorizing as is illustrated by the work of J. G. A. Pocock, Quentin Skinner, Stefan Collini and others.[48] Regrettably this

[44] Ibid., Chap. 1. See now W. Twining, *Rethinking Evidence* (Blackwell, 1990), Chap. 3.

[45] Ian Hacking, *The Emergence of Probability* (Cambridge, 1975); Barbara Shapiro, *Probability and Certainty in Seventeenth Century England* (Princeton, 1983).

[46] Op. cit. n. 43, at pp. 56–66.

[47] A few hints are dropped by R. F. McRae in his preface to the Toronto edition of *Mill's System of Logic* (1973).

[48] James Tully, op. cit, n. 24, Chap. 1., has usefully summarized Skinner's

movement has had only a marginal impact on the historiography of legal theory.[49] And Bentham scholarship has to date made

basic approach in the form of five questions: (a) What is or was an author doing in writing a text in relation to other available texts which make up the ideological context? (b) What is or was an author doing in writing a text in relation to available and problematic political action which makes up the practical context? (c) How are ideologies to be identified and their formation, criticism and change between political ideology and political action which best explains the diffusion of certain ideologies and what effect does this have on political behaviour? (e) What forms of political thought and action are involved in disseminating and conventionalizing ideological change? (ibid., 7–8).

These questions can with minor adaptations be applied to Bentham's *Rationale of Judicial Evidence*, viewed as an attempt to bring about a radical transformation in adjective law. The treatment of the *Rationale* in my *Theories of Evidence*, provides general answers to (a) and (b) and a partial answer to (c), in that it identifies and surveys a set of ideological conventions, provides a partial account of its development, but does not explain how and why it changed, and did not change, over time. I could have dealt more fully with (d) and (e). In particular, it would have been illuminating to ask more sharply: What aspects of conventional evidence discourse of the time did Bentham hold firm, while attacking other aspects? (A short answer might be: he confirmed the objective of pursuing 'rectitude of decision' through common-sense reasoning while attacking all technicality and non-utilitarian concerns with procedural fairness.) Why did some of Bentham's proposals become accepted as standard parts of evidence discourse and the Law of Evidence in the common law world, while others failed to become accepted? (The answer to this is probably quite complex and would involve detailed historical enquiries into developments and debates relating to the Law of Evidence and evidence discourse in several countries in the nineteenth century and beyond. So far as England is concerned, one hypothesis is that some of Bentham's proposals did not gain acceptance with ordinary judges and practitioners, who from self-interest or otherwise, managed to retain control over and preserve those aspects of the Law of Evidence that were perceived by reformers as 'lawyers' law' [when did that term come in and why?]. But this explanation is hypothetical and probably incomplete.) My essay did not attempt to deal in detail with particular topics. Again Skinner's approach would suggest some potentially fruitful lines of detailed historical enquiry into the ideological, political and linguistic contexts of a wide variety of topics of which jury nullification, safeguards of the accused, the uses and non-uses of writing in legal proceedings and the adversarial/inquisitorial distinction are obvious examples. One consequence of adopting a Skinnerian approach to Bentham's writings on evidence would be to extend enquiries into 'context' forward as well as backwards in time as part of a larger story about the development of evidentiary ideas and practices.

[49] In a recent symposium on *Philosophy in History: Essays on the Historiography of Philosophy*, ed. R. Rorty, J. B. Schneewind & Q. Skinner (Cambridge, 1984), philosophers of various kinds are joined by specialists in History, Sociology, and the History and Philosophy of Science, but not by a single jurist or legal philosopher. It is a striking fact that neither the Fontana Modern Masters nor the Oxford Past Masters Series had until recently included a work on a thinker

only a few tentative moves in this direction. A notable exception is David Lieberman's recent *The Province of Legislation Determined,* which attempts a fairly broad contextual interpretation of eighteenth-century legal theory in Britain, while remaining close to the texts.[50]

It must be obvious that I have considerable respect for this movement. Not only has it identified and effectively criticized some bad habits in dealing with past thinkers, but it has provided us with a rich range of fresh questions to ask of any text, for example about contemporary conventions and debates, the meaning and use of language, literary forms and functions, contemporary perceptions and assessments of the text and of its author; the pragmatic setting of its creation; and a host of other contextual factors. However, while a more puristic historiography can greatly enrich our study of political and legal theory, a balanced reception of these ideas should take note of three caveats: First, there should be no suggestion that focus on context should replace or dilute careful textual reading. Secondly, contextual reading does not invalidate certain kinds of conversational reading in which one considers the bearing of the text on questions that concern the reader, including public issues of his or her day. Thirdly, contextual, textual and conversational reading are not mutually exclusive genres. Many readings involve all of

who was treated first and foremost as a jurist. The only exception is John Dinwiddy's essay on Bentham (op. cit. n. 6). Legal ideas have been selectively explored by modern historians of ideas, such as John Pocock, Stefan Collini, and James Burns, but, by and large, very little genuinely historical work had been done on the development of Anglo-American jurisprudence until very recently. The publication of substantial monographs on John Austin, Sir Henry Maine, Sir James Stephen and others suggests that the situation is changing. The *Jurists* series was instituted in part to fill this gap. However, few, if any of these works, have been much influenced by the 'new intellectual history'.

The absence of a developed tradition of intellectual history within the discipline of law is not surprising. Law as a set of practices in the world of affairs is mainly concerned with the present and the future (or the immediate past). Legal scholarship is naturally responsive to the demands and expectations of judges, private practitioners, law reformers, contemporary-minded critics and vocationally-oriented students. Legal historiography, thanks to Maitland and his heirs (and more recently to those concerned with the social history of law), is by no means confined to a search for origins or crudely Whiggish interpretations. But legal history has been largely about doctrines and institutions rather than thinkers and theories. Legal theory has responded, often unconsciously and unselfconsciously, to the gravitational pull of 'contemporary significance' (see further below).

[50] D. Lieberman *The Province of Legislation Determined* (Cambridge, 1989).

them and they are related to each other in complex ways. Modern developments in intellectual history have provided us with a battery of new questions to ask of texts. But what questions are appropriate to put to a text depends on one's purposes. And I shall argue that there are occasions on which ahistorical interpretation and even non-reading have their uses.

Conversations, non-reading and 'contemporary significance'.

'What is the use of a book', thought Alice, 'without pictures or conversations?' (*Alice in Wonderland*, Chap. 1).

Contextual reading emphasizes the author and his contemporaries; textual reading focuses on the questions and answers and arguments embodied in the product of a given time and place. Both are oriented to the past and are in that sense historical. But the selection of texts and of ways of reading them is often governed, explicitly or implicitly, by considerations of 'contemporary significance'. The starting-point and the main emphasis shifts from the text and its historical context to the present-day reader. In one way or another the reader uses the text as an aid to pursuing his or her own concerns.

The term 'contemporary significance' tends to be used rather loosely, even by scholars.[51] In a discipline such as law, which is largely concerned with practical problems of the present and future, there is a natural tendency to give 'contemporary significance' priority over '(mere) historical interest'. There is also a tendency to take rather a lot for granted about the criteria of significance. In some contexts what is considered a significant question may be obvious, even self-evident. But sometimes the phrase may conceal questionable assumptions about a supposed consensus regarding the agenda of questions or 'the issues of the day (or age)' or it may represent an *ad hoc* reaction to some specific event or an unreflective response to a current intellectual fashion.

I shall refer to readings that take the reader's concerns as their starting-point as 'conversations'.[52] This may serve as a reminder

[51] *Mea culpa.* See my 'The Contemporary Significance of Bentham's Anarchical Fallacies', *Archiv fur Rechts-und Sozialphilosophie,* **61** (1975), 325, and *Theories of Evidence: Bentham and Wigmore* cit. n. 42, Chap. 4. which is entitled 'The Contemporary Significance of Bentham and Wigmore'. This self-criticism is not directed at attempting to answer questions concerning claims that a particular text or author deserves attention today, but at a lack of clarity about the precise meaning and status of such questions and answers.

[52] The term is borrowed from Richard Rorty, 'The historiography of philosophy: four genres', in Rorty *et al.* (eds), op. cit. n. 24, Chap. 3. My usage in this context is slightly broader than Rorty's.

of some fairly obvious points. First, there are many kinds of conversation which vary, *inter alia,* in the extent to which they are governed by strict or settled conventions. Just as the idea of 'conversation' is broad enough to cover the whole continuum from the formal 'disputatio' to casual, perfunctory exchanges, so too conversational readings are not governed by a single set of conventions. However, if one's purpose is to learn, one may be guided by some working rules of thumb. For example, one tends to learn more if one listens, if one gives due credit to the interlocutor's intelligence, and if one asks pertinent questions. Conversational reading has the advantage over live conversations in that the reader is in control. He or she need not be inhibited by considerations of fairness, courtesy or even historical accuracy. In entering into a dialogue with a text one is free to put the text to the question as sharply, brutally and persistently as one chooses. Yet one is usually likely to gain more if one gives due credit to the author's concerns and intelligence. Thomas Kuhn once wrote:

> 'When reading the works of (an) important thinker, look first for the apparent absurdities in the text and ask how a sensible person could have written them. When you find an answer, I continue, when those passages make sense, then you may find that more central passages, ones you previously thought you understood, have changed their meaning.'[53]

Kuhn was writing about historical reading. But, in so far as this is also good advice for serious conversational readings, it underscores the point that such conversations need not be ahistorical. Not only may careful attention to text and context illuminate the content of the text, but it may also clarify the reader's own situation and concerns through contrast with those of the author and the text. For example, Bentham's thoughts on torture assumed that its main institutionalized use was in the context of interrogation of a judicial or quasi-judicial kind. For he was writing before the development of institutionalized torture as an instrument of terror, deterrence and repression in which obtaining information often plays a minimal or marginal role.[54]

Not all conversational reading of past thinkers need be unscholarly. Indeed, our heritage of texts is one of our main resources for thinking about present day problems. Of all thinkers Jeremy Bentham, if he still exists, is estopped from complaining that his

[53] Thomas Kuhn, *The Essential Tension: Selected Studies in Scientific Tradition and Change* (1977), p. xii. I am grateful to Alex Stein for this reference.

[54] W. L. Twining & P. E. Twining, 'Bentham on Torture', *N.I.L.Q,* **24** (1973), 305, reprinted in M. James (ed.), *Bentham and Legal Theory* (Belfast, 1974).

works are being used for purposes other than those he intended or that commentators are treating him unfairly. Texts, like bodies, have many possible uses, and before summarily dismissing ahistorical or even atextual uses of Bentham's legacy we should consider each type on the merits. However, effective exploitation of such resources requires a reasonable degree of self-consciousness and discrimination regarding the purposes, methods and pitfalls of such readings.

That conversational reading is compatible with the highest standards of scholarship can be illustrated by considering the contributions of Herbert Hart to Bentham studies. For over thirty years, Hart has devoted almost as much time to studying Bentham as to doing jurisprudence.[55] Apart from editing three central texts, his essays and introductions have been rightly acclaimed as major contributions to Bentham studies. Hart approaches Bentham mainly from the perspective of an analytical jurist. In most of his essays he expounds, analyses and criticizes central concepts of Bentham's Jurisprudence: Law, laws and related concepts, such as commands, sanctions and sovereignty, legal rights, powers, duties and obligation, and of course, utility. Hart also compares some of Bentham's key ideas with those of John Austin, Beccaria, John Stuart Mill and others. The exposition is lucid and meticulously accurate; the analysis is both profound and exact. Much of the criticism exemplifies one form of conversation: Hart brings Bentham into contemporary debates with Dworkin and others and clarifies and develops his own position through dialogue with his predecessors.[56]

Hart first came into prominence largely by subjecting Austin's command theory to what all but a few have regarded as devastating

[55] See especially, H. L. A. Hart (ed.), *Of Laws in General* (CW, London, 1970); J. H. Burns & H. L. A. Hart (eds), *An Introduction to The Principles of Morals and Legislation* (CW, London, 1970), reprinted with a critical introduction by H. L. A. Hart (Methuen, 1982); J. H. Burns & H. L. A. Hart (eds), *Comment on the Commentaries and A Fragment on Government* (London, 1977). H. L. A. Hart, *Essays on Bentham*, cit. n. 14.

[56] Commentators on Hart tend to pay surprisingly little attention to his work on Bentham, given that some of his own ideas are developed in the greatest detail in these 'conversational writings' see, for example, P. Hacker & J. Raz (eds), *Law, Morality and Society* (Oxford, 1977); Ruth Gavison (ed.), *Issues in Contemporary Legal Philosophy: The Influence of H. L. A. Hart* (Oxford, 1987) and, most surprisingly, Robert Moles, *Definition and Rule in Legal Theory* (Oxford, 1987), a critique of Hart's use of Austin, which barely mentions Bentham. An exception is Neil MacCormick, *H. L. A. Hart* (London, 1981), but this was written before the publication of *Essays on Bentham*, Chap. 10, discussed below.

criticism and by advancing an alternative positivisitic conception of law.[57] Yet in his last essay on Bentham Hart finds a core of truth in Bentham's command theory in the notion of 'a content-independent and peremptory reason'.[58] The relevant texts by Bentham and Hart are, of course, susceptible to more than one interpretation. As I read them, Hart's criticisms are secondary to this core of truth. On this view, the leading critic of the command theory and our most eminent positivist has resurrected Bentham's theory of law, duly refined, at the centre of modern legal positivism.

I happen to have a significantly different conception of the enterprise of jurisprudence from Herbert Hart and a rather different vision of Bentham as jurist.[59] I shall develop this below. But this is more a matter of differences of perspective and concern than fundamental disagreement. And I consider that one of Herbert Hart's most valuable contributions has been to keep the analysis of 'fundamental legal conceptions' on the agenda at a time when a great deal of the attention of our leading legal philosophers has been directed to more abstract questions of normative theory. The most developed aspects of Hart's thought in this respect are to be found in his writings on Bentham.

The writings of Hart and Postema illustrate the point that conversational readings of past thinkers are quite compatible with meticulous scholarship provided that the nature of the enterprise is kept clear. In this I think that they are exceptional among contemporary jurists as I shall try to show below. But first let me make the case for giving priority to conversational reading in the educational context.

Many teachers of jurisprudence justify their courses in terms of helping students to clarify and develop their own views on significant general questions relating to law.[61] For this purpose students should be required to do jurisprudence (to theorize) rather than to learn *about* it and our heritage of texts is a means to this end rather than an object of study for its own sake. In my experience few jurisprudence courses fit this rationale in practice. There are no doubt many reasons for this, but one is a lack of clear distinction between historical and conversational readings

[57] H. L. A. Hart, *The Concept of Law* (Oxford, 1961).

[58] *Essays on Bentham,* cit. n. 14, Chap. 10, esp. pp. 243 and 261.

[59] See below pp. 133 ff.

[60] Above no. 56.

[61] See Neil MacCormick & William Twining, 'Theory in the Law Curriculum', in *Legal Theory and Common Law,* cit. n. 21, Chap. 13.

and a failure to equip students with a basic method for conducting reasonably disciplined conversations.

The paradigm case of an intelligent conversation with a text for the purpose of clarifying one's own views involves something like this: one asks of the text what questions does it address (or raise)? What answers does it offer or suggest? What reasons are advanced in support of the answers? And what might be the implications and applications of such answers and reasons? Then one asks: do I agree with the questions? Do I agree with the answers? Do I agree with the reasons? Do I accept all of the applications and implications? This intellectual procedure can be followed with different degrees of rigour and detail according to one's purposes. Similarly it can involve as much or as little contextual reading as seems appropriate. This general approach can be useful not only in developing one's own position on given questions, but also in determining what questions seem to be worth asking.[62]

There is no settled code of conventions for such readings, but there are a few working rules of thumb. For example, if a text is worth using in this way, generous interpretation usually pays. Treating one's interlocutors as intelligent friends or as worthy opponents tends to raise the level of conversation. Sometimes it pays to be ahistorical in this context. For example, it is one thing to ask: what version of utilitarianism did Bentham adopt in *An Introduction To The Principles of Morals and Legislation*? It is another to ask: what is the least vulnerable interpretation of utilitarianism suggested by a reading of this text?

Conversational reading is different in purpose from rigorous textual and contextual reading. But they are, of course, intimately related. Even the historical purist who seeks, in Skinner's terms, 'to recover intentions, to reconstruct conventions and to restore contexts'[63] is a creature of his or her time. Conversely one is usually not well-placed to judge which is the least vulnerable interpretation of a text before one has paid due attention to text and context. Conversation builds on text and context, but it need not be confined by them.

Thus entering into a dialogue with past texts for the purpose of posing and answering questions of contemporary significance

[62] This is developed in 'Talk about Realism', *N.Y.U.L. Rev.*, **60** (1985), 329 at pp. 336–8.

[63] Quentin Skinner, cited by W. Lepenies in Rorty *et al.*, op. cit. n. 24, at p. 155.

requires a delicate balance between careful textual and contextual reading on the one hand and less inhibited exploitation of the past for present purposes.

So much for scholarly conversations. Let me now deal briskly with some other types that need to be differentiated and seen for what they are. Some of these, I shall suggest, can be interpreted as examples of non-reading.

First, imaginary conversations. An intriguing literary genre is the imaginary conversation or dialogue, often in dramatic form, in which well-known historical figures converse anachronistically either with the author or with others from different eras. Landor's *Imaginary Conversations* and Oliver Wendell Holmes sr's *Breakfast Table* series are well-known, if unfashionable, examples.[64] This summer I came across a rather charming instance in Tanzania.[65] A versatile police officer and political commissar presented the basic ideas of fifteen leading political thinkers from Plato and Aristotle to Nkrumah and Nyerere in the form of a trial in which all of them were called upon to defend themselves against the charge of 'having vague and misleading ideas which have distorted the thinking of other people in the world' and of sowing confusion by disagreeing with each other.[66] As an exercise in popular education I found this engaging and effective. Since Jeremy Bentham was conspicuously absent from the fifteen defendants I spent a pleasant afternoon trying to remedy the omission. This exercise proved to be instructive as well as entertaining. On the one hand this literary form largely frees one from pedantic concern with both historical fact and textual accuracy; on the other hand one has to confront such questions as: How old is this Bentham? How much knowledge about the relevant time and place (e.g. modern Tanzanian conditions) is one to attribute to him? And what kind of character or mood should one give to him? Before one summarily dismisses such exercises as literary frolics that have no place in serious scholarship, one should perhaps bear in mind that Plato was one of the pioneers of the imaginary dialogue. And, one may ask, is not the standard practice of comparing the ideas of thinkers who lived at different times and in different contexts to some extent analogous to this form?

[64] Walter Savage Landor, *Imaginary Conversations*, ed. Havelock Ellis (London); Oliver Wendell Holmes Snr, e.g. *The Professor at the Breakfast Table* (1859).

[65] John Alfonso Nchimbi, *The Struggle of Ideas from Plato to Nyerere*, English translation from Kiswahili (Dar-es-Salaam, 1989).

[66] Ibid., p. 1.

Speculative conversations

Yet another kind of 'conversation' that obviously needs to be treated with caution is the speculative conversation. For example, it can be amusing, possibly even illuminating, to speculate about how Bentham might have reacted to the Lord Chancellor's proposals on the reform of the legal profession or the Civil Justice Review or the Official Secrets Act, 1989, to take three topical subjects on which he expressed strong views in his day.[66] Similarly, when the students in Tiananmen Square proclaimed repeatedly that 'the eyes of the world are upon us' (perhaps echoing American students in Chicago in 1968), one was tempted to interpret this in terms of Bentham's emphasis on publicity as the main safeguard against misrule and to ponder how far the subsequent tragic events might have undermined his faith in the Public Opinion Tribunal.[67] Such speculations can be more or less rigorously grounded in particular texts.[68] Sometimes they may be extensions of recognized forms of 'rational reconstruction'. For example, it is not beyond the realm of possibility that a selection of Bentham texts, or even the whole corpus when it is available, might be made the basis of an 'expert system' which could suggest the implications of Bentham's ideas for any question that was put to it. The point about expert systems is that they have the capacity to deal with new questions on the basis of disciplined extrapolation from a fixed body of knowledge.[69] The rigour, depth and reliability of such a system for Bentham or any other thinker would be a function of the quality and sensitivity of the programming. I am quite happy to leave questions about the feasibility and utility of any such development to a future generation of Bentham scholars. The immediate point is that *all* forms of conversational reading share to some degree a vulnerability to the pitfalls of anachronism, some of which are less obvious than others, and that all forms are to a greater or lesser extent conversational because no reading can be entirely passive.

[66] Ibid., p. 1.

[67] On the Public Opinion Tribunal see F. Rosen, *Jeremy Bentham and Representative Democracy: A Study of the Constitutional Code* (Oxford, 1983); see now the important treatment of the subject in Bentham's *First Principles Preparatory to the Constitutional Code,* ed. Philip Schofield (CW, Oxford, 1989).

[68] E.g. W. Twining, 'The way of the Baffled Medic: Prescribe First, Diagnose Later, if at all', *J.S.P.T.L.*, **12** (n.s.) (1973), 348 on reform of criminal evidence in 1972–3 with particular reference to misuses of Bentham's views on silence. See now *Rethinking Evidence,* cit. n. 44, Chap. 10.

[69] See generally, R. Susskind, *Expert Systems and Law* (Oxford, 1987).

One step away from the imaginery and speculative conversation involves postulating a modern disciple rather than a fictionalized historical figure.[70] Substitute for the young Marx, 'a modern Marxist' or for the octogenarian Bentham 'a modern Benthamite' and one is further liberated, by the device of indeterminate attribution,[71] from any concern for textual or factual accuracy at all. The use of isms, ists and schools as devices for designating views different from one's own is one of the most deeply entrenched and commonplace conventions of contemporary academic discourse in, for example, philosophy, political theory and jurisprudence. We thus have the paradox that much contemporary scholarship condones a practice which both in theory and practice is even less scholarly than imaginary conversations. That this practice is both widespread and regarded as respectable can be instanced by reference to John Rawls' treatment of classical utilitarianism in his *Theory of Justice;* Roberto Unger's treatment of 'liberalism' in *Knowledge and Politics;* and Ronald Dworkin's treatment of 'conventionalism' and 'pragmatism' in *Law's Empire.*[72] As this practice is free from almost any concern for textual accuracy one is perhaps justified in referring to it as 'non-reading'.

[70] Kipling admirably explores the vagaries of discipleship, ending:

'But his own Disciple
shall wound him worst of all'.

Rudyard Kipling's Verse (definitive edition, London, 1940), p. 774. An imaginary disciple may have an even more tenuous relationship with the original.

[71] That it is easy for a learned and meticulous scholar to shift unobtrusively from commenting on a particular text to discussing ideas attributed indeterminately to modern disciples is illustrated by an otherwise excellent paper by Gerald Postema, 'In Defence of "French Nonsense": Fundamental Rights in Constitutional Jurisprudence', in Neil MacCormick and Zenon Bankowski (eds), *Enlightenment, Rights and Revolution* Chap. 5. (Aberdeen, 1989). This is an explicitly 'conversational' (in Postema's terms 'philosophical') paper in contrast with the more historical *Bentham and the Common Law Tradition,* cit. n. 25. Postema quietly shifts between taking issue with the original text of *Anarchical Fallacies,* modern interpretations thereof, and (semble, modern) followers of Bentham (e.g. 'Benthamite critics of rights constitutionalism' at p. 109). One may ask: who precisely are these critics or what precise posture is to be attributed to such a disciple in respect of issues in which the context, the issues and the language of rights discourse have all changed significantly? For example, what knowledge and views does one attribute to a 'Benthamite' in the context of current debates about 'emergent rights' and 'third generation rights'? See further n. 85 and n. 100.

[72] John Rawls, *A Theory of Justice* (1972), e.g. Chap. 1.5 on classical utilitarianism; Roberto Unger, *Knowledge and Politics* (1975), p. 8 ('the liberal theory' as an ideal type) discussed in 'Talk about Realism', cit. n. 62, at p. 338 n. 21; Ronald Dworkin, *Law's Empire,* cit. n. 21. *passim.* Rawls, Unger and Dworkin all seek to set up recognizable targets and to avoid crude caricatures.

I have attacked some of the worst habits associated with non-reading on other occasions.[73] I have, for example, tried to show that most generalizations about American Legal Realism to be found in the literature are false or trivial or both; and that a great deal of discourse in contemporary jurisprudence involves false polemics based on a confusion between the idea of disagreement (advancing rival answers to the same question) and difference (answering different questions). While many examples of non-reading are vulnerable to such criticism, it is worth making the point that some kinds of non-reading and non-citation have benefits as well as costs.

One of the main uses of history, said Holmes, is to free us from the incubus of an irrelevant past.[74] Similarly when Herbert Hart took up the Chair of Jurisprudence at Oxford one of his concerns was to show that there was more to jurisprudence than repetitious exposition and criticism of dead thinkers.[75] By addressing questions directly, with relatively sparse references to other jurists, he gave a lead in making a switch from writing about jurists to doing jurisprudence. The uncluttered text came into fashion, especially in Oxford, and this undoubtedly helped to stimulate one of the most lively periods of legal theorizing in our history. That this style of discourse was embraced by followers and successors, some of whom were neither as well-read nor as meticulous as Hart himself, should not detract from his success in stimulating a major revival of theorizing as an activity within the discipline of law—of doing jurisprudence rather than reading or writing about it. Freeing jurisprudence from the incubus of second-rate intellectual history had its price, but few would doubt that overall the benefits have generally outweighed the costs. And Hart himself, especially in his work on Bentham, has shown by example that most of the bad habits associated with the uncluttered text are quite unnecessary.

Past thinkers, like bodies, have many potential uses. One kind which is both ahistorical and atextual is the symbolic use. This is

[73] E.g. 'The Great Juristic Bazaar', *J.S.P.T.L.*, **14** (n.s.) (1978), 185.

[74] O. W. Holmes Jr., 'The Path of the Law', *Harv. L. Rev.*, **10** (1897), 357.

[75] H. L. A. Hart, 'Analytical Jurisprudence at Mid-twentieth Century: a reply to Professor Bodenheimer', *U. Penn. L. Rev.*, **105** (1957), 953. MacCormick characterizes the situation at the time thus: 'Lawyers had stopped being interested in philosophy, philosophers in law. Jurisprudence in the universities had become a routine reading and re-reading of a canon of texts and text books. Except for a handful of brilliant exceptions the subject was moribund'. *H. L. A. Hart* (London, 1981), p. 19.

more like pictures than conversation, but it should not be condemned out of hand. Let us consider some uses of Bentham in this regard.

As you know, Bentham is unusual among dead thinkers in maintaining a physical presence among us. His auto-icon at University College is more often treated as an object of than as a participant in conversation. But it is entirely consistent with the Benthamite spirit to exploit it for pedagogical purposes.

In teaching, I uninhibitedly exploit the auto-icon as an ambiguous symbol: What is its message? Is this a literal-minded application of utility based on a dubious calculation of the value of bodies as ornaments, material for medical research or objects of veneration? What does it mean for a materialist to set himself up as an icon? Is this to be taken as a joke? Or as an example of extreme vanity? Or as a more subtle attack on taboos and fallacies about bodies and death? Did Bentham care about his reputation after death? If so, was that consistent with his articulated philosophy? Does he in some sense live on? Indeed is this really Bentham?

A different point is illustrated by Marx's treatment of Bentham. In a much-quoted passage in *Capital* Marx referred to him as 'the insipid, pedantic, leather-tongued oracle of the commonplace bourgeois intelligence of the nineteenth century'.[76] It is doubtful that Marx had read much Bentham in the original, no doubt because he would have thought he was wasting his time. He was probably acquainted with the clean linen of some of Dumont's *rédactions*.[77] Almost certainly he did not read those texts in which modern commentators have noted some remarkable affinities—for example, the theme of 'demystification' which is most prominent in Bentham's writings on Evidence, but which more generally underpins his satirical attacks on fallacies ... of left, right and centre ... most of which he saw as grounded in sinister interests of particular groups and classes such as 'Judge and Co', the Church and the aristocracy.[78] There are some remarkable affinities here with Marx's ideas about false consciousness and ideology. More significant still Bentham and Marx could be shown to have similar

[76] Marx, *Das Kapital* (Everyman edn), Vol. 2, p. 671, cf. ibid., p. 164.

[77] Dinwiddy, op. cit. n. 6, at p. 115.

[78] Examples of general comparisons include Hart, *Essays on Bentham,* cit. n. 14, Chap. 1; Mack, op. cit. n. 15, at pp. 85n., 217, 420; Twining, op. cit. n. 43, at pp. 75–9; Bahmueller, op. cit. n. 83, *passim.* See also George Brenfert, 'Marx and Utilitarianism', *The Canadian Journal of Philosophy,* 5 (1975), 421; Graeme Duncan, *Marx and Mill* (Cambridge, 1973).

concerns with conflicting interests and the rhetoric of rights;[79] and, one may ask, was not Marx himself both a materialist and a utilitarian? There are, of course, many significant differences. Indeed, part of the future agenda for Bentham studies is a fuller exploration of the affinities and differences of these two seminal figures.

To return to Marx's statement. If we apply the standard of seeking the least vulnerable interpretation of texts, the famous passage can be seen to serve a function irrespective of its fairness. In this context and elsewhere Bentham is used as a symbol of the limitations of petty bourgeois reformism and radicalism. The symbol is not inappropriate, if it is interpreted to refer to those aspects of Bentham and Benthamism which are quite contrary to the spirit and thrust of Marxian thought: for example, the emphasis on security and the consequent antipathy to all forms of revolution; and a pessimistic and somewhat mechanistic view of human nature. This is not a complete travesty of the historical Bentham, any more than Dickens's Gradgrind and Peacock's Mr MacQuedy were either unfair or worthless caricatures of some of Bentham's followers.[80] However, one suspects that the image projected by Marx has been widely accepted as sufficiently accurate to justify dismissing Bentham's writings as unworthy of detailed attention.

A rather more complex example of Bentham as symbol relates to the Panopticon. Even the most sympathetic Benthamists tend to be embarrassed by this aspect of his endeavours. Janet Semple has shown that the historical Bentham was not as inhumane nor as indifferent to the interests of suspects and criminals as has been suggested by Gertrude Himmelfarb and Michel Foucault.[81] I rather doubt whether Foucault had read even as much Bentham as had Marx.[82] I interpret Foucault as an example of one kind of inspired non-reader. Certainly he did not have access to the wealth of detailed material which has only been recently deciphered, only some of which has yet been published. For Foucault the Panopticon symbolized the murky side of the Enlightenment,

[79] See generally Jeremy Waldron (ed.), *Nonsense upon Stilts: Bentham, Burke and Marx on the Rights of Man.* (London, 1987).

[80] Charles Dickens, *Hard Times;* Thomas Love Peacock, *Crotchet Castle.*

[81] Janet Semple, 'Bentham's Haunted House', *The Bentham Newsletter,* **11** (1987), 35, commenting on Gertrude Himmelfarb, *Victorian Minds* (London, 1968).

[82] There is reported to exist a study of Bentham and Foucault in Portuguese by Mari, but I have not had access to it.

a hidden passion for dehumanizing social control that provides the central theme of his *Discipline and Punish*. One wonders how much of that haunting work would have needed to be changed in the light of detailed work that presents Bentham and the Panopticon scheme as more complex and in a rather more sympathetic light. In a sense the answer is to hand: for there has been some debate within Bentham scholarship concerning the forceful attacks by Himmelfarb, Bahmueller and others on this aspect of Bentham's ideas.[83] These discussions have centred on the question: in the light of meticulous examination of the texts and facts, how far do Panopticon, the National Charity Company and Bentham's ideas on related matters provide an appropriate general metaphor for authoritarian social control and seriously undermine his image as a progressive and humane reformer? In my opinion this is just one more aspect of Benthamic ambiguity.

I am conscious that in adopting a tolerant, mildly playful, mock-utilitarian approach to conversational reading and non-reading I may invite charges of fence-sitting pluralism. This might be justified if my argument had been that any kind of use or abuse of texts, however unscholarly, may have a place in Bentham studies provided that it can be justified on the basis of crude cost-benefit analysis. That is not my position. I believe that certain kinds of unscholarly practice and false polemics should be condemned as inimical to the pursuit of truth and understanding, an enterprise which can be justified on both utilitarian and non-utilitarian grounds. Since modern Bentham studies generally provide a model of the highest standards of meticulous scholarship, it is especially important that unscholarly practices should be exposed for what they are. My thesis is rather that in so far as Bentham studies extend beyond careful textual and historical scholarship to make claims or to seek justifications in terms of 'contemporary significance', we need to be self-consciously discriminating about such claims.

It is, however, my view that Bentham studies should tolerate, indeed welcome a plurality of perspectives and approaches, provided that the standards of care and accuracy set by recent

[83] C. Bahmueller, *The National Charity Company:* Jeremy Bentham's Silent Revolution (California, 1981); Himmelfarb, op. cit. n. 81; Semple, op. cit. n. 81; L. J. Hume, 'Revisionism in Bentham Studies', *The Bentham Newsletter,* **2** (1978), 12; Warren Roberts, 'Bentham's Poor Law Proposals', *The Bentham Newsletter,* **3** (1979), 28; Fred Rosen, 'Elie Halevy and Bentham's Authoritarian Liberalism', *Enlightenment and Dissent,* **6** (1987), 59.

Bentham scholarship are maintained. In some contexts the distinctions between textual, contextual and conversational reading, and refinements on these distinctions, have been the subject of protracted, sometimes acrimonious, dispute. Of course, when theories of interpretation are debated, especially in relation to authoritative texts, there is often much more at stake than academic fashion or prestige. Recent American debates about constitutional interpretation, for example, reflect sharp clashes of political interests and ideologies, as was dramatized by the episode of the Bork nomination.[84] Similar considerations apply to many theological and ideological debates. For the forseeable future Bentham scholarship is likely to be able to sustain a more tolerant pluralism than, for example, English literature, for three main reasons. First, Bentham studies are firmly rooted in a tradition of careful textual exegesis and particularistic history that serves to constrain excitable debate. Secondly, Bentham was too subtle a thinker, as is illustrated by the theme of Benthamic ambiguity, to be easily hijacked by doctrinaire extremists. Neither Mrs Thatcher nor a revolutionary of any kind could live comfortably with the label 'Benthamite'. Thirdly, in those areas where convincing claims can be made for Bentham's 'modernity' or 'contemporary significance', such as utility or human rights or legal positivism or the moral sanction or punishment or sexual or religious toleration, Bentham may be stimulating as a starting-point and admirable as a pioneer, but he rarely offers the last word on these topics.[85] He was essentially a product of the late eighteenth-century Enlightenment and since his day the context has changed and discourse and debate have advanced, often building on his contributions.

[84] E.g. R. Dworkin, 'The Book Nomination', *New York Review of Books*, **34**, No. 17, (1987) p. 3.

[85] A good example is human rights. Anarchical fallacies is still an excellent starting-point for critical consideration of contemporary discourse on the subject. However, in respect of particular topics, such as whether it is meaningful or useful to talk of 'a right to food', one is usually well-advised to move fairly briskly from Bentham's general discussion, including his aphorism 'want is not supply ... hunger is not bread' (*Anarchical Fallacies, Works,* Vol. 2, p. 501) and his treatment of the principles of subsistence and security, to more detailed contemporary writings, such as those of Amartya Sen and Onora O'Neill. Compare Peter Singer's simple, but effective, use of Bentham as the starting point for his *Animal Liberation* (London, 1975).

Bentham Redivivus

I wish to conclude by advancing some particular reasons why I consider that the time is ripe for the restoration of Jeremy Bentham to his rightful place as the Father of Modern Jurisprudence in the English-speaking world. I shall base my case on two arguments: first, the characteristics of his legacy that still make him worth reading and, secondly, the ideas of Universal Jurisprudence and the citizen of the world.

The first part of the case has already been made by implication: enough has been said to ground the claim that few, if any, thinkers, let alone jurists rival him in respect of reach, coherence, conceptual acuity, provocativeness, capacity to be puzzled, and the hallmark of a classic, openness to multiple interpretations. One can also add that although claims to 'modernity' need to be treated with caution, a remarkable number of Bentham's concerns and questions are still worth taking seriously today. For these reasons among others Bentham can be held out as England's most substantial jurist.

The second part of my argument brings us back to the themes of 'modernity' and 'contemporary significance'. In discussing 'conversational readings' I have already sounded a note of caution about our usage of such terms in relation to past thinkers. Both terms imply some affinity between the concerns, questions and ideas of a specified past and an unspecified present. There is no consensus or settled agenda concerning issues of the day or significant questions. So in making the case for one claim regarding Bentham's contemporary significance as a jurist it is incumbent on me to state a view about such matters.

Anglo-American legal theory has recently enjoyed a period of exceptional liveliness and richness. Yet I share with some colleagues a sense of dissatisfaction with a tendency to parochialism that runs through much of the work of our leading jurists. To put the matter briefly, in my view our stock of contemporary legal theorizing takes inadequate account of the phenomena of global interdependence[86] and legal pluralism[87]. One key to restoring

[86] See generally, Y. P. Ghai, R. Luckham & F. Snyder (eds), *The Political Economy of Law* (OUP, India, 1988). A very different attempt at global jurisprudence is W. Michael Reisman and Aaron M. Schreiber, *Jurisprudence: Understanding and Shaping Law* (New Haven, 1987). A useful corrective to exaggerated emphasis of global perspectives is Hedley Bull, *The Anarchical Society: A study of order in world politics* (London, 1977).

[87] A useful survey is Sally E. Merry, 'Legal Pluralism', *Law and Society Review,*

the balance is to revive the idea of General or Universal Jurisprudence.

Let me illustrate the concern with reference to my own undergraduate teaching. At University College in recent years we have set an exercise to our entering class to be done in the week before they arrive and to be discussed in their very first tutorial. They are asked to read every word in a non-tabloid newspaper published in that week in the light of a number of questions about the extent and treatment of 'legal' and 'non-legal' topics. The exercise has several pedagogical objectives, such as to stimulate interest, to raise some basic questions about the nature of law and to bring home the message that, far from being a new subject for them, their legal education started at birth, or possibly before. The exercise is also designed to make a point about law in today's world. This is that no law student can sensibly confine his or her attention exclusively or even mainly to domestic or municipal law. This point goes much further than making the case for studying European Community Law, Public and Private International Law, Foreign Legal Systems, Transnational Trade and the International Protection of Human Rights. One step beyond this is to show how interpreting yesterday's news from a legal perspective ... about the Hong Kong Treaty, or the Rushdie Affair, or an oil spillage or a hijack or a publishing takeover or even a package holiday that went wrong ... involves knowledge and understandings of much more than English or UK or national laws narrowly conceived. It reminds us that every citizen and every student is the subject of multiple systems of rules and social orderings, many or most of which, without semantic quibbling, could be called legal orders or legal systems. That even the most isolated individual or group or organization does not belong to only one community or society, but is inevitably involved in and affected by a multiplicity of semi-autonomous social fields, as Sally Falk Moore has called them.[88] That even the most localized legal

22 (1988), 869. The phrase 'legal pluralism' is out of favour in some quarters because it may 'carry connotations of equality that misrepresent the asymmetrical power relations that inhere in the coexistence of multiple legal orders. Various legal systems may coexist, as occurs in many colonial and postcolonial states, but the legal orders are hardly equal'. June Starr & Jane F. Collier (eds), *History and Power in the Study of Law* (Ithaca and London, 1989). In the present context the term carries no such connotations of equality.

[88] Sally Falk Moore, *Law as Process: An Anthropological Approach* (London, 1978), Chap. 2.

knowledge[89] in, let us say an industrial city such as Bradford or even a Hampshire village, such as Whitchurch, may include rules and orderings that emanate from Brussels or Strasbourg or Tokyo or Iran, as well as from Westminster, Whitehall, the Parish Council and local custom. And that any theory of law as a phenomenon or as a discipline has to accommodate and explain such facts.

The central messages of global interdependence and of legal pluralism may be truisms. Yet much of our stock of legal theorizing, and to only a slightly lesser extent, political theorizing, fails to accommodate them satisfactorily. Our first year students do not seem to be surprised or daunted by the lessons of the newspaper exercise. Yet when they come to study jurisprudence in their final year there appears to be a disjuncture.

The dominant theories in our contemporary canon of jurisprudence, despite their differences from each other, are largely parochial and monistic in tendency: that is to say they tend to treat the basic unit of law as the domestic legal system of a national state, they treat international law as being concerned primarily with relations between nation-states and they tend to be monistic in their interpretation of the phenomenon of co-existing rule-systems. Thus the theories of Austin and Hart are primarily concerned with municipal legal systems; John Rawls' theory of justice is primarily concerned with distributive justice within a political society that is bounded by the jurisdiction of a nation-state. As several critics have pointed out a major weakness of his book lies in the treatment of international relations: basing himself largely on the 1963 edition of Brierley's *Law of Nations,* Rawls treats both international law and international relations as a matter of relations between states and, strangely, that the basic principle of international law is that *peoples* organized as states have certain fundamental equal rights,[90] surely a questionable view of both international law and the transnational morality of human rights. Even those who, like Michael Walzer,[91] have addressed the problem of spheres of justice more directly, tend to treat independent political societies as the primary unit within which problems of justice can be meaningfully discussed. American jurisprudence, like American culture, has had an inbuilt tendency to parochialism, fortified by the emphasis placed

[89] Cliford Geertz, *Local Knowledge* (New York, 1983), esp. Chap. 8.

[90] John Rawls, *A Theory of Justice,* p. 378.

[91] Michael Walzer, *Spheres of Justice: A Defence of Pluralism and Equality* (Oxford, 1983).

on the courts as the focal point of a legal system. Even American Critical Legal scholars, with the exception of Roberto Unger, seem to outsiders to be largely inward-looking and parochial; they tend to interpret the legacy of American Realism as being significant only in respect of 'judicial process', which in my view misses much of its value.[92] One commentator has gone so far as to suggest that Ronald Dworkin's analysis of law as an interpretive concept challenges 'the possibility and value of general jurisprudence'.[93] This may be an overstatement, but it is nevertheless the case that the primary focus of Dworkin's work is common law municipal adjudication looked at from an internal, participatory point of view.[94] There are, of course, some notable exceptions, for example among the heirs of Maine, Marx and Weber, but by and large they are marginalized within our academic legal culture.

The argument that contemporary jurisprudence needs to take more account of the facts of global interdependence and local legal pluralism should not be conflated with idealistic pleas for world government or a general law of mankind. The argument relates more directly to ways of interpreting our situation than to strategies for ordering the world.

This point can be illustrated by recent trends in legal anthropology. The classic works in that field from Malinowski to Gluckman and Gulliver largely focussed on small-scale societies and tended to treat them as isolated and self-contained units. Recently this has been challenged at several levels. For example, at a symposium held in Bellagio in 1985 a general consensus emerged that, while it is in the nature of anthropological research to be both localized (geographically) and particularistic, most local phenomena cannot be adequately described and explained without reference to an ever-broadening circle of contexts: neighbours, the nation-state, regional and international groupings (the British Empire, the Arab world) and the world community. Context is, of course, not solely a matter of geographical space: legal anthropologists have also acknowledged that the classic local studies tended to neglect the dimension of time, and, perhaps surprisingly, by emphasizing the unique characteristics of each people to underplay the diffusion of cultures and belief-systems.

92 See 'Talk about Realism', cit. n. 62.

93 Ruth Gavison (ed.), *Issues in Legal Philosophy* (Oxford, 1987), Chap. 1. For Dworkin's response see *Law's Empire,* cit. n. 21, at p. 418 n. 29; cf. S. Burton, 'Ronald Dworkin and Legal Positivism', *Iowa L. Rev.*, **73** (1987), 109.

94 E.g. Dworkin, *Law's Empire,* pp. 14, 102.

Thus a plea for greater sensitivity to the facts of interdependence does not imply a move to some grandiose or optimistic form of internationalism nor does it necessarily involve replacing detailed microscopic studies by grand macroscopic theorizing. Indeed, this trend in anthropology challenges any sharp distinctions between microscopic and macroscopic perspectives.[95]

The theme of interdependence challenges the assumption that the nation-state, the civil society within its boundaries or the municipal legal system is the only or, in some contexts, even the main arena for legal discourse. They are of course important spheres of justice and of law and of economic and political ordering; but at best they should be seen as semi-autonomous social fields rather than as self-contained units.

The message of legal pluralism is that even within such a field, be it a national or provincial 'legal system', there is likely to be a multiplicity of orderings at work and these orderings often cannot be treated as being neatly subsumed under a single systemic structure, except for certain limited purposes such as adjudication. Local legal knowledge in Bradford, for instance, could not reasonably be confined to English law. Islamic Law, European Community Law, International Human Rights Law, the orderings (or otherwise) of multinational enterprises and the Mafia as well as more localized fields could all have a place in a rounded picture of Bradford's (or Whitchurch's) local legal culture. And it would be a peculiarly unreal kind of legal formalism that claimed that these existed or were to be taken account of only in so far as they are validated by the basic norm or rule of recognition or the sovereign of this nation state.

The Citizen of the World and Universal Jurisprudence

What, you may ask, has this to do with Bentham? I shall argue that by virtue of his standpoint and his conception of his juristic enterprise his work still provides the best starting-point, but not the last word, for resurrecting the concept of General Jurisprudence. I wish further to suggest that the story of Bentham's displacement by Austin and his successors provides one key to understanding the tendency to parochialism that I am questioning.

From his first published work until his death Bentham regularly (but not invariably) purported to adopt the standpoint of a (or the) 'citizen of the world' and to be concerned with humankind as

[95] Starr & Collier, op. cit. n. 87, Introduction.

a whole.[96] On 16 February 1831 the day after his 83rd birthday, he wrote in his Memorandum Book:

'J. B.'s frame of mind.
J. B. the most ambitious of the ambitious. His empire ... the empire he aspires to ... extending to, and comprehending, the whole human race, in all places ... in all habitable places of the earth, at all future time.
J. B. the most philanthropic of the philanthropic; philanthropy the end and instrument of his ambition.
Limits it has no other than those of the earth.'[97]

This standpoint is rooted in Bentham's conception of utility. One of the key dimensions of the felicific calculus is 'extent': whose happiness is in question? Bentham's answer is generally universalistic, indeed sometimes going beyond humankind to include all sentient beings.[98] Clearly his citizen of the world is not just a precursor of today's jet-setting technical expert peddling advice and constitutions to the rulers of nation states. This was indeed a role he presumed to, as when he offered his services or gratuitous advice to Tripoli, America, France, Scotland and Iberia.[99] 'Citizen of the world' means more than that. Bentham was persistently troubled by questions fundamental to any theory of individual ethics as well as legislation. With whose interests should we be concerned in our decisions and actions: members of our own community? All living persons affected by our actions? Humankind in general, including the unborn? All sentient beings? Is each of these really to count as one in all our moral and legislative deliberations? Do bonds of family or local or national or other loyalties or ties of membership not count except in terms of calculated consequences? Who are the proper objects of our benificence as individuals and rulers? Bentham was as concerned with such questions as are some modern philosophers, whether utilitarians, such as Peter Singer, or non-utilitarians, such as Onora O'Neill.[100]

[96] Ross Harrison, *Bentham* (London, 1983) at pp. 276–7.

[97] *Works*, Vol. 11, p. 72..

[98] *Introduction to the Principles of Morals and Legislation*, ed. Hart & Burns, 282–3n.; the passage includes the famous aphorism: 'the question is not, Can they *reason*? nor, Can they *talk*? but, Can they *suffer*?'

[99] See John Dinwiddy, 'Bentham and the Early Nineteenth Century', *The Bentham Newsletter*, **8** (1984), 15.

[100] E.g. Peter Singer, *The Expanding Circle* (Oxford, 1983); Onora O'Neill, *Faces of Hunger* (1986); W. Aiken & H. Lafollette (eds), *World Hunger and Moral Obligation* (1977). The philosophical literature is reviewed in David Gosling, 'Obligations to The Third World' in W. Twining (ed.), *Issues of Self-Determination* (forthcoming, Aberdeen, 1990).

Bentham was well aware of the tension between his universalist ethics and his ideas on sovereignty. In many passages he treats the extent of the legislator's concern to be his own community.[101] But he faced up to the problem squarely in writing about international law:

'If a citizen of the world had to prepare an universal international code, what would he propose to himself as his object? It would be the common and equal utility of all nations; this would be his inclination and his duty. Would or would not the duty of a particular legislator, acting for one particular nation, be the same with that of the citizen of the world? That moderation which would be a virtue in an individual acting for his own interests, would it become a vice, or treason, in a public man commissioned by a whole nation? Would it be sufficient for him to pursue in a strict or generous manner their interests as he would pursue his own? ... or would it be proper, that he should pursue their interests as he would pursue his own, or ought he so to regulate his course in this respect as they should regulate theirs, were it possible for them to act with a full knowledge of all circumstances? And in this latter case, would the course he would pursue be unjust or equitable? What ought to be required of him in this respect?'[102]

Such questions need to be addressed today by any theory of law and by any theory of justice. In my view, Bentham's specific answers are less interesting in 1989 than his questions. This also applies to his puzzles over sovereignty. In contrast with Austin he has at least struggled with questions of illimitability and divisibility of sovereignty and with how to erect securities against misrule by the sovereign and his subordinates.[103] Whatever one thinks of the answers, the questions, including conceptual questions, ought to be firmly on the agenda of contemporary legal theory. The context has changed, but the basic theoretical problems are more pressing than ever.

Much the same can be said of Bentham's treatment of non-legal rights. Debates about the meaning, scope and basis of discourses about rights are one arena in which claims about his 'modernity' are recognized to be well-grounded, if what is meant by this is that his concerns and questions are, or should be, shared by many of

[101] E.g. *Principles of International Law, Works,* Vol. 2, p. 561. This was unpublished in his lifetime. The Bowring edition contains a selection from manuscripts dated 1786–9.

[102] Ibid., at 537.

[103] See generally, Hart, *Essays on Bentham* (1982), esp. Chap. 9; J. H. Burns, 'Bentham on Sovereignty: An Exploration', in M. James (ed.), *Bentham on Legal Theory* (1973).

our contemporaries.[104] In my view, Bentham's most important contributions here are conceptual. Those who are concerned to promote human rights need to develop a vocabulary that clearly differentiates between discourses that belong to the spheres of political rhetoric, ethics, legislative recommendation, international relations and positivized international law. Bentham challenges the first two and makes constructive contributions in respect of the others. The charge of criterionlessness; the charge that talk of absolute rights tends to be self-contradictory; the charge that talk of claim rights without assigned correlative duties is meaningless; and the less convincing charge that all talk of non-legal rights is anarchical in tendency—all present challenges to modern rights theories. I have argued elsewhere that the draftsman of any modern declaration or convention or other statement that has more than a rhetorical function has to take account of these charges, but that this is not an impossible task.[105] However, a great deal of rights talk is vulnerable to Bentham's strictures. This applies especially to talk of 'emergent rights' such as the 'right to development' or 'the right to food' which can be interpreted as attempts to promote values to which Bentham also gave a high priority, while treating the mode of discourse as mischievous nonsense.[106]

The standpoint of the citizen of the world is fundamental to Bentham's conception of jurisprudence. The starting-point of modern legal positivism is often attributed to the passage in *A Fragment On Government* where Bentham distinguished between Censorial and Expository Jurisprudence:

> 'There are two characters, one or other of which every man who finds anything to say on the subject of law, may be said to take upon: that of the *Expositor* and that of the *Censor*. To the province of the *Expositor* it belongs to explain to us what, as he supposes, the law IS: to that of the *Censor*, to observe what it ought to be.'[107]

[104] E.g. Waldron, op. cit. n. 79; Hart, *Essays on Bentham*, Chap. 4; Postema, op. cit. n. 71.

[105] 'The Contemporary Significance of Bentham's *Anarchical Fallacies*', (1975) cit. n. 50; see the reply by Melvin Dalgarno in *Archiv fur Rechts-und Sozialphilosophie*, **61** (1975), 359, which offers a more sympathetic interpretation of Bentham's arguments than mine.

[106] The *locus classicus* is *Anarchical Fallacies*, but the theme is repeated in several other works, which are discussed in the writings cited in notes 104 and 105 above. For a recent defence of a 'right to development', see Philip Alston, 'Making Space for New Human Rights: The Case for a Right to Development', *Harvard Human Rights Yearbook*, **1** (1980), 3.

[107] *A Fragment on Government* ed. Burns & Hart (CW, 1977), at p. 397.

It has sometimes been overlooked that in the same passage Bentham continues:

'That which *is* Law, is, in different countries widely different: while that which ought to be, is in all countries to a great degree the same. The *Expositor,* therefore, is always the citizen of this or that particular country: the *Censor* is, or ought to be the citizen of the world.'[108]

In time Bentham devoted some attention to the influence of time and place on legislation. He made it clear from the start that his main concern was with censorial jurisprudence. This passage contains the basis of the distinction between General and Particular Jurisprudence which was later elaborated by Austin in the following terms:

'I mean, then, by General Jurisprudence, the science concerned with the exposition of the principles, notions and distinctions which are common to systems of law, the ampler and maturer systems which by reason of their amplitude and maturity, are pre-eminently pregnant with instruction.
Of the principles, notions and distinctions which are the subject of general jurisprudence some may be esteemed necessary.'[109]

Bentham's conception of the main part of jurisprudence was general, scientific and censorial. In his version of positivism the ought was anterior to the is. His concern with conceptual clarification, which later came to be called 'analytical jurisprudence', was part of his censorial jurisprudence, the main object being to construct a precise 'legislative dictionary'.[110] Strangely over time, analytical jurisprudence became expository rather than censorial, particular rather than general, and not very systematic. In the canon of English positivism the is was treated as anterior to the ought and, tragically, Austin supplanted Bentham as the Father of English Jurisprudence for nearly a century.[111] Today much juristic discourse hovers uncertainly between particular and general jurisprudence, on the one hand abstracted from technical detail of particular fields of law and, on the other hand, rather parochially concerned with localized debates in political philosophy. Even more strangely,

[108] Ibid., pp. 397–8.
[109] John Austin, 'The uses of the study of Jurisprudence', in H. L. A. Hart (ed.), *The Province of Jurisprudence Determined* (London, 1954), at p. 367.
[110] Mary Mack, op. cit. n. 15, esp. Chap. 4.
[111] This theme is developed in my 'Maine and Legal Education: A comment', in J. Lyons (ed.). [forthcoming] and '1836 and all that: Laws in the University of London 1836–1986', *Current Legal Problems,* (1987), pp. 261, 266–74.

positivism is both criticized and defended in terms that seem to be quite contrary to the spirit and substance of Bentham's concerns. Bentham was dethroned not merely in name, but also in spirit.

The Displacement of Bentham

The story of the displacement of Bentham by Austin as the Father of English Jurisprudence has often been sketched, but the puzzle remains: Why this extraordinary misjudgment? In particular, why instead of outright rejection was a close disciple, who was also a positivist, a utilitarian, and a systematic thinker, but who was clearly a lesser and derivative figure, embraced or set up in his stead?

Recently there has been a minor Austin revival, marked by the publication of no less than four books about him (and, in part, his rather more remarkable wife).[112] While these bring out some significant differences between Austin and Bentham and show that the former has in some respects been underrated in recent years, none makes the case for treating Austin as being a thinker of comparable stature in respect of originality, penetration, breadth or even readability. The most that could be said for him is that he took analysis of fundamental legal conceptions a bit further, he was more sympathetic to the common law than Bentham, and his simplemindedness was more congenial to practitioners, law students and critics than his more formidable mentor.

In a forthcoming article Philip Schofield gives a more plausible account.[113] In tracing the story of the eclipse of Bentham and the canonization of Austin within taught jurisprudence and legal scholarship in the late nineteenth century Schofield identifies a number of additional factors. First, Austin's conservative 'theological' utilitarianism was more congenial both to the legal establishment and the first generation of scholar-teachers of law than Bentham's secular, radical 'scientific' utilitarianism. Secondly, Austin's differentiation between expository jurisprudence and the science of legislation corresponded on the surface

[112] W. Morison, *John Austin* (London, 1982); W. E. Rumble, *The Thought of John Austin: Jurisprudence, Colonial Reform and the British Constitution* (London, 1985); L. & J. Hamburger, *Troubled Lives, John and Sarah Austin* (Toronto, 1985); and Robert Moles, op. cit. n. 56.

[113] Philip Schofield, 'Jeremy Bentham and nineteenth century English Jurisprudence', in W. Schrader & U. Guhde (eds), *Der Klassische Utilitarianismus: Einflusse—Entwicklungen—Folgen* (forthcoming).

to Bentham's distinction between expository and censorial jurisprudence. But whereas Bentham emphasized censorial jurisprudence as the basis of expository jurisprudence—for all of his thought was founded on utility—Austin's expository/analytical jurisprudence was treated as standing on its own and as being the foundation of the scientific study of law. '[Thus] law as a science was seen to be independent of any ethical basis. The censor disappeared entirely.'[114] Thirdly, Austin's successors interpreted him narrowly and used him selectively and it is this fact that gives some justification to the Austin revival. One might add that Bentham's attacks on the legal profession and the common law hardly endeared him to the bar and, its satellite, the nascent academic profession and that Austin's epistemology was more in tune with the 'commonsense' ideas of practitioners.

Austin radically narrowed down Bentham by concentrating on the law as it is, but he had nevertheless claimed to be doing general jurisprudence as part of a scientific approach to law. The first generation of full-time law teachers found in Austin a convenient text for the teaching of jurisprudence in the modest space allowed for it. This helped to certify their academic respectability. But in order to establish their credentials with the legal profession they concentrated on the exposition of English law and fairly rapidly Austinian analytical jurisprudence also became more particular than general, concerned with the interpretation of the basic concepts of the common law. This movement away from the conception of a general science of law was almost as significant as the sanitization of exposition from criticism and the freeing of positivism from utilitarianism.

It might be asked: What is the connection between my argument for a tolerant, but discriminating, pluralism in the next stage of Bentham studies and my plea for the restoration of Bentham as the Father of Modern English Jurisprudence? And, is not my account of his displacement an example of a Whiggish approach to the writing of history baccwards of just the kind that the new intellectual historians are concerned to attack?

A short answer to the first question is as follows: while a high proportion of current Bentham scholarship is understandably textual and historical in orientation, there is a natural tendency in the culture of academic law to be concerned with 'contemporary significance' and hence with conversational readings. The work of two leading Bentham scholars who are also legal philosophers,

[114] Ibid., text at n. 35–6.

Hart and Postema, illustrates this tendency. It also shows how conversational readings are compatible with, indeed gain from, textual accuracy and historical sensitivity. Hart combines conversational reading with intimate knowledge of the texts. Postema's *Bentham and the Common Law Tradition* is part of a broader enterprise which is explicitly 'critical and philosophical'.[115] The argument for the reinstatement of Bentham is a plea for giving his work, including some of the less well-known aspects, a more central place (some would say a privileged status) in the canon of texts that command attention both in taught jurisprudence and contemporary juristic debate. The idea of general jurisprudence is just one example of the many topics on which Bentham's concerns and questions are quite close to those of some modern jurists, including myself, who share an unease about certain tendencies in contemporary legal theorizing. The story of Bentham's displacement by John Austin and his successors helps to explain how such concerns and questions became marginalized within twentieth century Anglo-American jurisprudence. Far from being Whiggish, this argument is quite consistent with an historically sensitive approach to the interpretation and use of classic texts, including even the puristic approach of Quentin Skinner. Skinner's interests are focused on the history and historiography of political thought; but his arguments have important implications for contemporary juristic scholarship and debate, which has suffered from some of the bad habits that he and his colleagues have so effectively criticized.

Conclusions

1. Although less than a quarter of the texts of Bentham's *Collected Works* have been published, sufficient groundwork has been done and sufficient momentum has been built up that the end is in sight, provided that sufficient money can be raised to make it possible to complete the task within a reasonable time. It is right that this work should be done to the highest standards because Bentham, as a major international figure, deserves no less and because, unless the edition is accepted as definitive, scholars will insist on doing it again, as happened with the Bowring edition and the Economic Writings. The completion of the *Collected Works* must continue to have the highest priority for Bentham Studies.

2. In recent years a high proportion of Bentham scholarship

[115] Postema, op. cit. n. 25, Preface, p. viii.

has been textual and exegetical. Given the extent, the complexity and the difficulties of deciphering and editing the originals, such work too has rightly been given a high priority. Middlemen as well as editors have an important role to play in Bentham Studies.

3. It would be quite wrong to say that recent exegetical work has tended to be ahistorical or insensitive to context. However, it has tended to be rather specialized and cautious, concentrating on careful analysis of particulars rather than broader sweeps or fundamental criticism. In the next phase of Bentham Studies there will be more scope both for the detailed study of the contexts of particular works in the manner of modern intellectual historians and for more wide-ranging interpretations and re-interpretations that locate Bentham and his ideas and successors in broader historical contexts. There is also much work still to be done on the reception (and rejection) of Bentham's ideas in different parts of the world.

4. Strong claims can and will be made for the continuing vitality and 'contemporary significance' of some of Bentham's works. Bentham texts clearly have some potential for survival because of the 'modernity' of some of his concerns and ideas, his qualities of mind and his radicalism. However, it is clearly important not only to be discriminating about such claims, but also to distinguish between different ways of using and conversing with particular texts. In considering just a few kinds of 'conversation' I have not been arguing for a single kind of reading, but rather for a greater self-consciousness, especially in regard to conversational and critical approaches to such texts.

5. Bentham also has some particularly strong claims to be fully reinstated as the Father of Modern English Jurisprudence, a position regrettably held by John Austin for over a century, and to have a place in the canon of significant Anglo-American jurists who are read and critically discussed in the original. Apart from his historical importance as a jurist, and the reasons mentioned above, there are several reasons for this in respect of law. The most important is that at a time of increasing need to develop a global jurisprudence that is both genuinely interdisciplinary and international no other modern jurist has as strong a claim to fill the role of a classic forerunner many of whose works provide a suitable starting-point, though not the last word, for considering issues that are or should be of current concern in jurisprudence and beyond.

[8]
Imagining Bentham

In October 1995 President Mary Robinson delivered the John Galway Foster Lecture at UCL.[1] Her title was 'Imaginative Possessions', a phrase borrowed from W. B. Yeats. In an essay on Irish Theatre, Yeats had talked of Ireland as 'a community bound together by imaginative possessions'.[2] President Robinson started with England: she referred to the common law, the great eloquence of the English language, and the central place of land in our literature as examples of inspirational and artistic influences that have shaped our national identity. She emphasized how, far from being elements that separate us from the rest of the world, they have all served as bridges of international understanding. Many writers have emphasized the negative aspects of nationalism based on hatred, fear and alienation—'the pathology of modern developmental history, as inescapable as neurosis with the individual', wrote Tom Nairn.[3] President Robinson focused on the positive aspects, those features of our heritage in which we can take pride. Then, perhaps surprisingly, she chose the 150th anniversary of the great potato famine as her first example of a salient 'imaginative possession' of the Irish that could be turned to either negative or positive uses. She eloquently indicated how a sober commemoration of that tragedy could generate empathy and understanding with the victims of famines and other disasters in poorer parts of the world. Her second example was also a surprise: it was Seamus Heaney's celebration of his 'two-mindedness' as a member of the

[1] President Mary Robinson, 'Imaginative Possessions', John Galway Foster Lecture, 26 Oct. 1995 (unpublished).

[2] W. B. Yeats, (1902/3), see *Explorations* (ed. Mrs W. B. Yeats, London, 1962), Pt. II.

[3] Tom Nairn, *The Break-up of Britain* (London, 1977), 359.

minority in Northern Ireland who had been educated within 'the dominant British culture.'[4] President Robinson ended by describing another aspect of Irish 'two-mindedness', the sense of being simultaneously Irish and European. As she begins her new assignment as UN Commissioner for Human Rights, Mrs Robinson will have endless scope for further extending this concept of multiple identities in a single world.

1998 is the 250th anniversary of the birth of Jeremy Bentham. It is my job to help to introduce this celebration. As I pondered whether there is anything new to say about Bentham at a general level, I was reminded of President Robinson's lecture. Why should we value Bentham as one of our imaginative possessions? There is, of course, a literal sense in which we at University College possess Bentham—the auto-icon, his manuscripts, and his ghoulish head locked in the College strong-room. There are also moments in the College, and especially in the Bentham Project, when we seem to be possessed by him. To penetrate beyond the literal interpretations and the cruder images, we need to ask: who are we for this purpose? And who is Bentham? And this leads back to the notion of nested identities.

My thesis today is that we should be proud of Bentham, but it should be for the right reasons. For this purpose I shall adopt three standpoints: first, as a member of University College and as a member of the wider academic community; secondly, as a jurist; and, thirdly, as a citizen. As we shall see, each of these standpoints involves multiple nested identities that range from the very local to the global. Part of Bentham's greatness lies in the ease with which he transcends boundaries of time and space and specialism. Consider, for example, the identity of UCL: is it a London institution? Is it English? Is it British? Is it European? Is it cosmopolitan? The answer to all of these questions is unequivocally 'yes'. So too with academics, with jurisprudence, and with citizenship. And so too with Jeremy Bentham: he was a Londoner, an Englishman, British, an honorary citizen of France, a European, and a self-proclaimed citizen of the world.

Outside specialist circles, Bentham is mainly remembered today for three rather uncomplimentary images: the auto-icon; the panopticon; and Dickens' Gradgrind. I shall argue that these

[4] Seamus Heaney, *The Redress of Poetry* (London, 1995).

images are dangerously misleading. Each may contain a core of truth, but one is a distraction; one is an embarrassment; and one is a caricature. If Bentham is worth sustained celebration, it must be for other reasons.

First, the auto-icon. Jeremy Bentham sits in a cupboard in public outside the Provost's office in UCL. Some of us use this bizarre conversation piece as a teaching aid. What is the meaning of the auto-icon? Is this where utilitarianism leads? Is it an example of English eccentricity or of monumental bad taste or of extraordinary vanity? Or could it be a more subtle satire on sentimental attitudes towards bodies and death? What is a materialist icon? Is this really Bentham?[5] His physical remains raise interesting questions, but Bentham's significance lies in his ideas rather than his body. For Bentham is an imaginative possession. If we are to attribute any serious significance to him, what we have to imagine is not so much his physical appearance or even his rather uneventful life, but his ideas. It is Bentham the thinker rather than the relic or the amiable recluse whom we should honour in 1998.

The second popular image that fascinates the media is the Panopticon—Bentham's design for prisons, hospitals, asylums, and schools. This has done his reputation some harm. In *Discipline and Punish* Michel Foucault used it effectively as a symbol of repressive authoritarian control;[6] critics of Foucault's interpretation point out that transparency is designed to control those with power and not just those who are subject to it, and that Bentham was strongly opposed to all unnecessary

[5] Is the auto-icon really Bentham? In 1992 the College received a pressing invitation that Mr Bentham should travel to Essen as part of a major exhibition about London. If he went, this would constitute a precedent, for it would be the first occasion since his death that he would have ventured abroad. With proper caution, the College set up a multi-disciplinary committee to decide whether it was in the general interest that he should travel. The verdict was that the clothes, the cupboard, the wax head, Dapple (the walking stick), and some minor relics could proceed, but the skeleton was too brittle to risk on a venture abroad. So everything that we can see went to Essen, but nothing of the original body. 'Was it Bentham who went abroad?' I ask my students. 'And is it really Bentham who sits in the cloisters?' I have few doubts that the answer to these questions is 'yes'. There is a magnificent catalogue of the exhibition: Celina Fox (ed.), *London—World City 1800–1840* (New Haven, Conn., London, 1992).

[6] Michel Foucault, *Discipline and Punish: The Birth of the Prison* (trs. Alan Sheridan, Harmondsworth, 1977), esp. Pt. III, Ch. 3.

suffering.[7] But even his defenders have to concede that this is one of the least appealing of Bentham's contributions—although it is difficult to imagine a design for a prison at that time that would seem appealing today.

A recent example of a popularizing use of the panopticon is a book by a UCL graduate, Tim Willocks. His *Green River Rising* is a powerful novel, shortly to become a film. It has been described as 'maybe the best prison novel ever'.[8] The opening words are: '[a] million man-years of confinement had burnished the surface of the granite flags to a greasy smoothness ingrained deeply with grief and despair'.[9] It continues in similar vein. The prison governor, ironically called Hobbes, is a fanatic, obsessed by the ideas that his duty was to discipline and punish the inmates, and that this arcane hell-hole is the best that civilization can do. 'Green River was an architecture of power built upon the paranoid fantasies of the guilty.'[10] A bronze bust of Bentham sits on a plinth in the governor's office. Bentham is described by Hobbes as: '[t]he last mind of any real stature to devote itself to the problem of incarceration'.[11] The prison is based on the Panopticon, and in particular on the idea that if you can get people to believe that they are being watched all the time this will change their personality for the better.[12] Hobbes is mad; Bentham is his hero; the prison architecture and practice are based on Panopticon. The consequence is an approximation to Hell. Is this what we are about to celebrate?

This is hardly great public relations for Bentham or for UCL. Nor does it seem to me to be a serious distortion of Bentham. He did, indeed, call his panopticon 'a mill for grinding rogues honest'.[13] The conception of control through surveillance is basically accurate. Semple's valiant defence softens the Panopticon as a symbol of repressive control, but does not destroy it. She herself acknowledges that it is at best an ambivalent and at times an abhorrent institution.[14] I personally tend to agree with

[7] Janet Semple, *Bentham's Prison: A Study of the Panopticon Penitentiary* (Oxford, 1993); 'Foucault and Bentham: a Defence of Panopticism' (1992) 4 *Utilitas* 105.

[8] Review by James Ellroy, quoted on the cover.

[9] Tim Willocks, *Green River Rising* (London, 1994/5), 3.

[10] *Ibid.*, at 5.

[11] *Ibid.*, at 103.

[12] *Ibid.*, at 104.

[13] *The Correspondence of Jeremy Bentham* (ed. A. T. Milne, London, 1981), iv, 342.

[14] *Ibid.*, 117.

Margery Fry and Sir Stephen Tumim that Bentham's prison would have been 'a human disaster' and that we have rightly rejected it.[15] However, at a more general level I have a rather different interpretation of the Panopticon story. I have on previous occasions argued that Bentham studies can be characterised as the pursuit of the ambiguous by the ambivalent.[16] By this I mean, first, that Bentham is interesting just because—despite taking clear, sometimes extreme, positions—at key points he seems to cut across or transcend conventional differentiations. Benthamic ambiguity is illustrated by the fact that he is regularly praised for being an important forerunner of both *laissez faire* and the modern welfare state; that he favoured both strong government and strong democratic control; that he rejected some of the core features of the common law tradition, yet defended some its most salient institutions such as orality and cross-examination; and that there is a continuing puzzle within utilitarianism about the relationships between utility, justice, liberty, and equality.[17]

Conversely, far from being a sectarian enclave of rabid disciples, Bentham studies have attracted people of varied opinions and often mixed views about their subject.[18] I share this ambivalence, nowhere more so than on questions about punishment. Bentham's general ideas about the principles of punishment seem to represent the enlightenment at its most enlightened; yet the suggestion that the main reason why punishment of the innocent is to be avoided is that it generates alarm in others illustrates a serious flaw in utilitarianism.[19] I find the Panopticon abhorrent in design as well in respect of the dangers of abuse. But the underlying idea of visibility or transparency is less straightforward. Bentham was unequivocal in his belief in publicity as a security against misrule; he allowed few exceptions for state

[15] Stephen Tumim, review of Semple (1993), (1994) 6 *Utilitas* 135, at 137–98.

[16] William Twining, 'Hot Air in The Redwoods, A Sequel to The Wind in The Willows', 86 *Michigan L Rev.* 1523 (1988), at 1536–7.

[17] *Ibid.*, and William Twining, 'Why Bentham?', *The Bentham Newsletter*, No. 8 (1988), 34, at 44–7.

[18] For example, the modified utilitarianism of Herbert Hart and his treatment of the command theory.

[19] This interpretation is contested: F. Rosen, 'Utilitarianism and the Punishment of the Innocent: The Origins of a False Doctrine' (1997) 9 *Utilitas* 23; cf. 'Why Bentham?', n. 17 above, at 49, n. 35.

secrecy and, at least in the context of judicial evidence, gave a low priority to privacy.[20] In contemporary public life there seems to be a deep-rooted ambivalence about the twin issues of publicity and privacy: there are simultaneously strong movements (sometimes supported by the same people) for freedom of information and for a legally protected right of privacy. The roles of transparency and publicity in democratic theory are issues of contemporary significance where conversations with Bentham are still worthwhile.

The third popular image that needs to be challenged is that of Dickens' Mr Gradgrind:

> Now what I want is Facts. Teach these boys and girls nothing but Facts, Facts alone are wanted in life. Plant nothing else, and root out everything else.[21]

This image takes many forms: economics as the dismal science; utilitarianism as a philistine philosophy; positivism as involving an untenably sharp distinction between fact and value, often linked with an indifference to value; the bureaucratization of education in the interests of capital; extending out to rigid systematization of oppression of the poor.[22] This last point is illustrated by Dickens and was perhaps most vividly expressed by Marx, who referred to Bentham as 'the insipid, pedantic, leather-tongued oracle of the commonplace bourgeois intelligence of the nineteenth century'.[23] Such complaints all have resonance with the post-modern mood which challenges empiricism at its core.

This congeries of related images raises issues too varied and complex to pursue here. But it is not difficult to show that significant aspects are at the very least a caricature of Bentham's ideas. For example, his whole thought was founded on utility as a theory of value. It is completely misleading to suggest that he believed that '[f]acts alone are wanted in life' or that his legal positivism involves an indifference to moral concerns. His epistemology, as set out in his intriguing theory of fictions, shows that he was well

[20] Bentham's longest discussion of privacy is in the context of judicial evidence: he allows some scope for privacy, but the general principle is: publicity should be the rule, privacy the exception. (*Works,* VI, 351–80, cf. *Ibid.* 27–8).

[21] Charles Dickens, *Hard Times* (London, 1854), Bk. 1, 1.

[22] David Craig, Introduction to the Penguin edition of *Hard Times* (Harmondsworth, 1969).

[23] Marx, *Das Kapital* (Everyman edn., London, 1957), ii, 671; cf. *ibid.* 164.

aware of problems of describing and interpreting 'the world of fact'.[24] Marx, like Foucault, seems hardly to have read any Bentham and greatly underestimated his subtlety as a thinker.[25]

At the very least, the Gradgrind image is over-stated as a criticism. Indeed, one of the great strengths of Benthamite utilitarianism is its emphasis on the significance of social facts. In order to predict the social consequences of one's actions one needs to have good information about the situation that one is dealing with and the likely outcomes of particular courses of action; in order to evaluate decisions *ex post facto,* one needs to assess actual consequences and make informed judgements about causation. Bentham was a pioneer in respect of the census and other aspects of 'the statistic function'.[26] Utility serves as a counterweight to *a priori* moral theories that are indifferent to social facts and actual consequences and that are epitomized in extreme form in the dubious maxim: *fiat justitia, ruat coelum.* In politics and the social sciences generally Benthamism was a primary inspiration of the Fabian approach to social policy. In Jurisprudence Benthamite empiricism points to the importance of social context and a concern with the actual operation and impact of formal rules. It is clearly untrue that '[f]acts alone are wanted in life'; but it is also true that facts are central to rational decision-making. Some of Bentham's writings seem to be based on a banal common-sense empiricism; but, as we shall see in relation to fictions, his more arcane writings and his second thoughts are much more subtle.[27]

The auto-icon is an entertaining, possibly instructive, diversion; the panopticon is an embarrassment; and the Gradgrind image is a

24 N. 60 below.

25 On affinities between aspects of the thought of Bentham and Marx see H. L. A. Hart, 'Bentham and the Demystification of the Law', *Essays on Bentham* (Oxford, 1982), Ch. 1. Cf. William Twining, 'Reading Bentham', LXXV, Proceedings of the British Academy (1989), 97, 125–6 (hereafter RB).

26 *Constitutional Code* (Collected Works, ed. F. Rosen and J. H. Burns, Oxford, 1983), i, *passim* (see index).

27 An intriguing example is that in *The Rationale of Judicial Evidence* Bentham often adopts a simple common-sense empiricism that seems to be at odds with the much more complex views expounded in his ontology, which he worked on shortly after the writings on evidence. Whether this represents a development of his thought or merely that simple empiricism was adequate for the purpose of his main theses about evidence requires further exploration. A useful start has been made by Gerald Postema in 'Facts, Fictions, and Law', in W. Twining (ed.) *Facts in Law* (Wiesbaden, 1983).

caricature. So how should we imagine Bentham when we celebrate him? His significance is almost entirely in his thought. Past thinkers may be considered significant for a number of different reasons. They may be remembered for their originality; for their qualities of mind or vision; as outstanding representatives or advocates of ideas that they did not necessarily originate; for their influence on historical events or on the ideas of other thinkers or of influential actors; for being 'seminal', that is germinating ideas the implications of which were developed by others; or because their work still has significance for issues of contemporary concern;[28] or for a combination of these. Bentham has some claims to be remembered for each of these reasons, but they need to be differentiated.

For the sake of clarity I shall talk in terms of different characters: there is the historical Bentham, the actual person whom historians and biographers try to reconstruct; there is Bentham as object, the auto-icon as a material thing; there is Bentham as texts, the actual words that he himself wrote, to decipher which is the main concern of his editors; there is Bentham as ideas, reconstructed and interpreted from the texts; there is Bentham *redivivus*, an imagined Bentham transported to 1998 in order to comment on the present scene; and, most elusive of all, is the notional modern Benthamite, a disciple who can be constructed in myriad ways within the parameters of Benthamic ambiguity.

Bentham merits attention at all of these levels and in respect of an astounding array of subjects. For reasons of space and my own

[28] In respect of so-called 'contemporary significance', I have argued elsewhere that a distinction needs to be drawn between several kinds of uses of past thinkers, (*RB*, 116–28). One can enter into an anachronistic conversation with a classic text that speaks directly to current issues, perhaps because its significance transcends the time and place of its composition. Or one may enter into an imaginary conversation with a past thinker transported into the present (or with a follower, not an imaginary Bentham but a modern Benthamite (for examples, see *RB*, at 123 n.). For a light-hearted example of a visitation by Bentham see Lord Goff, 'A Visit from Jeremy Bentham' [1986] 41 *Current Legal Problems* (Presidential Address to the Bentham Club); cf. Hart, *Essays on Bentham*, n. 25 above, at 33–9. It is in this context particularly important to differentiate between genuinely historical readings, anachronistic readings of actual texts, and imaginary, text-free, conversations with an imagined Bentham or an imaginary modern Benthamite who is presumed to be familiar with present conditions. And, of course, readings vary within each genre. Past thinkers, their texts, and their ideas are a resource which may legitimately be used to clarify contemporary issues, but a disciplined approach needs to be sensitive to these distinctions.

limitations I must be selective. So I shall say almost nothing about his originality as a thinker, his qualities of mind, his style, the contentious question of his 'influence', nor about his particular contributions to philosophy, economics, public policy, or other subjects beyond my expertise.[29] Rather I shall give a personal view of why we should treasure him from the three standpoints: as an academic and member of this College; as a jurist; and as a citizen. In dealing with these three perspectives with a broad brush, I shall try to keep clear the distinction between historical, conversational and imaginary treatment of Bentham's ideas.

Bentham and University Education

Let us start with UCL. Most of us are familiar with Henry Tonks' picture in the Flaxman gallery of a portly Bentham inspecting the plans for the site of the new University of London, with several of his supporters very much in the background. It is an imaginative depiction of an imaginary event. Bentham gave his blessing and financial support to the new venture, but he did not actively participate in the foundation. The main initiative came from Thomas Campbell and Henry Brougham; the detailed planning was carried out by a committee which produced an institution which inevitably had some of the qualities of a camel. Campbell had been impressed by the religious toleration in German universities; Brougham had been involved with George Birkbeck in the founding of mechanics' institutes and the Society for Diffusion of Useful Knowledge. Increased educational opportunity was the cornerstone, but the foundation was a fee-paying institution targeted at middle class males. Scottish influence was particularly important: non-residential, non-tutorial, allowance made for attendance at single classes of lectures.[30]

[29] A representative range of such judgements up to about 1990 is collected in Bhiku Parekh's four volume anthology, *Jeremy Bentham: Critical Assessments* (London, 1993). My favourite is still John Stuart Mill's classic essay, 'Bentham', first published in 1838 in the *London and Westminster Review* and revised in 1859 in *Dissertations and Discussions*, i. This is a judicious mixture of praise and criticism, perhaps the classic example of ambivalence about Bentham. It may, inadvertently, have damaged his reputation by down-playing his originality.

[30] Brougham's biographer adds: '[l]ater generations of London students had reason to be thankful that Brougham and his associates, in taking Scotland for their model, imported to London's university an invigorating and adult atmosphere free from the cloying paternalism of its older and more celebrated English rivals'. Robert Stewart, *Henry Brougham: His Public Career 1778–1868* (London, 1985), 197.

Nevertheless, Tonks' image is quite appropriate. UCL was and is Bentham's College. Several of the founders, notably Henry Brougham and James Mill, were overt Benthamites. Bentham himself in a letter to Simon Bolivar refers to the committee as 'an association of liberals'.[31] Most important, several key ideas associated with Bentham have formed the core of UCL's ethos throughout its history. These include religious freedom, educational opportunity, freedom of speech and of enquiry, useful knowledge, and innovation. Although less explicitly proclaimed, one may add excellence.

Let us consider each briefly in turn. Bentham tended to maintain a certain diplomatic discretion about his own religious beliefs. He was himself almost certainly an atheist for most of his life. He was strongly opposed to the establishment of religion, but religious freedom was a central part of his political philosophy.[32]

The University of London was founded in reaction to the religious tests of Oxford and Cambridge which meant that only

[31] Bentham, letter to S. Bolivar, 13 Aug., 1825. The passage reads: '[t]he two great public nuisances—the government universities, Oxford and Cambridge, storehouses and nurseries of political corruption in its more baleful forms, are, by the rapid increase of the matter of wealth in this country, loaded with more scholars than they can hold: though the expense of maintenance there is swollen to such a pitch as to suffice of itself to shut the door against useful instruction and the general habit of application. At the expense of £300,000 (for that is the sum destined for it), an association of liberals are about to set up, in or near London, a seat of Instruction under that same name, for the sake of including the Sectarians, in which the pupils are to be left to pursue each his own notion in respect of religion. But Hazlewood School is at once an ordinary School, and a School of Legislation and Judicature in which, on the best principles, those branches of art and science are taught by practice: so that, as to those the most important of all, the London University will be inferior to the Hazlewood School, unless, as to those points, it does what is done there'. I am grateful to Dr Luke O' Sullivan for this reference.

[32] Bentham's position on religion is too complex to pursue here and much research remains to be done. The best account is Philip Schofield, 'Political and Religious Radicalism in the Thought of Jeremy Bentham' (forthcoming). The main thrust of most of his writings on the subject is to criticize it as an instrument of delusion abused by sinister interests. It has been suggested that he was out to destroy it by persuasion, but this view is controversial. He was clearly against religious discrimination, religious establishment, and indeed any association of religion with the state, but he was positively in favour of religious freedom (e.g. UC. Mss., Box 169, 113). See especially, *First Principles,* n. 69 below, index under Religion, Religious Sanction, Religious Establishment. It is significant that ch. 7 of *Constitutional Code Rationale* (below, n. 69) is entitled '[n]o power of government ought to be employed in the endeavour to establish any system or article of belief on the subject of Religion': *ibid.* 325.

members of the Church of England had access to university education.[33] It has long struck me as ironic that our godless institution, what Praed described as 'the radical infidel college',[34] was first founded in order to open university education to Catholics, Dissenters, Quakers, Jews, Muslims, and other 'infidels'. It is also apt that UCL should ban the teaching of Divinity in the name of religious toleration.[35]

The idea of a secular institution open to everyone regardless of class or creed, advanced by Campbell, espoused and promoted by Brougham, was not fully implemented at first. Fees had to be paid and higher education for women was not yet on the agenda.

However, over time London University has played a leading role in extending educational opportunity across lines of gender, race, and class, as well as religion. The London External System pioneered distance learning and further extended educational opportunity to the house-bound, full-time workers, and even to prisoners and prisoners of war on the dual principles of open access and open learning.[36]

Freedom of enquiry and freedom of speech are the twin pillars of modern notions of academic freedom. When the 12-year-old Bentham asked awkward questions about the Thirty-nine Articles he was told to respect the views of his elders and betters.[37] Thereafter one of his main aims in life was to replace authority by reason in the pursuit of enlightenment. Voltaire was his hero, fallacies of authority were one of the main objects of attack, and

33 At Oxford one had to subscribe to the Thirty-nine Articles in order to matriculate; at Cambridge one had to subscribe in order to graduate, which allowed a few jews and non-conformists to study, but they could not graduate.

34 W. M. Praed, 'A Discourse Delivered by a College Tutor at a Supper Party, July 1 1825', *The Morning Chronicle*, 19 July 1825.

35 On the historical background see Sydney Evans, 'Theology' in F. M. L. Thompson (ed.), *The University of London and the World of Learning* (London, 1990), 147–9.

36 On the External System see N. Harte, *The University of London 1836–1986* (London, 1986); Thompson (ed.), n. 35 above, *passim*. 'Open learning' in practice meant no teaching. One prepared for examinations at one's own pace with almost no help from the University, which merely claimed to be an examining body in this context. Naturally this has been a matter of controversy. Some maintain the idea that as a matter of principle higher education should be mainly a matter of self-education. Others, including students, cling to a more paternalistic view.

37 William Twining, *Theories of Evidence: Bentham and Wigmore* (London, 1985), at 20–1.

freedom of speech, especially freedom of the press, was one of the most important securities against misrule.[38]

A fourth idea was 'useful knowledge'. Suffice to say that 'useful knowledge' is a utilitarian idea and that the utilitarian tradition can take credit for opening up the study of technology, applied science, professional subjects, and modern languages at university level.[39] However, the idea is also closely associated with the Gradgrind image and with charges of anti-intellectualism and philistinism.

Anti-intellectualism is easily disposed of. Look at Bentham's works! One aspect of this requires comment. It is the unity of theory and practice rather than the elevation of practice over theory that characterizes Benthamism. This has been a keynote of UCL's ethos. Nowhere was this more clearly illustrated than in the original appointments in Laws: Andrew Amos, the first Professor of English Law, was a successful barrister with a decidedly practical orientation. But he was lively, engaging, learned, and wide-ranging—far from being banausic or anti-intellectual. John Austin, the first Professor of Jurisprudence, was an abstract philosopher of law, but in his lecture on 'The Uses of the Study of Jurisprudence', he not surprisingly emphasized the utility of his subject for adjudication, daily legal practice, and the development of juridical literature.[40] The importance of ideas and of the interdependence of theory and practice are utilitarian themes.

The charge of philistinism is less easy to counter. After all Bentham himself often questioned the value of poetry: he sometimes put it on a level with pushpin,[41] and, in planning a radical periodical which became *The Westminster Review*, he proposed '[o]ne-half consecrated to politics and morals, the other half left to

[38] See especially the indexes to the political and constitutional writings under 'Public Opinion Tribunal'; cf. *On the Liberty of the Press and Public Discussion* (*Works*, II, 275 (1821)).

[39] Eric Ashby, *Technology and the Academics* (London, 1963); F. M. L. Thompson (ed.), n. 35 above, *passim*.

[40] J. Austin, *The Uses of the Study of Jurisprudence* (1863, ed. H. L. A. Hart, London, 1954).

[41] As we have seen, even the accusation of philistinism needs to be tempered: take, for example, the much-quoted, or misquoted, dictum that '[p]rejudice apart, the game of pushpin is of equal value with the arts and sciences of music and poetry' (*Works*, II, 253); read in context this might be interpreted as a (possibly tongue-in-cheek) jibe against intellectual and social snobbery about 'higher pleasures'—after all Bentham loved music, was a reasonable performer, and is thought to have had a good ear, as Mill himself acknowledged. See Mary Mack, *Jeremy Bentham, An Odyssey of Ideas 1748–1792* (London, 1962), 246–8; Catherine Fuller's note on

literary insignificances'.[42] Furthermore, A. E. Housman's splendid introductory lecture delivered before the Faculties of Arts, Laws and of Science at UCL in October 1892 can plausibly be read as a defence of the Arts against crude interpretations of the idea of 'useful knowledge'. 'While the partisans of Science define the end of education as the useful, the partisans of Humanities define it, more sublimely as the good and the beautiful'.[43]

Crude utilitarianism is indeed vulnerable to charges of philistinism, but this need not concern us unduly. Bentham himself may have sometimes been dismissive of literature, but he was a lover of music and his version of utility purported to accommodate 'the good and the beautiful'. He poked fun at the intellectual snobbery involved in the idea of inherently 'higher pleasures', and much philosophical discussion has since revolved around this debate. Similarly Arts predominated in the original prospectus for the University of London. There were only two Faculties: Medicine, and Arts and Laws; under Arts were included Languages, Mathematics, Physics, the Mental and Moral Sciences, together with the Law of England, History, and Political Economy. One can readily concede that the concept of Arts was interpreted quite widely, including what was arguably the United Kingdom's first Professor of Engineering, that Literature found difficulty in establishing a foothold, and that Housman's lecture reminds us of a perpetual tension between the idea of 'useful knowledge' and love of learning for its own sake. However, I can leave it to my colleagues in Arts and the Slade School, and those who are pioneering a new programme in Law and Literature, to debate whether UCL has betrayed the intentions of its founding fathers by including such pursuits at the centre of our activities.[44]

'Bentham and Music' (unpublished, 1977). Moreover, Bentham may have had his own views on what gave him pleasure, but on this each person was the best judge for himself. Philip Schofield tells me that there is a splendid manuscript passage, that has contemporary resonance, on how the fine arts should not be publicly subsidised.

42 *Works*, X, 540 (1823) quoted in George L. Nesbitt, *Benthamite Reviewing* (New York, 1934), 34.

43 Introductory Lecture, 1892 (privately printed, reprinted in 1933).

44 The original Prospectus of the University in making the case for a university in London stated: '[n]o where else is knowledge more an object of desire, either as a source of gratification, a means of improvement, or an instrument of honest and useful ambition' (reproduced in Negley Harte and John North, *The World of University College London 1828–1978* (London, 1978), at 17). This text should, of course, be read in the same spirit as other fund-raising documents.

The Prospectus of the University stated that

> the Council trust, that they are now about to lay the Foundation of an Institution well adapted to communicate liberal instruction to successive generations of those who are now excluded from it, and likely neither to retain the machinery of studies superseded by time, nor to neglect any new science brought into view by the progress of reason.[45]

UCL was not only radical, but innovative. From the start it broadened and modernized the range of subjects offered at University level. Subsequently it pioneered many new subjects, including physiology, phonetics, and photogrammetry.

Religious toleration, free enquiry, educational opportunity, useful knowledge, and innovation have been core ideas in UCL's ethos throughout its history. They were emphasized and promoted by followers of Bentham. But, of course, one does not have to be a Benthamite to subscribe to any or all of them.

Bentham as Jurist

Bentham should be viewed above all as a jurist: his legal writings constitute the great bulk of his work; one of his first published works was his attack on Blackstone's Lectures on English Law;[46] among his last was *Constitutional Code* Volume I.[47] Jurisprudence is the most extensive, the most original and the most neglected part of Bentham's legacy. Yet he is better known as a philosopher, political theorist, and social reformer. Several factors explain this: within Jurisprudence he was for over a century supplanted by his disciple, John Austin, UCL's first Professor of Jurisprudence.[48] Remarkably, his general theory of law, embodied in *Of Laws in General,* was brought to light only in 1945 and was not published in definitive form until 1970.

[45] Negley Harte and John North, *The World of University College London 1828–1978* (London, 1978), at 19.

[46] *A Fragment on Government* (1776).

[47] *Constitutional Code* (1830), i.

[48] There are several explanations for this extraordinary displacement. Austin was more sympathetic to the common law, less critical of the legal profession, and less dangerously radical than his master. The cynic might add that his general ideas were also both easier to grasp and easier to criticize. Over time the focus of taught analytical jurisprudence also became more parochial or particular, focusing more on basic concepts of English legal doctrine than on fundamental conceptions of all advanced legal systems: Philip Schofield, 'Jeremy Bentham and Nineteenth Century English Jurisprudence', in W. Schrader and U. Guhde (eds.), *Der Klassische Utilitarianismus: Einflusse—Entwicklungen—Folgen* (Berlin, 1990); *RB,* 138–40.

Many of his legal writings have yet to be published; they now constitute the largest part of the buried Bentham. Related to all this, Jurisprudence is considered a rather esoteric subject even within legal circles. In the long term, Bentham and his successors failed to make Jurisprudence part of the mainstream of British intellectual life.[49]

Bentham's contributions to legal thought are generally underrated—both historically and in terms of contemporary significance. Here, I shall use just one issue to illustrate the point: his conception of and his agenda for Jurisprudence. Jurisprudence in this context is synonymous with legal theory, that is the more general aspects of thought and talk of and about law.[50] My thesis is, first, that Bentham's conception of legal theory is at once wider, richer, and more coherent than nearly all contemporary conceptions; and, secondly, that such a conception, revised and updated, is badly needed in an era of globalization.

In elucidating Bentham's conception of Jurisprudence I shall concentrate on his own thought derived from the more accessible texts, without having recourse to more speculative enterprises, such as following out the implications of his ideas or holding imaginary conversations with a resurrected Bentham or a modern Benthamite. Here, his actual words will be enough. However, in the final section, I shall indulge in a brief thought-experiment in relation to current debates about reform of the UK Constitution.

Bentham aspired to be to Jurisprudence what Luther was to Christianity[51] or Newton was to Science.[52] The extent of his ambition has often been remarked; but the nature of his vision of Jurisprudence has been only dimly perceived. The intellectual climate in England in the twentieth century has generally been quite hostile to grand theory,[53] and Bentham's more expansive vision has been dismissed as grandiose rather than treated as grand.

49 William Twining, *Blackstone's Tower* (London, 1994), Preface and ch. 1.

50 William Twining, *Law in Context: Enlarging a Discipline* (Oxford, 1997), chs. 6 and 7.

51 *Works*, VII, 270n.

52 Ross Harrison, *Bentham* (London, 1983), at 141.

53 See e.g. the articulation by Hugo Belfounder in Iris Murdoch, *Under the Net* (London, 1954), at 65–6.

What was that vision? I suggest that it is based on five main pillars: the principle of utility; the theory of fictions; his positivist command theory of law; the idea of a universal science of legislation; and, as a late, but crucial, addition, his democratic theory. The first three pillars have been the subject of an extensive, but uneven, secondary literature. The last two are generally less familiar. These five elements fit together in a single ambitious conception of the nature, agenda and uses of Jurisprudence. I shall comment briefly on each in turn.

First, Utility: the starting-point of all Bentham's thought was the principle of utility. Out of the massive secondary literature we can extract a few central themes.

Bentham refined his ideas on utility over time. The key texts are not the compressed early version in *Introduction to the Principles of Morals and Legislation,* but the much more sophisticated versions set out in general terms in the *Deontology* and some still unpublished manuscripts.[54] The more general aspects of utilitarianism were not new, although Bentham developed them in some significant respects; the originality and interest lie more in his applications of the basic ideas. For example, it is the principle of utility that gives coherence and bite to his very detailed treatment of evidence, the classification of crimes, the rationalization of punishment, and numerous other specific topics. He used utility as a weapon. His utilitarianism needs to be judged as much by its potential for illumination as an analytical and critical tool applied to concrete issues as by its philosophical defensibility as a general theory of value. One does not need to agree with Bentham's utilitarianism to find him continually challenging. As Herbert Hart put it: 'where Bentham fails to persuade, he still forces us to think'.[55]

Benthamic ambiguity begins at the very root of his thought: does pleasure refer to satisfaction or to preference? Was he a direct or an indirect utilitarian? Does Bentham's utilitarian actor maximize his own pleasure or is every human choice, in individual morality and collective decision-making, to be judged by its

[54] F. Rosen, 'Introduction' to *Introduction to the Principles of Morals and Legislation* (Oxford, 1996), at pp. li–lix.

[55] Hart, n. 25 above, 39.

tendency to maximize the general welfare? How far does the concept of 'extent' extend? In other words, does the general welfare always include all humankind and all sentient beings, or is the primary concern of the sovereign, his subordinates, and individuals rightly confined to one's own community, subject to certain exceptions? And so on.[56] Bentham's ideas developed and deepened over time, and he was not always entirely consistent.[57] Some excellent work has been done on aspects of Bentham's utilitarianism,[58] but we cannot have a comprehensive reconstruction of the core ideas of Bentham as utilitarian until the whole range of texts in which he purported to *apply* the utilitarian calculus in particular contexts is made available.

Nevertheless, some aspects of Bentham's position are tolerably clear. Of particular importance is the point that utility is a principle of both individual ethics and social and political morality, of morals and legislation. In Jurisprudence we are mainly concerned with utility as a principle of 'legislation' broadly interpreted. It is the basic principle to be used both in guiding practical social decision-making and in evaluating the actual consequences of such choices. At the core of Bentham's Jurisprudence is the idea of design: design of institutions, constitutions, codes, procedures, practices, and particular laws. Bentham's legal theory is not solely a design theory, because he is also concerned with such matters as interpretation, application, implementation, enforcement, and impact.

It is no coincidence that the most important modern grand theory in political philosophy, John Rawls' theory of justice, is

[56] My own view is that the most coherent rational reconstruction of Bentham's views makes him a preference-utilitarian and an act-utilitarian, concerned with the general welfare of humankind (and generally of all sentient beings) at the level of both individual morality and social philosophy. This does not fit all the texts, but neither does any other rational reconstruction.

[57] For example, in many places Bentham often restricted the application of utility to a single, impliedly enclosed community; but there are indications, especially in his later work, that he was concerned about the question whether any community could properly be treated as self-contained for this purpose—an issue of considerable importance as the world becomes more interdependent. See n. 97 below on extent.

[58] The best recent works are: Rosen, n. 54 above; Paul Kelly, *Utilitarianism and Distributive Justice* (Oxford, 1990); Gerald Postema, *Bentham and the Common Law Tradition* (Oxford, 1986).

also pre-eminently concerned with the design of institutions and their basic structure.[59]

Fictions: Bentham's theory of logic and language has been hailed by Ogden, Quine, Hart, and others as being philosophically original and ahead of its time. It anticipated in important respects key developments in English analytical philosophy over a century later. This contains his basic ontology and epistemology as they developed over a number of years. This is one of the most important sub-projects of the Bentham Project and it is splendid news that much of the key material has just recently been made accessible in English and French, based on a text established by Philip Schofield.[60] It is impossible to do justice to it here. But it is worth

[59] '[T]he guiding idea is that the principles of justice for the basic structure of society are the object of the original agreement. They are the principles that free and rational persons concerned to further their own interests would accept in an initial position of equality as defining the fundamental terms of their association. These principles are to regulate all further agreements; they specify *the kinds of social co-operation that can be entered into and the forms of government that can be established*. This way of regarding the principles I shall call justice as fairness': J. Rawls, *A Theory of Justice* (Oxford, 1972), 11, (italics added). See, generally, John Rawls, *Political Liberalism* (New York, 1993); Thomas Pogge, *Realizing Rawls* (Ithaca, NY, 1989), 8–9, 127, 136–7, and *passim*; J. Rawls, 'Justice as Fairness: Political not Metaphysical' (1985) 14 *Philosophy and Public Affairs* 223. Rawls is, of course, a leading critic of classical utilitarianism, which he locates with Sidgwick but associates with Bentham. I am not here concerned with the merits or otherwise of Rawls' own ideas, nor with setting up an imaginary conversation between two leading thinkers, who might be shown to have a greater affinity to each other than is generally perceived. The point in this context is that both are involved in the practical enterprise of designing principles, institutions, and practices of good governance.

Rawls' and Bentham's enterprises overlap substantially. But their situations and agendas as well as their ideas were not the same. One difference is that most of Bentham's energies were directed to applying the principle of utility rather than to establishing or elucidating it. (On Rawls' own 'epistemic abstinence' see Joseph Raz, *Ethics in the Public Domain* (Oxford, 1994, ch. 4)). Bentham did not attempt a proof of utility; his refinements largely took the form of afterthoughts; he used utility as a weapon for dealing with specific practical problems in what he considered, not always realistically, to be a realistic fashion. Like Marx he was more concerned to change the world than to understand it. Of our contemporaries, Peter Singer is closer to Bentham in spirit than is Rawls, focusing on the detailed application of utility to contemporary practical problems more than considering in depth its philosophical foundations (see, e.g., Peter Singer, *Practical Ethics* (2nd edn., Cambridge, 1993); *Animal Liberation* (New York, 1975). The fact that Bentham is still taken quite seriously as a moral philosopher, even in respect of individual ethics, can be as much a diversion as a compliment. Most of his jurisprudence is an application of utility as a principle of legislation rather than of morals.

[60] Jeremy Bentham, *De l'ontologie et autres textes sur les fictions* (ed. J.-P. Clero and C. Laval; trs. P. Schofield, Paris, 1997).

emphasizing two key points. First, Bentham's theory of fictions is a constructivist epistemology based on utility: we construct our knowledge of the world through the lens of language, itself a human construct, which is both necessary and dangerous. It is a theory which arguably has affinities with pragmatism, the sociology of knowledge, and even some kinds of post-modernism (e.g. Rorty). His conception of 'facts' is worlds away from that of Gradgrind.

Secondly, both construction and elucidation of abstract concepts are essential to jurisprudence and the science of legislation. Concepts are the basic tools. For almost a century an impoverished version of conceptual analysis, under the name of analytical jurisprudence, dominated legal theory in this country. It was impoverished in respect both of method and of the range of concepts treated as worthy of analysis. In the 1960s and 1970s a reaction set in, both as part of the general reaction against the excessive claims of so-called linguistic or 'Oxford' philosophy, in part because it was perceived that legal theory should address a much wider range of issues than elucidation of concepts. I am personally sympathetic to these concerns, but in retrospect there was an over-reaction and the balance needs to be adjusted. Bentham was quite right in treating the construction and elucidation of concepts as one of the main jobs of jurisprudence. Today there is a need for a revival of conceptual analysis as a key part of general jurisprudence.

Bentham's general positivist theory of law is probably that aspect of his jurisprudence that is most vulnerable to criticism. The notions of sovereign, command, and habit of obedience have all taken a hammering, especially in the Austinian version. Positivism versus anti-positivism is still treated by many as the main battle-ground of jurisprudence. My own view is that a modern Benthamite would need to re-conceptualize the basic phenomena of law within the framework of Bentham's general vision. And a sharp distinction between is and ought cannot be maintained across different contexts.[61] In short, this is the weakest of the five pillars of Bentham's science of legislation.

However, even here, we should not be too dismissive. For

[61] William Twining, 'Other People's Power: The Bad Man and English Positivism, 1897–1997' (1997) 63 *Brooklyn L Rev.* 189.

example, for his time Bentham was extraordinarily percipient about the conceptual problems of the notion of 'sovereignty' in respect of divisibility, limitability, and omnicompetence;[62] and towards the end of his life he posed acute questions about the extent of the duty of a particular legislator in the world arena: does utility require the sovereign to maximize the interests of his own people or should his duty be the same as that of the citizen of the world?[63] Bentham did not come up with clear answers, but he did pose some questions which lie right at the centre of contemporary international ethics.[64] On questions centring on the concept of 'rights' Bentham started a line of analysis that was later developed by Austin, Hohfeld, Hart, and others. And, of course, his famous attacks on natural rights and other non-legal rights still pose a challenge to rights talk.[65]

Even the notion of law as command is not entirely dead. It is one of the ironies of intellectual history that Professor H. L. A. Hart, who first made his reputation by destroying Austin's command theory, was later responsible for bringing Bentham's version of the theory to light; and in one of his last essays Hart even conceded that there is an important core of truth in Bentham's idea of law as command, as 'a content-independent peremptory reason for action'.[66]

This brings us back to Bentham's positivism. Whatever else one thinks of it, it is not apolitical or sterile or the basis for the idea that might is right or that law is simply a matter of brute fact, or some of other canards that are sometimes attributed to legal positivism. Bentham's idea of law is an instrument of power which ought to be, but often is not, exercised to maximize the happiness of the greatest number. The idea is still widely influential today and is, of course, perennially controversial. I personally sympathize with the view, most recently expressed by several contributors to

[62] These ideas are perceptively analysed in Oren Ben Dor, 'Constitutional Limits and the Public Sphere: A Critical Study of Bentham's Legal and Constitutional Theory', Ph.D. thesis (London, 1997), chs. 2 and 3.

[63] *Works*, II, 537, discussed *RB*, 133–8.

[64] Charles Beitz *et al.* (eds.), *International Ethics: A Philosophy and Public Affairs Reader* (Princeton, NJ, 1985). A contemporary example is whether prevention and succour of famines in poorer countries are only a matter of charity for richer nations and individuals.

[65] See n. 96 below.

[66] Hart, n. 25 above, 20, 261.

the volume on *The Autonomy of Law*, that much of the positivism *v.* anti-positivism debate is repetitious, trivial, and almost entirely pointless.[67] There are some genuine, sometimes profound disagreements and some differences of concern underlying controversies about positivism, but the range of disagreement is much narrower than decontextualized, obsessive discourse suggests. In my judgement, Bentham is here best treated as an important historical forerunner of modern positivism rather than as a good starting-point for considering contemporary issues. The debate has moved on.

General Jurisprudence: The Concept of a Universal Science of Legislation

Through the efforts of Hart and others several aspects of Bentham's jurisprudence have been explored in detail, for example: his version of legal positivism; a more flexible and subtle conception of sovereignty than Austin's; his penetrating attack on natural rights; his progressive ideas on punishment; and his theory of adjudication. These are all important topics, but they represent only a relatively small part of the whole. What is missing, above all, is a rounded account of the most comprehensive and radical vision of law in our intellectual history. Bentham adopted the standpoint of 'a citizen of the world' which is more in tune with modern globalizing tendencies than the perspectives of most of his successors. He propounded a universal science of legislation, which he worked out in great detail at a number of levels. Overall his grand vision included the five pillars mentioned above: a general theory of value, a theory of knowledge and of language, a theory about the nature of laws in general, a theory of institutional design, and, towards the end of his life, a theory of constitutional democracy. Subordinate to these were more or less developed sub-theories of codification, adjective law (evidence and procedure), rewards and punishments, and much else. No English-speaking jurist before or

67 Robert P. George (ed.), *The Autonomy of Law: Essays on Legal Positivism* (Oxford, 1996), e.g. Klaus Füsser, '[l]ast but not least, it is by no means clear that the battles about the Separation Thesis are not entirely pointless. The question of necessary relations between morality and law hinges crucially on the presupposition that the very concept of law itself does not unravel into different sets of convenient stipulations from different epistemological angles, each of which renders the question of necessary relations trivial', at 120, discussed in Twining, n. 61 above.

since has had such an ambitious intellectual agenda; indeed, it may be that British antipathy to 'grand theory' has been one of the obstacles to a full appreciation of his legal thought.

Philip Schofield in his lecture on 'Bentham: Legislator for the World', has dealt in detail with the idea of a universal science of legislation.[68] Let me just add one footnote: one reason for the modern tendency to shy away from general jurisprudence is a greater sensitivity to differences of history, tradition, language, culture, and circumstance that make us all chary of global generalizations, cultural universals, or universalizability, even if we hesitate on the path towards strong cultural or ethical relativism. But looking at law from a global perspective and constructing a general jurisprudence that looks at law in a global context involves no commitment to naïve universalism: rather it puts issues about interdependence, cultural and ethical relativism, multi-culturalism near the top of the agenda. Bentham was aware of issues of the influence of time and place on matters of legislation, but for my taste he underestimated the importance of history, language, and other factors that go to make up the complex matters that we tend to talk of in terms of 'culture' and 'identity'. In this instance, some of his less known texts may make a good starting-point for thinking about a revived general jurisprudence, but too much has happened in the world and the realm of ideas for them to be more than that.

Constitutional Reform and Democratic Theory

Jurisprudence is my subject, so I can claim to be a specialist, or at least a licensed dilettante. In respect of the fifth pillar, democratic theory constitutional reform, my standpoint is that of an interested citizen. However, as a member of UCL, I am near the hub of the current movement towards constitutional reform in which several of my colleagues—Jeffrey Jowell, Dawn Oliver, Rodney Austin—have played a prominent role. It is no coincidence that The Constitution Unit was to start with linked to the Faculty of Laws and that its Director, Robert Hazell, is now a member of our School of Public Policy. At the same time, the Bentham Project

68 See this volume, 115.

has been giving priority to Bentham's political and constitutional writings. Five splendid volumes have been published, with several more in active preparation.[69] In addition, the most important secondary writings on Bentham's constitutional ideas have been lucidly expounded by Fred Rosen, Philip Schofield, and Jimmy Burns—all members of UCL. As a non-expert surrounded by the world's leading experts in these two fields, I must tread carefully: but I want to report on a thought experiment involving bringing these two neighbours together.

Recently, under medical orders to rest, I decided to indulge in a reading binge on Bentham's constitutional ideas: so I took to my bed these five volumes, my favourite *The Book of Fallacies*, an anthology of critical writings about Bentham, and Fred Rosen's *Jeremy Bentham and Representative Democracy*[70]—a mere 4,000 or so pages out of a much more extensive whole.

Be assured: one does not expect ordinary citizens to read more than 1,000 pages of Bentham's constitutional writings and I did not read every word. In reading Bentham there are three primary rules of thumb: first, as Sydney Smith suggested, one needs to start with a middleman or secondary writer who presents the eminent philosopher 'washed, trimmed, shaved, and forced into clean linen'.[71] One does not usually start with the original in order to get the plot, and Fred Rosen in particular is an admirable guide to the general constitutional theory. Secondly, one does not read Bentham's works in the way one reads detective stories, starting at the beginning. Rather one reads and uses the superb analytical indexes of the relevant volumes in the *Collected Works* and the skimpier, but nonetheless useful, general index of the Bowring

69 Already published: *Constitutional Code* (ed. F. Rosen and J. H. Burns, Oxford, 1983), i; *First Principles Preparatory to Constitutional Code* (ed. P. Schofield, Oxford, 1989); *Securities against Misrule and other Constitutional Writings for Tripoli and Greece* (ed. P. Schofield, Oxford, 1990); *Official Aptitude Maximized: Expense Minimized* (ed. P. Schofield, Oxford, 1993); *Colonies, Commerce and Constitutional Law: Rid Yourselves of Ultramaria and other Writings on Spain and Spanish America* (ed. P. Schofield, Oxford, 1995); in preparation *Constitutional Code*, ii and iii; *An Essay on Political Tactics; Plan for Parliamentary Reform; Anarchical Fallacies and Political Fallacies*; and *'Legislator of the World': Writings on Law, Codification, and Education* (ed. P. Schofield and J. Harris, Oxford, 1998).

70 Bhikhu Parekh (ed.), n. 29 above, iii, 1019–20 (1993) and F. Rosen, *Jeremy Bentham and Representative Democracy* (Oxford, 1983).

71 Sydney Smith, 'Bentham's Book of Fallacies' (review), *Edinburgh Review*, 42, (1825), 367.

edition. Thirdly, one looks for a work or fragment in which Bentham summarized his basic ideas in his own words—in this instance *Constitutional Code Rationale of 1822*, a nutshell of just over 100 pages.[72]

I happily immersed myself for ten days in these primary and secondary works. Early on I got the idea that Bentham is like a fox in respect of administrative and logistical detail, but he is essentially a hedgehog in respect of constitutional design. He has one big idea: that the interests of the rulers, however they are chosen, are in all respects potentially opposed to the interests of the governed. It is the function of constitutional arrangements to bring about an identity of interests so far as is feasible, so that the greatest happiness of the greatest number will be maximized. The main solution is to give continuing and effective control over the exercise of power to the whole community, the people, and to provide a number of securities against misrule. By far the most important of these securities is publicity—a wide term which embraces such contemporary ideas as transparency, accountability, and freedom of information. The basic idea is embodied in three axioms:

1. 'The right and proper end of government in every political community is the greatest happiness of all the individuals of which it is composed'.[73]
2. 'The actual end of government is in every political community the greatest happiness of those, whether one or many, by whom the powers of government are exercised'.[74]
3. The Junction-of-interests prescribing principle: '[t]he nature of the case admitts but of one method, which is the destroying the influence and effect of whatever sinister interest the situation of the individual may expose him to the action of. . . .'—that is to divest rulers of virtually all sinister interest, so that the interest of the rulers is in accordance with the interests of the ruled.[75] This is mainly achieved by giving real and sustained power to the people to locate, to monitor, and to recall (or dislocate) and to punish almost anyone who is entrusted with political powers as their

[72] *First Principles*, n. 69 above, 227–331.
[73] *Constitutional Code Rationale*, n. 69 above, at 232.
[74] *Ibid.*
[75] *Ibid.*, at 235–6.

deputies.[76] Practically everything in the thousands of pages of constitutional and political writings stem back to this basic theme.

Even in clean linen, Bentham is not easy reading, and in time I drifted from thinking to day-dreaming to drowsiness to full-blown sleep to a real dream. Some years ago Ripley's 'Believe it or Not' depicted the auto-icon coming alive to haunt UCL with disastrous consequences.[77] It contained some egregious errors of fact and attributed to Bentham a malevolence that not even his severest critics accord him. In my dream the auto-icon came alive in 1998 in more benevolent mood and asked to inspect our institutions of governance. JB was in his late seventies, but looked pretty sprightly in a Bentham tee shirt and Reeboks. As with a similar tour allegedly referred to by Byron as 'Jeremy Bentham's cruise' and unkindly described by William Parry in 1825,[78] we 'set off jogging at the pace of a Highland messenger', but this time we were not ridiculed by prostitutes in Fleet Street or elsewhere, because jogging is a commonplace nuisance today as opposed to a sign of madness. Having completed our tour, Mr Bentham looked briefly at the current government's programme of reform, which as you know includes devolution, a government for London, a bill of rights, reform of the House of Lords, freedom of information, and possibly reform of the electoral system.[79] Asked for his reactions he started with a typical quadrifurcation: changes conducive to utility; changes adverse to utility; changes requiring further appraisal; and absence of significant change.

He grudgingly acknowledged a few improvements representing partial acceptance of his ideas: decolonization; a start in the direction of representative democracy; the House of Commons and local councils elected by secret ballot, on something approaching

[76] Bentham distinguished between appointment (location) and dismissal (dislocation) of administrators and judges: the electorate only directly chooses legislators, but it has powers to dismiss a wide range of officials, including judges (*Constitutional Code I*, ch. V, Art. 5, 31–2).

[77] *Ripley's Believe it or Not*, No. 87, Mar., 1979 (New York).

[78] W. Parry, *The Last Days of Lord Byron* (London, 1825). For a detailed account of 'Major' Parry and his connections with Bentham and Byron, see F. Rosen, *Bentham, Byron and Greece* (Oxford, 1992), ch. 10.

[79] See, generally, *Inquiry, The Constitution Unit Newsletter* (1995–7) and the series of reports published by the Constitution Unit.

universal suffrage—but not annual elections; relative freedom of the press and other media, despite ownership by a few sinister interests; a greater reliance on legislation, but resistance to codification;[80] a reasonable record on religious toleration and some progress on a trend towards secularization of the institutions of state; a system of bureaucratic public administration based in theory on utilitarian principles and, indeed, utilitarian thinking quite strongly, if patchily, operative in many areas of political and economic life; a salaried judiciary, albeit a bit too powerful, still drawn from the legal profession, and still operating under the common law; at least talk of privatization of prisons and an extensive use of conversation-tubes.[81]

The biggest changes are technological, and he expressed delighted amazement at the gadgetry connected with the communication revolution; but he was even more amazed that e-mail, faxes, mobile phones, electronic voting have not been harnessed in the service of securities against misrule and maximizing publicity and what we now call transparency and accountability.[82]

However, so far as constitutional affairs are concerned, his main comment was how little had changed in respect of fundamentals or how they had changed for the worse: in many respects the interests of the governors remain in direct and constant opposition to the interests of the governed—not least in their preoccupation with gaining and retaining power; patronage and waste pervasive: expense maximized, aptitude far from maximized; the hereditary principle still surviving as a basis of influence in the House of Lords and the Monarchy; the honours system and other examples of factitious dignity still surviving along with some new forms of corruption, such as the proliferation of undemocratic and unaccountable quangos;[83] too much power in the executive; and the fallacy of 'separation of powers' as opposed to subordination still in vogue; a rapacious legal profession still treating the legal system as largely its private preserve; judges still recruited from

[80] On codification, see Philip Schofield, 'Jeremy Bentham: Legislator for the World', ch. 4, this vol.

[81] On conversation-tubes, see *Constitutional Code I*, 442–43n.

[82] *Ibid.*; see also the discussion of the mimetic, or mimographical mode of registration: *ibid.*, at 230.

[83] Philip Schofield, 'Jeremy Bentham on Political Corruption: A Critique of the First Report of the Nolan Committee' [1996] 49 *Current Legal Problems* 395.

the band of advocates; and, perhaps most important of all, a style of political discourse that regularly and almost systematically is an instrument of mystification on behalf of the sinister interests of powerful groups and classes: jargon abundant; law dominated by the Technical System; regular use, mainly by the Ins, of most of the fallacies that he had so vigorously attacked: old favourites like The Chinese Argument, The Snail's Pace Argument, and Imposter Terms still in vogue; new fallacies developed and old ones refined: Cornford's Principle of Unripe Time, the Way of the Baffled Medic; and 'we need a Royal Commission' as a fallacy of delay. Finally, a survival, indeed a revival, of talk of inalienable natural or other non-legal rights and other mischievous nonsense. In short, mystifying nonsense-talk still pervasive in public discourse, largely furthering the sinister interests of the few.

Mercifully, my dream and Mr Bentham's visit were short: at the end I asked him what immediate constitutional reforms would he propose as priorities short of wholesale adoption of his Constitutional Code. Not surprisingly, all of his recommendations centred on bringing about a greater identity of interests between the People and those entrusted with power: his specific measures included the following:

(i) termination of surviving aspects of the hereditary principle—for example, abolition of the second chamber, removal of all remaining political power from the monarchy and the aristocracy, and extinction of all factitious titles;

(ii) strengthen democratic control over central and local government through more frequent elections, more offices subject to election, officials, whether elected or appointed, subject to recall by democratic vote between elections, popular control of the organs of public opinion, greater involvement of the public in legal matters through the Quasi-Jury, and legislation governing freedom of information;

(iii) the removal of Parliament, now a single chamber, to some more central and relatively unappealing location, such as Milton Keynes or Nuneaton;

(iv) a more systematic organization of democratically controlled regional government, with devolved powers, but subordinate and answerable to the central legislature.[84] This should include a Regional Government for London, located at Westminster, with an elected Supremo, called the Headman rather than the Mayor, chosen for his aptitude rather than his fame;

(v) a sustained war on all current forms of misrule, including waste in public expenditure, unnecessary punishment, patronage, and corruption—the latter defined much more widely than by the Nolan committee to include all practices that promote the particular interests of rulers at the expense of the governed;[85]

(vi) a computerized fallacy-spotting and publicizing machine monitoring all discourse in the central and subordinate legislatures, the news media, and other public arenas.

At this point I woke up and so failed to get a complete list of Mr Bentham's proposals. This was, of course, *my* dream. Other students of Bentham would no doubt have imagined such a visitation quite differently. It was not a nightmare, but it was mildly shocking because his recommendations were so much more far-reaching than anything that has been envisaged in recent debates on constitutional reform.

I have some doubts about the utility of such fanciful imaginings. But perhaps you will bear with me while I reflect briefly on what I learned from this thought-experiment.

First, we are experiencing what is presented as the most radical process of constitutional reform for over 150 years; yet Bentham's reaction is a reminder about how cautious, *ad hoc*, piecemeal, and in many respects unprincipled the current reform agenda is. This is hardly surprising. A distinction is sometimes drawn between traditional and contrived constitutions.[86] Bentham's Constitutional Code is a clear example of the latter: that is to say that it is, in Everett's words, logical and engineered, a single scheme, consciously designed, perhaps by a single mind, on the basis of articulated principles.[87] Contrived constitutions typically mark a

[84] Rosen (1983) Ch. 8.

[85] Philip Schofield, n. 83 above.

[86] e.g. Lord Hailsham, 'Is the British Constitution Wearing a Bit Thin?', *The Times*, 12 May 1975.

[87] C. W. Everett, 'The Constitutional Code of Jeremy Bentham' (1948), reprinted in Parekh, n. 29 above, iii, 501, at 503.

sharp break with the past. The American Constitution, of 1789, which influenced Bentham in some important respects, could be said to have been contrived; so too were independence constitutions in the period of decolonization after World War II, and more recently the new constitutions of South Africa and Uganda. The United Kingdom is often held up as being one of the clearest examples of a traditional constitution, even though it has a few contrived bits. Our constitution is said to be 'unwritten', and it has evolved over time in a series of fits and starts and barely visible transitions. It is true that in the past twenty years or so we have seen a speeding up of the pace of change and a slight move away from the traditional pole. But the current agenda of reform is qualitatively different in respect of both content and process from the Benthamic model. From that point of view, important as some of the changes are, they are in no sense radical. Tony Blair has promised 'the most extensive package of constitutional change ever proposed'[88]—except Bentham's *Constitutional Code*? From a Benthamic point of view devolution is incoherent; the incorporation of a rather shop-worn human rights document can only be seen as a quite cautious step in an evolutionary process rather than an historic break with the past or a new beginning; reform of the House of Lords may reduce, but will not eliminate, the hereditary principle; a Freedom of Information Act will almost certainly be a pretty cautious compromise; and, perhaps the most important change, a modification to the way votes are counted will leave unaffected the position of those who are elected, the frequency of elections, and the extent of direct control of the governed over the governors. Indeed, there is precious little about securities against misrule.

I make these points not by way of criticism: I personally think that most of these moves are improvements and that the Constitution Unit was right to emphasize considerations of feasibility—of practical politics—in respect of both substance and process. There is not a demand and there is not felt to be a need for a fresh start and a clear rejection of tradition. The Public Opinion Tribunal is silent, almost apathetic, on the matter. What these musings bring out is just how far from Bentham's model of a genuinely democratic polity we shall be even if the most ambitious planks of the present

[88] Labour Party Manifesto (1997).

reform agenda are implemented. Bentham revived would not be alone in thinking that the present reform agenda does not go very far towards reducing the democratic deficit.[89]

A second thought prompted by this exercise concerns the process. Bentham would have been quick to seize on the fact that our constitutional debates have been dominated by party politics. With the possible exception of the internal Scottish devolution debate, in which a lengthy cross-party process sought consensus and compromise, there has hardly been a constitutive process that was freed from marshalling opinion and votes along party lines.[90] Yet reading Bentham has left me unimpressed by his treatment of the process of constitution-making: on his analysis, why should any rulers sacrifice the opportunity to further their own interests through holding onto power? In his writings on Tripoli, and in a few other passages, he attempts to address the issue of how to obtain concessions from the existing ruler(s). He concedes that 'whatsoever may be the chance of such concession, blindness on the part of the sovereign to these its beneficial consequences is . . . a condition little less than indispensable to the existence of so felicitous a state of things'.[91] He goes on to suggest that '[t]he chance of the requisite concession is not equally minute in all imaginable cases' and, apart from hoodwinking the Sovereign, suggests that timidity, facility of yielding to advice, love of reputation, and sympathy for the people are among such conditions.[92] This looks like whistling in the dark. In several places he rules out violent revolution, but elsewhere he treats force, or at least the threat of force, as sometimes being necessary or justifiable.[93] Another example of Benthamic ambiguity?

[89] e.g. William Rees-Mogg, 'Can We Win Back our Democracy?', *The Times*, 24 Feb. 1997.

[90] On the Scottish Constitutional Convention (SCC), see *Scotland's Parliament* (Constitution Unit, London, 1996).

[91] *Securities Against Misrule*, n. 69 above, at 103.

[92] *Ibid.* 107.

[93] Bentham was generally against revolution and considered that change could and should generally be achieved without it: e.g. *First Principles*, n. 69 above, at 220–1; *Anarchical Fallacies*, n. 69 above; see Rosen n. 70 above, esp. 10, 223–5. *Per contra*, there are some passages where he appears to condone even violent revolution or its threat as a last resort: 'so universal and tenacious is the appetite for power, that the idea of any considerable change in this part of the field of legislation [i.e. Constitutional Code], affords little promise of being found endurable, unless when imposed by force or intimidation.' *Codification Proposal* s. 5 (1822); cf. *Securities Against Misrule*, n. 69 above, at 106–11, 138–40; *Works*, II, 286–7. Further research is needed to clarify his position and how far it changed over time.

Quite apart from the unlikelihood of the voluntary surrender of self-serving power, there may be another reason for Bentham's avoidance of discussing the constitutive process. His Constitutional Code is a complete blueprint which is not meant to be negotiable in respect of its fundamentals. How different has been the arduous process of democratic constitution-making through consensus and compromise in elected constituent assemblies that have characterized how the fresh starts in South Africa and Uganda have been worked out. Bentham could no doubt be defended on the ground that in respect of codification he allowed for extensive public discussion and amendment, especially in relation to adapting the substance to local conditions, but one wonders whether Bentham's fundamental constitutional principles can be treated as negotiable even within a democratic constitutive process.

My thought experiment did advance my thinking on a range of particular issues, including corruption, official aptitude, the education of public opinion, and its protection from manipulation. I also concluded that, far from rejecting the enactment of a positivized Bill of Rights with a provision for reference back to Parliament through a 'declaration of incompatibility' rather than full-scale judicial review,[94] Bentham might have argued that this provision does not go far enough: his objection was to talk of non-legal rights; not to enactment into positive law of enforceable legal rights. He could well have objected to a power of judicial review, but the present proposal for a declaration of incompatibility linked to a fast-track statutory instrument procedure seems more like admonitory instructions to Parliament—and, of course, for him sovereignty should lie not with Parliament but with the People.[95]

Bentham's attack on natural rights and the French Declarations of 1791–5 has sometimes been interpreted as an attack on all documents incorporating basic or constitutional rights. This is a mistake.[96] In *Anarchical Fallacies* he was mainly attacking a form

[94] Human Rights Bill, 1997, cl. 4, discussed in *Rights Brought Home: The Human Rights Bill* (Home Office, London, 1997, Cm 3782), ch. 2.

[95] See Ben Dor, n. 62 above, chs. 2 and 3.

[96] The arguments are dealt with at length in William Twining, 'The Contemporary Significance of Bentham's Anarchical Fallacies' (1975) 61 *Archiv für Rechts- und Sozialphilosphie* 325, and reply by M. Dalgarno, *ibid.*, at 357, pushing the argument even further. Both essays are reprinted in Parekh (ed.), n. 29 above, iii.

of discourse embodied in documents that in his view did not and could not have the force of law. His first line of attack was on the idea of non-legal rights, because rights are created by law—a non-legal right is like a son without a father. His second main line of attack was on the idea of inalienability or immutability: rights cannot be imprescriptable because it is not possible conceptually to limit the power of an omnicompetent sovereign. Thirdly, talk of absolute rights is self-contradictory, because rights can conflict with each other. Fourthly, much of his criticism was directed at specifics and style and content of the French Declarations. None of these criticisms apply to positivized conventions, and bills of rights, which have the force of law, can be changed by procedures established by law, and which are recognized as potentially competing with each other in specific contexts.

A modern Benthamite might well be critical of aspects of the style and substance of the European Convention or of the recently published Human Rights Bill. But none of Bentham's major criticisms apply to a law embodying legal rights, made by Parliament and specifically subject to future revision by Parliament. If the Bill had included a provision for judicial review on the American or Canadian model, there would be room for debate among Benthamists as to the logic of his position on this issue. But the current proposal for remitting potential clashes to Parliament has Benthamic echoes. The proposed Bill of Rights has as its main objective providing some securities against misrule: whether Bentham would have considered them adequate in respect of form, scope, or substance is an open question, but he would not necessarily have disapproved in principle of incorporating such values into law.

Imagining Bentham in this way, either dreaming of jogging around with the man or, more seriously considering our current constitution in the light of his texts, is highly artificial and of limited value, because it involves looking at late twentieth-century issues through early nineteenth-century lenses. So instead of imagining Bentham himself returning from the dead, one might substitute a contemporary Benthamite. That, too, requires interpretation and imagination, because within certain parameters there are many possible Benthamites to be imagined: combine Benthamic ambiguity with room for interpretation of our post-modern condition and one has plenty of leeway for constructing different visions.

A Jurist as Citizen of the World: A Modern Benthamite

So let me end by constructing my version of a possible Benthamite jurist at the end of this millennium, bearing in mind that this is my imagining and that I am not that committed disciple.

The main outlines of the agenda and ideas of such a person fit the five pillars of Bentham's jurisprudence, as I have interpreted them. She is an unequivocal utilitarian, a liberal democrat, a strong legal positivist, a feminist, a humanitarian, possibly ambivalent about endangered species; her epistemology treats knowledge and language as intimately related human constructs; and she aspires to recreate a general normative jurisprudence, that is concerned principally with the design and implementation of legal institutions, codes, laws, practices, and discourses. Knowledge, language and law should all be treated as tools created by humans for the maximization of utility. As a democrat, she believes that sovereignty must lie with the people at all levels, not only as a last resort, but in terms of continuing accountability of and control over those to whom power is temporarily entrusted as a matter of practical necessity. Her standpoint, less equivocally than that of Bentham, is that of a citizen of the world: that is to say the extent of her concern in respect of every important calculation is the welfare of all humankind, including future generations, possibly extended to all sentient beings. For her, with increasing interdependence and possible outreaches into space, the only self-contained community is the world.[97]

Such a global jurisprudence is both Utopian and intensely concerned with practicalities. It sets forth an aspirational ideal, but it focuses on the details of technology, the politics, and the means and barriers to the attainment of the ideal.

While true to the Benthamite spirit, one can envisage some adjustments in the light of developments since 1832. Let me just give a few examples: first, in an interdependent world 'legislation' in Bentham's broad sense must concern itself not just with the municipal legal systems of sovereign states and the relations between them (old style international law), but also with global, transnational, regional, and a variety of local and networked legal

[97] William Twining, 'Globalization and Legal Theory' [1996] 49 *Current Legal Problems* 1 at 28–31; cf. T. Pogge, n. 59 above, ch. 5.

orders.[98] This requires giving special attention to the concepts of sovereignty and of vertical hierarchical authority, and to problems of sanctions and enforcement. It does not, however, necessarily point in the direction of a monistic conception of world governance.

Secondly, within the utilitarian positivist tradition due account can be taken of refinements of utilitarianism in the light of criticism and controversy over the past 150 years. Our modern Benthamite might follow J. J. C. Smart or R. M. Hare at the level of philosophy and, more important, Peter Singer in respect of applied ethics.[99] Similarly in jurisprudence, Herbert Hart's substitution of the concept of 'rule' for command, habit, and a personalized sovereign can be accepted as a refinement within legal positivism, even though Hart himself was a modified, indeed ambivalent, utilitarian.[100]

Thirdly, our Benthamite jurist would fight for a revival of analytical jurisprudence as part of general jurisprudence, that is the elucidation, refinement, and construction of key concepts. In recent years this has gone into decline. For her, Bentham's notion of a legislative dictionary was not a naïve semantic obsession. Without concepts we cannot think. Rigorous rational thought involving a combination of a general vision and 'the method of detail' was the basis of his whole enterprise. In other words, there is a need for a sophisticated conceptual apparatus which can form both a meta-language for talking about laws in general and a toolbox for expressing laws with precision.

Fourthly, our jurist can take into account other developments in ideas within her basic theoretical framework: for example, she can try to accommodate criticisms of naïve conceptions of social engineering,[101] or of the significance of time, place, and culture in legislation,[102] or developments in the social sciences, especially

[98] Twining, n. 97 above, 5.

[99] e.g. J. J. C. Smart and Bernard Williams, *Utilitarianism For and Against* (Cambridge, 1983); Peter Singer (1975) and (1993), both n. 59 above, and *The Expanding Circle* (Oxford, 1981).

[100] See generally, Neil MacCormick, *H. L. A. Hart* (London, 1981).

[101] e.g. Roger Cotterrell, *The Sociology of Law* (2nd edn., London, 1992), ch. 2.

[102] See, especially, Bentham's 'Essay on the Influence of Time and Place in Matters of Legislation', *Works*, I, 169. Oren Ben Dor, n. 62 above, ch. 6, advances an interpretation which gives a much greater place to time and place and culture in Bentham's constitutional thought: 'constitutional limits are conceived as a medium through which a community might evolve from being a community of law into what Bentham called a 'community of sympathy', the latter being based largely on self-government'. (*ibid.*, at 1).

psychology, without abandoning the essentially rationalist, instrumentalist, and consequentialist vision of her subject.

She can find some support from contemporaries—for example, Peter Singer in applied ethics; David Held (although a Kantian) in respect of global democracy;[103] and, with some reservations, Harold Lasswell, Myres McDougal, and Michael Reisman in respect of law.[104] However, such support is limited and fragmented.

Nowhere will she find a conception and agenda for jurisprudence as comprehensive and ambitious as that envisaged by Bentham in his universal science of legislation and the pannomion. She might almost find illumination in the literature of economic analysis of law, but would cavil at the focus on common law doctrine within the confines of the nation-state and would consider subsuming all pleasures under 'wealth' to be an impoverishment. However, today many of the central tasks of a Benthamite jurisprudence remain only half-done or, as with the jurisprudence of the World Bank, seem half-baked, confused, and used largely in support of minority interests.

In the present condition of humanity, some obvious items might be at the top of her Benthamite agenda. Perhaps the most important is democracy at the global, international, regional, and transnational levels. If there is a democratic deficit at national level even in the most 'advanced' liberal democracies, how much greater is that deficit in respect of arrangements of governance and the control of power at supra-national levels.

I consider this to be both a grand and a challenging vision. However, I am not a committed Benthamite: I am not a utilitarian; I am only a weak positivist; and I would place more emphasis on history, tradition, intuition, and local knowledge than most Benthamites would accept. There is more complexity and pluralism in Isaiah Berlin's 'the crooked timber of humanity'.[105] I am the very model of an ambivalent Benthamist—viewing him with awe, but treating him variously as inspiration, formidable opponent, useful sounding-board, and as a crackpot. I am not here to

[103] David Held, *Democracy and the Global Order* (Oxford, 1995).
[104] e.g. Myres S. McDougal and W. Michael Reisman, *International Law Essays* (Mineola, NY, 1981).
[105] Isaiah Berlin, *The Crooked Timber of Humanity* (London, 1990).

expound my own views. Rather we are here to celebrate, and to praise Bentham, not to bury him. I hope that I have said enough to suggest that this extraordinary phenomenon is a magnificent fascinating, and underrated part of our imaginative possessions.[106]

106 I am grateful to Oren Ben Dor, Michael Freeman, Fred Rosen, Philip Schofield, Negley Harte, and members of the Bentham Project for helpful comments and guidance.

[9]
Globalisation, Post-Modernism and Pluralism: Santos, Haack and Calvino

'The symbolic cartography of law reinforces [my] conception of legal plurality – not the legal pluralism of traditional legal anthropology, in which the different legal orders are conceived as separate entities coexisting in the same political space, but rather, the conception of different legal spaces superimposed, interpenetrated, and mixed in our minds, as much as in our actions, either on occasions of qualitative leaps or sweeping crises in our life trajectories, or in the dull routine of eventless everyday life. We live in a time of porous legality or of legal porosity, multiple networks of legal orders forcing us to constant transitions and trespassings. Our legal life is constituted by the intersection of different legal orders, that is, by interlegality. Interlegality is the phenomenological counterpart of legal pluralism, and a key concept in a postmodern conception of law.' (Santos)

'The crucial question of how to reconstruct in postmodern architecture, the connections between the social and the legal finds a highly vague answer: interpenetrating, intertwined, superposed mutually constitutive, dialectical ... We are left with ambiguity and confusion. After all this is the very charm of postmodernism.' (Gunther Teubner)

'Only in Marco Polo's accounts was Kublai Khan able to discern, through walls and towers destined to crumble, the tracery of a pattern so subtle it could escape the termites' gnawing.' (Italo Calvino)

This essay is published here for the first time. Thanks are due to Terry Anderson, Christopher McCrudden and participants in seminars in Berkeley, London, Miami, and Warwick for comments on early drafts of the essay or particular sections, and especially to Susan Haack for patiently explaining her ideas and for saving me from error and imprecision, though not always from heresy.

1 INTRODUCTION

'Post-modernism', 'post-Marxism', 'post-structuralism' – such terms are boasts claiming superiority over the past. They imply: 'We know better now'. 'Globalisation' also suggests something grandiose. Post-modernism and globalisation are both in fashion. Combine the two and one has a dangerous liaison. But beneath these conceits may be some more modest truths that are worth rescuing.

In 'Globalisation and Legal Theory' I have attempted a preliminary exploration of how far the ideas of some mainstream Anglo-American jurists might be responsive to the challenges of globalisation and the need for a new general jurisprudence. The argument was essentially conservative in that it suggested that there is much in our heritage of canonical texts that is worth preserving and using in this changing situation.

This essay steps outside the canon to consider a rather different work, *Toward a New Common Sense* by Boaventura de Sousa Santos. This is perhaps the first major book to address directly central issues relating to globalisation and legal theory from a post-modern perspective. My essay has three main objectives: first, to try to make Santos's difficult, but important, work more accessible to non-specialist readers; secondly, to explore some ideas loosely associated with 'post-modernism' by considering Santos and Calvino in relation to one of the most trenchant critics of such ideas, Susan Haack;[1] and, thirdly, to clarify my own position in relation to some of Santos's main themes. This essay, then, is a 'conversational' reading of a work that I have found stimulating and irritating in almost equal measure.[2] I side with Haack in rejecting several of the more extravagant philosophical claims made by post-modernists, while being broadly in sympathy with some of their central concerns and ideas at less abstract levels. I shall argue that this does not quite amount to accepting Santos's conclusions while rejecting his premises, but there is a puzzle that needs teasing out.

'Post-modernism' is a notoriously vague label. Haack deliberately avoids using the term in her *Manifesto of a Passionate Moderate*. Calvino refused to be so categorised.[3] Santos, while acknowledging the ambiguity

1 The main works considered in this essay are Boaventura de Sousa Santos, *Toward a New Common Sense: Law, Science and Politics in Paradigmatic Transition* (1995) (hereafter *TNC*); Italo Calvino, *Invisible Cities* (tr W Weaver, 1974, hereafter *IC*) and *Mr Palomar* (tr W Weaver, 1985, hereafter *MP*); and Susan Haack, *Manifesto of a Passionate Moderate* (1998)(hereafter *Manifesto*).

2 On the distinction between historical and conversational reading see *RB*.

3 Calvino hated to be pigeon-holed, but some of his work, especially *Invisible Cities*, has several characteristics associated with post-modern style. It is playful, ironic, multi-layered, subversive of boundaries, and may even fit Santos's idea of the baroque.

of the term,[4] explicitly advances a 'post-modern theory of law.'[5] I shall treat Santos's ideas, as expounded in *Towards a New Commonsense*, as fairly representative of a congeries of ideas and attitudes now fashionable in academic law. I shall suggest that Santos combines two tendencies in post-modernism that need to be differentiated. First, *imaginative post-modernism* which emphasises the elusiveness of reality, the fallibility of what passes for established knowledge, the importance of attending to multiple perspectives and points of view, a resistance to closure, and a playful style that treats metaphor and imagination as necessary to understanding complex phenomena. Within certain limits, I find these tendencies both congenial and intellectually acceptable. However, these tendencies often spill over into *irrationalist post-modernism*, which seems to involve commitment to strong versions of cultural relativism, epistemological scepticism, anti-rationalism, and irrealism.[6] I say 'seems', because much of this kind of writing, illustrated by Santos's first two chapters, is characterised by a lack of clarity, so that one cannot tell whether what is being said is just meaningless or involves commitment to strong versions of scepticism or is an exaggerated way of expressing sensible ideas that can be articulated more clearly and simply.

In the next section I shall suggest that Santos combines both tendencies, that Italo Calvino can be interpreted as exemplifying imaginative post-modernism without being committed to anti-rationalist positions, and that Susan Haack convincingly steers a path between the two by robust debunking of the anti-rationalist version while allowing space for other strands, with some of which I am probably more in sympathy than she is.

In section 4 I shall suggest that Santos's views on many issues concerning globalisation and legal theory are quite close to mine, especially in emphasising the complexity, fluidity and elusiveness of legal phenomena, but that these views owe nothing to irrationalist post-modernism. Thus this essay can be read as an attempt to reconcile my rejection of some aspects of post-modernist metaphysics and epistemology with finding much affinity with Calvino's playful, sometimes melancholy, complexities and Santos's global perspective on law.

4 Eg at lx-x.
5 Eg at p 473.
6 Haack links 'irrealism' with Nelson Goodman (*Manifesto*, Ch 9). In legal contexts the term is used with a conspicuous lack of clarity, see eg Kenneth Graham Jr's 'Irrealist Theory of Evidence' in '"There'll Always be an England": The Instrumental Ideology of Evidence', (1987) 85 Michigan Law Review 1204 (a satirical critique of my model of the Rationalist Tradition of Evidence Scholarship in *TEBW*).

2. *TOWARD A NEW COMMON SENSE*

(a) Standpoints and Concerns: Santos and Twining

Although our views converge on a number of specific issues in legal theory, Santos and I have different starting-points and concerns. The main difference is that my standpoint is that of an English jurist concerned with the health of the discipline of law; Santos is concerned with the development of law itself, as well as its study. We are writing within very different time-frames: my interest is in the future development of the study of law in the medium-term – say the next 10 to 20 years. Santos deals with the long-term future of law itself. The closing words of the book are: 'The patience of Utopia is infinite'.[7]

At the time he wrote the book, Santos was Professor of Sociology at the University of Coimbra in Portugal and a regular visitor at the University of Wisconsin Law School. He studied law first at Coimbra, then in Germany, and in the late 1960s at Yale Law School. In chapter 3 he gives an engaging autobiographical account of an intellectual odyssey that took him through legal dogmatics and criminology to law and development, to field work in the squatter settlements in Brazil, eventually developing a position of a post-Marxist, post-modern, sociologist of law and social theorist.[8] Substantial parts of the book had been published before and, although they have been extensively revised, the work moves among a variety of levels and has a feeling of fragmentation that makes it difficult to read. Unity is imposed on the contents in the first and last parts by an intellectually ambitious and abstract statement of a general social theory. The result is rather like a gigantic sandwich containing a variety of succulent ingredients held together by a less appealing outer casing. I usually advise my students to begin with the filling and only to chew through the outer casing later, if they feel so inclined.

Santos's standpoint is that of a sociologist and social theorist advancing a thesis about the breakdown of modernity and the emergence of a new 'paradigm'. '[I]t is the purpose of the book as a whole to identify some of the constitutive elements of a postmodern understanding of law.'[9]

The aims of Part II are stated more concretely:

7 At p 519.

8 An earlier version of Santos's memoir was published in Robin Luckham (ed), *Law and Social Enquiry* (1981). This is a collection of research autobiographies and case studies. It sets Santos's intellectual development in the broader historical context of early efforts to do empirical fieldwork in the sociology and anthropology of law.

9 At p 5.

'My purpose is to show (a) that the legal field in contemporary societies and in the world system as a whole is a far more complex and richer landscape than has been assumed by liberal political theory; (b) that such a field is a constellation of different legalities (and illegalities) operating in local, national and transnational time-spaces; (c) and finally that, thus conceived, law has both a regulatory or even repressive potential and an emancipatory potential, the latter being much greater than the model of normal change has ever postulated; the way law's potential evolves, whether towards regulation or emancipation, has nothing to do with the autonomy or self-reflexiveness of law, but rather with the political mobilization of competing forces.'[10]

Santos advances his explicitly political thesis from the vantage point of a sociologist of law who has read widely in several other disciplines, especially political economy, legal anthropology, and international relations. He also enters boldly, perhaps rashly, into debates in the physical sciences, but pays rather little attention to micro-economics,[11] socio-legal studies and mainstream legal theory, which he tends to lump together under the tendentious label of 'liberal legalism'.

My standpoint is that of a mainstream English jurist interested in the implications of globalisation for legal theory and the discipline of law. Since I am writing from within the tradition of modernity, and in a more modest time-frame, I shall unabashedly adopt what Santos calls a 'subparadigmatic perspective'.[12] Santos's work is politically committed; the sociological analyses in Part II claim to adopt the perspective 'of the oppressed social classes and groups';[13] the overall objective is to proclaim and to advance a utopian dream. Set beside this my own standpoint may seem mundane, cautious and rather apolitical.[14] We have different

10 At p 111. I have strong reservations about the philosophical underpinnings (see below), but generally agree with the more concrete formulations in (a) and (b); and I am sympathetic to, but not fully persuaded by (c).

11 Santos also tends to gloss over sceptical views about globalisation, such as those of Paul Hirst and Grahame Thompson, *Globalization in Question* (1996).

12 Eg pp 121-122. On the misuse of the Kuhnian idea of 'paradigm shifts' see below, p 200.

13 xi.

14 Santos and I both have commitments to certain values, but we are involved in enterprises of different kinds. On my general position see *LIC* at pp 23-25. I agree with Santos that there is an intimate connection between law and power and so the study of law is 'political' in a broad sense. As a scholar my commitment is to a set of values embodied in Peirce's notion of 'the scientific attitude', that is open-minded pursuit of knowledge and understanding and a belief that truth and reason are important. I have considerable reservations about talk of capitalist or sexist or racist science, unless this means that actual enquiries have sometimes been used to bolster such ideological commitments – which is, of course, a denial of the scientific attitude.

projects. Our standpoints, concerns, time-frames, and objectives clearly differ.[15] The meeting-point is looking at law from a global perspective.

(b) The Plot of Santos's Book

Toward a New Common Sense is divided into four parts. Part I, headed 'Towards a Paradigmatic Transition in Science and Law', is an ambitious exercise in social theory. Part II consists of a series of sociological studies or forays that range from the very local to the global. This includes accounts of his fieldwork in Brazil and the fragment of autobiography already alluded to, interleaved in playful mode in his report on Pasagarda law. Part III uses the metaphor of mapping to present in more detail his theoretical reconstruction of the many landscapes of law within modernity and beyond. This part includes his best-known essay 'Law: A Map of Misreading', which will be discussed below. Part IV returns to the visionary level to give an abstract and openly Utopian account of 'the main parameters of the emancipatory struggles in the paradigmatic transition'.[16]

It is worth emphasising that by no means all of the text is lumbered with sociological abstractions and jargon. The book, especially Parts II and III, is much more readable than this brief summary suggests.

In the following sections I shall first set out why I do not accept Santos's version of postmodernism at the level of philosophy. I shall then explore more positively our respective, and largely convergent, views on globalisation, legal pluralism, mapping, and an alternative agenda for general jurisprudence, suggesting that mine is more modest and more cautious, but is not necessarily incompatible with some aspects of Santos's bolder vision.

15 This does not mean that I necessarily *disagree* with Santos's diagnosis of modernity or his vision of the future. Much of his analysis seems to me to be at least plausible, if rather abstract and often unclear. On some aspects I am agnostic. For example, I simply do not know whether we are coming to the end of the age of capitalism or of an era of modernity, or whether there is about to be a genuine revolution in law and legal theory.

16 At p xii. Throughout the book Santos uses the word 'emancipatory' without precisely specifying emancipation from what. The main thrust throughout seems to be 'the emancipatory struggles of oppressed social groups ... from a societal paradigm, based on an unequal and unfair capitalist world system ...' (p 477).

200

3 TWO STRANDS IN POST-MODERNISM

(a) Santos and Haack

'Post-modernism' is a term that originated in art, literature and architecture to designate a reaction against 'modernism'. Over time it has spread to most enclaves of intellectual culture, including law. 'Modernism' (or modernity) is a vague term and the reactions against modernism have been varied. In Jurisprudence, the term 'post-modernism', like 'positivism' and 'realism', is both vague and ambiguous. It has also been stretched and extended to cover almost any novel, or not-so-novel, idea. This leads to a tendency to bring together some incongruous bedfellows. It is sometimes claimed that we are all post-modernists now. If that means that all jurists participate in contemporary intellectual trends, that may be largely true, but is trivial. If it means that we are suckers for fashion, I hope that it is untrue.

Santos claims to be a post-modernist, but understandably distances himself from some of the ideas loosely associated with the term.[17] He explains his version largely in negative terms as representing a break from 'the socio-cultural paradigm of modernity'.[18] He gives a coherent, if rather abstract, account of 'modernity', and so defines in general terms what is being reacted against. Since his vision purports to be emancipatory, revolutionary, and utopian, the alternative is less specific. If, as I do, one deplores the current tendency to categorise almost any novel idea as a 'paradigm shift', one approaches his thesis with caution.[19]

For Santos 'modernity' is the label for the dominant mode of Western thought which began to emerge in the sixteenth century, received its greatest boost with the French Revolution and the Enlightenment, and remained dominant in the West until the middle to late twentieth century. Modernity preceded the rise of capitalism, but became closely associated with it. Modernity 'will disappear before capitalism ceases to be dominant'.[20] Santos claims that the main ideas associated with modernity

17 Eg he argues that 'the grain of truth' in post-modernity lies in the fact that in a period 'of paradigmatic transition' the new paradigm can only be defined inadequately *TNC* at p 1.

18 At p 1.

19 My personal ambivalence towards post-modernism is in part attributable to the fact that I assimilated some of the ideas associated with it from R G Collingwood over forty years ago in versions that now seem either more moderate or as cranky as those that are currently touted as 'novel' (see (1998) 25 Journal Law and Society 603). As I do not accept a reductionist concept of 'modernity', there seems to be no coherent 'ism' in the negative or reactive, let alone the positive, aspects.

20 Ibid.

are epistemological. They are rich, complex and internally 'contradictory':

> 'It is based on two pillars, the pillar of regulation and the pillar of emancipation, each of them constituted of three principles or logics. The pillar of regulation is constituted by the state, formulated most prominently by Hobbes, the principle of the market, developed by Locke and Adam Smith in particular, and the principle of the community, which presides over Rousseau's social and political theory. The principle of the state consists of the vertical political obligation between citizens and the state. The principle of the market consists in the horizontal self-interested or antagonistic obligation among market partners. The principle of the community consists in the horizontal solidary, political obligation among community members and associations. The pillar of emancipation is constituted by three logics of rationality as identified by Weber: aesthetic-expressive-rationality of the arts and literature, the cognitive-instrumental rationality of science and technology, the moral-practical rationality of ethics and the rule of law.'[1]

According to Santos, the rise of capitalism led to emphasis on instrumental-technical regulation in furthering an ideal of a social order based on science at the expense of the other two forms of rationality. In jurisprudence modernity is associated with legal positivism, liberal legalism, and the equation of legal science with legal dogmatics.[2] Under this paradigm law has had an important, but secondary place, as the main instrument of technocratic management of society. All of this looks like a nutshell of a vaguely familiar post-Marxist interpretation of the 'paradigm of liberal legal ideology'.

Santos's central argument is that modernity is in crisis. It has exhausted its potential and is in process of being replaced by a post-modern paradigm which could be built on the emancipatory possibilities of traditions and cultures that have been marginalised by the conjunction of modernity and capitalism. In Santos's view we now are in a position to diagnose this crisis in modernity in some detail. However, it is less easy to be precise about the likely characteristics of the new paradigm, since we are in a time of 'paradigmatic transition'. Santos's projection of the future is a remarkably optimistic and Utopian vision of the potential for a more democratic, just and communitarian world based on a '*paradigm of prudent knowledge for a decent life*' or 'a re-enchanted common sense'.[3]

1 At p 2.
2 At p 39 and Ch 2 *passim*.
3 Preface, p ix.

'Common sense' here refers to the forms of knowledge that individuals and communities create and use to give meaning to their practices. Santos emphasises that 'common sense' is not monolithic; under capitalism different 'common senses' have dominated in at least six different contexts or loci: the household, the workplace, the marketplace, the community, the citizenplace (nation state), and the world. Refreshingly, he distances himself here from the tendency to set common sense and science in opposition to each other. This accords with the view of 'general experience' (a society's 'stock of knowledge' or stock of beliefs) which has been developed within evidence theory as providing warrants for inferences in argumentation about questions of fact. The standard concept of 'general experience' includes generalisations accepted by the scientific community, 'horse sense' based on experience, more speculative beliefs, proverbs, stereotypes and myths.[4] Santos's categorisation could usefully be applied in this more specialised context.

Santos interprets the 'crisis of modernity' largely in terms of epistemology. For him, the crisis is most clearly seen in modern science. He draws on contemporary debates in some natural sciences and mathematics which suggest that traditional claims to authority and knowledge are as sharply contested as they are in the arts and social sciences. Einstein, Heisenberg, Gödel and others, as well as developments in fields such as astrophysics, micro-physics, neuro-science and socio-biology, are invoked to illustrate the challenges to modernity to be found within the natural sciences. Few lawyers, myself included, can judge how far this is an accurate or balanced interpretation of such developments. If this suggests that sustained challenges to institutionalised claims to the authority of science based on well-warranted results are new, this seems rather dubious. It is part of the enterprise of science that its authoritative claims should be always susceptible to challenge. If this involves a denial of cumulation of knowledge or, dare one say it, progress in science, one has one's doubts.[5] One is also left wondering whether this display of erudition is really necessary as a prologue to a post-modern theory of law. It locates Santos's vision in a broad intellectual context, but for a legal audience it may set up some unnecessary barriers.

Far from seeing this crisis in modernity as a quagmire, Santos presents an apocalyptic, eloquent, unspecific, and romantic vision of the possible

4 See William Twining, 'Civilians Don't Try', (1997) 5 Cardozo Journal of International and Comparative Law 69 and 'Generalizations and Narrative in Argumentation about Questions of Fact', (1999) 40 Southern Texas Law Review 101.

5 On progress in science, see *Manifesto*, Ch 5, especially pp 99-100 (steering a middle course between the excessive optimism of the Old Deferentialists and the excessive pessimism of the New Cynicism).

realisation of an emancipatory communitarian legal and political order. Santos imagines his utopia not in terms of a programme, but rather through three linked metaphors: the Frontier, the Baroque and the South.[6] Each represents a form of 'subjectivity' that has been repressed or, at least marginalised, by modernity. The frontier mentality is fluid, open to strangers, new ideas and the reinvention of tradition, mixing heritages and inventions, weak on hierarchy, and disdainful of boundaries. The baroque represents the aesthetic, playful, ironic, irreverent, given to rhetorical exaggeration that 'resides in disproportion, laughter, and subversion'.[7] The South, less clearly articulated, represents the rise of an emancipatory consciousness of the oppressed, exemplified by Gandhi, but not specified in advance as to the form it will take. Santos urges his audience to recognise the South, go South, and learn from the South.[8] Santos's utopia involves a conjunction of the three metaphors, so that none is privileged.

Some readers may dismiss this part of *Toward a New Common Sense* as incomprehensible. I personally find the metaphors intriguing, but frustratingly vague. As one commentator put it, Santos's 'evocation of the baroque is, well, a bit baroque'.[9] Others have pointed out that each of these metaphors, especially that of the South, is open to quite negative interpretations.[10] I read these chapters (and Santos's subsequent address) with enjoyment and scepticism in equal measure.

Santos's account of the crisis of modernity is a highly compressed piece of potted history. Such sweeping generalisations about broad intellectual trends are difficult to assess. They are so abstract and so hedged around with qualifiers that they are not specific enough to criticise. Like generalised accounts of schools or movements in legal or political thought, they may seem broadly true, yet misleading in their

6 Santos subsequently developed the metaphors in an address to the Law and Society Association in Toronto in 1995. This, together with six comments, is published in a symposium in (1995) 29 Law and Society Review 569ff. As I understand it, Santos's three metaphors are his way of articulating his vision of utopia: 'By utopia I mean the exploration by imagination of new modes of human possibility and styles of will, and the confrontation by imagination of the necessity of whatever exists – just because it exists – on behalf of something radically better that is worth fighting for, and to which humanity is fully entitled' (*TNC* at p 479).

7 At p 503.

8 Ibid at p 580. Here Santos follows Chomsky, but gives more emphasis to 'learning from the South'. However, in this context he only discusses Gandhi, and that quite briefly, and does not take the opportunity to suggest what 'unheard voices' among 'southern' jurists merit more attention.

9 Ie, per Webster's Dictionary: 'extravagant or farfetched arguments in scholastic syllogisms ... odd, bizarre, grotesque, exaggerated, and overdecorated', Rosemary Coombe (1995), Symposium, op cit, 599, at 603.

10 Eg Coombe, op cit, J. Brigham, p 589.

simplicity. However, in the second chapter Santos commits himself to some specific ideas that have been fashionable in post-modern writings, but which I believe can be shown to be bad philosophy.

Rather than go into great detail about the philosophical underpinnings of a book that I think is of real value at a different level, I shall briefly contrast Santos's main philosophical claims with Susan Haack's *Manifesto of a Passionate Moderate*.[11] This is a formidable philosopher's debunking of 'recent fads, fashions, and false dichotomies',[12] and of anti-scientific exaggerations and irrationalist tendencies in the current intellectual climate. Her position seems to me to dispose of the core ideas of anti-rationalist post-modernism, while leaving space for what I find attractive in imaginative post-modernism.

Haack depicts herself as an 'old-fashioned prig', 'an old feminist', and, engagingly, as 'the still small voice that whispers "bosh"'. An admirer of Charles Sanders Peirce, she is mainly concerned with philosophy. She distances herself from some of the standard targets of post-modernism, such as 'foundationalism',[13] metaphysical realism (that there is one true description of the real world, which consists of a fixed totality of mind-independent objects),[14] and what she calls the 'Old Deferentialism', or 'scientism', that is the belief that there 'must be a uniquely rational method of inquiry exclusive to the sciences'.[15]

Haack draws a clear distinction between metaphysics and epistemology.[16] Her *Evidence and Inquiry* is a work of epistemology.[17] In *Manifesto of a Passionate Moderate* she further adopts a metaphysical

11 Ibid.

12 The false dichotomies are revealing: '*either* scientistic philosophy *or* philosophy as "just a kind of writing"; *either* metaphor as an abuse of language *or* metaphor as ubiquitous and philosophy, even the sciences, as genres of literature; *either* the Old Deferentialism, *or* the New Cynicism; *either* scientific knowledge as a mere social construction *or* a denial of the internal organization and external context of scientific work; *either* the scholastic rigidities of analytic epistemology *or* wild and woolly "feminist epistemology"; *either* preferential hiring of women, etc. *or* the Old Boy network; and so forth and so on' (at p 5).

13 On the ambiguity of 'foundationalism' see below, p 206 n 4.

14 At p 153.

15 At p 3.

16 'Epistemology' refers to theories of knowledge: evidence, the justification of beliefs, more or less warranted claims, procedures and methods of enquiry, and foundationalist versus coherentist theories of justification belong here. 'Metaphysics' refers to theories of reality, truth, the problem of universals, realism versus anti-realisms etc. 'Innocent realism' is a theory within metaphysics. Haack's *Evidence and Inquiry* (1993) is a work of epistemology, as is her 'foundherentism' which convincingly, in my view, steers a path between foundationalist and coherentist theories of justification (*not* of truth). Questions about what is true, and how we know what truth is, belong to metaphysics. Questions about what we know and justifications for belief belong to epistemology. *Manifesto* includes arguments that belong to both domains. Post-

position that she labels 'innocent realism'.[18] Since this articulates simply and much better than I can a more plausible metaphysics than one finds in fashionable post-modernism or its standard targets, it is worth restating it briefly:[19]

1. There is one real world.
2. This world is largely independent of us.
3. Whether a synthetic description is true or false depends on what it says and how the world is.[20]
4. There are many true descriptions of the world; such descriptions can be combined into a single conjunctive description; but incompatible descriptions cannot be jointly true.[1]
5. Innocent realism can accommodate three concerns of Hilary Putnam's thesis of 'conceptual relativity': viz that vocabularies may vary and may change; that no one vocabulary is privileged; and that perception involves conceptualisation and interpretation.[2]

---

modernists seem to tend to run epistemology and metaphysics together, almost invariably committing 'the passes for fallacy', (ie the argument that because what 'passes for' truth is often no such thing, therefore there is no objective truth. See further below, p 217 n 8). Haack attacks Richard Rorty and Stephen Stich for proclaiming the end of epistemology and dismissing the idea of objective truth as meaningless. Santos distinguishes epistemology and ontology at the start of the book (*TNC*, p 7), but seemingly conflates metaphysics and epistemology for the rest of the first two chapters, claiming to focus almost entirely on a new epistemology. It is not clear to me whether he clearly is guilty of 'the passes for fallacy'. I am grateful to Susan Haack for help with this note, but I am responsible for the formulation. Of course, our views may not be identical on all of the issues referred to here, but any significant differences (some not yet resolved) are not germane to this essay.

17 Op cit.

18 Haack's realism is 'innocent' because it is simple, commonsensical and unspecific. It was meant to convey 'not unnecessarily complex and loaded with strange metaphysical commitments, but not naive, either' (communication to the author). The lack of specificity is deliberate, leaving space for a variety of ideas and positions. Haack suggests that amplification of the caveat that the world is *largely* independent of us would involve 'some loss of innocence' (p 158). This seems a neat way of postponing some of the central questions of interpretive sociology which has to concern itself with internal points of view (see below, pp 216-217).

19 This restatement is based on *Manifesto*, especially Ch 9. Haack's views are further developed in 'Realisms and their Rivals: Recovering our Innocence' (unpublished paper, adapted from 'Realism' in *Handbook of Epistemology* (eds I Niiniluoto et al, forthcoming, Dordrecht, 2000).

20 Haack's starting-point, like that of Peirce, is that a description is true if 'something is So ... whether you or I, or anybody, thinks it is true or not'. (C S Peirce, *Collected Papers* 2.135. 1902), cited in *Manifesto* at p 22.

1 At p 157.

2 Haack at pp 153-156, discussing Hilary Putnam, *Renewing Philosophy* (1992). Haack reports that Putnam subsequently revised his position.

6. That some statements are meaningful, but their truth-value is unknowable, and are epistemically idle if they are unknowable in principle.[3]

Haack's *Manifesto* is an eloquent defence and celebration of the values of reason, truth and the scientific attitude – especially open-mindedness, honesty, and 'the Will to Learn'. In *Evidence and Inquiry* Haack elaborates at much greater length a middle position between foundationalism and coherentism that she mischievously labels 'foundherentism' – in the process acknowledging that the supporters and critics of both positions make important points that need to be accommodated in a coherent epistemology.[4]

Haack's targets include feminist epistemology, deep philosophical forms of cultural relativism, and the excesses of some versions of the sociology of knowledge. She is especially harsh about those post-modernists, such as Richard Rorty, who claim to be 'pragmatists'. In an imaginary dialogue between Peirce and Rorty, she wittily shows Rorty's views on pragmatism to be almost the opposite of Peirce's.[5] While acknowledging that science is in an important sense a social enterprise,[6] she dismisses some of the claims made in the name of the social construction of knowledge:

> 'It is false that social values are inseparable from scientific inquiry; false that the purpose of science is the achievement of social goals; false that knowledge is nothing but the product of negotiation among members of the scientific community; false that knowledge, facts, reality are nothing more than social constructions; false that science should be more democratic; false that the physical sciences are subordinate to the social sciences.'[7]

In chapter 2, Santos makes a number of assertions that appear to be very close to Haack's targets. For example:

3 Ibid at p 164. At the level of philosophy, I am here prepared to follow Haack and Peirce, and hence to reject strong forms of epistemological scepticism, cultural relativism, and coherence theories of truth.

4 'Foundationalism' is another ambiguous '-ism'. Haack distinguishes three meanings, two of which she argues against, one of which she defends; *Evidence and Inquiry* (1993) Ch 9.

5 Ch 2 '"We Pragmatists": Peirce and Rorty in conversation.'

6 At p 3. Cf Ch 6, 'Science as Social? – Yes and No'.

7 At p 104. Cf 3. Haack also deplores the conflation of science, philosophy and literature, all of which she views as distinct enterprises with different primary objectives (Ch 3). Philosophy and science are both forms of *enquiry*; literature is not.

1. 'All Nature is Culture'.[8]
2. '... modern science, besides being modern, is also Western, capitalist, and sexist'.[9]
3. 'There are as many natures as there are cultures. This being the case, all natural-scientific knowledge is social-scientific'.[10]
4. 'The creation of knowledge in the emergent paradigm claims to be close to literary or artistic creation'.[11]
5. 'As the catalyst of the blending together of natural and social science, the neohumanities help us to look for global categories of intelligibility, warm concepts, capable of melting the frontiers from which modern science has divided and enclosed reality'.[12]
6. 'For postmodern emancipatory knowledge, truth is rhetorical, a mythic moment of rest in a continuous and endless argumentative struggle among different discourses of truth; it is the ever provisional result of a negotiation of meaning within a given relevant audience, which in the modern era has consisted of the scientific community, or rather, of a plurality of scientific communities'.[13]
7. 'Modern science built itself against common sense, which it deemed superficial, illusory and false'.[14]

8 Santos, p 30. On the ambiguity of 'culture' see Haack, Ch 8. Santos's claim is obscure, but Haack would probably reject all of the interpretations that can be most plausibly given to it.

9 At p 30, expanded at pp 30-32; contrast Haack, Ch 6.

10 Ibid, p 33. See Haack, Ch 9, especially p 156ff; cf ibid, Ch 6.

11 Ibid p 35, Haack explicitly distinguishes scientific enquiry from literary creation, Ch 3; cf n 7 above.

12 Ibid, p 36. The passage continues: 'Postmodern science is admittedly an analogical science that knows what it knows less well through what it knows better ... Other important seminal categories of the emergent paradigm are, to my mind, the ludic, the dramatic and the biographical analogies. The world is today either natural or social; tomorrow it will be both, and shall be looked at as if it were the text of a play, a stage or an autobiography'. Cf Haack, Chs 3 and 4.

13 Ibid p 38; contrast Haack, Ch 6. Elsewhere, Haack has considered the 'hard and tangled' question of the relationship between natural and social sciences, but would reject the passage in the text as 'romantic twaddle' (communication to the author). See below, pp 216-217.

14 Ibid p 46. In the context, Santos suggests that there has been a sharp epistemological break between science and common sense, which are interpreted differently from each point of view. Elsewhere (see p 202 above), Santos is more sympathetic to common sense than many critics and argues for 'a new, enchanted common sense' which is not sharply distinguished from science. Haack might agree that the ontology of, eg modern physics, is rather unlike commonsense physical objects, but would reject the suggestion that science is not continuous with everyday empirical enquiry in respect of method. Of course, scientific findings have often shown 'common sense' beliefs to be false, but they have also shown the same in respect of what have passed for warranted scientific truths. (see the 'Passes for Fallacy', below at p 217 n 8). On background beliefs see *Evidence and Inquiry* at pp 110-112 (see below, p 218).

8. 'All knowledge is self-knowledge';[15] ie the collapse of the traditional distinction between subject and object.

Taken at face value, these statements seem like a litany of post-modern mantras which Susan Haack could be expected to detonate, not with a whisper, but rather with a resounding 'bosh'. A preliminary complaint is lack of clarity. Of course, some of these quotations require elucidation in context. With charitable interpretation, some might even be found to have grains of truth that could be accommodated within Haack's position.[16] But nearly all of these statements, taken at face value, would be rejected.

In this essay I adopt Haack's distinction between metaphysics and epistemology, her 'innocent realism' (metaphysics), 'foundherentism' (epistemology), the traditional scholarly values that she passionately defends, and her main arguments in support of these views. I do this in order to outline a philosophical position that is significantly different from Santos's, but compatible with Calvino's (as I interpret him), without getting embroiled in complex philosophical arguments about the reasons for such differences as we have. The main point is to clarify my own position regarding two significant strands in post-modernism and to justify a significant convergence between Santos's and my views on globalisation, legal pluralism etc, despite differences in our starting-points and central concerns. I believe that some of Santos's theses, shorn of unnecessary philosophical baggage, make a lot of sense. For this purpose it is not necessary to enter into a detailed discussion of whether Santos can be defended against the kind of philosophical criticism that one might expect from Susan Haack.[17]

15 Santos, p 27, Contrast Haack, Ch 5.

16 *Manifesto*, Ch 9, 'Reflections on Relativism: From Momentous Tautology to Seductive Contradiction'. This essay contains a brief, but very illuminating, topography of different kinds of relativism. It deals with greater philosophical sophistication ideas that I tried to outline in 'Some scepticism about some scepticisms' (*RE*, Ch 4). On 'innocence', see above, p 205 n 18.

17 In an unpublished paper on *Manifesto*, entitled 'Rushing to Bosh?', I suggest that the trajectory of some of Haack's debunking, while philosophically sound, has unnecessarily conservative intellectual tendencies at a more applied level. *Manifesto* is sometimes too dismissive of the higher dismissiveness. For example, in an essay on multiculturalism (Ch 8) her main targets are (a) the idea that students should be educated exclusively in their own culture and (b) the idea that the 'opinions, practices, institutions, traditions' of other cultures are equally deserving of respect because all criteria of evidence and evaluation are culture specific. I reject such views, but these seem to me to be soft targets. When Haack concedes some value in exposure to or the study of other cultures she mentions tolerance (p 140), mutual respect (pp 140-141) and better and more critical understanding of one's own culture (p 139). She adds: 'And, yes, knowledge of the customs of minority communities within a multicultural society surely can contribute to the accomplishment of a mutually tolerable, or with good luck and good will, a mutually enriching, modus vivendi' (pp 139-140). This seems to me to understate,

I shall explore some of these issues in more detail in relation to multiple descriptions and perspectives. Here, it may help to clarify my position by giving a few brief examples. First, if the idea of 'feminist epistemology' suggests that what constitutes evidence and truth for women is different from what it is for men, then I agree with Haack that the idea should be rejected. If, on the other hand, it is an emphatic way of saying that very many women, by virtue of their experience, vantage points and position as women, have different perspectives, points of view, and beliefs about important aspects of life/the world/social phenomena and that these views, voices, narratives and so on have been suppressed or marginalised in male-dominated cultures, then such claims need to be taken very seriously indeed.[18]

When Raymond Williams or Edward Said challenges literary or scholarly 'canons' for excluding vast ranges of experience and points of view – typically, but not necessarily, those of the underprivileged or the colonised – their argument is mainly about exclusion.[19] Radical changes to a canon or to our perceptions of particular institutions or practices, may not only lead us to be more inclusive, but as our understandings are changed, so too may the standards underpinning the canon be challenged and be shown to be in need of adjustment.[20]

Similar considerations apply within the discipline of law. Legal pluralists can point out that many significant forms of 'non-state law' have been marginalised or ignored by legal theorists and mainstream legal scholars alike – they are treated as invisible or as not really being 'law'. In most Western countries Islamic, Hindu, Chinese, and Jewish legal ideas and traditions are not treated as 'Jurisprudence', in that they rarely feature in the canons of schools, texts and individual jurists that are considered as belonging to the mainstream. Similarly, I have argued elsewhere that the dominant 'Country and Western Tradition' of Western Comparative Law has focused, in respect of micro-comparison, almost exclusively on the municipal law of industrialised capitalist societies, typically emphasising what are referred to increasingly inappropriately as 'parent legal systems'.

---

if not to miss, the most important reason why engagement with other cultures is important, viz enlarging and possibly significantly changing both one's understandings, in respect of ideas and perceptions, as well and our experience of life regarding such matters as cuisine, art and the handling of conflict. See, however, the more positive formulation in Haack (1999) (*TLS*).

18 Cf Haack, 'Knowledge and Propaganda: Reflections of an Old Feminist', *Manifesto*, Ch 7.

19 Raymond Williams, *Culture and Society* (1958); Edward Said, *Orientalism* (1985).

20 The point about standards is illustrated by problems surrounding notions of 'merit' in university admissions and hiring, see *LIC*, Ch 13 (in which different meanings of 'affirmative action' are explored and arguing that preferential treatment may sometimes be justified, despite the costs, especially where there are no defensible criteria of merit).

210

One reason why Santos's work is important is because it presents a much broader and more complex view of legal phenomena than are to be found in orthodox Western legal theory and scholarship. His work opens up new perspectives, and fresh lines of enquiry. This vision seems to be directly related to his rejection of orthodoxies that have dominated 'modernist' treatments of law. However, to subvert an orthodoxy or to provide a fresh perspective does not necessarily need a change of metaphysics or epistemology or a new 'paradigm'. One can hold firmly to the simple truths of innocent realism and empiricism, while welcoming challenges to what has passed for knowledge in our dominant intellectual, including jurisprudential, traditions.

(b) Calvino and Innocent Realism

How can I reconcile my endorsement of Haack with my agreement with many of Santos's ideas and my attraction to Calvino, when the former looks like a direct attack on some of the philosophical positions adopted by Santos? My central argument is that Santos' juristic ideas and Calvino's visions of complexity make sense at a less abstract level than Haack's lean metaphysics and that, on my interpretation, some important ideas and perspectives of both Santos and Calvino are quite compatible with innocent realism.

There may indeed be a seeming tension between the robust simplicity of innocent realism and an emphasis on multiple perspectives, complex phenomena, and a generally anti-reductionist stance. I do not believe that these are incompatible. One clue to this is suggested by the imaginative post-modernism of Italo Calvino.

In earlier essays I have drawn on two of Calvino's later books, *Invisible Cities* and *Mr Palomar*, which have attracted me both personally and as a jurist.[1] The sense of affinity was initially intuitive, but it has grown, and it can, to some extent, be rationalised.[2] Both works are concerned with a

1 *IC* and *MP*, op cit, n 1. My interest in Calvino and 'realism' began with *If on a Winter's Night a Traveler*, See *RE* at pp 366-368. In addition to the themes discussed in the text, I like Calvino's antipathy to consumerism, his questioning of settled assumptions, his ambivalence towards technology, his linking of complexity and historical continuity, his lightness of touch, and his capacity to maintain a sense of humour despite a pessimistic vision of the human condition.

2 This section draws heavily on two works by Katherine Hume, 'Grains of Sand in a Sea of Objects: Italo Calvino as Essayist', (1992a) 87 Modern Languages Review 72 and *Calvino's Fictions: Cogito and Cosmos* (1992b), especially the Introduction and Ch 6. I have also learned from Sara M Adler, *Calvino: The Writer as Fable-maker* (1979); Albert H Carter, *Italo Calvino: Metamorphoses of Fantasy* (1987); and Beno Weiss, *Understanding Italo Calvino* (1993).

search for understanding and meaning in a universe that seems endlessly complex. As Sara Adler puts it, Calvino's central concern is to 'portray the diversity and at the same time the universality of human experience'.[3]

Calvino, while emphasising complexity, paradox, elusiveness, uses models, geometrical designs, and even Tarot cards to construct patterns of understanding. The central problem is that 'reality is granular',[4] like a sea consisting of ever more minute, isolated particles in constant flux.[5] When Mr Palomar, seeking the key to mastering the world's complexity, begins by trying to describe a single wave, he is defeated. When he attempts to subject one small part of his lawn to statistical analysis, his efforts prove absurd. In some ways, it is easier to see the moon, or his lawn, or an ocean as a whole from a distance than to describe one small part. Understanding requires both small scale and large scale enquiries.

In *Invisible Cities* Kublai Khan claims to have constructed in his mind a model city based on principles from which all possible cities can be deduced[6] – a conceit reminiscent of common law caricatures of the civilian mentality. Marco Polo replies that he has thought of an alternative model city 'made only of exceptions, exclusions, incongruities, contradictions' – a sort of urban hearsay rule – but if he proceeds to describe a particular city by subtracting exceptions and abnormalities from the ideal type, beyond a certain limit, 'I would achieve cities too probable to be real'.[7] Yet Marco Polo's accounts allow Kublai Khan to discern 'the tracery of a pattern so subtle it could escape the termites' gnawing'.[8]

Ironically, *Invisible Cities* is itself highly schematic, organised on a formal geometric structure. It both embraces patterns and undermines them. Calvino recognised both the value of models and their limitations in capturing complexity. Katherine Hume suggests that the exchanges between Marco Polo and Kublai Khan can be interpreted as a dialogue within a single, composite mind.[9] The reader is expected to embrace multiplicity and different levels of understanding reality, as is required of any 'intelligent human being facing the social world'.[10]

3 Adler at p 49.
4 Hume (1992a) op cit, p 72.
5 *The Literature Machine: Essays* (1987) at p 268, quoted by Hume (1992a) at pp 72-73.
6 *IC*, p 69.
7 Ibid.
8 *IC*, pp 5-6. Cf Ch 6.6 above.
9 Hume (1992b) at p 149.
10 Hume (1992a), p 75. Haack in a recent essay, discusses the added difficulties of description arising from the fact that 'human beings intervene in the world in various ways, and they, and their physical and mental activities are themselves part of the world'. Haack (2000) op cit, p 205 n 19.

In 'Mapping Law' I explored both geographical and metaphorical mapping of the variety of legal orders in the world and what is involved in giving an account of one legal order.[11] The first part was similar in content, but different in style, to Santos's map of the transnational legal field. In the second part I suggested that describing a legal order is rather like describing a city in that both are highly complex phenomena that can be depicted in many different ways from a great variety of vantage points and perspectives. I drew on Italo Calvino's *Invisible Cities*, in which Marco Polo gives 55 highly imaginative evocations of cities – all couched in metaphorical language – and all significantly different. These might be read as accounts of 55 different cities, or 55 accounts of one city, Venice, or, more plausibly, 55 accounts all of which implicitly use Venice as the reference point of comparison.[12]

At first sight, 55 accounts of one city sound rather a lot. However, Calvino's number seems modest when set against the report that there are approximately 25,000 works dealing with the history of London.[13] For even if one discounts repetition and overlap, the obviously inaccurate, and the tendentious, it should not be difficult to find well over one hundred substantially different accounts of the history of London which prima facie have the potential to add to our understanding of the city. One could in fact find a hundred different maps of Central London that would satisfy this test, and maps are one of the most abstract and thin forms of depiction.[14] Most or all of the differences between 100 accounts of a city or its history might be explained in terms of different vantage points, perspectives and concerns. For example, 50 kinds of specialist, from drainage engineer to mythologist, could each give an account from two or more vantage points in time or space. A further 100 inhabitants or tourists or other visitors could describe different experiences and impressions of the same city ... and so on. One of the central themes of post-modernism, but not exclusive to it, is its insistence on the value of looking at things from multiple points of view.

In a well-known passage about causation, R G Collingwood wrote:

> 'A car skids while cornering at a certain point, turns turtle, and bursts into flame. From the car-driver's point of view, the cause of the accident was cornering too fast and the lesson is that one must drive more carefully. From the county surveyor's point of view, the cause was a defective road surface, and the lesson is that one must

11 Above, Ch 6.

12 When Kublai Khan observes that there is one city of which Marco Polo never speaks, the response is: 'To distinguish other cities' qualities, I must speak of a first city that remains implicit. For me it is Venice'. *IC*, p 86.

13 Peter Ackroyd, London *Times*, 13 August 1998, at p 35.

14 Albert Carter, *Italo Calvino: Metamorphoses of Fantasy* (1987), pp 120-121.

> make skid-proof roads. From the motor-manufacturer's point of view, the cause was defective design, and the lesson is that one must place the centre of gravity lower.'[15]

This a graphic way of saying that different perspectives are appropriate for different kinds of enquiries. Here each person draws practical lessons relevant to their respective spheres of action. Someone trying to explain the crash might combine these answers to provide a multi-factored explanation. On the other hand, someone concerned to attribute responsibility, might select one element as 'the cause' for this purpose. For example, a court might hold the driver responsible because his act of cornering fast was a voluntary human act, subsequent in time to the other conditions and, if he was not exercising reasonable care, he might be held liable in negligence. Here the court selects one condition from a set of jointly sufficient conditions as 'the cause' in order to determine an issue of responsibility.[16]

It would not be difficult to multiply the standpoints from which this event might be viewed. The question that concerns us here is whether cumulating multiple perspectives on an event of this kind can generally add to or deepen our understanding. I believe that it can, though it will not always do so. Merely cumulating descriptions may be tedious and laborious, with a prospect of diminishing returns.[17] Obviously with a very complex phenomenon, such as a city, reading 20 different accounts could add to one's knowledge simply by adding new facts, but that is not the point. Metaphors, such as 'multiple lenses', convey the idea that one can understand better by looking at the same object in different ways. This is, of course, almost an article of faith for those who favour multi-disciplinary studies.

In addressing problems of depicting the cosmos, the human condition, or a single object, Calvino adopts three main strategies: narrative, the construction of models or systems, and literary mimesis (including metaphors).[18] These are treated as complementary rather than rival ways of trying to grapple with the complexities, multiplicity and fluidity of reality. Calvino had a strong sense of the limitations of language. At key

15 R G Collingwood, 'On the So-called idea of Causation', (1937-38) *Proceedings of the Aristotelian Society*, pp 85, 96.

16 H L A Hart and A Honoré, *Causation in the Law* (2nd edn, 1985). The authors rightly criticise Collingwood for over-emphasising pragmatic concerns with causation to the exclusion of other kinds of enquiry: 'Collingwood ... was prepared heroically to accept the conclusion that it is logically impossible to speak of discovering the cause of a disease unless we can use our knowledge to cure it' (at p 300).

17 On 'descriptivism', see below at p 237.

18 Ibid, p 73. On Calvino's complex treatment of models and mirrors in Palomar, see Hume (1992b), pp 143-144.

moments, in evoking cities, words fail Marco Polo and he resorts to gestures, emblems, images, silences and other indirections. When Kublai Khan asks him to describe Venice, Polo replies:

> 'Memory's images, once they are fixed in words, are erased. Perhaps I am afraid of losing Venice all at once, if I speak of it. Or perhaps, speaking of other cities, I have already lost it little by little.'[19]

Emphasis on the uses and limitations of language as a tool of description or depiction, and the value of narrative, fables, models, metaphor, images and silence as complementary ways of capturing aspects of reality fit comfortably with the idea of multiple perspectives. But what has this to do with jurisprudence? And can Calvino's approach to description be accommodated by innocent realism?

I have suggested that depicting a legal order is analogous in important respects to depicting a city.[20] One similarity is that the objects are extremely complex. Another is that their particularity tends to be rooted in history. A third is that cities and legal orders are experienced differently by different types of people. The standpoint of an urban planner, a mayor, a tycoon, a travel writer, a photographer, a poet, a tourist, a vagrant, a burglar, a historian, an ethnographer, and all the other kinds of visitor, inhabitant, or functionary tend to be significantly different. And, of course, there is not just one kind of tourist, poet, or planner. Similarly in law the standpoints of rule-maker, adjudicator, enforcement officer, bureaucrat, disputant, advocate, deviant, good citizen, bad man, professional adviser, expositor, and jurist in respect of a given legal order will all be different. There are many kinds of participants and many kinds of observers with different vantage points, concerns, perspectives, and particular experiences. For limited enquiries, limited perspectives may be adequate. A broader understanding of a city or a legal system involves taking account of multiple standpoints. The main purpose of the discipline of law is to advance knowledge and understanding of law; my primary objective as a scholar is to gain a better general understanding of my chosen specialism as well as to pursue particular lines of enquiry.

It might be objected that cities are extremely complex phenomena, especially when considered historically as well as spatially. Millions of people, relations, events, physical objects, and other phenomena may be suggested by the idea of 'London' or 'Venice'. Any account of such complexity must inevitably be selective and it is hardly surprising that different accounts select different aspects for different purposes. But do

19 *IC*, p 87.
20 On the the application of standard metaphors in urban sociology (bazaar, jungle, machine and organism) see above, Ch 6.6.

the same considerations apply to smaller, more specific or 'manageable' objects of study?

Of course, any city is immeasurably complex, but so is a legal order, let alone all law in the world, the subject-matter of a global discipline of law. A granular conception of reality, such as Calvino's, suggests that it consists of smaller and smaller particles in flux. Mr Palomar can move from considering the cosmos to his lawn, to one small part of it, to a blade of grass, and so on down to 'collections of collections'.[1] Marco Polo uses the wood of a chessboard as the jumping-off point for a potentially endless enquiry. This is like 'seeing a world in a grain of sand', except that a grain of sand is not an ultimate unit, as atoms were once thought to be.

I think that the general enterprise of trying to study and understand law is rather like that. One can move from trying to map law in the world, an exercise that has its uses, through profiling or giving some other account of a legal family or a single legal order, to more and more particular studies of legal phenomena and relations. Most of these phenomena are social and invisible, two features that complicate the task of depicting and interpreting them.

I do not see these points as causing difficulties for 'innocent realism'. Calvino's concern is with the complexity and the elusiveness of reality and with problems of description. As I read him, he accepts that there is a reality independent of our knowledge of it, but emphasises the difficulty of describing it. Conversely, Haack's epistemology is fallibilist and she explicitly allows for multiple descriptions, all of which can be true.[2]

I have already suggested that one of the tendencies of post-modernist thought is to conflate epistemology and metaphysics. A standard example is the claim that there are 'multiple realities'. This can be interpreted as a denial of the idea that there is one real world which is largely independent of anyone's knowledge of it.[3] In innocent realism the concept of reality belongs to what is (ontology), while the concept of knowledge refers to our apprehension of what is (epistemology). However, the term 'multiple realities' is sometimes used loosely to refer to different experiences or descriptions of reality or different perspectives or vantage points or subjectivities. Innocent realism acknowledges that there can be many different descriptions of an object, event or phenomenon, all of which may be true, provided that they are compatible.[4] It accepts that

1 *MP*, 'The Infinite Lawn'.
2 *Manifesto*, pp 146-147.
3 The phrase can be interpreted as a loose way of talking about multiple impressions or pictures of reality, but some post-modernists (including Santos, it seems) insist that reality is subjective.
4 Haack at p 157; 'incompatible descriptions, however, cannot be jointly true'. Compatibility is, of course, a necessary but not a sufficient condition.

216

one can look at an object from different points of view, but it is the points of view not the object that are different. Here, I think that Santos' philosophical views are generally incompatible with innocent realism, but, on my interpretation, Calvino's are not. For me, post-modernism is better treated as being more like a mood than a philosophy.

In legal contexts there is a particular danger of confusing three different meanings of 'pluralism': 'plural' – meaning diverse; 'pluralism' – meaning a plurality of perspectives or standpoints – and 'legal pluralism', which refers either to the co-existence of multiple legal orders in the same context of time and space or the recognition of different legal traditions and sources of law within a single legal system.[5] Confusing these terms can lead to trouble, for example, conflating the ideas of multiple legal orders and multiple descriptions of a single legal order. A further source of confusion arises from the fact that 'legal pluralist' is used sometimes to apply to those who advocate legal pluralism as against state centralism and sometimes to refer to those who study the phenomenon with relative detachment. In legal contexts such confusions can be avoided by using 'legal pluralism' in a neutral sense and by substituting for 'pluralism' in the general sense some other term such as 'multiple perspectives'.

How does innocent realism cope with the idea of 'multiple perspectives'? It denies that 'multiple realities' exist, but it accepts that there are many different true descriptions of reality all, of course, compatible. The innocent realist can accommodate notions of describing from different points of view, using different vocabularies, multiple perspectives, and – moving into metaphor – multiple lenses.

Susan Haack's main examples of multiple descriptions relate to simple physical objects such as rocks (natural) and paper-clips (human artefacts). The post-modern thrust towards multiple perspectives and pluralist descriptions is more closely related to studying social institutions, practices, and discourses, including law. Haack acknowledges that enquiry in the social sciences can be harder than in the physical sciences, partly because it involves enquiry into mental states. In a recent essay, she discusses the added difficulties of description arising from the fact that 'human beings intervene in the world in various ways, and they, and their physical and mental activities are themselves part of the world'. She concludes:

> 'There are many different truths about the world. All these many different truths must, somehow, fit together; there can't be rival, incompatible truths or "knowledges". But this doesn't mean that

5 On different conceptions of 'legal pluralism' see above, Ch 3.5 and below, section 4(b).

all the truths about the world must fit together by being reducible to a privileged class of truths expressed in a privileged vocabulary (that they must be "unified" in the logical positivists' strong sense of that term). A better analogy would be the way a road map can be superimposed upon a contour map of the same territory.'[6]

A popular theme in post-modernism, but not confined to it, is that certain ways of looking at things, certain perspectives, standpoints, discourses, views etc, tend to be 'privileged' (in a socio-political sense), while others get marginalised or suppressed. For example, sociologists are fond of debunking 'official views' and what passes for 'common sense';[7] feminists complain about the repression of women's points of view; critical scholars talk of 'unheard voices', 'suppressed narratives' and so on. I personally have a great deal of sympathy with some such complaints, provided that they are not expressed in terms of a new epistemology or metaphysics. I agree that what passes for knowledge or common sense in a given society may be shown to be partial, biased, or just plain false.[8] But such ideas presuppose rather than reject an ontology and some conceptions of evidence, inference and warranted conclusions.

Post-modern enthusiasm for 'the ludic' has often occasioned comment.[9] A hard-nosed empiricist may be inclined to disdain metaphor and be suspicious of playful treatments of serious issues. For her, Santos's enthusiasm for the Baroque or Calvino's humorous fantasies may be too fanciful, if not frivolous, for the responsible enquirer. However, respected traditionalist philosophers, including Susan Haack, have acknowledged an important role for metaphor in enquiry, especially in its early stages:

'Both the friends and enemies of metaphor, it seems to me, exaggerate. Metaphors are sometimes cognitively vital; not seldom

6 Haack (2000) op cit, above, p 205 n 19. 'Privileged' here refers to a vocabulary to which other vocabularies can be reduced, but which cannot be reduced to others. This usage should be distinguished from the socio-political usage that is now rather more common.

7 RE at pp 92-93 and references there.

8 One of Haack's targets is what she calls 'the passes for fallacy': '... the New Cynics disdain the notions of evidence and warrant, because, as they are at pains to point out, what has passed for warranted theory, relevant evidence, known fact, objective truth, has often turned out to be no such thing. This is true; but the conclusion that the notions of warrant, evidence, truth, fact, reality, knowledge, are ideological humbug manifestly doesn't follow' (at p 93). See now Haack, 'Staying for an Answer', TLS, 9 July, 1999. I agree with Haack that this is a fallacy; it is not clear whether it can be attributed to Santos.

9 Eg Santos at p 504. On the issue of post-modernist contributions to politics, see the debate in the Law and Society Review (1992) No 4 on Joel Handler's Presidential address to the Law and Society Association, 'Postmodernism, Protest, and the New Social Movements', (p 697). See also above, Ch 3.3.

> illuminating; perhaps more often than not harmless. Metaphors can also be feeble; can be exploited to the purpose of persuading by emotional appeal rather than strong evidence or good argument; can serve as lazy substitutes for adequate theoretical articulation; can lead inquiry into what turns out to be quite the wrong direction. Metaphor is neither a Good Thing nor a Bad Thing in itself; it is, rather, a linguistic device, capable of being put to good or bad use.'[10]

One can find metaphors cognitively useful, but still suspect that they may often be being used self-indulgently or as a cloak for laziness, lack of clarity, or even dishonesty. It is reasonable to ask of particular examples: Is your metaphor really necessary? Why don't you say what you mean? In what way exactly is the legal order of Xanadu like a city or a bazaar? Such questions can serve as a useful 'reality check' and help to differentiate the ludic from the ludicrous.

Furthermore, enquiry requires both imagination and checking out evidence. Haack's principal objection to the idea of 'studying {philosophy} in a literary spirit', is the suggested implication that imagination is not only necessary, but sufficient for serious enquiry and that checking out the truth by reference to evidence falls by the way.[11]

Haack's principal concern is to defend such values as intellectual integrity, disinterestedness, intellectual tolerance, respect for facts, and honest, open-minded enquiry. She sees these values as being under threat from 'the Higher Dismissiveness' and from tendencies that I have associated with irrationalist post-modernism. However, both Santos and Calvino purport to subscribe to such values, though less emphatically.[12] Conversely, Peirce's 'scientific attitude' can be viewed as being in much

10 *Manifesto*, p 72. One of Haack's most important ideas is that the structure of evidence is analogous to a crossword puzzle: '[A]n empirical proposition is more or less warranted depending on how well it is supported by experiental evidence and background beliefs (analogue: how well a crossword entry is supported by its clue and other completed entries); how secure the relevant background beliefs are, independently of the proposition in question (analogue: how reasonable those other entries are, independent of this one); and how much of the relevant evidence the evidence includes (analogue: how much of the crossword has been completed). How well evidence supports a proposition depends on how much the addition of the proposition in question improves its explanatory investigation' (*Manifesto* at p 106; cf pp 85-86). A fuller account is given in Haack's *Evidence and Inquiry* (1993), op cit. See also, 'staying for an Answer' (1999), op cit.

11 Haack, 'As for that phrase "studying in a literary spirit"', *Manifesto*, Ch 3.

12 Calvino's most eloquent statement is to be found in his posthumously published Charles Eliot Norton Lectures, *Six Memos for the Next Millennium* (tr Patrick Creagh, 1988). There may be a tension between some of Santos's rash philosophical claims and his commitment to scholarship, but I have no reason to believe that he rejects basic values of scholarly integrity.

the same spirit as post-modern resistance to 'closure'. There is nothing in Peirce or Haack that suggests that enquiry is easy or simple.[13] Nevertheless, seeking a complete rapprochement would be too glib. For Santos does appear to subscribe to some anti-rationalist views — such as the denial that objective truth is meaningful — that threaten central scholarly values.[14]

While Haack's defence of her views is passionate and robust, on some of the points that differentiate what I have called anti-rationalist and imaginative post-modernism she is clearly a moderate in relation to the latter, as the following statement illustrates:

> 'It is perfectly possible to acknowledge the short-comings of foundationalism and coherentism, human enquirers' pervasive epistemic dependence on one another, the social character of scientific inquiry, the complexity and fallibility of all human cognitive activity, the corruption of some claims to truth, without being obliged to grant either that epistemic standards are community- or culture-relative, or that inquiry is invariably political.'[15]

I have suggested that Calvino has no commitment to anti-rationalist post-modernism. But, it may be objected, is he not really a full-blooded post-modernist, especially in his later works? He was an admirer of Borges and Barthes. He indulged in baroque fantasy and fable. He emphasised the complexity and elusiveness of a cosmos in flux. Is not Marco Polo a paradigm case of post-modernism? And do not most commentators treat him as such? To me this illustrates the uselessness of such labels. The innocent realist starts with a simple premise and sticks with it: there is one world that is largely independent of our knowledge of it. Calvino stresses the complexity and elusiveness of reality and the difficulties in the way of knowing. I see no incompatibility here. In a lecture on multiplicity, published after his death, Calvino emphasised the continuity of our intellectual traditions. Writing of Flaubert, but also of Garda and Musil and Thomas Mann, he said:

> 'Flaubert's skepticism and his endless curiosity about the human knowledge accumulated over the centuries are the very qualities that are destined to be claimed for their own by the greatest writers of the twentieth century. But theirs I would tend to call active

13 See *Manifesto*, Ch 3.

14 See Haack's robust recent attack on 'the Higher Dismissiveness', see 'Staying for an Answer', op cit.

15 *Manifesto*, p 146.

skepticism, a kind of gambling and betting in a tireless effort to establish relationships between discourse, methods, and levels of meaning. Knowledge as multiplicity is the thread that binds together the major works both of what is called modernism and of what goes by the name of the *postmodern*, a thread – over and above all labels attached to it – that I hope will continue into the next millennium.'[16]

Why is emphasis on multiple standpoints and perspectives important? For me, law is an infinitely complex subject and understanding law is an endless and inevitably collective enterprise, a quest that will know no closure. In an essay written in 1967, Calvino asked 'Whom do we write a novel for? Whom do we write a poem for?'[17] He suggests that each new book is written so that it can be placed on a hypothetical bookshelf beside books that precede it and books that will inevitably succeed it. His answer applies as much to a jurist as to a poet or novelist. As Katherine Hume puts it:

> 'He weighs books and looks at the problems of the world and admits that the political weight of any book is extremely modest, and often not what the author intended. A book is only "un granello di sabbia", a grain of sand. However, an important book, literary or scientific, can raise consciousness to a new level by augmenting our instruments of understanding and imagining. Many books, many essays, are many grains of sand, and can be gathered in collections of sand. The claims made for any one must be minimal, but the number of potential grains is limitless and they may become significant.'[18]

On my interpretation, imaginative postmodernism, exemplified by Calvino and some strands in Santos' work, is quite compatible with innocent realism and Haack's critique of some fashionable fallacies associated with anti-rational post-modernism. Against this background, let us consider Santos's treatment of globalisation and law.

16 Italo Calvino, 'Multiplicity', in *Six Memos for the Next Millennium* (tr Patrick Creagh, 1993).
17 'Whom do we Write For? or The Hypothetical Bookshelf' (1967) in *The Uses of Literature* (tr Patrick Creagh, 1986).
18 Hume (1992a) at p 85.

4 SANTOS ON GLOBALISATION AND LAW

(a) Globalisation

> 'Far from being linear or unambiguous, the process of globalization is highly contradictory and uneven. It takes place through an apparently dialectical process, whereby new forms of globalization occur together with new or renewed forms of localization. Indeed, as global interaction and interdependence intensify, social relations in general seem to be increasingly deterritorialized, opening the way to new *rights to options*, crossing borders up until recently policed by customs, nationalism, language and ideology, oftentimes by all of them together. But, on the other hand, and in apparent contradiction with this trend, new regional, national and local identities are emerging that are built around a new prominence of *rights to roots*.
>
> The process of globalization is, thus, selective, uneven, and fraught with tensions and contradictions. But it is not anarchic. It reproduces the hierarchies of the world system and the asymmetries among core, peripheral and semi-peripheral societies. There is, therefore, no genuine globalism. Under the conditions of the modern world system, globalism is the successful globalization of a given localism. The English language, as *lingua franca*, is one such example.'[19]

Santos's interpretation of globalisation is quite close to mine. Indeed, I have found his analysis helpful in trying to make sense of these bewildering phenomena. We agree, for example, that the processes of globalisation have a long history, that they are not unilinear (but the flow is more from North to South), and that they are rapidly changing the significance of national boundaries. So far as the legal landscape is concerned, we also agree that no one can understand their local law by focusing solely on municipal domestic law of a single jurisdiction or nation state; that the range of significant actors and processes has been extended; and that the phenomena of legal pluralism are central to understanding law in today's world.

Santos distinguishes between four forms of globalisation as process: globalised localism (eg Coca Cola, the English language); localised globalism (eg structural adjustment programmes, and luxurious tourist facilities in poor countries); cosmopolitanism (defined as 'the networking of local progressive struggles with the objective of maximizing their

19 Santos at p 262 (italics in the original). See also, David Crystal, *English as a Global Language* (1997).

emancipatory potential *in loco* through translocal/local connections');[20] and the common heritage of mankind (struggles to cope with issues of genuine global significance such as nuclear proliferation, global warming, exploration and appropriation of other planets, and the protection of the environment). Santos interprets the first two categories as mainly involving impositions and flows from centre to periphery or, using a different taxonomy, from North to South. He explicitly confines the other two categories to 'counter-hegemonic forces' resisting the domination of the industrialised West/North and other capitalist centres of power.

This explicitly ideological categorisation is suggestive, but it is, perhaps, a bit too neatly schematic. For example, while there are clear instances of globalised localisms (eg CNN, Coca Cola), it is not clear why structural adjustment programmes and luxurious tourist facilities belong to localised globalism rather than *vice versa*. For example, structural adjustment typically involves the imposition of relatively uniform Western ideas on other countries – a form of cultural export. Similarly, while the idea of 'a common heritage of mankind' emanated largely from sources representing Third World interests,[1] it is strange to suggest that debates about such global issues are framed, let alone dominated, by 'counter-hegemonic' forces. Santos recognises that resistance to genuinely global solutions has come from Western powers, especially the United States. It is surely unduly optimistic to equate transformative practices with 'counter-hegemonic forces' and adaptive practices with hegemonic countries – the reverse is often the case. Similarly, it is unclear where international drug syndicates or the Mafia fit into this scheme, unless they are treated as 'progressive'. Again, the Internet, which originated in the United States, has the potential to be an instrument of cultural domination or a locus of transnational counterculture or, more likely a mixture of both, in ways in which it is impossible to foretell, especially in Santos's long and indefinite time-frame. Santos's neat scheme may fit his broad thesis, but for most other purposes it is important to recognise the complexity of interactions at all levels from the global to the local, including many intermediate ones.

Interpretations of globalisation range from the apocalyptic (both utopian and pessimistic) to the sceptical, exemplified by Immanuel Wallerstein and Kenichi Omae, on the one hand, and Paul Hirst and

20 At p 264.

1 The history of the idea of *ius humanitatis* is outlined in Mary Victoria White, 'The Common Heritage of Mankind: An Assessment', (1982) 14 Case W. Res. J. Int. L. 509. For recent discussions, see *Annale de Droit Aérien et Spatial* (Montreal).

Grahame Thompson, on the other.[2] Not surprisingly, as a prophet of paradigmatic change, Santos follows Wallerstein quite closely. Hirst and Thompson argue that 'rhetorical globalists' exaggerate the unity of the world economy, the importance of multi-national corporations, and the decline in importance of the nation-state as the key actor in transnational ordering. As a relatively short-term interpreter of the current scene, I find much of this cautionary argument persuasive, except that I think that it tends to underplay the qualitative significance of recent changes, especially in respect of communications and financial markets.[3]

The main difference between Santos's and my interpretations of globalisation seems to be largely one of time-scale. He readily concedes that in the medium- and short-term the nation state is likely to remain by far the most significant actor at nearly all levels and what he calls 'counter-hegemonic forces' are currently underdeveloped and weak.[4] Conversely, given the rapidity of change and the complexity of the processes, I do not feel capable of making confident predictions about the longer term. Where he is utopian and optimistic, I am agnostic and rather more pessimistic.

Traditional legal theory has focused almost exclusively on two levels of law: the municipal law of nation states and public international law. Santos recognises the multiplicity of levels of law, but largely focuses on three: the global, the national and the sub-national. These are adequate for his purposes. In a different context I have suggested that normative ordering reflects all levels of human relations (including legal persons, groups etc) and that, for general purposes, it may be useful to differentiate between global, international, regional, transnational, inter-communal, territorial state, sub-state, and non-state local.[5] This, essentially geographical, characterisation is just one rough and ready taxonomy among many. It has the advantage of drawing attention to various levels

2 Immanuel Wallerstein's writings are extensive; see especially, *The Capitalist World Economy* (1979); 'the Withering Away of States', (1980) 8 International Journal of Sociology of Law 369; *Unthinking Social Science* (1991). Wallerstein has been one of the most persistent critics of the tendency to treat societies and nation-states as self-contained: 'It is the world-scale structure and the processes of its development that provide the true subject of our collective enquiry' (at p 77). Kenichi Omae, *The Borderless World: Power and Strategy in the Interlinked Economy* (1990). Hirst and Thompson, op cit, pp 6-7.

3 Like Santos, Hirst and Thompson have an explicitly political agenda, in their case to attack the idea that the nation-state has lost the capacity to regulate most aspects of economic relations. John Gray, while conceding some of their points, dismisses their political prescriptions, such as European social democracy, as outdated and no longer viable (J Gray, *False Dawn* (revised edn, 1998), at p 64).

4 Eg pp 345-347.

5 Ch 6. 2.

of non-state ordering and emphasising the point that these different levels are not neatly nested in a single vertical hierarchy. Here, despite the different taxonomies, Santos and I are in broad agreement, especially on the point that the cross-cutting of normative orders puts the phenomena of legal pluralism at the centre of understanding law. This is the subject of the next section.

(b) Legal and Normative Pluralism[6]

Leading commentators, such as Merry and Griffiths, maintain that legal pluralism is a concept and a phenomenon rather than a 'school'. or perspective.[7] For them, as for me, the co-existence of multiple legal orders and multiple systems or bodies of rules are social facts. Their chief complaint is that these important phenomena are ignored or marginalised by orthodox legal theory and scholarship.

The concept has a long history and is often contested. Perhaps the conception that has been longest established refers to national or state legal systems that are 'pluralistic' in that they recognise as official sources of law bodies of personal or religious law belonging to different groups. This phenomenon is best-documented in relation to national legal systems in the colonial and immediate post-colonial periods.[8] For example, in Tanzania at the time of independence Muslim, Hindu and customary law were officially recognised as sources of state law, along with local legislation, supplemented by 'the substance of the common law, the doctrines of equity and 'statutes of general application so far as local circumstances admit'.[9] Anthropologists were quick to realise that there were often differences in scope, content and form between what was recognised as customary law by the courts and what was treated as

6 This section is an extension of the observations on pluralism made in Ch 3.5.

7 For references, see Ch 3.5.

8 For a general survey see Barry Hooker, *Legal Pluralism* (1975). 'Legal pluralism' in this sense has a long history, including the story of 'capitulations' (when colonists and other expatriate groups were allowed to be governed by their personal laws, often administered in special courts); the co-existence of alternative, sometimes competing, jurisdictions (as in England up to the nineteenth century); various kinds of involuntary receptions (see Sandra Burman and Barbara Harrell-Bond (eds), *The Imposition of Law* (1979)). Much of the history of law before the rise of the nation-state involved legal pluralism in a broader sense (see, for example, H J Berman, *Law and Revolution: The Formation of the Western Legal Tradition* (1983)).

9 The pre-Independence law was governed by the Tanganyika Order in Council 1920 (as amended) and continued, subject to local modifications, by the Interim Constitution (1965). On Sudan, see above, Ch 6.4. On immediate post-independence anglophone Africa, see A N Allott, *New Essays in African Law* (1970).

obligatory custom by the people subject to them.[10] In the period after World War II, academic lawyers who adopted a top-down perspective were concerned about practical problems facing the courts in ascertaining the content of customary law and in problems of choice of law or internal conflicts of laws.[11] These concerns led to proposals to codify, unify or 'restate' customary law at national level in order to assist the courts and other officials in ascertaining, interpreting, applying and enforcing the law as state law. Such proposals provoked quite sharp debates, for example in East Africa, the critics arguing that 'decontextualising' custom would lead to substantial changes in process, form and substance, while the proponents maintained that this was the only practicable way of incorporating and preserving traditional ideas and values within the official legal system.[12]

As jurists have become more conscious of 'multi-culturalism' and as societies have in fact become more plural, there has been increased recognition that all modern societies have to wrestle with the extent to which the state should recognise, make concessions to, or even enforce norms and values embedded in different religions, cultures, or traditions. Such recognition is exemplified by Federal Indian Law in the United States, the recent attention given to the position and rights of indigenous peoples in Australia, New Zealand and Canada, and the belated acknowledgement that there are issues relating to Muslim Law and that of other minorities within the United Kingdom.[13] Today, *state legal pluralism* is recognised as a fact in nearly all countries.[14] Some writers on the subject tend to be dismissive of state legal pluralism. In the context of a reaction against statist centralising interpretations this was perhaps

10 Eg Sally Falk Moore, *Law as Process: An Anthropological Approach* (1978).

11 Eg Allott (1970), op cit, Chs 4-7.

12 William Twining, *The Place of Customary Law in the National Legal Systems of East Africa* (1963); Eugene Cotran, 'The Place and Future of Customary Law in East Africa' in *East African Law Today* (1966); J Comaroff and S Roberts, *Rules and Processes* (1981); A N Allott, 'Hunting of the Snark or The Quest for the Holy Grail?: The search for customary law', in Ian Edge (ed) (SOAS Jubilee Lectures, forthcoming).

13 Eg David Pearl and Werner Menski, *Muslim Family Law* (3rd edn, 1998); Sebastian Poulter, *Ethnicity, Law and Rights: The English Experience* (1998) reviewed critically by Menski in (1999) 115 LQR 139.

14 John Griffiths in an important essay distinguishes between 'weak' and 'strong' concepts of legal pluralism, 'What is Legal Pluralism?' (1986) 24 Journal of Legal Pluralism 1. State legal pluralism is of increasing importance in the context of developing legal regimes, such as the EU, and the increased penetration of international human rights norms into municipal law (eg the Pinochet affair) and a possibly greater sensitivity to multiculturalism by legislatures and courts (for England see Poulter, and Menski and Pearl, op cit). Of course, cross-level interlegality involves not only interaction between different levels of 'official law' but also between state and non-state law.

justified. However, state legal pluralism has a continuing vitality, as was dramatically illustrated by the Otieno case in Kenya, in which litigation between the widow and the clan of a leading Nairobi lawyer about burial rights, dramatised, amid a blaze of publicity, issues about gender and culture, tradition and modernity, imported law and custom, tribalism, city and country, and a great deal else besides.[15]

However, 'legal pluralism' is more regularly associated with 'non-state law', a concept that is more problematic. Following Santos, one can distinguish between three main phases in the history of these concepts.[16] First, pioneers of the sociology of law, most notably Ehrlich, argued that a realistic depiction of the law in action had to take account of 'the living law' of sub-groups as well as 'the official law' of the state. They saw that these could diverge significantly and that sometimes one, sometimes the other would prevail. This was an important step not only in the direction of 'realism', but also away from the idea that the state has a monopoly of law-creation.

These ideas were developed in a number of directions. For example, Karl Llewellyn saw clearly that within a major group such as a nation-state, society or tribe, the basic functions or jobs of law, such as conflict prevention and dispute-resolution, could be performed at different levels by a variety of mechanisms in addition to rules – eg by education or the threat or use of brute force – and that different bodies of rules could co-exist without necessarily being ranked in a clear hierarchical order.[17] Kadish and Kadish developed the idea of legitimated interposition which in practice allows for departures from official law, even by officials.[18] For example, tax officials, health and safety inspectors, and environmental enforcement agencies typically develop more or less articulated norms that not only guide how formally authorised discretion is exercised, but sometimes go further to provide for waiving, ignoring, or even modifying

15 There is an extensive literature on the case. The best sources are S M Otieno, *Kenya's Unique Burial Saga* (Nation Newspapers, Nairobi, 1987) and J B Ojwang and J N K Mugambi (eds), *The S M Otieno Case* (Nairobi, 1989). More accessible are David William Cohen and E S Atieno Odhiambo, *Burying SM: The Politics of Knowledge and the Sociology of Power in Africa* (1992) and John W van Doren, 'Death African Style: The Case of S M Otieno' (1988) 36 American Journal of Comparative Law 329.

16 A different perspective with a longer time-frame is interestingly sketched by Massimo Corsale, 'Legal Pluralism and the Corporatist Model in the Welfare State', (1994) 7 Ratio Juris 95, linking pluralism to M Hauriou, Carl Schmitt and Santi Romano, among others.

17 The *locus classicus* is Karl Llewellyn, 'The Normative, The Legal and the Law-jobs' (1940) 49 Yale Law Journal 1355; see above, Ch 3.4(d).

18 M R Kadish and S H Kadish, *Discretion to Disobey: A Study of Lawful Departures from Rules* (1973). The concept is a complex one and arguably includes legal fictions, plea bargaining, refusal to prosecute even where there is a duty to do so, and 'perverse' jury verdicts.

official rules. These insights have been fruitfully applied and developed in empirical studies of regulation, among others.[19]

A second conception of legal pluralism was developed, mainly by legal anthropologists, in the late colonial and post-independence period. As anthropology began to escape from the idea that 'tribes' were self-contained units situated in a vacuum, there was increasing recognition that traditional norms, institutions and processes interacted with outside forces in complex ways. An early example, is Lloyd Fallers' classic account of Busoga law in Uganda, which brought out very clearly how traditional Soga ways of dispute-processing were linked to the colonial courts in a hierarchy. While the official legal system only recognised two or three levels of jurisdiction, disputants were generally required to move through two or more additional levels before reaching institutions that were recognised as courts of first instance.[20]

More recently, Sally Falk Moore, Martin Chanock and others have further glossed the idea of pluralism by showing that what passed for 'customary law' was often in large part an artificial creation of the colonial state, sometimes produced by negotiation between colonial officials and 'representatives' of the colonised – the result being a hybrid often bearing only a tenuous relation to traditional concepts, processes and norms, which might continue to survive and develop in different ways.[1] Chanock goes so far as to suggest that what has passed for 'customary law' in the discourse of both colonial administrators and post-Independence nationalist elites was 'a colonial myth based on need not knowledge' and 'an idealisation of the past developed in an attempt to cope with social dislocation'.[2] Indeed, what passed for customary law

19 Eg Keith Hawkins, *Environment and Enforcement* (1984); R Baldwin and J C McCrudden (eds), *Regulation and Public Law* (1987); and Julia Black, *Rules and Regulators* (1997).

20 'The "courts" held by parish chiefs, by village and sub-village headmen, and by lineage heads have never received legislative recognition, but the official courts have recognized their usefulness and have acted to maintain them ... From the point of view of the average villager, all these tribunals are a part of a single judicial system; all are nkiiko, with the authority "to cut cases",' Lloyd Fallers, *Law Without Precedent: Legal Ideas in Action in the Colonial Courts of Busoga* (1969) at p 59. Of course, such a phenomenon is not confined to traditional societies. In civil disputes in modern societies there are more or less formal, more or less voluntary, more or less institutionalised stages involving negotiation or mediation or some other 'alternative' means before a disputant gets anywhere near a court.

1 Sally Falk Moore, *Social Facts and Fabrications* (1986); Martin Chanock, *Law, Custom and Social Order* (1989).

2 At p 8 (citing Bloch); cf pp 236-237. The sceptical thesis about customary law being largely a product of colonial encounters can be over-generalised: in some places, eg today's Malaysia, there are well-documented examples of custom pre-dating colonisation and, of course, there were institutions and orderings in pre-colonial Africa.

was often a response to colonial rule, more modern than the imported law.

A third stage of development of the concept of 'legal pluralism' has evolved as the focus of attention moved back to 'non-state law' in modern or Western societies. Under this increasingly vague rubric, many empirical studies by socio-legal scholars, sociologists and others have been published, *The Journal of Legal Pluralism* has become established, and there have been some recent theoretical contributions – so that the field has become sufficiently diverse that it is dangerous to generalise.[3] There have been some stimulating contributions, but one is nevertheless left with a feeling of frustration about the literature: on the one hand the phenomena are important, on the other hand there is a worrying vagueness and lack of clear sense of direction about where this all leads. At this point, Santos appears to me to have made a very significant contribution.

Santos shares this sense of dissatisfaction. His own treatment of the topic advances the discussion in several important respects. First, until very recently nearly all discussions of 'legal pluralism' have focused on societies or sub-groups within them. Santos rightly emphasises the ways in which legal orders interact at all levels from the global to the very local. From a global perspective, the coexistence and interaction of legal orders at different levels is one reason why the phenomenon of legal pluralism must become central to general jurisprudence.

Secondly, the term 'legal pluralism' has some normative associations. Historically the term was often used rhetorically in political contexts as part of arguments against the centralisation of state power, its claims to having a monopoly of law, and the bogey of 'legal centralism'. So 'pluralism' has tended to be treated as a 'pro-word'. Santos identifies in the literature a tendency to nostalgia and romanticism. He is emphatic that 'To my mind there is nothing inherently good, progressive, or emancipatory about legal pluralism. Indeed, there are instances of legal pluralism that are quite reactionary.'[4] I agree with him that the term is more usefully treated as an analytical concept, without any necessary

3 A further development has been the introduction of the idea of 'legal polycentricity', but I agree with Gordon Woodman that, while some useful work has been done under this rubric, the concept is ambiguous and is of little or no analytical value (G Woodman, review of Hanne Petersen and Henrik Zahle (eds), *Legal Polycentricity: Consequences of Pluralism in Law* (1995) in (1997) 39 Journal of Legal Pluralism 155). See also Woodman (1998), op cit; cf Brian Tamanaha, 'The Folly of the Concept of Scientific Pluralism' (1993) 20 Journal of Law and Society 192. As was suggested above (Ch 3.5), most puzzles about normative pluralism are attributable to the complexity of the phenomenon; cf L Shelley, 'Transnational Organized Crime: The New Authoritarianism' in R Friman and P Andreas (eds) *The Illicit Global Economy* (1999).

4 At pp 114-115. For example, Santos describes the situation of pluralism in feudal society as 'complex, cumbersome, chaotic and arbitrary' (at p 58).

progressive connotations, that designates the co-existence of multiple orders, generally in a single time-space context.[5]

Thirdly, and probably most importantly, Santos develops the notion of 'interlegality' to refer to interactions between co-existing legal orders. It is a mistake to assume that because multiple legal orders co-exist they are necessarily self-contained, or in conflict with each other, or substantially different. Santos's case studies of squatter settlements in Brazil provide vivid illustrations of these points. For example, Pasagarda law – the internal legal order governing some social relations within a squatter settlement outside Rio[6] – borrowed some of its forms and rhetoric and concepts from 'asphalt law', ie state municipal law.[7] To some extent this regime was in conflict with the state, to some extent it was recognised as being an instrument of social ordering, so it served both as a brake on and an instrument of state control.

Santos's study of a series of disputes in Recife illustrates different aspects of legal pluralism in action: in a series of disputes between squatters and developers, both sides made use of the state legal system in different ways, but in two cases partial or total success was obtained by deploying other political and legal resources, including international human rights norms, constitutional law and natural law, as well as the media and the political influence of the Church. In both studies class conflict was central to the situation and the less privileged protagonists invoked a plurality of legal, political and ideological resources at a number of levels. In the case of Recife these ranged from the very local to the global.[8]

To capture the complexity of the relationships among legal orders and semi-autonomous legal fields, Santos introduces the concept of 'interlegality'. Using cartographic metaphors, he gives an ebullient account of his view in a passage quoted at the start of this essay. He claims to be presenting:

> '... not the legal pluralism of traditional legal anthropology, in which the different legal orders are conceived as separate entities coexisting in the same political space, but rather, the conception of different legal spaces superimposed, interpenetrated, and mixed in our minds, as much as in our actions, either on occasions of

5 Some legal orders apply to 'imagined communities' that are dispersed and whose members do not know each other – eg gypsy law, some versions of Islamic or Jewish law. See Benedict Anderson, *Imagined Communities* (rev ed 1991).

6 The Pasagarda study was done in 1970, that of Recife in 1980.

7 Ironically this 'illegal legal system' was primarily concerned with property relations – leasing, inheritance, disputes between landlord and tenant – notwithstanding that the basic norm is illegal from the point of view of state law.

8 Santos, Ch 5.

qualitative leaps or sweeping crises in our life trajectories, or in the dull routine of eventless everyday life.'[9]

This passage is dismissed somewhat mockingly by Gunther Teubner: 'We are left with ambiguity and confusion'.[10] Teubner's concern here is to find a basis for distinguishing the social and the legal; his remedy is autopoiesis. Here I am more convinced by Santos's picture, despite the ebullience, than Teubner's version of systems theory.[11]

The concept of interlegality could usefully be developed, especially at transnational and global levels to provide fresh analyses of such phenomena as legal transplants, imposed law, and regional legal regimes. One way of proceeding might be along the following lines. As a preliminary to systematic analysis of examples or to further empirical work, it would be useful to develop a conceptual framework, including the following:

(a) typology or typologies of norms;[12]
(b) a typology of agglomerations of norms (eg systems, orders, codes, collections, digests, muddles, melees);
(c) a typology of relations and of interactions between, among, and within agglomerations of norms (eg symbiosis, competition, conflict, prioritisation, imposition, imitation, convergence, subsumption, integration).

There is, of course, a massive, but diffuse, literature on (a) within jurisprudence and other disciplines (eg game theory, the emergence of norms). One suspects that (b) is less well developed (but see Sampford, Teubner and his critics, and Bentham's *Of Laws in General*). It is my impression that the literature on (c) is fragmented and uneven. There is relative sophistication in the legal literature on conflicts of laws and private international law, on legal pluralism, and on such topics as subsidiarity in the European Union and reception. But, so far as I am aware, there is little systematic analysis about different kinds of relation between normative orders (and other kinds of agglomeration). How far existing categories and differentiations developed in other contexts would be helpful in providing a more systematic framework for the study of

9 At pp 472-473. This passage is quoted at greater length at the start of this essay.
10 Gunther Teubner, 'The Two faces of Janus: Rethinking Legal Pluralism', (1992) 13 Cardozo Law Review 1443.
11 See above Ch. 3.5. On the futility of sharply distinguishing 'legal' and 'non-legal' orders, see Griffiths, op cit, at pp 29-39 and below, p 231.
12 'Norm' is used here in the broad sense of the generic term for prescriptions, of which categorical precepts, principles, guidelines, standards, and perhaps maxims (eg the maxims of equity) are sub-sets.

normative and legal pluralism is a large question.[13] Such preliminary, mainly conceptual, analysis is a task for analytical jurisprudence.

Santos rightly emphasises the increase of significance of legal pluralism as part of the process of uncoupling notions of state, nation, and law. Nevertheless, like Teubner, he feels the need to identify the defining characteristics of law.[14] Here, I side with Griffiths and Llewellyn, who reject general definitions of law as unnecessary and misleading, because the indicia of 'the legal' are more like a continuum or more complex mix of attributes, which it is not necessary to set off artificially from closely related phenomena except for pragmatic reasons in quite specific contexts.[15]

Strangely, Santos does not set his discussion of legal pluralism or legal plurality in the broader context of normative pluralism. There seem to me to be at least two advantages in doing this. First, everyone experiences normative pluralism as a fact every day of their lives. Lawyers' scepticism of the importance of legal pluralism, or even of its existence[16] is most easily countered by starting with this undeniable fact of the co-existence of normative orders or agglomerations which, from an individual point of view, are not necessarily linked hierarchically. Secondly, it is easier to deal with problems of defining the borders of legal/non-legal phenomena for different specific purposes, if one sees legal pluralism as a rather fluid sub-species of normative pluralism.

This justifies a digression into the broader topic. One of the puzzling features of legal pluralism is that everybody lives under and experiences normative pluralism in their daily lives, yet when lawyers or law students are presented with examples of legal pluralism they tend to find it surprising, or puzzling, or 'not really law'. To take a homely example: An outsider doing an ethnographic study of my law school, the Faculty of Laws of University College London, might ask: 'What norms apply to members of this community?' In order to answer this question, one would first need to distinguish between norms applicable to the community (and its constituent individuals qua members of the community) and the sum total of norms applying to each of the individuals who are members of the community.

To start with the former: a preliminary list would include international treaties relating to copyright, European Union Law, the European

13 Eg within jurisprudence, familiar distinctions between primary and secondary rules (Hart), rules and principles (Dworkin), rules expressed in fixed verbal form and rules not so expressed (Twining and Miers) and so on.

14 At p112. His general definition is reminiscent of Hoebel's attempt that Karl Llewellyn refused to include in *The Cheyenne Way*, see *KLRM* at pp 177-179.

15 Griffiths, op cit; Llewellyn, *Jurisprudence, Realism in Theory and Practice* (1960) at p 3ff.

16 See Woodman (1997) op cit (commenting on J Vansina).

Convention on Human Rights, the Constitution of the United Kingdom (if such exists), United Kingdom law, English law, the bye-laws and regulations of the Borough of Camden, Internet Law, the Charter and Statutes of the University of London, the statutes, rules, regulations and policies of University College, Faculty Regulations and rules, the ethical norms of the Law Society and the Bar and their rules relating to admission, the marking schemes and Examination Regulations and conventions of the University of London, rules created by the Faculty, the students' Law Society, and a host of unwritten norms of courtesy, university custom and practice, UCL tradition, and the customs and conventions of the Faculty of Laws. Other bodies of rules, regulations and other norms would impact on significant sub-groups within the law school, such as the norms of the Universities' Funding Council, the Association of University Teachers, and the National Union of Students. Members of Faculty spasmodically enforce English rules of grammar and spelling and principles of logic. Almost any behaviour within this community can be guided, appraised, or sanctioned by invoking one or more sets or systems of these and other rules.

Yet the norms operating within Bentham House (the Law School building) are much more complex than that. I sometimes ask my students to write down what bodies of norms they have been subject to or have invoked during the previous 48 hours. Naturally their answers are very varied. Our students come from different ethnic backgrounds, belong to different religions, play different sports and games, live in hostels or at home, join clubs, societies and political parties, watch television,[17] engage in sexual relations, queue,[18] travel abroad or indulge in other transnational relations, make rash promises, invoke proverbs, mantras and maxims, and visit night clubs, prisons, schools and other institutions.

Lawyers and law students encounter normative pluralism every day of their lives, in legal and non-legal contexts. Yet legal pluralism is generally marginalised and viewed with scepticism in legal discourse. Perhaps the main reason for this is that for over 200 years Western legal theory has been dominated by conceptions of law that tend to be monist (one internally coherent legal system),[19] statist (the state has a monopoly of law within its territory), and positivist (what is not created or recognised as law by the state is not law).

17 About half of them deny being subject to rules of television watching, the other half are not sure what theirs are (*HTDTWR* at pp 12, 143-144).

18 On queuing rules see Neil MacCormick, 'Norms, Institutions, and Institutional Facts', (1998) *Law and Philosophy*, pp 1, 3ff.

19 Though not necessarily as comprehensively monist as Kelsen who subsumed all national legal systems under international law (above, Ch 3.3).

A second reason is that law is conceived of as what lawyers think it is rather than what those subject to it think it is; but lawyers' conceptions of law are derived from their training and socialisation, from their claims to having a monopoly of certain kinds of knowledge and expertise, and these in turn are derived from or bolstered by underlying – largely statist – conceptions of law. Concepts such as 'non-state law', 'folk law', and 'customary law' are generally associated with anthropology and sociology, even though academic lawyers have contributed to their study as much as scholars from other disciplines. One of the pioneers of the study of the responsiveness of English law to customs and values of minority cultures, the late Sebastian Poulter, has been criticised for claiming that he was the only lawyer taking a legal approach to legal pluralism.[20] In my view, the criticism was just, for many of the pioneers of the study of legal pluralism have been academic lawyers. However, Poulter had a point. For few people practice or write manuals or train people to be skilled in the use of non-state law. On the whole, non-state law and the strong version of legal pluralism have been mainly thought and written about by scholars adopting the standpoint of observers rather than participants.

I have tried to show how Santos and I have slightly different 'takes' on legal and normative pluralism, but our differences are not great. Much more important is the point that we both treat pluralism as a central phenomenon of law, especially when it is viewed from a global perspective.

(c) Mapping

> 'Just like maps, laws are ruled distortions or misreadings of social territories. They share these characteristics with poems ... Though for different reasons, maps, poems and laws all distort social realities, traditions or territories, and all according to certain rules. Maps distort reality in order to establish orientation; poems distort reality to establish originality; and laws distort reality in order to establish exclusivity.' (Santos)[1]

Maps and mapping provide some of the most popular metaphors and analogies in many disciplines. One maps a field to provide an overview, to establish its contours, to chart relations between topoi, to set a context, or to serve as a guide to the terrain or the landscape for particular purposes. It has even been suggested that maps are *the* fundamental

20 Poulter, (1998), and the review by Werner Menski (1999), op cit, p 225n.
1 At p 458.

analogy.[2] Whether or not this is so, mapping as a metaphor is commonplace in law: Leibniz, Blackstone, Austin, and Wigmore, as well as many contemporaries, provide well-known examples.[3] In recent years, others have used geographical mapping as aids to giving accounts of the distribution of legal services, access to rural courts, patterns of crime and other spatial relations of legal phenomena.[4] There is even a nascent law-and-geography movement.[5]

Both Santos and I have long been interested in legal cartography. We have been concerned with both geographical and mental mapping *of* law. Santos has gone one step further to develop the idea of laws *as* maps. His main point is that laws, like maps, systematically distort reality rather than merely reflect it.[6] Chapter 7 of *Toward a New Common Sense* embodies a revised version of his well-known essay of the same title from which I, among others, have learned a great deal.[7] It is dense, richly suggestive and full of tantalising, sometimes obscure, aperçus that need clarification and further development.

I have dealt with legal cartography at length in Chapter 6. Here I shall deal with it quite briefly, without fully doing justice to Santos's

2 Santos, at p 351, citing A Robinson and B Petchnik, *The Nature of Maps* (1976). Susan Haack uses mapping analogies, including in relation to multiple descriptions: 'A heterogeneous true description of the world is no less true for its heterogeneity; any more than a map which superimposes a depiction of the roads on a depiction of the contours of the relevant terrain, or a map which inserts a large-scale depiction of a major city in a corner of a small-scale depiction of a state, is less accurate for its heterogeneity' (*Manifesto* at p 160; cf Peirce op cit, at p 35).

3 For references see above, Ch 6.3 at p 141n.

4 Eg Paul Wiles, 'A Future Research Agenda for Analyzing Crime in Cities' (1997) 31 Comparative Law Review 24; Keith D Harries, *The Geography of Laws and Justice* (1978); and *Serious Violence: Patterns of Homicide and Assault in America* (1990).

5 Kim Economides, 'Law and Geography: New Frontiers', in Philip Thomas (ed) *Legal Frontiers* (1996). See above, Ch 6.3 and 6.4.

6 Santos is attracted to cartography especially because he sees it as 'disproving' epistemological foundationalism and correspondence theories. This is unconvincing. Ironically, one of the most popular examples of ideological mapping, Peters's Projection, claims to provide 'the map which represents countries accurately according to their surface areas' in contrast to the Eurocentric maps based on Mercator's projection, which incorrectly showed the colonial powers as being larger than they really were, 'while the Southern continents Africa, South America, are shown as far too small' (New Internationalist edition, 1999). The argument is that Peters's map corresponds more closely to reality. Santos himself talks of maps as distortions of 'reality' – which seems to presuppose rather than refute a correspondence theory of truth. The fact that Santos makes some insightful points about cartography and law reinforces my argument that his sociology of law owes little or nothing to his dubious epistemology.

7 The full title was: 'Law: A Map of Misreading. Toward a Postmodern Conception of Law', (1987) 14 Journal of Law and Society 279.

ideas. My essay on 'Mapping Law' was stimulated by dissatisfaction with the Grands Systèmes tradition of comparative law. The issues seemed significant, but simplistic Cook's Tours and confused debates about taxonomy seemed inadequate. I used the idea of geographical mapping to suggest why developing total pictures of law in the world and particular legal orders is difficult. The main reason is the complexity of the phenomena involved and their inter-relationships. Constructing 'whole views' of law in the world is difficult because there are many kinds of normative ordering, with different histories, that coincide, overlap, and interact in complex ways in the same geographical spaces. Hence the centrality of the ideas of normative and legal pluralism in understanding legal phenomena.

A second theme was that maps presuppose reliable and comparable data, but such data in respect of law are sparse, uneven, and in many respects underdeveloped. This is illustrated by the relative scarcity of global and national statistics for law compared to such fields as economics, trade, health, and education. How far this is attributable to the cultural specificity of most legal phenomena or to the underdevelopment of our discipline, especially its empirical aspects, are issues for a revived general jurisprudence. Some legal phenomena, like Mr Palomar's lawn or waves, are not easy to describe empirically, let alone to subject to statistical analysis. Others may be amenable to this kind of treatment, but localised legal studies and the unempirical tradition of comparative legal studies have not produced much data or adequate concepts for data collection.

A third theme, introduced in relation to Calvino's *Invisible Cities*, is that understanding a legal order, like understanding a city, requires multiple viewpoints and perspectives.

In *Toward a New Common Sense* Santos uses the idea of mapping law to develop a number of points in relation to levels of law, legal pluralism, and globalisation. As we have seen, though our enterprises are rather different, our conclusions are remarkably similar. Santos provides one chart which neatly pictures his research agenda for the study of 'the Transnationalization of the Legal Field' (see p 236). This chart is useful, though a bit too schematic for my taste: the division into three levels (global, national, local) only begins to catch the complexity of types of relation and their ordering and, if it suggests that significant levels of relations are neatly stratified in a single geographical hierarchy, it is misleading.[8]

8 Above, Ch 7.2. Santos is well aware of such complexities, but, like other writers on globalisation, he is inclined to jump straight from the national to the global level without dwelling on other important intermediate and cross-cutting relations (eg regional, alliances, non-state networking in the Commonwealth or the Hispanic-speaking world).

Table 3 Structure–Agency Map of Capitalist Societies in the World System

Dimensions *Structural Places*	Social Agency	Institutions	Developmental Dynamics	Power Form	Legal Form	Epistemological Form
Householdplace	gender, generation	marriage, family, kinship	affection maximizing	patriarchy	domestic law	fatalism, familial culture
Workplace	class, nature as 'capitalist nature'	factory, corporation	profit maximizing, maximizing the degradation of nature	exploitation of 'capitalist nature'	production law	productivisim, technologism, professional training, corporate culture
Marketplace	consumership	market	utility maixizing, maximizing the commodification of needs	fetishism of commodities	exchange law	consumerism, mass culture
Communityplace	ethnicity, race, nation, people, religion	community, neighborhood, region, grassroots, organization, church	identity maximizing	unequal differentiation	community law	local knowledge, community culture, tradition
Citizenplace	citizenship	state	loyalty maximizing	domination	territorial (state) law	educational and cultural nationalism, civic culture
Worldplace	nation-state	interstate system, international agencies and associations, international treaties	effectivity maximizing	unequal exchange	systemic law	science, universalistic progress, global culture

Source: B Santos, *Toward a New Common Sense* p 417.

One particularly valuable insight is the idea that viewing law from multiple perspectives requires focusing not solely or mainly on the citizenplace (state-citizen relations) but also on five other fields of social relations: the household, the workplace, the marketplace, the community, and the global setting ('the worldplace'). These are not just different fields of state law (suggested by terms such as 'family law', 'labour law' etc), but rather are themselves domains of power, knowledge and ordering that may be more or less independent of the state. Under 'modernity', attention has been focused almost entirely on 'the citizenplace', obscuring the significance of these other loci:

> 'As there is a literary canon that establishes what is and what is not literature, there is also a legal canon that establishes what is and what is not law.'[9]

The idea of pluralism applies also to knowledge and power and there are important connections affecting how law, knowledge and power are in fact distributed at a given time.

Santos warns that it is not enough to redraw the map of law, or more broadly of social relations, solely by adding to the list of loci, actors and enclaves of ordering, or by cumulating descriptions, any more than it is useful to give purely chronological accounts of historical development:

> '[M]erely to recognize the existence of a plurality of legal orders, without grounding it theoretically, implies a triple fallacy: the fallacy of descriptivism (as far as it goes, the list of pluralities is complete; but it could be added on to indefinitely without any loss of coherence); the fallacy of triviality (the more complete the list, the greater the probability that it will defeat itself as a description of reality; if law, power and knowledge are everywhere, they are nowhere); and finally, if I may borrow Sartre's term, the fallacy of seriality (the list is practico-inert, the relationship among its elements – irrespective of their number – is never more complex than the relationship between people in a queue waiting for the bus).'[10]

Santos is emphatic that the plurality of law, knowledge and power 'far from being chaotic or infinite, is structured and relational'.[11] Theory needs to give some account of the structures and relations that affect

9 At p 473.

10 At p 403 (citing Sartre, *Critique of Dialectical Reason* (1976)). Queuing is not as simple as Santos suggests, see above, p 232 n 18.

11 At pp 403-404.

these distributions. For example, in assessing the relative importance of the power of the nation state and of other actors and enclaves of power in the global context, it is not enough to list the variety of actors or catalogue changes in the distribution of knowledge, law and power. One has to go further and offer some explanation of these matters, as Santos attempts to do in his account of modernity, capitalism and the emergence of a new 'paradigm'. One may not be persuaded by Santos's answers – I suspect that the nation-state has more staying power than he suggests – but the questions are worth asking.

Perhaps the most original part of this chapter relates to the idea of laws *as* maps. Santos' main thesis can be summarised as follows: Maps distort reality with three specific, related mechanisms: *scale*, *projection*, and *symbolisation*.[12] Laws are like maps because each presents ordered distortions of reality, the physical world for geographical maps, social relations for laws. In both cases there is a tension between representation (image maps) and orientation (instrumental maps). Laws not only represent reality, but also create it – 'the different forms of law create different legal objects upon the same social objects'.[13] For example:

> 'Large-scale legality is rich in details and features; describes behavior and attitudes vividly; contextualizes them in their immediate surroundings; is sensitive to distinctions (and complex relations) between inside and outside, high and low, just and unjust. ... On the contrary, small-scale legality is poor in detail and features. It skeletonizes behavior and attitudes, and reduces them to types of action. But, on the other hand, it determines with accuracy the relativity of positions (the angles between persons and things), provides sense of direction and schemes for shortcuts and, finally, is sensitive to distinctions between part and whole, past and present, functional and non-functional. In sum, this form of legality favors a pattern of regulation based on (and geared to) orientation and movement.'[14]

Santos gives convincing illustrations of large-scale and small-scale legality from his case studies in Brazil and from different levels of labour relations. For example, an industrial dispute will be perceived differently and will involve different distributions of power and knowledge on the shop-floor, in the local community, in national headquarters (of company

12 At pp 463-473.

13 Ar p 464. This may seem like a slide into dubious metaphysics; but that is not a necessary interpretation. For example, it is commonplace that murder, marriage and wills are in an important sense legal constructs. On law as institutional fact, see Neil MacCormick and Ota Weinberger, *An Institutional Theory of Law* (1986).

14 At p 465.

and union), at governmental level, and in the boardroom of a multi-national company.

Finally, Santos reiterates the point that maps inevitably involve selection and distortion based on value judgements. The choice of scale, projection and symbolisation similarly depend on the purpose of the map and the values of the map-maker. Maps in this sense are 'ideological distortions of reality'. These considerations apply to maps of laws and laws as maps. All of this is intriguing and potentially important, but in Santos's highly compressed presentation is no more than suggestive. These are themes that deserve more detailed development.

(d) Santos's research agenda

In a magisterial survey of what is involved in rethinking law from a global perspective, Santos identifies seven types of legal transnationalisation that particularly warrant attention. These are:

(1) *'The transnationalization of nation state law'*. for example movements to harmonise or unify branches of municipal law and programmes of structural adjustment, spearheaded by the World Bank, IMF, and Western donors, which use 'conditionality' as the lever for introducing 'modern', typically capitalist, ideas of commercial law, 'good governance, human rights and democracy'.

(2) The development of *legal regimes of regional integration*. European Union law is to date by far the most developed.

(3) *Transnational commercial regulation*, much of it involving non-state law, which Santos calls 'Global capital's own law'. Santos focuses on the contested topic of the development or 'revival' of a new *lex mercatoria* as a form of non-state law, but this important field of largely private justice also includes international commercial arbitration, the World Trade Organisation, and other more or less arcane institutions and processes through which transnational commercial relations are conducted.[15]

(4) *'The Law of People on the Move'*, that is the regulation and rights of migrants, refugees, and displaced persons. This usefully links together the problems of three categories of people whom conventional legal categories tend to treat as separate specialist areas of concern. Under this heading one might usefully add the situation of gypsies, pastoralists and other nomads.[16]

15 See, for example, Yves Dezalay and Bryant Garth, *Dealing in Virtue* (1996).

16 There is, of course, an extensive inter-disciplinary literature on migration and immigration, nomads, and so on. The legal literature seems rather uneven and tends to be confined within orthodox conceptions of municipal and public international law. However, that is changing. For example, the traditional

(5) Under the rubric 'Ancient Grievances and New Solidarities', Santos refers to *the Law of Indigenous Peoples*, an old issue that has gained a new prominence in the last two decades.[17] He rightly points to the beginnings of transnational linkages and coalitions between groups concerned with the collective rights of indigenous peoples such as Maories, Aborigines and native Americans. Informal networking and academic writings have begun to develop the potential for mutual learning and support on a South-South axis.[18]

(6) The topic of cosmopolitanism and *human rights* raises not only traditional issues about the development of international protection of human rights, but also fundamental issues about universalism, cultural relativism, self-determination, trade-offs between 'development' and human rights, and the emancipatory possibilities of a whole new post-modern portfolio or 'generation' of human rights.[19]

(7) Finally, Santos focuses on genuinely global law, so far only embodied in the vague and largely aspirational idea of a *common heritage of mankind* (*ius humanitatis*). This refers in first instance to the possible allocation of territories and resources on this and other planets that have not to date been appropriated by nation states or capitalist entrepreneurs. These issues surfaced most visibly in relation to the Law of the Sea, and to a lesser extent in relation to Antarctica, and the Moon Treaty of 1979.[20] So far they have tended to be viewed from the outside as relatively arcane and undeveloped aspects of public international law. But as Santos points out, there is enormous potential in the long-term for an expanded application of the principle of the common heritage of mankind, stretching beyond territory and mineral rights to a range of other issues. This relatively undeveloped area provides the clearest example of what he calls cosmopolitan law.

Santos sees the first three lines of enquiry as relating to global capitalism and the last four as providing key foci of attention for cosmopolitan, anti-hegemonic, and utopian legalities.[1] This agenda fits Santos's

distinction between refugees and displaced persons has been over-ridden in a UN-sponsored study: Francis M Deng, *Protecting the Dispossessed: A Challenge to the International Community* (1993).

17 *TNC*, p at 313.

18 Ibid, pp 313-327.

19 Ibid, p 358.

20 For a 'Southern' view on the Law of the Sea Conference, see N Rembe, *Africa and the International Law of the Sea* (1980). On Antarctica see Olav S Stokke and Davor Vidas (eds) *Governing the Antarctic* (1997). On the Moon Treaty see Stephen Garove, *Developments in Space Law* (1991) and Carl Q Christol, 'The Moon Treaty and Allocation of Resources', (1997) 22 Annals of Air and Space Law 31.

1 Santos, at pp 373-377.

particular ideological standpoint. It does not claim to be comprehensive: within his own framework, one might, for example, add communications and media (including copyright and the Internet),[2] nuclear proliferation, the arms trade, transnational crime, the internationalisation of legal practice, the regulation of financial markets, and transnational democracy as similarly deserving attention. Each of the areas he identifies is already or has the potential to become a distinct field of legal specialisation. What Santos does is to bring these together within a single framework of social theory and to suggest lines of enquiry about each as part of the sociology of law. He surveys this vast series of landscapes in a mere 120 pages. In the process he may have stepped on some specialists' toes, but he is surely right in suggesting that all of these areas need theorising both within a broad contextual framework and more locally. Some of these fields are under-researched and almost all are under-theorised. Mainstream legal theory hardly addresses any of the issues that they raise – a partial exception being human rights.[3]

Santos's specific agenda is less interesting than his use of theory. During the past year I have attended two conferences concerned with globalisation and law and heard of many others. Each has differed in emphasis and orientation, though not surprisingly there has been considerable overlap. It would be foolish to try to predict in detail what specific areas of concern will be on such agendas in ten years' time. Nearly all of the lines of enquiry identified by Santos and others have developed in response to perceived problems and other stimuli rather than being led by theory. This is likely to continue. My own preliminary forays into the literature of several transnational fields (comparative law, international law, the jurisprudence of the World Bank) suggest that the level of theoretical sophistication is at best uneven, in some cases non-existent. They have evolved with little regard to developments in legal theory, which in turn has paid them scant attention.

Comparative law is a good example of a field in which practice has outrun theory.[4] In practice comparative legal studies are no longer confined within the boundaries of the Country and Western model,

2 See, eg P. Bernt Hugenholtz (ed), *The Future of Copyright Law in a Digital Environment* (1996).

3 A reasonable conspectus of the massive literature on the philosophy of human rights, including issues of cultural relativism, can be obtained from, eg Jeremy Waldron, *Nonsense Upon Stilts* (1987); Abdullahi A An-Na'im and Francis M Deng (eds), *Human Rights in Africa: Cross-cultural Perspectives* (1990); Stephen Shute and Susan Hurley (eds), *On Human Rights* (1993); Martha Nussbaum, *Women, Culture and Development* (1995). Useful readers include, Henry J Steiner and Philip Alston (eds), *International Human Rights in the Context of Law, Politics, and Morals* (1996), Richard A Wilson (ed), *Human Rights, Culture and Context* (1997).

4 Above, Ch 7.

focusing largely on private law doctrine of 'advanced' or 'parent' common law and civil law systems of modern Western states. There has been a rich proliferation of subject-matters, perspectives and approaches. But there are still striking disjunctures between talk about 'comparative law' and best practice. The methodological problems of comparative work have been neglected; in many respects the focus has continued to be narrow, and departures from the Country and Western model have been ad hoc, fragmented, and uneven. There is an intellectual lag of about fifty years between the more reflective literature on comparative law and contemporary legal theory, which itself still focuses almost exclusively on the municipal law of nation states and typically outdated pictures of public international law.

What then can legal theory offer? My answer is all the standard services of theorising.[5] First a coherent 'total picture', or series of such overviews, of law-in-the-world (the synthesising function). Secondly, as a necessary element at this and other levels, the construction and clarification of important general concepts, including exploration of the extent to which it is feasible and desirable to develop cross-cultural meta-languages for legal discourse (a revived general analytical jurisprudence). Thirdly, the development of general normative principles, the clarification of values, and addressing questions about their universalisability. Fourthly, the generation of middle order empirical hypotheses and general working theories for participants, for example in such areas as constitution-making and dispute-processing and the methodology of various kinds of transnational enquiry. Fifthly, intellectual history of law as a discipline and of its specialised sub-disciplines, such as public international law and comparative law. Sixthly and perhaps most important, critical examination of assumptions underlying legal discourse in both general and quite specific contexts. In short, if one looks on legal theorising as the general part of law as a discipline, it can perform a number of functions concerned with the health of that enterprise. Occasionally, it may provide leadership with inspiring visions and grand designs or hypotheses, but more often it is reactive, setting contexts, sharpening tools, suggesting refinements, questioning assumptions, and generally tidying up.

5 CONCLUSION

Toward a New Common Sense is, in my view, the most important work to date to view law from a global perspective. One purpose of this essay has

5 Above, Ch 1.

been to make this difficult, sometimes infuriating, book more accessible to students of jurisprudence and others who are concerned with law and globalisation. For this purpose, my suggestion is that one should by-pass the first and last chapters, concentrate on the centre, and forgive the unevenness and aberrations of style. For there is a lot in the book that deserves attention.

My second purpose has been to clarify my own views in relation to those of Santos. Like many commentators, I find the more general parts of *Toward a New Common Sense* obscure, jargon-ridden and, in some instances, wrong. I resisted the temptation simply to dismiss Santos's philosophy as 'bosh', because this kind of 'post-modern' writing is now both fashionable in academic law and too important to be ignored. Santos can be treated as reasonably representative of one important version of this fashion. In this essay, I have tried to steer a path between two strands in post-modernism: on the one hand, an anti-rationalist stream that involves, or appears to involve, strong versions of epistemological scepticism and cultural relativism that I reject. On these issues I am prepared to side with the moderate, but passionate, empiricism of Haack and Peirce. On the other hand, there are aspects of imaginative post-modernism that I find attractive, stimulating, and quite compatible with innocent realism. This strand, exemplified by Calvino, emphasises the complexities and elusiveness of reality, the difficulties of grasping it, and the value of imagination and multiple perspectives in facing these difficulties. Here, it is not necessary for me to agree with Susan Haack on particular issues, for her thin metaphysics can accommodate a variety of views at lower levels of abstraction. Santos, it seems to me, embodies the vices of anti-rationalist and the virtues of imaginative post-modernism, but on a number of philosophical issues I just find him obscure.

Despite significant differences in our enterprises there is a strong convergence in our views on law. Santos presents a utopian sociological theory of law as part of a grand politico-social theory. I am a more orthodox jurist, an insider, concerned with the health of my discipline in the next 10 to 20 years. The point of convergence is a shared interest in viewing law from a global perspective. We both interpret the complex processes of globalisation along similar lines, except that I am more of an agnostic than Santos about the likely long-term implications. Santos and I both agree that legal pluralism is central to understanding law from a global perspective, that the phenomenon cuts across different geographical levels, that the existing literature on the subject is not very satisfactory and that 'interlegality' is a key concept in need of development. Santos tries at a quite abstract level to differentiate law, broadly conceived, from other forms of ordering, whereas, following Karl Llewellyn, I hold that precise general definitions of law tend to obscure the continuities between law and different kinds of ordering. There is too much fluidity for precise boundary-drawing to be appropriate in the abstract. For this reason, I prefer to treat legal pluralism as a species of normative pluralism, postponing the setting of criteria for differentiating between species (and sub-species) until a specific context and standpoint have been identified.

On mapping, Santos and I have long had a shared interest and my own views owe a good deal to his early classic essay on the subject. One of the strengths of *Toward a New Common Sense* is that it depicts in a single landscape a wide range of issues and topics that need attention in a period of rapid globalisation. Santos's specific agenda for research is not, and could not be, definitive, but it provides an admirable starting-point for mapping significant lines of enquiry and how they interconnect. In the Epilogue I shall outline a possible agenda for a new general jurisprudence.

The case for a revival of general jurisprudence is essentially a response to the challenges and opportunities presented to the enterprise of studying law as it inevitably becomes more cosmopolitan. The main difference between Santos and myself is that he is concerned with the aspirational development of all law over a long, and indefinite, time-frame, according to a particular utopian vision, while I am concerned with the healthy development of the study of law over the next decade or so, according to a traditional liberal conception of what is involved in the advancement and dissemination of learning.

[10]
Reviving General Jurisprudence

The literature on globalization is almost as confusing as the processes it attempts to interpret. There are those who speak in terms of revolutions and paradigmatic change. There are sceptics, like Paul Hirst, who consider most globalizing rhetoric to be overblown. There are Marxist, post-modern, free market, and religious interpreters. Within each of these groups there are optimists and pessimists. And there are agnostics who claim that the processes are too bewildering in their complexity and too rapid for it to be sensible to make firm judgements, let alone confident predictions. Yet, if one blows away

---

[1] This essay builds on and extends themes developed in William Twining, *Globalisation and Legal Theory* (Butterworth, 2000) (hereafter *GLT*) and *Law in Context: Enlarging a Discipline* (Oxford UP, 1997)(hereafter *LIC*). It was written as a prolegomenon to a series of lectures on 'General Jurisprudence' delivered at the Universities of Tilburg and Warwick in 2000-1. The main thesis is that there is a need for a revival of general jurisprudence as a foundation for an increasingly cosmopolitan discipline of law in response to the challenges of 'globalization'. This essay was written while I was a Fellow at the Center for Advanced Study in the Behavioral Sciences at Stanford. I am grateful for the superb support of the Center and its staff. Thanks for valuable comments and suggestions are also due to Michael Likosky, Terry Anderson, and to participants in seminars at University College London, Wolfson College, Oxford, the Australian National University, and Columbia, Griffith, Stanford, Sydney, Warwick and Tilburg Law Schools.

some of the froth from the excited and highly repetitive literature, there seem to be some givens that are widely accepted: that 'globalization' far from being a new phenomenon has a long history that stretches back for at least two centuries; that the interactions between the local and the global are processes of great fluidity and complexity; that in some areas, such as communications and ecology, we are indeed witnessing important developments; that the significance of national boundaries is changing; that nation states are not the only significant transnational actors, but it is unlikely that the nation state will wither away or be superceded by a world government in the foreseeable future.

'Globalization' in this context refers to those trends and processes which are making the world more interdependent. Whatever one's interpretation of the details of globalization – strong, weak or agnostic – it clearly has important implications for the discipline of law and for jurisprudence as its theoretical part. In earlier writings I have argued that globalization presents three specific challenges to traditional legal theory:

a. It challenges 'black box' theories that treat nation states, societies, legal systems, and legal orders as closed, impervious entities that can be studied in isolation;
b. It challenges the idea that the study of law and legal theory can be restricted to two types of legal ordering: municipal state law and public international law, conceived as dealing with relations between nation states;
c. It challenges the adequacy of much of the present conceptual framework and vocabulary of legal discourse (both law talk and talk about law) for discussing legal phenomena across jurisdictions, traditions, and cultures.[2]

These challenges all point in the direction of making law as a discipline more cosmopolitan. This in turn requires the revival of the idea of general jurisprudence. The purpose of this paper is to outline one vision of what might be involved in such an enterprise. It takes as its starting-point a broad conception of the subject matter of the discipline of law and a particular view of the role of jurisprudence as the general part of that discipline. These

[2] *GLT* Ch. 1.

assumptions may be controversial, but the case for them has been made elsewhere.

The main assumptions can be summarized as follows: Law is concerned with the ordering of relations between agents or persons (human, legal, unincorporated and otherwise) at a variety of levels, not just relations within a single state or society. One way of roughly characterizing these levels of relations is geographical. In terms of space they include the global, international, transnational, regional, inter-communal, municipal (nation state and subsidiary jurisdictions), sub-state local and non-state local.[3] These different levels are not simply nested in a single hierarchy of larger and smaller spaces. Rather, they co-exist, overlap and interact in complex ways. For this reason, normative pluralism, and legal pluralism as part of it, should be among the central concerns of a revived general jurisprudence.[4]

Jurisprudence can be viewed as a heritage, an ideology, and as the activity of theorizing, that is posing, reposing, answering, and arguing about general questions relating to the subject-matters of law as a discipline. As an activity within our discipline, theorizing has several functions: constructing whole views or total pictures (the synthesizing function); elucidating, constructing, and refining concepts; developing normative theories, middle order hypotheses, and general working theories for participants; intellectual history; and critically examining the underlying assumptions of different kinds of discourse of and about law.[5]

This paper is written from the standpoint of an English jurist, who is concerned about the health of the institutionalized discipline of law during the next ten to twenty years in the face of 'globalization'. I am based in London, I have worked in several countries, and I have travelled widely, mainly in the

[3] For detailed discussion see *GLT*, Ch.6.

[4] I here deliberately side-step traditional definitional issues concerning what counts as a 'legal order' and how legal and normative pluralism are distinguished. In this context, my conception of law is broad enough to include some kinds of non-state and religious law, e.g. a putative *lex mercatoria*, Dinka law, Islamic, Hindu, or Gypsy law, as worthy subject-matters of our discipline, but how one classifies borderline cases is not germane to my argument. Similarly, this characterization deliberately leaves open questions about the relative importance of different kinds of legal order. On general definitions of law, see *GLT* at 78-80, 224 ff.

[5] Id. Ch. 1.

United States and the Commonwealth, and in recent years in the Netherlands. My provenance, experience, and outlook are quite cosmopolitan, but my biases and culture are British, and my main language is English. A jurist from a different intellectual tradition approaching the same issues from another vantage-point would probably present a significantly different picture.

Given a broad conception of law and its study and a functional view of the role of jurisprudence within our discipline, let us look at what may be involved in the idea of general jurisprudence in the context of globalization.

General rather than Global Jurisprudence.

Globalization has implications for law and its study. It does not follow that what is needed is a global jurisprudence, if that means looking at law solely or mainly from a global perspective. That is too narrow. A good World Atlas does not contain only maps of the world. Rather it has a combination of large scale, small scale, and intermediate maps with a multiplicity of projections and perspectives. The old term 'General Jurisprudence' is broader and more flexible than 'global' just because it refers to discourse about two or more jurisdictions or legal orders from the micro-comparative to the universal. One task of general jurisprudence is to construct overviews of legal phenomena in the world as a whole – global mapping of law – but legal theory needs to be concerned with all levels of legal ordering and their inter-relations.[6] Viewing law from a global perspective has its uses, not least in providing context, but understanding law will continue to require detailed focus on particulars at all levels.

In the nineteenth century the term particular jurisprudence referred to the study of the concepts and presuppositions of a single legal system; general jurisprudence referred to the study of two or more legal systems and was quite often confined to advanced or 'civilized' systems; universal jurisprudence was more like global jurisprudence, but was often restricted to the law of sovereign nation states. Generality and particularity are relative matters. Here I shall use 'general jurisprudence' to refer to the theoretical study of two or more legal orders (including ones within the same legal tradition or family).[7] This conception has some affinity with nineteenth century usage, but differs from it

[6] Problems of mapping law are explored in *GLT* Ch. 6.
[7] On 'comparative common law' see below.

in three important respects. (i) it treats generalization about legal phenomena as problematic; (ii) it deals with all levels of legal ordering, not just municipal and public international law; (iii) it treats the phenomena of normative and legal pluralism as central to jurisprudence.

During the nineteenth century English jurists normally assumed that jurisprudence is general. The Natural Law Tradition was universalistic. Bentham developed a universal science of legislation. Austin, more cautiously, developed a general analytical jurisprudence for maturer nations. Holland claimed that jurisprudence was a science and therefore must be general. Leaders of the Historical School, such as Maine, advanced sweeping Darwinian generalizations about law and social change.[8] However, during the early days of academic law in both England and the United States the focus became more particular. One reason for this was that the study of the fundamental legal conceptions of one's own legal system was seen to be more practical and relevant to the rest of the curriculum. Austin, Pollock, Gray, and others explicitly emphasized practicality. There were also signs of a tacit legal relativism, exemplified by W. W. Buckland.[9]

The story in the United States is more complex. Like his English counterparts, John Chipman Gray emphasized that for pedagogical purposes particular jurisprudence was more practical and relevant to the rest of the first degree curriculum. Hohfeld focused on Anglo-American concepts while emphasizing the importance of broad perspectives. Roscoe Pound was a generalist at heart, but normally confined his jurisprudence teaching to postgraduates. During the first decades of the twentieth century Pound, Wigmore, Kocourek and others were cosmopolitan in outlook and pioneered important projects, such as the Continental Legal Philosophy series, which unfortunately did not last long enough to become established as a regular Trans-Atlantic conduit for European legal thought. From the 1930s, talented refugees from Nazism provided an important antidote to potential isolationism, but nevertheless for most of the twentieth century the study of foreign and comparative law, international law, and other transnational subjects tended to be marginalized in the first degree curriculum and the professional examinations. This had a profound impact on the focus of most American legal scholarship. However, from the perspective of general jurisprudence

[8] For details see *GLT* Ch. 2

[9] Ibid.

there was one crucial difference between the academic cultures of the United States and most European countries, including Great Britain. The rise of the national law school in the United States led to nearly all American legal education and scholarship being *multi-jurisdictional*. General jurisprudence is concerned with theoretical aspects of law across jurisdictional boundaries; so too is comparative law. In important ways nearly all American academic law has been multi-jurisdictional and comparative, without being transnational. This fact has considerable significance for the theory and practice of comparative law.[10]

For most of the twentieth century the focus of much Anglo-American legal theory has either been quite parochial or else geographically indeterminate.[11]

---

[10] See below.

[11] Ibid. There have, of course, been some notable exceptions. For example, H. L. A. Hart consistently claimed that his *The Concept of Law* was a contribution to general jurisprudence. Some of his writings, e.g. on causation and on criminal responsibility, were more local, but he did not generally draw a sharp distinction between general and particular jurisprudence. In the Postscript to *The Concept of Law* (1994), he tried, unsuccessfully in my view, to revive the distinction in order to suggest that he and Ronald Dworkin were involved in different enterprises (*GLT* Ch. 2).

Why do I talk of 'reviving' general jurisprudence, when some prominent contemporary jurists claim to be continuing the tradition of theorizing about law across legal cultures and traditions? A brief answer is that my conception of 'general jurisprudence' is much broader than theirs and harks back to a time when jurists as different as Bentham, Austin, Maine, Holland, and followers of Natural Law were all conceived as pursuing different aspects of 'jurisprudence'. The label itself is unimportant, although it has sometimes been misused. Furthermore, contemporary jurists who consistently do general jurisprudence are exceptional, for the great bulk of legal theorizing in the Anglo-American tradition is confined to modern western legal systems, often very largely to the United States and the United Kingdom. Second, my concern is to break away from the strong tendency to confine the concept of law to municipal (state) law and, often reluctantly, public international law narrowly conceived. Religious law, chthonic (traditional) law, and other candidates deserving consideration as significant subject matters of the study of law are regularly excluded or marginalized. Finally, my conception of general jurisprudence is intended to challenge tendencies (often latent) to project parochial or ethnocentric preconceptions onto non-Western legal orders, cultures, and traditions. See further, 'The Province of Jurisprudence Re-examined', (Julius Stone Memorial Lecture, Sydney, 2000) (forthcoming).

In his inaugural lecture as Professor of Comparative Law at Oxford F. H. Lawson, echoing a wider suspicion of both grand and abstract theory, said: 'Nowadays to be universal is to be superficial'.[12] This was the keynote of most Anglo-American legal theory for much of the twentieth century.[13]

In the last decade of the twentieth century we have witnessed two conflicting tendencies: on the one hand, a particularistic tendency that emphasizes difference, the uniqueness of history, culture, and identity, sometimes even cultural and ethical relativism. On the other hand, awareness of globalization points to the changing significance of national boundaries and the need for academic law and legal theory to take account of multiple levels of social and legal ordering.

Rather than assume universality we need to consider difficult issues of the feasibility and desirability of general discourse about law at all these levels. A central question for general jurisprudence is: how far is it possible and desirable to generalize about legal phenomena – conceptually, normatively, empirically etc. – as part of understanding law? So questions of cultural, legal, and ethical relativism become crucial.

Legal theory is concerned with a variety of conceptual, normative, empirical, and interpretive issues. Rough distinctions between concepts, values, and facts have provided the basis for conventional ways of classifying jurisprudence into different approaches – analytical, philosophical (or normative), historical, sociological and so on. Such taxonomies were convenient and had some use as indicators of differences between lines of enquiry or of emphasis; but they were sometimes misleading in suggesting disagreements among rival 'schools' about a shared agenda of issues. For the purpose of exposition, and in order to indicate some links with tradition, I shall consider the idea of a revived general jurisprudence in relation to these conventional categories, but it must be emphasized that it is not intended to present them as designating distinct branches or sub-disciplines. Indeed, most particular legal studies involve conceptual, normative, interpretive, and empirical dimensions.

---

[12] F. H. Lawson, 'The Field of Comparative Law', (1950) 61 Juridical Review 16.

[13] *GLT* at p. 144. On the differences between 'parochialism' in respect of focus, audience, sources, perspectives, and potential significance, see id Ch 5.

Analytical Jurisprudence[14]

The term 'analytical jurisprudence' is sometimes treated as co-extensive with 'linguistic analysis', or with elucidation of abstract concepts. This is a mistake. For example, Herbert Hart explicitly included as part of analytical jurisprudence the study of the form and structure of legal systems, problems of legal reasoning, problems of definition of law, and analysis of legal concepts.[15] He considered that the critical analysis of assumptions and presuppositions of legal discourse was one the main tasks of legal philosophy. He also emphasized that distinctions between different branches of jurisprudence and philosophy of law were matters of convenience, reflecting 'no very firm boundaries'.[16] In this view, the relationship of analytical jurisprudence to jurisprudence is similar to the relationship between analytical philosophy and philosophy in general: it gives an approximate indication of a style and approach that involves the application of a range of techniques of analysis to legal discourse and its concepts. Analytical method here includes not only linguistic and conceptual techniques developed by analytical philosophers, but also tools of analysis such as ideal types, models, metaphors, and deconstruction developed in neighbouring disciplines.

The identification of analytical jurisprudence with conceptual analysis has some basis in history. Elucidation of abstract concepts was the main focus of attention of most Anglo-American analytical jurists from Austin through Hart, including Holland, Hohfeld, Kocourek, and Salmond. This has been criticized as narrow in two respects. First, insofar as analytical jurists concentrated on such questions rather than on 'substantive' issues of normative, sociological, or historical jurisprudence, they could rightly be accused of being over-concerned with conceptual analysis or even with mere semantics. At its height the leaders of 'the revolution in philosophy' in Oxford, associated with J. L.

---

[14] This section is a condensed version of the second Tilburg Lecture, entitled 'Have Concepts, Will Travel: Analytical Jurisprudence in a Global Context' (forthcoming).

[15] H. L. A. Hart, 'Problems of Legal Philosophy' P. Edwards (ed.), 6 *Encyclopedia of Philosophy* 264-76 (1967), reprinted in Hart's *Essays in Jurisprudence and Philosophy* (1983) Ch.3.

[16] ibid. But Hart revived the distinction between general and particular jurisprudence to differentiate his views from those of Dworkin in the posthumously published Postscript to *The Concept of Law*, discussed in *GLT* Ch. 2-3.

Austin's circle, gave the impression that they believed that most philosophical problems could be solved, or the underlying puzzlements could be dissolved, by careful examination of language, especially ordinary usage. Despite denials that they made any such claim, there is little doubt that in the first flush of enthusiasm some analytical tools were overused.[17] In both England and the United States there was such a strong reaction that 'linguistic analysis' became a by-word for narrow, sterile, over-abstract logomachy.[18]

Some leading mainstream jurists of the next generation, for example Dworkin, Rawls, Raz and MacCormick, quietly assimilated some of the specific techniques of analysis developed by Oxford analytical philosophers, while making clear that they considered themselves to be dealing with issues of substance.[19] However, conceptual analysis as a distinct enterprise largely went out of fashion in political theory and jurisprudence to be replaced by interest in 'substantive philosophical issues', exemplified by the work of Rawls and Dworkin.[20] This was generally a welcome development, but there was, in my view, an over-reaction against sustained conceptual analysis. In taught jurisprudence an almost exclusive focus on analysis of 'fundamental legal conceptions' was indeed narrow; but something was lost when applied

[17] A good example was T D Weldon's *The Vocabulary of Politics* (Penguin, 1953) which had almost cult status when I was an undergraduate. On my own experience of the related disease of 'Korzbyskian paralysis' and Llewellyn's cure, see Twining, *The Karl Llewellyn Papers* (U. Chicago Law School, 1968) pp. 5-8. I described my own symptoms as 'an obsession with the definition of terms in seemingly endless regress, a shying away from concrete factual detail in favor of abstract generalizations and an all-or-nothing approach which masquerades as precision.' (ibid 6).

[18] E. Gellner, *Words and Things* (1959).

[19] E.g. Ronald Dworkin on drawing the semantic sting in *Law's Empire* (Fontana, 1986) Ch.2. Dworkin classifies Hart as a semantic jurist; this seems to me to be a caricature.

[20] This move is associated with the distinction between 'concept' and 'conceptions' (See, e.g., Dworkin, id., at pp. 71-2) and the challenge to the sharp distinction between 'analytic' and 'synthetic'. Rawls advances his conception of justice in the form of substantive principles and devotes little time to the concept of justice. In the view of some, Hart's book might have been more accurately labeled 'A/My Conception of Law'.

analysis of concepts was almost entirely replaced by more abstract discussions on the borders of political philosophy.[21]

A second charge of narrowness bites deeper. Most analytical jurists from Bentham through Hart have focused on a narrow range of 'legal concepts' that is to say the basic terms for expressing or reconstructing legal doctrine and their underlying concepts (such as right, duty, legal person, ownership, and possession) or the concepts presupposed by such discourse (such as command, rule, sovereignty, sanction and legal system). This focus is associated with a conception of law and of its study that is largely confined to legal doctrine or rules. Analytical jurists hardly ever brought their techniques to bear on concepts such as dispute, process, institution, function, and group.[22] One way of expressing this is to distinguish between 'law talk' (the discourse *of* rules and its presuppositions) and 'talk about law' (discourses *about* any legal phenomena).

Jurists in the Anglo-American tradition of analytical jurisprudence have largely confined themselves to analyzing law talk, and have tended to neglect the much wider field of talk about law. This is partly attributable to the fact that this kind of work was associated with a rule-oriented picture of law and of its study. Also the concepts of law talk were considered to be distinctively legal, while many concepts associated with talk about law belonged to, or were at least shared with, other disciplines, such as sociology, economics, ethics, and political theory. This essay adopts a broad conception of the subject-matters of law as a discipline and proceeds on the assumption that the need for conceptual elucidation applies as much to any discourse about law as to the more traditional 'law talk'.

---

[21] *GLT* 33-4.

[22] W. Twining, 'Academic Law and Legal Philosophy: The Significance of Herbert Hart', 95 LQR 557 (1979) op. cit. ; cf. *GLT* at pp. 34-7. Hart himself often expressed the view that his kind of analysis was applicable to these broader inquiries, but in practice he very largely confined his attention to concepts of law talk. 'No very firm boundaries divide the problems confronting these various disciplines from the problems of the philosophy of law. This is especially true of the conceptual schemes of classification, definition, and division introduced by the academic study of law for the purposes of exposition and teaching; but even the historical and sociological statements about law are sufficiently general and abstract to need the attention of the philosophical critic.' (Hart (1983) p.89. Cf. Preface to *The Concept of Law* (1961) ('essay in descriptive sociology').

Elucidation and construction of concepts are not a subject apart, but are typically one part of any inquiry. If the methods of conceptual analysis suitable for legal discourse are little more than the principles and techniques of logical analysis and clear thinking, is there any justification for treating analytical jurisprudence as a distinct enterprise? I think that there are good reasons for keeping it as a focus of attention, but not as a separate sub-discipline.[23] Just as it is useful to consider legal reasoning about questions of law or of fact at a higher level of generality than particular fields of law, so too with conceptual analysis.

Analysis of concepts is only one part of analytical jurisprudence, but it may have a special importance in the coming years. A cosmopolitan discipline of law needs a vocabulary and conceptual apparatus that can be used confidently across jurisdictions and cultures. If jurisprudence is to be general, its vocabulary and concepts need to travel well.[24]

At first sight, we seem to be a long way from having an adequate meta-language for this purpose. The literature of analytical jurisprudence and comparative law both send out strong cautionary messages. The early analytical jurists observed that there were only a few 'fundamental legal conceptions' that form part of general jurisprudence.[25] Comparative lawyers from Buckland to the present day have regularly warned of the many pitfalls of translation and comparison because of differences between the conceptual schemes of different legal systems. The dominant movement within

---

[23] In his important address on 'A Vital School of Jurisprudence and Law' (*Proceedings* of the Association of American Law Schools (1914) 76 ff), Hohfeld acknowledged that students could pick up basic techniques of analysis in the ordinary professional courses through what is now known as 'the pervasive approach', provided that their teachers were reasonably proficient as analytical jurists. But budding teachers needed a separate course on analytical jurisprudence to obtain 'a systematic and extensive grasp of the matters involved.' (at pp. 98-99). My own view is that laying the foundation for basic skills is best acquired by direct study, reinforced in other courses, rather than by optimistic 'pick-it-up' approaches (*LIC* at pp. 85-6, 188-9).

[24] The metaphor of 'travelling well' is useful in catching the dynamic nature of language and its adaptability to different contexts; but, of course, concepts, like languages, disperse and spread without necessarily leaving their original homes.

[25] Bentham, Austin, Hohfeld and other analytical jurists recognized that most legal discourse was specific to a given legal culture and hence belonged to particular jurisprudence. The lists of general legal concepts were quite short.

mainstream comparative law, represented by Rabel, Kahn-Freund, and Zweigert and Kotz emphasized that convergence between civil and common law systems is normally a convergence of outcomes or solutions to 'shared problems', often reached by different conceptual routes.[26] Within legal anthropology there has been a well-known debate about the extent to which the 'folk concepts' of one culture can be translated or even elucidated in the language of another.[27] The debate ended in a near-consensus that one needs both analytic and folk concepts to give an adequate account of Tiv or Barotse or Cheyenne law-ways and institutions.[28] And, echoing Shaw, Atiyah and Summers have reminded us that 'England and America are two countries separated by the same language.'[29] Not only do we use words like 'trunk', 'boot', 'pint', and 'quite' differently, but we do not even have a shared conception of 'rule'.[30]

Some other considerations can be set against these salutary warnings. Globalization is not new, nor are transnational legal relations. Trade, diplomacy, and commerce have been transnational for centuries and they have developed usable ways of communicating, for example through the recognition of one or other *lingua franca* ('the language of diplomacy', 'the

---

[26] This 'functionalist' approach has attracted growing criticism in recent years. See, e.g., Jonathan Hill, 'Comparative Law, Law Reform, and Legal Theory' (1989) 9 OJLS 101; cf. *GLT* 177.

[27] For a summary of the debate and references see the Preface to Paul Bohannan's *Justice and Judgement among the Tiv* (Oxford UP, Revised edn. 1968). This is sometimes linked to the 'emics/etics debate' in social anthropology, but I have been persuaded by my colleague Kit Woolard that the analogy with phonetics tends to muddy the waters.

[28] Gluckman's position can be interpreted as a claim that the Barotse had flexible concepts that were functionally equivalent to the English concept of 'the reasonable man'; Bohannan's book on the Tiv was written mainly in English, using standard concepts from social anthropology in addition to his careful elucidation of Tiv terms. Interestingly, Hoebel acknowledged that he and Karl Llewellyn did not pay sufficient attention to Cheyenne vocabulary and concepts in their classic study, *The Cheyenne Way* (Oklahoma UP, 1941) (Private communication to the author).

[29] The dictum is often attributed to Bernard Shaw, but *The Oxford Dictionary of Quotations* states that it is not to be found in his published writings.

[30] P. S. Atiyah and R. S. Summers, *Form and Substance in Anglo-American Law* (Oxford UP, 1987) at pp. 264-6, 418-20,

language of science') or through the development of specialized vocabularies and conceptual schemes. So have public international law and transnational business. Regional groupings such as the European Union, the Council of Europe, and the Organization of African Unity have long experience of struggling with problems of transnational legal communication. Furthermore, the tendency of analytical jurisprudence and mainstream comparative law to concentrate on legal doctrine (law talk) may have obscured the fact that a great deal of talk about law is multi-disciplinary. More or less sophisticated transnational vocabularies have been developed in neighboring disciplines. Those social sciences that have been particularly influenced by strong conceptions of 'science' have for that reason been concerned to develop general discourses. For example, much of the specialized vocabulary of economics, psychology, and geography claims to be transnational. Even anthropology, which has strong particularistic tendencies, has always claimed to be a comparative enterprise.[31] Thus while the revival of general jurisprudence presents enormous challenges, we are not starting from scratch. But there is a need to take careful stock of the extent to which our existing vocabulary and concepts are adequate for general discourse and how much they are obviously or subtly culture-specific, local, or even ethnocentric.

As a first venture into the exploration of the usability of our stock of concepts in cross-cultural and transnational legal discourses I undertook preliminary case-studies of four groups of concepts: (i) Hohfeld's analytical scheme as one of the highlights of traditional analytical jurisprudence. (ii) Transnational discourse about prisons as an example of a body of concepts that seems to travel remarkably well. (iii) Corruption as an example of a topic that was thought to be quite culture-specific, (but on examination this turned out to be over-simple). (iv) Transnational comparison of lawyers, legal professions, and legal education as an area which is notoriously problematic in respect of usable concepts.[32] My provisional conclusions are as follows:

Hohfeld's analytical scheme for 'rights' travels far and travels well for many purposes. It fits, and can be used in rationally reconstructing, almost any

---

[31] E.g. Paul Bohannan, *Social Anthropology* (Holt, Rinehart and Winston, 1963) Ch.1.

[32] This is a report on work in progress, which has not yet been completed. This brief summary is included here merely to illustrate the idea of what might be involved in taking stock of the applicability and transferability of existing groups of concepts and vocabularies as part of an expanded conception of general analytical jurisprudence.

normative system. It moves between different levels of legal ordering and, more controversially, can be applied to moral systems[33] and even games, such as chess. It is useful for removing ambiguities and for rational reconstruction of legal rules and many other kinds of norms. However, it is only a starting-point for analysis of discourse about 'rights'. For example, it does not deal with different kinds of 'duty' or 'power', it does not consider whether there is some underlying connection between the four uses of 'right', nor the relation of rights to other concepts such as interest, benefit, or need.

A second case-study examined transnational terminology relating to state prison systems, as illustrated by the Standard Minimum Rules for the Treatment of Prisoners (SMR), Human Rights Watch's national and global reports on prisons, and Vivian Stern's *A Sin Against the Future: Imprisonment in the World*.[34] The concepts and terms used in these texts seemed to travel remarkably well, given the great variety in prison conditions, populations, and policies worldwide. For example, the SMR has been widely used in assessing prison conditions and regimes in many countries and has had some influence on standard setting within some state prison systems.[35] The underlying philosophy (essentially based on rehabilitation) is no longer widely accepted, the application of these standards by foreigners is often resented, and few prison systems meet these minimum standards in fact; but there appear to be relatively few *conceptual* difficulties about applying these standards world-wide. One interesting feature is that the Standard Minimum Rules are expressed in non-technical English, which appears to travel better than the terminology of prison laws.

In her powerful survey and polemic about imprisonment as a global phenomenon, Vivien Stern makes a number of sweeping factual generalizations about the state of prisons and shared problems in the world today. As descriptions of conditions these seem at least to represent testable descriptive hypotheses.

The normative generalizations of SMR and Stern's empirical ones refer mainly to prison conditions and prison regimes. They apply less clearly to

[33] E.g. Alan Gewirth, 'Ethical Universalism and Particularism', 85 Jo. Philosophy 283 (1983).

[34] Vivien Stern, *A Sin Against the Future: Imprisonment in the World* (Penguin, 1998).

[35] E.g. it is used in several of Human Rights Watch's recent reports on prison conditions in nearly twenty countries.

prison ideology and policies. The main reason for this is probably that 'the modern prison' developed as one of the first institutions of the modern bureaucratic state to be the subject of significant transnational networks of bureaucratizing professionals. Prison ideology, rationales, and policies are more closely entwined with local politics, history and culture. They may be harder to compare or subject to generalization.

Corruption, bribery, and related concepts used to be considered strongly culture-specific. Since the early 1990s a powerful transnational campaign against 'corruption' has gained ground.[36] It is based largely, but not entirely, on the ideology of the Washington consensus concerning 'democracy, good governance, and human rights' and on free market and related ideologies concerning 'development'. The main target of this campaign is various kinds of deviation from bureaucratic norms of impartiality, efficiency, and 'service', especially financial dealings. The focus is primarily on 'public servants' of state bureaucracies. When the campaign is extended to the private sector and 'traditional' contexts it encounters many more gray areas, for instance in respect of nepotism, patronage, tipping, and traditional forms of gift-giving that tend to be more local and culture-specific. Thus corruption and related concepts seem to travel reasonably well in respect of the modern sector of nation states, especially state bureaucracies, but are more problematic outside this specific context. The strongly emotive language of 'corruption', 'bribes', 'sleaze' and the like seems to fit sensational journalism rather than detached analysis. This sententious discourse tends to direct attention towards individual ethics and personal integrity rather than structural and institutional conditions of large-scale systemic practices.[37] One suspects that here the language often skews both diagnosis and prescription.

Concepts associated with legal education, legal professions, and lawyers on the whole do not travel well, even within the same 'legal family' or between contexts in a single jurisdiction. For example, who counts as a 'law student' is

---

[36] A good recent assessment by an economist who is a strong supporter of the fight against corruption is Susan Rose-Ackerman, *Corruption and Government: Causes, Consequences, and Reform* (Cambridge UP, 1999); cf. Robert Klitgaard, *Controlling Corruption* (U California Press, Berkeley, 1988).

[37] See, e.g., Philip Schofield, 'Jeremy Bentham on Political Corruption: A Critique of the First Report of the Nolan Committee', 49 Current Legal Problems, vol. 2, 395 (1996).

problematic within a single jurisdiction, England, and no definition seems to provide a sensible basis for comparison between mass university systems, like Italy, multi-stage processes of professional formation, such as England's, and professional law school programmes in the United States. If 'law student' is defined as someone registered for a 'first degree in law', there are serious doubts whether this is a sensible unit of comparison.[38] If the definition is extended to include anyone involved in a professional training programme or in the process ending in initial certification, the problems of comparability are more complex. Any comparative statistics about numbers of law students under any of these definitions are almost meaningless, generally misleading, and often false. That is only the start of the difficulties. Similar considerations apply to terms like 'lawyer', 'legal profession', 'legal services' and 'legal work', and to a lesser extent to 'judge', 'court', and 'trial'. These conceptual difficulties have been a serious obstacle to the development of comparative studies in this area.[39]

This modest pilot study illustrates the artificiality of trying to maintain sharp distinctions between different branches of jurisprudence. Any transnational study of prison conditions or anti-corruption measures or legal education is likely to involve conceptual, normative, interpretive and empirical dimensions. In the case of prisons and corruption the discourses have travelled as part of a complex process of diffusion. Hohfeld provided some powerful analytical tools for studying normative orders, but how well they fit 'radically different cultures' or all normative systems are questions that still require quite complex empirical and interpretive investigation. The same theme will recur when we look briefly at some implications of globalization for normative and historical-empirical jurisprudence.

---

38 W. Twining, 'Thinking about Law Schools: Rutland Reviewed' 25 Jo. Law and Society 1 (1998)

39 The comparative study of legal professions is one of the most developed fields of transnational legal sociology. The extent to which it is still bedevilled by basic conceptual problems is clearly illustrated in John J. Barcello and Roger C. Cramton (eds) *Lawyers' Practice and Ideals: A Comparative View* (Kluwer, 1999).

Normative Jurisprudence

> 'Some think that all justice is of this sort, because that which by nature is unchangeable, and everywhere has the same force (as fire burns both here and in Persia), while they see change in things recognized as just. This, however, is not true in an unqualified way, but is true in a sense.' (Aristotle)[40]

Normative jurisprudence encompasses general questions about values and law. It deals with the relations between law, politics and morality, including debates between and among positivists and others about the relationship between law and morality, whether law is at its core a moral enterprise, and about political obligation and civil disobedience. It includes questions about the existence, scope and status of natural, moral and non-legal rights, theories of justice, and standards for guiding and evaluating legal institutions, practices and decisions. Whether normative theories of reasoning and rationality and questions of scepticism and relativism about them are subsumed under normative or analytical jurisprudence is largely a matter of convenience.

Issues about universality and generality in respect of values have concerned philosophers throughout history. Western jurisprudence has a long tradition of universalism in ethics. Natural law, classical utilitarianism, Kantianism, and modern theories of human rights have all been universalist in tendency. In jurisprudence, most of these ideas have been discussed mainly in relation to the municipal law of nation states. In recent times liberal democratic political and legal theory have tended either to be geographically indeterminate or to place some limits on their geographical claims. A great deal of recent Anglo-American normative jurisprudence has been relatively local in respect of provenance, audience and even focus. For example, most writings about the new communitarianism, critical race theory, and republicanism have been explicitly or implicitly or unselfconsciously American.[41] Feminist jurisprudence has only recently begun to be genuinely transnational. John Rawls limits his theory of justice to self-contained liberal societies and in

---

40 *Nicomachean Ethics* (trs. Ross), Book 5, Ch.7 (1134b24-28)

41 Critical legal scholars have quite recently turned their attention to to comparative law, international law, and Latin America ('Lat-Crits') and issues of globalization, but it is too early to assess the significance of these develoipments.

regard to international relations to relations between 'liberal and decent peoples'.[42]

There are some important exceptions to the trend towards greater geographical particularity. The field of international ethics, exemplified by Peter Singer, Onora O'Neill and Amartya Sen, addresses transnational issues from a global perspective.[43] There have been lively debates about human rights and cultural relativism and universalism versus contextualism.[44] In practice, the most politically influential, are probably the ideological assumptions underlying the 'Washington Consensus' which links free market economics to the seductive catch-phrase 'human rights, good governance, and democracy'.[45]

The long tradition of universalism in ethics and the cosmopolitanism of the last three examples suggest that our heritage of normative jurisprudence may have to make fewer adjustments in the face of the challenges of 'globalization'. This may be partly true. But casting a critical eye on that heritage, especially the work of mainstream or canonical jurists leads to the conclusion that some rethinking is called for. Let us consider two examples by way of illustration.

First, most juristic discussions of positivism, law and morals, and obedience to law have been almost exclusively concerned with the municipal law of nation states. For the most part they barely address questions of value in relation to other levels of legal ordering (public international law is a partial exception) nor the phenomena of normative and legal pluralism.[46] A particularly clear example is Rawls' theory of justice, which is explicitly, and unconvincingly, limited to nation states as notionally self-contained

[42] John Rawls, *The Law of Peoples* (Harvard UP, 1999), Ch. 1

[43] E.g. Peter Singer, *Practical Ethics* (2nd edn., Cambridge UP, 1993), Onora O'Neill, *Faces of Hunger* (1986, Allen and Unwin), and *The Amartya Sen and Jean Dre'ze Omnibus* (Oxford UP, 1999).

[44] A convenient introductory anthology is Richard A. Wilson (ed.), *Human Rights, Culture and Context* (Pluto Press, 1997).

[45] A good example of the burgeoning literature challenging the sincerity, coherence, and realism of this ideology is Amy Chua, 'Markets, Democracy, and Ethnicity: Toward a New Paradigm for Law and Development', 108 Yale L. Jo. 1 (1998).

[46] On normative and legal pluralism, see *GLT* pp. 82-8 and 224-33..

communities, and, as a secondary matter, to relations between such states.[47] Just because Rawls' theory is concerned with basic practical principles of institutional design, questions about its extension or adaptability to institutions concerned with ordering at other levels (e.g. regional integration or the regulation of exploitation of unappropriated minerals on this or other planets) is of particular significance

Second, nearly all modern normative jurisprudence is either secular or explicitly Christian. Post-Enlightenment secularism has deep historical roots in the intellectual traditions of Western Christianity. Even those theories which claim universality have proceeded with only tangential reference to, and almost complete ignorance of, the religious and moral beliefs and traditions of the majority of humankind.[48] When differing cultural values are discussed, even the agenda of issues tends to have a stereotypically Western bias.[49] A genuinely general jurisprudence will need to do better than that.

---

[47] Rawls uses such phrases as 'more or less self-sufficient' (*A Theory of Justice* (Harvard UP, 1967) at p. 4), 'self-contained national community' (id, p. 457), and 'a closed system isolated from other societies'. (id. at p. 8). The fullest critique of this aspect of his theory is Thomas Pogge, *Realizing Rawls* (Cornell UP, 1992). See *GLT* pp. 69-75. Rawls gives a partial, and in my view, inadequate response to his critics *in The Law of Peoples* (Harvard UP, 1999).

[48] It is notoriously difficult to estimate the numbers of adherents of world religions. With the normal *caveats, The Oxford Atlas of the World* (1994) estimates that Christian 'adherents' represent about 40-43% of the world population, Muslims about 25%, and other religions the rest. No figure is given for atheists and agnostics.

[49] This tendency is well caught in Ahdaf Salouf's novel, *The Map of Love* (Bloomsbury, 1999) at p.6. An Egyptian woman, Amal, is expecting an American visitor: 'Wary and weary in advance: an American woman – a journalist, she had said on the phone. But she said Amal's brother had told her to call and so Amal agreed to see her. And braced herself: the fundamentalists, the veil, the cold peace, polygamy, women's status in Islam, female genital mutilation – which would it be?'

Legal Reasoning

Whether one subsumes 'legal reasoning' under analytical or normative jurisprudence is largely a matter of convenience. However, locating the subject within general jurisprudence brings to the surface some neglected issues.

A Cook's Tour of the heritage of Western literature on 'legal reasoning' might include the following: (a) a remarkably sophisticated, obsessively repetitive body of normative theorizing about justification of judicial decisions on questions of law in 'hard cases', and, especially in civil law systems, the rationalization of systematic exposition of legal doctrine ('legal science'); (b) a largely separate, less developed, and rather more diverse literature on reasoning about disputed questions of fact in adjudication, especially contested jury trials in the United States; (c) an intermittent and even more diverse body of literature subjecting actual discourse, especially the discourses of argumentation in adjudication, to analysis and criticism from a variety of perspectives;[50] (d) very little sustained work, normative, empirical, or interpretive, on the modes of reasoning and argumentation employed in other legal operations (e.g. sentencing, negotiation, mediation, rule-making, enforcement); (e) even less about the relationship between reasoning about questions of law, questions of fact, and other law-related questions, except occasional indications that all kinds of rational argumentation in legal contexts may possibly be subsumed under a single model of practical reasoning or of problem-solving;[51] (f) very little about the similarities, differences, and relations between the various modes of reasoning and argumentation employed in modern municipal legal systems, on the one hand, and other kinds of legal orders, (including transnational, religious, and traditional legal orders) on the other; (g) a nascent, but rapidly burgeoning, literature about expert systems and other applications of Artificial Intelligence to law; (h) a spectrum

---

[50] 'Argumentation' is used here to refer to actual discourses used in advancing arguments, including both 'rational' and 'non-rational' means of persuasion. For a recent survey, dealing mainly with (a) and (c), see Eveline Feteris, *Fundamentals of Legal Argumentation* (Kluwer, 1999)

[51] *LIC* pp. 194-5, 334-5.

of sceptical and relativist views of varying degrees of strength challenging one or more of the above.[52]

In contemporary mainstream jurisprudence the enormous literature on legal reasoning tends either to be explicitly particular to a given legal system (e.g. American constitutional interpretation), limited to a 'family' or tradition (e.g. common law reasoning), or else geographically indeterminate (Is Ronald Dworkin's Hercules a role model for the German judiciary, the European Court of Justice, or an Islamic jurist?). There are a few studies that seek for deep structures underlying Western legal thought in general, but these are exceptional.[53] A largely unexplored question is how far theories of legal reasoning, such as those of Aarnio, Alexy, MacCormick, or Dworkin can be generalized across legal cultures and traditions. Most such theories assert or assume universal principles of logic and/or general principles of practical reasoning, but typically they are set in some more or less local institutional context, such as a country's highest court, or American or common law adjudication. Take the question: 'What constitutes a valid, cogent, and appropriate argument on a question of law?' Some criteria of validity may be general, others (such as rules relating to authoritative sources or evidence) may be local; criteria of cogency may be a mixture of general and local, but criteria of appropriateness tend to be context-specific.[54]

The concept of 'questions of law' is also context-dependent. It is a familiar theme in comparative law and legal history that whether an issue is categorized as being a question of law or of fact or of something else (e.g. disposition) varies both within and among jurisdictions. In English law 'questions of fact' are classified differently for purposes of allocation of functions of judge and jury, precedent, appeals, statutory interpretation and so on. Dezalay and Garth have shown how, in the context of international commercial arbitration, there are marked differences between common

---

52 This paragraph anticipates the entry on 'Legal reasoning and argument' in the new *International Encyclopedia of the Social and Behavioral Sciences* (forthcoming, 2002).

53 E.g. Geoffrey Samuel, *The Foundations of Legal Reasoning* (Maklu, 1994) which 'reflects upon the structural nature of legal reasoning in the perspective of a *ius commune*; focusing on Roman, English and French law...'(cover).

54 On appropriateness in relation to institutional context, standpoint, and style, see William Twining and David Miers, *How to Do Things With Rules* (4th edn, 1999, Butterworth) at 366-70 *et passim*.

lawyers and civil lawyers as to how they frame the issues in terms of disputed questions of fact or law.[55] If legal theory is to be genuinely trans-national and cross-cultural, it must address questions of generalizability not only about legal reasoning in the narrow sense, but also about other reasonings in legal contexts about facts, policy, law-making, sentencing, negotiation and so on.

Historical, Social Scientific and Interpretive Enquiries

Analytical jurisprudence has been primarily, but not exclusively concerned with concepts and the most stable relations have been with analytical philosophy; normative jurisprudence has been concerned with values and the most stable relations have been with ethics and political theory. Other theoretical lines of enquiry concerned with interpreting, describing, and explaining actual legal phenomena in 'the real world' are sometimes assigned to Historical Jurisprudence and the Sociology of Law.[56]

Such labels are misleading. 'Historical Jurisprudence' came to be associated almost exclusively with the idea of legal evolution, and in the Anglo-American tradition with the rather odd kind of history practiced by Sir Henry Maine.[57] This is an important tradition that is due for a revival, but it is only one strand in the complex relations between legal theory and historiography. General jurisprudence also needs to take account of intellectual history, comparative or world history, as well as more particularistic kinds of historical enquiry. Similarly, in some contexts terms like 'Sociology of Law', 'Sociological Jurisprudence', 'Law and Society', and 'Socio-legal Studies' may suggest that the main, or even the only, important relationship between law and social science is with sociology. That is, quite obviously, wrong.[58]

---

[55] Yves Dezalay and Bryant Garth, *Dealing in Virtue* (Chicago UP, 1996).

[56] 'Sociology of Law' has generally replaced 'Sociological Jurisprudence', which came to be identified quite narrowly with the 'social engineering' perspective of Roscoe Pound and others.

[57] Peter Stein, *Legal Evolution: The Story of an Idea* (Cambridge UP, 1988) gives an excellent account of the rise and decline of 'the Historical School'.

[58] For example, in the United Kingdom the term 'socio-legal studies' was originally coined for bureaucratic purposes to designate those kinds of cross-disciplinary research

One function of jurisprudence is to map the relations between law and other disciplines. Professor Julius Stone called Jurisprudence 'the lawyer's extraversion'.[59] This has sometimes been interpreted as encouraging dilettantism and eclecticism. A more positive interpretation is that jurisprudence can have a useful role as a kind of Foreign Ministry for our discipline in keeping track of relations with other academic tribes and territories. Professor J. L. Montrose used to bewilder and impress beginning law students in Belfast by presenting a picture of law in the context of all learning. This may have served a useful purpose by setting particular studies in a broad context, analogous to the Grands Systemes approach to comparative law.[60] The idea is attractive, provided that is not interpreted in a grandiose or a reductionist fashion. What is needed is not a monolithic synthesis, but rather occasional maps of the main interdisciplinary lines of enquiry that are being or might be pursued and the connections between them. Such maps would need to deal not only with the state of relations between law and the sub-disciplines and enclaves of every social science, but also with the humanities (including literature and theology) and the physical and applied sciences (including medicine, genetics, and engineering).

I cannot attempt to do justice to the details of law's relations with other disciplines here. In the run-up to the Millennium there were a good many overviews, critical stocktakings, and programshrifts that can be consulted.[61]

---

about law that qualified for financial support from the then Economic and Social Research Council in respect of research that involved perspectives, methods or concepts from any of the social sciences, including anthropology, business studies, criminology, economics, geography, linguistics, penology, politics, psychology, social history, and some aspects of statistics. Each of these disciplines has its own complex history, culture, feuds, traditions, external relations, and fashions. Their relations to law are correspondingly complex. On the whole, such points have been well understood by those involved in socio-legal research, but this diversity has sometimes been obscured at the level of theory.

[59] Julius Stone, *Legal System and Lawyers' Reasonings* (Stanford UP, 1964), p. 16.

[60] *GLT* Ch. 6.

[61] Useful sources include the introductions to the relevant volumes in the International Library of Essays in Law and Legal Theory, entries in a range of new scholarly encyclopedias, such as Denis Patterson (ed.), *A Companion to Philosophy of Law and Legal Theory* (Blackwell, 1996), Christopher Gray (ed) *Philosophy of Law: An Encyclopedia* (Garland,1999) and the planned new edition of the *International*

The overall picture is diverse, complex, dynamic and uneven. Here I shall confine myself to two brief points.

First, every area of inter-disciplinary work needs to consider the implications of globalization and the challenges outlined above. This is a task for specialists. It has already begun in some areas, but not in a very coherent fashion. Second, I have suggested that problems of generalizability should be central to a revived general jurisprudence. Here contrasts between particularistic and scientistic disciplines are quite suggestive. For example, the cultures of anthropology or history tend to be particularistic, emphasizing 'thick description', uniqueness, complexity, 'granularity', layers of meaning, multi-factorial causation, and the importance of local knowledge. By contrast, 'harder' social scientists, striving to generalize, invoke Occam's Razor, use simplifying assumptions, stress measurability, look for patterns, trends and correlations. 'How can a historian 'explain' an event outside a universe of cases?', ask the scientists. 'How can such thin descriptions, or such unreal assumptions, be the basis for true generalizations?' counter the qualitative scholars? Of course, 'soft' and 'hard', 'qualitative' and 'quantitative' are poles at the ends of a spectrum, with most scholars somewhere in-between looking both ways. The tension can be quite creative, as lawyers well know, because the complexities of relations between the general and the particular – between general rules and concrete cases – are a central part of legal culture.

The Role of Comparative Legal Studies

A cosmopolitan discipline of law will need to be quite general in regard to sources and perspectives, even when the audience is quite local. The appropriate level(s) of focus of a line of inquiry will depend in large part on its

---

Encyclopedia of the Social and Behavioral Sciences (forthcoming, 2002). See also, on socio-legal studies, P. A Thomas (ed.) *Legal Frontiers* (Dartmouth, 1996) and *Socio-Legal Studies* (Dartmouth, 1997), and Volkmar Gessner, Armin Hoeland, and Csaba Varga (eds) *European Legal Cultures* (Dartmouth, 1996).

purpose and context. To what extent it is feasible and desirable to generalize about a given subject of study will be among the central issues of legal theory.

Here comparative law will have a crucial role. John Stuart Mill treated observation, description, abstraction, comparison, naming, classification, and induction as important stages in the process towards generalization.[62] Without necessarily following Mill's model of scientific inquiry, comparative work in law should play a crucial role in the process of enlarging our understandings of legal phenomena beyond national boundaries en route to exploring problems of generalizability. The idea of general jurisprudence includes study of two or more legal orders; so do comparative legal studies. Comparative law and legal theory should be conceived as interdependent. Only detailed comparative work can provide the essential concrete raw material for constructing and testing general propositions – conceptual/ analytical, normative, empirical, and prescriptive.

In the Anglo-American tradition 'comparative law' has tended to be treated as a subject apart, peripheral, 'academic', and somewhat given to dilettantism. The mainstream of the institutionalized sub-discipline has in the past tended to be rather narrowly focused on comparing private law doctrine of 'parent' common and civil law systems.[63]

In addition, mainstream comparative law has been criticized for generally being formalistic and atheoretical.[64] However, mainstream comparative law has attracted many outstanding scholars, especially from the extraordinarily influential generation of refugees from Nazism. Taught comparative law may have been narrowly focused for pragmatic reasons, but figures such as Ernst

---

[62] J. S. Mill, *A System of Logic Ratiocinative and Inductive* (1st edn. 1843, J. M. Robson, Toronto, 1973) Book IV Of Operations Subsidiary to Induction.

[63] This statement is subject to two caveats: first, it applies to micro-comparative law, which has been the dominant approach especially in the common law tradition. Second, I have gently satirized the dominant *conception* of comparative law as 'the Country and Western Tradition'; the practice, especially in respect of research, has been much more diverse in recent years. See 'Comparative Law and Legal Theory: The Country and Western Tradition', in Ian Edge (ed.), *Comparative Law in Global Perspective* (Transnational Publishers, 2000) and *GLT*, Ch. 7.

[64] E.g. Pierre Legrand, 'Comparative Legal Studies and Commitment to Theory', 58 M. L. R. 262 (1995) and *Fragments on Law-as-Culture* (Deventer: WEJ Tjelnik Willink, 1999); William Ewald, 'What was it Like to Try a Rat?', (1995) 143 U. Penn. L. Rev. 1889.

Rabel, Max Rheinstein, Wolfgang Friedman, and Otto Kahn-Freund were the opposite of narrow-minded, intellectually as well as geographically. Indeed several of them played a major role in broadening the discipline of law in the United States and the United Kingdom.[65]

Comparative law as an institutionalized sub-discipline has diversified and expanded in many ways in recent years. More important, if ever there was a time when a serious legal scholar could concentrate entirely on a single jurisdiction in respect of sources and focus, that time is past. Legal orders are interdependent. Almost all legal scholarship draws on transnational sources, is informed by ideas from other disciplines and legal traditions, and even when the focus is highly local, either implicitly or explicitly makes comparisons with legal phenomena elsewhere. In short, to a significant extent we are all comparatists now.

At this point, let us pause to note two near paradoxes. First, few experienced comparatists compare. By this I mean that even within mainstream comparative law sustained explicit molecular comparison is wholly exceptional. Of course, juxtaposition, parallel studies, outsider perspectives, and ad hoc contrasts all abound. But systematic analysis and explanation of similarities and differences between legal orders and particular legal phenomena are both rare and fragile. The reasons for this are obvious. The theoretical and practical problems of sustained strict comparison are enormous. Experienced comparatists, usually acutely aware of many of these difficulties, tend to skirt the pitfalls, make disclaimers, and lower their sights.[66] Few comparatists compare, for they know the difficulties.

---

[65] E.g. K. Lipstein in J. Carlebach et al., *Second Chance: Two Centuries of German-speaking Jews in the United Kingdom* (J. C. B. Mohr, Tubingen, 1991) 221 and Bernard Grossfield and Peter Winship, 'The Law Professor Refugee', 18 Syracuse Jo. of Int. and Comp. L. 3 (1992).

[66] A good example is Chapter 1 of David Downes' excellent *Contrasts in Tolerance: Post-war Penal Policy in the Netherlands and England and Wales* (Oxford UP, 1988) which sets out the main difficulties of comparing criminal justice systems and explicitly disclaims that it is a comparative study of post-war criminal justice policy in the two countries (at p.5). I have been involved in a number of transnational comparative projects in which at an early stage we abandoned any pretensions to be doing systematic comparison, see, e.g., R. Dhavan, N. Kibble and W. Twining (eds) *Access to Legal Education and the Legal Profession* (Butterworth, 1989) and M.

A second near-paradox is that what is frequently perceived to be the most insular tradition in academic law may have the most sophisticated culture involving sustained comparison. American legal scholarship and legal education are frequently accused, by both locals and foreigners, of being 'inward-looking' or 'parochial' or 'isolationist'. Yet it is probably the most experienced and adept at handling issues, sources and relations that cross jurisdictional borders. I am one of those foreigners who on occasion have chafed at the American tendency to focus 'almost exclusively on American law, American ideas, American institutions (especially courts and law schools) and local American hang-ups.'[67] I am not about to recant. But viewed from another perspective, where in the world has there been a scholarly tradition that has had to deal routinely with interpreting, comparing, and generalizing about relations, problems, sources, and 'solutions' that involve over fifty jurisdictions, often simultaneously?[68] The facts behind the images of the United States as 'a melting pot' or 'a laboratory' reinforce the thesis that all American legal scholarship, and much of its legal practice, is a sub-branch of comparative law.

It might be objected that studies of state probate law in Illinois and Michigan,[69] or Federal Jurisdiction, or Native American Law, or the Common Law Movement of the militias (in the prairie states or the United States as a whole),[70] do not involve 'real comparison', for this term should be reserved for analyzing similarities and differences across legal families or cultures. The basic impulse behind such views is obvious and healthy: law students and lawyers need to be made aware of a wider world. Nevertheless, this conception of 'real comparison' should be treated as a dangerous fallacy. Any comparatist should know that not only is it *easier* to compare and contrast phenomena that

---

Malsch and J. F. Nijboer (eds) *Complex Cases: Perspectives on the Netherlands Criminal Justice System.* (Amsterdam, Thela Thesis, 1999).

[67] *GLT* at p. 59.

[68] The closest approximation might be large empires, but none that I am aware of could match the sophistication of American lawyers in dealing with interstate commerce, choice of law issues, federal jurisdiction and the like.

[69] I was taught by Max Rheinstein in a course entitled 'Decedents' Estates' in Chicago. We focused on Illinois probate law; I leave it to the reader to imagine the geographical and historical range of his examples.

[70] See, e.g., Susan Koniak, 'When Law Risks Madness', (1996) 8 Cardozo Stud. in Law and Literature 65.

are closely related or otherwise similar in important respects, but such comparisons are less likely to be *invalid*. In other words, comparability presupposes some affinity. Psychological research supports this elementary truth.[71]

In this view, comparative legal studies took a wrong turn historically when 'comparative common law' and 'comparative civil law' were excluded from the sub-discipline.[72] For this had the implication that the pioneers of comparative law were not only starting with more difficult kinds of comparison – for which there were some good reasons – but they were excluding from conscious consideration all the accumulated experience, techniques, and wisdom that could be found in existing 'best practice' involving more local comparative work. They further increased their own difficulties by trying to exclude the study of 'foreign law' from comparative law.[73] Collectively they purported to run before they had considered what walking involved. The lesson is that comparison begins near home.

This argument is presented here in a deliberately provocative way. If it is broadly correct it has implications for theory and methodology in comparative law. The mainstream tradition of comparative law has been criticized as being atheoretical[74] and the leading textbook on the subject quotes Gustav Radbruch as saying 'sciences which have to concern themselves with their own methodology are sick sciences'.[75] Max Rheinstein used to suggest that comparative law was more like a way of life than a method.[76] Scepticism about methodology may have been reinforced by a judgement that the theoretical literature about the subject has been rather unhelpful. My own

---

71 Dedre Gentner and Arthur B. Markman, 'Structural Alignment in Comparison: No Difference Without Similarity', 5 Psychological Science 152 (1994).

72 E.g. Harold Gutteridge, a pioneer of comparative law in England, wrote: 'No special form of technique seems to be called for if the comparison is, for instance, between Australian and Canadian law and the law of the United States.' Preface to *Comparative Law* (Cambridge UP, 1946). Compare Atiyah and Summers (1987) op. cit. See further *GLT* 145-8.

73 Discussed *GLT* pp. 187-88.

74 E.g. Legrand and Ewald, op. cit.,

75 K. Zweigert and H. Kotz, *An Introduction to Comparative Law* (3rd edn., trs. Tony Weir, Oxford, 1998) at p. 32.

76 In conversation; cf. M. Rheinstein, 'Comparative Law __ Its Functions, Methods, and Usages', 22 Ark. L. Rev. 415 (1968)

preliminary explorations suggest that there have been many reflective practitioners but almost no outstanding theorists. On the whole comparatists have preferred to get on with the job.

In a participant-oriented discipline such as law, practice very often outstrips theory. But there may be something about the subject matters of law, other than the general impatience with theory of practitioners of an art, that accounts for the reluctance of comparatists to theorize. Insofar as many legal phenomena are embedded in specific histories and cultures, one does not have to be a strong relativist to have doubts about comparing and generalizing about them. Some may just not be susceptible to valid comparison at appropriate levels for significant purposes. Yet globalization and the seeming confidence of the ideologues of a global economy and of free market policies present direct challenges to such doubts. That is one important reason, among many, why we need a revival of general jurisprudence.

[11]
The Great Juristic Bazaar

Down the Rabbit-hole

"What is the use of a book" thought Alice "without pictures or conversation?"

ONE of my first memories of what might be categorised as a philosophical puzzlement occurred on a walk with my father. "What are flowers for?" he asked me unexpectedly. "What indeed?" I parried, more defensive than Socratic, and the matter dropped. Even a wise child can have problems with repartee.[1] I came in time to realise that the question was open to a rather splendid variety of responses:

It depends what you mean by "for."

There are many kinds of flowers and they have many uses: for example, courtship, decoration, dandelion wine. . . .

An acorn knows its mission; so why not a flower?

Are you not committing the intentionist fallacy?

A silly question: they happen to be there.

Let many flowers bloom, but don't ask why.

I was reminded of this lost opportunity shortly after I received an invitation to attend the World Congress on Philosophy of Law and Social Philosophy. A friend was reading the tentative programme for the Congress. He did not pose the relatively straightforward question "What is a World Congress of Legal and Social Philosophers for?"—to which there are some obvious and pleasing answers; instead, he asked "A General Theory of Law for the Modern Age? What would that be for?". Then, like Senator Borah, he just leered and went off to embarrass the administration.[2]

I had been casting about for a topic to earn my airfare. Semi-abashed by his question, I decided to take it semi-seriously—which is perhaps a good deal more seriously than either he or the conference organisers had intended. But seriousness is in the air. *A* general theory of law for the modern age? Only one? A *general* theory of law? General as opposed to particular? General as contrasted with complete? General as contrasted with singular? A general *theory* of law? Why theory rather than philosophy, science, model, programme or panacea? *Of* rather than about? Of *law* rather than for law or lawyers or persons regularly involved with law? *For* the modern age? Are theories *for* as flowers are or are not for? . . . I began to day-dream.

[1]Ogden Nash "The Strange Case of the Wise Child" in *Good Intentions* (1942).
[2]*Ibid.*

Consumers, Customers and Clients

"Such and so various are the tastes of men". Akenside.

I found myself in a milling throng, such as that described by Herman Melville:

> "Natives of all sorts, and foreigners; men of business and men of pleasure; parlor men and backwoods men; farm-hunters and fame-hunters; heiress-hunters, gold-hunters, buffalo-hunters, bee-hunters, happiness-hunters, truth-hunters, and still keener hunters after all these hunters. Fine ladies in slippers, and moccasined squaws; Northern speculators and Eastern philosophers; English, Irish, German, Scotch, Danes; . . . modish young Spanish Creoles, and old-fashioned French Jews; Mormons and Papists; . . . In short, a piebald parliament, an Anacharsis Cloots congress of all kinds of that multiform pilgrim species, man".[3]

The crowd was in holiday mood; ambling and jostling, joking and arguing, they appeared to be converging at different speeds on a single destination. As we got nearer I saw that we were making for a gateway with two enormous towers from which was hanging a huge banner that read:

THE GREAT JURISTIC BAZAAR

A GENERAL THEORY OF LAW FOR THE MODERN AGE

I had a momentary sense of *déja vu. One* general theory for all these people? This line of enquiry was interrupted by a commotion in the crowd. Some marshalls had appeared and were trying to divide us into two. Performers to the left, spectators to the right. The performers were admitted at once to set up their stalls, side-shows, platforms, pulpits and exhibits. The spectators were marshalled into a queue. Although this was a cosmopolitan event, clearly Anglo-Saxon influence predominated. I joined the queue and, as we had some time to wait, I decided to take the opportunity to find out something about my immediate neighbours and what it was they expected to find in the bazaar. So I began to engage them in conversation.

The people in the queue had one thing in common: they were "laymen," that is to say people who are not jurists. Otherwise they were more remarkable for the diversity of their appearance and their interests than for any shared characteristic. First in line was a group of students. I went up to them and asked what had brought them to the bazaar. "I need a certificate of attendance," said the first, "that's the only reason." "I have come to see if there is anything that will help me to become a good lawyer," said the second. "I've been told that everyone has a legal philosophy, whether or not they acknowledge it," said the third, "I have come to find out what a legal philosophy is and what mine is or might become." "I want answers to some questions," said the fourth, "what *is* justice? what *is* law?

[3]Herman Melville *The Confidence Man.*

and so on. I shall be disappointed if I don't get them." "I am a student of bourgeois mystification," said the next mysteriously. Of all the groups of consumers this was by far the largest, no doubt because they were not here by choice. It was not possible to question all of them; in any case, most were reticent, whether from bewilderment, ignorance, resentment, apprehension or torpor I do not know. Only a small minority were actually looking forward to going in, for the advance publicity for the bazaar among students had not been good.

Standing slightly apart from the students was an unlikely looking pair. A middle-aged man, immaculately dressed, with a predatory look and a well-practised posture of distinction stood next to a person of very different aspect: a thirty-year-old unsuccessfully disguised as a teenager, whose ruminative stare might easily have been mistaken for reflection—but that would be to confuse thinking with meditation. Both were impatient at having to wait. Their wants were also not very different. Each was seeking concentrated wisdom at the fount of Continuing Legal Education. The Successful Practitioner—for such he was—needed aphorisms, anecdotes, and adages for Law Day addresses, after-dinner speeches and other platforms for aspiring statesmen. His companion was also looking for some instantly usable material, identical in form, if not in content, but to be used for chanting rather than speaking. They knew what they wanted and how to get it quickly and cheaply.

The next lot of consumers looked as if they would be less easily satisfied. A polyglot group, these were persons all regularly, usually professionally, involved in legal processes as practitioners, participants, victims or voyeurs: private practitioners of law, magistrates, journalists, judges, policemen, officials, tycoons, ponces, businessmen, middle-Mafia executives and others. Although the most sceptical and the most philistine had presumably stayed away, the main characteristics that this group had in common were the indiscriminate use of the word "practical" as a term of praise and rather low expectations of what they would find in the bazaar. A sensible impressario does not probe too deeply into the wants and expectations of his theatre audience. He does not worry too much about their reactions to *Waiting for Godot;* for him it is enough that they are there. The same may be true for organisers of juristic bazaars, but such considerations did not inhibit me from making some inquiries. These were an almost total failure, for most of the members of the group either did not know what they wanted, did not want anything or seemed confused, inarticulate, or ambivalent. Insofar as they stated any needs, these seemed to be varied and sometimes contradictory. Their attitudes contained such a strange mixture of awe and scorn, romanticism and scepticism, impatience and submissiveness, that it was difficult to conceive what kind of product would please them. Pity the poor advertiser who has to produce copy designed to attract such a public:

"The whitewash that makes it all worthwhile."

"The Elixir from the garbage dump."

"The most charming battering-ram."

There were, however, some exceptions. A dyspeptic judge had come to find out why the academics squabbled interminably over what gratuitous advice to give him about cases of a kind which hardly ever arise, while remaining silent about his daily routine of finding facts and disposing of offenders. There was a group of legislators, among whom one stood out: he was clearly from the West and he had the bearing more of a technocrat than of a Pericles. "I am here to find out if anyone has improved and updated Jeremy Bentham's Science of Legislation, with a comprehensive working theory which is detailed, precise and appeals to practical men like myself." This statement seemed to provoke an almost uniformly adverse response from his companions, who called him a genius of bourgeois stupidity, a dangerous radical, and other names, but were less clear, when asked, as to what precisely it was they were looking for themselves.

Standing slightly apart from this group was a rather lonely figure, who looked both sad and quizzical. He was treated rather patronisingly by the rest, who referred to him as the Third Man, because he was poor. He knew what he was looking for. He wanted, *inter alia*, to know whether law necessarily impedes economic development, what would constitute a healthy legal system in his country in the period after decolonisation, and what principles of justice should govern the relations between rich nations and poor nations. He did not know how helpful the bazaar would be in suggesting answers to these and many other questions, but he was prepared to listen.

Behind the Third Man was a group of academics. There was an unusually modest law teacher who said simply that he wished to obtain a better understanding of his subject. There was a sociologist who claimed that he had come to study jurists as phenomena; he was quite put out when I suggested that this was also my intention: "Science is one thing, journalism another and Narcissism a third," he said irritably. Behind him were scholars from a variety of disciplines, who had recently heard that Law might have something interesting to offer after all and beyond them were many other people, including professional politicians, professional criminals, professional revolutionaries and even a few ordinary citizens, although considerably less than the hundred thousand that one optimist had predicted. I was not able to pursue my inquiries with these other groups, for the gates were suddenly thrown open and the crowd surged forward. We entered the bazaar.

The Entrance

From the entrance we could see the whole bazaar laid out before us. More expansive than Disneyland, more confusing than Wonderland, less systematic than either, all attempts to impose some kind of order on this lavish, sprawling, anarchic scene had proved quite fruitless. This was not for want of trying. From time to time first one planner then another had tried to organise the participants into schools, movements, -isms and -wasms, traditions, ideologies, areas, fields, geographical regions, sub-disciplines, specialities, periods, fashions, styles, trends. Here and there were small, often temporary, enclaves of order, but they were as elusive and evanescent as ripples on an ocean. A few optimistic organisers were still trying to draw some sort of plan as a rough guide for students and other tourists, but the enterprise was like trying to map the surface of a turbulent ocean and, as we shall see, only one such marine cartographer seemed to have succeeded in satisfying a significant number of clients.

A brief glance at the scene from above was enough to show that the "performers" (which category includes peddlers, preachers, exhibitionists, craftsmen and a variety of stall-holders) were at least as diverse and extensive as the original dockside crowd. It was also clear that they outnumbered the spectators. Indeed, some sections of the bazaar were reminiscent of some large jamboree of amateur sportsmen, where the game is the thing, the participants being content to take it in turns to play with and to each other or themselves and to form an audience to conspicuously ignore, applaud, consume or destroy their colleagues.

Although the bazaar stretched out beyond the horizon in every direction, the distribution of the participants was very uneven. There were areas which were very crowded, with many performers bunched into confined spaces, and there were large expanses which were unoccupied and uncultivated; some had been worked for a time, but had then been neglected; others had never been fashionable enough even to be the subject of preliminary exploration. For a moment I had a vision of bands of nomads huddled together at oases and encampments of varying size, surrounded by a vast and largely unfertile desert. Occasionally a solitary figure, having spotted a mirage, would break away only to be pursued by the others, gesticulating and shouting. In chasing mirages, jurists tend to travel in groups. But the vision quickly faded, for it too was a mirage, and I saw that the bazaar was in fact really quite cosy and intimate despite its complexity.

Faced with this rather confusing scene some of my friends from the queue decided to form a group and to stick together, at least to start with. These included the Legislator, the Third Man, the Law Teacher, some of the students and practitioners and myself. Without the help of either an adequate map or guide, we decided that there was no alternative but to plunge in.

The Pavilion of the Apprentices

"If you wish in the world to advance,
Your merits you're bound to enhance,
You must stir it and stump it,
And blow your own trumpet,
Or, trust me, you haven't a chance!"

W. S. Gilbert.

Nearest to the entrance was a large marquee, decorated in eye-catching, indeed gaudy, colours and sporting a banner proclaiming that it was the Pavilion of the Apprentices. We entered. If I had thought about the matter beforehand, I would have expected to find statues or facsimiles of great jurists around the walls, with groups of young persons sitting at their feet, studying their works in the original, occasionally assisted by acolytes, as a preparation for climbing onto the shoulders of their chosen master, perhaps in order to stab him in the back. Instead we found a gymnasium at once more systematic and banausic: every apprentice followed essentially the same course (although there were a few specialised options); this was organised in a series of lessons, each of which had a title. The object was unequivocal and sincere: to provide plain, direct, familiar instruction in the arts of attracting attention and getting on.

The first lesson was entitled Cocktail Party. Each student was provided with a list of 100 jurists and, associated with each name, a single word or phrase—for example, Kelsen—basic norm; Savigny—*volksgeist;* Hart—union of primary and secondary rules. As the title suggested, students were required to circulate and engage in interchanges which took the form of student A dropping the name of a famous jurist and student B responding with a key word, or *vice versa.* There was a strict system of scoring. For a correct reply, according to the list, a student would be awarded one mark. But if, for example, a student in response to the key word "principles" were to say Pound, Llewellyn, or Bentham, instead of the correct answer, Dworkin, he would be fined 3 marks. Conversely, if any other idea than that listed were mentioned in connection with a named jurist, the same fine was imposed, for, as we have recently been reminded, there is only one right answer to even the hardest question. Copies of the list were on sale in the pavilion and were specially recommended for reluctant teachers of jurisprudence. I noted that the Distinguished Practitioner was among those who bought one.

It would be tedious to give a full description of all the lessons included in the course. Most of them were commonplace, although some had intriguing titles: Indeterminate Attribution, Ignoring (destroying a rival by pretending he does not exist), Conduit (a crash course in the language of other countries or other disciplines), Labelling Theory (the artificial inflation of small and commonplace notions into full-blown theories), Twining (the risqué practice of inventing catchy titles), Innovation (the coining of new words for old ideas), Ismatizing (the formulation of vulnerable propositions attributable only to others), Balance (riding two horses at once) and Debate (repetitious exaggeration of minute differences).

Most of these techniques could, of course, be learned in any academy and are not specialised to Jurisprudence. However, there were certain skills which appear to have been developed to a higher stage of refinement by jurists than by others. One sequence of lessons on the conduct of polemics is worth describing briefly. The first lesson in the sequence deals systematically with the manufacture of artificial targets. The simplest type, commonly known as a school, was fashioned by pasting together barely recognisable caricatures of the more vulnerable parts of a dozen or more individual jurists to form a target so large that it would be virtually impossible to miss even at a great distance. The only remarkable feature of this was that a high proportion of students, although armed with the equivalent of blunderbusses that scatter their shot, managed to miss it completely. From Schools, students moved on to make artificial targets, variously known as Aunt Sallies or Straw Men, the art being to create an object which is at once vaguely familiar and very easy to destroy.

I would gladly have lingered in this section for the variations and refinements of the target-makers were numerous and sophisticated, but some of my companions were becoming impatient and so we moved on to the class on Posture. Here what is normally picked up and developed naturally without much thought had been formalised and systematised in a manner not dissimilar to the *Kama Sutra* or modern manuals on sex. The general principle appeared to be that apprentices should become adept at adopting positions which were at once improbable (or eye-catching in other ways) and yet not quite as precarious as they might seem. Whilst we were there a student was called on to demonstrate the Jerry Frank posture, which was held out as a model of its kind. By ingenious contortion he managed to get himself in a position where he appeared to the spectator to be standing on his head on an apple on a tightrope with a bucket of cold water immediately underneath. He was pelted by the other apprentices with an extraordinary variety of missiles. Once again their aim was rather wild, but eventually one missile hit the apple and removed the apparent support from the target, whereupon instead of falling into the bucket of water he assumed an upright position and revealed that he had had both feet planted firmly on the ground all along.

From Posture we moved on to Perpetual Debate. This was a small group activity, different in kind and quality from anything we had seen before. Clearly reserved for advanced students, it appeared to combine elements derived from some aristocratic and graceful game with something of a ritual dance, performed gracefully and in slow motion. The players appeared to be of very similar background, outlook and manner; the action took the form of tapping an invisible ball or shuttlecock back and forth with many minute variations, each shot being designed to place the imaginary object at a point which would stretch the opponent without putting it out of his reach, so that the rally could continue indefinitely. From time to time players would be substituted and would even occasionally change sides. Throughout the participants complimented each other in a manner which appeared exceedingly gracious and recondite. Once again I could have watched for a long time, fascinated by the intricacies and variations of this elegant activity. My companions, at once more impatient and more purposive, maintained that they could not see the point of it and insisted that we proceed. I left wondering whether this was a game which was destined to be understood only by the players themselves.

Our departure was so hasty that we by-passed entirely the advanced classes on Book-of-the-Moment, Revival, Popularization and, the most advanced of them all, Silence. But it is my impression that these had all been ruthlessly plagiarised from other disciplines and were still at a relatively underdeveloped stage within Jurisprudence. On the way out we overheard the class on Radical Polemics, which contrasted sharply with Perpetual Debate in that it was both robust and easy to understand. Its fairly straightforward use of a limited number of simple set pieces and rhetorical ploys attracted large numbers of the apprentices, some of whom lacked the finesse even to distinguish it from vulgar abuse. With their incantations pounding on our ears, we left the pavilion.

The Academy of Legal Science

"If law be not a science, a university will best consult its own dignity in declining to teach it."

Langdell

It is, of course, a truism that academic respectability is confined to those engaged in Science. Art is for trade schools, Action is for the arena, Science is for the academy. Why else the persistent pressure for accreditation, as field after field of enquiry proceeds from -ics to -ology to science? Why else political science, policy science, police science, domestic science, and legal science? Why else are budding broadcasters subjected to classical rhetoric, cooks to chemistry, and lawyers to logic?

It would have come as no surprise to find many persons at the bazaar claiming to be scientists—indeed who can claim to be a Jurist who claims to be neither a scientist, nor a philosopher, nor a prophet? —but it was unexpected to come across a separate palace called the Academy of Legal Science. Admission proved to be a formality and on entering we found it to be, for the most part, a temple dedicated to false analogies invented in the quest for respectability.

The atmosphere was primarily, though not exclusively, Germanic. But all Western nations were represented at the exhibition. Italian phrenologists, Swedish astrologers, French Euclideans, Finnish logicians and Austrian polymaths all sported the badge of "legal scientist." There were rather few Englishmen. The American display included a range of analogies as lavish as their conceptions of the various sciences were simple. As anthropologists appropriate tribes on a first-come first-served basis, so there was a time when American jurists, mistranslating "wissenschaft" as "science," claimed particular scientific analogies as their own. Langdell claimed zoology and botany, Holmes, science in general; Pound, horticulture and engineering; Corbin, Darwinian biology; Hohfeld, chemistry; Cook, physics; Moore, behaviourist psychology; Beutel, experimental science. Such early appropriations made things difficult for the late-comers, some of whom had to content themselves with such barely accredited fields as economics, cybernetics and psychoanalysis.

The American exhibit was dominated by a gargantuan structure entitled The Great Observing Machine. Disdainful of analogies, this engine appeared to be a product of its own technology. The name was a trap for the unwary: for all who were lured onto the platform marked "observers" immediately found themselves swallowed up into the machine as participants, to help keep going manually the elaborate gadgetry which might have been designed by the late Heath Robinson. Indeed the machine was used for manufacture rather than observation, for there was nothing to be seen from within except the mangled effigies of all past jurists and the machinery itself, out of which issued a steady flow of large rectangular objects of considerable weight, imposing appearance and expansive titles.

The other major American exhibit, the Micro-Analyzer, made the Great Observing Machine look both old-fashioned and cumbersome beside it. "Invented" in the mid-west, this had the appearance, the size, the flexibility, the cheapness and, indeed, the functions of a pocket calculator. Rumour has it that after a prolonged and well-planned sales drive it has also had a comparable success in the American market, and this is hardly surprising since its more enthusiastic salesmen claim (despite explicit disclaimers in the guarantee) that it can solve all problems including Crime, Love, Charity and the existence of the God of Efficiency. I noticed, however, that when the Third Man enquired whether the machine would work in the tropics, the salesman snapped back: "I'm playing economics, not politics."

The European stalls appeared rather staid and old-fashioned alongside these products of American ingenuity. Indeed, to the casual observer, European legal science, at least in respect of exposition, did not seem to have changed very much since it was described by Ihering. This, however, may be a false impression, for we were not able to find out. Whenever any of my companions asked a non-dogmatic question related to his concerns, he was turned away with a polite smile and the uniform response: "Very interesting, but that is not a *scientific* question."

This, too, was the fate of a rather depressed band of sociologists and lawyers who were trying to set up a stand within the Academy. Keen to dissociate themselves from something they referred to as "Sociological Jurisprudence," they carried a placard proclaiming "Scientology of Law." On all other matters they appeared to be in irreconcilable disagreement. They had with them a large Map of Knowledge which they spread out on the floor and, then, rather in the mode of nineteenth-century colonial powers, they proceeded to argue about how some of the various unexplored and inaccurately charted regions should be carved up between them. However, before they had the chance to settle into the gentle rhythms of Perpetual Debate, a steward would come up to them and say politely, but firmly, "This is not Legal Science; I must ask you to leave." They would shuffle on a few yards and try to spread out their map once more, only to be moved on again. By the time we left they had not yet found an assured place within the Academy, nor indeed within the whole bazaar, and some were beginning to argue that they had come to the wrong place and so they should change their name.

As we proceeded through the Academy we passed a number of familiar sights: Purists perpetually shooting at targets out of reach; simple seekers after the Absolute; Counters counting the unquantifiable or, with their blinkers on, studying only minutiae which could be quantified; Seven-day Sciences; one-man sciences for the get-wise-quick; innumerable guerillas and evangelists poorly disguised as scientific researchers; and persons of modest intellect immodestly claiming to have established a new paradigm or to have overturned an old one.

At the far end of the Academy a large space had been left clear. The floor, the walls and the high-domed ceiling had all been whitewashed. In front of it was a notice which stated categorically:

The One True Legal Science
No entry without Purification.

It turned out that, unlike being washed in cynical acid, purification was a relatively painless process: it merely involved putting on a pair of spectacles similar to those used by opticians for testing vision, the only difference being that the sides and both lenses had been completely blocked, so that no light whatsoever could enter. We were told that if we put on the spectacles, sat on the floor and gazed at the ceiling we would be in absolutely no danger of falling into error. This claim turned out to be fully justified for, since we could see nothing, there was no possibility of misperception. I was reminded of the Bellman in the Hunting of the Snark who had kept his crew happy by bringing a map of the sea that they could all understand:

"Other maps are such shapes, with their islands and capes!
But we've got our brave Captain to thank"
(So the crew would protest) "that he's brought us the best—
A perfect and absolute blank."[4]

So long as we stayed within the confines of the enclosure with our spectacles on we were quite safe; there were none of the navigational risks associated with the Bellman's steering, for we were not moving; and even the danger of softly and silently fading away should the Snark prove to be a Boojum was slight, since it was very unlikely that we would actually discover anything at all in this place. The only dangers were boredom and blindness. It was not long before my companions, especially the Third Man, began to be restive. "Did not someone say that knowledge does not have to be scientific to be useful and important?" he asked. We decided to leave for less safe, but more varied, scenes. Brushing aside the blandishments of yet another salesman of pocket calculators, we left the Academy.

The Avenue of Disappointed Expectations

Outside the Academy we entered a tortuous road which seemed to turn in on itself in a spiral. We were immediately set upon by

[4]Lewis Carroll *The Hunting of the Snark.*

numerous hustlers who tried to importune us, with promises of many delights and spectacles, to enter into their particular version of inter-disciplinary intercourse. It was not clear from their sales-talk whether they saw themselves more as pimps or marriage brokers and their establishments as brothels or registry offices; but the more experienced members of our group wearily maintained that such promises offered little real hope of consummation or fulfilment and that we would merely be presented with a frustrating ritual alternation of clarion calls and babble about budgets.

This scepticism was not confined to my companions. In full view of the protagonists of interdisciplinary intercourse was an enclosure, dominated by a large placard which pointedly advocated: "Do-It-Yourself". As one who had been taught at Oxford to believe that a man with a First in Greats could get up science in a week, I was pleased to find that our American cousins had transformed this into the maxim: A person who has been to the Yale Law School can fix anything. De Tocqueville would have been delighted. The D.I.Y. enclosure was very crowded, despite an admirable insistence on confining it to theory. It was by no means monopolised by true blues and ivy leaguers. Indeed, the only requirement was that the participant should have no formal qualifications in any discipline other than law. Here lawyers were not only diagnosing problems-in-the-round and studying Society, Context and Action, but they were also actually professing other disciplines. For on close inspection it transpired that such banners as Sociology of Law, Psychoanalysis and Law, Law and Economics, Legal Philosophy, and Law and Art were somewhat misleading, for they contained no Law whatsoever. It would have been more accurate if "by Lawyers" were substituted throughout for "of Law" "and Law" "Law and . . ." and "Legal"—so that they read "Sociology by Lawyers," "Psychoanalysis by Lawyers" and so on. For this was the Lawyers' extraversion in its purest form: from here they sallied forth onto uncharted seas and other people's territories, never to return.

A very clear example of this was the Legal Philosophers' Circle, a spherical balloon, floating high above the enclosure, kept up by a combination of warm air and long supple stilts. In sharp contrast with the previous exhibits, ordinary tourists were discouraged from entering, for serious philosophers prefer to speak only to or past each other. The ascent was arduous and, in order to gain admission, an applicant had to undertake to observe certain conventions: to think before speaking, to speak before listening, to write before reading, to confine himself to philosophical questions and, much to the disappointment of the serious student, never to expect any answers. Furthermore no heavy books or footnotes were admitted, in case the balloon might become weighed down and descend to earth. Despite these restrictions a number of lawyers had gained entry, and had settled down for good, seemingly content to address themselves only to philosophers. The attractions to them were obvious. Here the lawyer could not only forget all the law he ever knew, but also need no longer trouble himself with particular instances taken from real life. The Contracts scholar could forget about the banal realism of slippery poles, peanut races, and agreements to pay existing debts and could concentrate on the conceptual complexities of promises to come to lunch or to get up at eight in the morning on a desert island. The Torts lawyer could puzzle over the problems of attributing causation and responsibility in simple road accidents without being diverted by the implausible fact situations of *Palsgraf* or *The Wagon Mound.* Moreover, the activity sounded like a very agreeable party, with much good-natured badinage and the cares of the world largely forgotten. From below it was not possible to tell whether what was being said was sense or nonsense, for the stilts were so tall as to put the speakers out of earshot, even if they had not all been speaking simultaneously.

Despite the lighthearted sounds from the balloon overhead, there was an air of malaise in the D.I.Y. enclosure. So many adventurers who had set out, had never been heard of again or had lapsed into mere dilettantism; so many pioneering efforts had not reached take-off point, either for lack of funds or lack of commitment; so many leaders had failed to find followers. And then there was the matter of the next round of the Queen of the Sciences contest. Law had not really had a look-in since Justinian had made his bold claim on behalf of Jurisprudence.[5] For most of the Middle Ages Theology's position had not been challenged. And when at last Theology began to fade, Law had missed its chance and was overtaken by some of the upstart physical sciences. It was really not until the 1920's, thanks largely to the efforts of the American D.I.Y. brigade, that the chances of Jurisprudence began to revive, at least so far as the regional contest for Queen of the Social Sciences was concerned. The finest moment had been when an attempt was made to put forward the lawyer as the supreme policy-maker in society, but this had proved abortive and it was now generally acknowledged that Henry Kissinger had probably never read a Jurisprudence textbook, nor had Spiro Agnew, although he might be said to have written one. The present prospect for Law now looked bleak, and the talk in the D.I.Y. enclosure was about the relative claims of Sociology and Biology to the crown, with Scientific Materialism as a hot outsider if they could only agree on who was to represent them.

There was one further disappointment in store for us. Tucked away to one side, hidden by more lavish exhibits, was a large marquee which was in a very poor state of repair. The notice outside read: Theories of the Middle Order. Several members of our group made for this eagerly, hoping that here they might find what they had been looking for. But the marquee turned out to be almost empty, with only one or two old-fashioned exhibits standing forlornly on their own. We asked the doorman for an explanation of this neglect. He was not sure, but said he thought it was partly a matter of fashion, partly of prestige. He had the impression that more work was being done than the exhibition suggested, but the more pretentious considered it beneath their dignity to be seen in this setting and the more modest felt it to be arrogant to claim that what they had been doing deserved the name of "theory." Thus the level of theorising

[5]Digest 1.10.

which might have proved most useful to some of the clientele, turned out to be the one which was the least cultivated.

The Souk

We came at last to the very centre of the bazaar, which was aptly called the Souk. Here down twisting lanes, blind alleys and narrow byways were to be found hundreds of small shops, stalls and other establishments in which individual craftsmen, peddlers, zealots, pick-pockets and merchants of various kinds went about their respective businesses. Even an inhabitant of this maze, who had or had not grown up there, would find it difficult to describe in a clear and systematic way the rich variety of sights, sounds, smells and wares that were to be found there. I shall only attempt to give a few fleeting impressions. There were numerous craftsmen, beavering away at producing objects, exquisite or grotesque, quaint or ordinary, useful or useless; there was much repetitive junk for the tourist and, here and there, hidden delights for the connoisseur. Among the motley collection of carpenters and charlatans, fashion-mongers and fishmongers, sages and butchers, two categories are worth a brief mention: the locksmiths and the puffers.

In the Middle Ages many alchemists sought the philosophers' stone which they believed would change base metals into gold and guarantee eternal youth. This was the Single Right Answer to all the Great Questions. The advent of modern science put paid to that absurd myth, so that no-one—well, hardly anyone—believes that such stones exist. Elixirs and Essences are also recognised as mere wishful imaginings. It was accordingly comforting to find that a modern substitute is readily available: the master key that unlocks all puzzlements.

In Locksmiths Lane competition was hot. Dozens of vendors proclaimed loudly that they offered the one and only true key. The keys came in all shapes and sizes and colours; blue keys and red keys, simple keys and difficult keys, invisible keys and unspeakable keys, some intricately wrought and needing the lightest touch, others big, bold and bludgeoning—they had only one thing in common: at each stall each and every vendor chanted of his product "The Key, This is the Key."

The problem of deciding which key, if any, was the true one appeared at first sight to be rather more straightforward than judging between false and genuine nails from the true cross and other religious relics. For surely keys are susceptible to empirical testing: all one has to do is to sit down with a collection of them and go on trying them until one is found that actually works. But, of course, that assumes the existence of something to be unlocked. The problem in Locksmiths Lane stems from the fact that there were many keys, but no locks. On one point all the vendors were in agreement: there is only one lock to be opened, so only one key is needed, for Jurisprudence is a one question subject. Once upon a time all were agreed that "what is law?" was *the* question of Jurisprudence. But since it was first pointed out that this question is misposed, and is not worth asking anyway, confusion has reigned. There is no longer any consensus as to what the central question is: some maintain that it concerns the concept of a legal system; others that it relates to the nature of judicial discretion, others to the unique characteristics of legal reasoning; yet others that it has to do with validity or legitimacy, and so on. In Locksmiths Lane they are still making keys against the day when someone poses the Single Right Question. All are agreed that a theory of law is an answer to the central question of Jurisprudence, and the vendors continue to chant: "The Key, This is the Key"—but what is the question? Perhaps Auden provides a clue: maybe Law, like Love, laughs at locksmiths.[6]

In Puffers' Alley we encountered a different problem of the market—what is known in the trade as the Overspill Effect. Caveat Emptor! Everyone knows about standard form contracts and exemption clauses, but the consumers still persist in failing to read the small print. The process is a familiar one: the manufacturer goes to a great deal of trouble to spell out the limitations of his latest product and the conditions under which it may safely be used, and rightly disclaims any responsibility for harm resulting from the misuse or abuse of the article. Any civilised system of jurisprudence would ensure that such disclaimers are sufficient to relieve him of any duty to the ultimate consumer. It is a proposition that I venture to suggest that no-one would for one moment doubt. It is hardly T. S. Kuhn's fault if foolish enthusiasts apply his notion of paradigms to the social sciences or fail to distinguish between paradigms and mere trends or tendencies; John Rawls cannot be fairly taken to task if his principles of justice are rashly applied to actual societies or to the world community, when the conditions for the application of his theory are obviously not satisfied; it is surely improper to blame the inventors of the Micro-Analyzer if over-zealous converts try to use it to solve problems in the real world, instead of confining it, where it belongs, to such questions as whether it is preferable to spend a million years in Hell and the rest of eternity thereafter in Heaven or to take things in the reverse order. Surely theorists should not be held responsible for the excesses of their disciples any more than Anthony Burgess can be held to account for any alleged social effects of *A Clockwork Orange*. If it is there in the small print, the manufacturer should be exempted. *Caveat Emptor*.

It is, of course, true that the untutored customer, who does not, will not, or cannot read the small print, is also in need of protection. He needs to be protected not only from the unscrupulous or over-enthusiastic salesman, but also from any contact whatsoever with products unsuited to his needs. But responsibility should be placed where it belongs: not on the manufacturer who never intended his product to reach the ultimate consumer, but on the real villain, the middle-man. If manufacturers are not protected from consumers and consumers from manufacturers, chaos will ensue. And so we found it in Puffers' Alley. Here the most exquisite and intricately conceived ornaments were being marketed by loud-mouthed salesmen as if they were the most pedestrian and useful household gadgets—to be *used* rather than admired! Imagine a Sèvres soup tureen being sold

[6] W. H. Auden "Law, say the gardeners, is the Sun".

as a washing-up bowl or a Louis XVI musical box as a teasmaid! In the short time we were there we witnessed a number of aberrations: one salesman tried to sell a copy of Hart's *Concept of Law* to an anthropologist about to embark on field-work; another tried to off-load Dworkin's *Hard Cases* onto an actual judge; the salesmen of pocket calculators buzzed everywhere with their improbable claims; and, although it is difficult to believe, one vendor even tried to impose Rawls' principles of Justice, ripped from their context, on the Third Man!

Pity the poor craftsman, but spare a thought for the bewildered consumer. Such exquisite talent wasted, such simple needs unsatisfied. Clearly the wicked middle-man is to blame for this dual disservice. It is his fault for bringing this ill-assorted pair together: if a customer wants a washing-up bowl, let him shop elsewhere. If there is no market for the craftsman's works of art, let him console himself with the thought that it is enough that they exist. Every effort must be made to eliminate all middle-men and to protect our more exquisite theories from spilling over into the world outside and from being wasted on the banal problems of everyday existence.

Exit

The time had come to leave the bazaar. I had, of course, inspected only a small part of it. Hindu, Islamic, Russian, Chinese, Melanesian, African, Latin American and many aspects of European Jurisprudence had been omitted. I had concentrated, though not exclusively, on the Anglo-American exhibits and I had only been able to cover some of these. This report, too, is incomplete: I have said nothing of The Museum of Sporting Metaphors, The Palace of Fallacies, and the Fullerian Collection of Ingenuous Hypotheticals, to mention only three that may merit special consideration on some other occasion. But rather than impose any more on the patience of my readers, I shall conclude by reporting briefly on my observations of the customers as they left the bazaar by the main exit.

Some looked elated, some despondent, others bewildered; some were loaded down with purchases, others left empty-handed. A few had decided to stay on as performers. First to go were the Successful Practitioner and his companion, still together, each with a neat packet of purchases—the cocktail party list, a nutshell, *Great Sayings by Famous Lawyers* (or is it *vice versa?*), a little red book and a big blue one. At least they had known what they had wanted. Next came some students, empty-headed and eager to leave, followed by the Third Man who looked as bemused and quizzical as ever. Some new converts looked complacent, others aggressive. Some sported the latest fashions and follies, others looked pleased at having met old friends. Most of those who had made purchases looked satisfied; carrying their neatly wrapped parcels and pocket calculators they hurried home to play or do battle with their new toys or weapons. Maybe they had not yet had time to read the fine print and disclaimers. One or two were practising new postures or the ploys of Perpetual Debate.

Many of the customers seemed dissatisfied. Those who had wished to get wise quick, had not. Some looked disgusted or bored—but who knows what would have pleased them? The judge seemed none the wiser and as dyspeptic as ever; the legislator had received no answer and the earnest student had found progress to be slow. The demystifier thought it all a conspiracy and a rip-off. Saddest of all were those who had learnt to hate their subject and would for ever be condemned to be legal masochists. But by far the largest number were not affected one way or the other. For a brief instant some stall or sideshow may have caught and held their attention, but they had wandered on, tossing off the memory with a shrug or a laugh or a yawn. What was in it for them? Who remembers last week's T.V. programme? What was different about this? Was it not just another spectacle, just one more slice of the human tragicomedy?*

**Note:* This paper was written for the World Congress on Philosophy of Law and Social Philosophy, held in Australia in August 1977. It is published here with permission of the Organizing Committee of the Congress. To avoid misunderstanding the author wishes to point out that neither the World Congress nor any other particular event was the subject of his dream. There is a difference between a conference and a bazaar.

[12]
Lawyers' Stories

I understand that his strength as an advocate lay not in his powers of oratory, but in the reasoning and persuasiveness of the arguments by which he tried to bring the court round to his point of view. He continued to use his powers of persuasion when he was sitting as a Lord of Appeal and would come home and say that he thought that he had won his 'brothers' over to his side or 'so-and-so is still not convinced but I think he may be tomorrow.' He certainly persuaded his family that he was right. When he gave us the facts of a case and asked us what we thought about it, his way of presenting the problem was such that there was never any suggestion in our minds that the other side could have a leg to stand on.

E. Cockburn Millar on her father, Lord Atkin[1]

Might it be suggested that the central act of the legal mind, of judge and lawyer alike, is the conversion of the raw material of life ... into a story that will claim to tell the truth in legal terms?

James Boyd White[2]

Introduction

Once upon a time, Rhetoric was central to the humanities and forensic oratory was central to Rhetoric. In the long and complex story of rhetorical studies, the forum ceased over time to be the main arena and persuasive oratory was displaced as the main object of study. Conversely, the discipline of law lost touch with Rhetoric. Demosthenes, Cicero and Quintilian are almost entirely ignored in contemporary legal studies.[3] When jurists cite Aristotle, it tends to be the *Ethics* or *Politics* rather than the *Rhetoric*. Of course, practising lawyers still practise advocacy and they elicit, translate, construct, narrate, distort and attack stories as part of their art of persuasion. Legal theorists, on the other hand, have written a great deal about the reasoning of judges, especially appellate court judges, but have paid remarkably little attention to the argumentation of advocates, especially where it is the facts or the sentence rather than the law which is in dispute. 'Narrative' features hardly at all in discussions of legal reasoning; 'rhetoric' when applied to the discourse of a judge or even an advocate usually implies criticism.[4] One might infer from this that rhetoric and narrative have little or nothing to do with legal reasoning and so, by implication, are consigned to the dubious sphere of 'irrational means of persuasion'. On such a view, Lord Atkin's daughter's account of her father may be interpreted as an example of a skilful advocate, either through conscious trickery or unconscious bias, winning his family over by non-rational means. Is that the only or even the most plausible interpretation?

This essay is one of a series of exploratory studies of the role of narrative in general culture. It challenges any suggestion that narrative has a marginal role of dubious legitimacy in legal discourse; it also challenges the converse idea that constructing stories is 'the central act of the legal mind' as White and others have suggested.[5] The essay focuses mainly on one class of legal discourse, forensic advocacy in modern Anglo-American courts. In particular, it addresses the question: What, if any, are legitimate functions of narrative in *rational* argument by advocates on disputed questions of law and disputed questions of fact? In the course of what is a preliminary exploration, I shall suggest that narrative probably plays a variety of roles in advocacy: some of these roles are unavoidable and legitimate, but are more to do with communication than with rational argument and persuasion; that narrative can be used in ways that would be considered to be illegitimate or dubious, judged by conventional standards of ethical advocacy; but that narrative also has some important, legitimate contributions to make to rational argument by lawyers and that some of these roles fit uneasily with some standard accounts of lawyers' reasonings. The focus is normative rather than empirical; the examples used are illustrative rather than representative.

The discourse of advocates in court is only one kind of legal discourse. A wide variety of actors and commentators participate in law talk and talk about law in an even wider variety of contexts. Judges, law-makers, office lawyers, legal scholars, teachers of law, historians, journalists, novelists and all citizens regularly produce and consume legal discourse.[6] It is widely accepted by contemporary legal scholars that litigation is just one species of legal and law-related action and that what happens in open court is only one, often atypical, phase of the total process of litigation. There is debate among legal theorists as to how far the contested trial, the dialectics of adversary proceedings and the reasoned judicial decision are paradigmatic, or representative, or central forms of legal life and discourse. We need not enter these debates here, but it is relevant to state that I am personally sceptical of such claims.[7] For one message of this essay is a reminder of complexity. There are many kinds and contexts of legal discourse; there are many kinds and phases of litigation; any litigated case is likely to prove on examination to be an extremely complex kind of social process. It would be unwise to start on an exploration of the role of narrative in legal discourse by anticipating that there will be global or reductive answers.

My colleagues in law may think it surprising, even eccentric, to begin such an exploration by focusing on the discourse of advocates. For there are other types of legal discourse that are much better documented and more extensively studied and analysed. We have in reported judgments, in legislation, in legal textbooks and secondary writings about law, for example, a rich treasury of accessible and familiar texts. Compared to these, advocates' arguments are only spasmodically documented and, at least in modern times, they have been relatively under-theorized.[8] I accept that a systematic narratology of legal discourses, especially one that is to have a sound empirical base in concrete and representative examples of such discourses, has to engage with our general heritage of texts of different kinds and our stock of theorizing about them.[9] There are, however, two related reasons for using a different starting-point. Firstly, the situation, purposes, role and audience of the advocate in court are typically clearer or less problematic than those of the judge or the jury or the expositor.[10] *The primary task of the advocate is to persuade this tribunal to decide in favour of this client in respect of previously defined issues of law and/or fact and/or disposition.* By focusing on a relatively uncontroversial kind of actor one may be able to skirt, rather than plunge directly into, the morass of controversies surrounding theories of adjudication and other familiar areas of juristic debate. We shall not be able to avoid getting our feet wet, but we may be able to paddle before trying to swim.

A second reason is that a central concern of narratology is the role of stories in rational argument. While some aspects of the advocate's role are considered relatively unproblematic, questions about what constitute 'rational' and 'irrational', legitimate or illegitimate techniques or modes of persuasion are central, sharply posed questions in any theory of advocacy. In order to keep matters simple, I shall concentrate on three tasks of the advocate that are generally regarded as distinct: arguments about disputed questions of fact; arguments about disputed questions of law; and arguments about sanctions, such as arguments about the amount of damages to be awarded in a civil action or pleas in mitigation of sentence in criminal proceedings.

In legal theory the distinction between questions of fact and questions of law is recognized to be analytically problematic.[11] It is also recognized that determinations of fact and law in particular cases have an artificial all-or-nothing character (guilty/not guilty, liable/not liable). The winner takes all.[12] By contrast, the determination of sanction tends to be more open-ended, involving a choice between a range of possibilities within varying limits, such as maximum (and less frequently, minimum) penalties.

These distinctions have practical consequences for advocates. Whether a question is classified as one of fact, law or disposition may determine the arena, the audience, the timing and the style of presentation. In simplified form, questions of law are for judges; questions of fact are for the jury or other triers of fact; questions of sentence are usually for the judge. Elaborate rules govern which kinds of issue are subject to appeal or review in a higher court. There are reasons for adopting the working assumption that these three kinds of argument represent three different kinds of task, each with a distinct kind of discourse appropriate to it. Later we shall need to consider the relations between them.

222 *Lawyers' Stories*

A lexicon of advocacy

The discourse of advocacy, as found in manuals, trial records and informal conversation, contains relatively few terms of art. In so far as there is a distinctive vocabulary, much of it has recognizable roots in the formal rules of procedure and evidence, in classical and medieval rhetoric and in drama. Contemporary Anglo-American manuals of advocacy[13] contain a number of key terms that are useful for present purposes: theory, story, situation, scene, scenario, theme and thelema. Even the best English and American manuals tend to adopt an informal, often chatty, style in which precision is sometimes sacrificed to readability. A rather more exact vocabulary is needed for purposes of theoretical analysis. Accordingly, I propose to stipulate some definitions and make some distinctions that are more precise than ordinary usage.

Theory An advocate's 'theory of the case' is his argument about the case as a whole.[14] It should be capable of being expressed in the form of a logical and coherent statement of the reasoning supporting the desired conclusion. A summary statement of such a theory should take the form of a précis of a complex argument. To take some simple examples:

1 Where the only issue is a question of fact:
   (a) 'The prosecution has failed to produce sufficient evidence that it was the accused who committed the alleged crime'; or
   (b) 'The evidence shows that my client was in another city at the time of the murder and therefore he could not be the murderer'; or
   (c) 'The evidence shows that the deceased was killed accidentally during the course of a struggle in which he was trying to stop the accused from committing suicide by shooting herself.'[15]
2 Where the only issue is a question of law:
   (a) 'Authority, principle and reason support the proposition that a professional person owes a duty of care to a non-professional in respect of advice given in circumstances X, Y and Z. The facts of this case are a clear example of this type of situation';[16] or
   (b) 'This case is new. It should be approached on principles applicable to modern conditions rather than on outmoded nineteenth-century precedents and values. Authority, principle and policy based on modern values support the proposition that the public interest should prevail over the private interest where there is a conflict between reasonable and long-established uses of land in the interest of the public at large (such as village cricket), and the private interest in enjoyment, without interference or risk of injury, or damage to adjacent property which has recently been developed.'[17]
3 In a plea in mitigation:
   'Notwithstanding the seriousness of the offence, the facts that my client has an unblemished record, has shown contrition, is unlikely to repeat the offence, has good prospects of employment and has a dependent family combine to support the conclusion that a custodial sentence would be inappropriate and could serve no useful purpose in this case.'

Manuals of advocacy, especially those concerned with trial techniques, stress the importance of developing and maintaining a clear and cohesive theory of the case as a whole: 'It is essential to develop a theory of the case before trial and act in accordance with it throughout the trial itself.'[18] The theory provides the basis for the advocate's strategy which will guide all his choices and actions throughout the proceedings.

This conception of 'theory' serves the function of isolating that aspect of advocacy which is concerned with rational arguments from other aspects, such as commanding attention, communication, questioning, persuasive presentation and various courtroom tactics. The conception is also analytically convenient in that it provides a convenient connection with theories of legal reasoning.

In standard, but not entirely uncontroversial, accounts of legal reasoning, the paradigm example of 'a case as a whole' takes the following form: 'If X then Y; if Y then Z.' Here X represents the *circumstances* governed by the rule; Y represents the *legal effect* (guilt or liability); and Z represents the *sanction* or consequence. For example, 'Whenever a person intentionally and with malice aforethought causes the death of another without lawful justification, that person is guilty of murder. Where a person is guilty of murder, that person shall be condemned to death (unless ...).' On this view, the paradigm case of a disputed question of law is: 'What is the scope of X?' Or 'Do circumstances a, b, c, constitute a case of X?' The paradigm case of a disputed question of fact is: 'Does the evidence support the conclusion that X happened?' The paradigm case of an issue in sentencing is: 'Given X and Y, and in view of M_1, M_2, M_3 (mitigating factors) what is the appropriate punishment in this case?'[19]

Story In the discourse of advocacy the word 'story' tends to be used rather loosely to encompass a party's or witness's version of what happened; or a chronological statement of a sequence of events; or a statement of 'the facts' of the case by a judge or advocate; or the formal allegations (the material facts) set out in the pleadings; or even the advocate's theory of the case.[20] In considering the role of narrative in forensic argument, it is important to give the term 'story' a more precise, restricted meaning. Adapting Ricoeur, I propose the following definition: 'A story is a narrative of particular events arranged in a time sequence and forming a meaningful totality.'[21] In this formulation particularity, time, change and connectedness are all necessary ingredients. But the connections between the events which make the story a totality need not be causal. In this usage, adapting E. M. Forster, 'The King died and then the Queen died' is not a story, but merely a chronological statement; 'the King died and then the Queen died of grief' has the necessary element of connectedness.[22] But so does the following: 'The King was reported to have died; the Queen died of grief; in fact the report was false, for the King had been feigning death in order to evade an assassination attempt.' Although this last narrative does not follow a strict chronological order and its connectedness does not depend on causation alone, it counts as a story. For the rest of this essay I shall equate narrative with story-telling: one narrates stories, but describes situations.[23]

There is an intimate relationship between 'theories' and 'stories', but it is important to keep them conceptually distinct. The distinction and the relationship can be illustrated by the closing speech for the Crown by Archibald Bodkin in the case of George Joseph Smith (the 'Brides in the Bath Case'). Smith was accused of murdering Bessie Mundy by deliberately drowning her in a bath in a rented house in Herne Bay. The crux of the case was whether her death was caused by accident or design. The defence theory was that she drowned during an epileptic fit. The evidence concerning the cause of death was circumstantial and inconclusive. In Bodkin's opening speech, and during the trial, the jury had been presented not only with the story of the course of the relationship between Smith and the deceased and of its aftermath, but with two other stories of deaths of Smith's 'brides' who had died in similar, unexplained circumstances. Bodkin's closing speech takes up only four paragraphs in the record. The last half reads as follows:

> The prisoner and the woman being alone in the house, he had the opportunity of committing the crime. The motive of the prisoner has been demonstrated, the opportunity admitted, and the exclusion of accident proved. You are entitled to look at the evidence as to the two other deaths to see whether the death of Miss Mundy was accident or designed, and, if designed, for the benefit of whom? You can also look at that evidence to see whether the death was part of a system or course of conduct – horrible as it is to think so – of deliberately causing people's deaths in order that monetary benefit might ensue to him.
>
> The three cases are of such a character that such a large aggregation of resemblances cannot have occurred without design. In each case the prisoner went through the form of marriage; in each case the ready money of the woman was either realized or drawn out of whatever deposit bank it might have been in; in each case there was a will drawn in favour of the prisoner absolutely; in each case the will was drawn by a stranger to the testatrix; in each case the victim insured her life or was possessed of property which did not make it necessary to insure her life; in each case there was a visit to a doctor shortly before the death, which, we contend, was unnecessary from the physical condition of the patient; in each case the women wrote letters to relatives the night before, or on the night on which they died; in each case there was an inquiry as to a bathroom drowning, and the prisoner was the first to discover it; in each case the bathroom doors were unfastened and the water was not drawn off until after the doctor had been; and in each case the prisoner was putting demonstrably forward the purchase of either fish, or eggs, or tomatoes to show that he was absent from the house in which his wife was lying dead; and in each case there was the prisoner's subsequent disappearance and the monetary advantage resulting or attempted to be made to result.[24]

This is generally regarded as a classic of advocacy. It is misleading to treat it as an example of narrative discourse. Rather it is more accurately described as an argument directed to a single issue (design). It proceeds by analysing and comparing three stories in order to fill a crucial gap in one of them, the story of the death of Bessie Mundy. Bodkin was *arguing* about one part of a story rather than narrating. The argument supports the prosecution 'theory' that Smith intentionally caused the death of Bessie Mundy. We could not give an account of the case without some notion of story – for it is a reasonably clear example of a jury having to choose between competing stories – but that is different from saying that Bodkin was here using story-telling as a technique of persuasion.

It may be objected that such notions as telling stories, stating the facts and narrating as they are ordinarily used in the discourse of advocacy do not correspond with the notion of 'story' as it was defined above.[25] For example, the predecessors of the serjeants-at-law were the '*narratores*' or 'counters' whose primary task was to present the plaintiff's *narratio* to the Court of Common Pleas. But the '*narratio*', far from being a story, was a formal statement of claim that fitted a strictly limited set of categories. The primary skill of the *narratores* was 'in fitting the facts alleged by their clients into the appropriate mould'.[26] The art was not to tell stories, but to translate them. It was a sophisticated form of classification, more like form-filling than story-telling.

Similarly, in an argument on a question of law 'stating the facts' of the case before the court, or 'stating the facts' of some precedent used in argument does not necessarily involve telling a 'story' *stricto sensu*. For example, the material facts may concern a situation or state of affairs rather than a sequence of events; or the facts may be stated in a way which corresponds precisely with the elements of a crime or tort or other cause of action. Although typically presented less formally than the medieval *narratio*, a statement of the material facts of a case is only one step away from form-filling, especially in the case of written pleadings.

This line of argument raises two important issues. First, it can be readily conceded that there are many cases in which advocates are not involved in explicit story-telling at all. An argument about interpretation of a statute conducted at a general level; a defence based on a simple alibi; a plea in mitigation which emphasizes factors other than the accused's version of and attitude to the crime are all simple examples. Whether stories are necessary elements of an argument about 'a case as a whole' will be considered below.[27]

Secondly, can a sharp distinction be drawn between form-filling and story-telling? 'On 5 March X intentionally and with malice aforethought stabbed Y, who died from his wounds on 6 March' contains all the ingredients of the crime of murder and satisfies the formal definition of a story, viz. it is a sequential narrative of particular events that forms a whole. We normally expect stories to be more detailed, colourful and interesting, but analytically the bare-bones statement of alleged facts in a statement of claim or an indictment will often (but not always) satisfy the requirements of a 'story'.[28] Indeed the element of configuration or connectedness that make this account into a story is that the events narrated amount to a legally significant action, such as a murder.

Situation A situation is a state of affairs at a given moment of time. An account of a situation is like a snapshot or a picture. It is a configuration, but neither chronological sequence nor change are necessary ingredients. The distinction between 'situation' and 'story' is important in law, because the law is often concerned with momentary or static states of affairs. For example, someone may be responsible for a car with defective brakes or driving without a licence or owning a factory that violates Health and Safety Regulations irrespective of how the state of affairs came about.[29] Again, a plea in mitigation may focus wholly or in part on the situation of the defendant at the time of sentence and his or her likely future behaviour, without regard to his version of the story of the crime. Stories and descriptions of states of affairs have some shared features; but there are also important differences. However, most of what I have to say about stories in this context applies *pari passu* to descriptions of situations.

Scene, scenario, context Advocates often talk in terms of 'setting the scene', 'developing a scenario', 'painting the canvas', and the like.[30] Sometimes what is meant is covered by or overlaps with the notions of 'story' and 'situation', as they were defined above. However, such talk typically suggests something additional in the way of 'background' or 'contextual' elements which are not essential parts of the story or situation, but which may nevertheless be helpful in understanding or grasping it. In fiction or drama or painting it is often difficult, if not impossible, to distinguish sharply between background and foreground, between scene and scenario, between context and substance. Legal argument on questions of law and of fact is supposedly characterized by strict and generally well-understood criteria of relevance which provide a basis for such distinctions.[31] One hypothesis, which we shall explore later, is that one function of narrative in advocacy is to allow in much more by way of context and background than is technically permitted in explicit argument.

Theme 'Theme' is another term that is used ambiguously in the literature on advocacy. Sometimes it is used to refer to the overall characterization of the situation or story or some element of it that appeals to a popular stereotype. For example: 'This is an example of a grasping landlord exploiting a helpless tenant'; or 'This is a case of property developers needlessly desecrating the countryside.' Another, more precise usage, which is useful in the present context, refers to any element that is sufficiently important to deserve emphasis by repetition. An English barrister gives a vivid account of what he calls 'the mantra', as follows:

> In almost all cases there will be a key factor which has played a dominant role in the case from your point of view. It may be 'stupidity', 'fear', 'greed', 'jealousy', 'selfishness'. Pick your word, inject it into your opening. Put it on a separate piece of paper. Repetition will have a lasting effect. If you have hit the right note and have repeated it often enough, it will echo in the Jury's mind when they retire. It will be the voice of the 13th Juror. Try to hit the note as soon as possible in opening.[32]

Thelema A constant refrain of manuals on advocacy is the importance of winning the trust and sympathy of the tribunal and of providing them with the means of reaching the result you want: '[A]im from the outset to capture and keep the sympathy of your audience.'[33] 'Aim to be the honest guide.'[34] 'You have got to be trusted.'[35] 'Maintain your status.'[36] 'Show them the way home.'[37] These are just some of such precepts set out in a recent introduction to *Advocacy at the Bar*. Such advice, typically presented in the form of discrete precepts, is usefully encapsulated by an American judge in a single concept:

> Thelema is a generic term denoting the universe of things which can combine to create, in judge or jury, the desire to help. I pick an unknown word, which can precisely be defined without pruning away the semantic accumulations of similar words, such as; favor, appeal, sympathy, motive, beneficence, empathy and the like. The meaning of thelema, in Greek, is all of these things.[38]

Presentation and argument I suggested earlier that the advocate's role in court is less problematic than that of other legal actors. It is to persuade this tribunal to decide in this case in favour of his or her client. It does not follow that the job is either simple or easy. In a contested trial it can be extremely complex, involving multiple tasks or sub-roles. In the popular metaphor of drama, the advocate may have to combine the roles of producer, stage-manager, actor, narrator and even, within limits, script-writer. In appellate cases and pleas in mitigation there are fewer participants, but the task is not necessarily easier. Indeed, Shapland reports that some barristers consider that 'doing a good mitigation is one of the higher tests of advocacy and is often very much harder to do than to do a successful contested fight.'[39] In so far as adjudicators are meant to decide on rational grounds, the task of the advocate is to persuade by rational means. On this view, the role of the advocate is to *present an argument* and that is implicitly recognized both in the notion of 'the theory of the case' and in the key role accorded to it in organizing and guiding the advocate's performance. However, especially in contested trials, the argument is not presented solely in terms of explicit argumentation. The story of a case is not merely told in the speeches of counsel: the evidence is typically presented by a succession of witnesses through direct examination, cross-examination and re-examination. Sometimes witnesses are allowed to 'narrate' their testimony, but often they are confined to answering questions. Some complain that they were prevented from telling their story.[40] In disputes on points of law the advocate has a much more straightforward role in presenting explicit argumentation, but even then part of the argument may proceed by question and answer. Similarly pleas in mitigation may involve not only a speech but also testimony and comments on written reports (such as social enquiry reports, medical reports, antecedent reports).[41]

In the present context this has a two-fold significance. First, an advocate's 'argument' may be more or less implicit and may have to be reconstructed from material that has been presented to the court. Secondly, the notion of argument needs to be distinguished from the manner and style of its presentation. Manuals of advocacy tend to devote far more attention to presentation than to construction of cogent arguments.[42] They emphasize the importance of attracting and retaining attention; of being clear, comprehensible and succinct; of body language and other non-verbal communication and of all that is encompassed by the notions of theme and thelema. There is, as we all know, much more to the art of persuasion than making logically cogent arguments. Clearly stories have a role to play in arousing interest, in maintaining attention, in winning thelema and in setting the context for argument. But, one may ask, what role, if any, do they play in *rational* persuasion? And, closely related to this, by what standards are we to determine the legitimacy or otherwise of the uses of narrative in advocacy?[43]

We have seen that not all arguments by advocates involve explicit story-telling. However, it is generally thought that story-telling is indeed a central skill of advocacy in respect of each of the three standard tasks with which we are concerned. Thus in a contested trial on disputed facts the prosecution is typically required, and the defence has the opportunity, to outline their respective 'cases' and very often this consists of presenting the facts in narrative form. At later stages in the trial counsel for each side may re-tell the story, or part of it, directly or have it told through witnesses. It is commonly said that in contested trials in the adversary system juries have either to choose between two competing stories or to construct a third from what has been presented to them.[44] In many criminal trials the defence takes the form of attacking or casting doubt on the prosecution 'story' without offering an alternative account.

Less obviously, narrative is recognized to be of critical importance in appellate advocacy (or other cases involving questions of law). 'The statement of facts is the heart' is a well-known dictum. Perhaps the classic statement is by John W. Davis, a highly respected leader of the Bar in the United States: '(I)n an appellate court, the statement of the facts is not merely a part of the argument, it is more often than not the argument itself.'[45] The precise meaning and significance of such precepts will have to be considered in some detail.

The role of stories in pleas in mitigation is recognized to be more problematic. Officially the prosecution's story has already been accepted and cannot openly be challenged. Where the accused has pleaded not guilty and has been convicted, he/she has already had an opportunity to tell his/her story and it has been rejected. The plea in mitigation has to be made in the context of an already defined version of what happened. Some mitigating factors may gloss or supplement the existing story, but others may relate to 'extraneous' matters such as the accused's past record, his present attitudes or situation and the likelihood of repetition of the offence. Where, however, the accused has pleaded guilty the situation is rather different. Although the truth of the prosecutor's allegations is acknowledged, it has only been in bare-bones form. The accused has not yet had a chance to present his/her version to the court and may wish to do so. While the truth of the charge(s) may not be directly challenged, there is generally some scope for putting the story in a different light by re-telling all or part of it in person or through the advocate.

Thus it is claimed that stories feature in all three kinds of advocacy, though with differing degrees of frequency and importance. However, it cannot be assumed that their role in each context is identical. Let us, then, look at some of these claims in more detail.

Arguments about Questions of Law: Stating the Facts

On the orthodox view a contested question of law involves a disagreement about the *general* scope of a rule or norm or principle (interpretation) or whether a *particular* set of facts fits within it (application). By convention, an argument about an issue of law is conducted on the basis that the facts are given – it proceeds *as if* the facts are true. Conversely, an argument about a disputed issue of fact proceeds *as if* the applicable law is settled. Both legal theory and legal practice recognize that these conventional distinctions are not unproblematic.

If in an argument about interpretation or application of law the facts are treated as given, what are we to make of the claim that the statement of the facts is 'not merely a part of the argument, it is more often than not the argument itself'?[46] The best-known, and probably the most theoretically sophisticated, explanation was advanced by Karl Llewellyn:

> It is trite that it is in the statement of facts that the advocate has his first, best, and most precious access to the court's attention. The court does not know the facts, and it wants to. It is trite among good advocates, that the statement of the facts can, and should, in the very process of statement, frame the legal issue, and can, and should, simultaneously produce the conviction that there is only one sound result. It is as yet less generally perceived as a conscious matter that the *pattern* of the facts as stated must be a *simple* pattern, with its lines of simplicity never lost under detail: else attention wanders, or (which is as bad) the effect is submerged in the court's effort to follow the presentation or to organize the material for itself.[47]

This explanation contains at least three elements: securing the court's attention; framing the issue; and producing conviction. In the context of Llewellyn's wider theory of appellate judging and advocacy, there are two other points. First, he makes it clear that he considers that skilful statement of the facts is an element of *good* advocacy in the sense that it is legitimate and ethical and a hallmark of excellence. Llewellyn was much concerned with the ethics of advocacy and he was careful to distinguish those techniques which were, in his view, clearly legitimate from those which were illegitimate or of dubious legitimacy.[48] Secondly, Llewellyn maintained that what constituted a good argument by an advocate (on questions of law) and a good justification by a judge are to be evaluated by the same criteria. The role of an advocate is to advance the best justification for a decision. The statement of facts by the judge as much as by the advocate is (part of) the 'heart' of the argument.[49]

Let us, for the sake of simplicity, treat some elements of Llewellyn's theory as uncontentious. We can accept that it is both legitimate and important for an advocate to seek to secure the attention and interest of the court. We are not concerned here with examples of techniques of advocacy that Llewellyn would treat as clearly illegitimate, such as lying, deliberately misleading the court, inventing facts, or adopting diversionary or consciously obfuscatory tactics.[50] Our concern is with excellence, not just with effectiveness. Finally, let us proceed on the basis that there is at least a sufficient overlap between standards of excellence in argument, by judges and advocates, to justify looking at examples of statements of facts in reported judgments.[51] This is convenient, because texts of reported judgments are more accessible, extensive and familiar than verbatim reports of appellate arguments by advocates.[52]

If these points are accepted, at least two aspects of Llewellyn's explanation require clarification. What is the role of the statement of facts in framing the issues? And, why is the statement of facts considered so important in producing conviction about the answer to a question of law? The answers to both questions depend on one's view of the relationship between the general and the particular in legal argument in the common law tradition. Llewellyn's answer to the first question looks like a restatement of a familiar and orthodox position. His answer to the second has occasioned both puzzlement and controversy among jurists.

Llewellyn's position on the first question can be restated as follows:[53] it is a general principle of common law adjudication, subject only to a few exceptions, that courts will decide only questions arising out of actual disputes. Generally speaking, they will not give rulings on hypothetical facts or answer questions of law posed in general terms, divorced from some concrete fact-situation. The essence of case-by-case adjudication is to respond to problems that arise from some particular real life situation. Before legal argument begins the issues have been 'limited, sharpened and phrased in advance'.[54] But, as every common lawyer knows, there is considerable leeway as to the precise level of generality at which a question of law is posed and answered. In Llewellyn's terms the issues are *'reasonably but not rigidly clarified in advance'*.[55] The initial statement of facts, by advocate or judge, provides an opportunity for suggesting the categories to be used and the appropriate levels of generality for formulating with greater precision the problem or issue that arises from the facts. How one characterizes the problem depends upon how one characterizes the facts. To put the matter in formal terms: the statement of facts takes the form 'X happened'; the question of law is: If X happens, what is the legal effect? The answer to that question (one usage of the term *ratio decidendi*) takes the form: 'If X, then Y'. X is a common factor linking statement of facts, the question of law, and the applicable rule (the answer to the question of law). How X is characterized is crucial.

Up to this point this looks like a restatement of a familiar and orthodox view of common law reasoning.[56] But Llewellyn introduced a new concept, 'situation sense', which has occasioned a good deal of puzzlement and controversy. Some have adopted the term uncritically, but used it rather loosely; some have viewed it as impenetrably obscure or meaningless; some have rejected it as introducing an irrational or subjective or metaphysical element into theories of legal reasoning. I have explored some of the problems associated with Llewellyn's account of 'situation sense' elsewhere. Here I wish to concentrate on its function in respect of the claim that 'The Statement of Facts is the Heart'.[57]

What kind of statement of the facts of a case by a Grand Style judge or advocate satisfies the requirement of 'situation sense' and, because of this, 'can produce the conviction that there is only one sound outcome'?[58] The first requirement is that the facts of the particular case are stated in terms of categories that are directly translatable into a recognizable 'type-fact-pattern'.[59] The facts are categorized in such a way as to form a clear example of the situation seen as a *type*. Secondly, the type-fact- situation, so characterized, appeals to 'sense', 'reason' and 'justice' in such a way as to suggest a general solution to the problem raised by the particular case.[60] Factors in the unique story which are likely to arouse sympathy or antipathy – 'the fireside equities' – are filtered out or given a secondary role.[61] Thus X is a constituent in the process of translation from the statement 'X happened' to the statement 'This is a case of type X' and again to the statement 'Whenever X happens, Y ought to happen.'

But, it may be asked, what makes one particular characterization of X appeal to 'sense, reason and justice'? And, why should there be any difference in the persuasiveness or the cogency of an argument by presenting it in the form of a statement of the facts of the particular case rather than explicitly as a formulation of a general fact-pattern or as a rule?

Let us consider three possible ways of answering those questions that represent three different interpretations of the claim that 'the statement of the facts is the heart'.

The first, and weakest, answer acknowledges that there is no analytical difference in the characterization of X in statements of the kind 'X happened', 'This is a case of type X' and 'Whenever X happens, Y ought to happen.'[62] However, the advocate who takes care to formulate his statement of the facts in such a way achieves two things: First, a good foundation for the argument is laid at the very beginning. What is initially implicit can be made explicit by subsequent elaboration. Secondly, it ensures that there is complete harmony between the initial statement of the facts and the general proposition of law that is being argued for. The facts and the rule are not merely consistent; analytically they are the same. On this interpretation, the precepts we have been considering contain sound advice in exaggerated form. For the statement of facts is not 'the heart' of the argument, nor is it 'the argument itself'; rather it anticipates one crucial step in the argument, the formulation of the applicable rule.

A second interpretation is that the statement of facts allows implicit appeals to values or 'sense' (whatever that is) in a way which would be either less effective or perhaps even impermissible if it were done explicitly at a general level. Gerald Lopez puts the matter thus:

> While debate over what the facts mean (argument) is encouraged to be more explicitly persuasive than debate over what the facts are (story-telling), argument as an act of persuasion is constrained in most cultures in a way that story-telling is not ... stories by their very nature can appeal to what is, by convention, still taboo in a culture. Because facts themselves capture and reflect values, what cannot be argued explicitly can be sneaked into a story. Indeed the genius of story-telling as an act of persuasion is that it buries arguments in the facts. Stories can thereby circumvent the existing constraints on the meaning that can be given to the facts as found. Put differently, relevance is for a story a much looser standard than it is for argument.[63]

This is a perceptive account of some reasons why advocates consider the statement of facts to have an important role in the task of persuasion. But is this consistent with an ideal of argument that is legitimate, ethical, fair? Lopez acknowledges that 'this sounds very much like hypocrisy ... Yet in some ways hypocrisy is necessary to civilized life.'[64] On the other hand, jurists of an earlier generation have tended to emphasize articulation, explicitness and openness as important safeguards of honest and wise argument. 'Covert tools are never reliable tools', wrote Karl Llewellynn.[65] John Henry Wigmore, as we shall see, emphasized the utility of articulation of the implicit as a check on the validity and cogency of arguments about evidence.

A third interpretation makes a positive virtue of appeals to implicit, unexpressed or dimly perceived factors. In this view, far from being a matter of 'sneaking in' such factors or of licensed hypocrisy, narrative has a positive role to play in generating a pressure towards 'the inexpressible, the inexplicable'.[66] The most articulate proponent of the role of the inarticulate in legal argument is James Boyd White, a professor of both literature and law, who has developed a sophisticated, if somewhat idealized, view of the role of narrative in legal discourse.[67] Others talk in terms of appealing to intuition, emotion, or the imagination. Some rationalize this in terms of giving a legitimate place to appeals to 'irrational' considerations; others advance this in terms of differing conceptions of rationality.

Even Llewellyn's views fit this third interpretation. His glorification of the common law tradition and of the Grand Style of judging is based in part on the idea of courts being responsive to the nuances of complexity and change through a special sensitivity to facts that reaches beyond existing legal categories. I have argued elsewhere that one can only make sense of 'situation sense' by including in it some notion of 'judgment' that outruns our capacity to construct articulate and logical justifications for what is felt to be 'just' or 'wise' or 'to make sense'.[68] It is beyond the scope of this paper to explore whether Llewellyn can be rescued from charges of inconsistency in giving a place to such factors while emphasizing the value of articulation and explicit rationalization. Suffice it to say here that I believe that such a defence is possible because, in my view, there is no necessary incompatibility between rational reconstruction and giving play to the legal imagination in normative theories of advocacy and judging.

The judge as advocate: Lord Denning as hero and as deviant

A brief consideration of two of Lord Denning's most famous judgments may cast further light on the notion that 'the statement of facts is the heart'. No English judge in modern times has so regularly and so openly observed the precept that the manner of stating the facts of a particular case has a significant role to play in justifying decisions in disputed questions of law of general significance. His statements of fact have been highly praised, sharply criticized and treated with uneasy ambivalence by fellow judges and by academic commentators.[69]

In *Candler* v. *Crane Christmas* Denning MR (as he then was)[70] delivered a dissenting judgment which presented an interpretation of the duty of care that was, in due course, accepted by the House of Lords almost exactly in terms of his formulation.[71] It is widely regarded as a great dissent by a Grand Style judge that made legal history. The most famous passage in the judgment reads as follows:

> ... Did the defendants owe a duty of care to the plaintiff? If the matter were free from authority, I should have said that they clearly did owe a duty of care to him. *They were professional accountants who prepared and put before him these accounts, knowing that he was going to be guided by them in making an investment in the company. On the faith of those accounts he did make the investment, whereas, if the accounts had been carefully prepared, he would not have made the investment at all. The result is that he has lost his money.* In the circumstances, had he not every right to rely on the accounts being prepared with proper care, and is he not entitled to redress from the defendants on whom he relied? I say he is, and I would apply to the present case the words of Knight Bruce LJ in *Slim* v. *Croucher* (1860) 1 DeG. F. & J. 518, an analogous case ninety years ago, where he said: 'A country whose administration of justice did not afford redress in a case of the present description would not be in a state of civilisation' [italics supplied].[72]

This is widely regarded as an example of Lord Denning at his best. Before considering why this should be so, it is worth noting that this passage does not come at the start of the judgment. It contains Denning's third formulation of the facts of the case. The judgment begins with a statement of the facts in a single paragraph.[73] This is quite succinct, but more detailed than the version in the passage quoted above. It is a summary statement which through its language and emphasis seems calculated to win sympathy for the plaintiff. Someone reading it for the first time should have no difficulty in predicting the judge's decision; they may also find it quite persuasive. However, its ostensible function is to lay a foundation for a statement of the issue; for those facts 'raise a point of law of much importance'.[74] After framing the issue, Lord Denning proceeds to a much longer restatement of the facts in a narrative that takes up more than two full pages of the *All England Law Reports* (about 1,500 words). This very careful and detailed examination contains few 'rhetorical' flourishes; its main function is to make clear that in this case the accounts were intended to induce the plaintiff to invest in the company; and that the plaintiff's loss was 'caused' by this negligent advice. Few 'fireside equities' sneak into this detailed narrative. Its primary function is to establish that there is no doubt that this case does in fact constitute a clear example falling within the general rule for which Lord Denning is arguing.

Lord Denning next considers the decision in the court below, before restating the question of law ('of general importance')[75] to which this case gives rise. The passage quoted above comes at the start of his consideration of 'the law' on the matter and the authorities which, allegedly, support the defendant. His statement of the facts here is a third re-formulation. It is explicitly part of an argument, the gist of which might be rendered: 'Were it not for authority, I should have said that reason and justice and sense dictate that a duty of care exists in this kind of situation.'

He then turns to consider 'Authority'. Professor Patrick Atiyah has observed: 'When Lord Denning begins like this, one can be sure that he will then analyse the authorities in order to come out where he wants to, and this case was no exception. Skilful examination of the cases showed them to be either distinguishable, or else inconsistent with the principles of *Donoghue* v. *Stevenson*.'[76] This, however, involved a bold reinterpretation of authority, rather than a 'timorous' analysis of the cases,[77] 'not designed to lead to a pre-determined conclusion, but to see what the cases had originally stood for'.[78] In this view, creative interpretation was required in order to ensure that reason and sense prevailed over a settled view of authority. Despite his hints at impropriety, Atiyah calls this 'one of the great dissenting judgments in the history of the common law'.[79]

What is the basis of this claim to greatness? The power of the argument lies not in any direct appeal to emotion through 'sneaking in fireside equities' or choosing emotionally laden terms. Rather it is persuasive because it suggests grounds both for extending and limiting liability in a type of situation which has the following elements: *reliance* by a *non-expert* on a *professional* in a relationship of *proximity* in which the professional gives *negligent* advice which he *expected* and *intended* would be followed by this plaintiff. The element of reliance links this to a general principle that is widely accepted as justifying liability; but, equally important, the other factors (professional, non-expert, negligence, proximity, expectation, loss) *limit* the scope of the situation and close the door on 'the floodgates argument' which had worried 'the timorous souls'. In short, Denning's formulation characterized and circumscribed the type of situation in which justice, reason and sense suggested that there should be liability. Most of the rest of the judgment is taken up with interpreting (or re-interpreting) earlier precedents and setting strict limits to the scope of the doctrine that he is advocating.

At first sight, Lord Denning's highly persuasive categorization of the facts in his third formulation neither violates any taboos nor expresses in particulars what is inexpressible at a general level. Rather it introduces and neatly encapsulates in simple and concrete terms the gist of an argument that is thereafter explicitly elaborated at a general level. On this reading, it seems to fit the first interpretation of 'the statement of facts is the heart', better than those of Lopez and White. This, I think, is too simple. For, I shall argue that, read as a whole, Denning's judgment gains some of its force from factors suggested by the other two interpretations.

In the first place, Denning saw this as a case of a conflict between justice and sense, on the one hand, and authority (as conventionally interpreted) on the other. 'The lawyer who argues from justice has a weak case'; but the lawyer who appeals to justice, sense and reason implicitly through the facts is often very persuasive. By judicious use of thelema and theme (*three* statements of the facts!) Denning's judgment appeals to 'reason, sense and justice' before he ever considers a single precedent. Anyone who doubts that his statements of the facts had a key role to play in his argument should try reading the judgment without these passages. 'Grand Style' or 'creative' or 'innovative' judges typically find themselves in situations in which all or most of the authorities seem to be ranged against them. It is a standard technique for them to use careful statements of the facts of the case at hand as part of their arguments for changing or re-interpreting the law. They tend to be at their most effective when, as in *Candler*, there is a high degree of consensus among 'laymen' as to what would be a just or sensible result in the particular case.

At first sight, *Candler* v. *Crane Christmas* looks unpromising as an example of a judge or advocate conveying more through a statement of the particular facts than can be captured by a purely abstract statement. For surely part of Denning's achievement was to identify and articulate the ingredients (professional and non-expert; proximity; reliance etc.) that constitute the new rule in an acceptable way. Undoubtedly that is part of the appeal of the famous passage. However, I wish to suggest that this is a good example of the appeal of the particular. For something *is* changed if we translate Denning's categorization of the facts into a statement of a general rule, as follows: 'A duty of care exists whenever a professional accountant prepares and puts before [a layman] accounts, knowing that he is going to be guided by them in making an investment and on the faith of these accounts he makes the investment and as a result he loses his money.' Analytically no change has been made in the course of translation. 'X happened and Y ought to happen' has become 'Whenever X happens, Y ought to happen.' But, whereas the particular statement seems unexceptionable, the general statement of the rule is likely to make lawyers uneasy. In this instance, the reason is clear. The formulation of the rule is too narrow: surely the rule, even in 1951, was not to be restricted to preparation of accounts for the purposes of investment by professional accountants. What of other professionals? Other forms of statement? Other purposes? Other kinds of loss? How far should the duty of care extend? In *Candler* Denning persuasively argued that there should be liability in this case, he suggested a general rationale for liability, and indicated some limits to the scope of the rule. But he left many details of the precise scope of the rule to be determined in future on a case-by-case basis. In an important sense, the general rule governing the situation was 'inexpressible' in 1951. For there is a difference between saying, 'This is a clear case of X', and providing a general definition of X.[80]

Miller v. *Jackson* Lord Denning's dissenting judgment in *Candler* v. *Crane Christmas* won almost universal acclaim and made legal history. A much later dissenting judgment, in *Miller* v. *Jackson*, is almost as well known, but represented a partial defeat.[81] The judgment is too long to reproduce here. Some of its flavour and the reasons for its notoriety can be gleaned from the opening paragraph:

> In summer time village cricket is the delight of everyone. Nearly every village has its own cricket field where the young men play and the old men watch. In the village of Lintz in County Durham they have their own ground, where they have played for these last 70 years. They tend it well. The wicket area is well rolled and mown. The outfield is kept short. It has a good club-house for the players and seats for the onlookers. The village team play there on Saturdays and Sundays. They belong to a league, competing with the neighbouring villages. On other evenings after work they practise while the light lasts. Yet now after these 70 years a judge of the High Court has ordered that they must not play there any more. He has issued an injunction to stop them. He has done it at the instance of a newcomer who is no lover of cricket. This newcomer has built, or has had built for him, a house on the edge of the cricket ground which four years ago was a field where cattle grazed. The animals did not mind the cricket. But now this adjoining field has been turned into a housing estate. The newcomer has bought one of the houses on the edge of the cricket ground. No doubt the open space was a selling point. Now he complains that, when a batsman hits a six, the ball has been known to land in his garden or on or near his house. His wife has got so upset about it that they always go out at weekends. They do not go into the garden when cricket is being played. They say that this is intolerable. So they asked the judge to stop the cricket being played. And the judge, much against his will, has felt that he must order the cricket to be stopped; with the consequences, I suppose, that the Lintz Cricket Club will disappear. The cricket ground will be turned to some other use. I expect for more houses or a factory. The young men will turn to other things instead of cricket. The whole village will be much the poorer. And all this because of a newcomer who has just bought a house there next to the cricket ground.[82]

When I ask first-year students to read *Miller* v. *Jackson* as an example of Lord Denning's later writing, it stimulates a mixed reaction. Nearly everyone finds it enjoyable and interesting. Some find it persuasive, others think that it is 'over the top' or in some undefined way unjudge-like. Some see it as exhibiting prejudice or bias – in favour of cricket, against the Millers personally, or against property developers, or private property. When I point out that Lord Denning seems to have invented some facts (e.g. 'the animals did not mind the cricket'), omitted relevant facts (e.g. the Millers had a child,[83] they were not alone in complaining), and was guilty of exaggeration ('village cricket is the delight of everyone' – including the Millers?), most students agree that this is inappropriate behaviour for a judge. Would it be inappropriate for a barrister? Opinion tends to be divided. When I point out that in the course of the judgment he makes an elementary misuse of statistics,[84] they agree that invalid arguments are inappropriate for advocates as well as judges.

What of those who find it persuasive? The story as he tells it, does suggest that the Millers were being unreasonable, whereas the cricketers had in every respect behaved reasonably. Moreover, the Millers were newcomers who were trying to put a stop to a popular community activity that had been going on for seventy years ('newcomer' used five times; 'seventy years' six times – a clear example of 'theme');[85] 'thelema' is apparent too – is not the first paragraph alone calculated to win the sympathy of cricket-lovers, environmentalists, conservationists, ecologists, and lovers of tradition?[86]

There are some similarities between *Miller* v. *Jackson* and *Candler* v. *Crane Christmas*: in each Lord Denning perceived a conflict between what he calls 'the merits' and outmoded precedent;[87] in each he used his statement of facts as a foundation for framing the issue, for winning sympathy for one side and for weakening the force of prior adverse precedents before dealing with them explicitly. In each case he pinpointed the elements which provided a rationale for what he believed to be the right result. Reliance, proximity, negligence in *Candler*; long-established community activity; reasonable steps taken to minimize risk to neighbours; private individual purchasing adjoining property with notice of the activity and of the risk. However, whereas his performance in *Candler* is masterly, there are some weaknesses in *Miller*. It is not so much that in *Miller* he too overtly assumed the mantle of advocate, as that his argument is spoiled by poor advocacy. This is not merely because of the lapses which are even less acceptable from a judge than an advocate: inventing facts; not mentioning an awkward fact;[88] misusing statistics; and giving an impression of being unfair to the opposition. Nor is the essential weakness an unsuccessful striving after literary effect (law students, I find, are amused but not impressed). Rather he fails to make the strongest possible argument. There are two crucial weaknesses: first, he fails to meet head-on the main argument of substance (as opposed to authority) for the other side; is it reasonable for people living next to a sports field, whether newcomers or not, to bear the risk of injury to person or damage to property caused by cricket balls? Cumming-Bruce LJ found a *via media* by awarding damages, but refusing an injunction to prevent the playing of cricket.[89] Secondly, Lord Denning became so immersed in the particulars of the Millers' story, that he failed to step back sufficiently to satisfy Llewellyn's ideal of a Grand Style judge who categorizes the case in terms of the situation seen as a type in a way that suggests a solution. This could have been done along the following lines: 'This is a case of a long-established popular community activity which, despite all reasonable efforts to minimize risk of injury or damage to people and property on the adjoining land, cannot continue without an element of such risk.' One solution is to allow the activity to continue, but to make those involved bear the risk of damage.[90] This was in fact the final result.

Statement of facts

To conclude: the claim that 'the statement of facts is the heart' in arguments about questions of law is an example of an exaggerated statement that contains an important core of truth. It is exaggerated in two different ways: first, many statements of 'the facts' by advocates, as well as judges, are deliberately non-argumentative: that is to say that they set out to be 'impartial' or 'unbiased' or 'dispassionate'. Most judgments aspire to such relative neutrality; in proceedings by way of case stated a court will attempt a formulation which fairly raises the issue to be resolved by a superior court; in some jurisdictions both sides will agree on a statement of the facts; even some of Lord Denning's most colourful openings are designed to dramatize what he sees as a genuine dilemma rather than to lay the foundation for an argument justifying his decision one way or the other.[91] Of course, a skilful reader may be able to identify hidden clues or unconscious biases in the language of a purportedly fair statement of the facts. But that is very different from claiming that such a narrative is the heart of the argument.

The precept is exaggerated in another respect: even when narrative statements are clearly part of an advocate's argument or a judge's justification, it is wholly exceptional for this to be the main part of the argument, let alone 'the argument itself'. Legal argument typically consists of a mixture of authority reasons and substantive reasons.[92] Even those theories of legal reasoning which discount the importance of pure fiat – of authority unglossed by interpretation that spills over into 'substance' – would treat as wholly exceptional a case in which the gist of the argument is that the facts speak for themselves. At the very least, explicit argumentation will seize on one or two elements in the story for emphasis as key points in the argument – for instance, as a ground for distinguishing this case from others or for proceeding by analogy or for grounding a general reason of principle or policy. The facts at most are a component of the argument.

The analysis of *Candler* v. *Crane Christmas* and *Miller* v. *Jackson* suggests a further point. For these are examples of a judge using narrative to ground an argument appealing to 'substance' in a context where arguments based on authority appear to support an opposite conclusion. The judge who justifies his decision entirely or mainly on 'authority reasons' is likely to have less need to use his statement of the facts as an important part of his argument. In short, narrative is more likely to be important for advocates and judges who are concerned to attack, undermine or re-interpret authority (whether precedent or statute) than for those who can invoke it in a more straightforward fashion.

However, the precept contains an important core of truth. This goes much further than the mere claim that how the story of the particular case is told plays an important part in strengthening substantive reasons in some arguments on questions of law in path-breaking or historic or particularly hard cases. Rather my suggestion is that narrative can play many different kinds of roles in legal arguments.

The three different interpretations of the precept illustrate three such roles, without in any way claiming to be exhaustive. A statement of the facts of a case may do little more than anticipate in concrete terms what will later be explicitly formulated as a general rule: 'The facts are X' precedes 'wherever X, then Y.' Or, a formulation of the facts may appeal to 'reason, sense or justice' in a way that is rhetorically more persuasive than overt general argument.[93] The formulation in *Candler* appealed in a way that could be rationalized at a general level, but it was a statement of a clear example falling within a less clear general rule. The formulation in *Miller v. Jackson* involved some dubious appeals to 'fireside equities' – the particular plaintiffs were depicted as unattractive and unreasonable. In both of these cases narrative accounts of the facts of the particular case were being used, *inter alia*, as indirect means of weakening the force of adverse precedents. None of this is incompatible with the claim that focusing on the particular may also be a way of capturing 'the unexpressed' or 'the inexpressible'. *Candler* is an example of a common law judge in effect saying: 'This is clearly a case in which there should be a remedy. It is neither necessary nor desirable for me to delineate precisely the bounds of the general rule which should govern this and analogous kinds of situations.' The appeal of a case-by-case method of proceeding has appealed to most common lawyers and some philosophers over the centuries.[94] Narratology draws attention to the significance of the way in which we describe or characterize particular particulars.

Disputed Questions of Fact: Holism and Atomism in Arguments about Evidence

The distinction between questions of law and questions of fact is problematic at the level of analysis; it has important consequences in legal practice. Contests about facts are governed by different procedures, involve different actors and, in contested jury trials, multiple audiences – for the respective functions of judge and jury are governed by quite elaborate rules. In our legal culture decisions on questions of law are generally required to be supported by public justifications, whereas there is no such general requirement for determinations of fact. Thus, lawyers have good reason for treating argumentation about questions of law and questions of fact as quite different kinds of operation. Conventional legal discourse adds a further twist: when lawyers talk of 'appellate cases' this generally implies that the issues are related to questions of law; when they talk of 'trial practice', it is assumed that typically what is at stake is a dispute about the facts.[95] Such talk sometimes masks a much more complex reality.

This artificial separation of two intimately related spheres of legal discourse is reflected in secondary treatments. The massive theoretical literature on 'legal reasoning' deals almost exclusively with reasoning about disputed questions of law, sometimes without any acknowledgement that legal practice involves arguments about several other kinds of issues.[96] Discussions of reasoning about questions of fact – exemplified by recent debates about probabilities and proof – are largely dealt with in a separate body of literature, which belongs to a different intellectual tradition.[97] This artificial segregation has been maintained by a kind of fiction: just as arguments about questions of law proceed as if the facts are given, so arguments about questions of fact proceed as if the law is settled.

The complexities of the relations between narrative and argument are rather vividly exemplified in theorizing about judicial proof. Some of these can be illustrated by looking briefly at three apparently contrasting perspectives on the subject: Wigmore's account of the logic of proof;[98] a recent book entitled *Reconstructing Reality in the Courtroom*;[99] and the thesis, advanced by Abu Hareira and others, that many judgments about the evaluation of evidence are 'holistic' rather than 'atomistic' – and properly so.[100]

The great American Evidence scholar, John Henry Wigmore, developed a 'Science of Judicial Proof as given by Logic, Psychology and General Experience'. In his view there are two methods of organizing and analysing a mixed mass of evidence, 'such as is commonly presented in a judicial enquiry': the Narrative Method and the Chart Method:[101] 'The Narrative Method rearranges all the evidential data under some scheme of logical sequence, narrating at each point the related evidential facts, at each fact noting the subordinate evidence on which it depends; concluding with a narrative summary.'[102]

The Chart Method, which was Wigmore's own invention, involves restating the arguments about the evidence as a whole in the form of a list of propositions and depicting the relations between all the propositions in a single chart. The method is in essence an elaborate and rigorous form of rational reconstruction (or construction) of arguments in a manner which involves articulating every step of an argument and mapping the relations between all the parts.

Questions about the validity and the uses and limitations of Wigmore's Chart Method have been extensively canvassed elsewhere.[103] What is interesting in the present context is that Wigmore saw the Narrative and Chart Methods as alternatives, the former being in effect a more primitive and less rigorous version of the latter. 'The Narrative Method ... is the simpler method, more readily used by the beginner, and more akin to the usual way of describing an evidence problem.'[104] The Chart Method, by contrast, 'may not commend itself to some types of mind. It is the only true and scientific method.'[105] Wigmore made two main claims for the Chart Method: it enables one to see an argument as a whole and, through a process of disciplined articulation, it makes it easier to spot fallacies, unwarranted jumps and other weaknesses in a complex argument.

Wigmore saw narrative as no more than a rather casual form of analysis, organization and presentation of evidence. Story-construction and story-telling had no significant role to play in his 'Science of Proof'. In sharp contrast, the most extensive modern account of the role of narrative in contested trials maintains that 'The American criminal trial is organised around story-telling'.[106] Bennett and Feldman's *Reconstructing Reality in the Courtroom* explores in great detail and with some sophistication the theme of presenting and interpreting competing versions of reality in jury trials. The authors conducted a number of empirical studies about how cases are presented to and assessed by jurors in criminal trials in the United States. The underlying theory is based on the work of ethnomethodologists, such as Garfinkel, Cicourel and Saks, and on the ideas of Kenneth Burke.

Bennett and Feldman argue that the advocates and jurors typically use stories to organize the otherwise disjointed bits of evidence that are presented to them. This helps them to select, interpret and assess what would otherwise be a confusing and unmanageable mass of data. 'Stories organize information in ways that help the listener to perform three interpretive functions': to locate the central action of the story; to construct inferences about the relationships among the elements surrounding the central action; and to test the story as a whole for 'internal consistency and descriptive adequacy or completeness'.[107] The authors suggest that Kenneth Burke's 'pentad' of elements of social action – scene, act, agent, agency and purpose – provides an appropriate standard in this context: this general social frame of reference helps us to organize and evaluate the relations between the five elements in terms of their completeness and consistency.[108] Bennett and Feldman state their main conclusion as follows:

> Judgments based on story construction are, in many important respects, unverifiable in terms of the reality of the situation that the story represents. Adjudicators judge the plausibility of a story according to certain structural relations among symbols in the story. Although documentary evidence may exist to support most symbolizations in a story, both the teller and the interpreter of a story *always* have some margin of control over the definition of certain key symbols. Therefore, stories are judged in terms of a combination of the documentary or 'empirical' warrants for symbols and the internal structural relations among the collection of symbols presented in the story. In other words, we judge stories according to a dual standard of 'did it happen that way?' and 'could it have happened that way?' In no case can 'empirical' standards alone produce a completely adequate judgment, and, there are cases in which the structural characteristics are far and away the critical elements in determining the truth of a story.[109]

In this account stories perform several functions: they serve as aids to *selecting* from a superfluity of information and to *filling in gaps* in that information; they are a vehicle for introducing judgments of value; and, above all, they provide essential *frames of reference* for organizing, evaluating and interpreting evidence. In this view, empirical evidence and logical analysis have a secondary role as checks on completeness and consistency. To put the matter simply in terms of our lexicon: Wigmore subordinates story to theory in his account of the logic of proof; Bennett and Feldman appear to subordinate theory (and even evidence) to story in their account of reconstruction of reality in the courtroom by advocates and triers of fact.[110]

A similar tension between narrative and argument, story and theory, underlies a new debate between 'holists' and 'atomists' in the theory of proof. In the Anglo-American tradition of discourse about evidence, by far the predominant view of what is involved in organizing and evaluating judicial evidence has been 'atomistic'. That is to say, the construction and criticism of arguments about evidence, involves logical analysis of the relations between individuated items of evidence. In the extensive debate between Baconians led by Jonathan

Cohen, and Bayesians (and other 'Pascalians'),[111] both sides have assumed that it is (in principle) possible and meaningful to combine judgments of probability (conjunction, corroboration, convergence), to construct 'chains of inferences' and to evaluate evidentiary propositions. What has been at issue has been questions as to what are the applicable criteria for making and evaluating judgments about probabilities in the context of judicial proof.

Recently, however, M. A. Abu Hareira suggested that much evaluation of evidence is, and is rightly, configurative or holistic. For example, in evaluating the probative force of a 'mass of evidence' we do not and should not proceed by analysing the mass into separate 'items' and giving each item an independent probative value. Rather we consider the mass as a whole, as a gestalt or configuration, and assess its total probative force or plausibility in a manner which defies analysis.[112]

A rather different version of 'holism' is summarized by Peter Tillers as follows:

> For our own part, we are inclined to believe that the effort to state systematically and comprehensively the premises on which our inferences rest may produce serious distortions in the factfinding process, in part (but only in part) because such systematic statement obscures the complex mental processes that we actually employ and should employ to evaluate evidence. It is not true that we can say all we know, and the effort to say more than we are able to say is likely to diminish our knowledge and our ability to use it. In our daily lives, we confidently rely on innumerable premises and beliefs that we often cannot articulate or explain, but our inability to express these premises and beliefs does not necessarily make them illegitimate or unreliable. The same may be true of many beliefs relied upon in the assessment of evidence by a trier of fact in the courtroom.[113]

These brief accounts of some very different perspectives on judicial evidence illustrate how questions about the role of narrative and stories are of considerable significance in this context. They should also serve as a warning against over-simplification. It is beyond the scope of this essay to explore these issues in detail. But it is relevant to the argument in the next section to outline a position that suggests, *inter alia*, that these apparently different perspectives have rather more in common than appears on the surface. Each contains elements lacking in the others. The 'holistic' approaches of Tillers and Abu Hareira have yet to be presented in the form of rounded theories. Each, in different ways, usefully directs attention to the relevance of fundamental philosophical issues about conceptions of 'rationality' and the place of notions such as configuration and coherence in rational argument. But we await a fully developed 'holistic' account of the role of analytical techniques in the evaluation of evidence.[114]

Wigmore's Chart Method is open to the criticism that, by failing to develop the notions of 'theory' and 'story', he gives the impression that his 'Chart Method' involves an almost mechanical application of ordinary principles of inductive logic. Anyone who tries to apply the method to a mass of evidence soon learns that Wigmore's theory provides almost no guidance in making *strategic* choices in constructing or criticizing a complex argument. He had a very crude view of narrative and he was surely mistaken in seeing 'the narrative method' as an alternative rather than as complementary to his method of analysis.

Bennett and Feldman's account has a converse weakness. They exaggerate the importance of stories in trials and underestimate the sophistication of good trial lawyers. Unfortunately they did not pay sufficient attention to the standard accounts by lawyers of how problems of selection, incompleteness and inconsistency are supposed to be tackled. In particular, by ignoring almost entirely such lawyers' notions as facts in issue, materiality, relevance, burdens of proof, presumptions and, most surprising of all, the advocate's notion of 'the theory of the case', they fail to reach a point where issue is squarely joined with standard legal accounts. Ignoring 'theory' leads them to exaggerate the role of stories in structuring understandings and decisions about disputed facts. Moreover, a Wigmorean can point out that general impressions are no substitute for meticulous detailed analysis in checking stories for consistency, coherence and completeness. Relying on stories to 'fill in gaps' could be interpreted as licensing just such unwarranted jumps and mere speculations that Wigmorean analysis can be used to expose. Finally, perhaps the best way of testing the plausibility of an argument or theory or story is to spell out in detail what precisely is being claimed. One of the best ways of exposing weaknesses in an argument is to articulate clearly what that argument is. This may be the main value of the Chart Method.[115]

All the theories mentioned here accept similar criteria of the credibility or plausibility of a theory or story: it must be compatible with uncontested or established particular facts; it must be internally consistent; it must be coherent; and it must be in conformity with what is variously referred to as 'general experience', 'the common course of events', 'common sense generalizations' or 'the stock of knowledge' in a given society. There may be scope for disagreement about the meaning and role of 'coherence' in such evaluations, and about the relative importance of these various criteria. But all of the views considered are open to interpretation as non-sceptical, cognitivist theories that treat the enterprise as one of enquiring about the correspondence of some version of events with a notionally external reality.[116] In this respect they may be out of tune with some of the more sceptical tendencies of post-modernist thought.[117]

In sketching a perspective that treats these seemingly different perspectives as to some extent convergent or complementary, I do not wish to give a false impression of consensus in this area. There are many unresolved questions and ample scope for genuine disagreements and differences at many levels in the theory of judicial proof. Rather I am suggesting that both narrative and explicit argument are almost bound to have a place in any prescriptive theory about arguing towards, arriving at, justifying and evaluating adjudicative decisions on disputed questions of fact. What precisely are the functions of narratives in this context and what are the proper relations between narrative and argument are open questions. My hunch is that the functions are diverse and the relations complex, but that they are closely analogous to those that we considered in connection with questions of law. My reasons for this are explored in the next section.

Making Sense of the Case-as-a-whole: Law, Fact, Value and Outcome

> [W]e can say that both the history and the tapestry are in this respect like a law case: the lawyer knows that to prove his (or her) case he must not only demonstrate the truth or probability of certain propositions of fact; he must present to the judge or juror a way of looking at the case as a whole that will make sense; and it must 'make sense' not merely as a matter of factual likelihood, but as a predicate to judgment, as a basis for action. While a case can in a technical sense be refuted by disproving one element or another, in practice the lawyer knows that he must do more than that: he must offer the judge or juror an alternative place to stand, another way of making sense of the case as a whole. To do his job, that is, the lawyer must both engage in an accurate retelling of the facts and make his own claim for what they mean.
>
> James Boyd White, *Heracles' Bow*[118]

So far I have followed legal convention by dealing separately with argumentation about questions of law, questions of fact and questions of disposition. The *basis* for the distinctions causes difficulty in legal practice as well as in legal theory, but the distinctions have important practical *consequences* in respect of allocation of functions between participants (e.g. judge and jury), rights of appeal, the doctrine of precedent and other matters.[119] The question arises whether such sharp distinctions make sense from the perspective of narratology or whether they break down within some such concept as the story of a case as a whole. I propose to argue that these differentiations are not merely artificial technicalities within legal discourse; they are relevant in the present context for identifying some differences both within and between stories of (or about) cases. But there is no escaping traditional juristic puzzlement about relations between law, fact and value.

One of the most powerful images in legal history is Holmes's Bad Man, an amoral citizen who is indifferent to the morality of his behaviour, the niceties of legal argument and procedure, or any questions about obligation to obey the law.[120] The Bad Man washes lawyers' discourse in cynical acid in order to arrive at a clear answer to a single selfish question: 'If I do this, what will happen to me?' The Bad Man is concerned only with what the organs of the State will do to him in fact, if he is caught. For him, 'the bottom line' is the outcome of the case. Imagine, for example, a petty criminal with a record of previous convictions, who has been arrested and charged with theft in circumstances in which the law is unclear, the evidence against him is problematic and sentencing practice for this kind of offence is indeterminate or variable. He meets his lawyer and tells her that his main concern is to keep out of jail. From his perspective, decisions whether to contest on the facts or on the law or both or to petition for leniency via a guilty plea are secondary considerations which he may leave to his lawyer.

From the lawyer's point of view there are some tactical choices to be made. The prosecution case is: 'If X, then Y, then Z. This is a case of X, therefore Y, therefore Z.' The defence can contest X and/or Y and/ or Z. What is involved in contesting on the facts, on the law or on sentence is very different in each instance, procedurally and in other ways. This is not just a matter of preparing and presenting three different kinds of argument, possibly to different audiences (judge, jury, magistrates, appellate court). One possibility might be a tacit or open plea-bargain: in exchange for not contesting X or Y, the prosecution (or the court) might agree to a non-custodial sentence, which is the lawyer's primary goal. In considering the case as a whole the lawyer might develop three very different kinds of theories: a theory of the law relating to the type of offence (Y); a theory about the evidence concerning the alleged incident (X); and a theory about mitigating circumstances (Z). While it would be unwise to have radical inconsistencies between these three possible lines of argument (for example to plead alibi in respect of X, and depression in connection with Z – 'my client was elsewhere at the time; he was depressed when he did it'),[121] the three theories could in principle have little or no overlap; in practice they are more likely to fit together as three fully integrated components of a single whole. The three lines of argument are all means to the same end (securing an acquittal or, at least, avoiding a jail sentence) in a single case and can be used to support each other. From the standpoint of the Bad Man's lawyer the distinctions between questions of fact, questions of law and questions of sentence are of practical importance. However, even from her standpoint, these distinctions and the decisions they entail operate within the context of some notion of the case as a whole. Conversely, the Bad Man may not be the only participant who is primarily concerned with the outcome; the prosecutor, in deciding to prosecute,[122] or the jury, in deciding whether to convict, may in practice base their decision on some global judgment about the Bad Man's deserts or the merits of the case rather than on a more differentiated approach that might restrict their role or the factors that they are meant to take into account. For example, the jury may return a 'perverse' or 'protest' verdict one way or the other because they think this law is an ass or that this prosecution should not have been brought or because they have taken against the accused.

How distinctions between law, fact, value and outcome break down in practice is vividly illustrated by Diana Trilling's account of the trial of Jean Harris, who was indicted for murdering her lover, Dr Herman Tarnower.[123] The case originally attracted attention because the accused was the headmistress of a well-known school near Washington DC (Madeira) and the victim was even more famous as the author of a best-seller, *The Complete Scarsdale Medical Diet*. It is likely to continue to attract attention for many years to come, not least because many people believe that Mrs Harris was wrongly convicted. From the standpoint of the lawyer the case contained almost no questions of law. The crucial issue related to intention: did the evidence support beyond reasonable doubt the proposition that Jean Harris intentionally caused the death of Herman Tarnower? The prosecution argument was that Dr Tarnower's four wounds could only have resulted from deliberate shooting. Mrs Harris's story of the shooting was that she had come to Tarnower's house in order to have a last conversation with her lover before committing suicide in his garden; the conversation had gone badly wrong and Tarnower had been shot accidentally as he struggled to disarm her when she tried to shoot herself in his bedroom. There was no dispute that the pistol was Mrs Harris's. The issue of intent essentially turned on what happened in the space of less than five minutes in Tarnower's bedroom.

Diana Trilling suggests that Mrs Harris's lawyer, Joel Arnou, employed four different strategies in her defence: 'an old-fashioned compassionate defence; a defence based on social defence; what might by a stretch of definition be called an ideological defence (it dealt with Mrs Harris's dilemmas as a woman); and a defence based on physical evidence'.[124] Conspicuously absent was a psychiatric defence.[125]

The theory behind each of these strategies might be rendered by a Wigmorean analyst as follows:

1 Mrs Harris deserves your sympathy, therefore she should be acquitted;
2 Mrs Harris is a fine lady, therefore she did not commit murder;
3 Dr Tarnower deserved all he got. Mrs Harris acted rightly on behalf of all women. Therefore, the killing was justified;[126]
4 Dr Tarnower was accidentally shot in the course of a struggle in which he was trying to prevent Mrs Harris from committing suicide.

Diana Trilling claimed to be 'considerably estranged' by the first three strategies; 'I respected only the last of them.' Lawyers will recognize the first three as quite common courtroom tactics. They could point out that the second goes to Mrs Harris's credibility as a witness ('She is a good headmistress, renowned for her veracity; such people tell the truth; therefore you should believe her story').[127] However, they would agree that only (4) is legitimate and cogent as the main theory of the case. It is probably fair to say that this was the defence's theory and, in so far as the other strategies played a part they were ancillary. However, over a week of the trial was taken up with a parade of 'character' witnesses from Mrs Harris's school who, on Trilling's interpretation, were testifying on behalf of the school more than for the accused: 'They have no public choice except to treat the shooting of Dr Tarnower as "the tragic accident" that Arnou calls it, a temporary block in the otherwise unimpeded onward and upward march of education.'[128]

Perhaps even more significant is the lack of emphasis given in the closing speech for the defence to an account of the shooting itself: 'The story has taken no more than a minute or two, if that much, of Arnou's three-hour summation.'[129] On this interpretation the great bulk of the defence was taken up with attempts to secure thelema in terms which Wigmorean analysis quickly reveals to be based on defective logic. But it also suggests that the core defence theory relating to the fatal few minutes was wrapped up in the context of a story spread over several years and presented in a way which mixed fact, value and speculation within rather generous conceptions of relevance. It is reported that the jury focused almost entirely on the immediate circumstances of the shooting and decided that not all the shots could have been fired by accident.[130]

Some further complexities about the notions of 'case', 'case-as-a-whole', 'case-studies' and 'case-stories' can be illustrated by switching from the standpoint of the advocate to that of some outside observer, such as a student of law.[131] It is a common criticism of academic law in the Anglo-American tradition that it suffers from 'appellate court-itis';[132] law students and legal scholars pay too much attention to reports of appellate cases, whereas records and accounts of trials represent neglected materials of law study. In this context the distinction between 'leading cases' and '*causes célèbres*' is illuminating.[133] 'Leading cases' are precedents which have become landmarks in the development of legal doctrine either because they created or consolidated or gave authoritative approval to some resolution of a question of law of general significance. A few, for example, *Brown* v. *Board of Education*[134] or *R.* v. *Dudley and Stephens*,[135] are well known outside the legal profession; but these are exceptional. Most such cases are considered 'leading' only within the specialized culture of law. Most *causes célèbres*, on the other hand, whether famous or notorious or otherwise 'celebrated', are known to a much wider audience; for example *Dreyfus* or *Sacco and Vanzetti* or *Bywaters and Thompson* or *Alger Hiss* or *Jean Harris*. Almost all leading cases at common law were decided by appellate courts and feature in the law reports. Many *causes célèbres* have involved dramatic, much-publicized trials; most have little or no 'legal' significance; it is a matter of contingency whether they feature at all in the law reports. When they do, the report tends to give a rather thin account of the story of the case.[136]

Only a minority of cases featuring in the law reports count as leading cases. But, generally speaking in jurisdictions with selective law reporting, cases are selected for inclusion only if they have precedent value, that is they raised significant *questions of law*. The manner in which the reports are constructed, including the stories they tell, is determined in nearly every respect by this criterion of significance. *Candler* v. *Crane Christmas* and *Miller* v. *Jackson* are marginal examples of 'leading cases'. *Candler* paved the way for a later change in the law, but itself only reaffirmed the orthodox position that there was no duty of care for negligent misstatement. *Miller* v. *Jackson* is notorious because of Denning's performance, but its significance as a precedent is rather limited: it did little more than confirm the nineteenth-century doctrine. The law reports give us 'the facts' of *Candler* and *Miller*, but they do not tell us the complete stories of particular disputes. We do not know from that source what happened to Mr Candler or the Millers or the Lintz Cricket Club after their cases were decided. Nor, from the reports alone, can we tell what part these cases played in the story of the development of the law of negligence and nuisance.

Even on the most orthodox view of leading cases and other precedents, three different kinds of story are relevant to a reported case. The story of the original event or dispute which gave rise to the proceedings; the story of the litigation itself; and the story of the development of an area of law in which this precedent featured. We can rely on reports of cases *regularly* to tell only the first kind of story (the facts); even then the reported story may consist solely of allegations that have never been established by evidence – it is trite that the most famous of all English leading cases, *Donoghue* v. *Stevenson*, may be a monument to a mythical snail.[137] Yet, it is rather exceptional for a law report to be criticized for being incomplete. Judged by orthodox criteria of significance, law reports generally tell us all we need to know about a particular 'case'.[138]

This last point should prompt us to take a further look at the notion of 'a case as a whole'. An adequate report of a 'case' in the sense of a legally significant precedent does not need to give a full account of the proceedings nor of the dispute; it often does not even tell us the end of the story of the episode between the parties. Yet, from the point of view of legal significance, what is reported is the whole 'case'. What constitutes 'a case as a whole', even in a loose sense, depends on one's point of view and why the case is considered significant.

Some lawyers may think that this is belabouring the obvious. But a recent trend in legal scholarship suggests that the implications of this are not as obvious as they should be. The last decade has seen the publication of a number of notable contextual studies of leading cases. A conspicuous example is Brian Simpson's *Cannibalism and the Common Law*.[139] Such studies explore the historical context of the case in great detail and, in most instances, examine its aftermath and impact. Typically they cover all three kinds of story mentioned above: the story of the original facts; the story of the legal proceedings; and the story of the aftermath, including the legal aftermath.

They tend to make for good reading and they often change one's perception of the original case. Almost invariably they make the point that leading cases tend to become abstracted from their original historical context and take on a life of their own. Yet, as I have argued elsewhere, the significance of such studies is often unclear.[140] The reason is simple: leading cases are leading because they are legally significant. In-depth studies of the background of such cases, however scholarly, entertaining or illuminating they may be as slices of legal life, may add very little to our understanding of the general doctrine they produced. Their significance lies elsewhere and is sometimes obscure or unfocused. Law reports are centripetal; contextual studies are often centrifugal.

Contextual studies of leading cases are no different from other case-studies in lacking settled criteria of significance.[141] Indeed, it is leading cases and precedents which are exceptional in this respect. There are, of course, many different kinds of reasons why *causes célèbres* may be celebrated. They may have involved famous people or sensational events or dramatic trials or politically significant issues. Many retain their interest mainly as unsolved mystery stories. Some are significant as unequivocal or ambiguous symbolic events. America's leading *cause célèbre*, the *Sacco–Vanzetti* case provides a striking example.[142] It originally attracted attention as a potential miscarriage of justice.

Niccola Sacco and Bartolomeo Vanzetti, both Italian immigrant workers, were accused of murdering two men during a payroll robbery in South Braintree, Massachusetts, in August 1920. They were tried and convicted in April 1921. After a lengthy legal and political campaign to save them, they were eventually executed in August, 1927.

Few *causes célèbres* have generated such an extensive literature. The full transcript of the trial and subsequent proceedings has been published in several volumes. Lawyers involved in the case and prominent legal scholars, including Felix Frankfurter, John Henry Wigmore, Edmund Morgan and Karl Llewellyn published studies, including detailed analyses of the evidence. Many prominent figures were involved in the international protest. The case became the subject of so many novels, plays and poems that it prompted the comment that it was the only major literary event in the United States between two world wars.[143]

What is the legal, political and literary significance of the story of Sacco and Vanzetti? It has never been seriously doubted that a payroll robbery and murder took place in South Braintree on 15 August 1920. The central issue in the trial was a single question of fact concerning identity: were Sacco and Vanzetti (or one of them) involved in the crime? There were no substantial questions of law in the case, but many questions have been raised about the fairness of the proceedings, including some concerning admissibility of evidence. Legal opinion is split on these issues: 'The trial judge, the trial jury, the Supreme Judicial Court, and the Advisory Committee each and all decided every vital issue against [the accused].'[144] Most, but by no means all, legal commentators maintain that the trial involved serious violations of due process and that such evidence as there was linking the accused to the crime did not satisfy the standard of proof beyond reasonable doubt. There is still scope for disagreement about evaluation of the evidence relevant to the question whether as a matter of historical fact either or both were participants in the hold-up. From an orthodox legal point of view this does not differentiate the case from many other alleged miscarriages of justice. Karl Llewellyn, who campaigned actively on behalf of Sacco and Vanzetti, argued that the case was important not because it was unique, but because it was typical. It revealed serious institutional deficiencies in the administration of criminal justice in the United States.[145]

That is not why the story of Sacco and Vanzetti is 'celebrated'. Nor is it generally regarded as just another example of a mystery story. Rather it was treated (somewhat belatedly) and has continued to be perceived as a major political event. Sacco and Vanzetti became symbols of injustice. The significance of their story has, not surprisingly, been variously interpreted.[146] It has been taken to represent capitalist oppression of the working class; the non-acceptance of immigrants in American society; the persecution of political radicals; and conspiracy and corruption in 'the establishment', or just blind prejudice. In many commentaries, and in nearly all fictional accounts, it is assumed that this is a clear example of wrongful conviction of individuals who were innocent in fact as well as in law. Such interpretations often ignore distinctions between three kinds of miscarriage of justice in the courts: a person may be wrongly convicted because the court made a mistake of fact (in this case, that they got the wrong persons); or, whether or not as a matter of historical fact the accused did commit the crime, there was insufficient evidence to justify conviction according to the criminal standard of proof; or, whether or not the accused did commit the crime, the procedures followed were unfair. Many 'non-legal' interpretations of the *Sacco–Vanzetti* case tend to ignore these distinctions or treat them as trivial or irrelevant. On this view the important fact is that Sacco and Vanzetti were wrongly convicted and wrongly executed. The point of their story is the outcome: whether or not that outcome is attributable to factual error or insufficient evidence or procedural irregularity or other technical niceties or a combination of these is beside the point. They were victims of a great injustice.

This view needs to be taken seriously by lawyers as well as others. For the reasons for treating this case as important seem to be independent of such lawyers' distinctions. Surely, what matters is who they were (Italian, working-class, anarchists) and what happened to them (wrongful conviction and execution). Some of what is at stake here in this difference of views may be illuminated by considering Vanzetti's letters.

Bartolomeo Vanzetti's letters are among the classics of prison literature.[147] Written in touchingly fractured English, they have moved many readers with their combination of constant reiteration of his innocence with simplicity, concern for others, political awareness, and dignified acceptance of death. If one reads them on the assumption, or indeed as evidence, of Vanzetti's complete innocence, they constitute a powerful human document. If, however, one tries to read them on the contrary assumption that he was in fact one of the robbers, does this transform the collection into a work of monstrous hypocrisy? I do not think so. It could be that Vanzetti had come to believe in his own innocence and that this is a pathetic or tragic example of self-delusion. Or one can discount the protestations of innocence – perhaps as tactful, perhaps even necessary, white lies – and still respect his courage and dignity and concern for others. Or, is it perhaps the testament of a committed political activist who, well aware of his significance as a symbol of injustice, is consciously making his courageous last contribution to the cause? Opinions may differ on the plausibility of these different readings. But, I would suggest, the brute question of fact of his involvement in the hold-up is a central element in almost any interpretation of the story of Bartolomeo Vanzetti. Whether the 'point' of the story concerns the workings of American courts or political persecution of aliens and radicals or just an extraordinary person, it makes a qualitative difference whether the story proceeds on the basis that he was not in fact at South Braintree or that he was wrongly convicted because there was a reasonable doubt on the evidence or because unfair procedures were followed or because there were technical irregularities in the proceedings. Injustice established as a matter of historical fact is qualitatively different from miscarriages of justice that are solely deviations from the law's own standards.[148]

Jurisprudence and Narratology

Jurisprudence, viewed as the theoretical part of law as a discipline, is centrally concerned with the nature of legal discourses and their underlying assumptions. Legal discourses are of many kinds. This essay has principally been concerned with two specific kinds: 'arguments' by advocates and judges in court on questions of law and questions of fact. The conceptual difficulties associated with distinctions between 'law', 'fact' and 'value' are much debated in jurisprudence. On one view, with which I have some sympathy, arguments about questions of fact and questions of law are both species of practical reasoning with similar, but not identical, criteria of validity, cogency and appropriateness. However, the distinction between 'questions of fact' and 'questions of law' has very significant consequences for the discourse of advocates. How an issue is classified affects who addresses whom in what arena according to what procedural conventions and practices.

The modes of discourse in argumentation about questions of law and questions of fact in court are accordingly very different. Nevertheless there are some important structural and other similarities. In this essay I have tried to illustrate some of the variety of functions that narrative can play in both types of discourse and to a lesser extent in pleas in mitigation. It should not be a matter of surprise that in law, as in other parts of our culture, there are recurrent tensions between general and particular, fact and value, logic and rhetoric, and reason and intuition or imagination.[149] Nor should it come as a surprise that narrative plays a variety of roles in legal discourse or that in advocacy the relations between story-telling and rational argumentation are problematic. What may be more surprising to the outsider is to find that legal theory has almost entirely forgotten its roots in classical rhetoric; that theorizing about arguments on questions of law, questions of fact and sentencing occupy three largely disconnected bodies of literature; and that, in recent years, contacts between literary and legal theory have largely been confined to concern with the first kind of question. In considering what jurisprudence and narratology may currently have to offer each other in the Anglo-American context during the next few years, all of these factors are relevant.

The first message of the essay has been a warning of complexity. Not only are there many different contexts and kinds of legal discourses, but the specific context of advocacy – litigation – is itself extremely complex. Proceedings in court are of many different kinds and any particular example of courtroom discourse by lawyer, or judge or other participant, needs to be set in the context of the total process – the story of that particular piece of litigation. We have seen how even orthodox readings of the most familiar kind of legal text, 'cases' in the law reports, typically require differentiation of at least three kinds of stories: the story that gave rise to the proceedings ('the facts'); the story of the litigation (the proceedings); and the story of the development of the law which gives the case its significance (the case as precedent). Yet, as every lawyer knows, but we sometimes forget, law reports are highly selective, incomplete accounts of atypical cases, selected because they were 'hard', i.e. there was a doubt about the law. Quite often one does not learn of the final outcome of the proceedings, that is the resolution of the story of that particular litigation. The texts on which we draw for examples of arguments about disputed facts are more variable, less accessible, and even less likely to be typical of contested trials than the standard law report. Narratologists, beware!

The second lesson of this preliminary exploration is that it is easy to exaggerate the importance of narrative (*stricto sensu*) in legal argument. It plays important and multiple roles, sometimes in the foreground, sometimes as background. But some claims made for it are overstated: 'The statement of facts is the heart'; 'Juries choose between competing stories'; 'the central act of the legal mind . . . is the conversion of the material of life . . . into a story that will claim to tell the truth in legal terms' – these are all overstatements that exaggerate the roles of story-telling in legal argument, let alone other legal discourses. It is probably fair to say that 'story' and related notions have been neglected in legal theory. In so far as this is so, 'narratology' has something potentially significant to contribute – not least in stimulating lawyers to re-examine their conceptions of rationality. But it is unlikely that Law will become part of Narratology's Empire.

Thirdly, this essay has been almost entirely concerned with prescriptive theories of advocacy and argumentation. The focus has been on issues relating to what constitute legitimate, valid, cogent and persuasive modes of reasoning on disputed questions of law and fact. We have only touched incidentally on modes of persuasion in advocacy that may be perceived as clearly or arguably illegitimate or irrational. Narrative is no doubt sometimes used 'to sneak in' irrelevant or improper considerations, to conceal or divert attention from gaps or weaknesses in an argument, and in many other ways. Here, narratology may help to remind jurists of important issues about the ethics of argumentation. Such issues were central concerns of classical rhetoric, but have been relatively neglected in Anglo-American jurisprudence at least from this kind of perspective. These are just some possible lines of enquiry within normative jurisprudence.

Legal theorizing should not be and is not confined to normative questions. It is also concerned with understanding and interpreting law in the real world. In recent years actual examples of legal texts of different kinds have been subjected to scrutiny from a variety of perspectives. Ethnomethodologists, phenomenologists, semiologists, structuralists of many fashions, deconstructionists, literary theorists, hermeneuticists, and other inelegantly labelled academic entrepreneurs have exploited the rich heritage of legal texts with many fanfares and mixed success.

This essay is one of a series of explorations of the place of narrative in general culture. Can one expect to find something particularly illuminating or distinctive from the study of legal texts? Apart from the dual warnings about diversity and complexity, I have dropped a few hints about my own tastes. I happen to think that much of legal life and legal discourse is a part of general culture, far less distinctive, peculiar or unfamiliar to 'laymen' than is often suggested. So, for many purposes, legal texts can be treated as just one standard kind of cultural artefact which happens to be at hand. For example, just as social historians cull legal records as standard, relatively accessible sources of evidence about this or that aspect of social life, so one can find in the law reports an extraordinarily rich, well-documented anthology of 'real life' stories which can be analysed for all sorts of reasons unconnected with why they were originally preserved, constructed and published. However, if I had to settle for one reason why narrative in legal discourse has a special significance in culture, I would focus on the key factors of power, decision, publicity and argumentation. In no other sphere of social life are there to be found in such abundance practical decisions by powerful officials that have had to be argued for and justified in public and recorded in texts. Whether those texts are statutes, law reform documents, records and reports of trials, law reports or formal agreements, they share the elements of power, decision, recording and, to a lesser extent, public accountability and justification. Such legal texts are not unique in having these characteristics – witness for example election manifestos, (non-legislative) parliamentary debates, company reports – but as a body of literature they are unrivalled in their extent, detail and availability. Narratology seems to me to offer a fruitful lens for studying such texts; and, if legal narratology develops as a flourishing sub-discipline, it may even help to reunite legal theory with rhetoric. But that is another story.

252 *Lawyers' Stories*

NOTES

This essay was originally presented at the Seminar on Narrative in Culture organized by the Centre for Research in Philosophy and Literature, University of Warwick, in 1987. I am particularly grateful to Christopher Nash, Martin Warner and John McEldowney for stimulating my interest in the topic and for their guidance and comments on the original version. Later versions of the paper were presented, *inter alia*, at legal seminars at University College, London; the University of Miami; York University and the University of Windsor, Ontario. I am grateful to all those who participated in these seminars. The current version was largely completed in September 1987. I have profited enormously from discussions with or writings by, among others, Terry Anderson, Clarence Bennett and Martha Feldman, John Dewar, Reid Hastie, John Hoffman, Bernard Jackson, Gerald Lopez, Nancy Pennington, Stephen Penrod, Kim Lane Schepele, David Schum, Peter Tillers, James Boyd White and Steven Winter. Joanna Shapland's *Between Conviction and Sentence* was particularly valuable on pleas in mitigation. I have also made extensive use of manuals of advocacy; this revealing body of literature has been traditionally ignored by academics, perhaps because it tends to be 'anecdotal' and 'unscientific'. It has recently begun to be 'academicized' in the United States. However, Karl Llewellyn appears to be the only major theorist to have bridged the gulf between practitioners' cook-books and middlebrow legal theorizing. I have learned much from some writers on narrative, in particular Ricoeur, Danto and Rimmon-Kennan – but I have again been struck by a gap between this type of work and aspects of legal literature that deal with closely related, if not identical, questions.

So many issues and lines of thought have been suggested by these exchanges that it has been impossible to do justice to most of them in this essay, which is only my first venture into an enormous and seductive field. Some of the more significant writings are included in the bibliography. In the summer of 1987 Lord Denning very kindly agreed to be interviewed at his home by four of us on his conceptions of story-telling in advocacy and judging. The section on 'Lord Denning as hero and as deviant' was written before that interview and the text has not been altered, but a few points are mentioned in the notes. It is hoped that it will be possible in due course to report on that memorable occasion.

1 Millar (1957), 14–15.
2 J. B. White (1973), 859. Compare the claim of Fredric Jameson (1980): '[t]he all-informing process of narrative [is] the central function or instance of the human mind', cited by Nash (1987), 2.
3 The main exception is the 'New Rhetoric' of Chaim Perelman and his associates. See especially Perelman and Olbrechts-Tyteca (1971) and, more recently, Goodrich (1986, 1987), Bernard Jackson (1985, 1988) and others working in legal semiotics.
4 A notable example is Lord Diplock's rebuke, in criticizing Lord Denning's arguments in his dissenting judgment in *Gouriet* v. *Union of Post Office Workers*, as revealing 'some confusion and an unaccustomed degree of rhetoric', [1972] AC 1027, 1054.
5 White, op. cit., n.2; cf. Bennett and Feldman (1981).
6 Discussed, Twining (1984), 264–5.
7 Twining (1984), esp. 299.
8 In canvassing the literature of advocacy I have gained an impression of fragmentation rather than total neglect. The scene is the not unfamiliar one of bodies of literature talking past each other. In considering the role of narrative in arguments about disputed questions of law I have learned a great deal from the insights of Karl Llewellyn and James Boyd White. Despite a sense that White sometimes overstates his case (rhetorical exaggeration?), I am generally in sympathy with his impressive efforts to develop a humanistic rhetoric of law.
9 Non-lawyers should be warned that the great bulk of the jurisprudential literature on reasoning about questions of law (e.g. MacCormick, 1978) and on questions of facts (e.g.

Wigmore, 1937) is normative rather than empirical, and tends to be highly selective in its use of examples. See further, B. Jackson (1988), ch. 1.

10 I am here postulating that canons of ethics and the status of 'officer of the court' operate as side-constraints on this role of advocates in common law litigation to represent the interests of their clients. Although not unproblematic, the primary role is more easily grasped than the perennially controversial roles of the judge and jury. On the heuristic value of adopting the standpoint of advocate as a device for differentiating puzzlements about role from other concerns see Twining and Miers (1982), 286–91.

11 See generally Zuckerman (1986) and Jackson, Ockleton, White and Summers in Twining (ed.) (1983).

12 Ehrenzweig (1971).

13 This section draws on Du Cann (1964), Evans (1983), Jeans (1975), Mauet (1980), Rumsey (1986) and Stryker (1954). These are, of course, mainly examples of discourse *about* advocacy.

14 See *Analysis* ch. 3 and at 194–5, and below, 274 ff.

15 A reconstruction of the defence theory in the case of *Jean Harris*, below 245.

16 A reconstruction of a possible theory of the case for the plaintiff in *Candler* v. *Crane Christmas* [1951] 1 KB 164, discussed below, 232–5.

17 A reconstruction of a possible theory of the case for the defence in *Miller* v. *Jackson* [1977] QB 966, discussed below, 235–7.

18 Mauet (1980), 8. Recent research in Ontario suggests that manuals of advocacy and advocacy training have tended to underplay the importance of developing strategic plans as a basis for effective advocacy (N. Gold in Gold et al. 1989, 323).

19 Twining and Miers (1982), 136–40. Typically, determinations of X and Y take an all-or-nothing form, whereas (absent a fixed penalty or tariff) the appropriate sentence has to be selected from a range of possibilities. Orthodox theory recognizes deviations from the paradigm. For example, mixed questions of fact and law; judicial discretion in respect of application of a rule (e.g. discretion to exclude evidence) or of remedies (e.g. equitable remedies); interlocutory questions of procedure and so on.

20 These are different *usages* of 'story' commonly found in lawyers' talk. There are, of course, many *kinds* of stories, as the term is used in this essay. In the present context, it is especially important to distinguish between several types. First, stories about the events, or rather the alleged events, that gave rise to the proceedings ('the facts of the case'). Secondly, the story of the legal proceedings which may, of course, be one phase of some longer process, such as a long drawn-out dispute or feud. Thirdly, a party's or witness's version of events of which they have first-hand knowledge. There is an extensive literature about the ways in which our adversarial system of procedure can prevent or make it difficult for witnesses to tell 'their story' in their own way and in their own words (see below, n. 40). Fourthly, there are stories about the development of the legal doctrine applicable to the case. Such 'legal stories' sometimes form part of an argument by an advocate or judge *in* the case. (See e.g. Lord Denning in *Central London Property Trust Ltd* v. *High Trees House Ltd.* [1947] 1 KB 130.) Stories can also be told *about* the case, for example, explaining its significance as a precedent by setting it in the context of an account of the historical development of an area of law. Finally, the 'life-story' of a central participant, in more or less abbreviated form, may be treated as relevant in one phase of a legal proceeding (e.g. sentencing), but may be treated as irrelevant or inadmissible at a different stage (for example, there are complex rules governing the admissibility of evidence of character or disposition, including prior convictions, in relation to determination of guilt, but not of sentence). That this is not a comprehensive list of lawyers' stories can be easily seen by consulting the *Oxford Book of Legal Anecdotes* or *Great Legal Disasters* or any legal biography or collection of *causes célèbres*. In lawyers' clubland one can expect to hear a fairly predictable mix of war stories, anecdotes, jokes, gossip, legends, tales and myths. We are here mainly concerned with narrative accounts of the facts of a case and the use of narrative in legal argument ('legal stories', types 1–4).

21 Ricoeur (1981), 278–9.

22 Forster (1949), 82–3, discussed Rimmon-Kennan (1983), 16–19. Forster defines 'plot' explicitly in terms of causality; I have modified this in order to include narrations that are arguably totalities independently of notions of 'cause': in the third example, causation plays a part but is, arguably, not the 'point' of the story. Some writers, e.g. James Boyd White (1985), Kim Lane Schepele (1988) and Italo Calvino (1982), appear to maintain that all stories need a resolution or ending. While I am sympathetic to this view I have not included resolution as a necessary element in my conception of a story because in legal contexts there seem to be counter-examples: e.g. the facts of a case may raise an unresolved question, or an account of the development of a doctrine through a series of precedents may be presented as 'the story so far'. In both instances the telling of the story has a point, but not a resolution, as I understand that term.

23 'Narrative' is sometimes used more broadly to include accounts that are not stories. This paper is concerned with stories and story-telling in legal discourse; much of what is said here may also be true of other kinds of accounts.

24 *Trial of George Joseph Smith*, Watson (ed.) (1915), 261–2; cf. Bodkin's opening speech, 73–4.

25 See above 223.

26 Milsom (1967), 5–6. This probably over- simplifies the functions and discourses of *narratores*.

27 Below, 243 ff. Lawyers use the word 'case' in several different senses: one can bring a case (action), read a case (report), argue a case (argument), state a case (problem), win a case (action), or rely on a case (precedent). We have been considering reports of cases and case-studies. Let us call the genus 'case-accounts'. Such accounts share several features with stories: they have a unity; and they are supposed to have a point or meaning or significance. To say of a story or a case-account that it is pointless or meaningless or insignificant is generally to criticize it. Many case-accounts lack the time element of stories – they may concern situations or states of affairs; they may differ from stories in containing non-narrative materials – for example, arguments or diagnosis or solutions. But the elements of construction, configuration and of particularity linked to general significance make the analogy a close one. Stories and case-accounts *impose* beginnings and endings and resolutions and meanings on situations and events (but see above, n. 22). Within legal discourse, especially in the common law, different kinds of case-accounts play a prominent and varied role. For a different perspective on the concept of 'case' as a unit of discourse see below, ch. 11.

28 The use of stereotyped or mechanical or reconstructive stories, in e.g. traffic courts, may serve to simplify and speed up the process through 'typification'. See Brickley and Miller (1975), 693; Carlen (1976). I am grateful to an unidentified commentator at York University for this point.

29 Even in cases of strict liability, an account of how the situation came about may be relevant, for example, to ground a specific defence or as a mitigating or aggravating factor. It is, however, important to bear in mind that while attribution of legal responsibility normally relates to acts and omissions of identified legal persons, this is not always the case.

30 E.g. Patrick Bennett QC in Rumsey (1986); K. Evans (1983).

31 On whether lawyers have a peculiar notion of relevance, see Holdcroft and Zuckerman in Twining (ed.) (1983).

32 Bennett in Rumsey (1986), 3.

33 K. Evans (1983), 25.

34 Id., 36.

35 Id., 37.

36 Id., 43.

37 Id., 79.

38 The Hon. Charles L. Weltner in Rumsey (1986), 6. The primary meaning of θέλημα

(thelema) in classical Greek is 'will'; compare θέλγω (thelgo) 'to stroke with magic power, to charm, enchant, spell-bind, Lat. mulceo: to cheat, cozen', Liddell and Scott, Greek Lexicon (abridged).

39 Shapland (1981).

40 E.g. Danet (1980), 514–19; O'Barr (1982), 76–83, 137–48.

41 Shapland (1981).

42 E.g. K. Evans (1983), Du Cann (1984). American manuals tend to place more emphasis on preparation. The distinction between 'argument' and 'presentation' is related to, but does not quite correspond with, Aristotle's categories of logos, pathos and ethos. An 'argument' belongs to the sphere of logic in a broad sense; its validity and cogency are to be judged by whatever are achieved by the applicable principles of correct reasoning. Presentation refers to the method, style and techniques of communicating with an audience or audiences and, in relation to persuasion, is judged by its effectiveness in fact. Many of the precepts of advocacy relating to presentation, such as the importance of arousing and maintaining attention, of winning trust and of ensuring that one is understood are quite compatible with notions of 'rational persuasion'. To what extent such matters as thelema, themes, ethos and pathos belong to the sphere of persuasion by non-rational means is central to the theory of advocacy. See generally, J. B. White (1973), 810–21.

43 The concept of legitimacy is, of course problematic: see further below, 229–32.

44 E.g. Bennett and Feldman (1981), Preface and ch. 1.

45 J. W. Davis (1940, 1953), 181. Steven Winter has suggested to me the hypothesis that the 'best' advocates are more inclined to follow Davis's dictum in higher than lower courts. This corresponds with the notion of 'typification' as a means of speeding up the process in lower courts; see above, n. 28.

46 J. W. Davis, id.; cf. Paterson (1982), 52–65.

47 Llewellyn (1962), 341–2; cf. (1960), 238. The passage immediately preceding the quotations reads:

> [The] real and vital central job is to satisfy the court that sense and decency and justice require (a) the rule which you contend for in this *type* of situation; and (b) the result that you contend for, as between these parties. Your whole case, on law and facts, must make *sense*, must appeal as being *obvious* sense, inescapable sense, sense in simple terms of life and justice. If that is done a technically sound case on the law then gets rid of all further difficulty: it shows the court that its duty to the Law not only does not conflict with its duty to Justice but urges along the exact same line.
>
> The great change during these last few years in the approach of the best advocates lies here. As little as twenty or even ten years ago [i.e. before 1945], leading appellate advocates were still apologizing in private for that necessity of their profession that they termed 'atmosphere' ... It is no longer a question of 'introducing atmosphere'. It is now a question of making the facts talk. For of course it is the facts, not the advocate's expressed opinions, which must do the talking. The court is interested not in listening to a lawyer rant, but in seeing or discovering, from and in the facts, where sense and justice lie. (Id., 341)

On sense, wisdom and justice see Llewellyn (1962), 59–61.

48 E.g. Llewellyn (1962), 85ff., 192, 256–60.

49 E.g. 126–8, 238.

50 Twining (1973), 261–3.

51 See below, n. 88.

52 One must, of course, beware of what Llewellyn called 'the threat of the available' (1962), 82–3. In this context, it is worth repeating that the examples used in this essay are not meant to be representative of day-to-day practice, in which, one suspects, explicit story-telling plays a more limited role than these illustrations suggest. Most lawyers and judges are more formalistic than Lord Denning and Karl Llewellyn.

53 See further, Twining (1973).
54 Llewellyn (1960), 29.
55 Ibid., note.
56 Twining and Miers (1982), ch. 7.
57 Llewellyn (1960), 238; Twining (1973), 216–27, 257–64.
58 Llewellyn (1960), 238.
59 Id., 59–61, 426–9.
60 Id., 60–1, 238, discussed Twining (1973), 216–27, 262–4.
61 Ibid.
62 Discussed Gottlieb (1968), chs. 3–4.
63 Lopez (1984), 32–3. This article illuminatingly explores stories and story-telling in order to illuminate 'the connections between how we perceive the world, how we persuade others, and how we make difficult choices ...' in problem-solving by lawyers seen as instances of human problem-solving (10, 2). The article centres on an example in which lawyers' sharp distinctions between questions of fact, law and disposition do not apply. The thrust of section IV of this paper is very much in sympathy with Lopez's analysis.
64 Id., 34.
65 Llewellyn (1960), 365, discussed Twining (1973), 227–9.
66 J. B. White (1973), 863–5; cf. J. B. White (1985), ch. 2 and 118–19. This idea may find some confirmation in psychological research on 'telling more than we can know', e.g. Nisbett and Wilson (1977).
67 J. B. White (1973), (1984), (1985). Some indication of White's perspective – he would not accept it as a definition – is expressed in this dictum: '[L]aw can be best understood as a set of literary practices that at once create new possibilities for meaning and action in life and constitute human communities in distinctive ways' ('The Judicial Opinion and the Poem: Ways of Reading, Ways of Life', 1985, 107). For an excellent critique of White's views see Sherwin (1988).
68 Twining (1973). There is now an extensive literature on Llewellyn's concept of 'situation sense'. One of the best discussions is Whitman (1987).
69 See especially, Jowell and McAuslan (1984), esp. 17–19, Robson and Watchman (1981), Harvey (1986). Lord Denning's own discussions of his style are also revealing, e.g. *The Family Story* (1981), 206–20. It is important to emphasize that the two cases discussed here are among the most striking of Lord Denning's judgments, and so cannot be taken as representative judgments of his output as a whole: still less can Lord Denning as story-teller be treated as typical of the style of English judges. See further note 52.
70 [1951] 2 KB 164, [1951] 1 All ER 426.
71 *Hedley Byrne and Co. Ltd* v. *Heller and Partners Ltd* [1964] AC 465. Lord Denning has denied that his judgment was written to persuade the House of Lords to overrule prior precedents on negligent misstatement (interview, July 1987). Nevertheless he is generally given credit for having persuaded them (e.g. Atiyah and Waddams, in Jowell and McAuslan, 1984, 57, 468).
72 [1951] 1 All ER at 428.
73 In the *Law Reports* the first paragraph is omitted. The paragraph reads:

> In September 1946, the plaintiff invested £2,000 in a company called Trevanance Hydraulic Tin Mines, Ltd. (which I will call 'the company'), and he has lost it all because the company turned out to be a failure. He now brings this action against the defendants, who are the company's accountants and auditors, claiming that he was induced to invest the money because of erroneous accounts put before him by them and on the faith of which he invested his money. The judge had found that the accounts were 'defective and deficient' and presented a position of the company which was 'wholly contrary to the actual position', that the accountants were 'in fact extremely careless in the preparation of the accounts', and that the damage suffered by the plaintiff was 'plain', but,

nevertheless, the judge dismissed his claim because, in his opinion, there was no duty of care owed by the accountants to the plaintiff.

On the phenomenon of judges restating the facts (or doctrine), using different words see Llewellyn (1951), 47; Twining (1973), 235.

74 428.
75 Ibid.
76 Atiyah, op cit., 57.
77 The famous passage on 'timorous souls' and 'bold spirits' is at 432; Asquith LJ's riposte is at 442.
78 Atiyah, op cit.
79 Ibid.
80 cf. John Wisdom's account of 'case-by-case procedure' in his Virginia Lectures, discussed by D. C. Yaldon-Thomson in Bambrough (ed.) (1974), ch. 3.
81 *Miller* v. *Jackson* [1977] 3 All ER 340. This passage is discussed by Bernard Jackson (1988), 94–7, where he glosses but does not undermine my interpretation.
82 Id., 340–1.
83 [1977] 3 All ER at 346 (per Geoffrey Lane J), 350 (per Cumming-Bruce LJ).
84 'Despite these measures, a few balls did get over. The club made a tally of all the sixes hit during the seasons of 1975 and 1976. In 1975 there were 2,221 overs, that is, 13,326 balls bowled. Of them there were 120 sixes hit on all sides of the ground. Of these only six went over the high protective fence and into this housing estate. In 1976 there were 2,616 overs, that is 15,696 balls. Of them there were 160 six hits. Of these only nine went over the high protective fence and into this housing estate' (341). Later he states: 'He could not complain if a batsman hit a six out of the ground, and by a million to one chance, it struck a cow or even the farmer himself' (344). Innumerate lawyers and narratologists are invited to spot the fallacy.
85 At 340–5. In a recent interview (July 1987) Lord Denning indicated that at the time there was a lot of sympathy for the Millers and that he was concerned to right the balance. He graciously conceded that if his audience feels that he has overstated his case, then this is not good advocacy.
86 See B. Jackson (1988), 94–7 for a different interpretation.
87 In *Candler* the main, but not the only, adverse precedent was *Le Lievre* v. *Gould* [1893] 1 QB 491; in *Miller* v. *Jackson* it was *Sturges* v. *Bridgman* (1879) 11 Ch. D. 852.
88 J. B. White (1985), 116, says: 'An opinion that simply adopted one side's brief would not be worthy of the name.' This, however, underestimates the notion that the most persuasive advocate is the one who confronts the difficulties and surmounts them. Cf Llewellyn (1960), 241–5.
89 [1977] 3 All ER at 351.
90 Ibid.
91 E.g. *Lim Poh Choo* v. *Camden and Islington Area Health Authority* [1979] 1 All ER 332 (CA), 9.
92 Summers (1978), Fuller (1946).
93 Cf. Lord Atkin, op. cit., n. 1; B. Jackson (1988), 94–7.
94 See above, n. 80.
95 See e.g. Mauet (1980), Jeans (1975); cf. Weiner (1950).
96 A notable exception is MacCormick (1978, 1984).
97 See bibliographies in *TEBW* and Twining (1983) and Tillers and Green (1988).
98 Wigmore (1913, 1937).
99 Bennett and Feldman (1981).
100 Abu Hareira (1984, 1986); Schum and Martin (1982); cf. Tillers (1983), cited below, 241.
101 Wigmore (1937), 821.
102 Ibid.
103 *TEBW* (1985); Anderson and Twining (1987); Schum and Martin (1982).

104 Wigmore, op. cit., 821–2.
105 Ibid.
106 Bennett and Feldman (1981), dust jacket and preface. For a more moderate account see Hastie, Penrod and Pennington (1983), in which they develop a psycho-linguistic 'story model' of juror decision making.
107 Id., 41; cf. 67.
108 Id., 62–3.
109 Id., 33; cf. 65.
110 It could be argued that Wigmore and Bennett and Feldman are engaged in very different enterprises. Wigmore's Chart Method is a recommended intellectual procedure for analysing, criticizing and constructing arguments based on evidence. It is part of a prescriptive 'logic of proof'. Bennett and Feldman purport to be presenting a sociological analysis of how lawyers, judges and jurors in fact 'reconstruct reality in the courtroom'. As such it is a contribution to an empirical, or interpretative, sociology of law. However, the connections are closer than appear on the surface. For Wigmore claims that what he is recommending is a usable, practical tool that reflects the practices of the best lawyers. His Chart Method is a systematization of good practice. Conversely, Bennett and Feldman, while primarily concerned with description and explanation, imply that the kinds of story-telling that they found in their data represent both inevitable and legitimate procedures for decision. They use their ideal types of 'case construction strategies' to explain (and by implication to criticize) deviant practices, such as disruptive and diversionary tactics (125–31) and the intrusion of bias into trial process (ch. 8). Accordingly, like Wigmore, they provide standards for criticizing the actual practices of advocates and triers of fact.
111 See n. 97 above.
112 Abu Hareira (1984, 1986).
113 Tillers (1983), 986n.
114 See works cited in n. 100 above and *TEBW* 183–5. Neither Abu Hareira nor Tillers denies a role to analysis and logical testing of the validity and cogency of arguments about disputed questions of fact. Like Bennett and Feldman, Abu Hareira appears to give such analysis a secondary place, as providing subordinate tests in a process in which attempts to individuate items of evidence in the process of evaluation involves an artificial, unwarranted and often dangerous attempt to dissolve the indissoluble. His theory echoes the traditional suspicion of practising lawyers of 'over-logical' approaches. Tillers, on the other hand, is self-consciously appealing to a different philosophical tradition in challenging the conceptions of rationality espoused by Wigmore and most participants in recent debates about probabilities. See now MacCormick (1980, 1984) and B. Jackson (1988).
115 See further Anderson and Twining (1987), *passim*.
116 There are two further points of agreement in all of the theories mentioned. All agree that one of the most important tests of the plausibility of a story or theory is its compatibility with uncontroversial or incontrovertible particular facts. It is a basic precept of advocacy (and detection) that one should confront uncomfortable facts (or evidence) both in constructing one's theory of the case and in presenting an argument. On the whole it does not pay to ignore or gloss over or try to divert attention from undisputed or credible facts. Rather one should explain them away or re-interpret them or acknowledge them, but seek to show that one's account is consistent with them. This is a different kind of 'consistency' from the internal consistency of the story considered apart from this evidence. Novels are generally supposed to be 'consistent', without having any direct connection with actual events in the real world. For a stronger version of a coherence theory see now B. Jackson (1988). Of course, many stories appeal to a community's stock of stories.
117 See generally, chapter 4 above and B. Jackson (1988).
118 J. B. White (1985), 160; cf. 174.

119 See generally, Summers and White in Twining (1983), Zuckerman (1986) and Guest (1987).

120 Holmes (1897), White (1985) warning against over-emphasizing the importance of outcome.

121 Cf. the morality tale of the lawyer's son who was charged with breaking the schoolroom window: 'In the first place, sir, the schoolroom has no window; in the second place, the schoolroom window is not broken; in the third place, if it is broken, I did not do it; in the fourth place, it was an accident' (*Punch*, cited Williams, 1973, 21).

122 On decisions to prosecute, see Mansfield and Peay (1987).

123 Trilling (1982). The following passage is an analysis of Diana Trilling's report of the Jean Harris trial as she observed it. The accuracy of the report is not in issue here. For a different view of the trial see Harris (1986). Diana Trilling's book about the case is a piece of impressionistic and imaginative reporting of the trial, presented as 'a work of social criticism'. 'My initial response was one of unqualified sympathy for the headmistress and I conceived the book in a spirit of partisanship' (9). As she sat through the trial and pondered what she had read and seen and heard, the work became transformed as she tried to make sense of the case. Her account needed a resolution, not just an outcome: 'Whatever one's judgment of Mrs Harris's guilt or innocence, or one's reaction to her as an individual, she was the person in this story who unmistakably had a fate, like a character in fiction. Dr Tarnower hadn't a fate; he had only an outcome, a conclusion to his life' (23). 'This story' is, of course, Mrs Trilling's story of Mrs Harris and her case. There have been, and no doubt will be, many others built on the same historical events. The point of the story in this particular interpretation is not the killing of Dr Tarnower nor the outcome of the trial nor the picture of American criminal process in action, but the character of Mrs Harris that was revealed by the courtroom drama and how it explained her behaviour before and during the trial. For Diana Trilling,

> Mrs Harris has star quality ... without the armature of fiction, she can all too easily become a clinical study. She belongs to imaginative writing, where, as I say, Freud learned, as we learn, about character in conflict. Mrs Harris was unable to bring her inner contradictions into reliable working agreement, but our interest in her derives precisely from the unresolved opposition between her conscience and her impulses. She belongs to the novel in the way that Emma Bovary does, or Anna Karenina. They too were characters in contradiction. (435, 431)

What started 'as a story of sexual and social politics' (blurb) became transformed into 'faction', an imaginative and speculative interpretation of an interesting character. This, it seems, is the only way in which Mrs Trilling could make sense of her story-as-a-whole.

Mrs Harris's recent book *Stranger in Two Worlds* (1986) is also an account of herself. It covers her early life, her career as headmistress and her experiences in prison. Only two chapters deal in any detail with the events immediately surrounding the death of Dr Tarnower and with her trial.

124 Trilling (1982), 422.

125 Id., 414–20.

126 The first three 'arguments' can be extrapolated from Trilling's account at 356, 233, 216–17; cf 420–38. Possible feminist interpretations of the case are only lightly touched by Trilling, e.g. 9–12.

127 Id., 422–3.

128 219–20, cf. 226.

129 Id., 357.

130 Newspaper reports.

131 On the different uses of 'case' in legal discourse see above n. 27 and below ch. 11.

132 The *locus classicus* is Frank (1949).

133 This theme is developed in Twining (1986).

134 *Brown* v. *Board of Education* 347 US 483 (1954), 349 US 294 (1955)

135 *R.* v. *Dudley and Stephens* 14 QBD 273 (1884), affirmed 14 QBD 560 (1885).

136 Compare the treatments of *Dudley and Stephens* in the law reports and by Simpson (1984).

137 The questions of law in *Donoghue* v. *Stevenson* [1932] AC 562 were decided by the House of Lords on the basis of the averments which were never put to the proof, i.e. the case was settled before 'the facts' were determined by a court.

138 Sykes and Heywood (1987) report that psychologists who have studied the phenomenon of story-understanding and recall, report that story grammar comprises four elements: setting, theme, plot and resolution. Reports of cases in the law reports can be readily analysed in these terms: the setting (S) represents the procedural context of the case; the theme (T) represents the issue of law which the court was called upon to determine and which is the basis for treating the case as a precedent (the point of the case); the plot (P) is the facts of the case; and the resolution (R) is how the court decided that issue of law for this and future cases. Thus a précis of *Candler* v. *Crane Christmas* could be rendered as follows:

S: In *Candler* v. *Crane Christmas* the plaintiff in an action for negligence appealed to the Court of Appeal against a decision of the Queen's Bench.

P: The defendants in the action were professional accountants who had negligently prepared a statement of accounts which gave a misleading picture of the financial position of the company. The accounts were prepared with the intention and expectation that the plaintiff would be guided by them in deciding whether to invest in the company. On the faith of the accounts he made the investment and as a result he lost his money.

T: The issue was whether a duty of care for negligent mis-statements is owed to the plaintiff in such circumstances.

R: The Court of Appeal decided that no such duty exists (Denning MR dissenting), but this decision was later overruled in *Hedley Byrne* v. *Heller* and the modern law of negligent mis-statement was born.

In this rendering, there are at least three stories. The story *in* the case (the facts); the story *of* the case as reported in [1952] All ER, and the story of the development of liability for negligent mis-statement, in which *Candler* v. *Crane Christmas* and Lord Denning's judgment in particular played an historic role. Each of these three stories can readily be made to fit the grammar (S), (T), (P), (R).

139 Simpson (1984).

140 Op. cit., n. 133.

141 Twining (1986c).

142 The literature on the *Sacco–Vanzetti* case is massive. The main sources of the discussion here are Joughin and Morgan (1948), Felix (1965) and Frankfurter (1927, 1961).

143 The remark has been attributed to H. L. Mencken, but I have been unable to trace the source.

144 Felix (1965).

145 Discussed Twining (1973), 341–9.

146 Felix states: 'The Sacco–Vanzetti case became a legend of innocence betrayed. It became more: a parable about betrayal in American society' (op. cit., 240). I would suggest that this is only one of many different, but overlapping, interpretations.

147 *The Letters of Sacco and Vanzetti* were published in 1924, edited by Marion Frankfurter and Gardner Jackson; the latter was in charge of the public relations of the Sacco–Vanzetti Defense Committee. Felix, whose interpretation of the case and of Vanzetti himself is less sympathetic than mine, commented: 'the published edition of the letters is a carefully edited fraction of the prisoner's epistolary production, which is crueler, rawer, less grammatical, more violent and more vital' (op. cit., 256).

148 Some writers argue that 'legal truth' is different from 'historical truth' and that trials are not concerned with historical truth. This is a mistake. One consequence of this view would be to deprive legal discourse of strong conceptions of 'mistake' or 'miscarriage of justice'. I may believe that Sacco and Vanzetti or Dreyfus or Luke Dougherty were victims of injustice on one or more different grounds:

1 There were technical irregularities in the proceedings which should, according to the rules, have been grounds for questioning the conviction. For example, an inadmissible confession or hearsay was admitted.
2 Unfair procedures were followed. For example, the trial was conducted in an atmosphere of prejudice against the accused.
3 The evidence adduced at trial did not satisfy the standard of proof beyond reasonable doubt.
4 As a matter of historical fact the accused was (were) innocent. For example, there was a mistake of identity; the crime was committed by someone else.

These are all four examples of miscarriages of justice. But accounts of great injustices would nearly always be qualitatively different, if claims of type (4) were ruled out. Legal discourse needs the categories of historical truth and historical error.

149 The suggestion that stories are one means of resolving such tensions fits in with the thesis of Clifford Geertz that the Western polarization of fact and law (and similar dichotomies) misleads us about the reality of our own processes. These may not be so very different from notions of judgment in other cultures that are expressed by such concepts as *dharma, haqq* and *adat* (Geertz, 1983, esp. chs. 4 and 8).

[13]
Anchored Narratives: A Comment

In 1992 three Dutch psychologists published *Dubieuze Zaken: De Psychologie van Strafrechtelijk Bewijs*. *Anchored Narratives*, by the same authors, is a sequel addressed to an international audience and purporting to deal with some universal problems faced by criminal justice systems.[2] The book is very close to *Dubieuze Zaken* in that it is based on analysis of the same 35 Dutch cases and presents essentially the same argument, but it is much shorter. Its relationship to the original is roughly comparable to that of Dumonts *Traite des preuves judiciares* to Benthams *Rationale of Judicial Evidence*: it is a *redaction* rather than a translation, addressed to a foreign rather than a domestic audience.

This is a comment rather than an orthodox book review. *Dubieuze Zaken* 'caused much uproar in our country, both in and outside the legal community.'[3] The authors had criticized the practices of the police, prosecutors, the judiciary and defence lawyers in many of the cases they analyzed and had made sweeping proposals for reform. They were accused of misunderstanding Dutch law, of misinterpreting some of the cases, and of making unwarranted generalizations from a small, biased and unrepresentative sample. They were treated like ignorant outsiders trespassing on others' territory with insufficient local knowledge.

In this kind of controversy it is often difficult to differentiate between resentment at the fact of criticism, resistance to incursions from other disciplines and genuine airing of differences and correction of errors. An English jurist, commenting on a book by three psychologists, based on material in a foreign language and on a legal culture in which he has been no more than a tourist, is similarly vulnerable to charges of lack of local knowledge. In the present instance, aware of the controversy and of some of the prior criticisms of the work, I cannot even claim to have approached the book with the fresh eyes of a reviewer.

However, the English version is presented as a general critique, dealing with universal problems of the administration of criminal justice:

> 'Virtually every criminal justice system of which we have any knowledge appears to disregard the many documented fallibilities of human judgment'.[4]

---

1. Quain Professor of Jurisprudence, University College London; Visiting Fellow, NIAS 1994-95.
2. *Anchored Narratives; The Psychology of Criminal Evidence* by W.A.Wagenaar, P.J. van Koppen, and H.F.M. Crombag, London, Harvester Wheatsheaf (1993), (hereafter AN). This comment builds on ideas developed in three prior works by the author: *Theories of Evidence: Bentham and Wigmore* (1985) (hereafter TEBW); *Analysis of Evidence* (with Terence Anderson, 1991) (hereafter AE); and *Rethinking Evidence* (1990,1994) (hereafter, RE).
3. AN, Preface.
4. *Ibidem*.

The Dutch cases are presented as merely illustrative. Moreover the authors purport to draw on a body of theory that is largely Anglo-American in origin, to apply that theory to Dutch examples, and to advance a general thesis about anchored narratives. In the process they make some bold claims that are worth examining from the point of view of general theories of evidence and proof in legal, especially criminal, processes. The book also raises some difficult questions about the comparative study of legal cultures. This comment, then, relates both to the book and the controversy it generated, but is concerned with its general rather than its local (Dutch, legal) significance.

The general theory of anchored narratives may be summarised as follows: This is a psychological theory about how judges in fact think in dubious cases involving questions of fact.[5] It applies to other triers of fact, such as juries, because all fact-finders have to rely largely on common sense reasoning.[6] Building on American empirical research, notably by Bennett and Feldman[7] and Pennington and Hastie,[8] the authors suggest that instead of arguing from evidence to conclusions (as is suggested by bottom-up 'logical inference theories') judges follow a top-down, hypothesis-testing approach.[9] The hypotheses take the form of narratives or stories, because 'evidence derives its meaning from the story context'.[10] A credible story satisfies two tests: is it a good story? Is it true? A good story is one that has 'a readily identifiable central action; and a context (setting) that provides an easy and natural explanation of why the actors behaved in the way they did.'[11] A good story lacks both missing and contradictory elements – it forms a coherent whole. But a story not only has to be good, it has to be true,, that is to say it needs to be supported by 'anchors' that satisfy the relevant standard of decision: in criminal cases proof beyond reasonable doubt (the common law phrase) or conviction of the trier of fact (civil law). 'Stories are anchored in common-sense rules by means of chains of embedded sub-stories.'[12]

The authors maintain that stories are necessary to thinking about questions of fact, but they are also dangerous. They are dangerous in legal contexts because a good story may create an illusion of veracity, with only a few details anchored;[13] or because the court will tend to prefer evidence which supports the prosecution's account rather than contradicts it. Similarly, police and prosecution may be tempted only to look for inculpatory evidence or even to ig-

5. *Idem* at p. 18.
6. *Idem* at p. 16.
7. W.Lance Bennett and M. Feldman, *Reconstructing Reality in the Courtroom* (1981). For a critical discussion, *see* RE at pp. 144-145.
8. *E.g.* N. Pennington and R. Hastie 'Evidence Evaluation in Complex Decision Making,' *Journal of Personality and Social Psychology* (1986), pp. 242-258. For further references *see* the bibliography in AN and N. Pennington and R. Hastie, 'A Cognitive Theory of Jury Decision-making: The Story Model', *Cardozo Law Review* (1991), p. 519.
9. The contrast between 'bottom-up' and 'top-down' approaches can be overdrawn: first, detectives, prosecutors, defence lawyers and judges all have to work with hypotheses and to relate clues, information that is potential evidence, and judicial evidence to allegations, probanda, facts in issue etc. Such propositions represents 'the top' in this context. Secondly, the process of constructing and criticising arguments about questions of fact is typically reflexive, involving movement from top to bottom and back again. Wigmorean analysis is both top-down and reflexive (AE at pp. 120-129). The main point that the authors wish to emphasise is the temptation on prosecutors and judges not to look for exculpatory evidence and to be too easily satisfied by looking at evidence that supports the allegations.
10. AN at p. 33.
11. *Idem* p. 36.
12. *Idem* p. 40.
13. *Idem* p. 225.

nore or suppress falsifying or exculpatory evidence;[14] or because the court will select evidence, but not give reasons for discounting or disregarding other evidence; or the court may rely on unarticulated generalizations, which might be shown to be dubious or unsatisfactory if articulated and subjected to critical examination.[15]

> *'All parties involved in criminal proceedings, with the possible exception of the defence, have a strong preference for suspect-driven search and verification, both in the investigative stage and during the construction of proof.'*[16]

While the theory of anchored narratives claims to be mainly predictive, it has prescriptive implications.[17] In general terms it suggests that given the dangers inherent in the way that judicial reasoning proceeds in practice, there is a need for safeguards against systematic or common errors in order to secure the validity of judicial reasoning.[18] The final chapter sets out ten 'universal rules of evidence' that the authors claim follow from their theory.[19]

At a very general level, a good deal of this is familiar and not particularly controversial. It is widely acknowledged that stories play a significant role in fact-finding in adjudication and that 'the logic of proof' is founded in common-sense reasoning in which background generalizations ('general experience') play an important part.[20] In regard to some topics, such as confessions, identification evidence, reliability of witnesses, and experts, the book confirms and illustrates well-established bodies of psychological research without claiming to be a major theoretical advance.

Anchored Narratives can thus be interpreted as an application and extension of an important body of theory. At the very least, it adds to the literature by applying the theory in a fresh context, the Netherlands, and by illustrating and testing it with a quite rich collection of detailed case-studies. If the accounts of the cases are accepted as fair, on the whole they serve well as illustrations of the general points.[21] On some topics, such as the importance of distinguishing between the uses of evidence at the investigative and adjudicatory stages, suspect-

14. *Idem* pp. 96-97.
15. One of the main claims made for Wigmores chart method is that it articulates a whole argument, making explicit many steps that are left implicit in ordinary discourse, and thereby facilitating judgments about strong and weak points.
16. *Ibidem.*
17. *Idem* p. 18.
18. *Idem* pp. 18-19.
19. *Idem* p. 232.
20. The traditional phrase used in common law accounts is 'general experience', which is rather broader and, in this context more useful, than 'generalizations' (*see* below notes 37 and 38). *See*, in Netherlands Law, Article 339, s.2., of the Code of Criminal Procedure (WvSv), which is analyzed in J.F.Nijboer, *Strafrechtelijk bewijsrecht* (1994), pp. 88ff and 249ff.
21. Ironically, the authors' use of cases illustrates the difference between good stories and true stories: most of the authors' accounts of Dutch cases satisfy the test of a good story: that is they are coherent, internally consistent and (seemingly) complete. A few seem implausible, judged by my stock of background generalizations: for example, I find it barely credible that a Dutch prosecutor or judge gave any weight to hearsay evidence by an eight-month old baby related by his two-and-a-half year old sister and relayed in a police report in a child abuse case (Castelyn at pp. 199 and 220); or that some cases were decided on the basis of identification of suspects in parades when the perpetrators had worn masks during the commission of the crimes (Haaknat, Neeringh, and Rotweiler, p. 243). The authors have been accused of misrepresenting or misinterpreting some of the cases: that is they misunderstood the legal context (general) or they misrepresented or were too selective in summarizing the record. I do not have access either to the relevant legal information nor to the particular evidence which might suggest that these stories, even if good, are untrue.

driven enquiries, on the kinds of reasons courts in the Netherlands do and do not give in justifying decisions, and on defence tactics, they have some interesting things to say, especially in the specifically Netherlands context. The idea of focusing on the wider category of 'dubious cases' rather than on alleged miscarriages of justice is potentially fruitful.[22] The category is a bit vague, for it could include almost any case that involves a serious dispute about the facts; but, like Ronald Dworkins concept of 'hard cases', there are advantages in widening the focus of the enquiry and the category is less contentious than miscarriages of justice. In fact, despite their criticisms of Netherlands practice, the authors conclude that probably only one of their 35 cases ended in a wrongful conviction.[23]

Whether or not some of the authors criticisms of practice in the Netherlands are overstated, *Anchored Narratives* addresses issues which are important for any legal system. In many jurisdictions some of these issues have tended to be neglected by legal scholars, at least until recently. For example, in England most of the literature on miscarriages of justice, including some of the best, has been by crusading journalists rather than scholars.[24] *Anchored Narratives* is written in a clear, readable and polemical style that is in some respects closer to 'the higher journalism' than more 'scientific' publications. The authors have been conspicuously successful in being provocative, but the general theory needs to be refined and developed if it is to provide a usable basis for further research on an important range of issues. It is in the spirit of constructive criticism that I draw attention to some weaknesses in the theory and make some suggestions for its future development.

TERMINOLOGY: STORIES, GENERALIZATIONS, AND RULES

The first need is for a more precise terminology. Let us focus on three key terms in the theory.

First, 'narrative' has recently become a fashionable focus of attention in many disciplines. In the process terms like 'story', 'scenario' and 'narrative' itself have been used somewhat loosely, sometimes so broadly as to be indistinguishable from discourse in general. But the explanatory power of the theory of anchored narratives is in part dependent on a more precise terminology, which distinguishes, for example, between story, chronology, scenario, situation, theory and a charge in an indictment.[25] In particular, in the present context, it is important to distinguish clearly between a story and an argument or at least to clarify the relationship between the concepts, for at least two reasons: within the theory of anchored nar-

22. *Idem* p. 11.
23. *Idem* p. 16. The idea that 'the process is the punishment' is clearly illustrated by the sexual abuse case of Donker in which the accused was eventually acquitted (p.195); cf. the English case of the politician Peter Hain, who convincingly claimed that he was a victim of misidentification even though he was eventually acquitted, RE p. 171. *See* generally, M. M.Feeley, *The Process is the Punishment* (1979), which focuses mainly on plea-bargaining.
24. Prominent English examples include, L. Kennedy, *Ten Rillington Place* (1961), P. Foot, *Who Killed Hanratty?* (1973), C. Mullin, *Error of Judgement* (1986); *see* more generally, B. Woffinden, *Miscarriages of Justice* (1987). Recently the subject of miscarriages of justice has attracted more sustained official and academic attention. The American literary tradition is somewhat different from the British in respect of treatment of *causes celebres* and alleged miscarriages of justice, but it is similar in respect of the point that this has generally not been an area of sustained scholarly attention; one exception is the literature on the Sacco-Vanzetti case, discussed RE, pp. 247-249 (*see* further the forthcoming book by J.Kadane and D.Schum).
25. RE Ch.7; *see below* note 27.

ratives an implicit distinction is drawn between a story and its anchors – that is between the elements which constitute a good story and the justification for claiming that each element is 'anchored' and that the story as a whole is true. Secondly, it is important to distinguish between a story and an argument, because story-telling and narrative are sometimes presented as alternatives to argument[26] or as challenging prevailing conceptions of rationality.[27]

A thin definition of story, adapted from Paul Ricoueur, is:

> *'A story is a narrative of particular events arranged in a time sequence and forming a meaningful totality.'*[28]

This is a significantly different form of discourse from an argument conceived of as a number of propositions related to each other within some inferential structure in such terms as 'tends to support/ tends to negate.' Time, particularity and coherence are defining characteristics of stories in this thin sense; arguments are monochronic, they are not necessarily restricted to particulars, and the role of coherence within argumentation is notoriously problematic.[29]

In *Anchored Narratives* the failure to distinguish between two distinct spheres of discourse leads to some basic confusions. For example, the authors state:

'Every piece of evidence, that is offered to prove the truth of a story, is itself a sub-story in need of an anchor, which takes the form of a generally accepted common-sense rule'.[30]

Evidence is a means of proof within an *argument*; it may take many forms, but in the classical theory an evidentiary fact is a *factum probans* if it tends to support or tends to negate, *i.e.* is relevant to, a *probandum.* A 'piece of evidence' can often be stated in the form of a simple proposition, such as: 'X saw Y enter Z's house at 3p.m. exactly' or 'Y's blood matches the bloodstains'. A simple fact of this kind is not a story, although it may easily be made part of one (or more). We often have to deal with 'simple facts' – a trace, a bullet, a single assertion by a witness – which are not stories in themselves; nor do they always need to be woven into a story in order to form part of an argument.

The authors suggest that 'evidence derives its meaning from a story context.'[31] In this passage the authors imply that stories are the only form of context to give 'loose facts' meaning. We can agree that '[w]ithout a context any evidence is meaningless'.[32] The classical rationalist theory of evidence treats evidence as a term of relation:[33] it accepts that evidence takes its meaning from context. The context, however, is traditionally seen as an argument, rather than a story. One reason why modern narrative theories are significant is that they appear to pro-

26. *E.g.* J.H.Wigmore, *The Science of Judicial Proof* (1937), ch. XXX-XXXI, discussed in AE at p.155ff.
27. *E.g.* M.A.Abu Hareira, discussed in RE, pp. 77 and 241.
28. RE at pp. 223-225; for example, many, but not all. criminal charges contain the ingredients of a story (temporality, particularity, connectedness); but some relate only to states of affairs at given moments of time (*e.g.* being drunk in charge of a vehicle or violation of some health and safety standards) and some may lack connectedness (*e.g.* where a proponent has to prove the identity of the accused and the fact of death of the victim and the evidence relating to these two probanda is unrelated). It is worth noting that one condition for applying Bayes theorem in evaluating evidence is that the information to be combined must be independent or conditionally independent, *i.e.* not connected, *see* AE pp. 421-424 (P.Dawid).
29. D. N. MacCormick, , 'Coherence in Legal Justification', in W.Krawietz *et al.*, eds., *Theorie der Normen* (1984).
30. *Idem* p. 40.
31. *Idem* p. 33.
32. *Ibidem.*
33. *E.g.* TEBW, pp. 126-127.

vide an alternative context for 'homeless facts'. Whether, in the context of advocacy and adjudication, stories and arguments are alternatives or complementary is an important issue in the theory of evidence. Wigmore believed that his analytical approach was superior to 'the narrative method'; I agree with the authors that narrative and analysis are more plausibly regarded as complementary.[34] But the distinction between the two remains significant.

Another potential source of confusion is the way in which the authors seem to equate 'generalizations' and 'rules'. For example, they list a number of examples of 'rules, empirical or legal, that are often found to underlie the acceptance and rejection of evidence.' [35] These include 'confessions are usually true', 'Police-officers do not commit perjury' and 'all drug addicts are thieves'. In ordinary usage these would all be treated as examples of empirical generalizations rather than rules.[36] In the immediate context, where the authors are questioning reliance on such crude 'common-sense generalizations' they may be rescued by suggesting that they have used the wrong term; but later, when they advance 'universal rules of evidence', they seem in some cases to have jumped straight from factual findings to recommending binding rules based on them It does not follow that because there is a great deal of research showing that eyewitness identification evidence or confessions are often unreliable, particularly under specified conditions, that there should be a general requirement of corroboration of these kinds of evidence. Indeed, it is striking that after giving due consideration to the research on eyewitness identification evidence, to the best of my knowledge, no common law jurisdiction has prescribed a general rule requiring corroboration of such evidence, precisely because such a rule would be over-inclusive; instead, as in England, the most common prescription is admonitory, a duty to warn of the dangers of convicting on this kind of evidence alone.[37]

The loose terminology in *Anchored Narratives* leads to another dubious feature of the theory: it is said that narratives are either anchored in sub-narratives or in common-sense rules. But anchoring is both much more complicated and more reassuring than that. For typically, we try so far as possible to anchor in specific, concrete, particular evidence rather than in mere generalizations which may be speculative, prejudiced, vague, or just plain untrue.[38] In the classical rationalist theory the role of generalizations is twofold: first, to fill in gaps in the absence of particular evidence; and, secondly, to *justify* inferences from particular to particular.[39]

In their analysis of actual cases the authors use such ideas; but their general formulation of

34. *See* AE at pp. 155-171. The exact nature of the relationship is complex, depending in part on context. The issues are too complex to pursue here. At a very general level one may say that narrative is the dominant mode in presentation, but analysis is important in preparation of an argument and in justification of decisions and conclusions. Some of the complexities of the relationship between narrative and story in literary theory are usefully explored in S.Rimmon-Kenan, *Narrative Fiction: Contemporary Poetics* (1983).
35. At pp. 42-43.
36. 'Rule' is used here in its primary, normative, sense. The *locus classicus* for insisting on clear distinctions between 'rule' (normative) and 'habit' , 'prediction' and other empirical concepts is H.L.A.Hart, *The Concept of Law* (1961).
37. The likelihood of formal rules being either over-inclusive or under-inclusive in the evidentiary context is one of the main foundations for Benthams 'anti-nomian' thesis, his attack on *all* formal rules of evidence; TEBW, pp. 69-75.
38. Like stories, generalizations are both necessary and dangerous. On some of the problems relating to generalizations in this kind of context *see* AE, pp. 66-69,367-384; RE, pp. 284-285, 290-293.
39. On the role of generalizations as 'glue' in an argument *see* D.Schum, *Evidential Foundations of Probabilistic Reasoning* (1994), pp. 82-83, 109-110.

the theory of anchored narratives oversimplifies the nature of anchoring, and obscures some of the complexities of inferential argument.[40] In particular, it says surprisingly little about problems of relevance, weight and combining evidence.Furthermore, the distinction between 'good' and 'true' stories applies as much to sub-narratives as to master-narratives and they too need to be warranted by specific evidence.

THE ROLE OF STORIES

The authors give a convincing account of the seductive nature of stories and point to some of their dangers. I agree that stories are both necessary and dangerous, but I think that the authors underestimate the range and significance of the dangers: the eloquent or glib story-teller can, for example, sneak in unproved or irrelevant facts, proceed by innuendo, or switch the focus of attention from specific events to the character of the actor, (thereby subverting the precept 'judge the act not the actor).[41] Even Bennett and Feldman, the prime story enthusiasts, acknowledge that one of the main roles of story-telling is *to fill in gaps* in the evidence.[42] Configuration and confabulation enable us to see patterns from incomplete evidence. In other words they quite explicitly acknowledge that one reason why jurors resort to stories is to make up for the absence of evidence: stories help us to make sense of the world by enabling us to jump from fragmented, incomplete data to believable or familiar patterns when the anchors are missing. Nancy Pennington has elegantly illustrated how story-telling typically proceeds by confabulation and innuendo: if one knows ones audience, one need only present a few fragments of information and one can usually rely on the listeners to fill in the picture from their own background without making any specific allegations. That is why, in adjudication, every element of a story needs an anchor.

The authors of *Anchored Narratives* are no doubt aware of many of these points, but they do not really give us a coherent account of *why* stories are important in the context of investigation and adjudication: this is an area ripe for further research. Possible hypotheses include laziness; to cover gaps in available information; because particularities are easier to grasp than generalities; because a significant part of our stock of beliefs takes the form of stories rather than bare propositions; or because in certain circumstances relying on 'holistic' intuition is a better way of making judgments about what happened than proceeding analytically.[43]

40. For a masterly survey, *see* Schum, *ibidem, passim.*
41. RE ch. 7, especially, pp. 231, 243-245, 259 No. 123.
42. W. Lance Bennett and M. Feldman, *op. cit.*, pp. 33, 62-65.
43. These are not mutually exclusive. This is an area in which our understanding of legal decision-making could be greatly advanced by further psychological research.

UNIVERSAL RULES OF EVIDENCE

The point on which I most strongly part company with the authors is in respect of their recommended 'universal rules of evidence'.[44] We have seen already that they make no clear distinction between empirical generalizations and rules and that they seem to jump too fast from establishing certain points and embodying them in legal rules. On a very charitable reading, they can perhaps be rescued by Jeremy Bentham, the arch anti-nomian. Bentham distinguished between rules (categorical precepts) addressed to the will and instructions addressed to the understanding.[45] By instructions he meant something even weaker than guidelines, more like admonitions to take into account certain known dangers, such as the unreliability of certain kinds of evidence. Bentham argued that triers of fact should not be bound by any rules in considering and weighing evidence, but that triers of fact could be 'instructed' about the lessons of experience (which includes scientific findings) in the difficult task of fact-determination in particular cases. While some of the recommended rules might be acceptable as general admonitory instructions or guidelines in some systems, I know of no common law jurisdiction that adopts any one of the rules as a mandatory precept (although we might find some approximations). I believe that there are good reasons for this, but it is not possible to go into detail here. Suffice to say that most are far too simple and over-generalized to be workable.

However, there is a different ground for objection to these universal rules. This relates to differences in the procedural contexts of different legal systems and cultures. For example, the precept 'The prosecution must present at least one well-shaped narrative' assumes that the role, tasks and position of prosecutors are universal. They are not. While some of these general precepts have wide application, much more detailed local knowledge is required to test out their fit to any particular context. It is true that what constitutes a valid, and cogent argument on a disputed question of fact should be subject to general principles of logic that may claim universality; there may also be psychological generalizations about decision-making that could be found to transcend legal cultures. But what is appropriate or workable in a

44. Table 12.1 (at p.232) summarises the 'Ten universal rules of evidence' as follows:
'1: The prosecution must present at least one well-shaped narrative.
2: The prosecution must present a limited set of well-shaped narratives.
3: Essential components of the narrative must be anchored.
4: Anchors for different components of the charge should be independent of each other.
5: The trier of fact should give reasons for his or her decision by specifying the narrative and the accompanying anchoring.
6: A fact-finders decision as to the level of analysis of the evidence should be explained through an articulation of the general beliefs used as anchors.
7: There should be no competing story with equally good or better anchoring.
8: There should be no falsifications of the indictment's narrative and nested sub-narratives.
9: There should be no anchoring onto obviously false beliefs.
10: The indictment and the verdict should contain the same narrative.'

It is not possible here to consider each of these 'rules' in detail; while sympathetic to most as informal guidelines or 'instructions' to decision-makers, I would modify or qualify most of them, would reject No. 4 and would oppose the enactment of any of them as formal rules in my own jurisdiction. No.5 raises controversial issues for those common law jurisdictions in which the jury survives as an important institution and is prohibited from giving reasons. This is a good example of why it is difficult to prescribe universal rules of this kind without regard to context.

45. TEBW, pp. 43-44, 67-68.

given context is much more complex. Whether one crosses disciplinary or national boundaries, it is important to be sensitive to local knowledge.[46]

To conclude, I am in general agreement with the general thrust of *Anchored Narratives* and I believe that it adds significantly to the literature by focussing attention on relatively neglected issues and sources and by offering many stimulating and highly provocative hypotheses. The tone of the book may appear to be more controversial than it needs to be, especially at the level of theory. If some of the criticisms made here seem sharp, it is just because more research is needed in this area on the basis of quite sophisticated theory.

In English academics colloquially, and only semi-seriously, sometimes distinguish between 'good-bad' and 'bad-good' books; the latter give defective answers to important questions; the former offer attractive, elegant or palatable answers to trivial or meaningless questions. Perhaps we might say of *Anchored Narratives* that it is an uneven, good book: the questions it raises are very important, but the answers are in need of refinement.[47]

46. This theme is developed in W. Twining, *Blackstone's Tower: The English Law School* (1994), ch.7, especially at pp. 177-184.
47. I am grateful to Terry Anderson, Jelte Hielkema and Hans Nijboer for advice and comments, but they are not responsible for, and do not necessarily agree with, my opinions and conclusions.

[14]
Good Stories and True Stories

Over the past decade I have visited the Netherlands many times. On almost every occasion Hans Crombag has been a significant presence. On a personal level, he has been a friendly, welcoming host and a quietly nuanced guide to what it means to be Dutch. Intellectually, he has been an important presence. Even when he did not say much, he has provided a subtle reminder of different perspectives and a questioning attitude. And, of course, how often was he silent? I consider Hans to be a friend and it is a great pleasure to contribute to this *liber amicorum.*

In the English-speaking world, Hans Crombag is best known as a co-author of *Anchored Narratives.*[2] I make frequent reference to this text and I have felt a frustrated by not being able to consult the much more substantial *Dubieuze Zaken*,[3] of which the English version is a redaction. As a foreign observer, I have been surprised to learn that *Dubieuze Zaken* caused such a stir and such hostile reactions. It is refreshing to find a much closer link between academic and general public debate about legal matters in the Netherlands than in my own country. However, although the tone of the book was polemical, many of the basic ideas were well grounded in Anglo-American evidence scholarship. The originality lay in applying these ideas in detail to a civil law jurisdiction, the Netherlands, and in extending them at a theoretical level, in some instances quite adventurously. I have commented on *Anchored Narratives* at length elsewhere, broadly agreeing with most of its central themes, but dissenting from some particulars.[4] This paper elaborates briefly on just one topic, the distinction between good stories and true stories.

1. Faculty of Law, University College London.
2. W.A. Wagenaar, P.J. van Koppen and H.F.M. Crombag (1993) *Anchored narratives: The psychology of criminal evidence.* London: Harvester Wheatsheaf, further: *Anchored Narratives.*
3. H.F.M. Crombag, P.J. van Koppen and W.A. Wagenaar (1994) *Dubieuze zaken: De psychologie van strafrechtelijk bewijs.* Amsterdam: Contact (2e herziene druk).
4. W. Twining (1995) Anchored narratives: A comment. *European Journal of Crime, Criminal Law and Criminal Justice, 1995*(1), 106-114; W. Twining (1999) Necessary but dangerous? Generalizations and narratives in argumentation about 'facts in criminal process'. In M. Malsch and J.F. Nijboer (eds.), *Complex cases: Perspectives on the Netherlands criminal justice system* (pp. 69-98). Amsterdam: Thela Thesis.

A central theme of *Anchored Narratives* is that in criminal process in the Netherlands there is a danger that 'good' stories will be accepted without being anchored in particular evidence and background generalizations. Stories may play an important, possibly even a necessary, part in the psychological processes involved in fact-investigation and fact-determination, but for the purposes of criminal justice they must be true, that is all the material allegations must be warranted or anchored. Seductive 'good' stories often push out true stories. In criminal process, stories may be necessary, but they are also dangerous.

Quite apart from serious literacy criticism, a story can be considered 'good' for many different reasons. It may good for a particular purpose: for example, in teaching it may be a good vehicle for making a point interestingly, clearly, or memorably. In other contexts it may be 'good' because it has a strong moral, or is amusing, or is a vehicle for a fecund metaphor. From the point of view of a hearer a story may be 'good' because it appeals to the imagination or some strong emotion, such as fear or lust or hope. And so on. In adjudication stories may appeal because they arouse interest, are persuasive, plausible, reassuring, or familiar.

In *Anchored Narratives* it is acknowledged that stories may be good for many different reasons, but the focus is on 'well-formed' stories, that is ones that are believed to be true because they have "a readily identifiable central action; and a context that provides an easy and natural explanation of why the actors behaved in the way they did."[5] In this context stories are considered important because they help the decision-makers 'make sense' of the events under consideration.[6] Similarly, in *Anchored Narratives* 'true' is treated as empirically true. In the immediate context of exploring the theme that 'good stories push out true stories', it was probably adequate to define 'true' and 'good' quite narrowly. However, I shall suggest that for purposes of future psychological research on the role of stories in criminal process, more complex notions of goodness and truth may be required.

I believe that the thesis that good stories often push out true stories is generally correct. In my own writings I have extended the argument about the dangers by suggesting that in practice narrative provides a wonderful vehicle for subverting some of the cherished values of adjudication – for example by sneaking in irrelevant facts, by suggesting unproven facts through innuendo or confabulation,[7] by shifting attention

5. *Anchored Narratives*, pp. 35-37.

6. Of course, in adjudication the main task of the fact-finder is to decide what happened in fact, without necessarily explaining it. For example, in most criminal cases motive is not a material fact. As every lawyer knows, in practice motive is nearly always treated as important and this corresponds to psychological literature. This suggests that human beings feel a strong need to understand 'why?', even if it is not strictly part of their immediate task.

7. Webster's Dictionary defines to confabulate as "3. To fill in gaps in memory by fabrication". The term is used in American case law, see, for example, Blackmun J. in Rock v Arkansas 483 US 44 (1987): "to fill in details from the imagination to make an answer more coherent and complete." Psychologists sometimes prefer the more differentiated terminology

from the specific events in issue to the character(s) of the main protagonist(s) (thereby subverting the principle 'judge the act, not the actor'), and by playing on unspoken biases and prejudices through the choice of emotionally laden terms or by the suggestion of dubious unspoken generalizations.[8]

In teaching about the role of narrative in legal processes, I introduce some of the main themes by telling a series of stories. I hope that they are all pedagogically 'good' in the sense of being interesting and in making a 'point', but not all are good in the narrow sense of being well-formed. Here I shall consider four examples with specific reference to the distinction between 'good' stories and 'true' stories.

1. Relevance

> Once upon a time, I walked into a law school. The place was Boston. The institution was the New England Law School, formerly known as the Portia Law School, then is was an all-women's institution. I was due to give a public lecture. The ground floor of the law school is made of plate glass and owing to a trick of the light I had walked nose-first into a plate glass window. I had had a good lunch, but I was quite sober.
>
> When I picked myself up from the pavement I was dazed and my nose was bleeding. I found my host's room and lay down on the floor. By the scheduled time my head had cleared and the worst of my nosebleed was over, but there was blood all over the front of my suit and I still had to dab my nose with a bloody handkerchief. With a stiff upper lip, I decided to give the lecture. At the start I explained the reason for my condition. I have never had such a sympathetic audience and my lecture was unusually well received.

This story is generally true, and can be vouched for by my host, Peter Tillers, a leading evidence scholar. When I tell it in class, I may embellish it a little, acting it out and possibly exaggerating the amount of blood. One might say that this is a moderately good story that is largely, but not wholly, true. I make it better in the telling in order to illustrate some points about relevance – in particular the point that a good story can be persuasive without being in the least relevant to the merits of the argument. Note that in this version I omit to mention the subject of the lecture (Wigmorean analysis) and the fact that the audience was potentially very sceptical, if not hostile. The information about Portia may be interesting, but it is entirely irrelevant to the point of the story.

associated with "schematic processing". The best account of the literature relating to law is to be found in R. Hastie (ed.). (1993) *Inside the jury: The psychology of juror decision making.* Cambridge: Cambridge University Press.

8. Ibid.

2. 'Holism'

> Once upon a time, the Inner London Education Authority was approached by a man who claimed that he had a programme for teaching skills of facial recognition in a very short time. The core of the technique was a protocol for asking a series of questions designed to classify the features of a face, first horizontally (hairline, forehead, eyebrows, eyes, nose, mouth, chin etc.) and then vertically (ear-shape and so on). The Authority expressed cautious interest, perhaps because it thought that such skills might enhance the employment prospects of school-leavers, for instance, as security guards or immigration officials. However, they felt that the programme should be validated, so they asked a psychologist to test it. The psychologist conducted some controlled experiments involving two groups that took the course and two control groups that did not and evaluating their facial recognition skills at the end. The results suggested that those who had not taken the course were better at facial recognition than those who had taken it.

This story is based on fact.[9] I think that it is a good story, not only in the sense that it is well formed, but also because it makes a point in a nicely ironic and quite memorable way. The point is that in ordinary life we make some judgements 'holistically' rather than analytically and that sometimes analysis can impede good judgement. The story is useful both in discussing ideas of coherence and in raising questions about the role of analytical techniques and stories in making judgements based on evidence, a theme close to the core of *Anchored Narratives*. This seems to me to be an example of good story that is probably true (though not well-anchored) which is useful in raising questions about holism and atomism in a vivid way, whether or not it is correct in all its details.[10]

3. Confabulation

> *"Once upon a time, John Went to Sam's Party. Sam Blew out the Candles."*[11]

9. See A.D. Baddeley and M.M. Woodhead (1983) Improving face recognition ability. In S.M.A. Lloyd-Bostock and B.R. Clifford (eds.), *Evaluating witness evidence: Recent psychological research and new perspectives*. Chichester: Wiley, at pp. 126-127.

10. On holism and atomism, see T.J. Anderson and W.L. Twining (1998) *Analysis of evidence: How to do things with facts based on Wigmore's science of judicial proof*. Evanston: Northwestern University Press, at pp. 165-171, 278-289. This is a field ripe for further psychological research into the relationship between stories and 'good judgement'.

11. This story is borrowed, with grateful acknowledgement, from Nancy Pennington, who uses it to great effect in explaining the idea of confabulation.

When I tell this story to a class or other legal audience in Britain or the United States, I then ask how many of them did not imagine a cake. Hardly anyone claims that they did not. One gets similar, but less uniform responses, if one asks about the ages of Sam and John (English audiences tend to assume that this was a children's party).

This is a work of fiction. It is untrue (empirically) and it can hardly claim to be well formed. But it is an excellent vehicle for illustrating the idea of confabulation in a vivid way. The hearer or audience instinctively fills in the gaps from their own stock of background knowledge and beliefs. If one knows one's audience one can be reasonably confident not only that they will go beyond the information in the story, but also about what information they are likely to supply. However, that depends on a shared cultural experience or 'stock of knowledge.' On at least two occasions, when I have addressed groups of young lawyers from the Commonwealth, those from the Indian sub-continent have claimed they did not imagine a cake. Instead they assumed that there had been a power cut, because back home candles are associated with electricity failures. This neatly illustrates the point that people's 'general experience' or background beliefs vary across time, place, and culture – a crucially important theme in the theory of evidence.[12]

Clearly confabulation offers rich opportunities for 'cheating' in legal contexts, especially by advocates who are confident of their audience. It does not necessarily even involve overt innuendo. In adversary proceedings, where both sides are represented, an alert advocate can, at least in theory, counter dangerous examples of this kind of trap. For example, s/he can ask about the ages of Sam and John or whether there was in fact a cake. But, in practice, this will not always be easy. Again there is plenty of scope for research into the extent and varieties of confabulation in legal proceedings, for example as a means of introducing implicit, 'unanchored facts'.

4. Parables as Evidence

My final story concerns the parable of the Prodigal Son. I have written about this at length elsewhere in relation to the idea of the 'moral' or 'point' of a story.[13] Here I consider it from a somewhat different point of view.

I regularly use *In Re the Estate of James Dale Warren, Jr.* as a vehicle for detailed analysis and construction of arguments about questions of fact.[14] This simulated case,

12. See futher, W. Twining (1999) Necessary but dangerous?: Generalizations and narratives in argumentation about 'facts in criminal process'. In M. Malsch & H. Nijboer (Eds.), *Complex cases: Perspectives on the Netherlands criminal justice system* (pp. 106-114). Amsterdam: Thela Thesis.

13. W. Twining (2000) The ratio decidendi of the case of the prodigal son. In K. O'Donavan and G.R. Rubin (eds.). Oxford: Oxford University Press (forthcoming).

14. The case is reproduced in full in Anderson and Twining, 1991, *op. cit.*, at pp. 305-27. This is a hypothetical case that originated as a simulated problem in the American National Trial

set in the United States in 1980, concerns a contested will executed by James Dale Warren, Sr. in a nursing home on the afternoon of his death. This new will purported to leave almost all of his estate to his son, James Dale Warren, Jr., who had been estranged from him for most of his life, but who had been recently reconciled with him. He had assiduously attended his father during the last three days before he died. The effect of the will, if valid, would be essentially to disinherit his only daughter, Susan, and her two children. Susan had lived with her father in his home during his last years until she felt that his medical condition required transferring him to a nursing home. James Sr. may have resented the transfer, but otherwise there was little evidence of any serious rift between father and daughter and convincing evidence that James Sr. adored his grandchildren for whom his house was the only home they had known. Unfortunately for Susan, she had been involved in a road accident a few days before her father's death and had stayed away for fear that her injuries might upset the old man. Unknown to Susan, James Jr. had stepped into the breach and was in attendance while his father wrote the new will. Susan contests the will on two grounds: (1) that the testator lacked testamentary capacity at the time of execution of the new will; and (2) that the will was made under the undue influence of James Jr., the principal beneficiary. The main issues are factual.

In the context of a mock trial counsel for each party are asked to develop persuasive 'theories' and 'themes' to support their case. In this case each side latches on to fairly obvious competing images: counsel for Susan regularly develop a Dickensian image of grasping relatives fawning over a dying man; the other side counters with the parable of the Prodigal Son. [15]

On one occasion, in an American law school, before assigning roles, I asked the class to discuss what themes might usefully be developed in this case. As usual, the Prodigal Son was the first suggestion. However, at this point the discussion took a surprising turn. The exchange can be reconstructed in the form of an imaginary dialogue:

WLT: Which side does the parable help?

Student 1: The son, of course.

WLT: Why?

Student 2: because it is natural for a father to be generous after reconciliation with a long lost son.

WLT: Is that the moral of the original parable?

Competition in the 1980s. It is particularly well designed in that the documentation is thorough, and the evidence is difficult to analyze, is evenly balanced and raises interesting problems of trial tactics and presentation.

15. In teaching, Anderson and I challenge the appropriateness of both of these images in this context.

Student 3: It could be about repentance and forgiveness. That still helps James Jr.
WLT: Are you suggesting that a story from the New Testament is *evidence* of how fathers behave in twentieth century America?
Student 2: No. But it does support the proposition that this is *reasonable* behaviour on the part of the father, therefore he was not behaving irrationally.
WLT: Is that not inferring an 'is' from an 'ought'?
Student 1: Well, the story sets out a familiar model of how good fathers do and should behave, like 'best practice'.
WLT: Again, is that evidence?
Students (in chorus): Yes.
WLT: Have you read the original text of St Luke's Gospel?
Students 1 and 2 (abashed): Well, not recently.
WLT (meanly producing the text and circulating copies from the St James' version): Look, the father, in responding to the elder son's complaint, explicitly says: "Son, thou art ever with me, and all that I have is thine." (Luke 16. V. 31). In other words: "I am not disinheriting you. I am only throwing a party to celebrate." Surely, that helps Susan.
Student 4: That's pedantic. The popular image of the story makes it out to be about reconciliation and forgiveness and generosity. It is the image rather than the text that will have resonance with the jury. So it does help James Jr.
WLT: Is that rational?
Student 1: Counsel for Susan can point this out, if counsel for James Jr. tries to use it...
(The dialogue continued).[16]

This is, of course, an idealized construction of the behaviour of both teacher and students. The original incident stimulated me to think further about the roles of theories and themes in argument about questions of fact and about the analogy between biblical parables and precedents in the common law.[17] Here I want to pursue a different issue: how can a secondhand report of a parable (presumably presented as a fictitious story) be *evidence* of what happened in a particular situation in Middle America in 1980? The students wanted to use the biblical story to support two propositions: (i) that James Warren Sr at the time of the making of his deathbed will had testamentary

16. Subsequently, students alerted to these points have usually shied away from using both the Prodigal Son and Martin Chuzzlewit as the explicit basis for themes in presenting their arguments.
17. *Op. cit.* above. On the role of stories in arguments about questions of law and about questions of fact and their inter-relationship, see W. Twining (1991) *Rethinking evidence.* Evanston: Northwestern University Press, at pp. 228-249.

capacity to make a valid will,[18] (ii) that James Dale Warren did not intend to disinherit his daughter and grandchildren.

A reasonable reconstruction of the two lines of argument might be as follows:

1. For James Warren Jr.

1. At the moment of reconciliation between a father and his son, it is appropriate for the father to be forgiving and generous in celebrating the return of the lost sheep/prodigal.
2. James Dale Warren Sr. was forgiving and generous in his treatment of his son at the moment of reconciliation.
3. James Dale Warren Sr.'s behaviour was natural and appropriate for a father in such circumstances.
4. James Dale Warren Sr.'s behaviour was not unreasonable or irrational in the circumstances.
5. Either (a) James Dale Warren's behaviour does not support the proposition that he lacked sufficient mental ability to make a valid will. Or (b) James Dale Warren's behaviour was rational and reasonable and supports the proposition that he had sufficient mental ability to make a valid will.

2. For Susan

1. At the moment of reconciliation it is appropriate for a father to celebrate, e.g. by throwing a party and killing the fatted calf, but it is not appropriate for him to disinherit loyal children who have stayed at home and supported him.
2. James Dale Warren Sr's deathbed will disinherited his loyal daughter who had stayed at home and supported him.
3. James Dale Warren Sr's deathbed will effectively disinherited his grandchildren whom he loved dearly.
4. James Dale Warren Sr's treatment of his daughter and grandchildren was not reasonable in the circumstances.
5. This supports the propositions that at the time JDW lacked testamentary capacity, in that:
   a. JDW was not able to know the natural objects of his bounty and their claims upon him

18. In this context 'testamentary capacity' means that "such person at the time of execution of the will must have had sufficient mental ability to understand the business in which he is engaged, the effect of his act in making the will, the nature and extent of his property; he must be able to know his next of kin and the natural objects of his bounty and their claims upon him; he must have memory sufficient to collect in his mind the elements of the business about to be transacted and to hold them long enough to perceive at least their obvious relation to each other and to be able to form a reasonable judgment as to them."

b. JDW did not have sufficient memory to collect in his mind the elements of the business about to be transacted and to hold them long enough to perceive at least their obvious relation to each other
c. JDW did not make a reasonable judgement as to any aspects of the effects of his will

The story of the Prodigal Son supports propositions 1.1 and 1.3 and 2.1 and 2.4 – in other words it can be invoked by both sides. But what is the relationship between a biblical parable and *a question of fact* in America in 1980? One answer is that the parable provides a model for behaviour by fathers in the situation of reconciliation with prodigals. There is scope for differing interpretations of the precise scope of the moral(s) of the parable,[19] but two points are clear from the text: (i) it is reasonable for the father to be generous, forgiving and to celebrate, but (ii) it is not reasonable for him to be so generous as to disinherit loyal, stay-at-home offspring.

The key point is that the 'question of fact' here involves judgements of reasonableness, the parable provides a standard or model for the behaviour of fathers in this kind of situation, and the parable has been absorbed into American culture to the extent that people do appeal to the New Testament for standards and models for good or appropriate parental behaviour. Accordingly, St Luke's gospel is relevant, and indeed quite cogent in its support for both lines of argument.[20] If the concept of 'questions of fact' includes normative judgements, for instance about reasonableness, as it clearly does, then appeals to the Bible for standards of reasonableness are relevant and can be quite cogent. Whether one wishes to call the Bible 'evidence' in this context is a secondary matter of semantics. The point is that it can be a source of valid, relevant, and potentially cogent arguments.

What is the implication of this for the distinction between good and true stories? Clearly, the parable of the prodigal son is a 'good story' in several senses, including the narrow one of being 'well-formed'. But is it true? No claim seems to have been made that it was presented as an account of an actual historical event and Luke's version is a secondhand account of Jesus telling a story – hearsay upon hearsay about a work of fiction. So it is not true in a narrow empirical sense. Almost certainly it never happened. But is it 'a true story' for the purposes of *Anchored Narratives*?

19. See above note 14.
20. At first sight, on the interpretation given here, it gives stronger support to Susan's case than to her brother's. However, it should be borne in mind that the burden of proof is on Susan and the probanda require that she shows that he lacked ability and memory, i.e capacity, not that he made a mistake, or forgot, or acted unreasonably on this occasion, i.e there is an additional inferential step from this occasion to general capacity.

Conclusion

There is a great deal of scope for further psychological research into the role of narrative in criminal process and other legal contexts. For example, what psychological needs are stories satisfying in particular legal contexts? When and how do 'good' stories push out 'true' stories? What do different decision-makers consider to be good? It is for psychologists to frame the precise questions and the best methods of approaching them within their discipline. But lawyers have a role in providing accounts of the specifically legal contexts that are both realistic and sensitive to the complexities. So let me end with a cautionary tale.[21] In the Anglo-American tradition an enormous amount of time, energy, ingenuity and money has been spent on research into the design and staging of identification parades ('line ups' in American usage). Nearly all of this research proceeds on the assumption that the only or main function of such staged events is to produce admissible and, as far as possible, reliable evidence. But this assumption is sociologically dubious. It may well be the case that in practice identification parades may serve other functions, such as persuading the suspect that 'the game is up' and that, in the common law system, it would be sensible to plead guilty; or that no positive identification is expected and that the absence of a positive identification may be used to eliminate a suspect or to provide a justification for closing an enquiry for lack of evidence; or there may be other latent functions. Similarly, further research into the role of stories in criminal process needs to have a sociologically nuanced and realistic picture of the complexity of these processes. Such research should not be confined to contested trials, let alone American juries, but should extend to other stages, including the investigative stage, where 'suspect-driven inquiries' are a real danger, as *Anchored Narratives* convincingly illustrates. Such a nuanced set of assumptions needs to include the ideas that stories may be considered 'good' in particular contexts for many different reasons and that in law almost all determinations of 'fact' combine both normative and empirical elements that are difficult to keep separate.

21. For further details see W. Twining (1991) *Rethinking evidence.* Evanston: Northwestern University Press, Chapter 5; G.M. Stephenson (1989) *The psychology of criminal justice.* Oxford: Blackwell, Chapter 9.

[15]
Narrative and Generalizations in Argumentation about Questions of Fact

A familiar feature of academic life is the phenomenon of two or more bodies of literature "talking past each other," even though the problems and issues they address seem to be closely connected. Within the discipline of law, a striking example is the almost entire separation of literature and debates concerning argumentation about questions of law on the one hand, and questions of fact on the other. The term "legal reasoning" has been imperialistically hijacked for the former by jurists who seem to know little or care less about the latter, which has been variously referred to as "the logic of proof," "evidence and inference," "fact determination" and so on. Ronald Dworkin does not concern himself with Bayes Theorem; Bayesians and inductivists alike do not concern themselves much with Dworkin or other theorists of legal reasoning. Yet every lawyer knows distinguishing between "questions of law" and "questions of fact" is problematic, contingent, and often unsustainable. Surely issues about the validity, cogency, and appropriateness of reasoning about questions of law and questions of fact are intimately related aspects of

---

* This paper is one of a series resulting from an ongoing project of an international group of scholars that worked together at the Netherlands Institute of Advanced Study on Criminal Justice in Wasenaar in 1994–1995. Other members of the group are Professor Hans Nijboer (Leiden), Dr. Jelte Heilkema (Rotterdam), Dr. Marijke Malsch (Leiden), and Professor Terence Anderson (Miami). The paper grew out of many discussions in the group. This version is adapted from an essay published in UPPSALA, FESTSKRIFT TILL STIG STRÖMHOLM (Åke Frändburg ed. 1997). It draws in part on earlier papers, especially William Twining, *Civilians Don't Try: A Comment on Mirjan Damaska's Rational and Irrational Proof Revisited*, 5 CARDOZO J. INT'L & COMP. L. 69 (1997) [hereinafter *Civilians Don't Try*] and William Twining, *Anchored Narratives—A Comment*, 3 EUR. J. CRIME, CRIM. L. & CRIM. JUST. 106 (1995) (book review) [hereinafter *Anchored Narratives—A Comment*]. Further, it anticipates parts of William Twining, *Necessary but Dangerous: The Role of Stories and Generalizations in Legal Proof in* COMPLEX CASES (Hans Nijboer & Marijke Malsch, forthcoming 1999) which explores the same themes in more detail, with special reference to the Netherlands.

"lawyers' reasonings,"[1] which in turn is part of the more general topic of practical reasoning.[2]

Within evidence scholarship, a similar, but less sharp, bifurcation can be discerned between the literature on "the logic of proof" (including debates about probabilities and proof) and the largely empirical literature on the role of narrative and stories in fact determination. Here the divide is not so great, for some writers have acknowledged a place for both in the study of evidence in legal contexts.[3] However, many puzzles remain about the relationship between stories and reasoning in argumentation in legal contexts. This paper attempts to explore one aspect of this relationship and to further undermine the separation of discussions about questions of law and questions of fact.

It may be helpful to set my topic in a historical context. A brief overview of the development of "the new evidence scholarship"[4] might be restated as follows: Questions about the nature of evidence and inference in law can be traced back at least to the eighteenth century, and beyond that to the convoluted history of rhetoric.

The modern Anglo-American debates about "the logic of proof" could be said to have begun about 1970.[5] In retrospect one can

1. The useful term "lawyers' reasonings" was coined, or at least popularized, in JULIUS STONE, LEGAL SYSTEM AND LAWYERS' REASONINGS 325 (1964). Unfortunately, Stone followed convention in confining his attention largely to reasoning about disputed questions of law in hard cases. *See id.* at 301–37. The term can usefully encompass and draw attention to the relationships between, for example, reasoning in negotiation, sentencing, rule making, other lawyers' operations, and the two more standard topics of questions of law and questions of fact.

2. *See* WILLIAM TWINING, LAW IN CONTEXT: ENLARGING A DISCIPLINE 348–50 (1997).

3. *See generally* TERENCE ANDERSON & WILLIAM TWINING, ANALYSIS OF EVIDENCE (1998) (exploring the uses of logical analysis and story telling in the fact finding process); DAVID A. BINDER & PAUL BERGMAN, FACT INVESTIGATION (1984) (outlining the uses of empirical proof and story telling in the fact finding process).

4. The term "New Evidence Scholarship" was coined by Richard Lempert, *The New Evidence Scholarship*, *in* 109 PROBABILITY AND INFERENCE IN THE LAW OF EVIDENCE: THE USES AND LIMITATIONS OF BAYESIANISM 61 (Peter Tillers & Eric D. Green eds., 1988) (referencing specifically the debates about probabilities and proof). Since then, it has been expanded to cover a much wider range of topics relating to evidence and information in law. *See* WILLIAM TWINING, RETHINKING EVIDENCE 350–52 (Northwestern Univ. Press 1994) (1990) [hereinafter RETHINKING EVIDENCE].

5. The phrase "the logic of proof" was coined by Wigmore (1913) to depict that part of the field of Evidence dealing with what constitutes valid, cogent, and appropriate arguments about disputed questions of fact in adjudication. *See* RETHINKING EVIDENCE, *supra* note 4, at 351. It is used here to include inductivist, Bayesian, skeptical, and other perspectives on analysis and argumentation about questions of fact in legal contexts. While Wigmore focused mainly on contested jury trials, his successors have extended the application of the basic ideas to other kinds of proceedings, other phases of the legal

distinguish five main phases. There was, first, a quite practical concern that lawyers were generally innumerate and as such were unable to cope with the rapidly increasing use of statistics in litigation, especially in areas involving expert evidence with respect to such matters as paternity, discrimination, antitrust, and insurance.[6] This problem was dramatized by the difficulties encountered in dealing with even the most elementary misuse of statistics by an alleged "expert" in the famous case of *People v. Collins*,[7] which involved identification of an interracial couple in California. The first commentators stressed the potential of statistical analysis in evaluating evidence—provided that it was properly used.[8]

The second phase, led by Professor Laurence Tribe of Harvard, was directed at curbing the enthusiasm of mathematicists.[9] Tribe and others argued that even if all reasoning about disputed questions of fact is in principle mathematical, it would be both inappropriate and dangerous as a matter of policy to encourage or allow explicit quantification of such matters as the criminal standard of proof or the likelihood of guilt in identification cases.[10] Three main reasons were advanced for this: (1) as a matter of communication, as long as judges and juries can be assumed to be innumerate, they should be addressed in a language they can understand; (2) mathematical arguments are likely to be overly seductive or prejudicial because seemingly "hard" quantified variables will tend to push out "soft," non-quantitative variables; and (3) it is politically improper to quantify certain matters, such as an acceptable level of risk of conviction of the innocent.[11]

In the next phase, the debate moved to a quite different, more

process (including police investigation, which Wigmore dealt with briefly in an appendix), and non-common law systems, in this case the Netherlands. *See id.* at 349–50.

6. *See* DAVID W. BARNES, STATISTICS AS PROOF 33–34 (1983).

7. 438 P.2d 33 (Cal. 1968). In recent years it has often been argued that lawyers and judges can no longer afford to be innumerate. *See* DAVID W. BARNES, STATISTICS AS PROOF xv (1983); SIR RICHARD EGGLESTON, EVIDENCE, PROOF AND PROBABILITY PREFACE 1–7 (1983); John Kaplan, *Decision-Theory and the Fact-Finding Process*, 20 STAN. L. REV. 1065, 1092 (1968). For more details, see RETHINKING EVIDENCE, *supra* note 4, at 118–19. For anthologies of contributions to the debates *see generally* EDWARD J. IMWINKELRIED & GLEN WEISSENBERGER, AN EVIDENCE ANTHOLOGY (1996) (combining numerous authors' works regarding various evidentiary subjects); EVIDENCE AND PROOF (William Twining & Alex Stein eds., New York Univ. Press 1992) (bringing together the leading trends and thoughts concerning legal fact finding).

8. *See* RETHINKING EVIDENCE, *supra* note 4, at 70.

9. *See* Laurence H. Tribe, *Trial by Mathematics: Precision and Ritual in the Legal Process*, 84 HARV. L. REV. 1329, 1329–30 (1971).

10. *See id.* at 1332–38 (giving examples of cases where mathematical probability confused the juries).

11. *See id.* at 1334–38.

philosophical plane with the intervention of Jonathan Cohen, a logician from Oxford. He challenged the assumption that all arguments about probabilities are in principle mathematical or, as he termed it, Pascalian.[12] Law, he suggested, provides one of the paradigm examples of non-Pascalian inductivist reasoning.[13] Cohen stimulated controversies in several disciplines, notably law, medical diagnosis, and psychology.[14] Although it was based on philosophical arguments, Cohen's thesis clearly had political implications.[15] It served as a warning against "the cult of the expert" and provided theoretical support for the belief in the cognitive competence of ordinary citizens to make sound judgments based on everyday practical reasoning.[16] This is particularly significant in jurisdictions that place a high value on lay participation in the administration of justice. In this view, innumerate judges and ordinary jurors are competent to adjudicate disputed questions of fact and are usually justified in relying on "common sense." Cohen's thesis provoked sharp attacks from jurists in England, Australia, and especially the United States.[17]

A fourth phase has seen strong challenges to the rationality of the kinds of propositional logics espoused by both mathematicists and inductivists. These challenges have taken several forms: practicing lawyers, especially in England, remain highly skeptical about the scope of mathematical reasoning and formal logic in legal contexts.[18]

---

12. *See* L. JONATHAN COHEN, THE PROBABLE AND THE PROVABLE 38–39 (1977) (arguing that lawyers use non-Pascalian inductive reasoning about questions of fact).

13. *See id.* at 44.

14. *See id.* at 258–63.

15. *See generally id.*

16. *See id.* at 120.

17. *See* RETHINKING EVIDENCE, *supra* note 4, at 92–141. These three strands in the probabilities debate continue to command attention in the common law world. For example, a lawyer and a statistician based in New Zealand have recently published a practical manual directed toward forensic scientists and lawyers outlining a Bayesian approach to scientific evidence. *See* BERNARD ROBERTSON & G.A. VIGNAUX, INTERPRETING EVIDENCE: EVALUATING FORENSIC SCIENCE IN THE COURTROOM 17–18 (1995); *cf.* C.G.G. AITKEN, STATISTICS AND THE EVALUATION OF EVIDENCE FOR FORENSIC SCIENTISTS 34–36 (1995) (discussing Bayes' theorem and the evaluation of evidence). Similarly, at both theoretical and practical levels, the debates between Bayesians, frequentists, inductivists and others have continued. Developments such as DNA testing and evidence have naturally attracted the attention of statisticians, and I have learned that many of the applied problems my colleagues in statistics are studying have implications for forensic contexts, police investigations and other legal processes. *See* JOSEPH B. KADANE & DAVID A. SCHUM, A PROBABILISTIC ANALYSIS OF THE SACCO AND VANZETTI EVIDENCE 121–31 (1996); DAVID SCHUM, EVIDENTIAL FOUNDATIONS OF PROBABILISTIC REASONING 243–61 (1994).

18. *See, e.g.*, CROSS AND TAPPER ON EVIDENCE 173 (8th ed. 1995); *contra Regina v.*

Skeptics, relativists and subjectivists of various kinds question traditional conceptions of rationality or even the very possibility of rationality in fact determination.[19] Also, there seems to be as great a chasm between the mathematicists and even the most moderate of the growing mêlée of post-modernists.[20] Most immediately relevant in the present context is the work of empirical social scientists, notably Pennington, Hastie, Bennett, and Feldman, who have produced compelling evidence that in practice, jurors and other triers of fact reach judgments about particular past events by assessing the plausibility of stories.[21] Jurors, it is said, proceed "holistically" by comparing competing stories, by deciding on the plausibility of the story offered by the prosecution (or other proponent), by reconstructing their own version of events from the material presented to them.[22]

In the last few years, "the New Evidence Scholarship" could be said to have entered a fifth phase. Scholars from the Netherlands, led by Professor Hans Nijboer of Leiden, have introduced recent Anglo-American ideas into Continental Europe, and in the process, have stimulated a revival of interest in the study of the theory and practice of proof in civil law systems.[23] More recently, three psychologists from

---

Adams (No. 2) (C.A.), TIMES, Nov. 3, 1997 (rejecting the use of Bayes' theorem by the English Court).

19. *See* RETHINKING EVIDENCE, *supra* note 4, at 92–93.

20. *See id. See also* Donald Nicolson, *Truth, Reason and Justice: Epistemology and Politics in Evidence Discourse*, 57 MOD. L. REV. 726, 729–30 (1994) (recognizing the two sides in that fact finding involves more than substantive law, and no matter how formally the law is looking at factual truth, ethics, justice and politics play a part in the legal process); Michael L. Seigel, *A Pragmatic Critique of Modern Evidence Scholarship*, 88 NW. U. L. REV. 995, 995–96 (1994) (noting that evidence scholarship has been distorted by foundationalism and legal positivism).

21. *See* W. LANCE BENNETT & MARTHA S. FELDMAN, RECONSTRUCTING REALITY IN THE COURTROOM 4–5 (1981); REID HASTIE ET AL., INSIDE THE JURY 22 (1983); Nancy Pennington & Reid Hastie, *A Cognitive Theory of Juror Decision Making: The Story Model*, 15 CARDOZO L. REV. 519, 530–31 (1991). Bernard S. Jackson has added a semiotic dimension to these studies. *See* BERNARD S. JACKSON, LAW, FACT AND NARRATIVE COHERENCE 7–12 (1988); BERNARD S. JACKSON, MAKING SENSE IN LAW: LINGUISTIC, PSYCHOLOGICAL AND SEMIOTIC PERSPECTIVES 140–93 (1995). For a balanced appraisal of these developments see generally SCHUM, *supra* note 17 (discussing such developments).

22. *See* HASTIE ET AL., *supra* note 21, at 22–23; Pennington & Hastie, *supra* note 21, at 556.

23. In addition to his own extensive writings on the subject, Professor Nijboer has organized a series of conferences, the first being in Amsterdam in 1992. *See generally* FORENSIC EXPERTISE AND THE LAW OF EVIDENCE (J.F. Nijboer & N. Kwak eds., 1993) (a symposium on expert evidence). Professor Nijboer was also the team leader of the NIAS group project mentioned in note *.

the Netherlands have analyzed and criticized the criminal process in their own country on the basis of a theory of "anchored narratives" that draws heavily on American literature.[24] This suggests the story model is not confined to juries or common law adversary proceedings.

There is an apparent tension between psychological accounts of "holistic" story telling in decision making involving reconstruction of particular past events and "atomistic," analytical accounts of reasoning about questions of fact. This paper deals with one aspect of this relationship. The problem can be restated as follows: The logicians assert that background generalizations are necessary in reasoning about questions of fact, and the psychologists tell us that stories are necessary in the process of decision making in this context. Yet, it is quite easy to show both are potentially subversive of orthodox rationalist conceptions of fact determination. In short, both generalizations and stories are necessary, but dangerous in this context. There seems to be a pattern, but what is the exact relationship between the normative thesis of the logicians and the empirical findings of the psychologists? Let us first look briefly at the standard accounts.

GENERALIZATIONS: NECESSARY BUT DANGEROUS

Mainstream evidence theory gives a central place to the role of generalizations in "rational" fact determination. Every inferential step from particular evidence to particular conclusion—from *factum probans* to *factum probandum*—requires justification by reference to at least one background generalization. In David Schum's phrase, generalizations constitute the "glue" of inferential reasoning.[25] They can also be used in the formation of hypotheses, to fill in gaps in stories, and, as a last resort, as anchors for parts of a story for which no particular evidence is available.[26] They are necessary as providing the only available basis for constructing rational arguments. This orthodox view is in line with theories developed by Toulmin, Perelman, the Amsterdam School of Argumentation, and most recently by David Schum.[27]

24. *See* HANS CROMBAG ET AL., ANCHORED NARRATIVES 20–43 (1993). This was condensed and translated into English from *Dubieuze Zaken* (1992), *discussed in Anchored Narratives—A Comment, supra* note *, at 106–14.

25. *See* SCHUM, *supra* note 17, at 82–83, 109.

26. *See* CROMBAG ET AL., *supra* note 24, at 20–43.

27. *See generally* FRANS H. VAN EEMEREN & ROB GROOTENDORST, ARGUMENTATION, COMMUNICATION, AND FALLACIES: A PRAGMA-DIALECTICAL PERSPECTIVE (1992) (explaining the pragma-dialectical approach to argumentation); CH.

It is widely recognized that such generalizations may be more or less indeterminate, unarticulated, vague, or precise. They may be backed by scientific evidence, "general knowledge," sheer speculation, or prejudice. They are often overtly or covertly value laden. They are said to be rooted in what passes for common sense or knowledge in a given society (or sub-group) at a given time. Thus, judgments of fact are rooted in and justified by a society's "stock of knowledge" or stock of beliefs. The Rationalist Tradition, at least in its more sophisticated forms, explicitly recognizes that knowledge and beliefs change over time.[28] In short, the "glue" for arguments on questions of fact is often historically contingent, culturally relative and value laden.

Generalizations are dangerous in argumentation about doubtful or disputed questions of fact because they tend to provide invalid, illegitimate, or false reasons for accepting conclusions based on inference. They are especially dangerous when they are implicit or unexpressed. For example:

(i) the warranting generalization may be *indeterminate* with respect to:

(a) frequency or universality (all/ most/ some);

(b) level of abstraction;

(c) defeasibility (exceptions, qualifications);

(d) precision or "fuzziness";

(e) empirical base/confidence (accepted by scientific community; part of everyday firsthand or vicarious experience; speculative etc.);

(ii) it may be unclear as to identity (which generalization—there may be rival generalizations available to each side in a dialogue) or source (whose generalization—male/female experience in a domestic violence case);[29]

PERELMAN, THE IDEA OF JUSTICE AND THE PROBLEM OF ARGUMENT (John Petrie, trans., Routledge and Kegan Paul 1963) (1963) (containing all the author's most important writings on justice); CH. PERELMAN & L. OLBRECHTS-TYTECA, THE NEW RHETORIC: A TREATISE ON ARGUMENTATION (John Wilkinson & Purcell Weaver trans., Univ. of Notre Dame Press 1969) (1958) (suggesting Perelman's theory of argumentation will help develop the justification for actions when justifications cannot be based on objective truth or reality); SCHUM, *supra* note 17 (discussing a theory in line with such an orthodox view); STEPHEN TOULMIN, THE USES OF ARGUMENT (1958) (suggesting jurisprudence rather than mathematics should be the model in analyzing rational procedures, and that logic should not be a purely formal study but rather a comparative one).

28. *See* RETHINKING EVIDENCE, *supra* note 4, at 71–72.

29. *See* Donna Martinson et al., *A Forum on Lavallee v. R: Women & Self-Defence*, 25 U. BRIT. COLUM. L. REV. 23, 36–44 (1991).

(iii) there may not in fact be a "cognitive consensus" on the matter, especially in a plural society;

(iv) value judgments (including prejudices, racist or gender stereotypes) may be masquerading as empirical propositions;

(v) when articulated, a generalization may be expressed in value laden language or in loaded categories.[30]

Thus, generalizations are dangerous because, especially when unexpressed, they are often indeterminate with respect to frequency, level of abstraction, empirical reliability, defeasibility, identity (i.e., which generalization), and power (i.e., whose generalization). They are powerful vehicles of prejudice and bias that may be concealed. In the process of articulating an unexpressed generalization, there is scope for using emotive language, giving a misleading impression of precision or confidence, or presenting value judgments as if they were empirical facts. Such tendencies are seen as dangerous in the sense that once it has been clarified what precisely is being argued, it may be shown the argument is invalid or weak because the generalization or its application in this case may be subject to rational criticism.[31]

STORIES NECESSARY, BUT DANGEROUS

As we have seen, another recent tributary in the same mainstream is the idea that stories and story telling are central to fact determination. The second thesis is that stories and story telling are psychologically necessary to decision making in legal contexts, but are dangerous in that they often can be used to violate logical standards, appeal to emotion rather than reason, and subvert legal principles and conventions.

Empirical research by Bennett and Feldman,[32] Pennington[33] and others suggests that American juries determine "the truth" about alleged past events mainly by constructing and comparing stories rather than critically evaluating arguments from evidence. These findings have been confirmed in other disciplines (e.g., medical diagnosis and history) and extended to fact determination by legal

30. For examples of these "dangers," see ANDERSON & TWINING, *supra* note 3, at 66–69, 367–84.

31. One of the main uses of Wigmore's chart method of analysis is to clarify precisely what is being argued by forcing into the open the articulation of steps in the argument, especially generalizations, which are usually left implicit or unstated, thereby making them more easily subject to critical scrutiny. *See id.* at 112–31.

32. *See* BENNETT & FELDMAN, *supra* note 21, at 10–18.

33. *See* HASTIE ET AL., *supra* note 21, at 20–23.

professionals and the police.[34] Simply put, the widely accepted thesis is that human beings need stories in order to make certain kinds of decisions and, more generally, to make sense of the world.

The literature is less clear about the functions of story construction and comparison. Bennett and Feldman say they are used to fill in gaps; others suggest in order to be satisfied, triers of fact need to explain human motivation and action, even when motive is not a material fact, or when the facts to be determined relate to a static situation or a single "simple" fact such as identity.[35] There is scope for disagreement as to whether stories are psychologically necessary in all situations involving fact determination in legal contexts (e.g., identity in a motiveless murder), but there seems to be a consensus they are in practice felt to be very important a great deal of the time.

Story telling can also be shown to be dangerous in legal contexts in that it can be, and is often, used to violate or evade conventional legal norms about relevance, reliability, completeness, prejudicial effect, etc.[36] It is widely regarded as appealing to intuition and emotion and as a vehicle for "irrational means of persuasion." Examples of such dangers include:

(i) sneaking in irrelevant facts;

(ii) sneaking in invented or ungrounded facts;

(iii) suggesting facts by innuendo;

(iv) focusing attention on the actor rather than the act;[37]

(v) appealing to hidden prejudices or stereotypes;

(vi) telling the story in emotionally toned language;

(vii) telling a story that may win sympathy for the speaker or the victim but is irrelevant to the argument;

(viii) making use of dubious analogies;

(viii) subverting lawyers distinctions between fact, law, and disposition and, more generally, fact and value; and

(ix) good stories pushing out true stories.[38]

34. *See generally* CROMBAG ET AL., *supra* note 24 (discussing the use of narratives in fact finding situations).

35. In private discussions, Terence Anderson and I have differed on whether stories are "necessary" in all cases, my own view being they undoubtedly play an important role in most cases, but in some instances simple facts (e.g., alibi, illegally parked car) may suffice and a story is not required.

36. Such norms include: judging the act not the actor; considering only relevant evidence; arguing from evidence; and keeping separate questions of fact, law and disposition. *See* RETHINKING EVIDENCE, *supra* note 4, at 219–61.

37. To give a simple example: In English law, evidence of disposition or bad character (such as prior convictions) is not normally admissible to support a criminal charge, but character is often an important but implicit part of a story.

THE RELATIONSHIP BETWEEN STORIES AND GENERALIZATIONS

It might be objectionable that the two theses apply to different spheres of discourse. Generalizations are logically necessary in the context of rational argument; stories are psychologically necessary in the context of human decision making. The logical "dangers" are different from the dangers of poor "judgment."

The relationship between logic and psychology in relation to decision making is a very large subject. Here, I shall confine myself to two points. First, I accept that some of the functions of story telling are to do with human interaction and communication, and are not performing a function in an argument. For example, in oral presentation by an advocate, stories may legitimately be used to attract and retain interest, set a comprehensible context, and provide concrete illustrations to assist understanding. They may, of course, be used to distract attention or win sympathy for the speaker or the victim independently of what is at issue and so on. So, some of the dangers are to do with communication rather than argumentation.

However, stories also seem to have a place within arguments and questions can be asked about the legitimacy, validity or cogency of their place in this context. Some of the allegations about the dangers

38. For further analysis and examples see RETHINKING EVIDENCE, *supra* note 4, at 219–61. For a useful development of the distinction between good and true stories see CROMBAG ET AL., *supra* note 24. In fact, the notion of a good story is ambiguous. It can mean just a well formed story, which relates to its internal structure and coherence, or it can relate to fitness for different purposes or the actual effect on an audience. I may exaggerate some incident in order to make people laugh, win sympathy, or justify my part in it; an audience may find a story good because it is interesting, intriguing, unexpected, or reassuring. In a battle of narratives, there will often be two competing versions of events, and in order to bolster one side, there may be a temptation to embroider or stretch the facts so as to strengthen the case. It may also happen that a story is considered not good because it ends in an anti-climax, ceases to have a point, or is not memorable—yet it may be true all the same. In criminal cases, one danger is that the trier of fact may be tempted to believe a story because it suggests a crime has been solved or because some other version of events might be threatening, inconvenient, or disturbing in some other way. *See id.* Finally, a story may be appealing because it is *familiar* and fits into a schema that one recognizes. *See generally* NECESSARY BUT DANGEROUS, *supra* note * (developing this point in relation to the case of *Warren* and the parable of the Prodigal Son). The tension between truth and entertainment value for journalists is candidly articulated by Janet Malcolm in her account of her first interview with Sheila McGough, an attorney who had been convicted of a number of charges relating to trust accounts: "[McGough] talked almost incessantly for the two hours of our meeting. [But she] was not interested in telling a plausible and persuasive and interesting story. She was out for the bigger game of imparting a great number of wholly accurate and numbingly boring facts." JANET MALCOLM, THE CRIME OF SHEILA MCGOUGH (1998), *reviewed by* Daniel Max, MIAMI HERALD, Feb. 21, 1999.

of stories seem to be appealing to standards of rationality. For example, a story winning sympathy for the speaker independently of the issue can be criticized as irrelevant to the argument; where a good story pushes out a true story, it can be criticized on the ground its attraction is to do with something other than truth (e.g., excitement, reassurance, titillation), and undue weight is being given to it. Where a story is used to fill in gaps in the evidence, its justificatory force may be little or none, and it seems odd to claim that an argument about a question of fact is bolstered by claiming the situation is analogous to a work of fiction or a parable.[39] One version of this position may be restated as follows: In ordinary life and in making important decisions we need stories in order to "make sense" of the world and of particular past events; in factual inquiries, including adjudication, for a story to be accepted as true it needs to be warranted by (or anchored in) evidence. A well formed story needs to be coherent, but to be true, it must be both plausible and backed by particular evidence. Plausibility is tested by background generalizations; the truth of specific factual conclusions is tested by reasoning from particular evidence.[40]

There are also important examples, mainly in the Anglo-American literature on advocacy and adjudication, of claims that stories play a crucial role not merely in respect of presentation and rhetoric, but analytically as part of an argument. For instance, in a much cited paper, John W. Davis maintained, "in an appellate court the statement of the facts is not merely a part of the argument, it is more often than not the argument itself."[41] Similar statements have been made by Karl Llewellyn, James Boyd White and other American jurists.[42] The precise meanings of such statements are not always clear, but it is reasonable to interpret them as maintaining that such notions as stories need to be accommodated within a conception of rational argument in legal contexts. Such claims are controversial, but if, for the sake of argument, we accept them as plausible, the question remains: What is the relationship between stories and generalizations in this context?

Perhaps the main link between stories and generalizations in this context lies in the idea of "a stock of knowledge." A

39. *See* RETHINKING EVIDENCE, *supra* note 4, at 240–42.

40. *See generally Anchored Narratives—A Comment*, *supra* note * (refining the view advanced by CROMBAG, ET AL., *supra* note 24).

41. John W. Davis, *The Argument of An Appeal* (1940), *reprinted in* JURISPRUDENCE IN ACTION 181 (1953).

42. For examples, see RETHINKING EVIDENCE, *supra* note 4, at 228–32.

"stock of knowledge" does not consist of individual, empirically tested, and readily articulated propositions; rather, both individually and collectively, we have ill defined agglomerations of beliefs that typically consist of a complex soup of more or less well-grounded information, sophisticated models, anecdotal memories, impressions, stories, myths, proverbs, wishes, stereotypes, speculations, and prejudices. Fact and value are not sharply differentiated. Nor are fact, fantasy and fiction. Nor can one take for granted either consistency or coherence within an individual's or a society's "stock of knowledge."

The content of a "stock of knowledge" does not consist solely or mainly of ready-made generalizations, still less of empirical laws. Beliefs may be embedded in stories, examples, and experiences that are particular and may not have been articulated in general terms. There is often considerable indeterminacy about what moral or general lesson or other generalization(s) may or will be extrapolated from such material.

A high degree of consensus about the contents of the social "stock of knowledge" or beliefs cannot be taken for granted, especially in a plural or a stratified society.[43] Moreover, so much of "common sense" that is indeed common in a given society is relative to time, place, and subject matter. Beliefs vary and beliefs change. We may treat ideas such as "story" and "stock of beliefs" as cultural near universals, while recognizing their fluidity over time and space. Even within subgroups, this gives plenty of scope for diversity and hence "relativism," at least in a weak sense.

X=X=X

Generalizations may be indeterminate as to their application; stories may be indeterminate as to their significance. There is an intimate interaction between the general and the particular in all arguments about questions of fact. One aspect of the relationship between generalizations and stories can be usefully analyzed with greater precision. Generalizations are, by definition, general; stories are particular.[44] There is, as every lawyer knows, an intimate

43. *See generally* MCCORMICK ON EVIDENCE (John W. Strong ed., 4th ed. 1992) (discussing the relationship between cognitive consensus and a plural society); *cf.* COHEN, *supra* note 12, at 274–76 (placing more emphasis on cognitive consensus as the basis for common sense reasoning). For a criticism of this passage, see ANDERSON & TWINING, *supra* note 3, at 371–72.

44. Following Ricoeur, I would stipulate that particularity, temporality, and

relationship between general rules and particular cases. Similarly, as every theologian and moralist should know, there is an intimate relationship between parables (and other morality tales) and their significance. That significance can be expressed in such terms as the point or the moral or some other general lesson or idea that it illustrates. Stories appeal strongly to the imagination. Part of that appeal lies in their concreteness and their particularity. That power can be undermined if the moral or point is spelled out or otherwise made explicit. Why this should be so, is crucial in the present context.

The idea of precedent as a source of law is an especially clear illustration of the interaction between the general and the particular. Because precedents are especially important in the common law, there has been much theorizing and controversy about the relationship.

We need not venture into that old controversy here because on several relevant points there is widespread agreement. "The facts" of a case are particular. The facts, at least in a hard case, give rise to a question of law. Such questions of law should be expressed in general terms, not "is the defendant guilty or liable?," but "in circumstances of this type, is the defendant guilty or liable?"[45] In deciding the particular case, the court gives an authoritative answer to the question(s) of law. That answer may be explicit or implicit.[46]

The relationship between the facts, the issue(s), and the answer can be formally restated as follows: the facts = X happened; the issue = if X happens, then what? (legal consequence); the answer = whenever X happens, then Y.

In this formulation X is a constant despite the transition from particular to general. This transition from a particular situation to general questions and a general answer involves a shift from "this was the situation" to "in situations of this type, the law prescribes . . . ." The crucial point in this context is that X is a constant. In short, X=X=X.

One of the main problems in interpreting cases is the level of generality of X is indeterminate. The same applies to "the moral" of parables and morality tales. But if the facts are known, and if X=X=X, how can X be clear at the particular level, but unclear at the

connectedness are all necessary elements in the concept of a "story" *stricto sensu*. *See* RETHINKING EVIDENCE, *supra* note 4, at 223.

45. *See id.* at 221.

46. One area of controversy surrounds what weight to give actual words used by a judge in this context. Few consider that courts are formally bound by the precise wording, but in practice great weight is quite often attached to such formulations.

general level? The answer is, of course, that how exactly the facts are to be categorized is also indeterminate. X represents a particular situation seen as a type. How precisely that situation should be interpreted, what elements are material, and what is the best or an appropriate description of the situation is a matter of interpretation. And, since X=X=X, the problem of interpreting X is almost constant.[47]

Descriptions of situations are typically expressed in language. The choice of language is not significant solely because of the more or less obvious rhetorical potential of emotive or value laden terms. For example, a categorization may be judged appropriate because it reflects the way a significant reference group thinks or talks (for instance, using the concepts of a particular trade to describe the situation in a commercial case), or because it corresponds with or fits, explicitly or implicitly, some general principle or policy (for example describing a situation in a way that brings out that a non-expert was relying on the judgment of an expert in a reasonably proximate relationship).[48] This idea of choosing appropriate categories to describe particular fact situations is at the core of Karl Llewellyn's important, but elusive, idea of "situation sense."[49]

Some of the alleged "dangers" of stories shared with generalizations include, for example, presenting unsupported facts as if they were anchored or appealing explicitly or implicitly to biases or prejudices. Perhaps the most obvious common element is indeterminacy: Indeterminacy as to what exactly is being argued or is the general significance of the particular example. For example, what

47. I say "almost" because as a practical matter there are some differences. For example, in teaching beginning law students how to write a precis or note of a case, one advises them to adopt as a rule of thumb: "In respect of the facts, when in doubt include." The reason for this is that it is easier to edit out unnecessary detail than to add extra facts at a later stage. So a student's preliminary note of a case contains not a definitive statement of "the facts," but a provisional formulation of potentially material facts. *See* WILLIAM TWINING & DAVID MIERS, HOW TO DO THINGS WITH RULES 307–08 (4th ed. 1999).

48. This example is based on Lord Denning's famous "persuasive" categorization of the facts in Candler v. Crane Christmas & Co., [1951] 1 All E. R. 428, which was concerned with whether there is ever a duty of care in respect of negligent misstatements causing financial loss.

> They were professional accountants who prepared and put before him these accounts, knowing that he was going to be guided by them in making an investment in the company. On the faith of those accounts he did make the investment, whereas, if the accounts had been carefully prepared, he would not have made the investment at all. The result is that he has lost his money.

Id. at 431.

49. *See* KARL N. LLEWELLYN, THE COMMON LAW TRADITION: DECIDING APPEALS 230–34 (1960), *discussed in* RETHINKING EVIDENCE, *supra* note 4, at 230–32.

precisely is the moral of the parable of the prodigal son? Indeterminacy is generally presented as a weakness in an argument. But, as John Wisdom points out, one of the attractions of case by case argument is that one is not forced to define the boundaries of X in advance.[50] It can be valid and sensible to say "this is a clear case of X" without *defining* X. That is part of the key to understanding the attraction of precedent at common law. It is a form of argument by analogy which does not commit the arguer to a position beyond what is needed for the case at hand. This may be why in theology, emphasis in moral education and precedent at common law on particular stories often treat indeterminacy as a virtue. But that, as they say, is another story.

50. *See generally* JOHN WISDOM, OTHER MINDS (1956) (discussing case by case argument). *See also* JOHN WISDOM: TWELVE ESSAYS 38–40 (Renford Bambrough ed. 1974) (containing discussion of the problematic effects of arguing inferentially from a static premise).

[16]
The *Ratio Decidendi* of the Parable of the Prodigal Son

MORAL

A Respectable Family taking the air
Is a subject on which I could dwell;
It contains all the morals that ever there were,
And it sets an example as well.
(Hilaire Belloc, 'F is for Family')[1]

Legal scholars and law students are not the only people who should be grateful to Brian Simpson. He has made important contributions to legal history, legal theory, and the study of the common law. He has also been one of the few academic lawyers of his generation to convey to a wider audience the message that the study of law can and should be part of the humanities and of general intellectual culture. Contextual studies of leading cases are Simpson's special genre, as we have seen in the other chapters of this book. These demonstrate how our subject can not only illuminate many things other than law, but can be fascinating and enjoyable as well.

The purpose of this chapter is to add a gloss to Simpson's insights into the role of 'cases' in our legal culture. People sometimes ask: What lessons or morals can be drawn from Brian's accounts of *Rylands v. Fletcher*, *R v. Dudley and Stephens*, or *Liversidge v. Anderson*? What is the point?

My argument is that it is limiting to think of contextual studies of common law cases or Biblical parables, or the contents of the law reports as being only or mainly like morality tales. 'What is *the* point?' may not be the best question to ask.

Simpson's *Rylands v. Fletcher* essay shows that today's perception of it as the leading case on strict liability in torts is different from perceptions at the time which took it to be a partial response to the immediate problem

* University College London. I have benefited from discussions of this topic with classes in Boston, Miami, and London and with members of the Forensic Expertise Group at the Netherlands Institute for Advanced Study. I am grateful for comments and suggestions by Terry Anderson, Zenon Bankowski, David Miers, Hans Nijboer, and Katherine O'Donovan.

[1] Hilaire Belloc, *Cautionary Verses: The Collected Humorous Poems* (London: Duckworth, 1939; Folio Society, 1997), 76.

of bursting reservoirs.[2] It is also a vivid example of the process by which a decision originating in response to one situation can have little impact on the original problem, but may survive as part of the armoury of the common law, or of its mythology, in quite different social contexts. Like his other studies, it illustrates what the law reports do not tell us. These interpretations are not incompatible with each other, for the essay does not have a single point.

Cannibalism and the Common Law also speaks of many things: disaster cannibalism; nineteenth-century sailing ships; how a case can be staged and managed; relations between elite and popular opinion; moral dilemmas—and so on. It has been suggested that the main point of the book is that leading cases become detached from their original context and take on a life of their own; or that *Dudley and Stephens* was about control of merchant shipping rather than moral condemnation of cannibalism or the defence of necessity; or that it merely provides a vivid illustration of how the main protagonists in a case can all cheat under the veneer of legality. Brian Simpson is a fox rather than a hedgehog. His case studies are centrifugal rather than centripetal. Or to put it differently: *Cannibalism and the Common Law* does not have one *ratio decidendi*.[3]

The concept of the *ratio decidendi* seems rather like the 'moral' of certain kinds of story or 'the point' of a parable. And questions about how to determine a *ratio* are at first sight analogous to questions about interpreting stories and parables. The most obvious link is that they concern *particular* events (real, fictional, stipulated, or hypothetical) that are considered to have *general significance*. But how close are the analogies between reported cases at common law and parables and other kinds of stories? Can consideration of parables (and the vast theological literature about them) throw any light on 'the problem of the *ratio decidendi*'?

I was stimulated to think about the question by an incident in a class on evidence. The case we were studying mainly concerned disputed questions of fact, but as I have argued elsewhere, stories play similar roles in arguments about questions of fact, and questions of law and tend to be subversive of artificially sharp distinctions between fact and law and fact and value.[4] The discussion centred on the relevance of the parable of 'The Prodigal Son', which occupies in theology a place similar to *Donoghue v. Stevenson* in the literature on precedent.[5]

[2] A. W. B. Simpson, 'Legal Liability for Bursting Reservoirs: the Historical Context of *Rylands v. Fletcher*', 13 *Journal of Legal Studies*, 249 (1975).

[3] The themes in this paragraph are explored in William Twining, 'Cannibalism and Legal Literature', 6 OJLS 423 (1986).

[4] William Twining, 'Lawyers' Stories' in *Rethinking Evidence* (Chicago: Northwestern University Press, 1994), 228–49; 'Narrative and Generalizations in Argumentation about Questions of Fact', 40 S. Texas L. Rev. 101 (1999).

[5] 'The Prodigal Son . . . . continues to produce more secondary literature than any other parable.' Craig L. Blomberg, 'The Parables of Jesus: Current Trends and Needs in Research',

I am not sure when I was first introduced to the parable of the Prodigal Son, but for as long as I can remember I was vaguely perplexed and even disturbed by it. What does it mean? Is it a *nice* story? Is the point that forgiveness trumps justice? That repentance pays? That one loses out if one stays at home with one's parents? Or merely that reconciliation warrants a celebration? I now realize that I had tended to identify with the elder son who, having stayed at home helping his father and carrying out his filial duties, finds that it is his no-good brother who has been rewarded. The father's reply did not seem to me to meet the charge of unfairness.

I was led to reconsider this view after a discussion in a class on Analysis of Evidence. I regularly use *In Re the Estate of James Dale Warren, Jr* as a vehicle for detailed analysis and construction of arguments about questions of fact.[6] This simulated case concerns a contested Will executed by James Dale Warren, Sr in a nursing home on the afternoon of his death. This new Will purported to leave almost all of his estate to his son, James Dale Warren, Jr, who had been estranged from him for most of his life, but had been recently reconciled with him. He had assiduously attended his father during the last three days before he died. The effect of the Will, if valid, would be essentially to disinherit his only daughter, Susan, and her two children. Susan had lived with her father in his home during his last years until she felt that his medical condition required transferring him to a nursing home. James Sr may have resented the transfer, but otherwise there was little evidence of any serious rift between father and daughter and convincing evidence that James Sr adored his grandchildren for whom his house was the only home they had known. Unfortunately for Susan, she had been involved in a road accident a few days before her father's death and had stayed away for fear that her injuries might upset the old man. Unknown to her, James Jr had stepped into the breach and was in attendance while his father wrote the new Will. Susan contests the Will on two grounds: (1) that the testator lacked testamentary capacity at the time of execution of the new Will; and (2) that the Will was made under the undue influence of James Jr, the principal beneficiary. The main issues are factual.

In the context of a mock trial counsel for each party are asked to develop persuasive 'theories' and 'themes' to support their case.[7] It is hardly

in Bruce Chilton and Craig A. Evans, *Studying the Historical Jesus: Evaluations of the State of Current Research* (Leiden and New York, E. J. Brill, 1994) at 250.

[6] The case is reproduced in full in Terence Anderson and William Twining, *Analysis of Evidence* (London: Butterworths, 1991; Chicago: Northwestern University Press, 1999) at 305–27. This is a hypothetical case that originated as a simulated problem in the American National Trial Competition in the 1980s. It is particularly well-designed in that the documentation is thorough, and the evidence is difficult to analyse, is evenly balanced and raises interesting problems of trial tactics and presentation.

[7] In this context 'theory' means a strategic argument concerning the case as a whole and 'theme' is an element in the argument that is considered sufficiently important to deserve emphasis by repetition. On the relations between theory, theme, and story see Anderson and

surprising that counsel for Susan regularly develop a Dickensian image of grasping relatives fawning over a dying man. It is no more surprising that the other side counters with the parable of the Prodigal Son.[8]

On the occasion in question, in an American law school, before assigning roles I asked the class to discuss what themes might usefully be developed in the case. As usual, the Prodigal Son was the first suggestion. However, at this point the discussion took a surprising turn. Let me try to reconstruct the exchange in the form of an imaginary dialogue:

WLT: Which side does the parable help?

Student 1: The son, of course.

WLT: Why?

Student 2: Because it is natural for a father to be generous after reconciliation with a long lost son.

WLT: Is that the moral of the original parable?

Student 3: It could be about repentance and forgiveness. That still helps James Jr.

WLT: Are you suggesting that a story from the New Testament is evidence of how fathers behave in 20th-century America?

Student 2: No. But it does support the proposition that this is reasonable behaviour on the part of the father, therefore he was not behaving irrationally.

WLT: Is that not inferring an 'is' from an 'ought'?

Student 1: Well, the story sets out a familiar model of how good fathers do and should behave, like 'best practice'.

WLT: Again, is that evidence?

Students (chorus): Yes.

WLT: Have you read the original text of St Luke's Gospel?

Students 1 and 2 (abashed): Well, not recently.

WLT: (*meanly producing the text and circulating copies from the St James' version*):[9] Look, the father, in responding to the elder son's complaint, explicitly says: 'Son, thou art ever with me, and all that I have is thine.' (LUKE 16: 5, 31.) In other words: 'I am not disinheriting you. I am only throwing a party to celebrate.' Surely, that helps Susan.

Student 4: That's pedantic. The popular image of the story makes it out to be about reconciliation and forgiveness and generosity. It

Twining, op. cit., at 166–8, 278–80 *et passim*. See also, Twining, *Rethinking Evidence*, chs 7 and 8.

[8] In teaching, Anderson and I challenge the appropriateness of both of these images in this context. See *Analysis of Evidence, Teachers' Manual*, at pp. 55–60.

[9] See Appendix.

is the image rather than the text that will have resonance with the jury. So it does help James Jr.

WLT: Is that rational?

Student 1: Counsel for Susan can point this out, if counsel for James Jr tries to use it . . .

(The dialogue continued).[10]

This is, of course, an idealized construction of the behaviour of both teacher and students. The original incident stimulated me to think further about the roles of theories and themes in argument about questions of fact.[11] I also started thinking more seriously about the parable. I re-read St Luke's Gospel and dipped, though not very deeply, into some of the theological literature about the Prodigal Son and parables generally. This suggested that there might be some illuminating analogies between jurisprudential discussions of precedent and theological discussions of parables. Here I confine myself to possible analogies between debates about 'the point' of parables and about determining the *ratio decidendi* of a case, with particular reference to the Prodigal Son.

CASES AND PARABLES AS TEXTS

On a first reading of a small part of the theological literature it becomes obvious that there appear to be striking analogies between discussions of parables and of cases at common law.[12] Both involve particular instances with potential general significance. Both are associated with 'authority', but in different ways. Theologians as well as lawyers have dabbled in literary theory.[13] There are analogous patterns of difference about emphasis on original intent, text, context, and reader response. Terms such as 'exegesis' and 'hermeneutics' have found their way into juristic literature. However, further consideration suggests the differences may be at least as significant.

The *Oxford English Dictionary* lists 14 primary meanings of the word 'case' (*et casus*), including an event, a chance, an instance or example of the occurrence of an event or the existence of a thing, and the actual state or

[10] Subsequently, students alerted to these points have usually shied away from using both the Prodigal Son and *Martin Chuzzlewit* as the explicit basis for themes in presenting their arguments.

[11] On the role of stories in arguments about questions of law and about questions of fact and their interrelationship, see *Rethinking Evidence*, above, n. 4, 228–49.

[12] I have relied heavily in this section on Blomberg, above, n. 5, whose survey concentrates on the period 1980–94. See also Dan Otto Via Jr., *The Parables: Their Literary and Existential Dimension* (Philadelphia: Fortress Press, 1967); J. Ellsworth Kallas, *Parables from the Back Side: Bible Stories with a Twist* (Abingdon, 1992); Joachim Jeremias, *Rediscovering the Parables* (New York: Scribner, 1966); Eta Linneman, *Jesus of the Parables* (New York, 1964).

[13] A useful survey is Anthony C. Thistleton, 'Hermeneutics, Biblical', in *The Routledge Encyclopedia of Philosophy* (London, 1997/8).

position of matters. It lists six uses in Law under the general rubric of 'the state of facts juridically considered', including: (a) a cause or suit; (b) a statement of the facts of any matter *sub judice* drawn up for consideration by a higher court (as in case stated); (c) a cause which has been decided, including a leading case [and] a precedent; and (d) an argument (the sum of grounds on which [one of the parties] rests his claim).[14] Here, then, we are mainly concerned with cases-as-precedents, but also with cases-as-examples (as in Simpson's case studies), and cases-as-arguments.

Cases-as-precedents and parables are both embodied in texts, in the narrow sense of writings in fixed verbal form.[15] When lawyers read or cite cases, we are in fact referring to a particular kind of document or text—a law report. When we read the Parable of the Prodigal Son 'in the original', we are typically reading a translation of St Luke's account of Jesus telling a story. The authenticity, accuracy, and reliability of each text are not the same, but both are treated as authoritative.[16] A law report contains the *ipsissima verba* of each judge; St Luke's account is at best hearsay. Modern law reports follow a standard form; the Gospels are freer-flowing. Nevertheless both texts are treated as primary and authoritative, though in different ways.

Keeping in mind the differences between the texts, it is interesting to compare two standard definitions of parables and cases-as-precedents. C. H. Dodd advanced the following account of New Testament parables, 'At its simplest the parable is a metaphor or simile drawn from nature or common life, arresting the hearer by its vividness or strangeness, and leaving the mind in sufficient doubt about its precise application to tease it into active thought.'[17]

Theologians differ about the nature of parables. In my preliminary reading I have found suggestions that a standard parable, or a particular one, should be viewed as a metaphor, an allegory, an 'example story', a lesson (providing insight rather than a 'moral'), an analogy, an argument, a conundrum, or a morality tale.[18] These are not all necessarily incompatible, but some lead to profound differences of interpretation. If by 'moral-

[14] Paraphrased from the *OED*.

[15] Here the important point is that both the New Testament and the law reports are in (relatively) fixed verbal form (though translations differ), but interpretations of parables and cases are not. On the distinction between rules in fixed verbal form (such as statutes) and rules not in fixed verbal form (such as customary or common law rules) see William Twining and David Miers, *How To Do Things With Rules* (4th edn, London: Butterworths, 1999) ('HTDTWR') at 131–2, 137, 218–19.

[16] On the differences between authenticity, veracity, accuracy, and reliability see David Schum, *Evidential Foundations of Probabilistic Reasoning* (Chichester and New York: John Wiley, 1994).

[17] C. H. Dodd, *The Gospel Parables* 5 (Manchester: Manchester University Press, 1932)) quoted by John R. Donahue S.J., *The Gospel in Parable* (Philadelphia: Fortress, 1988).

[18] Several of these, and possible differences between them, are discussed by Blomberg, above, n. 5.

ity tale' is intended a story with a specific 'moral' that can be articulated as a normative proposition, I would contest that interpretation. However, if the term is taken to mean a story that belongs to the general sphere of moral discourse, broadly interpreted, then 'morality tale' can encompass all, or almost all, of these different conceptions.

For example, if the main point of the Prodigal Son is interpreted as providing an insight into the nature of God's love (lesson) or, alternatively, as Jesus' indirect justification for consorting with sinners (argument), both interpretations fit within a broad conception of 'morality tale'. One of the main differences between commentators relates to the appropriateness of thinking of 'the point' as being expressible in the form of a proposition.[19] Similarly, cases-as-precedents, cases-as-examples, and cases-as-arguments are all concerned with normative discourse. To what extent and how a case can be interpreted as authority for, or as an example of, an identifiable, articulated proposition of law is in part what is at issue in 'the problem of the *ratio decidendi*'.

Dodd's definition is contested, but is often treated as fairly representative. It is interesting to contrast this with a well-known American definition of a reported case:

> A case is the written memorandum of a dispute or controversy between persons, telling with varying degrees of completeness and accuracy, what happened, what each of the parties did about it, what some supposedly impartial judge or other tribunal did in the way of bringing the dispute or controversy to an end, and the avowed reasons of the judge or tribunal for doing what was done.[20]

These two formulations, if treated as reasonably representative, bring out some differences and similarities between New Testament parables and reported cases. Dodd's account stresses four aspects of parabolic language: (a) its poetic and metaphoric quality; (b) its realism; (c) its paradoxical and engaging quality; and (d) its open-ended nature.[21]

One might say of reported cases that they are (a) prosaic rather than poetic; (b) realistic in the sense of being close to actual events (though not necessarily confined to everyday life); (c) dialectical rather than paradoxical; and (d) although they may engage attention, that is not their primary purpose or characteristic. The most important similarity is that there are leeways for interpreting the general significance of both cases and parables, but within constraints imposed by text and context. Thus the main point of comparison is the room for interpretation of the general significance of an account of a particular event or situation. One might add that narrative plays a major role in both types of account.[22]

[19] *ibid.* at 237–40.

[20] Adapted from N. Dowling, E. Patterson, and R. Powell, *Materials for Legal Method* (2nd edn, Chicago: Foundation Press, 1952), pp. 34–5.

[21] Based on Donahue at 6, see n. 17.

[22] *ibid.*; cf. Twining (1994).

The *OED* definition of a 'case' cited above brings out some further differences: the law reports follow a uniform format and typically contain standard ingredients: facts (particular) giving rise to a disputed question of law (general), culminating in a decision (both particular and general) backed by a reasoned justification. Parables differ from cases in that issues are not always sharply framed (what was the issue in The Prodigal Son?); no decision is involved; nor is a reasoned justification for the conclusion necessarily articulated. The absence of precisely-framed issues and of explicit justifications may leave parables a bit more open-ended in respect of interpreting their general significance, but this difference could be exaggerated. Similarly, the fact that a case involves a final decision on a particular dispute does not affect the problem of interpretation of its general significance. Precedents have direct practical effects both on the immediate dispute and beyond it. The practical effects of theological and literary texts are less easy to pinpoint. Both parables and cases are authoritative in quite similar ways at a general level.

THE RATIO OF A CASE AND 'THE POINT' OF A PARABLE

As Simpson rightly pointed out in an early essay, it is important to distinguish between the meaning of the term '*ratio decidendi*' and the problem of determining the *ratio decidendi* of a given case.[23] From the extensive literature on the topic, five different definitions or usages of '*ratio decidendi*' can be singled out:

1. The rule(s) of law explicitly stated by the judge(s) as the basis for the decision (the explicit answer(s) to the question(s) of law in the case).
2. The reason(s) explicitly given by the judge(s) for the decision (the explicit justification for the decision).

[23] A. W. B. Simpson, 'The *Ratio Decidendi* of a Case and the Doctrine of Binding Precedent' in A. G. Guest (ed.), *Oxford Essays in Jurisprudence* (First Series, Oxford: Clarendon Press, 1961) 148, at 159, 168. Simpson restricts the concept of *ratio* to binding precedents. This stems from the idea that it is the binding part of a binding precedent. This is a legitimate use, but not the only possible one. The idea of the *ratio* as the proposition of law (principle, rule or rule-fragment) for which the case can be treated as authority, whether binding or persuasive, has two advantages: it (i) separates the puzzling idea of 'bindingness' from other problems of interpreting cases. The meaning of a precedent and its status as precedent can usually be treated as separate issues; (ii) allows for the possibility that the same or closely related methods of interpretation apply both to cases that are binding on the interpreter and to those that are not. Consider the interpretation of Case A, a decision of the Court of Appeal, at a particular moment of time by both the House of Lords and a lower court. The latter is bound, but the former is not; yet the proposition for which it is authority will usually be the same. See, however, some more subtle variants in the standpoints of the House of Lords and lower courts in regard to the Court of Appeal's decision in *Davis v. Johnson* [1979] A. C. 272, discussed in HTDTWR (see n. 15 above) at 266–8. On the difference between Simpson and myself on the issue whether a *ratio* can change over time, see below, n. 28.

3. The rule(s) of law implicit in the reasoning of the judge(s) in justifying the decision (the implicit answer(s) to the question(s) of law in the case).
4. The reason(s) implicitly given by the judge(s) for the decision (the implicit justification for the decision).
5. The rule(s) of law for which the case is or can be made to stand or is cited as authority by a subsequent interpreter (the imputed answer(s) to the question(s) of law in the case).[24]

In ordinary legal usage the term is used quite loosely and, even in jurisprudential debate, each of these usages has its supporters.[25] All five notions have a place in legal discourse and legal reasoning: explicit rule-statements, implicit propositions of law, explicit and implicit justifications for a decision, and imputed propositions of law, are all used by subsequent interpreters of cases-as-precedents and in other contexts. For present purposes it is sufficient to note, first, that the term is ambiguous and does not have one settled usage; and, secondly, that in the first four usages the *ratio* is treated as being embodied in the text and therefore does not change over time, whereas in the last usage the *ratio* can change over time.

Given the ambiguity of the term and the variety of contexts in which it is used there is some doubt as to whether it is a useful concept.[26] I have argued elsewhere that the fifth usage is the most useful because it links the concept of *ratio* more closely to interpretation and use of past precedents: if and only if interpretation of cases involves reading the text of each case in isolation can any of the first four usages fit this context.[27] Since neither theory nor practice precludes interpreting precedents in the context of prior and subsequent cases, legal developments, and other factors, there is no such self-denying rule of interpretation.

The first four usages apply to the context of *justification*, for example from the standpoint of the original judge or someone rationally reconstructing the arguments in the case, but not in most contexts of subsequent *interpretation and use*.[28] The fifth usage is more realistic here because (i)

[24] Adapted from HTDTWR (see n. 15 above) at 334, where the definitional question is discussed in more detail.

[25] For references, see *ibid*.

[26] William Twining, 'Il Precedente Nel Diritto Inglese: Una Demistificazione', in *La Giurisprudenza Per Massime e Il Valore del Precedente* (Padova: Cedam, 1988), 461–6 (arguing that the terms *ratio decidendi* and *obiter dictum* obfuscate what is involved in using and interpreting precedents). Sir Rupert Cross arrived at a similar conclusion by a different route, *Precedent in English Law* (2nd edn, Oxford: Clarendon Press, 1968) at 77–8.

[27] *ibid*. Of course, the reasoning of a judge in a prior case cannot only be cited as authority but can also be used as raw material for constructing an argument. In this context citing a passage from a judgment often involves two implicit claims: 'This is a strong argument and look who said it.'

[28] Neil MacCormick refers to the 5th (imputation) definition as *ratio-scepticism*. 'Why Cases Have Rationes and What These Are', in L. Goldstein (ed), *Precedent in Law* (Oxford: Oxford University Press, 1987), 155. He implies that adopting such a usage involves radical indeterminacy or other versions of 'free interpretation'. This is incorrect. Subsequent interpreters often give weight to the text as well as to other factors and such other factors may

different interpreters use cases as part of their arguments on questions of law in significantly different ways: there are, for example, appropriately cautious and bold interpreters;[29] (ii) a single precedent is normally interpreted in the light of other precedents and other contextual factors; (iii) the conditions giving rise to doubt in interpreting a prior precedent also change over time:[30] texts are fixed, but interpretations change.

Within theology there is much debate about whether the interpretation of parables can and should change over time. Clearly the perspectives, techniques, and situations of interpreters vary according to time and place, but the divine origin of the text naturally makes for greater emphasis on 'original intent'. There are fewer possibilities for authoritative interventions between reader and text than in the common law; even an authoritarian church does not typically claim to overrule, reverse, limit, modify, or otherwise change the original text.[31] Despite this powerful constraint, even a cursory glance at the theological literature of any religion shows how much scope there is for differing interpretations of parables and other religious texts. For example, the relevance of changed social and other conditions to such interpretations is, of course, a central issue in Islam and Judaism as well as in Christianity.

The usages of '*ratio*' (1, 3, and 5) which identify it with propositions of law (principles, rules, or rule-fragments) suggest a close analogy between precedents and stories with 'morals' that can be expressed as propositions. Both involve the extraction of general normative propositions from

limit rather than extend the leeways for interpretation. e.g. there is much less scope for differing interpretations of the *ratio decidendi* of *Donoghue v. Stevenson* in 1999 than there was in 1933 just because other contextual factors, especially later decisions, have narrowed the range of plausible interpretations. We now know that 'the neighbour principle' is too broad and that the duty of care in negligence is not confined to manufacturers of goods. MacCormick's own account is more concerned with justification than with later interpretation and use. Simpson (1961: see above n. 23), attacks as 'perverse' 'the theory that the *ratio decidendi* of a case is a rule which is constructed by a later court when called on to consider the case' (168). This is not the same as definition 5., which relates to the standpoint of an interpreter rather than to someone commenting on another court's interpretation. There is nothing perverse or odd about interpreter D saying: 'Case A has been interpreted differently in cases B and C.' D may prefer one of the two interpretations or construct another; D may argue that each interpretation was plausible at the time, but neither is plausible today, and so on.

[29] HTDTWR (see n. 15 above) at pp. 336–7.

[30] *ibid.*, ch. 6.

[31] Joachim Jeremias (1966; see n. 12 above) concludes, 'The parables have a twofold historical setting. First, the original historical setting, not only of the parables, but of all Jesus' sayings, is their individual concrete situation in his earthly life. Secondly, they went on to live in the primitive Church. We know them only in the form that they were received from the primitive Church, and so we are faced with the task of recovering their original form as far as we can' (at 87). Jeremias suggests that the meaning may have changed because of the evangelizing concerns of 'the primitive Church' and its propensity to add generalizing conclusions. On the tendency of earlier commentators, such as Julicher and Jeremias, to lose interest in the story once they have extracted the point, see Zenon Bankowski, 'Parable and Analogy: The Universal and Particular in Common Law' *Acta Juridica* (1998), 138; see also Zenon Bankowski and Claire Davis, 'Living In and Out of the Law', in *Faith in Law*, Oliver, Douglas-Scott, Tadros eds. (Oxford, 1999).

accounts of particular events. Parables are often treated as morality tales in the narrow sense. This was my assumption before I looked into the theological literature. There one finds that searching for a 'moral' is sometimes challenged as superficial or simplistic. Without going very deeply into the theological debates one can identify a variety of positions on the interpretation of parables. These include propositions that:

1. *A parable may be intentionally polyvalent: the audience is deliberately left to draw its own moral or point from the story.* On this view, it is within the spirit of the genre that different audiences at different times and places should interpret the text differently. This position does not necessarily involve a commitment to radical indeterminacy or to 'the death of the author', because constraints may be put on the range of interpretations: e.g., an interpretation may be treated as only being acceptable if it 'fits' the text or takes due account of what is known of the historical context or the background beliefs of the original audience. On this view, the fact that there are multiple interpretations of the Prodigal Son can be treated as a strength rather than a weakness.
2. *Even if one gives weight to 'original intent', it does not follow that a parable has only one 'point'.* The significance of the Prodigal Son varies, e.g., according to how much one focuses on the prodigal, the father, or the elder son. There is no good reason why a parable or other story need have only one 'point'.[32]
3. *If by 'point ' is meant 'the important or essential thing' (e.g. the point of the matter or 'the salient feature of a story, epigram, or joke ' (e.g., 'he missed the point'),*[33] *the idea need not be confined to a 'moral'.* For example, the point may be an insight or lesson (e.g., about the nature of God's love); or an argument (the Prodigal Son was Jesus' way of justifying his association with publicans and sinners);[34] or a conundrum (how should the elder son behave?);[35] or a way of challenging some taken-for-granted assumption (the father flouted convention by *running* out and embracing the prodigal *before* he had declared his repentance and by treating him as an honoured guest).[36] *All of these may have an evaluative dimension, but they are not the same as a 'moral' in the form of a moral rule or principle.*
4. *Parables may also be viewed as metaphors or allegories that communicate indirectly, by powerful images, ideas that cannot be adequately expressed in propositional form.*[37] The parable of the Prodigal Son has a powerful hold on

[32] Blomberg, n. 5, pp. 237–40.

[33] Adapted from *The Random House Dictionary of the English Language* (unabridged edition, 1966). The *OED* devotes over 10 pages to 'point', cataloguing many nuances and analogies; the closest to the idea in the present context is: '28 . . . The precise matter in discussion to be discussed; the essential or important thing.' Cf. '29b. *to make a point*: to establish a proposition, to prove a contention.'

[34] Linneman, see n. 12 above, at 23.

[35] Kallas, above n. 12, at pp. 79–80.

[36] Blomberg, above n. 5, at pp. 232–3.

[37] *ibid.*, at 237–9

people's imaginations that may be quite different from the impact of an articulated general proposition. Often, to spell out a point or a moral may spoil a story.

This list could be extended considerably.

At first sight, only some of these ideas seem to fit reported cases. But the idea of the *ratio decidendi* is only significant, if ever, in the context of one way of reading and using cases, that of extracting propositions of law from them. One can, of course, read cases for many other purposes: as examples of judicial style or as historical responses to immediate problems (as Simpson does); to identify judicial values or biases; to deconstruct the reasoning; or to provide raw material for substantive arguments.[38] The concept of '*ratio*' has little or no relevance to such readings.

Conversely, one can read and use parables for their 'morals', but many theologians do not consider this to be the primary use. Here the theological literature is suggestive in reminding us that there are other uses of cases in addition to their being treated as authoritative sources of normative propositions.

INTERPRETATION, STANDPOINT, THE POWER OF THE PARTICULAR, AND CONDITIONS OF DOUBT

Ronald Dworkin has developed the idea of interpretation as making a text 'the best it can be'.[39] This fits some contexts better than others. It generally fits the production of a play or conducting a symphony, or texts with alternative endings; it fits legal contexts, especially where the interpreter is participating in the legal system and, for example, is in a relationship of co-operation with the originator of the text or subscribes to the system's basic principles. However, Dworkin's conception of interpretation does not comfortably include a hostile critic of a book or other artifact, a straight historical account of the origin of some text, or an attempt to 'deconstruct' it.

In legal contexts it would be odd to say that a tax consultant representing a taxpayer, or an advocate trying to limit or bury an adverse precedent, Holmes' 'Bad Man', or a member of a Law Commission considering the reform of a controversial statute are trying to make each text 'the best it can be'. What is most appropriate for particular interpreters may be best for their purposes, and perhaps for the system as a whole, but hardly for every text they are called upon to interpret. Hostile interpretations do not

[38] Above, n. 14.

[39] R. Dworkin, *Law's Empire* (London: Fontana, 1986), Ch.2, discussed HTDTWR (see n. 15 above) at 377–9. Dworkin's notion of 'integrity' transfers quite easily from legal to theological interpretation; the idea of precedents being like chapters in a chain novel is less obviously analogous.

necessarily involve uncharitable readings, or distortions, or non-reading of the text—though in practice they often do.[40]

Dworkin's usage probably fits most contexts of theological interpretation of parables. Even so, in order to explain divergent interpretations of parables, one needs to differentiate between standpoints. A preacher using the story as an illustration in a sermon, a Sunday school teacher instructing 10-year-olds, a biographer of Jesus, a theologian trying to construct a coherent interpretation of Luke's Gospel, may have significantly different vantage points, roles, objectives, and interpretive resources. They may also have different theological theories. Similarly, what is the best interpretation of a precedent may be different for a legal historian, counsel for the prosecution in a criminal case, an appellate judge, and the writer of a student textbook according to their context and purposes.

Interpretation is an activity that involves complex relations between interpreter, text (or other object of interpretation) and, indirectly, the originator(s) of the text. Interpretation is relative to the standpoint of the interpreter because the activity takes place in a given historical situation or context. Interpreters can have different vantage points, background assumptions, beliefs, interests, roles, resources, and immediate objectives.

As we have seen, puzzles about the *ratio decidendi* belong mainly to contexts involving reading cases as authoritative sources of law within a legal system rather than for other purposes.[41] In such contexts precedents seem like morality tales in that their significance lies in the general normative answers they give to questions raised by the story. So, for some interpreters, are parables. But, as we have seen, there are disagreements as to when, if ever, it is appropriate to express the moral or point of a parable in propositional form.

Precedents are reported mainly because they raise and purport to answer general questions of law. In the context of interpretation of precedents as authoritative sources of law, it is usually fairly straightforward to identify the question(s) of law raised by the case. The main doubts about interpretation relate to the level of generality at which the question(s) and answer(s) can be most appropriately formulated.[42] The facts, the issue(s)

[40] William Twining, 'Other People's Power', 63 *Brooklyn L. Rev.* 189 (1997).

[41] For such purposes, Dworkin's concept of interpretation may be appropriate for most official participants, even if we do not accept, fully or in part, his particular theory of legal interpretation and argumentation. However, as argued elsewhere, it is useful to distinguish puzzlement about role from other puzzlements about interpretation of texts. HTDTWR (see n. 15 above) at 335–7. Thus it is easier to identify what is involved in interpretation of a precedent from the standpoint of an advocate (relevant precedents are either adverse or supportive of an argument) than from the standpoint of a judge just because 'the role of the judge' is more problematic.

[42] Doubts about the most appropriate level of generality of a precedent are not the only ones, but they are the most common. E.g. doubts can arise about the precedent value of a case (is it strongly or weakly persuasive?; Has it been overruled or narrowed down?); and about the appropriateness of the classifying concepts used to categorize the situation (e.g. at

and the answer(s) to the question(s) are all intimately related, for the paradigm example of a single-issue case fits the following format:

Facts:	X happened (particular)
Issue:	If X happens/ in situations of type X then what? (general)
Answer:	Whenever X happens, then Y (general).[43]

X is a constant, i.e. X = X = X. Typically the main doubt in interpreting a case relates to how X is characterized, especially the level of generality of X.

X = X = X suggests one way in which parables and precedents are quite closely analogous. In both, particularity is a key source of their appeal. Why is this? Three different, but possibly complementary, answers may be suggested.

1. *As John Wisdom pointed out in discussing case-by-case argument, there is an important difference between saying 'this is a clear case of X' and giving a general definition of X.*[44] This is because it is often easier to make confident judgments in specific circumstances than to articulate a precise general rule or principle. Case-by-case decision can be easier than the formulation of general rules.
2. *Telling a particular story without articulating its general significance may be a matter of not crossing bridges before one comes to them.* But it may also be a matter of giving more leeway to subsequent interpreters to draw their own conclusions or to make their own choices. At common law the practice of treating the result of a particular case as settled, but not according the same weight to the reasoning and articulated rule-formulations of the judges in the case also has the effect of leaving some leeway for future interpreters, perhaps somewhere between weak and strong discretion.
3. *Explicit, propositional moralizing may be too intellectual and may tend to cut down the scope for the role of intuition and imagination in making judgments.*[45] Child psychologists tell us that indirect story-telling may have a greater impact on children in moral education than explicit moralizing or articulating the morals of stories. Perhaps this was what Belloc was satirizing in his *Cautionary Tales*. Stories are easier to grasp and to remember than abstract principles, but they also, as Dodd suggests, tease the hearer into active thought. They also more readily grip the imagination.

various times there have been differences of view as to whether the facts of *Donoghue v. Stevenson* raised issues of privity or duty of care in negligence or product liability, concepts which do not differ solely in respect of levels of generality).

[43] 'If X' is the protasis, 'then Y' the apodosis of a rule of law. Y typically relates to liability or responsibility (guilty/not guilty; liable/not liable).

[44] See D. C. Yalden-Thomson, 'The Virginia Lectures', in Renford Bambrough (ed.), *Wisdom: Twelve Essays* (Oxford: Blackwell, 1974), discussing John Wisdom's lectures on 'Proof and Explanation' (1957).

[45] See above, nn. 32–7.

Thus the power of the particular narrative lies in: (a) combinations of factors that make for clear cases and confident judgments in particular circumstances; (b) allowing leeways for subsequent interpreters to make their own choices; and (c) avoiding over- intellectualization of judgments.

There are therefore some suggestive analogies between parables and reported cases, including cases-as-precedents. But there are also some very significant differences between interpreting parables and precedents. Such differences become clearer if one considers what are the main conditions of doubt in respect of each genre. When a difficult problem of interpretation arises, it can be helpful to try to diagnose the problem by asking: *what factors are contributing to puzzlement or doubt in this situation*?[46] On the basis of the analysis so far, I suggest that there are at least five reasons why interpreting parables tends to be less straightforward than interpreting precedents. These can be restated as follows:

1. *The text*: there are more problems about establishing biblical texts than modern law reports in relation to authenticity, accuracy, reliability, and translation, especially in respect of what Jesus actually said.[47] Moreover, modern law reports follow a standard format which generally distinguishes clearly between primary material (e.g. the *ipsissima verba* of the judgments) and secondary 'furniture'.
2. *The genre*: precedents are generally reported because they provide authoritative determinations of disputed questions of law. The 'what' of cases-as-precedents is more clearly defined than that of parables as a genre.[48] They have a formal quality as dispositive of previously unanswered questions of law.
3. *Standpoint*: both parables and reported cases are read and used by a variety of kinds of interpreters in a variety of contexts. However, in interpreting and using cases as authoritative precedents the standard participant standpoints of judge, advocate, legal adviser, and expositor generally belong broadly to the same interpretive community, even if their roles, purposes, etc., may be different.[49] Some of these roles and purposes are quite precisely defined. Readers of the Bible and people who cite, retell, or use parables are more numerous and diverse than readers of law reports. They may not have such clearly-defined roles. Perhaps the closest analogies in respect of standpoint are between biblical scholars and jurists in their role of exegetists or expositors of doctrine. But both these standpoints are quite problematic. Furthermore, legal and biblical exegesis are not identical activities. Most of the other legal actors who use precedents—such as judges, advocates, advisers—

[46] HTDTWR (see n. 15 above), ch. 6. [47] Above, p. 154. [48] Above, p. 155.

[49] I skirt over the issue of whether all those who read and use law reports, especially non-participants who consider them from an external point of view, can be said to belong to one interpretive community.

are typically mainly concerned with the context of interpretation of precedents in legal argumentation concerning the relationship of particular to particular, more than particular to general. This is probably less common in theology.

4. *Issue-posing*: in parables, the question(s) to which it may be treated as giving an answer is often not determinate, e.g., the Prodigal Son could be interpreted as raising such different questions as: What is the nature of God's love? Why was Jesus justified in consorting with sinners? What is the relationship between repentance, forgiveness, and justice? One might say that parables do not fit as easily into a question-and-answer framework as do reported cases; or alternatively, what questions one imputes to a parable depend on one's theory of parables. That cases are selected for reporting because they involved previously unresolved questions of law is not seriously disputed in the theory of precedent.[50] Given that the questions addressed by parables are often less determinate than for precedents, if indeed parables address questions, it is hardly surprising that the range of plausible interpretations for a parable does not operate solely or mainly on a single continuum of levels of generality.[51] Different kinds of questions invite different kinds of answer. And we cannot be as confident about treating parables as raising and answering questions as we can with precedents.
5. *Changing conditions and the status of precedents*: the relevance of changed social and other circumstances (including theories of interpretation) is problematic in theology. Nevertheless the status of the New Testament as an authoritative source is relatively constant. Interpreters of precedents, on the other hand, have to take account of new precedents, other legal developments and other changed circumstances: precedents may be abolished by legislation, overruled, limited, extended, and so on. Changed conditions may raise doubts about the status or scope of a precedent or they may narrow or settle doubts: e.g., the scope and significance of the House of Lords' decision in the recent *Pinochet* case is likely to be much clearer in 5 years time than now, both as a precedent and as a historical event.[52]

[50] Katherine O'Donovan rightly points out that in some specialist series of law reports, as in family and medical law, cases may be selected other than for their value as precedents and that the proliferation of reported cases may be attributable to commercial reasons that do not restrict selection to cases of 'precedent value'. My remarks here therefore refer to paradigm examples of general, selective law reports for which the criteria have traditionally been mainly related to their value as precedents.

[51] Above p. 159. Of course, there may be doubts about the scope or level of generality of 'the moral' of a morality tale (see below), but this is not the main source of doubt in respect of parables.

[52] *R v. Bow Street Metropolitan Stipendiary Magistrate, ex p Pinochet Ugarte (Amnesty International intervening) (No 3)* [1999] 2 All E. R. 97.

These five points suggest that interpreting cases-as-precedents—as authoritative sources or supports for propositions of law—is a good deal easier than interpreting parables. There are, of course, some special difficulties in regard to precedents, such as multiple judgment decisions, but by and large the conditions of doubt are more significant in biblical interpretation. This, I hope, may help to demystify precedent.

However, this modest venture into theology also reminds us that there are other significant ways of looking at reported cases in addition to or instead of solely considering them as authoritative precedents. The recent explosion of interest in literary theory within biblical hermeneutics may be more illuminating in regard to other ways of reading the law reports than to reading cases-as-precedents.[53]

THE *RATIO DECIDENDI* OF THE PARABLE

Can lawyers' approaches to interpretation throw any light on a parable? For example, can one argue plausibly that there is a main point or moral of the Prodigal Son that can be extracted by combining juristic method and theological insights? In order to keep this simple, let us assume that the St James' translation of Luke's account of Jesus' parable is an authentic and reliable primary source. My standpoint is that of a lay person, with a common law background, using scholarly commentaries to clarify my understanding of the meaning and significance of the parable out of general interest rather than for some specific purpose.

First, context. The text suggests that Jesus was responding to the Pharisees' complaint that he was consorting with publicans and sinners. The primary audience consisted of scribes and Pharisees and of the people with whom Jesus was consorting. There is some historical evidence about the background beliefs and attitudes of these two audiences. For example, it was not unusual for a younger son to emigrate, taking his share of the inheritance in advance.[54] The Pharisees had clear ideas (rules?) about repentance and forgiveness, so there was nothing new or surprising about a father forgiving his son.[55] But this father's behaviour was unconventional, perhaps shocking, in that he *ran* out to greet his son, embraced him *before* he had expressed contrition, and went *beyond* mere forgiveness to treat him as *an honoured guest* and to order a special feast in *celebration*. It would have been even more shocking if he had reduced the share of the elder son, but he did not do this. Rather he admonished him for putting concerns of merit above the joy of finding a lost sheep. The same chapter in Luke includes two other parables that also deal with the theme of rejoicing over repentance: the parables of the lost sheep and the lost piece of

[53] Thisleton, above, n. 13. [54] Otto Via (1967) at pp. 169–70 (citing Linneman).
[55] Linneman (1964), op. cit., at pp. 74–6.

silver. There is even an articulated moral for the second parable: 'Likewise, I say unto you, there is joy in the presence of the angels of God over one sinner that repenteth.' (LUKE 15: 10).

The textual and historical contexts considerably reduce the scope for interpretation. They tell us about the audience, what they would have taken for granted and what was new. They pinpoint a central question that Jesus was addressing: why are you consorting with sinners? The previous parable explicitly identifies rejoicing at repentance as a central theme. Indeed, one might ask: with all these aids to interpretation, what is the problem? Yet this is the most debated parable in theological literature.[56]

What then are the conditions of doubt? Some of the puzzles and disagreements relate to the status of the text, to its relation to the St Thomas' Gospel, and to the standpoints of different users, such as preachers and evangelists. I have eliminated these as sources of doubt for my purposes and concentrated on scholarly theological commentaries. The range of interpretations is still quite wide. How can this be?

One set of difficulties relates to genre. Is a parable an allegory, a metaphor, an argument, a conundrum, or what? Doubts arising from these nuanced differentiations surround questions like: should a parable be treated as having a single main point or moral?; should such morals be appropriately articulated as 'propositions'?; should the significance of a parable be treated as changing over time, and if so, to what extent?; and, related to that, how much emphasis should be placed on 'original intent'? Here the analogies with legal interpretation are quite resonant.

It seems to me that some of these doubts can be settled quite easily. Take, for example, the suggestion that the moral of the Prodigal Son depends on which of the three main characters is the main focus of attention. The repentance of the son and his hope that he would be accepted back, albeit in a lowly position, contain some lessons for prodigals. But the context suggests that the basic ideas were familiar and that the son's behaviour and attitude did not provide an answer to the question posed by the Pharisees. So I would suggest that this could not be the main point of the story.

The behaviour and attitudes of the father are more striking. In his treatment of the prodigal, he provides a fresh and powerful role-model for compassionate fathers. One may also learn something about the nature of God's love from this. However, the story does not end there and this suggests that, on its own, the father's treatment of the prodigal is not the only point.

The elder son's reaction and the interaction between father and son provide a third focus. I disagree with Kallas' suggestion that the parable ends

[56] In contrast, contextual histories of leading cases in the genre originated by Simpson tend to illustrate how far later interpretations may stray from the original context, which may not limit or even affect the scope for interpretation.

with a conundrum: how should the older son (and by analogy the Pharisees) behave?[57] For it seems clear from the context that, *in the circumstances of this case*, the father is implying that the only correct course of action is to join in the celebration wholeheartedly. A strong argument can be advanced to support the suggestion that the elder son represents the Pharisees and that his fault lay in being too legalistic. He had played by the rules and thought that he deserved to be rewarded. One can take the interpretation one step further and suggest that Jesus is implying that salvation depends on faith rather than on works. But this is not the only possible interpretation, and it may be reading too much into the parable. Suffice to say here that even if one accepts that the main point relates to the final exchange between father and elder son, it still leaves open such questions as: what precisely is the best interpretation of this exchange, and can it adequately be expressed in propositional form?

Rather than pursue this hare, let us make a lawyer's move. Let us assume that we are persuaded by the parable about the appropriateness of the behaviour of the prodigal and of his father's treatment of him, and the inappropriateness of the elder brother's response in the circumstances. What if we vary the facts a bit?

Suppose the prodigal had not already repented—would it be appropriate for the father to treat him in exactly the same way, in respect of forgiveness, *and* a special welcome, *and* a celebration? Suppose the father had been even more generous and had given the repentant prodigal part of the elder son's inheritance (or, like James Warren Sr, all of it)? What if the elder son later had further grounds for a sense of grievance, for example, that the younger son continued to be treated with special favour or was perceived to be exploiting his father's generosity? Were the elder son's obedience and good works irrelevant to his prospect of salvation or is it that works alone are not enough? Prior repentance, unconditional forgiveness, and a celebratory party (but no more) are potential limiting factors regarding the scope of possible morals about forgiveness, repentance, and justice.[58] One or more such factors might provide a basis for distinguishing the original situation from some future one. Or they might not. On all these matters the parable is open-ended. In the specific context of justifying consorting with sinners, such issues do not arise. Maybe the original parable presents an easy case. On the facts this was a clear case of X, but it is indeterminate as to the general scope of X.

[57] Kallas, above, n. 12.

[58] Cf. the use of such limiters in leading cases: 'the neighbour principle' in *Donoghue v. Stevenson* was presented as setting limits to the scope of the duty of care; similarly, in *Candler v. Crane Christmas*, Denning MR (dissenting) was careful to emphasize proximity, the expert–non-expert relation, and reliance as *potential limiters* as he tried to extend the scope of the duty of care to negligent misstatements involving financial loss. The classic formulation of the rule in *Rylands v. Fletcher* also contains such limiters.

LESSONS

What have I learned from this exercise? First, I have long felt that problems of interpreting legal texts are closer to theology than to literary theory. My first venture into theological scholarship has strengthened this view.

However, the differences between interpreting parables and precedents are as significant as the similarities. Like all analogies this one could easily be pushed too far. Nevertheless, there is scope for further fruitful cross-disciplinary exchanges in this area. Perhaps because of the greater difficulties it has to deal with, the theological literature on parables seems generally more extensive and sophisticated than the juristic literature about precedents, not least in respect of hermeneutics and the relevance of literary theory. The benefits may be reciprocal, because lawyers' treatments on such matters as issue framing, relevance, materiality, and the use of hypotheticals might throw some light on theological puzzlements.

Secondly, this exercise has underlined the difference between routine and problematic readings of texts.[59] The nuanced differences between the various uses of the term *'ratio decidendi'* and some of the subtleties of the theoretical literature do not have much bearing on routine reading and using of cases-as-precedents. Similarly, most of us have read or heard parables and other Bible stories without any elaborate theological apparatus. My students adopted a cavalier attitude to the original text. I may have missed the main point of the Prodigal Son until now, if it has one, but it still said something about repentance and forgiveness. When genuine puzzlements or disagreements arise in respect of hard cases, clarification of standpoint, diagnosis of the conditions of doubt, and distinctions between ratio-as-rule, ratio-as-reason, reconstruction of arguments, and imputation are important tools.[60] Similar considerations apply in theology.

Thirdly, my understanding of the Prodigal Son has changed. I no longer consider it to be solely or mainly about reconciliation and forgiveness. Focus on the context narrows the range of plausible interpretations in two main ways. Historical knowledge is helpful in differentiating between what would have been familiar to the original audience and what would have been novel, surprising, or even shocking. The context also helps to identify one, perhaps *the*, central issue: how did Jesus justify consorting with sinners? The answer includes the ideas that the souls of sinners are as important as those of the righteous and that there is special reason for rejoicing when a lost soul is 'found'. However, even if one can formulate a clear central issue, there is still some indeterminacy about the answer to the question and the scope and meaning of the justification. The parable, on its own, leaves open the range of circumstances to which the answer or

[59] HTDTWR (see n. 15 above) at 207–8. [60] *ibid.*, chs 6 and 9.

moral might apply. This is clearly illustrated by the limiters included in the story: prior and genuine repentance by the son; the interests of the elder brother not materially affected by the celebration; and it is not clear whether there were absolutely no conditions attached to forgiveness.

These, in the language of precedent, relate to the level of generality of the governing norm or principle. But, of course, there are other potential levels of meaning and this may be a legalistic and superficial way of reading the story. I had instinctively identified with the older son, who is often interpreted as representing the legalistic Pharisees. Now that I see this, I can empathize more with both the prodigal and the father. However, for me the parable still leaves unanswered some questions about justice.

Finally, despite significant differences between parables and cases-as-precedents, the analogies are illuminating. As mentioned above, the theological literature on parables is sophisticated and quite suggestive. For example, it reminds us that parables, like cases, are read and interpreted in many different contexts for quite varied purposes. Multiple perspectives have been brought to bear on parables. Some are familiar in jurisprudence, others are less so.[61] This exercise has stimulated me to reflect further on cases-as-precedents. It has in some respects confirmed or fortified my prior views, for example, on standpoint, conditions of doubt, and the use of 'what if . . .?' questions. It has also led me to reconsider others: for example, whether attempting to formulate potential interpretations of precedents in propositional form within a framework of question-and answer may not be too intellectual.

There may be many other lessons. But rather than spoil my story by articulating a moral, I leave it to readers to tease out their own conclusions.

[61] For useful surveys of the range of perspectives see Blomberg and Thisleton, op. cit.

Appendix

ST LUKE CHAPTER 15 (KING JAMES' VERSION)

1. *Then drew near unto him all the publicans and sinners for to hear him.*
2. *And the Pharisees and scribes murmured, saying, This man receiveth sinners and eateth with them.*
[3.–10. parables of the lost sheep and the lost silver]
11. *And he said, a certain man had two sons:*
12. *And the younger of them said to his father, 'Father, give me the portion of goods that falleth to me.' And he divided unto them his living*
13. *And not many days after the younger son gathered all together, and took his journey into a far country, and there wasted his substance with riotous living*
14. *And when he had spent all, there arose a mighty famine in that land; and he began to be in want.*
15. *And he went and joined himself to a citizen of that country; and he sent him into the fields to feed swine.*
16. *And he would fain have filled his belly with the husks the swine did eat: and no man gave unto him.*
17. *And when he came to himself, he said, 'How many hired servants of my father's have bread enough and to spare and I perish with hunger! '*
18. *I will arise and go to my father, and say unto him, 'Father, I have sinned against heaven and before thee',*
19. *And am no more worthy to be called thy son: make me one of your hired servants.*
20. *And he arose, and came to his father. But when he was a great way off his father saw him, and had compassion, and ran, and fell on his neck, and kissed him.*
21. *And the son said unto him, 'Father, I have sinned against heaven, and in thy sight, and am no more worthy to be called thy son.'*
22. *But the father said to his servants, 'Bring forth the best robe, and put it on him; and put a ring on his hand, and shoes on his feet:*
23 . *And bring hither the fatted calf and kill it; and let us eat, and be merry:*
24. *For this my son was dead, and is alive again; he was lost, and is found.' And they began to be merry.*
25. *Now the elder son was in the field: and as he came and drew nigh to the house, he heard musick and dancing*
26. *And he called one of the servants, and asked what these things meant.*
27. *And he said unto him, 'Thy brother is come; thy father hath killed the fatted calf, because he has received him safe and sound.'*
28. *And he was angry, and would not go in: therefore his father came out, and intreated him.*
29. *And he answering said to his father, 'Lo, these many years did I serve thee, neither transgressed I at any time thy commandment: and yet thou never gavest me a kid, that I might make merry with my friends:*

30. *But as soon as this thy son was come, which hath devoured thy living with harlots, thou hast killed for him the fatted calf.*
31. *And he said unto him, 'Son, thou art ever with me, and all that I have is thine.*
32. *It was meet that we should make merry, and be glad: for this thy brother was dead, and is alive again; and was lost, and is found.'*

Index